Aboriginal Autonomy and Development in Northern Quebec and Labrador

Colin H. Scott

Aboriginal Autonomy and Development in Northern Quebec and Labrador

UBC Press · Vancouver · Toronto

Printed in Canada on acid-free paper ∞

ISBN 0-7748-0844-6

National Library of Canada Cataloguing in Publication Data

Main entry under title:

Aboriginal autonomy and development in northern Quebec and Labrador

Includes bibliographical references and index.
ISBN 0-7748-0844-6

1. Native peoples – Quebec (Province) – Nord-du-Québec.* 2. Native peoples – Newfoundland – Labrador. I. Scott, Colin.

E78.C2A124 2001 971.4'1100497 C2001-910261-5

This book has been published with the help of a grant from the Humanities and Social Sciences Federation of Canada, using funds provided by the Social Sciences and Humanities Research Council of Canada.

UBC Press acknowledges the financial support of the Government of Canada through the Book Publishing Industry Development Program (BPIDP) for our publishing activities.
Canadä

We also gratefully acknowledge the support of the Canada Council for the Arts for our publishing program, as well as the support of the British Columbia Arts Council.

Set in Stone by Darlene Remus
Printed and bound in Canada by Friesens
Copy editor: Joanne Richardson
Proofreader: Jacqueline Wood
Indexer: Patricia Buchanan

UBC Press
The University of British Columbia
2029 West Mall, Vancouver, BC V6T 1Z2
(604) 822-5959
Fax: (604) 822-6083
E-mail: info@ubcpress.ca
www.ubcpress.ca

Contents

Figures / viii

Preface and Acknowledgments / ix

Part 1: Perspectives on the General Issues

1 On Autonomy and Development / 3
Colin H. Scott

2 Healing the Past, Meeting the Future / 21
Peter Penashue

Part 2: (Re)defining Territory

3 Shaping Modern Inuit Territorial Perception and Identity in the Quebec-Labrador Peninsula / 33
Ludger Müller-Wille

4 Writing Legal Histories on Nunavik/ 41
Susan G. Drummond

5 The Landscape of Nunavik/The Territory of Nouveau-Québec / 63
Peter Jacobs

6 Aboriginal Rights and Interests in Canadian Northern Seas / 78
Monica E. Mulrennan and Colin H. Scott

7 Territories, Identity, and Modernity among the Atikamekw (Haut St-Maurice, Quebec) / 98
Sylvie Poirier

Part 3: Resource Management and Development Conflicts

8 Voices from a Disappearing Forest: Government, Corporate, and Cree Participatory Forestry Management Practices / 119
Harvey A. Feit and Robert Beaulieu

9 Conflicts between Cree Hunting and Sport Hunting: Co-Management Decision Making at James Bay / 149
Colin H. Scott and Jeremy Webber

10 Becoming a Mercury Dealer: Moral Implications and the Construction of Objective Knowledge for the James Bay Cree / 175
Richard T. Scott

11 Media Contestation of the James Bay and Northern Québec Agreement: The Social Construction of the "Cree Problem" / 206
Donna Patrick and Peter Armitage

12 Low-Level Military Flight Training in Quebec-Labrador: The Anatomy of a Northern Development Conflict / 233
Mary Barker

13 The Land Claims Negotiations of the Montagnais, or Innu, of the Province of Quebec and the Management of Natural Resources / 255
Paul Charest

Part 4: Community, Identity, and Governance

14 Community Dispersal and Organization: The Case of Oujé-Bougoumou / 277
Abel Bosum

15 Gathering Knowledge: Reflections on the Anthropology of Identity, Aboriginality, and the Annual Gatherings in Whapmagoostui, Quebec / 289
Naomi Adelson

16 Building a Community in the Town of Chisasibi / 304
Susan Jacobs

17 Cultural Change in Mistissini: Implications for Self-Determination and Cultural Survival / 316
Catherine James

18 The Decolonization of the Self and the Recolonization of Knowledge: The Politics of Nunavik Health Care / 332
Josée G. Lavoie

19 Country Space as a Healing Place: Community Healing at Sheshatshiu / 357
Cathrine Degnen

20 The Concept of Community and the Challenge for Self-Government / 379
Hedda Schuurman

21 The Double Bind of Aboriginal Self-Government / 396
Adrian Tanner

Part 5: In Conclusion

22 Ways Forward / 417
Colin H. Scott

Contributors / 427

Index / 428

Figures

1.1 Territories of First Nations represented in this volume / 2
3.1 The socio-cultural region of Nunavik and the administrative region of Kativik / 38
6.1 Territorial lands and seas of James Bay Cree and Northern Quebec Inuit / 82
8.1 Waswanipi moose harvests vs. forest area cut and burned, 1969-85 / 139
12.1 Conceptual framework / 234
12.2 The Quebec-Labrador Peninsula / 236
12.3 Comprehensive land claims / 238
12.4 Resource use and development initiatives in Labrador / 240
12.5 Regional distribution of public submissions commenting on the first (1989) and second (1994) Goose Bay Environmental Impact Statements / 246

Preface and Acknowledgments

This book stems from collaborative research undertaken by members of the AGREE (Aboriginal Government, Resources, Economy, and Environment) research program from 1991 to the present as well as by others who, in one way or another (e.g., through symposia, workshops, or informal consultation) became involved with our examination of common issues. In responding to the sometimes incremental, sometimes sudden, subordination and dispossession imposed by macro-political and economic orders, northern First Nations are compelled to negotiate "space" for themselves across a broad spectrum of territorial, institutional, and symbolic practices. While these interconnected aspects cannot easily – and indeed should not – be compartmentalized, they cluster around certain cultural priorities, political flashpoints, persistent conundrums, and hopes for transcendence and reconciliation. These have provided some direction for organizing the chapters of this book into five parts.

Part 1, Perspectives on the General Issues, offers an overview by the editor of the volume, followed by the ground-level insights of a prominent First Nations leader. Both chapters perceive inherent connections between political subordination, territorial dispossession, and suffering; and between re-entitlement, autonomy, and community healing.

Part 2, (Re)defining Territory, addresses the all-important issue of reinforcing authority over homelands and waters – an issue so basic to Aboriginal cultural and political identity, and a seemingly inarguable prerequisite for material improvement and autonomy. The chapters in this part address how Aboriginal collectivities seek to redefine the effects of "Crown" property, political boundaries, and the jurisdictional claims of the state; they also address how the strategic redefinition and hybridization of territorial forms reciprocally reshape Aboriginal conceptions and practice.

Part 3, Resource Management and Development Conflicts, follows quite logically from Part 2. Here the cut-and-thrust of renegotiating jurisdictional and property rights is explored across a representative range of contests over natural resources and the institutional instances through which these issues are mediated – litigation, media campaigns, protest and direct action, scientific authority, environmental review, co-management, and claims negotiation. It is here that the political factors motivating the state and state-sponsored economic interests are cast in sharpest relief. From the composite of cases considered, there emerges a strong sense of the conditions and prospects for Aboriginal action with regard to structural change.

Part 4, Community, Identity, and Governance, expands the view of local development dynamics to emphasize how communities are coping with debilitating burdens of social dislocation and suffering through processes of relocation, social healing, and cultural renewal. It is this part that offers the most explicit views of the problem of constructing and maintaining community; of relations between women and men, young and old, those with a vision, and those who have lost heart; of the human effects of the chronic contradictions between indigenous and externally imposed orders.

Part 5, In Conclusion, considers the imperative of structural reform, and conditions for achieving it – reform that would reaffirm Aboriginal possession of homelands and waters, authentic political self-determination, and room for cultural self-definition. Particular attention is drawn to key recommendations of the recent Royal Commission on Aboriginal Peoples, unwisely neglected by current federal and provincial governments.

AGREE co-investigators include professors in anthropology, geography, and law from McGill University (where AGREE is headquartered) as well as from several other universities in Quebec, elsewhere in Canada, and abroad. Numerous graduate students, both former and current, have contributed immensely to this research and are richly represented in this book.

The research program developed around a partnership with northern Aboriginal communities and leaderships to tackle priority problems in self-government and development. The original partners in this venture were the Grand Council of the Crees of Eeyou Istchee (GCCEI) (Eeyou Istchee meaning "people's land"), Makivik Corporation for the northern Quebec Inuit, the Innu Nation of Labrador, and the Lubicon Cree First Nation in northern Alberta. Each of these organizations nominated a member to an advisory board for the AGREE research. We are grateful for the guidance and support provided in this capacity by Bill Namagoose (GCCEI), Robert Lanari (Makivik Corporation), Peter Penashue (Innu Nation), and Bernard Ominayak (Lubicon). Although the geographic focus of this book is northern Quebec and Labrador, Lubicon participation provided our discussions with an immensely valuable comparative dimension.

Several political, administrative, and scientific members of the aforementioned organizations, their constituent communities, and allied administrative entities advanced our collaboration with the partner organizations: Peter Armitage, Daniel Ashini, Abel Bosum, Robert Beaulieu, Lorraine

Brooke, Brian Craik, Rick Cuciurean, René Dion, Sam Gull, Suzanne Hilton, Ginette Lajoie, Fred Lennarson, Matthew Mukash, Basil Penashue, Alan Penn, and Katie Rich, among many others. Some of these individuals have contributed chapters to this volume.

Between 1992 and 1997, we organized several workshops to bring together researchers and Aboriginal partners. These included an initial planning workshop in the Department of Anthropology at McGill University in 1991, consultation between some of the researchers and Aboriginal partner representatives at the community of Little Buffalo (Lubicon) in 1992, a full team workshop at the community of Oujé-Bougoumou (Quebec Cree) in March 1994, and a thematic workshop (Negotiating Nationhood: An Intercultural Dialogue on Contemporary Native Issues) at McGill University in December 1996.

We also organized a series of team symposia at several professional academic meetings to share work-in-progress and exchange ideas: the Canadian Anthropology Society Meetings, Université de Montréal, May 1992; the First International Congress of Arctic Social Sciences, Université Laval, Quebec, October 1992; the Canadian Anthropology Society Meetings, York University, Toronto, May 1993; and the Learned Societies Meetings, Université du Québec à Montréal, May 1995. Smaller sub-sets of the team also presented together on the issues of this volume at the Learned Societies Meetings, Memorial University, St. John's, June 1997; at the Seventh Conference of the International Association for the Study of Common Property (IASCP), University of British Columbia, Vancouver, June 1998; at the Eighth International Conference on Hunting and Gathering Societies (CHAGS), National Museum of Ethnology, Osaka, Japan, October 1998; and at the conference, In the Way of Development: Indigenous Peoples, Civil Society and the Environment, McMaster University, Hamilton, November 1998.

Regina Harrison and Jonathan Salsberg served as editors for the AGREE Discussion Paper Series, through which earlier versions of several of the chapters in this volume were developed. Several other graduate students and colleagues contributed to the vetting of drafts. Kate Degnen, Kreg Ettenger, Liz Fajber, Tara Goetze, Hedda Schuurman, and Audra Simpson took leading roles in organizing workshops, producing the newsletter, and getting our documentation resources in order. Special thanks are also due to Nicola Wolters, who served a three-year term running our office, as well as to Karine Bates and Brian Thom for more recent administrative support. AGREE has benefited greatly from our participation in the Centre for Society, Technology and Development (STANDD), directed by John Galaty, and the Programme in the Anthropology of Development (PAD), directed by Laurel Bossen.

The original source of funding for our research and deliberations was a strategic grant from the Social Sciences and Humanities Research Council of

Canada (SSHRCC), 1991-4 (principal investigator C. Scott; co-investigators H. Feit, C. Lambert, L. Müller-Wille, and A. Tanner), for the project "Aboriginal Government, Resource Management, and Resource-Based Economic Development in Provincial Northern Regions." Subsequent team funding (1994-7) was granted by Quebec's Fonds pour la formation de chercheurs et l'aide à la recherche (FCAR) (principal investigator C. Scott; co-investigators C. Lambert, M. Mulrennan, L. Müller-Wille, and J. Webber; with out-of-province associates H. Feit, D. Soyez, and A. Tanner). Numerous individual and supplementary team grants also contributed to the funding base for research and conference symposia. This book has been published with the help of a grant from the Humanities and Social Sciences Federation of Canada, using funds provided by the Social Sciences and Humanities Research Council of Canada.

A most gratifying aspect of working on this book has been the opportunity to include case material from Aboriginal areas additional to those of the original Aboriginal partners in our research. Thus, we are able to incorporate experience from Quebec Innu and Atikamekw. We are beholden to those authors, and to the Aboriginal communities who have sponsored their research, for contributions that materially enhance the scope and comparative significance of the research program.

Jean Wilson, Emily Andrew, Ann Macklem, and others on the team at UBC Press provided faith, wisdom, and meticulous assistance throughout the publication process. Two anonymous peer reviewers, for UBC Press and for the Aid to Scholarly Publications Program, offered encouragement and invaluable advice.

We hope that this book may contribute to the understanding and enhancement of Aboriginal autonomy and self-determined development and reciprocate, in some measure, the support received from so many quarters – above all from the Aboriginal participants and their communities.

Part 1
Perspectives on the General Issues

Figure 1.1 Territories of First Nations represented in this volume

1
On Autonomy and Development

Colin H. Scott

Fundamental to the idea of development is the notion of improvement, the imagining of bettered lives, and the enactment of those imaginings in social practices that convert dreams and visions into durable, lived realities. Development is not managed or understood by privileged reference to a particular subset of economic, political, or cultural practices. If the pressures experienced by northern Aboriginal societies due to other peoples' development are commonly portrayed by narrow measures of economic or political power and interest, then Aboriginal strategies for opposing and converting them involve a calculus more subtle and complex than is generally recognized. In northern Aboriginal societies, the projects of a hunter or an entrepreneur, homeland ties of sentiment, knowledge and responsibility, the blockage of a forestry road, and steps towards community healing are inextricably intertwined aspects of development. As Aboriginal societies elaborate strategies for autonomous development within myriad contexts, usually against daunting odds, they are actively challenging and revising commonplace theories about the necessities inherent in mass market economies and state monopolies of power.

Autonomy implies, by definition, that collectivities enact self-generated futures, defending and creating lives that include but are not simply reducible to hegemonic forms or counter-hegemonic responses.[1] Otherwise, such terms as "cultural survival" and "self-determination" – important as they are in winning political allies and making moral claims against the state – would amount to little more than the affixing of Aboriginal identities onto progressively "mainstream" lifeways. Is there scope within the state to accommodate the "potential radical alterity" (Povinelli 1998, 587) of Aboriginal social and cultural orders? Public and scholarly interest in northern Aboriginal societies is due, in significant measure, to the perception that, notwithstanding increasingly complex and intensive involvement with mainstream economy, politics, and culture, these societies are composed of peoples who have a fighting chance to define themselves and to live in substantially unique ways.

The chapters in this book ask by what means and in what forms Aboriginal societies resist domination and dependency to negotiate self-determined paths of development in the contemporary world. Thus posed, it is a broad question, demanding a broad-spectrum response. The paths negotiated cut through all domains of social life: property and territory, law and governance, ecology and resource management, economy, knowledge, health, schooling, gender relations, identity, and spirituality. Throughout, Aboriginal cultural *difference* is an implicit condition and explicit symbol for institutional innovation and societal restructuring. The accommodation of difference demands a new relatedness – one that is enacted through multiple interconnected strategies: sovereignty shared between Aboriginal and central state governments (Asch 1988, 1993; Scott 1993; Tully 1995); more equitable distribution of Aboriginal and non-Aboriginal rights and titles (Slattery 1987; Asch 1997; Culhane 1998); resource co-management arrangements (Feit 1988; Pinkerton 1989; Berkes et al. 1991; Usher 1996); creative articulations of subsistence and cash economies (Duhaime 1990; Scott and Feit 1992); more engaged conversations between Western science and local environmental knowledge (Freeman and Carbyn 1988; Johnson 1992); enhanced cultural and institutional syncretism in medicine, justice, administration, and education (Ross 1992; Niezen 1993; O'Neil 1993; Haig-Brown 1995); and redefined and realigned collective identities and alliances (Dyck 1985; Beckett 1988; Tanner 1993).

This, at least, is the optimistic vision and expectation. Sceptics will argue that the reality is a revised subordination of Aboriginal peoples, token accommodation in the guise of a disingenuous "multiculturalism" whose function is to lubricate the ongoing rearrangement of Aboriginal lives to fit the imperatives of capitalism and liberal state hegemony. Yet the Aboriginal demand for collective material and political equity – promoted in discourses of social justice, Aboriginal rights, cultural relativism, pluralistic power sharing, and environmental responsibility – persistently contradicts (and exposes the contradictions of) mainstream social orders. Northern Aboriginal societies, whose marginalization can produce fierce oppositional cohesion, are often staging grounds for change according to alternative societal premises. As they confront and renegotiate their relationship with the state, the fracture lines dividing the resisters from the resisted admit the eruption (and irruption) of new (inter)cultural forms – new internal orders, and new external articulations. In making space for themselves, they seek no less than to transform all of "us."

Cases at Hand

The Aboriginal peoples represented in this book comprise a significant proportion of Canadian subarctic and arctic peoples. The eastern Cree, Innu, and Atikamekw occupy the eastern one-third of a subarctic Algonquian cultural continuum that stretches from Labrador to the Rocky Mountains. This continuum is marked by numerous cultural, organizational, and linguistic shifts; however, historically, throughout the length and breadth of their distribution, each adjacent community has had ties to the next via relations of kinship and production. The Inuit of northern Quebec belong to an arctic distribution of similar character and even broader geographic sweep. While the political-territorial relations between Inuit and neighbouring Algonquians in the eastern North American Arctic/Subarctic were often hostile, the boundaries between these primary cultural/language groups were also significantly permeable.

These hunting peoples reflect considerable heterogeneity with regard to culture and history. They have responded in variable ways to distinctive local and regional ecologies, distinctive colonialist interventions, and uneven contemporary opportunities for fashioning "mixed economies" of subsistence and cash and for navigating the increasing complexity of their material and political environments.

The land and water – and associated economic and cultural activities – remain critically important to the social animus and self-definition of all. However, all are located in areas that central governments and corporate capitalist developers regard as resource extractive "frontiers." The Aboriginal homelands and waters examined in our cases were annexed to contemporary "provinces." As such, federal, one or more provincial, and sometimes territorial governments must be dealt with in negotiating rights to land, water, and resources; self-government jurisdiction; and development opportunities. Several groups (Innu, Inuit, and Cree) have homelands and populations that are cloven by provincial and territorial boundaries – a circumstance that significantly complicates the ethno-political identities, organizations, and strategies of these First Nations.

For the past few decades, the pace of intruding industrial "development" projects has accelerated: hydroelectric and mineral extraction affecting Cree, Atikamekw, Innu, and Inuit peoples; extensive forest clear-cutting of Cree, Atikamekw, and Innu territories; low-level military overflights of Innu homelands in Quebec and Labrador; proliferating road networks; and increasing competition with recreational hunting and fishing. These forms of development, which are familiar throughout the Canadian provincial north (Waldram 1988; Ashini 1989; Richardson 1989; Goddard 1991; McCutcheon 1991; Wadden 1991; Ferreira 1992; Gagné 1994; Henriksen 1994; Notzke 1994; Niezen 1998), have caused substantial erosion of Aboriginal resource areas and interference with land-based subsistence and commercial activities, and bring inadequate alternative employment and entrepreneurial opportunities to local communities. All are struggling to a greater or lesser extent with problems of social stress and dysfunction that are a legacy of domination and dependency; all are engaged in determined efforts at social healing and cultural revitalization.

An important trend in the history of the last one-quarter century has been the emergence of regional political organization out of formerly band-organized communities. Opposition to Hydro-Québec's program for hydro-electric development at James Bay, among other factors (see Salisbury 1986), precipitated the relatively vigorous and focused Grand Council of the Crees of Quebec (GCCQ) (as they were then known) in the early 1970s. Something parallel emerged among Quebec Inuit with the formation of Makivik Corporation, though a few so-called dissident communities did not accept the legitimacy of either Makivik or the James Bay and Northern Québec Agreement (JBNQA). The regional organization of the Innu Nation of Labrador includes two communities, separated for many practical political purposes from other Innu communities by the Quebec-Labrador border. On the Quebec side of the border, Innu (Montagnais) communities allied for a number of years with Atikamekw in the Conseil Attikamek-Montagnais (CAM), but they separated before a joint regional comprehensive claim settlement was concluded (see Paul Charest, Chapter 13, this volume).

All groups share a commitment to maintaining themselves within, and caring for, community and homeland. All are determined to make it possible for a substantial proportion of their young people to stay home. To secure the economic means to maintain their populations on their home territories, Aboriginal leaders must convince central governments to increase public spending and/or win a significant share of the resource rents from their home territories.[2] Uncompromising Aboriginal campaigns to block unfavourable development have sometimes been the only way to demonstrate de facto, if not de jure, ownership of the resources in question. And even if rights to a share of royalties, employment, and entrepreneurial benefits from industrial extraction are won, then there still remains the need for the pro-development negotiation of resource extractive projects to be balanced with protection of adequate lands and waters for hunting, fishing, and trapping.

Aboriginal agendas for autonomous development demand a major redefinition of the state-imposed regimes of political jurisdiction and property that now severely restrict the right of Aboriginal societies to regulate or share in the benefits of development. The pathways towards this redefinition are variable. The JBNQA, signed by Quebec Cree and Inuit in 1975, is the longest-standing example, within provincial borders, of a comprehensive modern treaty negotiated with peoples not formerly covered by late nineteenth- and early twentieth-century treaties. The agreement addresses areas that intersect broadly with state authority – lands, resource and environmental management, self-government, financial compensation, economic development, education, health and social services, and so on.

But as many of the chapters in this collection show, the JBNQA has produced mixed results. While this undoubtedly will be true of all comprehensive settlements, including those in exclusively federal territories, the necessity of dealing with both provincial and federal layers of central government introduces special obstacles and complexities.

Geo-economically and geo-politically, most provinces in Canada are similarly constituted. The basic model includes (1) a southern industrial and agricultural region that is quite densely settled by immigrant majorities who have long since displaced Aboriginals from the vast majority of that land base and (2) a northern resource extractive hinterland supporting forestry, mineral and petroleum extraction, and hydroelectricity. In these northern regions, extensive land use by Aboriginal occupants remains (or has remained until very recently) an option – but one under mounting pressure from the aforementioned industrial activities.

The tenurial configuration of provinces is a straightforward expression, in legal proprietary terms, of the power structures imposed on northern Aboriginal peoples. While in the South the great majority of lands are in private freehold, the vast majority of the North is designated Crown land, ostensibly for the general benefit of the provincial "public-at-large." To achieve the erasure of Aboriginal property in northern as well as in southern areas, either late nineteenth- and early twentieth-century treaties of cession and surrender were signed (in Alberta, Saskatchewan, Manitoba, and Ontario) or Aboriginal rights and titles were outright denied and ignored (as in Quebec and Newfoundland-Labrador). In the mid-1970s, the James Bay Cree and northern Quebec Inuit turned surviving Aboriginal title to their partial advantage when they negotiated a comprehensive settlement that was, in several respects, more satisfactory (if only because less ambiguous and more enforceable) than were the historical treaties. The JBNQA represents, for better and for worse, something of a benchmark to such groups as the Labrador and Quebec Innu and Atikamekw who, not having signed historical treaties, have for many years been seeking to come to satisfactory arrangements through comprehensive negotiations.

Redefining Territory

Political survival demands a dual, seemingly contradictory, strategy. On the one hand, First Nations are impelled to enlighten and persuade outsiders about the character and meaning, in Aboriginal cultural terms, of their relationship to homelands and waters. On the other hand, in order to create legal and constitutional space for the defence and autonomous development of their territories, they are forced to negotiate Aboriginal cultural and political landscapes in relation to Euro-Canadian concepts of property and jurisdiction. The culturally defined and locally experienced realities of social and natural "community" are primary; yet, paradoxically, struggling to maintain a political space for them threatens to see them overhauled by European conceptions of sovereignty and ownership (see Susan Drummond, Chapter 4, this volume; Susan Jacobs, Chapter 16, this volume; and Ludger Müller-Wille, Chapter 3, this volume). Still, Aboriginal definitions remain, in significant measure, the raison d'être of northern politics and a major source of legitimacy for Aboriginal rights.

For northern hunting peoples, land and sea spaces are configured as "itineraries" of significant places and events that are networked and registered in sensory experience, knowledge, memory, and imagination (see Sylvie Poirier, Chapter 7, this volume). The hermeneutics of home place, culturally invested and experience-laden,[3] put the lie to the abstract cartography of territorial spaces defined by state boundaries – tools of centralized orchestration and surveillance that function to order capitalist inequalities (Lefebre 1991). Home places (or, in the sense used by Peter Jacobs [Chapter 5, this volume], "landscapes") and state territoriality, then, are readily counterposable tropes for political struggle. In Aboriginal sovereignty, we imagine the defence or creation of political spaces, through reconfigured rights and relationships, in which Aboriginal societies might resist intrusion and subordination. Such spaces are of course hybridized – ordered in part by Aboriginal definitions of home place yet simultaneously transformed in negotiation with mainstream canons of jurisdictional and property rights. The coercive power backing state definitions is beyond direct challenge; hence, Aboriginal conceptions and institutions must gain recognition and legitimacy through terms of agreement. Enlarged recognition of Aboriginal title involves, inevitably, an intersystemic negotiation of meanings.

Euro-intrusions on Aboriginal lands clash with different "modes of experiencing territory, founded on strongly contrasting cultural ontologies, knowledge systems, practices," values, and cartographies (Poirier, Chapter 7, this volume). The perceptions of the North held by Canadian politicians, planners, and most citizens – that it is a wide open, empty terrain; that it is demarcated principally by abstract jurisdictional lines enclosing provincial Crown land; that it is a resource frontier for railways, mining and forestry companies, and energy utilities; that it is available to pioneer settlement wherever feasible – are sharply at odds with the Aboriginal cultural experience of homeland.[4]

The fracturing of home territories by state jurisdictional boundaries is one of the most blatant effects of colonial policies. For many Cree and Innu, as for Inuit, the land and the sea are a continuous scape – in resource use and management, in customary tenure, and in the construction of social identities. But because of the provincial boundary, "the Territory," as defined by the JBNQA, ends at the seacoast. The result of this is that a different regime of Aboriginal rights and titles, as yet unmodifed by treaty, applies to the offshore area. The seashore itself, together with the beds and shores of the principal lakes and rivers in the region, is excluded from even the limited lands set aside by the JBNQA for collective ownership by the Cree and Inuit, along with a 200-foot strip backing the shores of the sea, lakes, and rivers. These exclusions are held by the Crown in the right of Quebec.[5]

The marine space and offshore islands of the Cree and Inuit of northern Quebec are appropriated within the boundaries of the new territorial jurisdiction of Nunavut, carved out of the former Northwest Territories. As Susan Drummond (Chapter 4, this volume) observes, this line does not exist in Aboriginal spatial perception; in the seasonal expansion and contraction of land-fast sea ice; in the migrations of fauna; or in the continuous networks of place names, stories, and environmental knowledge that inform local use and relationships. It can be added that the division between land and sea has no existence for Aboriginal tenure systems. Contiguous land *and* sea spaces, for example, are integral to every coastal hunting territory of the James Bay Cree. Monica Mulrennan and Colin Scott (Chapter 6, this volume) argue that substantial Aboriginal control of coastal and marine resources offers the best prospect for reconnecting the fractured and increasingly redundant jurisdictional domains of territorial, provincial, and federal agencies in the Hudson Bay-James Bay basin.

It cannot be doubted that externally imposed "administrative delimitations and modes of resource development have contributed to transforming and indeed alienating" northern people's relationships to ancestral territories (Poirier, Chapter 7, this volume). And yet, despite "the continual shrinkage of their territories and the decline of resources" (ibid.), for Atikamekw, as for other groups throughout the Subarctic, social links to the land remain shaped by systems of "values, knowledge and practices which derive from hunter society traditions" (ibid.). Regardless of externally imposed administrative delineation and fracturing, and despite industrial damage to their territories and relationships, Algonquian people throughout the Subarctic have maintained and persistently reaffirmed their role as guardians, stewards, and trustees of extended family territories. As one Atikamekw elder at Manawan insists, "even if it's levelled, it will always be my territory" (ibid.).

In some areas where customary territories have fallen into relative disuse there has been a movement to reassert active presence in a variety of ways. Some recent community relocations have been motivated, in part, by the wishes of senior territory stewards to move back to the land in order to protect it (Abel Bosum, Chapter 14, this volume). Hunters' associations throughout the Arctic and Subarctic have been expanding their capacity for environmental monitoring and land management, and they have been reinforcing their authority to speak for the land by supplementing Aboriginal knowledge and practices with modern technologies of remote sensing, geographic information systems, and so on.

In all of this, the regional redefinition of northern First Nations territories is a strategic compromise, both defensive and opportunistic, born of the conflict between Aboriginal and non-Aboriginal powers, perceptions, and agendas. It involves: the containment and dissection of Aboriginal homelands and waters by legally described provincial and territorial boundaries (in which jurisdictional rights are claimed by the state); the emergence of regulatory institutions bound to these new territories; and the counteractive assertion by First Nations of symbols of their own spatial integrity in concert with emergent regional ethnonational identities.

This raises questions of cultural capitulation. Regionalized and newly named homelands, like the Inuit territory of Nunavik, the Cree territory of Eeyou Istchee, or the Innu territory of Nitassinan, indicate a reworking of Aboriginal identities "from autonomous to enmeshed status" (Drummond, Chapter 4, this volume). And yet it is a strategic and subversive capitulation and enmeshment. For these territorial entities – as aggregates of culturally established networks of Aboriginal place names, stories, knowledge, and experience – insist on an appropriation of political space that is in line with local environmental perception, as in the counter-discourse of Inuit place names (Müller-Wille, Chapter 3, this volume). Aboriginal representations of these regions challenge and *deny* the authority and/or legitimacy of provincial and municipal boundaries sketched arbitrarily along high- or low-tide marks or lines of longitude and latitude. They provide the socio-cultural substance of demands for shared sovereignty, to be worked out through intercultural compromise and engagement.

If claims are to be legitimated through the people's cultural definition and social experience of the land, can the pitfall of subordinating rights to legally codified representations of culture be avoided? The goal must be the creation of autonomous spaces within which Aboriginal peoples can give full play to their own cultural dynamics, reproduce their own social orders, and engage in innovations according to their own cultural genius. In its recent judgments, the Supreme Court of Canada has, in some respects, attempted to loosen the dependence of Aboriginal rights on static views of culture, allowing some reinterpretation of culture-based rights according to their practical exercise in modern contexts. But the contradictions of tying rights to specific cultural forms for courtroom adjudication remain troublesome. Where, between hunting with firearms for subsistence and cutting trees with chainsaws for the market, for example, does cultural change run out of bounds, disqualifying Aboriginals from developing their homeland resources?

In the *Delgamuukw* decision, in certain areas a range of non-traditional resource use and development is now explicitly admissible under Aboriginal title.[6] But the Supreme Court now shifts to another device to ensure that Aboriginal title does not obstruct the interests of non-Aboriginals. If Aboriginal title-holders have the right to develop homeland resources, then the Crown has the right to authorize such developments as forestry, mining, and hydro as well as to create new human settlements – in some cases perhaps on condition of Aboriginal consent, in others after consultation and compensation for losses. The Court's intent appears to be to increase pressure on central governments to negotiate in earnest, but power remains far from symmetrical in this procedure, as recent confrontations over commercial forestry and fisheries have shown.

To argue ownership and territorial jurisdiction in this setting (and in policy debate more broadly), Aboriginal peoples must contend with the claims and interests of a much larger non-Aboriginal public beyond (and present as a minority within) their borders. In so doing, they respond to criteria of political legitimacy that transcend their Aboriginality and cultural distinctiveness. These critera include, inter alia, the notions that those who have invested or can invest labour and capital, or who can and will use resources to the economic benefit of society at large, or who will serve most effectively as stewards of essential resources should have primary rights. In arguing their own eligibility according to these criteria, Aboriginal peoples face well-established opposing interests, major asymmetries of wealth and power, and lingering racism.

Resource Management and Development Conflicts

The JBNQA established institutional linkages between Aboriginal resource users/managers and central governments, while promising compensation for losses of traditional resources to external development (Feit 1989). These linkages included, centrally, environmental review and wildlife co-management bodies. Among our cases, through the JBNQA, the Cree and Inuit of northern Quebec are those whose experience with such bodies is longest-standing.

All northern groups, however, have become very familiar with environmental impact assessment procedures, whether pursuant to comprehensive settlements or under federal and provincial legislation. These procedures have become important forums for voicing Aboriginal grievances, forming alliances with environmental and other activist groups, confronting adversaries, and soliciting public support (see Mary Barker, Chapter 12, this volume). They have brought into focus the culturally relative nature of the environmental values and traditions of knowledge involved in gauging past and probable impacts as well as the inevitable politicization of knowledge (scientific and local) when resource development is at issue. They have also sometimes driven corporations, central governments, and Aboriginal parties into more rigorous negotiation of common interests and more proactive attention to issues of regional planning.

In practice, however, environmental impact assessment has demonstrated major limitations. It tends to be undertaken primarily to get specific project approval rather than as part of any sustained or coherent strategy for understanding the composite effects of development in a region. The existence, for nearly one-quarter of a century, of an environmental regime under the JBNQA has not resulted in systematic or adequate strategies for documenting and understanding, let alone countering, the deleterious industrial impacts of hydroelectricity, large-scale forestry, and the extensive development of roads infrastructure; rather, the JBNQA, as "authoritative" and ambiguous text, has become the locus of proliferating claims and counterclaims in the public media – to which enormous energies have been devoted by both Aboriginal and Quebec government parties – contesting the legal necessity of environmental review and the parameters within which it must be conducted (see Donna Patrick and Peter Armitage, Chapter 11, this volume).

The construction of scientific knowledge about environmental impacts, and its bearing on public health policy, is the locus of a subtler politics. The management of the crisis of mercury contamination by governmental, corporate, and research communities has involved a major focus of resources on related research and public information campaigns. This episode reveals a great deal not only about the elusive task of achieving responsible health policy standards, but also about the profound involvement of scientific research in the moral economy of compensation that accompanies the imposition of development projects on Aboriginal communities (see Richard Scott, Chapter 10, this volume).

Co-management of living resources, through structures and processes linking Aboriginal and state authorities, constitutes a contemporary movement in global political and environmental relations. This has come about not only because of the growing international prominence of Aboriginal and human rights concerns, but also because it is increasingly understood that the knowledge and participation of Aboriginal communities is fundamental to devising strategies for sustainable resource use and to coping with environmental changes that are both local and global (see, for example, Brundtland 1987). The last decade has seen the development of numerous wildlife management boards that provide a voice for Aboriginal northerners (e.g., the Beverly and Kaminuriak Caribou Management Board; the Porcupine Caribou Management Board; the Nunavut Wildlife Management Board; the James Bay and Northern Québec Hunting-Fishing-Trapping Coordinating Committee [HFTCC]; and several others). Such experiments are testing the limits of state systems to achieve genuine decentralization, sharing of powers, and the accommodation of Aboriginal knowledge and social priorities.

To date, these limits have proven to be rather narrow. The Quebec government has maintained tight restrictions on the HFTCC's jurisdictional scope. The Cree, for example, have faced provincial stonewalling in their attempts to get forestry issues discussed in the HFTCC. Yet the quality of forest habitat, wildlife harvests, and the ability of Cree to sustain hunting-fishing-trapping as a way of life as guaranteed under the JBNQA are patently interconnected issues, and they can only be managed as such (see Harvey Feit and Robert Beaulieu, Chapter 8, this volume). The Quebec government's eagerness to impose its policies through the manipulation of voting procedures (rather than through genuine efforts at consensus) and through reliance on the threat of ministerial veto have severely limited the HFTCC's value as a joint management body (see Colin Scott and Jeremy Webber, Chapter 9, this volume). JBNQA provisions for protection of the natural resource base, regional economy, and Cree decision making are under continuous pressure to be subordinated to Quebec's "right to develop" and its presumption of sovereignty.

This pressure marks the primary cleavage in contested power between Aboriginal peoples and the state. The state seeks to relegate Aboriginal involvement in environmental assessment and co-management arrangements to consultation without decision-making power and to participation with a subordinate role in decision making. Feit and Beaulieu (Chapter 8, this volume) explore manoeuvres by central governments to gain legitimacy for their policies and decisions through procedures for Aboriginal participation while at the same time limiting more critical forms of public involvement. For their part, the Cree people of Waswanipi have been attempting meaningful participation in forestry decision making since the 1960s. According to Feit and Beaulieu, Cree strategies neither originate with nor simply respond to mechanisms of participation established by governments. They are multi-pronged, including dialogues with foresters, negotiation of special provisions in the JBNQA, direct negotiations with companies, public protests, and court actions. Feit and Beaulieu find that, while the Cree have not achieved broadly effective participation, their autonomy has been maintained and partly enhanced through these initiatives.

The achievement of Aboriginal control in transborder resource management faces obstacles of a special nature (see Mulrennan and Scott, Chapter 6, this volume). In principle, Aboriginal rights to such territories and resources; their institutions of tenure, resource use, and management; and their environmental knowledge present the opportunity to transcend jurisdictional squabbles between central governments and to bring greater coherence to transborder environmental management. This will depend, however, on the resolution of the substantial business left unfinished by contemporary comprehensive settlements, which tend to confine regimes of rights within provincial and territorial boundaries.

Paul Charest (Chapter 13, this volume) offers a detailed perspective on the complexities of negotiating a comprehensive settlement in matters of ownership, control, and management of resources. The protracted and ongoing struggle of the Atikamekw and Montagnais for the viable recognition of their rights illustrates the jurisdictional jealousy of central governments and how, for Aboriginal peoples whose territories have been subject to relatively greater urban and industrial activity (and correspondingly more diverse and entrenched "stakeholder" competition for resources) the obstacles to agreement are compounded. The Atikamekw-Montagnais case also illustrates the cleavages that can develop in Aboriginal political alliances that face government intransigence. For many Aboriginal people, the experience of northern Quebec Cree and Inuit with regard to the unfulfilled terms of the JBNQA reinforces the view that existing Aboriginal rights and titles, unabridged by a comprehensive settlement, may be the wiser option, at least in view of the terms of settlement presently acceptable to central governments. For others, ongoing losses and damage to lands and resources – the result of the difficulty of enforcing Aboriginal rights that are undefined by treaty – are strong pressures to conclude comprehensive agreements, even if unjust concessions are demanded.

It is certainly not clear that resource rights and compensation monies under the JBNQA model provide a sufficient base to support regional social orders and economies. True, the negotiation of jurisdictional and proprietary rights to homeland resources has enabled the Cree and Inuit to gain some relief from the "welfare colonialism" (Paine 1977) and "third world in the first" (Young 1995) conditions that still beset many northern Aboriginal communities. An innovative income support program for Cree hunting/fishing/trapping under the JBNQA (Scott and Feit 1992), together with substantial new wage employment in local and regional government services and in the variety of enterprises stimulated by public expenditure, temporarily created full employment in Cree communities from the late 1970s to the early 1980s. Yet by 1990 unemployment levels had increased markedly, as growth in available jobs failed to keep pace with the large numbers of young Cree coming to working age (LaRusic et al. 1990; Scott 1992; Simard et al. 1996) – a problem that has since worsened. The situation of most Atikamekw and Innu communities, in the absence of comprehensive settlement of their claims, is proportionately more desperate.

This economic crisis occurs in areas from which, typically, there are massive net outflows of wealth in natural resource extraction. The precarious socio-economic circumstances of First Nations that this book addresses have dual, simultaneous origins: (1) erosion of the traditional economy and (2) a paltry share of industrial resource rents resulting from central governments' minimal recognition of Aboriginal property or territorial jurisdiction. The frank reality is that central governments return to northern regions only a tiny fraction of the economic value extracted from them.

Development, then, hinges on enhanced political control of homeland resources and institutions.[7] Adequate recognition of Aboriginal jurisdictional and proprietary rights demands the restructuring of relations with the state on a scale generally surpassing the concessions that central governments have offered in existing comprehensive agreements.

Community, Identity, and the Dynamics of Resistance

The impetus for this restructuring originates in the lives and communities of those who have the most at stake, both materially and culturally. Much in the social dynamics of Aboriginal communities reinforces their capacity for solid resistance and sustained action: the generally egalitarian cast of subarctic and arctic cultures, an ethos of perseverance in the midst of hard circumstance, high respect for individual autonomy and variability combined with a keen sense of responsibility towards extended kin and the wider community, a knack for consensus building, and vibrant oral histories and mythologies that provide alternative standpoints and still afford (the mass media notwithstanding) some insulation against mystificatory capitalist and state ideologies. There are also the intangible but unmistakable reserves of humour and spirit, which, as many outsiders privileged to live in northern Aboriginal communities have come to appreciate, are key resources for the renewal of hope and courage in the midst of suffering.

And local suffering, to greater and lesser extents, is endemic within provincial resource frontiers. Cathrine Degnen (Chapter 19, this volume) and Peter Penashue (Chapter 2, this volume) provide eloquent local testimony to this distress as well as to the grim resolve of many communities to halt the destruction of lands and lives – damage all too commonly inflicted by state authorities and corporate developers. Local testimony holds a particular power. The voices of those who speak, from everyday experience, of the damage inflicted are not easily muted by official excuses. That central governments impose miserly terms on Aboriginal communities and that the consequences of this are local demoralization and despair becomes clear – and is exposed as clearly immoral.

As Penashue explains, political intervention and protest among Innu must be accompanied by measures to deal with their social distress. Degnen shows that community healing, a familiar movement in Canadian Aboriginal communities, is not simply about mending physical ailments or addictions. Healing is a forum for negotiating Innu identity, a search for new social meaning and coherence. Traditional life "in country" (*nutshimit*) provides a symbol for community healing and identity renewal. Similar dynamics are described by Naomi Adelson (Chapter 15, this volume) for the Whapmagoostui Cree. She takes as her focus an annual summer gathering – a ritual of identity and cultural renewal, and a forum for introspection regarding social suffering and healing, that is gaining widespread currency in northern communities. Cree aboriginality, Adelson finds, is at once rooted in contemporary circumstances and enacted through modern interpretations of the past.

The perceptions and experiences of youth provide a particularly active window on processes of identity formation and change. Catherine James's (Chapter 17, this volume) research on teenage pregnancy reveals an increasingly pluralistic notion of Cree identity and culture at Mistissini. Imported ideologies of gender, methods of birth control, the category of adolescence, and expectations associated with the wage economy have all altered "traditions," but youth frequently regard ensuing norms and practices as reconcilable with "being Cree." James finds that cultural survival is less the preservation of the traditional than the creation of Cree, or Aboriginal, approaches to the world; and she makes the crucially important point that cultural loss, or threats to cultural survival, occur not when cultures change but when the community is powerless to debate and control the changes occurring.

Self-determination requires that communities coalesce as functional collectivities able to give pragmatic institutional shape to their definitions of culture and identity. Abel Bosum (Chapter 14, this volume) discusses how one Cree community in Quebec, Oujé-Bougoumou, came together and charted a course of collective action after years of dispersal for the purpose of establishing a new village. Bosum recounts the long process of political negotiations, much of it under his leadership, that the band pursued in order to secure a viable agreement from the provincial and federal governments. Community solidarity and political participation were paramount throughout the protracted negotiations, and Bosum sheds light on both the consensual processes of unity and the tactics that were effective in dealing with central governments.

"Community" is a quality that cannot be taken for granted. As Hedda Schuurman (Chapter 20, this volume) shows, settlements created through both voluntary and involuntary relocation and sedentarization do not automatically function as communities. Several formerly distinct territorial hunting groups comprise present-day Sheshatshiu (also correctly rendered "Sheshatshit"), and abrupt social changes have, in some regards, entrenched the divisions between them. As Adrian Tanner (Chapter 21, this volume) also shows, the principles of social exchange between life in the settlement and life in country demand quite a fundamental reworking within the context of regional ethno-national polity.

The role of women has been pivotal in building community, maintaining solidarity against the invasion of Aboriginal lands and resource bases, and sustaining political action while coping with the challenge of social healing. Susan Jacobs (Chapter 16, this volume) examines a setting within which changes to the life of the eastern Cree community of Chisasibi are both fundamental and rapid: relocation to a new town, deterioration in natural surroundings due to hydroelectric projects, and rapidly evolving institutional orders both locally and regionally. Cree women, like Innu women, have assumed central responsibility for rebuilding families and community while also, increasingly, occupying executive positions in local and regional governance.

Suffering, resistance, and the drive for self-determination present Aboriginal communities with a series of paradoxes and, as Adrian Tanner (Chapter 21, this volume) refers to them, "double binds." One such conundrum is that counter-hegemonic resistance, so obviously essential for cultural survival, demands strategies that tend to mirror hegemonic forms and risk cooptation. This risk is perhaps most clearly illustrated where authority for existing state institutions is transferred to, or shared with, Aboriginal communities.[8] In Nunavik, Josée Lavoie (Chapter 18, this volume) finds that provincial health planners envision northern health care as a subset of the Quebec system, while Inuit perceive it as a vehicle that will enable them to transcend conventional health objectives. Each party uses the discourse of self-determination in community health to negotiate divergent positions, with the result that it both promotes and limits community self-determination.

Indeed, the fact that Aboriginal practices do not move towards state-endorsed institutions becomes an aspect of the Aboriginal community's "dysfunctionality" (Tanner, Chapter 21, this volume). In recent decades, this particular double bind has fed into a variety of personal dysfunctionalities, such as addiction and domestic violence, which, in turn, hinder (while making all the more apparent the need for) assertive self-determination. Hence the urgency with which healing and self-government are pursued in tandem. The power of the state, however, remains; the goal of self-government forces a choice between a sovereignty that is largely rhetorical and symbolic or subordination to state structures. Tanner poses the fundamental question: is self-government within the framework of the state ever reconcilable with the ideal of self-determination? Innu, in common with other northern groups, seek a radical redefinition and renewal of community – one based on Aboriginal cultural values yet acceptable to the wider society. If that acceptance is to entail anything other than the capitulation of Aboriginal ways of life, then the relationship between the state (and its mainstream economic interests) and Aboriginal peoples must be radically reinvented.

Notes

1 Cultural invention and the creation of social and cultural variety are ongoing, but, as Asad (1992, 333) comments, this variety "everywhere responds to, and is managed by, cate-

gories brought into play by modern forces." The conditions within which cultural difference is generated, the ideologies of economic growth and progress to which it responds, now involve the ubiquitous interaction of local and global forces.

2 Asch (1987) discusses the relative merits of resource rents for economic development.

3 For example, see Basso (1988, 1996); Cruikshank (1990); Jackson (1995); Layton (1995); Morphy (1993, 1995); Myers (1991); Povinelli (1993); Rose (1992); Thorton (1997).

4 Willems-Braun (1997) provides an instructive portrait of such contrasts.

5 Charest (this volume) notes similar exclusions in the proposed settlement of Atikamekw-Montagnais claims (i.e., the beds and banks of rivers and streams, lakes, and reservoirs).

6 However, by injecting the proviso that Aboriginal rights cannot, by definition, be exercised in such a way as to undermine the cultural connection of an Aboriginal group to its land, the Court retains a toehold in its anachronistic role as arbiter of rights-compatible culture change. And more Aboriginal rights in areas no longer claimable as Aboriginal title lands have been tied more explicitly than ever, in decidedly fragmentary fashion, to culturally distinctive Aboriginal institutions.

7 This view is corroborated by research elsewhere in Aboriginal North America. Cornell and Kalt (1990, 121), for example, conclude that political sovereignty is a fundamental precondition for building viable economies: "To the extent that federal [United States] policy reinforces the legal, political and institutional foundations of tribal sovereignty, it increases the chances that tribes can find their own pathways out of poverty."

8 For, as Kulchyski (1994, 121) sees it, "regardless of the level of power provided to Aboriginal governments, every decision that is made following the dominant logic, in accordance with the hierarchical and bureaucratic structures of the established order, will take Aboriginal peoples further away from their own culture. Every decision that is made in the form appropriate to traditional cultures will be another step in the life of that culture."

References

Asad, T. 1992. "Conscripts of Western Civilization," in *Dialectical Anthropology: Essays in Honor of Stanley Diamond*, Vol. 1, 333-51. Gainesville: University Press of Florida.

Asch, M. 1987. "Capital and Economic Development: A Critical Appraisal of the Recommendations of the Mackenzie Valley Pipeline Commission." In *Native People, Native Lands: Canadian Indians, Inuit and Metis*, ed. B. Cox, 232-40. Ottawa: Carleton University Press.

–. 1988. *Home and Native Land: Aboriginal Rights and the Canadian Constitution*. Scarborough: Nelson.

–. 1993. "Aboriginal Self-Government and Canadian Constitutional Identity: Building Reconciliation." In *Ethnicity and Aboriginality: Case Studies in Ethnonationalism*, ed. M. Levin, 29-52. Toronto: University of Toronto Press.

–, ed. 1997. *Aboriginal and Treaty Rights in Canada: Essays on Law, Equality and Respect for Difference*. Vancouver: UBC Press.

Ashini, D. 1989. "David Confronts Goliath: The Innu of Ungava versus the NATO Alliance." In *Drumbeat: Anger and Renewal in Indian Country*, ed. B. Richardson, 43-70. Toronto: Summerhill Press/Assembly of First Nations.

Basso, K. 1988. "'Speaking with Names': Language and Landscape among the Western Apache." *Cultural Anthropology* 3, 2: 99-130.

–. 1996. "Wisdom Sits in Places: Notes on a Western Apache Landscape." In *Senses of Place*, ed. S. Feld and K. Basso, 53-90. Santa Fe: School of American Research Press.

Beckett, J. 1988. "The Past in the Present, the Present in the Past: Constructing a National Aboriginality." In *Past and Present: The Construction of Aboriginality*, ed. J. Beckett, 191-217. Canberra: Aboriginal Studies Press.

Berkes, F., P. George, and R. Preston. 1991. "Co-management: The Evolution in Theory and Practice of the Joint Administration of Living Resources." *Alternatives* 18, 2: 12-18.

Brundtland, G.H. 1987. "Empowering Vulnerable Groups." In *Our Common Future: The World Commission on Environment and Development*, 114-17. Oxford: Oxford University Press.

Cornell, S., and J.P. Kalt. 1990. "Pathways from Poverty: Economic Development and Institution-Building on American Indian Reservations." *American Indian Culture and Research Journal* 14, 1: 89-125.

Cruikshank, J. 1990. "Getting the Words Right: Perspectives on Naming and Places in Athapaskan Oral History." *Arctic Anthropology* 27, 1: 52-65.

Culhane, D. 1998. *The Pleasure of the Crown: Anthropology, Law and First Nations*. Burnaby, BC: Talon.

Duhaime, G. 1990. "La chasse inuit subventionnée: Tradition et modernité." *Recherches sociographiques* 31, 1: 45-62.

Dyck, N., ed. 1985. *Indigenous Peoples and the Nation-State: Fourth World Politics in Canada, Australia, and Norway*. St. John's: Institute of Social and Economic Research, Memorial University of Newfoundland.

–, and J. Waldram, eds. 1993. *Anthropology, Public Policy and Native Peoples in Canada*. Montreal/Kingston: McGill-Queen's University Press.

Elias, D. 1991. *Development of Aboriginal People's Communities*. North York/Lethbridge: Captus Press/Centre for Aboriginal Management Education and Training.

Feit, H. 1988. "Self-Management and State-Management: Forms of Knowing and Managing Northern Wildlife." In *Traditional Knowledge and Renewable Resource Management*, ed. M. Freeman and L. Carbyn, 72-91. Edmonton: Boreal Institute for Northern Studies.

–. 1989. "James Bay Cree Self-Government and Land Management." In *We Are Here: Politics of Aboriginal Land Tenure*, ed. E. Wilmsen, 68-98. Berkeley: University of California Press.

Ferreira, D. 1992. "Oil and Lubicons Don't Mix: A Land Claim in Northern Alberta in Historical Perspective." *Canadian Journal of Native Studies* 12, 1: 1-35.

Freeman, M., and L. Carbyn, eds. 1988. *Traditional Knowledge and Renewable Resource Management in Northern Regions*. Edmonton: University of Alberta Press.

Gagné, M.-A. 1994. *A Nation within a Nation: Dependency and the Cree*. Montreal: Black Rose Books.

Goddard, J. 1991. *Last Stand of the Lubicon Cree*. Vancouver: Douglas and McIntyre.

Haig-Brown, C. 1995. *Taking Control: Power and Contradiction in First Nations Adult Education*. Vancouver: UBC Press.

Henriksen, G. 1994. "The Mushuau Innu of Labrador: Self-Government, Innovation and Socio-cultural Continuity." *Proactive* 13, 1: 2-22.

Jackson, M. 1995. *At Home in the World*. Durham: Duke University Press.

Johnson, M., ed., 1992. *Lore: Capturing Traditional Environmental Knowledge*. Ottawa: Dene Cultural Institute, International Development Research Centre.

Kulchyski, Peter. 1994. *Unjust Relations: Aboriginal Rights in Canadian Courts*. Toronto: Oxford University Press.

LaRusic, I., S. Bouchard, A. Penn, T. Brelsford, and J.-G. Deschênes. 1990. *Socio-Economic Profile of the Cree Communities in Northern Quebec, 1989*. Produced for the Grand Council of the Cree/Cree Regional Authority by Norman D. Hawkins and Associates, Inc., Montreal.

Layton, R. 1995. "Relating to the Country in the Western Desert." In *The Anthropology of Landscape: Perspectives on Place and Space*, ed. E. Hirsch and M. O'Hanlon, 210-31. Oxford: Clarendon Press.

Lefebre, H. 1991. *The Production of Space*. Trans. Donald Nicholson-Smith. Oxford: Blackwell.

McCutcheon, S. 1991. *Electric Rivers: The Story of the James Bay Project*. Montreal: Black Rose Books.

Morphy, H. 1993. "Colonialism, History and the Construction of Place: The Politics of Landscape in Northern Australia. In *Landscape: Politics and Perspectives*, ed. B. Bender, 205-43. Oxford: Berg.

–. 1995. "Landscape and the Production of the Ancestral Past." In *The Anthropology of Landscape: Perspectives on Place and Space*, ed. E. Hirsch and M. O'Hanlon, 184-209. Oxford: Clarendon Press.

Myers, F. 1991 [1986]. *Pintupi Country, Pintupi Self: Sentiment, Place, and Politics among Western Desert Aborigines*. Berkeley: University of California Press.

Niezen, R. 1993. "Telling a Message: Cree Perceptions of Custom and Administration." *Canadian Journal of Native Studies* 13, 2: 221-50.

–. 1998. *Defending the Land: Sovereignty and Forest Life in James Bay Cree Society*. Toronto: Allyn and Bacon.

Notzke, C. 1994. *Aboriginal Peoples and Natural Resources in Canada*. North York/Lethbridge: Captus Press/Centre for Aboriginal Management Education and Training.

O'Neil, J. 1993. "Report from the Round Table Rapporteur." In *The Path to Healing: Report of the National Round Table on Aboriginal Health and Social Issues* (Royal Commission on Aboriginal Peoples). Ottawa: Ministry of Supply and Services.

Paine, Robert. 1977. *The White Arctic: Anthropological Essays on Tutelage and Ethnicity.* St. John's: Institute of Social and Economic Research, Memorial University.

Pinkerton, E. 1989. *Co-operative Management of Local Fisheries: New Directions for Improved Management and Community Development.* Vancouver: UBC Press.

Povinelli, E. 1993. *Labor's Lot: The Power, History and Culture of Aboriginal Action.* Chicago: University of Chicago Press.

–. 1998. "The State of Shame: Australian Multiculturalism and the Crisis of Indigenous Citizenship." *Critical Inquiry* 24: 575-610.

Richardson, B. 1989. "Wrestling with the Canadian System: A Decade of Lubicon Frustration." In *Drumbeat: Anger and Renewal in Indian Country*, ed. B. Richardson, 231-64. Toronto: Summerhill Press/Assembly of First Nations.

Rose, D. 1992. *Dingo Makes Us Human: Life and Lands in an Australian Aboriginal Culture.* Cambridge: Cambridge University Press.

Ross, R. 1992. *Dancing with a Ghost: Exploring Indian Reality.* Markham, ON: Octopus Books/Butterworths.

Salisbury, R. 1986. *A Homeland for the Cree: Regional Development in James Bay, 1971-1981.* Montreal/Kingston: McGill-Queen's University Press.

Scott, C. 1992. "Political Spoils or Political Largesse? Regional Development in Northern Quebec, Canada and Australia's Northern Territory." In *Centre for Aboriginal Economic Policy Research Discussion Paper Series*, no. 27, 38 pp. Canberra: The Australian National University, Centre for Aboriginal Economic Policy Research.

–. 1993. "Custom, Tradition and the Politics of Culture in Aboriginal Self-Government." In *Anthropology, Public Policy and Native Peoples in Canada*, ed. N. Dyck and J. Waldrum, 311-33. Montreal/Kingston: McGill-Queen's University Press.

Scott, C., and H. Feit. 1992. *The Income Security Program for Cree Hunters: Ecological, Social and Economic Effects.* PAD Monograph Series. Montreal: Programme in the Anthropology of Development, McGill University.

Simard, J.-J., J.-F. Langlais, J.-P. Garneau, M. Gaudreault, S. Proulx, and R. Robitaille. 1996. *Tendances nordiques: les changements sociaux 1970-1990 chez les Cris et les Inuit du Québec.* 2 vols. Québec: Groupe d'études inuit et circumpolaires, Université Laval.

Slattery, B. 1987. "Understanding Aboriginal Rights." *Canadian Bar Review* 66: 727-83.

Tanner, A. 1993. "History and Culture in the Generation of Ethnic Nationalism." In *Ethnicity and Aboriginality: Case Studies in Ethnonationalism*, ed. M. Levin, 75-96. Toronto: University of Toronto Press.

Thorton, T. 1997. "Know Your Place: The Organization of Tlingit Geographic Knowledge." *Ethnology* 36, 4: 295-307.

Tully, J. 1995. *Strange Multiplicity: Constitutionalism in an Age of Diversity.* Cambridge: Cambridge University Press.

Usher, P. 1996. *Contemporary Aboriginal Land, Resource, and Environment Regimes: Origins, Problems, and Prospects.* Unpublished report prepared for the Royal Commission on Aboriginal Peoples, Land, Resource and Environment Project. Ottawa: Royal Commission on Aboriginal Peoples.

Wadden, M. 1991. *Nitassinan: The Innu Struggle to Reclaim Their Homeland.* Vancouver: Douglas and McIntyre.

Waldram, J. 1988. *As Long as the Rivers Run: Hydroelectric Development and Native Communities in Western Canada.* Winnipeg: University of Manitoba Press.

Weinstein, M., A. Tanner, and D. Denton. 1993. *An Inhabited Wilderness: The Land Use of the Whapmagoostui Cree of Great Whale River, Québec.* Whapmagoostui Band Council/Grand Council of the Crees of Quebec.

Willems-Braun, Bruce. 1997. "Colonial Vestiges: Representing Forest Landscapes on Canada's West Coast." *BC Studies* 112: 5-37.

Young, E. 1995. *Third World in the First.* London and New York: Routledge.

2
Healing the Past, Meeting the Future
Peter Penashue

The Labrador Innu represent less than one-fifth of the total population of 10,000 Innu on the Labrador Quebec Peninsula. The 1,500 Labrador Innu include the population of both the communities of Sheshatshiu and Davis Inlet (Utshimassit) and are represented by the Innu Nation. The larger population of Innu in Quebec are represented by the Counseil Attikamek-Montagnais (CAM). In 1927 the Privy Council decided to draw a line between what was Quebec and what was Newfoundland, thus ensuring that most of the Innu population ended up in Quebec. Their second language is French, and we speak English as our second language. At some point the whole Innu population would have encompassed the area of James Bay and what is now known as Labrador. There are a lot of similarities in our customs, language, and spiritual beliefs. At one point we were one big nation, but because of the way these boundaries were drawn we are now separated by linguistic and provincial boundaries.

Questions of Federal and Provincial Jurisdiction

In 1949, when Newfoundland joined Confederation, bringing Labrador with it, there was a discussion as to how to deal with the Innu population in Labrador. At that time, the federal government wanted to transfer the responsibility for Aboriginal peoples to the Province of Newfoundland. Newfoundland and the federal government decided that they would implement this policy, which had recently been developed but had not yet been implemented in other regions. So, as Aboriginal peoples, we came under Newfoundland's jurisdiction. We were not included in the Indian Act, and there was no reserve system. Under the Canadian Constitution, everyone in Newfoundland is a citizen of that province. This includes Aboriginal people. Thus there is no special recognition for Aboriginal people, and this results in all kinds of problems.

Newfoundland and Canada signed funding agreements to provide supplementary financing for services that the province agreed to provide to the

Innu population. Newfoundland enjoyed this agreement because it benefited from the transfer of funds. In other words, it was able to use federal funds to support everyone in Labrador, not just the Aboriginal people. So the provincial government turned what was supposed to be an Aboriginal program into a Labrador program.

Under this program we were educated in the Newfoundland system. The Innu had adopted Roman Catholicism before this, and we were under a Roman Catholic School Board. The way in which Newfoundland and the Department of Indian Affairs set up the education system and social programs effectively destroyed the spirit of the Innu people. We believe that by providing "free money" under social services, the provincial and federal governments damaged our self-esteem and self-worth. They created dependency. Under the traditional Roman Catholic education system the provincial government was able to teach whatever it wanted to the Innu people. So, in our view, it controlled what we thought and how we perceived our world. Many people believe that, through this form of social engineering, the federal and provincial governments attempted to make Innu people become full Newfoundlanders under the Constitution. Of course, this attempt has been a total failure; it has not worked and the result has been social chaos and collapse within our society. The province maintains that we are just citizens of Newfoundland. So we were caught because there were no special funding programs for Aboriginal peoples.

Social Problems

The Roman Catholic Church played an important role in this social experiment of which we were a part. The Church, in my view, condemned our culture, our language, and our way of life. Today there are elders who say that when they went to sit down to play the drum and to dance the priest would come and tell them that they were worshipping Satan, and he would take the drum. When the priest condemned these traditions the Innu people were very humiliated and very scared. So a lot of people stopped practising these traditions, and of course the priest became a respected person and continued to control all these practices.

Due to the degree of social collapse we are facing, we have come to the point where we need to identify the causes of the current problems in our community. We believe that the Church and the government attempted to change our people; this being the case, they are responsible for creating our problems. Our responsibility now is to address these problems.

In the last few years we have been working on trying to educate the Innu people and to change their attitudes towards and perspectives on many things. Now people are starting to share things that they were afraid to talk about before. For example, a friend of mine who is now about thirty-two had been sexually abused by a priest when he was seven years old. But, because of the power the Church had in our communities, when this boy came home and told his parents what had happened, his mother said, "Don't be crazy, this is a priest you are talking about!" He did not discuss the matter again until last year. This is an example of the type of power these priests had. The teachers coming from Newfoundland and other places also influenced us, and there was a lot of sexual and physical abuse for which these people must take responsibility. We have to take responsibility for changing the social problems with which, as a result of these past experiences, we are now faced.

We have been trying to change the school system so that we can start to change attitudes. Then we will be able to teach history and some of the facts of the past and so explain why we are in our current situation. I was taught to believe that Innu people were inferior and that I would have to change if I wanted to fit into this new world. If children are taught this constantly, they will start believing it; and this is what has been happening and continues to happen. So, in the end, what you have is a boy or girl, a man or a woman, who is absolutely confused as to who he or she is. These people do not fit into the Canadian environment and they do not fit into their own. They are somewhere in between. Most of us believe that is why we have children who sniff gas. That is why we have a very high rate of sexual abuse. That is why our society is falling apart on a large scale.

People are not generally bad. As Innu people we are not born bad. What happens is that something in our life experience affects the way we think and the way we look at things. If we suffer from a lot of pain and refuse to look at it, then we have look for ways to escape from it. So we turn to bingo, gambling, drinking, drugs, and gas sniffing. The Innu, like people everywhere, do not do this because they love it; they do it because they are runners. Kids who sniff gas, given the choice, would choose to drink alcohol. But because they are children and do not have access to alcohol, they turn to gas. Gas is readily available, can be stolen in the middle of the night, and gives you a high. If you say to a young person in Davis Inlet, "Look, what you are doing is dangerous," he or she might say to you, "Well, I want to die."

Media Attention

Last year, around January or February, a few people in Davis Inlet took a camcorder and videotaped kids sniffing gas, thus capturing the effects of gas sniffing. We discussed whether or not we should release that film to the media. Some of us were worried that we would be exploiting the children, and others were worried that if we did not do something soon, nobody would listen to us and then we would never have access to the resources needed to tackle these problems. We also knew that releasing the video to the media would give us access to a larger audience, so in the end we decided to release it. That is what started the whole media event that was centred around Davis Inlet. The community really opened itself up to the Canadian public, and it was very hard to do this because it allowed people to put us down. This was especially true in nearby communities like Goose Bay, where racism towards the Innu is already quite serious. But because we exposed ourselves in this way to Canada, Europe, and the world, it is now possible for us to address a larger audience and so advance our cause. We have had invitations to speak at the United Nations and have had ministers return our calls. People have started responding to our issues.

A lot of young people are now starting to get involved in fighting for change. When we occupied the outside of the Parliament buildings to protest against low-level flying, the young people were saying how empowered they felt. If they did something in Davis Inlet, they would be thrown in jail. But at the Parliament buildings they were breaking the laws and could not be arrested individually because they were working together as a group. There was a real strength in that. If one person were to be arrested, then we would all have to be arrested. We have also learned to use the media to our advantage – well, most of the time it is to our advantage. We know that the general Canadian population does not want to see elders being thrown in jail, especially for protesting at the Parliament buildings. So we had elders with us. We knew that young people would go to jail much more quickly than would the elders. We then agreed to be prepared to spend at least three weeks in jail so that our plight would become an issue and we would not lose media coverage.

Young people from Davis Inlet and Sheshatshiu learned a lot from the protests against low-level flying. We started learning that if we managed the media well, and if our actions were powerful and we worked together as a group, then we could make a difference. For example, a few years ago in Sheshatshiu there was a logging company that came in and started logging. We just blocked it and said: "Look, arrest us all." There were elders and young people there. So the logging companies just pulled their equipment out. The government ordered them out; they did not want to arrest us and thus have to deal with the public relations disaster that such an act would have created.

Seven Point Plan

We put out a plan in response to the publicity generated around the problems surrounding Davis Inlet, and we called it the Seven Point Plan. This plan outlines how we want to address the social problems of the Innu people. We discuss the need for a cultural renewal centre, which is essentially a treatment facility for our people. We emphasize the need to teach people to be proud of who they are, to learn the facts about their history. We want to begin counselling services for groups, families, and individuals. We want to begin a process of reconciliation with people in the community. After more than forty years of difficulties, people have begun to fight with each other because there are deeper issues under the surface, and these are not being talked about.

Relocation of Davis Inlet

The Seven Point Plan also addresses the need for relocation. The population of Davis Inlet is 550. When the Innu were asked by the government to move to the present site it was 1967, and the community was not consulted. The only people involved in making the decision were the government representatives, the missionary, and the chief. The government promised to supply better housing, with water and sewer facilities. In all those years since 1967 none of the promises has been fulfilled. Now the Innu people are saying: "What happened to all these promises made by the government of Newfoundland?"

The present site of Davis Inlet does not have any land for the necessary expansion of the community. It is not suitable for water and sewer, and there is no water to supply the community. The people of Davis Inlet are hunters and feel as though they are prisoners on the island because, during break-up and freeze up, they have no way of getting to the mainland. This has led to a lot of drinking problems and suicides. Almost all the deaths since we moved have been alcohol-related: everyone has lost close friends and relatives from alcohol-related violence and suicides. About three years ago, there was a house fire in February; it took the lives of six children, all under the age of ten. Their parents had been drinking and had left them on their own. That is when the Innu realized that they had to stop for awhile and think about the problems facing Davis Inlet. So we asked the federal government for money for an inquiry. It turned us down, and we did it on our own. From this inquiry came the book *Gathering Voices*. The process of conducting this inquiry helped bring all our problems into the light. The Innu want to leave this island and leave behind the losses and the problems that have plagued them here.

The community wants to be relocated to Sango Bay, which is about fifteen kilometres away from the present site. Because the community chose to move fifteen kilometres away from the island to the mainland, where there is water and the capacity for sewer facilities, the government talks about isolation! The government's view is that we should not move the community to an isolated spot. It has suggested that we move the community to Goose Bay in order to merge with a larger urban centre, where there would be more economic opportunities for people. However, we believe that, this time, the people, who have already suffered from several forced relocations, have to decide where they want to move.

In 1948 the Innu of the Davis Inlet region were moved to the Inuit village of Nutak, where they were encouraged to work with the Inuit to develop the fishery. However, this was an arrangement that neither the Innu nor the Inuit liked. The Innu did not like the coastal environment of this northern area, and, after a while, they just disappeared, showing up five months later in Old Davis Inlet. In 1967 they were moved from the mainland site of Old Davis Inlet to the present site. In 1969 some of the people were moved to Sheshatshiu. It is our view that this time people must decide for themselves. The choices that the government made for them in the past were all wrong. So now the federal government is saying, "Okay, we will look at Sango Bay, unless a technical study says there is no water or something like that." The provincial government says that it cannot get involved. But behind closed doors the federal government is saying that it wants the province in on this. So it is trying to please the provincial government and bring it in line so that it will not jeopardize the relocation process.

Negotiating with the Federal Government

When I met with the minister of Indian Affairs a few months ago in Halifax, he put forward a document that he wanted to take to Cabinet before coming to Davis Inlet. There were some good things in the document as well as a lot of things we did not like, so we made some suggestions. He appeared to take down our suggestions, but in the end the document went to Cabinet unchanged. So we told the government that this was a document of the federal government rather than a negotiated document, so we should not be expected to sign anything. The document does address some aspects of the Seven Point Plan we put forward, so if we had given them a flat "No" they could have killed us in terms of publicity; instead, we said, "This is your document, let's try to work with it, but don't expect us to sign it." Behind closed doors the minister of Indian Affairs said, "Look, you have got to sign it, we want you to sign it." They were really pressuring us to sign that document. They said they would not be able to implement it if we did not sign it. What they really wanted was to have us sign the document in front of the television cameras so that they could say, "We've got their concurrence regarding the problems addressed, let's move on." Though there is nothing stopping us from proceeding to work with the document now, there are a lot of political currents behind the scenes.

This document addressed several issues. It addressed the issues of jurisdiction, and it brought us under the Indian Act. In 1979 we were caught in the tension of federal-provincial politics, and we decided that we wanted to be placed under the Indian Act. But the federal government refused our request at that time. In 1987, when the issue of low-level flying was front and centre, the federal government wrote us a letter and said: "You want the Indian Act? Okay, here it is. Just sign it and we will give it to you." We said "No" then because, at that time, it was something that other Native groups were talking about and trying to get out of.

Again, we put more pressure on the federal government last year when we went to Ottawa and occupied the area outside the Parliament buildings. It responded by saying, "We'll give you all the things you want if you just accept the Indian Act." We said, "No, we are not going to accept the Indian Act." Now the document that came up from the federal government [in February 1994] states that we do not have to be under the Indian Act and that it will give us all the programs and services.

There is a lot of work involved in establishing your own foundations and starting to work as a community. I have found it to be a very difficult process. Many people have gone to jail over the protests on the runways. It has been hard at Parliament, with the high levels of stress involved in negotiations, but I think it is paying off. As Abel Bosum has previously stated, "When there is action there is a reaction." But there is always more work to be done.

We are going to be relocated to Sango Bay. I have no doubt that this will happen, but it will take some work. We have learned a lot over the last ten years. One of the things that we have learned is that you never get anything for free. However beautifully we argue our point of view, that is not enough. What we have learned is that if we want it badly enough we have to shake the system. For example, a few years ago, as a result of the low-level flying protests, we started to get non-insured health benefits even though we did not fall under the Indian Act. When we began stirring up problems for the government, it started offering us things. That is why I believe we always have to take a stand, and that is why I am very confident that relocation is going to happen.

Meeting Our Future

Relocation on its own will not solve the social problems of Davis Inlet. It will solve water and housing shortages, and it will solve employment problems for five or six years. There will also be other spinoffs from economic development. Social problems, however, are a different issue. There is still a lot of work that needs to be done in this area, and we are now taking responsibility for that. The funding for a proposed treatment centre, or cultural renewal centre, has been approved for two years. But that is not enough; we need funding for at least ten years. Nevertheless, work will begin with about ten families. People who sniff gas or drink are usually in a lot of pain. These addictions are just symptoms of larger problems. You have to go deeper to find the real problems.

One of the saddest things is that some of our people have no respect for themselves or their families. Within the last three years the social development work that we have done has had some really positive impacts, and I can see changes taking place in the people. More and more people are sobering up, and more and more people are taking responsibility for healing themselves.

Three years ago, when I got elected as president of the Innu Nation, I had my first meeting in Davis Inlet. David Nui was the vice-president, and we could not even have our meeting because so many people there were drunk. Now when you go to Davis Inlet it is unusual to see any person who is drunk during our meetings. Things are changing because people are taking responsibility for their problems and their pain.

Going into the country provides great therapy for people. In Sheshatshiu, during the spring and fall about half the population go into the country. This is a really positive thing to do – to go out on the land and practise a way of life that we understand, surrounded by friends and family members of our choice. This time is very important to us. The government would like us to build institutional treatment facilities because this is a standard type of service – one with which they are familiar and which they could easily provide. But we have stated that what we want is a country program, a cultural renewal centre, a place in the country where people can go. We are generally hunters anyway, so we know what we are doing. We are very fortunate that people still want to go into the country and practise this way of life. So many of our problems are community-based, and going into the country gives us an opportunity to deal with them in a more effective way.

In addition to working on establishing a cultural renewal centre for counselling, and a place where people can reconnect with their culture and spirituality, we also want to change our education system so that it reflects our culture and values. The issue of sexual abuse is really one of the most difficult. There is still a lot of anger in this area. We are trying to bring families together who are dealing with incest so that we can stop the cycles of violence. We have approached the government about diversion programs so that we can avoid channelling everything through the courts. We want these problems dealt with in the community, where we can actually start the healing process. If someone does not want to use this healing process, then she or he is free to go through the court system. Some cases that are currently being dealt with in the community were not even raised with the courts. We felt that we could deal with the problems in our community. We want to avoid being constantly put under the policies of the government and the Church. It is as though they have taken our souls, and now we have lost our values and our vision. Many people say they do not want to get up in the morning because there is nothing to get up for. People end up fighting their own loved ones, their families, their children. I grew up in that type of violent environment and so have many other people in my community and in this country. I think we have learned now that when people are oppressed, when people are not involved in determining the direction of their lives, they are deeply damaged.

Note

This chapter, transcribed by Hedda Schuurman, is based on a presentation delivered by Peter Penashue at an AGREE workshop in Oujé-Bougoumou in March 1994. Penashue was then, and is now, president of the Innu Nation, the political body for the 1,500 Innu who reside in Labrador. Over the past ten years the Innu Nation has been working with the communities of Davis Inlet and Sheshatshiu to bring about change through political interventions, protests, and efforts to deal with desperate social problems. The relocation of the Davis Inlet people to Sango Bay is one attempt to take local control and institute needed changes, including programs to address economic dependency and social distress (which accompanied the transition from nomadic to sedentary life) through community healing and reconnecting with the land and cultural traditions.

Part 2
(Re)defining Territory

3

Shaping Modern Inuit Territorial Perception and Identity in the Quebec-Labrador Peninsula

Ludger Müller-Wille

In Canada, as elsewhere, toponymy mirrors the country's cultural history and socio-economic and political structures, and it represents the various aspirations and goals of the different components that have shaped this particular spatial entity. The Canadian toponymic landscape, along with its glossary, is continuously evolving and thus also functions as a barometer for rapid changes that have occurred throughout the Canadian territory. Since the 1960s, these changes relate predominantly to the assertion of cultural and territorial rights by either Aboriginal or Québécois populations, using, among other elements, toponyms as strong cultural and political symbols to express distinctness.

These socio-spatial processes have been given increasing attention in the highlighting of relationships between place or space and regional identity (cf. Paasi 1995, 1996; Poole 1994). In most cases newly emerging regional identities are a reaction to socio-economic and political changes that require a reassessment of one's own spatial position. New terms and names quite often become a focal point of the impact of these changes on the particular positions of local residents relating to land, power, and control.

The northern regions of the Quebec-Labrador peninsula in arctic Canada serve here as an example of how territorial perception and identity have been shaped by different approaches to the issues of rights to land. On the one hand, the Aboriginal inhabitants, the Inuit, base their position on inalienable rights obtained and maintained through their close relationship with the land (cf. Csonka 1995; Collignon 1996), defining their cultural and regional identity through the symbolism of Nunavik, a newly created spatial concept (Gordon 1993; Müller-Wille 1987). On the other hand, the emerging national identity of Quebec, whose judicial territory within Canada includes Inuit lands, also seeks its assertion and recognition through toponymic symbolism by expanding its linguistic inclusion of places and spaces in Nouveau-Québec (cf. Brochu 1962). The success of such processes, as demonstrated here by the case of Nunavik, lies ultimately with the people who shape their own identities as related to culture, language, and land (cf. Nieminen 1998).

Concept of Land

As a framework for the discussion of territorial perception and identity I have deliberately chosen the rather broad theme of the relationship between humankind and land or, rather, space; that is, the attachment and commitment of people to the area around them. By "land" I mean the space around us, not only the actual landmass or territory occupied and used by people, but also water, ice, and air – all spatial dimensions that humankind has integrated into its realm of activities. By definition, there are many aspects of land that affect human beings.

I intend to focus on the cultural and socio-economic dimensions of land, combining interpretations that have been put forward in disciplines such as geography (both human and political) and cultural anthropology. This is not to say that political and, in particular, legal aspects of land are of less importance. Clearly, these aspects have paramount implications for the rights of peoples in their own lands. However, sovereignty and ownership issues have dominated the recent discussions of rights to land, its occupancy, and use; this, to some degree, has led to the neglect of the strong connection between culture and land.

Spatial Perception and Organization

Let me first turn to the concepts of territory (land) and spatial relations, which are generally combined under the term "spatial (environmental) perception." Spatial perception varies from people to people, from culture to culture, and definitely from individual to individual. It relates to our identification with feelings and attitudes towards, and philosophies about, land and its contents. Philosophers and geographers have analyzed human-spatial interaction and have proposed models of spatial perception. I refer here to the model of spatial perception proposed by the French geographer André-Louis Sanguin (1977). Sanguin points out that all peoples have a notion of the spatial environment surrounding them. This integration of the perceived and experienced environments is guided by three components: (1) distance, (2) direction, and (3) accessibility.

According to Sanguin, these components establish the "field of perception" of a society or individual in a spatial sense; this, in turn, is influenced by several variables that have a bearing on the spatial perception of society and individuals within it. These variables relate to cultural, socio-economic, and political circumstances in conjunction with ideological motivations and economic possibilities. Spatial perception is thus also a reflection of the intensity of human environmental relations in a particular territory expressed through, for example, land-use practices. In his model (which has society/individual at its centre) Sanguin (1977, 47) distinguishes between the actual physical space (combining the natural and anthropogenic environment) and the fields of operations, the perceived environment, or, as he also called it, behavioral space. These operational fields are comprised of human activities and their implicit results and impacts on the land.

Thus land does have different meanings and values for different peoples and their cultures. It is, therefore, necessary to identify the central pivot around which different spatial perceptions turn, and we do this by looking at the integrity and significance of territoriality, the link between people and land, and people's identification with land (referred to in geography as regional or local identity).

Territorial Integrity

Human history tells us that evolving societies – both larger and smaller ones – have developed patterns and practices of occupancy and land use that outline territories whose boundaries or, rather, fringes were more or less respected by neighbouring societies; that is, the Others. Still, conflicts related to land have always arisen over sought-after resources. Such conflicts have resulted in warfare and territorial annexations, entailing both extinguishments and expansions of territory. The notion of basic mutual respect for territorial rights (i.e., their inclusion within human rights) has led to the creation of diplomacy and international relations to alleviate spatial and other conflicts – a successful exercise at times but often, it seems, futile (cf. Gottmann 1973).

Borders delineate spaces and territories, although they might not always be exactly defined, thus allowing for buffer zones among different spheres of interest. Certainly, borders are, necessarily, the seams connecting spaces whose defining human elements (be they laws, regulations, land-use practices, social behaviour, education, etc.) extend to them. Clearly, the emergence of rigorous institutions such as the central state have strengthened these aspects of territory by creating standards and maintaining them through systems of control (i.e., sovereignty or territorial integrity).

Significance of Land

The significance of land to humankind has been highlighted by a number of philosophers and geographers. The German philosopher Otto Friedrich Böllnow (1980), in his treatise on "Mensch und Raum" (People and Space), discusses the intimate relationship that humankind has with space; that is, with the area that humans integrate into their routine activities, the "ecumene" versus the "anecumene" (i.e., the area beyond perception, the unknown and, thus, supposedly unlivable space). According to Böllnow (1980, 33), to human beings land is an "organized space" that can be understood and comprehended. More important, environmental knowledge can be and is transferred from human to human as cultural heritage, an important prerequisite for the maintenance of spatial and environmental integrity (cf. Hügin 1996).

The French geographer Jean Gottmann (1973) looked at the gradual historical development of the significance of territory to humankind. Different political, socio-economic, cultural, and religious systems established varying definitions of territory and its boundaries. Gottmann focused on "traditions in Western civilization" and the concept of "homeland," which was derived, he argues, from the process of urbanization and socio-economic differentiation. The resultant concentration and density of populations demanded the spatial delineation of "spheres of interest" in order to avoid conflict and to allow the flow of goods across boundaries.

This is not to say that hunter-gatherer and herder societies, for example, did not recognize territories or organized lands as such. In the case of the Inuit in the Canadian Arctic, at least until recently, the existence of sparse populations within vast lands allowed for spatial avoidance whenever there were conflicts over territory. Still, territories were clearly recognizable by markers and symbols in the landscape, whether they were physical (cairns) or mental (geographic names). Such markers indicated that the land belonged to a particular group.

Gottmann (1973) argues that, through time, the human organization of space has gone through various stages based on different circumstances. He identifies at least four distinct phases:

(1) The delineation of areas based on the interest in economically valuable resources and areas of strategic interest, beginning with urbanization;
(2) the development of "universal empires" based on economic and military power cutting across cultural lines;
(3) the concept of culture-nation and state-nation, combining the perceived, if deceptive, notion of "one state, one culture, one language and one contiguous territory" with all its implications; and
(4) the assumption that "nations," based on power and control, harbour rights to expand their territories, thus creating colonies by disregarding the territoriality of other peoples.

These stages clearly extend to the oceans, air, and outer space, thus creating complex networks of spatial perception and territoriality that encompass all dimensions accessible to humankind at any given point in time.

Kativik or Nunavik: Land, Consciousness, and Identity

Recently, the discussions of spatial perception in geography and, in particular, political geography have turned away from the focus on the nation-state and its impact on humankind. More attention has been given to the territorial consciousness and identity of local people. Since the early 1980s, the Finnish geographer Anssi Paasi (1995, 1996), by concentrating on examples from various areas in Finland, has raised the issue of the dynamic process of regional identification among local populations. The results of his studies confirm that local regional identification is very strong and stable. This consciousness of, and identification with, "the land," the surrounding space, the "homeland" is supported and enhanced by the level of socio-cultural well-being as well as by the extent of knowledge of markers and symbols (Paasi 1996).

Let me illustrate this point by taking an example from northern Canada, more precisely, from northern Quebec, where two different regional concepts – Kativik (a legal-administrative regional construct connected with land rights) and Nunavik (a cultural-linguistic concept based on geographical names and other cultural elements) – have emerged as territorial markers. The two regions overlap considerably in territory and include the same population – Inuit – yet each has a quite different history (see Figure 3.1).

In the early 1970s the Province of Quebec proposed the immense James Bay hydroelectric power development, which would occur on Aboriginal, Cree, Naskapi, and Inuit territory. The execution of this proposal led to a major court case and finally to negotiations between Canada and Quebec, industrial corporations, and Aboriginal nations over territorial rights and ownership. The negotiations resulted in the James Bay and Northern Québec Agreement (JBNQA), which extinguished Aboriginal title to lands under dispute and created special Aboriginal rights to specific categories of lands, financial compensation, and subsidy programs. The JBNQA became the law of the land in 1977 and created a complex administrative structure that included "Kativik Region" as the spatial reference for the territory in which the law applied. The spatial extent of this territory was, in a sense, arbitrarily chosen so that its southern interior land boundary, the 55th parallel, cut through Cree/Naskapi and Inuit lands and into Labrador (CANOMA 1988: 36 and Figure 3.1). Along the coast of the Quebec-Labrador peninsula, the boundary of the Kativik Region was defined by the legal borderline between the Province of Quebec and the Northwest Territories – the average water line at low tide. This line is certainly a distinct and defining natural phenomenon, but it is quite unmanageable from an administrative and political point of view. It is even more nonsensical from the Inuit point of view because these people have always perceived the coastal zone – land and water – as a unified realm used, for diverse purposes, according to an annual seasonal rhythm (Gordon 1993; Makivik Corporation 1991).

It is obvious that the creation of Kativik Region and its geographical extent was an outgrowth of legal and technical negotiations that did not

Figure 3.1 The socio-cultural region of Nunavik and the administrative region of Kativik

have much to do with the region's cultural and socio-economic realities. Even the name "Kativik" – "meeting place" in Inuktituk – was formulated in an office.

Quite different is the process that produced a "new" region and an identity to which the inhabitants – cultural "stakeholders," to apply an oft-used modern term – could far more easily relate. In fact, in this instance, they created the concept themselves. During the immediate aftermath of the JBNQA, Inuit elders rallied around issues they deemed essential to the continuation and development of their culture and language. In the early 1980s the Inuit Elders' Conference, through its Avataq Cultural Institute, defined priorities and strategies to enhance Inuit cultural identity and integrity. Part of this strategy was to foster environmental knowledge and geographical perception through documenting locally known Inuit place names. These efforts resulted in large-scale toponymic surveys that involved all Inuit communities with their elders. The product was a full-fledged gazetteer of Inuit place names (Müller-Wille 1987), which was approved by the Inuit Elders' Conference in 1987. In the 1990s this was followed by the publication of Inuit place name maps (Müller-Wille 1990-4). Through precise geographical identification, the surveys established the places named throughout the spatial extent that had been occupied and used by Inuit for as long as their own experts remembered. Moreover, the amalgamation of these various areal surveys produced the outlines of a contiguous toponymic and linguistic region for the Inuit of northern Quebec.

The gazetteer presented, for the first time, place names from various local areas in one volume. For the Inuit, a trans-local territory comprised of their combined toponymic knowledge emerged in the idiom of their own language. A newly perceived cultural region was created whose cohesiveness was already partially understood based on linguistic similarities, kinship ties, and common socio-economic and political conditions. However, this space did not have a single name to serve as a symbol of spatial integrity. The solution proposed by the Inuit elders was to hold a referendum on the choice of a regional name to serve as a unifying symbol for all Inuit living within the area defined by the distribution of their place names.

In late 1986, from among eight proposals, this referendum produced "Nunavik" (the great land) as the regional name. Local Inuit acceptance of the new regional name was swift and complete. This name clearly answered a contemporary need pertaining to the socio-cultural representation of Inuit land – a land whose content and boundaries needed focus. In April 1988, the Quebec government recognized Nunavik as the name for the socio-cultural region of the Inuit existing within its own legal jurisdiction (Figure 3.1) (i.e., up to the line of the average low tide). Since then, Nunavik has obtained precedence over Kativik as a strongly unifying symbol for the Inuit region, and it serves as an external image builder through its inclusion in travel publications (cf. Michelin 1992, 247-55; Nunavik Tourist Association 1994).

Today, as a space defined by Inuit, Nunavik straddles three political entities within Canada (i.e., Quebec, Newfoundland-Labrador, and the Northwest Territories or, as of 1999, Nunavut). It also overlaps with Cree territories on its southern fringe.

Conclusions

In discussing territorial perception and identity, socio-cultural dimensions of land give rise to clearly competing notions – in this case, Kativik versus Nunavik. Kativik is the defining legal, administrative, and socio-economic term, while Nunavik is the spatially broader and more popular socio-cultural term.

As is so often the case in matters of identity and spatial allegiance, a wide range of choice is available. Still, Aboriginal nations do not, in most cases, have the control over legal, administrative, and political institutions that would enable them to make their own decisions regarding their land. They often find that their cultural perspectives on territorial identity and integrity are in conflict with the superimposed ideas and concepts of nations and states whose majority citizenries relate quite differently to space. For the Inuit, Nunavik is a spatial concept that emerged at a juncture of internal and external forces, and it motivated a reshaping of identity by redefining space so that it responds to their current conditions as an Aboriginal nation.

Note

Revised version of a presentation given at the symposium on "Economic, Social and Cultural Rights of the Sami, the Maasai and the Ogoni." This symposium was organized by the Northern Institute of Environmental and Minority Law, University of Lapland (Rovaniemi, Finland), 12-14 September 1997.

References

Böllnow, Otto Friedrich. 1980. *Mensch und Raum*. Stuttgart: Kohlhammer.

Brochu, Michel. 1962. *Le défi du Nouveau-Québec*. Montréal: Éditions du Jour.

CANOMA. 1988. "News from Quebec. Nunavik: A New Regional Name." CANOMA 14, 1: 36. Ottawa: Energy, Mines and Resources.

Collignon, Béatrice. 1996. *Les Inuit: Ce qu'ils savent du territoire*. Paris and Montréal: L'Harmattan.

Csonka, Yvon. 1995. *Les Ahiarmiut: À l'écart des Inuit Caribous*. Neuchâtel: Éditions Victor Attinger.

Gordon, Michael. 1993. "The Relationship of Land and Inuit in Nunavik." Essay, McGill University Northern Studies Program. 12 pp.

Gottmann, Jean. 1973. *The Significance of Territory*. Charlotteville: University of North Carolina Press.

Hügin, Urban. 1996. *Individuum, Gemeinschaft, Umwelt: Konzeption einer Theorie der Dynamik Anthropogener Systeme*. Bern: Peter Lang.

Makivik Corporation. 1991. "Filing a Claim to Nunavik's Offshore." *Makivik News* 20: 20-3.

Michelin Tires (Canada) Ltd. 1992. "Nunavik." In *Quebec*, 247-55. Dorval: Michelin Tires (Canada) Ltd.

Müller-Wille, Ludger. 1987. *The Gazetteer of Inuit Place Names in Nunavik (Québec, Canada)*. Inukjuak: Avataq Cultural Institute.

–, ed. 1990-4. *Inuit Place Name Map Series of Nunavik*. Inukjuak: Avataq Cultural Institute. (various issues)

Nieminen, Anna. 1998. "Cultural Politics of Place Naming: Toponymic Negotiations and Struggle in Aboriginal Territories." PhD diss., Department of Geography, University of Ottawa.

Nunavik Tourist Association. N.d. [ca. 1994]. *Nunavik: Friendly, Beautiful and Wild*. (brochure)

Paasi, Anssi. 1995. "Constructing Territories, Boundaries and Regional Identities." In *Contested Territory: Border Disputes at the Edge of the Former Soviet Empire*, ed. T. Forsberg, 42-61. Aldershot: Edward Elgar.

–. 1996. *Territories, Boundaries and Consciousness: The Changing Geographies of the Finnish-Russian Border*. Chichester: Wiley.

Poole, Peter. 1994. "Geomatics: Who Needs It?" *Cultural Survival Quarterly* 19(4): 1.

Sanguin, André-Louis. 1977. *La géographie politique*. Paris: PUF.

4
Writing Legal Histories on Nunavik

Susan G. Drummond

Nunavik

> In 1988, Avataq Cultural Institute ... requested of the Commission de Toponymie du Québec the acceptance of Nunavik as a regional name for the Inuit homeland in northern Québec ... Nunavik is the contiguous land and sea area occupied and used by the Inuit who, today, live in permanent and temporary settlements along the coastline of mainland Nunavik. The limits of Nunavik represent the outer geographical reach of those areas and places which the Inuit have named and used. Thus ... Nunavik represents the Inuit homeland based on continual land use and occupancy and on the congruous and contiguous naming of places and spaces.[1] (Müller-Wille 1987: 19)

In a recent article, Arjun Appadurai summarizes a shift in anthropological epistemology away from "trait" geographies to "process" geographies.[2] The former conceptualization of cultural space is driven by an imagery of coherence bound together by some list of traits (values, languages, material practices, ecological adaptations, marriage patterns, and the like). This way of rendering cultural coherence sees cultures as characterized by relatively enduring properties and as contained by more or less stable historical boundaries. Process geographies, on the other hand, construe manifestations of human cultural organization as outcomes of various kinds of action, interaction, and motion (trade, travel, pilgrimage, warfare, proselytization, colonization, exile, and the like). These latter conceptions of human geography are more fluid, broader in spatial scope (less specifically local), and less permanent than are the former. They are also much more the result of broad historical forces, much more the result of contest and strategy, and much more intercultural than narrowly local.

Much of this recent shift in anthropological thinking has focused on how the construction of culture ought to be conceived in less bounded and self-contained terms than has heretofore been the case. Not as much emphasis has been placed on the ways in which the spatial boundaries themselves (of nations or of peoples) have been historically and culturally constructed. The idea of culture has been parasitic on a geographic imagery of containment that is now proving to be unhelpful; however, the cultural props of spatial thinking have not been unpacked. In this chapter I want to focus on the ways in which the notions of space and territory are themselves grounded in cultural and intercultural understandings, negotiations, and strategies. The implications for a rich and diverse intercultural understanding of law emerge out of this enterprise. I focus on a not-always-fixed swath of land that has, in recent history, been variously invoked by the labels "Nunavik," "Nouveau-Québec," "Northern Quebec," and "Rupert's Land." Not only do I recast cultures and nations as unfixed, nebulous, negotiated phenomena, but I detach the borders used to hold the idea of culture and nation in place from naturalized constructions of the Real. I begin with the most recent toponymic transformation relating to how the area is conceptualized: with the history of how the spatial entity "Nunavik" came to be born. I end with the stable but unfixed nature of intercultural negotiations around (and with) borders.

Nunavik is a recent construct. Prior to 1988 Nunavik did not exist in the imagination of the Québécois, the Canadians, the British, the French, or any of the other *Qallunat* (non-Inuit) groups whose paths crossed the land. Nor, it must be added, did it exist in the imagination of the Inuit prior to the referendum that preceded the proposed name change. Once the members of the Inuit Place Names Project had collected, transcribed, and organized the place names for the area that is now called Nunavik, they realized that they did not have a name to represent the entity as a whole. The entity only exists, however, in contradistinction to perspectives that lie outside of it. Those perspectives include the awareness of cultures, provinces, nations, and peoples as bounded entities; aerial and naval perspectives; historical and anthropological prejudices about when and where a people begin and end; and the perspective of the cartographic enterprise itself.

The cartographic perspective is also political. Nunavik exists as a way of defining an Inuit territory against the encroaching interests of outsiders. The notion of Nunavik, then, is thoroughly imbricated with realities originally outside (and now inside) its boundaries. It is an intercultural object. It no more represents the way that the Thule Inuit (forbears of contemporary Inuit) saw the land than a glass-bottomed boat reveals the perspective of the fish being observed.

What do we make of the new, intercultural object known as Nunavik? From one perspective, it might symbolize the degeneration of Inuit history, culture, and autonomy. From this point of view, Nunavik stands as a toponymic monument to all that the Inuit have lost. It represents their contemporary inability to define, on their own terms, the content and limits of who they are. This evocation of loss and degeneration fits well with trait geography. The corpus of traits of a conceptually enclosed people are eroded by every encroachment from "beyond" the enclosure. This way of viewing culture might be endorsed by a particular reading of what the place name project brought about. The idea that the project compromised Inuit culture rather than achieved a compromise between Inuit and non-Inuit cultures finds justification in the following kinds of construals.

The methodology of the Inuit Place Name Project and the demands of the Commission de Toponymie du Québec might be said to illustrate the compromised nature of the Inuit homeland. The project gathered information from interviews with elders. That information had been transmitted orally from generation to generation. As the culture was transformed from a nomadic to a sedentary orientation, the oral basis of transmission was transformed along with the uses of land. Place names survive with familiar usage, not just of the names, but also of the land. If the relation between human and land shifts – as happened, for example, with the use of motorized vehicles for hunting, fishing, and trapping – then the use of once familiar place names changes. An intact body of names from one system of usage is rendered redundant, and its transmission is no longer guaranteed. If one no longer does the things that originally gave places their names, then some other usage must be developed to preserve the historical names. Qallunat human geography forms such a new usage.

The new usage, however, comes with its own criteria of correctness. Guidelines are developed to "facilitate the transition from orally transmitted and preserved information to written, standardised and politically accepted information" (Müller-Wille 1984, 5). However, with such usage, the place names no longer stand on their own ground. "Any contemporary toponymic study, if it is to result in official approval and legal status, now has to be conducted within the legal constraints concerning place names in a political territory" (7).

This demarcation of place names within a political territory is not a mere peripheral, post hoc activity. It *locates* the Inuit homeland within Qallunat territory and within Qallunat usages, within a Qallunat political body and within Qallunat epistemological categories. The Inuit homeland is part of a reworking of the Inuit identity from autonomous to enmeshed status. Acquiring official approval and legal status supports the existence of the Inuit as a "cultural entity" within the modern state or as a "people" in international law. As Müller-Wille (1984, 8) notes, "in adapting to modern western society and written tradition [Native societies] would be wise to follow the established procedures of recording names established by the majority society." In classical anthropological terms, the menacing choice is between established procedures and the obliteration of the history concealed behind the names – between extinction and salvation.

What if the Inuit should balk at the apparent redundancy of the legal concept of "officialization," reasoning that "indigenous names have always been used as long as man can remember" (8)? With the change in procedure from oral to written transmission, from popular usage to official usage, there is also a change in transmission, and this has the same inevitable necessity as does the former; without such benevolent intervention, the names will no longer be used as they have been used historically. They will not be used at all.

Just as the change in procedure is no longer wholly within the control of this newly located people, so the change in transmission is no longer wholly within their control. The Inuit will need to be taught the new usage. Facilitating the translation of spatio-temporal perceptions into the visual expression of a map will require "educating and training the native users to apply their place-name inventory within their own culture areas in the context of modern communication applications" (5). To facilitate their preservation as a collectivity or a people, the Inuit will need to be taught who they are within its context and within its conventions.

These are the arguments that sustain trait geography's conception of space and territory. Nunavik is not so much an Inuit entity as it is something born of a certain self-consciousness that did not wrinkle the Inuit worldview before exchanges with Qallunat became commonplace. On the trait geography model, which construes cultures as a nexus of spatially bounded values, material practices, and ecological adaptations, Nunavik is a compromised entity. It is already massively encroached upon by southern conceptions of territory and land use. It has already been translated and thereby transformed. Nunavik has been constructed – translated, schematized, and officialized – in such a way that it does not radically impair Qallunat consciousness. As an area constituting an object of history, the disputes it provokes do not do violence to southern historical consciousness (another spatially conceived nexus of traits). But it does distress an Inuit historical consciousness. Nunavik, as a homeland entity for the Inuit, asks that familiar Southern usages of maps be extended. It does not ask that they be transformed altogether.

Rather than dismissing Nunavik as a compromised entity, I want to explore how it may, indeed, be only the most recent manifestation of a polemical *intercultural* history. The perspective elaborated above is not the only way of characterizing Nunavik. The stark opposition between an unperturbed past and an anomic, inexorable march towards one monolithic and global historical consciousness does not capture all of the nuances that dwell behind the name. On another reading, Nunavik is one historical instant in a shifting dialogue between Inuit and Qallunat historical consciousness.

There is a way of connecting Nunavik to its pre-contact historical consciousness. This depiction of historical continuity is not so much about a discrete displacement of one sensitivity by another as it is about an ongoing dialogue over a spectrum of pasts (albeit refracted through an asymmetrical configuration). Nunavik bears witness to the tenacity of the dialogue as it generates a toponymic counter-discourse.

Nunavik is not completely contained by Western epistemological categories. It insists on its own version of recognition, even if that version is intercultural. Although its imagination may be constrained by things like two-dimensional schematization, officialization, and contemporary usages, it suggests a world not imagined by those practices. It suggests a world beyond the boundaries that Nunavik would represent on a conventional two-dimensional map if only because the place name project had to make contact with the coherencies of this world in order to make sense of what it was doing. This contact lingers even in the pasteurized official versions of place name maps.

The subversions suggested by Nunavik may be noted in the fact that the circuit court recognizes the boundaries that stop at the water's edge. After the James Bay Agreement in 1976 and until the Nunavik name change, this region was called, for administrative purposes, the Katavik Region north of fifty-five degrees of latitude, or, for electoral purposes, Nouveau-Québec. Neither designator fully represents the area used by the Inuit of the communities along the coast of northern Quebec. The boundaries of the Kativik/Nouveau-Québec jurisdictions end mainly in the offshore area at the tidal low water line between the Northwest Territories and Quebec. According to Inuit spatial perception, these lines do not exist. These lines do not reflect the four-dimensional seasonal expansion and dilation of the ice floe that Nunavik incorporates into its whole. Nunavik is represented by the continuous Inuit place name system that embraces both the coast and the offshore region – a territory consisting of land, water, and ice as a spatial network.

Furthermore, Inuit place names do more than render a previously fixed boundary (Kativik/Nouveau-Québec) more fluid and seasonally dependent. The network that makes up the Inuit place name system is not only based on human-land relations, but also on inter-species relations. The flux of Inuit territory is thus not only dependent on seasons, but also on the seasonal and annual movements of animals over the land, over and under the ice, and under the water. Humans and animals are subtly and intricately interwoven through mutual dependence on land and sea. This interweaving is reflected in human understanding of the habits, interrelationships, and movements of animals. The patterns of land use that have evolved throughout the region's history are rooted in these understandings. Hence the two- or even three-dimensional officialized maps of the South are doubly notional, not only for failing to represent the temporal shifts in the ice floes, but also for failing to capture the complex changes in the movement of species and seasonal distribution. Lines drawn on maps might represent a complex, interwoven summary of land use per species hunted, but the lines are neither fixed nor absolute. These lines form neither a natural frontier nor the absolute limit to which animals are pursued. In the case of the white fox, which has a four-year population cycle, the lines may change quadri-annually; in the case of the beluga whale, which has been decimated in arctic waters, the lines may change for generations.

Even Nunavik, then, as a geographical entity, pushes the spotlight beyond the mundane spectacle of southern legal justice. Jurisdictional questions of whose police would be obliged to pursue a criminal onto the ice arise. On whose territory is a crime committed if it is committed on the ice over the sea and not the ice over the land that, until 1988, was Nouveau-Québec? This anxiety renews the anxiety of the Québécois in the early 1960s, concerned to assert administrative sovereignty over Nouveau-Québec. Michel Brochu, a Québécois cartographer unabashed about the urgency and primacy of the Québécois territorial agenda, thus rang the alarm:

> Les conséquences de ces limites absurdes peuvent se faire sentir jusque dans le domaine policier: en effet, des Esquimaux ayant commis un délit ou un crime, justiciables devant les tribunaux du Québec, pourraient échapper à la police du Québec simplement en se réfugiant sur une île à quelques centaines de mètres de la rive. Il faudrait alors, soit que le Québec demande à Ottawa l'autorisation de poursuivre un individu passible d'arrestation, soit encore que la Police Montée de Frobisher, ou de Cap Dorset, se déplace sur des distances considérables et vienne arrêter les prévenus qu'elle déférera au parquet de Québec.
>
> The consequences of these absurd limits can affect even the policing: in fact, Eskimos who have committed an offence or a crime within the jurisdiction of the courts of Quebec could evade the Quebec police simply by taking refuge on an island just a few hundred metres offshore. It would then be necessary for Quebec to ask Ottawa for the authorization to pursue the suspects, or for the Mounted Police of Frobisher or Cape Dorset to travel considerable distances to arrest the accused and hand them over to Quebec. (Brochu 1962, 19)

The humiliation of dependency on other administrative centres is the least of the problems to which Nunavik gives rise, however. For Nunavik, as a homeland entity, conjures up new and more perturbing questions of sovereignty – not only political, but also historical. If the Inuit perception of space is to be valorized, then why not the Inuit perception of history? If the Inuit historical perspective on the Court is favoured, then might not the very stability of the legal order be rendered that much more uncertain? Once the Court's legitimacy is rendered more contingent, the question of whose police pursue whom onto whose territory becomes simultaneously more complex and more redundant. The very legitimacy of these Western institutions – police, Court, territory – may be subverted.

The idea of capturing Inuit place names as one form of writing Inuit history and the concomitant implications for sovereignty are not beyond the scope of the Inuit Place Names Project. The network that makes up the Inuit place name system is composed of a complex cultural, linguistic, historical, and epistemological labyrinth of relations. Place names do not exist in isolation. Inuit linguistic schemes represent Inuit forms of geographical knowledge. Imbedded in the language is a whole way of ordering reality, of ordering social and natural relations, of ordering historical events. Qallunat give the name "Helicopter Island" to the island where a helicopter landed in 1953, and "Cape Bernard Shaw" to a contour that resembles, from the air, the profile of George Bernard Shaw. The Inuit give the name *Tiluq* to the place where two men exchanged blows over some eggs, and the name *Nigukuk* (meaning "a slimy place") to the place where people used to fish for cod (their hands would get slimy from working with them), or the name *Tasiujalugasak* (meaning "it looks like a pond that nobody likes") to a saltwater pond (Brice-Bennett 1977; Müller-Wille 1985). Place names constitute a descriptive record of the landscape, and these descriptions reflect particularized, local sensibilities and practices.

The place names are also interrelated. They constitute a system and relate to each other in terms of description and orientation. Inuit places have different names depending on the direction from which they are approached; this is because they have different aspects from each direction. Having different perspectival aspects, they serve as different landmarks for future journeys, depending on the direction of approach. As part of a system encoding spatial behaviour, place names "enable hunters to construct oral maps by which they can visualise areas, approximate distances, and recognise travel routes" (Brody 1977, 195).

But place names have more than this functional use. Indeed, this functional use by individual hunters is reliant on a more systematic background. Individuals occupy and use the land as representatives of a social and cultural system. Place names thus provide a sense of cultural and historical continuity over the land. They are a nominal testament to a complex web of social, natural, and historical relations. They are a record of how the Inuit organized space, rendering aspects of it salient and identifying and valorizing its particular assets. As a record, they are interwoven with a cultural form of inscribing history. Place names are, for the Inuit, a way of speaking about who they were and who they are. As historical records, however, they do more than merely identify a people.

The more subversive vocation of place names dwells in their attestation to the integration and appropriation of space into the environmental perception of the Inuit. Through the continuous use and application of place names, a system of spatial organization was created and maintained. Therein lies Nunavik's most provocative defiance. As a system of spatial organization, place names represent aspects of territoriality and sovereignty.

This connection between place names, territoriality, and sovereignty is one of the legal bases for grounding Inuit claims to autonomy. Just as Inuit place names had to be "officialized" in order to be recognised as more than a cultural penchant, the Inuit conception of land use and territorial, cultural, and social autonomy had to be translated into non-Inuit legal discourse in order to represent a legal interest entitled to claim relief upon violation.

Lex Loci[3]

There are minimally two ways of approaching a dialectic between local Aboriginal law and non-Aboriginal law: from outside state coherencies in international legal orders and from inside state coherencies in domestic law. There is some interplay between the orders, with international law constrained by domestic tropes and domestic legal systems configured by international rhetoric. However, just as Nunavik repeats elements from both Inuit and Qallunat sensibilities, elements of domestic and international law can repeat the tension between Aboriginal and non-Aboriginal sensibilities. This can be seen in international arguments about territorial sovereignty and domestic arguments about Aboriginal title. These arguments most often exploit an orthodox toponymy. At times, however, they are attentive to an unfamiliar spatial imagination. The reconstructed Nunavik has a part to play in exoticizing conventional cartography.

Conventional toponymies are reflected in what it means to stake a proprietary claim within southern legal systems. Parties must satisfy the Court that they enjoy an appropriate legal interest in a given piece of land. "Piece of land" is presumed to be a culture-neutral concept. It is not conceived of in the four-dimensional, interspecies-dependent sense understood by the Inuit; rather, it refers to the kinds of precise, two-dimensional Cartesian vectors that made up the Kativik/Nouveau-Québec region.

The Cartesian schematization of land is not an insulated cartographic exercise. It reflects a labyrinth of interrelated values and practices. A division into "metes and bounds" reflects a distinctive way of relating to the object so divided as well as a distinctive way of relating to other human beings within a social nexus. If aspects of Inuit history compel them to claim relief upon violation of a legal interest, then not only must they frame their claim in foreign spatial terms, but they must also translate their ways of relating to the land and to each other into a foreign idiom. They must convert their conception of possession into a practically antithetic notion of ownership.

The Inuit did not historically share the civil law notion of the exclusive right of the individual owner of the land to its *usus, fructus,* and *abusus.*[4] Traditional Inuit land use held that everyone was free to live and hunt wherever he or she wished. Everyone shared the animals. Every hunter had free access to game. As put by an Inuk elder:

> I was happy if there were other people at my place because there were a lot of animals and because they came. I was happy to have other people because we were not going to be alone. I never heard anyone say, "He is going to get the animals that I should get from my place." People were happier and liked it better if there were others going to their place because animals are always moving, they are always coming ... I never heard any Inuk say "This is my land." (Brice-Bennett 1977, 165)

That set of ideas is far-removed from the notion of ownership in civil law. Yet it is not the Qallunat notion of ownership that must be inverted to make sense within the Inuit lex loci of land use. The Inuit conception of land use, antithetical as it is to ownership, must be translated into Qallunat vernacular in order to ground the new claim: "this is Inuit land."

Again, that translation carries with it the risk of obliteration. Inuit territory must be articulated in foreign terms or it will be consumed by non-Inuit uses. In the face of arguments claiming that, without individual ownership by the Inuit, Qallunat own all the land and are free to use it on their own terms, such an articulation could suggest ways of preserving Inuit land for Inuit uses in audible and credible terms. As with the Inuit Place Names Project, rendering Inuit claims audible and credible suggests not just a recasting of Inuit usages, but also an extension of the boundaries of southern legal imagination. Inuit uses may have been misshapen, but this deformation was carried out so that Qallunat legal uses would expand to accommodate them. This expansiveness was not emblematic of the way that law courts historically construed Aboriginal land rights. Indeed, it existed at the margins of legal argument.

With the arrival of Europeans in the Americas, there arose a series of legal and political manoeuvres between the imperial powers that were meant to justify claims to sovereignty and ownership of enormous tracts of land. Vis-à-vis each European nation, rules of territorial sovereignty were argued, settled upon, and reargued. Discovery was asserted as a basis of valid title, but it was only valid vis-à-vis other European claimants. In the face of the presence of Aboriginal peoples, Europeans, at the moments of original contact, did not regard the lands as terra nullius.[5] Discovery, then, would not ground claims to sovereignty vis-à-vis Aboriginal peoples. Europeans needed another way of understanding their territorial relationships with the Natives.

One tack followed by the British Crown with regard to territory that it acquired beyond the realm of England was the argument from lex loci. On that argument, the rights of the people inhabiting the territory under their own customs and usages were presumed to survive the change in sovereignty. Their customs and usages were said to amount to a lex loci, which the Crown is bound, as a matter of law, to respect. In contested cases, however, this respect is not automatic. In order for a court to be obliged to take cognizance of the system and rights arising under lex loci, they must fall within the ambit of the rules of recognition laid down by the Judicial Council of the Privy Council. If there is no recognized lex loci, then the land is considered, for all purposes, unoccupied – a waste and desert land. The land is then open for peaceful settlement – an alternative form of possession giving title.

One approach to this roadblock to outright non-Aboriginal possession, raised to a principle of law in such American cases as *Tee-Hit-Ton* v. *The United States* (1954; 348 US 272, hereinafter *Tee-Hit-Ton*), was to argue that Aboriginal peoples had no settled system of law. Their land use was not just different, it was primitive and pre-legal. As such, it had no basis upon which it could be recognized by an Anglo-American court of law. On that argument, Aboriginal peoples were lacking the kind of social coherency and relationship with land requisite to attaining the status of nation. The land was sparsely peopled by savage and nomadic tribes who were, as a collective entity, denied international legal personality.

There was, however, another legal argument that did not retroactively void the land of human presence prior to European arrival. This argument sought to render Inuit land use in the categories of Western law, to bring the Inuit land-use system within the Privy Council's various rules of recognition. There is an obvious problem of fact for this argument in that the Inuit do not have commensurate conceptions of property. There is, however, a series of Privy Council cases that indicate that this deficit is not fatal to their claim.[6] The principles laid down in these cases place emphasis not on individual ownership but on the presence of a *system* of land use and occupancy. This system of usage makes up a lex loci that is, in theory, knowable to lawyers who then produce it as evidence in court to ground a claim. The scope of the Inuit land system determines the boundaries between Inuit and non-Inuit jurisdictions. Under Canadian law, what falls within this land system is governed by Aboriginal law unless those rights have been extinguished with clear and plain language by a piece of federal legislation.[7]

It is here that place naming serves as evidence for the integration and appropriation of space into the territorial perception of the Inuit. More than just serving as a written record of historical Inuit land use and occupancy, the existence of a place naming system, now transcribed and organized in Western cartographic categories by the Inuit Place Names Project, establishes a legal presumption of an Inuit lex loci that is the requirement for recognition by a court of common law.

It is this aspect of Nunavik that renders the legitimacy of the court's historical consciousness precarious. The entity Nunavik suggests ways of making oppositions and contrasts between Inuit conceptions of sovereignty and Qallunat conceptions of sovereignty that were not possible before Nunavik took on its present contours. Nunavik is a shorthand that allows the Inuit to be fortified with the same geographical, linguistic, and legal armaments that Qallunat use to stake their claims.

Inuksuit and the Contingency of Maps

> [Inuksuit:]
> Plural for inuksuk, which means "to act in the capacity of a human."
> (a) a person-like thing
> (b) a special stone object or figure constructed by a person in a variety of ways so as to:
> - assist in hunting
> - serve as a message, sign, or signal
> - function as an indicator, locator, marker, or co-ordination point
> - serve as a symbol
> - act as a memorial
> - be an object of power or veneration
> - have a purpose known only to its builder
> - have astronomical significance. (Hallendy 1994)

I have intimated what place naming and map making mean to the contemporary Inuit. I have not outlined a complementary Qallunat compulsion to name places and draw up maps. Clearly, part of that compulsion is a need, very similar to that of the Inuit, to record who the Qallunat are, who they were, and how they relate to the land and to each other. However, if Qallunat needs were so contained, it would not be incumbent upon the Inuit to frame their geographical history in terms opposable to territorial encroachment.

Place naming and map making are as much dimensions of dominion for Qallunat as they are dimensions of a historical and social imagination. This affiliation of maps with territorial aspirations suggests their ideological contingency. Inasmuch as maps constitute one version of the historical and social imagination, such an affiliation with desire and aspiration also suggests, at best, a mediated fit between historical consciousness and its object. I will return to the implications of Qallunat map making for the land and for the historical record.

First I want to contextualize maps and place naming within the Qallunat realm of dominion. The idea that the mere act of naming a place gives one title to it is not a new one, and it is clearly not an Inuit idea. It is also not an idea that has enjoyed persistent international acclaim. Hence lawyers who argue for Inuit sovereignty by invoking a place name system do not do so on the basis of the existence of Inuit place names alone but, rather, on the surer basis that place name systems are evidence of a lex loci.[8] They shrewdly make this distinction because of the legal history of the formal requirements of sovereignty under international law.

The idea that one could name a place and thereby gain title to it enjoyed a chequered history in the protean struggles for domination between the three main imperial powers in North America: Britain, Spain, and France. It is an idea that fits with one conception of sovereignty; namely, symbolic sovereignty, which is currently somewhat outdated. It is a concept that has a compulsion of its own, however, and it is only reluctantly that it is ever completely abandoned.

The notion of naming as ground for title was invoked in the North as recently as 1962 by Brochu, the Québécois cartographer mentioned above. In 1939, the *Re Eskimos* case between the federal and Quebec government over administrative control of the territory determined that "Indian," under head 24 of s. 91 of the Constitution Act, 1867, included "Eskimo" inhabitants of the Province of Quebec.[9] The Inuit were not a mere collection of individuals, indistinguishable from other individuals in the province: they were an Aboriginal *people*. As social service programs became widespread across Canada after the Second World War, the federal government inherited the delivery of welfare resources in northern Quebec as part of its jurisdiction. Brochu awoke in 1962 with the rest of the Québécois to the realization that the administration of northern Quebec was wholly within the control of the federal government. As the federal government controlled Northern schools, the language of instruction was not Inuktitut. More significantly for Brochu, the language of instruction was not French. With alarm, Brochu further noted three distressing facts:

(1) Quebec had no effective administrative presence in northern Quebec;
(2) due to English being the language of instruction at school and hence the second language of Inuit "le sort des Esquimaux ne diffère en rien de

celui des Esquimaux habitant les Territoires du Nord-Ouest proprement dits (the future of the Eskimos is in no way different from that of the Eskimos living in the Northwest Territories proper)"; and

(3) the complete absence of the official use of the French language in the territory, in light of which "Il faut nous rendre compte du fait, qu'actuellement, plus de la moitié du territoire du Québec, le Nouveau-Québec, échappe à peu près complètement au contrôle effectif de la province de Québec (we have to realize that, at the moment, more than half of Quebec territory, Nouveau-Québec, escapes the effective control of the province of Quebec)" (Brochu 1962, 53).

The solution to the problem that more than half the territory of the province escaped the effective control of Quebec City was twofold. First, the Québécois were to take over the administration of the northern territory immediately. Thus the way to counter the fact that the Inuit were not entitled to instruction in their own language (combined, of course, with the fact that French was not being taught at school) was that "le Québec, prenne complètement et totalement en main le système d'instruction des Esquimaux (Quebec take complete and total control over the Eskimos' education system)" (51). Further, in order that French become, within five years, the language of communication in Nouveau-Québec (while still acknowledging the intangible rights of the Eskimo language), "il parait évident que la condition essentielle d'un contrôle effectif et efficace du Nouveau-Québec est la présence d'au moins trois administrateurs officiels et permanents du Québec dans ses territoires du Nord (it seems that the presence of at least three official and permanent administrators from Quebec in the northern territories is an essential condition for the effective and efficient control of Nouveau-Québec)" (48).

In addition, however, to these acts of administrative control pertaining to northern Quebec, Brochu promoted the adoption of a complete system of name changes for the region, which, on official maps, was dominated by titles such as Wakeham Bay, Cape Wolstenholme, Payne Bay, George River, Port Harrison, and Diana Bay. In 1961, the provincial minister of lands and forests announced the official adoption by the Comité de Toponomie du Québec of a list of new French names (sometimes with odd constructions, such as "Notre-dame-d'Ivujivik") for the reclaimed territory of Nouveau-Québec.[10] As Brochu noted, "cette politique symbolise la détermination bien arrêtée de la province de Québec de marquer sa présence française dans ces régions nouvelles (this policy symbolizes Quebec's determination to make its French presence known in these new regions)" (126). And with this symbolic ritual of renaming, the Québécois affected a repossession of Nouveau-Québec.

But if naming is such an effective ground for sovereignty, then how did the rituals of the Commission de Toponomie du Québec unknot the strings that attached "Wakeham" and "Payne" and "Harrison" to the ground, leaving them to float off into name heaven, while securely and irrevocably tying "Maricourt" and "Notre-dame-d'Ivujivik" in their places?

Naming does not, in fact, enjoy, in the various rituals of sovereignty, a very hallowed place. It is only one of a number of symbolic acts relied upon in the history of international law to fortify claims to sovereignty over a territory. Among themselves, Europeans accepted that title could be validly acquired on the basis of discovery. But discovery on its own was not necessarily recognized as a sufficient basis for sovereignty unless it was accompanied by an act of possession. It was the nature of possession that was contested between the three imperial powers.

Juricek (1970) has postulated that there were, historically, two competing conceptions of the acquisition of effective title to a territory in international law: one acquired title either through pre-emption or through domination. On the pre-emptive model, discovery was a mental act. Legal possession was a separate act from discovery; however, it did not require much greater effort than the act of declaring that something new had been discovered. Legal possession was effected symbolically and consisted of actions not directed towards the inhabitants of the territory in question but at the other imperial powers, broadcasting that the new state was now sovereign in that particular region. Such symbolic sovereignty consists chiefly of a series of gestures, demonstrations, and other actions, such as the performance of ceremonies on the beachhead, the unfurling of a national standard, the recital of various ritual legal or religious formulae, or the erection of a stone cairn or wooden cross. Possession, on this view, was as quick as the duration of the ritual. It was also final and decisive.

Spain, being (along with Portugal) the first to "discover" the Americas, cleaved firmly to the pre-emptive model of acquisition of title. Symbolic possession was all that was required to render title complete. By the mental act of the intention to embrace the territory within the ambit of the ritual, those countries were able to lay claim to fantastic swathes of land and to effectively eliminate potential claims from the other imperial powers.

Not unexpectedly, imperial powers coming latterly onto the land contested the efficacy and legality of that method of acquisition. Rather than symbolic possession being sufficient to give title, they argued that possession had to be "actual," "real," or "effective." That model of sovereignty is the dominative model, which maintains a distinction between what is symbolic and what is real. In virtue of the greater energy expended in taking "effective" possession, the acts involved in the latter imputedly have a reality beyond mere intention. They have a reality that establishes them in international law and sets them in opposition to other claims to sovereignty, both deeply and veridically. "Real" possession is supposed to be an alternative to the transparently self-serving and solipsistic devices of symbolic sovereignty.

It is this dominative code that has gradually taken precedence over the pre-emptive code, especially in its contemporary formulations of "developmental sovereignty" or the "consolidation of sovereignty" (Morrison 1986, 247). These latter forms of sovereignty are said to be achieved when a government formulates policies for the development of the territory under its control. It is this latter form of sovereignty that can be seen at work in Brochu's desire to dispatch at least three official and permanent Quebec administrators to the northern territory.

While "real" sovereignty can, if approached from a different direction, sometimes appear to be a rather symbolic thing, arguments from symbolic sovereignty can also have a real compulsion. Because of the relative and contextual basis of prescriptive sovereignty, drawing a line between actual and symbolic sovereignty is not a simple declaratory exercise. In the first place, the standard for the amount of energy required to assert effective control is not easily measured as it changes according to the landscape and environment it is measuring. As noted in the *Legal Status of Eastern Greenland Case*, "the tribunal has been satisfied with very little in the way of actual exercise of sovereign rights, provided that the other State could not make out a superior claim. This is particularly true in the case of claims to sovereignty over areas in thinly populated or unsettled countries" (*Denmark* v. *Norway* [1933] PCIJ Ser. A/B, No. 53). The geographical and social context underlying the claim could render substantial what would be, in other contexts, insubstantial and solipsistic.

Another implication of the transition from nominal symbolism to nominal realism is that a claim that would be sufficiently dense in the absence of a superior claim becomes thin and loses its efficacy in the face of a relatively thick claim. In other words, the effectiveness of the claim does not inhere in the claim itself but, rather, in the claim's relationship with other claims. What is at one moment "real" and "effective" possession becomes chimerical when faced with more gripping attachments. The threshold is a moving target, as a "real" claim can be demoted to a mere symbolic claim by a further, more compelling, claim.

A claim could also fail if it were not coherent within received customary understandings of what constitutes legitimate signals of sovereignty. Thus, in the 1928 *Island of Palmas Case,* not only did there need to be a continuous and peaceful display of state authority, but the display also had to be "open and public, that is to say that it [had to be] in conformity with usages as to exercise of sovereignty over colonial states" (*Netherlands* v. *United*

States [1928], 2RIAA 829; hereinafter *Netherlands*). What constitutes "open and public" is not unilaterally determined, but it must pertain to more than the party making the claim.

The conjunction of these three conditions – context, relative density of claim, customary agreements in judgment – indicates that an apparently tenuous claim (such as the erection of a stone cairn) might not be symbolic if the physical and social landscapes did not call for greater effort, if there were no parties with more substantial claims, and if there was customary agreement that such an act constitutes a display of sovereignty. Conversely, a claim generally associated with the consolidation of sovereignty, such as the establishment of a post office, would pass into the realm of mere symbol if the physical and social context required more, if there were thicker claims to factual control, and if there was a customary agreement in judgment that post offices are impoverished displays of sovereignty.

Ultimately, there are implications from the plasticity of the symbolic/real distinction that have some bearing on the Inuit people. First, if the Inuit can be shown to have been historically more responsive to the physical and social exigencies of the land, then an Inuit claim to sovereignty would have weight in international law.[11] Second, while the claims of Europeans vis-à-vis each other might have required very little in the way of consolidation of sovereignty, those claims would be relatively insubstantial in the face of a continuous and peaceful Inuit presence. Third, if an agreement in judgment about what constitutes public and open use has excluded the Inuit from the agreement, then that agreement passes into the merely symbolic for want of "conformity with usages as to exercise of sovereignty over colonial states" (*Netherlands*, 829). The acts fail to conform with Aboriginal usages that are, within the postcolonial context, highly relevant in determining the appropriate exercise of sovereignty over colonial states. What constitutes "real and effective" title as between European nations and their offspring could well become symbolic and ineffective vis-à-vis the Inuit.

The relativity of the distinction between real and symbolic sovereignty can be seen in cameo in the struggles between the imperial powers over names. Historically, the existence of a custom of recognizing the legitimacy of place naming as a method of grounding title was a matter of dispute. As a result, place naming as a display of sovereignty enjoyed a not wholly disreputable history.

The British Crown was notable in being unsettled about the type of sovereignty upon which it was going to stake its claim to title. France persistently based its claims to title on "real" possession, supplementarily adorned with the requisite trappings of symbolic sovereignty. Britain acquired, over the reign of King James I (between 1610 and 1620), a new incentive to embrace the quick and decisive finality of the pre-emptive code. It was at this time that the British Crown was on the verge of having an empire of its own in North America. Given the spectacular mass of land over which King James was claiming a monopoly, it was inconceivable that the entire entity could be effectively occupied and possessed by the British. Rather than modify his claims, the king modified his taste for symbolic sovereignty and allowed that it gave effective title against other discovering nations. British place naming played a crucial role in this renewed fondness for symbolic acts.[12]

The use of place naming as a message, sign, or signal of sovereignty in the region now called Nunavik, then, has a much deeper history than does the Commission de Toponomie du Québec. That region was the object of the British expansion of empire through the pre-emptive code of naming. It was also the site of a series of confrontations between the French and British Crowns over the validity of rival codes. During the late seventeenth century, the dispute between the two imperial powers over the legal status of rival codes was incarnated in disputes between the Hudson's Bay Company and the French.

The British, in their search for a sea route to Asia, dispatched Henry Hudson to find a northwest passage. In 1610 he sailed into a vast body of water and down its edge into the land of the Cree. His ship was approached by a lone Cree who exchanged furs for a mirror, a knife, some buttons, and a hatchet (Crowe 1974). On behalf of the British king, Hudson named the bay after himself. Forty years later two French traders, Radisson and Groseilliers, travelled overland to reach the same land of the Cree. Shored up by the symbolic acts of possession performed by a chain of British explorers, including Cabot, Frobisher, Foxe, Button, and Hudson himself, the British claimed title to all of Hudson Bay and its hinterland – Rupert's Land. In 1670, Charles II granted a colonial charter to the Hudson's Bay Company (HBC) over this land, thereby granting it a monopoly on the fur trade in the region, empowering it to exclude every European outsider from the bay, and thus consolidating the king's title. The French, not awed by these rituals, attacked the HBC post at Fort Nelson in 1682, thereby triggering a series of diplomatic exchanges between Britain and France to determine, as between themselves, who had valid title and how. The authority of place naming had a prominent position in these exchanges, which ricocheted between the pre-emptive and dominative codes of possession.

The British, by now well enamoured of the pre-emptive code, traced the HBC's chain of title back to the symbolic acts of the explorers. The French, consistently adhering to the dominative model, retorted that the explorers had but an evanescent presence on the land and that their rituals were solipsistic; rather, they insisted that, "for Establishing the Right upon the possession of a Country [it] is not sufficient to have Discovered the Same and to have lived there some time but there must be an Ancient possession and a Continued habitation or a least a Trade maintained[,]" adding that

"Tis well knowne that Collony's cannot bee wholly established but by time & the Care & paines of those who have the managemt. of it" (Lester 1979, 61). The British, recognizing that they could not possibly have had "real" possession of the whole of Hudson Bay, relied instead on the fact that "all the Rivers Lakes Streights Islands Capes and Promontoryes are called by English names and are soe denominated even in Sanson's Mapps which hee lately dedicated to the Dauphin" (62). A web of English names had been spread out over representations of the land, and this was testimony to the care and pains required to ensnare the whole within one's title. British place name maps were not proof in and of themselves of title; rather, "the names which they Generally give to Country's are Convinceing marks of the Propriety." The British retreated from their obstinately pre-emptive position and subsumed place naming under the auspices of dominative title, with names serving as evidence of possession rather than being effective in terms of their own force. Ultimately the British, in the face of scathing French disdain, fortified their argument from place naming with other claims to symbolic possession.

Before leaving this particular seventeenth-century diplomatic dispute I want to emphasize France's scorn for the invocation of maps (even those dedicated to the future king of France) because it sets up nicely the epistemological quandaries involved in writing a history of the area. In response to the British argument from maps, French diplomats responded in 1687 that, "if one would admit these sorts of Profes the French will make appeare by Divers priviledged Relations printed at London, that all the country's in Question, did belong to them before the English knew them, and this alone would end the Contest" (Lester 1979, 64). If all that is required for sovereignty is the production of a representation of the land accordingly labelled in one's mother tongue with culturally pertinent referents, then anyone, by the simple act of transcribing names onto a page, can thereby claim title. To what do maps serve as testimony apart from the private intentions of the parties? What is the difference between a map and a heap of rocks on the landscape that might serve as a message, sign, or signal – but might also be just a heap of rocks on the landscape?

Map making not only sets up the problematics of the history, it also reveals some of the philosophical knots that tie up the entire history-writing enterprise. If maps are a form of writing history, then all forms of writing history might be corrupted by the same ideological solipsism. Writing history might amount to the reproduction and reinforcement of dominion. If writing history is like map making, then accounting for history's intelligibility and claims to veridicality becomes as confounded as does accounting for the catholic aspirations of maps.

The magical allure to the Western imagination of the idea that maps are capable of addressing questions of sovereignty is evident. It speaks to the belief that one can capture "the real" – the belief that one can perform a series of magical gestures over a "piece of land" or, indeed, a *representation* of a "piece of land" and that these rituals will have a singular and universal meaning for all the "pieces of land" that are contiguous to it and that make up, by contiguous addition, the whole world (which surely has an indisputable and universal solidity and reality).

The idea that a map has a "real" referent is by no means easy to formulate. The very terms that go into its component parts – "piece of land" for example – have no singular, universal, culture-neutral meaning (apart from the ones we have agreed to give them). Even the category of the "real" is one that is historically and culturally conditioned.

The epistemological difficulties of cartography stand on their own. However, they also have implications for other Western discourses, most notably the discourse of history. If maps are contingent, then how exactly does one tie a history of Inuit and Qallunat presence in Nunavik to the ground? Topographical referents are one of the principal means of distinguishing conventional history from fiction.

One answer to this epistemological dilemma is that the practices that we engage in determine the criteria for determining what constitutes "reality." So, for example, a pile of rocks on the land is not an indicator, locator, marker, or coordination point – is not an inuksuk – outside of the Inuit custom of building Inuksuit on the land. The rocks do not indicate which direction a hunter is to go unless the hunter participates in the custom of inuksuk building, which, like all customs, is essentially an arbitrary convention. The pile of rocks could just as easily be a pile of rocks as an indicator. However, the conventionality of the system of signification does not prevent the Inuit from giving adequate directions to each other. The Inuit do not explicitly agree to use piles of rocks as Inuksuit any more than historians agree to use written texts as historical records; rather, the custom is held in place in spite of, and even as a result of, the continual challenges of regular usage.

The convention of place naming (and, by implication, map making) as an act of sovereignty is further illustrative of the point. If there had been the same agreement in judgment between the French and British with regard to place naming giving title that there was with regard to discovery having to be accompanied by at least one form of possession, then the matter would have been settled by Sanson's Mapps. As it was not agreed between the parties that place naming was a sufficiently realistic way of determining possession, its legitimacy was contested in a volley of diplomatic exchanges. But the very arguments about the legitimacy of place naming could only make sense within the context of a customary practice of acquiring territory beyond one's realm and determining acquisition by the conventions of discovery and possession. The diplomatic exchanges could only take place if there were an agreement in judgment between the parties that some things were not arbitrary, some things were not matters for discussion, and that some things were the ultimate criteria for determining realistic thinking.

Postcolonial critiques have shifted some of the complacencies that enabled the diplomatic exchange to get off the ground in the first place. The fixity of the conceit of acquiring territory beyond one's realm is becoming unhinged; it has become open to argument and diplomatic exchange. These newer disputes are held in place by the gravitational pull of other conventions – conventions that have not been subject to doubt and that hold larger worldviews in place.

Just as the French and British foregrounded their particular disputes against a common background of international conventions, which belonged to each nation separately and to both nations together, disputes about Aboriginal title and sovereignty are the foreground of a tenuously settled intercultural practice. This intercultural zone enables the dialogue – even the dialogue that continually challenges the scope of the zone – to get off the ground. While commanding rhetorical attention requires a prerequisite acceptance of the terms of the dialogue, the terms are not eternally fixed. They are set by agreements in judgment between participants in a shared practice, who, along with other people, have also learned to use words and objects grouped around a common activity. This common activity – not infrequently intergroup and intersocietal conflict – suggests the existence of an intercultural zone of shared sovereignty that is ill-reflected in state legal practice.

Questions about what conditions would have to prevail for one people to consider *sharing* sovereignty with another might provide the outlines of the criteria of legitimacy of modern governments. Nunavik, as an entity, was essentially created so that those questions might arise. Nunavik was created to challenge the notion of sovereignty *over*. It was created out of this postcolonial discourse as much as it was created via the agency of the Inuit Place Names Project. As such, it both arises out of intersocietal conflict and intimates a path of transcendence through continued intercultural compromise and engagement. It is out of these diverse processes that an alternative geography continues to emerge. It is also out of these processes that an alternative conception of geography, frontier, and culture continues to emerge.

Notes

1 In 1981, the Northern Québec Inuit Elders Conference passed a resolution to institute a project to preserve Inuit place names. In 1983, Avataq Cultural Institute and Indigenous Names Surveys of the Department of Geography, McGill University, implemented the Inuit Place Names Project to systematically collect all Inuit geographical names in the Arctic region of the Quebec-Labrador peninsula. The toponymic maps, as well as a description

of the surveys and methodology, can be found in the *Gazeteer of Inuit Place Names* (Müller-Wille 1987).

2 Arjun Appadurai, "Grassroots Globalization and the Research Imagination," *Public Culture* 12, 1 (2000): 7.

3 Local law.

4 The rights of *usus, fructus*, and *abusus* are, respectively, the right to use the land, the right to its fruits, and the right to alienate it.

5 That lands occupied by tribes were not terra nullius and, hence, were not open for acquisition through occupation was confirmed in the *Western Sahara Case,* Adv. Op. [1975] ICJ Rep. 12.

6 Notably *Tamaki* v. *Baker* (1901) AC 561; and *Amodu Tijani* v. *Secretary, Southern Rhodesia,* (1921) 2 AC 399.

7 *Calder* v. *A.-G.B.C.* (1970) 13 DLR 3d, 64; *R.* v. *Sparrow* [1990] 1 SCR 1075.

8 See Lester 1979.

9 *Re Eskimos*, SCR 104 [1939].

10 In 1912, the Québec Boundary Extension Act, 2 George V, 1912, ch. 45 (hereinafter the Boundary Extension Act) enlarged the territory of Quebec and gave underlying title to the Province of Quebec. The territory was still burdened by Aboriginal title. The federal government needed to effect an absolute surrender of the land from the Aboriginal inhabitants before the province's title could be perfected. This happened with the James Bay and Northern Québec Agreement in 1975. Although the 1912 act did not alter the residual federal jurisdiction to deal with "Indians, and Lands reserved for the Indian" under s. 91.24 of the Constitution Act, 1867, the Boundary Extension Act reiterated the burden of Aboriginal title over the land in s. 2(c): "The province of Québec will recognise the rights of the Indian inhabitants in the territory in the same manner as the government of Canada has heretofore recognised such rights and has obtained surrender thereof." While the province had underlying title to the territory since 1912, in effect it did not administratively occupy the territory until the 1960s. Prior to that time the federal government provided basic services to the Inuit, including education, social services, policing, and health care. Effective control of the territory escaped the province. It is in this sense of acquiring political and administrative control of the territory that it can be said that the provincial government was claiming Nouveau-Québec.

11 I mean, by sovereignty, both self-government and the larger claim to shared territorial sovereignty implicit in the fact-driven approach to the acquisition of sovereignty. By the latter I mean that, as a matter of fact, it may be found that more than one peoples have peacefully and continuously occupied a territory and thus merit a more nuanced territorial arrangement. By "Inuit sovereignty" I do not mean exclusive territorial sovereignty amounting to statehood. The latter would be considerably attenuated by the continuous and peaceful, public and open display of Canadian territorial sovereignty. The public to which this display of Canadian sovereignty has been addressed has historically included the Inuit, at very least in the James Bay and Northern Québec Agreement, and is signalled by both Inuit consent and acquiescence to Canadian sovereignty.

12 For an excellent account of the diplomatic exchanges that were triggered by disputes between the Hudson's Bay Company and the French, see Lester (1979, 1977).

References

Brice-Bennett, C., ed. 1977. *Our Footprints Are Everywhere: Inuit Land Use and Occupancy in Labrador.* Ottawa: Labrador Inuit Association.

Brochu, M. 1962. *Le défi du Nouveau-Québec.* Montréal: Éditions du Jour.

Brody, H. 1977. "Permanence and Change among the Inuit and Settlers of Labrador." In *Our Footprints Are Everywhere: Inuit Land Use and Occupancy in Labrador*, ed. C. Brice-Bennett, 311-47. Ottawa: Labrador Inuit Association.

Crowe, K. 1974. *A History of the Original Peoples of Northern Canada.* Montreal: Arctic Institute of North America.

Hallendy, N. 1994. "The Last Known Traditional Inuit Trial on Southwest Baffin Island in the Canadian Arctic." Background paper no. 2 in Places of Power and Objects of Veneration in the Canadian Arctic. Prepared for the World Archaeological Congress 3.

Juricek, J. 1970. "English Claims in North America to 1660: A Study in Legal and Constitutional History." PhD diss., University of Chicago.

Lester, G. 1979. "Aboriginal Land Rights: The Significance of Inuit Place-Naming." *Études Inuit Studies* 3, 1: 53-75.

–. 1977. "Primitivism versus Civilization: A Basic Question in the Law of Aboriginal Rights to the Land." *In Our Footprints Are Everywhere: Inuit Land Use and Occupancy in Labrador*, ed. C. Brice-Bennett, 351-74. Ottawa: Labrador Inuit Association.

Morrison, W. 1986. "Canadian Sovereignty and the Inuit of the Central and Eastern Arctic." *Études Inuit Studies* 10, 1-2: 245-59.

Müller-Wille, L. 1987. *Gazeteer of Inuit Place Names in Nunavik*. Inukjuak: Avataq Cultural Institute.

–. 1985. "Une méthodologie pour les enquêtes toponymiques autochtones: Le répertoire inuit de la région de Kativik et de sa zone côtière." *Études Inuit Studies* 9, 1: 51-66.

–. 1984. "The Legacy of Native Toponyms: Towards Establishing the Inuit Place Name Inventory of the Kativik Region (Québec)." *Onamastica Canadiana* 65: 2-19.

5
The Landscape of Nunavik/ The Territory of Nouveau-Québec[1]

Peter Jacobs

> On the orders of Minos, King of Crete, an elaborate labyrinth was constructed by Daedalus following a victorious war against the Athenians. Minos demanded of the vanquished that a tribute of seven young women and seven young men be sent every nine years as a sacrifice to the Minotaur, a ferocious bull hidden at the center of the labyrinth.
>
> As fate would have it, Thesius, an Athenean Hero, finding himself amongst the designated tribute, resolved to kill the Minotaur and thus to liberate his City from the ignominy of the cyclical reminder of defeat. Ariadne, the daughter of Minos, enamoured of Thesius, sought council from Daedalus who advised her to provide him with a spool and woolen cord with which the hero might retrace his path through the labyrinth. Arriving at the center of the labyrinth Thesius kills the Bull and, retracing his steps with his young companions, escapes his intended fate.[2]

The labyrinth, and, more specifically, Ariadne's magic cord, serves as a metaphor for the development process and the reversible transformations of territory and landscape. It informs our understanding of the process that occurs in moving from captivity to liberty, from captured territory to the promise of inhabited landscape. The essential mechanism in achieving this transformation is the infrastructure of development, the magic cord of Ariadne that allowed Theseus to penetrate the corridors of the labyrinth and then to regain his freedom.

Development is culturally charged; it is grounded in and informed by our myths, and it tends to reinforce them though the transformations that are effected through development. Development in the northern region of Quebec serves as one example of this process. In particular, the proposed development of a network of large dams in the North to provide increased hydroelectric energy in the South illustrates the interplay of at least four such cultural perspectives – those of the Inuit, the Cree, and the northern and southern populations of Euro-Canadians.

For the vast majority of Canadians, the North is perceived as a virgin and empty territory, "the true north strong and free" of our national anthem. In contrast, for those who live in the region it is a homeland, a very real landscape charged with meaning, a source of sustenance and social structure. Notwithstanding these two visions of the North, the North is in the process of changing.[3] This process is perceived quite differently, depending on whether it is being viewed by the South or by the North (Mulvihill and Jacobs 1991).

The history of northern development, particularly as it relates to changes initiated by the South, tends towards strategies more appropriate to the development of a territory than a landscape. Even the names given to the region – "Nouveau-Québec" as opposed to "Nunavik" – reflect these attitudes.[4] My use of a classical Greek metaphor reflects the cultural orientation of the primary audience to which this chapter is addressed. The multiple meanings suggested by the narrative of the labyrinth and Ariadne's strategy, it is hoped, may inspire a deeper consideration of the northern development process. The perspective that I offer on the none too subtle distinctions between landscape and territory in the North is informed by twenty years of community-based conservation and development work in the fifteen villages that dot the coastal landscape of Nunavik.

All development induces transformations to the receptor environment. When development is embraced by a community that shares a common set of values, the impact of the project is usually perceived as positive. When the project is destined for an environment that consists of a number of value systems, development is frequently discussed in terms of the equitable distribution of benefits and risks. These perceptions of equity are informed by the respective value systems at play, and, in many cases, the "golden mean" is not easy to discern. But when a development project is introduced into an environment that is entirely different from the one that has generated the need for such a project, questions of equity are supplanted by more visceral reactions – reactions that question whether the project should proceed under *any* circumstances. Such is the case of an immense development project proposed for a large region 1,000 kilometres north of Montreal. The project in question involves harnessing and exploiting the hydroelectric potential of the Great Whale River and its tributaries in order to meet the projected energy demand in southern Quebec and the northeastern United States (Hydro-Québec 1991).

The project to develop infrastructure for hydroelectric power to be transported by a network of towers and lines and supported by roads, airports, and maritime docking facilities that would link the Inuit communities to the South raises important issues. These concern the nature and meaning of development and, more specifically, the continuing role that development infrastructure plays in the progressive (or retrogressive) transformation of landscape into territory, of homeland into resource, that has characterized northern development to date.[5]

Infrastructure serves as a means to organize the development process. It is the backbone of the newly configured landscape – or territory – depending on your perspective. Two conditions can be envisaged: the first involves the infrastructure and the territory being intimately related (e.g., as they are along the coastal landscapes where the Inuit have fished and hunted for millennia); the second involves the infrastructure being comprised of, for example, new roads, rails, air routes, and maritime installations designed to transform and restructure the territory, which, perhaps, will emerge later as a new and cherished landscape or, sadly, as a vanquished homeland.

Insofar as infrastructure (such as, for example, that associated with the Great Whale project) serves to link two or more destinations and thus to establish some form of communication between or amongst them, it is reasonable to ask in which direction and with what force the flow of information is being propelled – particularly if we wish to avoid the consequences of colonialism that all too frequently accompany the establishment of new links to the North. Given these stakes, therefore, it seems reasonable that, before launching into an extensive development program, we should have an understanding and appreciation of the needs and desires of all those involved.

The linkages of infrastructure and territory are joined in the matrix of an existing landscape, where they provide the potential to form new landscapes. Territory, in this sense, is simply a spatial dimension, whereas landscape represents home and habitat; thus infrastructure can serve to establish links between a spatial extent and a homeland. Depending on the development strategy retained, however, it can also act to decompose and transform a landscape into a territory that is open to exploitation.

Daedalus transformed a natural labyrinth into one conceived and constructed by a human being. According to Ovid, insofar as Minos charged Daedalus with the task of hiding the Minotaur in the built form of a labyrinth, "he multiplied false paths and dead ends without number. With the construct of Daedalus the labyrinth was objectified, became an object and passed from symbol to concept" (Bord 1975, 45). The labyrinth is continually reconstructed, and the exit from one is the entry to the next – a strategy adopted by James Joyce in recounting the adventures of Stephen Dedalus within the built labyrinth of the City of Dublin (Joyce 1934). Dedalus held his fate in his own hands – the paradigm of Western development from the Industrial Revolution to the present.

Landscape and Territory

What, then, is "landscape," and what is the meaning of "territory"? Numerous origins may be found for the term landscape (Seddon 1986; Turner

1982/3), which modern dictionaries continue to define "as an expanse of natural scenery seen by the eye in one view."[6] Contemporary concepts of landscape extend well beyond the picturesque to embrace the memory of natural process and human action – the expression of who we are and what we wish to become. It is the expression of culture and how we choose to live with nature (Jacobs 1991). Mitchell (1994) suggests that, like money, the landscape serves as a social hieroglyph that masks the real basis of its worth.[7]

The idea of territory can be approached from two directions: (1) either it consists of the water and land that fall under the jurisdiction of the nation, state, or king or (2) it is a part of a nation or homeland that does not have the same status and rights as does the rest of the state. It is interesting to note that, with regard to the second category, the two largest territories are found in northern Canada and northern Australia. Both are inhabited, in very large part, by Aboriginal peoples – the Inuit and the Aborigines, respectively.

In its most noble expression the landscape is sacred, invested with a spirit that supports a profound, holy sense of belonging.[8] Indivisible, it is the place of sharing and of social exchange. There remain, even in our day, societies that work the land and the seas as common property regulated through a system of sharing and of collective management.[9] At its most banal, landscape is the land to be modelled and shaped according to the perceived needs of the prince; this has been the typical, but not exclusive, situation since the Industrial Revolution.

The landscapes of Australia, many of which are less than hospitable to the Western visitor or settler, have been the homeland of the Aborigines for millennia. When this landscape is perceived as a territory that is not occupied or claimed, or as occupied but by people clearly inferior (i.e., more primitive) than those more newly arrived, then, consistent with imperial and colonial models, such a territory becomes, ipso facto, available for development. It was in Australia and within this framework that one of the more barbaric of legal fictions – terra nullius – was developed.

This fiction postulates that Aboriginal peoples have no legal status and that, therefore, their territory may be regarded as uninhabited. This provided the newly developed colonies the widest margin of manoeuvre with respect to the use and abuse of territory. Terra nullius ignores the tangible evidence that these "primitive" peoples survived the most cruel and unforgiving of landscapes for 40,000 years or more, developed an exhaustive understanding of their environment, and developed an artistic legacy second to none. Only recently has the celebrated legal case of an indigenous Torres Strait Islander, Mabo,[10] served to annul this fiction in Australia, which is certainly not the only place in the world where it occurs.[11]

Within this context, development reflects a considerable, even devastating, play of power that can and does transform landscapes into territories, homelands into claim sites. Nor is this transformation limited to the exotic landscapes of the North. In *Landscape and Memory*, for example, Simon Schama remarks that the choice of development projects that focus on the control of water courses is anything but arbitrary. In describing development as a means of transforming landscape into territory, it is evident that the most certain of strategies is to install the appropriate infrastructure as a base of operations – the latter being a military metaphor that is both apt and accurate.

Schama (1995, 260-1) notes that a long line of sociologists, from Karl Marx to Karl Wittfogel, has seen "hydrological societies and despotism as functionally connected ... The colossal dam and hydro-electric power stations as emblems of omnipotence were for modern despots what the Nile irrigation canals were for the Pharaohs ... and by pressing ahead with the titanic project of the Three Gorges Dam, the most famous icon of all China's river landscapes, Deng Xiaping tried to present himself in succession to the founder of the very first dynasty, around 2200 BC, the semi-legendary emperor Yu whose authority was established on his mastery of the flood, and the establishment of intensive, irrigated agriculture." Ivan Illich (1985) bemoans the loss of natural stream and river courses, particularly in the city, where water has been accorded a sterile and antiseptic role rather than the symbolic and fertile one that it fulfilled in the past. Bachelard (1942) treats water as a rich source of inspiration – one that lends itself poorly to the grand gestures of hierarchical control.

Notwithstanding these views, and depending on societal objectives, other changes can be effected through the provision of development infrastructures that are either cataclysmic or catalytic with regard to transforming traditional landscapes into new landscapes, some of which, in turn, will become traditional. Such is the case of Western Europe over the last 500 years – a modest period of time relative to that of the Inuit and Aborigine. In this regard, it may be instructive to review the process of transforming old landscapes into new ones before returning to the landscapes of northern Quebec.

Transformation of Landscape to Landscape

Between 1612 and 1635 the citizens of Holland risked at least ten million guilder to drain some 26,000 hectares (100 square miles) of swamplands, adding one-third to their existing landbase – this in addition to the immense amount of land reclaimed from the sea fifty years earlier between 1560 and 1610. These new landscapes were typically located adjacent to the original land profile contained by new dike walls. The polders so formed were flat and, at regular intervals, were traversed by canals, one of which inevitably marked the seam between the old and new landscape.

Ann Jensen Adams, in her excellent analysis of seventeenth-century Dutch landscape painting, remarked on the virtual absence of pictorial representation of this transformation. She speculates that the nostalgic themes of the paintings of this period may have served to diminish a collective sense of guilt with regard to the commercial transformation of the traditional Dutch landscape (Adams 1994). Yet, the transformed landscape is what we now consider the traditional landscape, as did the Dutch themselves by the eighteenth century.

In France, the minister of finance, Fouquet, built Vaux-le-Viscomte and, in so doing, changed the very basis from which the French landscape was viewed. Fouquet believed that, by regulating the flow of water in the form of canals, we affirm the power of humanity with respect to nature. This is illustrated by the statue of Hercules at the terminus of the principal garden axis. This same theme was reprised by Louis XIV after he disposed of Fouquet and integrated his team of Le Nôtre, Le Vau, and Le Brun at the Palace of Versailles.

The Grand Canal at Versailles was, in many respects, the paradigm of the entire network of canals that was in the process of being constructed by the king's military engineers throughout Provence and Bourgogne. The entire enterprise was necessary in order to compete with the system already established in Holland. The form of the canal was the perfect expression of the absolute control the Sun King exercised over the waters of his realm – straight, linear, obedient, and foreseeable. The formal vocabulary derived in large part from these two palace gardens was to mark the entire French countryside around Paris, transforming, once again, a traditional landscape into the more formal and structured landscapes of Louis XIV. These, in turn, became the traditional landscape of the next generations of Parisians.

Two hundred years later, in the New World, 31,000 miles of rail linked the eastern United States by the beginning of the American Civil War, and, on 10 May 1869 a golden spike marked the successful completion of the transcontinental railroad, forever transforming the notion of the American frontier landscape.[12] The consequences of this transformation were foreseen by the celebrated painter Thomas Cole in his series of five canvases entitled "The Course of Empire."[13] The first illustrates the virgin natural landscape inhabited only by Native-Americans; the second depicts the pastoral landscape of the early European settlers; the third portrays the rise and glory of the Industrial City; and the last two show the demise and ruin of this transformation, with nature once again reclaiming its due.[14]

And, at the beginning of the twentieth century, John Ruskin remarked at the wonders of the Industrial Revolution: "I sometimes watch a locomotive take its breath at a railway station, and think what work there is in its bars and wheels." He noted, however, that there was a price to pay. "We are forced, for the sake of accumulating our power and knowledge, to live in Cities: but such advantage as we have in associating with each other is in great part counter-balanced by our loss of fellowship with Nature." He continued with the complaint that "the changes in the state of this country are now so rapid ... that I must ask how much of it do you seriously intend within the next fifty years to be coalpit, brickfield, or quarry" (Herbert 1964, 145-51). Given his attitudes towards the city, industrialization, and nature, it is not surprising that Ruskin was horrified at the possibility that the beauty of the English countryside, as depicted by Turner, might simply be eradicated. He foresaw the arrival of electricity transported by lines strung across the landscape like so many clotheslines, and he pleaded with his government to at least have the decency to bury them where they would traverse national parks and other sensitive landscapes. All this before the magic cords of Ariadne were ever suspended between the lighthouses of Rhodes.

Ruskin's desire to hide these cords that would carry electricity to the very cradle of the new industrial city implies an aesthetic. This aesthetic views such cords as wounds that cut across and transfigure the landscape, and it recalls the nostalgia of the seventeenth-century Dutch landscape painting. This nostalgia continues to inform our development strategies, which seek to hide or absorb these lines within the landscape in both the South and the North.

Transformation of Landscapes into Territories

> A struggle erupted between a crow [representing the Inuit] and a gull [representing the Whites] over a piece of meat. Days turned into weeks, and weeks into months, as the contestants grappled and tore at one another. In the end, it was the gull who triumphed, establishing Whites as the stronger and better-off people. But when finally the gull took flight with his prize, the meat had grown putrid. (my condensation; refer to Metayer 1972; Melzack 1970)

The Great Whale River Hydro-Electric Project consists in the construction of three hydroelectrical power plants some 1,200 kilometres north of Montreal. Each power plant has its own reservoir, and all are linked to a regulating reservoir formed by enlarging Lac Bienville in the interior of the watersheds associated with the project. The installed power produced by the three power plants will approach 3,168 megawatts (Hydro-Québec 1991). In order for the Great Whale project to be achieved, an important network of marine, airport, and road infrastructure is essential to support the numerous sites that will be required to build, operate, and convey power to the South. As a consequence, the project opens a gateway that serves as an entry to, as well as an exit from, the territory. The paths provided by the infrastructure associated with the project are anything but the neutral artefacts of the development process. Their raison d'être consists in delivering energy from the North to the South, and this raises the question as to who benefits from the development of the territory in question and at whose risk.

Ariadne's cord, cutting across the territory of northern Quebec that is now regulated by the James Bay and Northern Québec Agreement (JBNQA), is very tangible and real.[15] The cord consists of the multiple strands of wire transporting energy across the northern territories to the urban landscapes of the South. Suspended, these cords are carried by immense towers of steel that march at regular intervals of 100 metres for 1,200 kilometres – conceptually, a distance comparable to that between London and Paris. The cord carries energy from one homeland to another, or from a territory to a landscape, depending on one's viewpoint. The critical factor is that the magic cord is perceived and valued differently by the North and by the South, and its role within the different cultures is at once an opportunity for, and a constraint on, their respective development (development itself being a term largely defined by the values and social structure of the communities concerned).

The Minotaur that lies in wait within the labyrinth of landscapes that stretch from North to South is, variously, the insatiable urban place or the rich resources of the northern territories. Theseus is either the skilled engineer or the Aboriginal hunter, Ariadne the economist or the anthropologist, depending, as always, on one's point of view.

While the traditional values of the Euro-Canadian and the Inuit have much in common, they are distinguished, in part, by notions of justice that are collective rather than individual and hierarchical, an economy that focuses on sharing rather than on the accumulation of wealth, an emphasis on holistic health rather than on absence of disease,[16] and on cooperation rather than on competition. In the South, time is linear and sequential; in the North it is cyclic and repetitive. Space, too, is linked to our heritage. Ever since the first military engineer set foot in the New World we have divided and subdivided space. It is an integral part of the way we conceive of space and render it legally operational. But how can we define and operate within a region whose limits change radically from winter to summer, where frozen ice extends the land surface along thousands of kilometres of coastline? Where the substance of space shifts from solid to liquid form?[17]

Obviously, information is shaped by culture.[18] Our tendency is to simplify complex systems, to order them with respect to discrete and objectively verifiable categories in order to better understand them. It is unlikely, however, that the knowledge and information pathways of the Inuit follow the same trails. It is both foolish and arrogant to marginalize the fund of knowledge called traditional that has served a culture for thousands of years in an effort to distinguish it from our own, particularly as it reflects on our own civilization and its tendency to exclude rather than to include.

Ariadne's cord is a virtual one, and it allows us to imagine the flow of energy and ideas that can be shared by a people whose landscapes are adjacent to, and have formed the substrata of, those we now call home. The cord provides the medium through which we might renew the rite, ritual, and rhythm of the daily and festive aspects of each other's lives. Insofar as the cord retains its integrity, exchange is possible. Once the cord ruptures, we are confronted with a discontinuous flow of information that leads to systems failure. The cord carries a further message for our ears, however – that we are losing a rural arcadia in order to extend the urban realm.[19]

The proposed Great Whale project in northern Quebec was the source of enormous anxiety for the resident Cree and Inuit populations. The principal issues of concern included, but were not limited to, the health of all human and animal communities in the region; continuing access to the territory by all human and animal populations, including the caribou; the availability of resources; the maintenance of social cohesion at the local, regional, and national levels; and respect for values. This last issue includes the concern for preserving the ecosystem, the preservation of unique and remarkable sites, the maintenance of cultural diversity, and the improvement of the region's quality of life.

Needless to say, the task facing the team charged with the mandate of reviewing the environmental and social impacts of the proposed hydroelectric project was daunting, both because of its temporal and spatial extent and because of its social and cultural complexity. The evaluation process consisted, first, in a "scoping" exercise designed to develop the basic guidelines against which the environmental impact assessment (EIA) would be written (Commission de la qualité de l'environnement Kativik 1992). The project proponent then provided the evaluation team with an environmental impact statement (EIS) (Hydro-Québec 1993) that was reviewed for its conformity with the directives (if necessary, the statement would be revised to conform more closely to them). The EIA would then be submitted for public review and comment, and, finally, the evaluation team would render its decision as to whether or not, and under what conditions, the project might proceed. Given the issues raised with respect to the very nature of development, and in particular with respect to the infrastructure of development, the task of writing the guidelines was critical. A few of these guidelines will serve to illustrate our attempt to provide equitable treatment to the cultures of both the North and the South.[20]

Amongst the directives issued to the project proponent for the Great Whale project, particular attention was focused on the consequences of providing a road from the South to the community of Great Whale, which had, to this point in time, been accessible only by air. The directive reads as follows:

> The Proponent shall evaluate how the construction of access routes to the installations would contribute to the opening of the territory as a whole through the creation of transportation links with the rest of the continent. The Proponent shall also indicate the extent to which needs for access (both northward and southward) would be met and to which needs for isolation would be compromised (potential users, frequency, seasons, methods of transportation, reasons for use, changes in travel costs between the host region and the rest of the country) for each affected population. Again, collaboration with the communities of Kuujjuarapik and Whapmagoostui and analysis of other instances where territories were opened (including Chisasibi) are recommended. The Proponent shall be particularly attentive to the sense of identification with the territory on the part of both local populations and those of other regions. (Commission de la qualité de l'environnement Kativik 1992, Directive 528)

But of which territory or landscape are we talking? The Great Whale River is perceived by the engineers in terms of cubic metres of water flow per second; the fishing and hunting community of southern Quebec views the river as a recreational resource without equal; the Cree and Inuit see the river as a source of sustainable food and as a sacred landscape. The choice lies in maintaining the wild river or in submitting to the dams, turbines, and raceways that would define the river as a source of energy. For this and other similar reasons, the directives insisted that the project proponent characterize the social and environmental impacts on the landscapes and inhabitants of the region from a number of different cultural perspectives:

> Local residents' knowledge of their biophysical and social milieu is essential to an adequate assessment of the impacts of a development project. Furthermore, each cultural group has its own conceptual and symbolic system that reflects the group's image of itself and of its communities, this environment and its past and future. Since this conceptual and symbolic system partly determines the group's reaction to change, it is an intrinsic element of the environment itself and must be thoroughly understood before the impacts of a development project can be assessed. In the case of the proposed Great Whale project, the Proponent must be particularly attentive to the conceptual and symbolic systems and knowledge of the populations affected. (Directive 126)

> Considering this diversity of cultures, it is to be expected that the ecosystem components which are identified and given value may well vary from one culture to another, and even if they are similar, that the reasons for which they are valued may be different. In the same way, since points of view concerning the proposed project and its impacts are based on different values and knowledge, it is quite likely that they will vary from one culture to another. The Proponent shall take this diversity into account both in its description of the environment and in its impact analysis, through the notion of valued ecosystem component. (Directive 127)

In addition, the directives insist on "the right of local communities to decide their future and their own societal projects and not to be forced to risk the quality or sustainability of the resources that form the economic basis of their region's landscape" (Directive 113).

With specific reference to the economic organization of the Cree homeland, the traplines define family limits for harvesting wildlife within the collective landscape of the Cree Nation. The policies of compensation for impacts occasioned by the proposed project outlined by the project proponent create a dependency on the municipal services that would be supplied by the proponent and that would inevitably affect the nature of the indigenous villages of the region (Penn 1995).

Whose strategies and whose plans will shape the northern landscape of Quebec? Clearly, the Great Whale project would dominate use of the territory. In the process of implementing the network of dam sites, reservoirs, airports, and roads, the nature and meaning of the area affected would be profoundly marked. Transportation from one community to the next and from northern communities to those in the South is not simply a question of moving freight efficiently and effectively. The social dynamic between communities in the North and the impact of movement and access from the South to the North is neither trivial nor of obvious benefit to the latter in the absence of transitional strategies. Planning for tourism, housing, and natural resource harvesting cannot be seen as a subset of a hydroelectric project. In the absence of integrated planning, it is difficult to see how the landscape of Nunavik could be anything other than a territory.

Conclusion

Projects as vast and encompassing as the Great Whale project challenge our ability to understand the implications of project implementation – to foresee the consequences, both positive and negative, over the long term. When these projects occur within multicultural contexts, as many do, they frequently result in alienation and the erosion of cultural diversity. When this does occur, one culture's landscape becomes another's territory. The opposite ideal is expressed in the following short tale: "A biblical midrash (adam v'adama) suggests that Adam was formed of yellow sand, red clay, black soil, and white chalk in order that he be received back into the earth anywhere that he died."[21] The relationship between the North and the South serves to teach us prudence and caution, particularly when a landscape and homeland is treated as a territory and resource, when we pretend that Adam has no home in this place.

The model of development that one chooses can dominate the landscape, transforming it into a territory, or it can serve to link it with others over time and space, transforming landscapes into new ones, adding layers of meaning and purpose to a homeland.[22] The first strategy is one of dominance; the second is one of sharing and of partnership. To believe that the choice is objective is to deny the rich patina of values that reside in our concepts of landscape and of territory and their relationship to each other.

There is an interesting view of the labyrinth contained in one of the Hasidic tales recounted by Martin Buber (1955, 11):

> A king once built a great and glorious palace with numerous chambers but only one door was opened. When the building was finished, it was announced that all princes should appear before the king who sat enthroned in the last of these chambers. But when they entered, they saw that there were doors open on all sides which led to winding passages in the distance, and there were again doors and again passages, and no end arose before their bewildered eyes. Then came the king's son and saw that all the labyrinth was a mirrored illusion and he saw his father sitting in the hall before him.[23]

Some of the development instruments of our age have become part of a common cultural toolbox. An Inuk in the Village of Quartaq can watch surfers in California while we eat caribou and ptarmigan in the restaurants of Montreal. But when homeland becomes independent of culture of place and all landscapes are transformed into territories, both real and virtual, is it not time for us to retrace our steps with the aid of Ariadne's magic cord?

The question of dependence, independence, and interdependence of landscape and territory within the framework of development raises critical issues concerning our relationships between each other and between ourselves and place, between young and old, between lifestyles and individual and collective values.[24] How can we continue to develop a sense of belonging to time, place, and culture when we are less and less attached to landscape, while, simultaneously, we travel the world with ease on the Internet?

The strategy of hiding the infrastructure of development, of considering it as a scar across the landscape, as outlined by Adams and reinforced by Ruskin, now rings hollow. Perhaps it is time to celebrate strategies that link landscape to landscape and to support their successive transformations in ways that are sustainable and equitable. Perhaps we should view ourselves as charged with the vital mandate of Theseus – to liberate territory and return it to landscape and homeland.

Notes

This chapter originally appeared in French, as "Paysage de Nunavik, territoire du Nouveau-Québec," in *Le paysage territoire d'intentions,* ed. P. Poullaouec-Gonidec, M. Gariépy, and B. Lassus, 115-31. Paris and Montreal: L'Harmattan.

1 The Inuit of Northern Quebec refer to their homeland as Nunavik, while the Government of Quebec refers to the region as "le Nouveau-Québec" (New Quebec).

2 See, amongst other renditions of this well known fable, Bullfinch (1898). Note that a variant rendering required that the tribute be paid every year. See also Bord and Lambert (1977, 45).

3 For an excellent overview, see the three-volume study by Freeman (1976).

4 Nunavik, named by the Inuit who have inhabited the region for at least 5,000 years (see Müller-Wille, Chapter 3, this volume), has become a theatre of development in every sense. As a member and chairman of the Kativik Environmental Quality Commission with a mandate to evaluate development proposals in the region over the last twenty years, I have had the opportunity to travel through this enchanted landscape. The Kativik Environmental Quality Commission was created by virtue of Chapter 23 of the James Bay and Northern Québec Agreement. The mandate of the commission consists in examining and evaluating the environmental and social impacts of projects situated northward of the fifty-fifth parallel in Quebec. The commission decides whether or not a proposed project should proceed and, if so, under what conditions. As a direct function of these trips, and the numerous discussions I've had with my Inuk and southern colleagues, I have gradually formulated a perspective on the issues involved in the development of the northern landscape – a landscape that reveals its secrets slowly and in direct proportion to our understanding of the "genius of the place."

5 These issues were reviewed by the Kativik Environmental Quality Commission, the Evaluating Committee, the Federal Review Committee North of the 55th Parallel, and the Federal Environmental Assessment Review Panel (henceforth referred to as the Kativik Environmental Quality Commission et al.). These groups were acting conjointly within the framework of the environmental review of the Great Whale River Hydro-Electric Project.

6 *Webster's New Twentieth-Century Dictionary*, unabridged, 2nd ed. (Philadelphia: William Collins Publishers, 1979).

7 Mitchell (1994, 5) states that "landscape is a medium of exchange between the human and the natural, the self and the other. As such it is like money, good for nothing in itself, but expressive of a potentially limitless reserve of value."

8 The idea is best expressed by the Hebrew concept of "Makom," which encapsulates the idea of a holy place.

9 See the extensive literature on common property management, beginning with Berkes (1989).

10 For a summary and discussion, see Havnen (1994).

11 The same thesis of the availability of a territory for resource exploitation is developed for the Northwest Territories of Canada. See Richardson (1993).

12 The National Parks service brochure on the Golden Spike National Historic Site in Utah notes: "More than economically, the railroad tied the west to the eastern states. They altered the very pace of life, putting people on a schedule who had always geared their activities to natural rhythms."

13 The perception of the transformation of the New World of the nineteenth century is treated by Sweet (1945). For the philosophic debates, see Weiner (1962).

14 Alain Roger (1989) remarks that the very idea of the aesthetics of the picturesque or the sublime, invented by Baumgarten at the end of the eighteenth century, is difficult to imagine beyond the specific references to the landscape types he uses.

15 See James Bay and Northern Québec Agreement; the Environmental Quality Act, Section 23; Laws of the Government of the Province of Quebec.
16 Adelson (1992) explores a parallel theme among neighbouring Cree.
17 Independent of the spatial division of territory, Mulrennan (1994) questions the relevance of the concept of "land" itself in a cultural system where the coast is seen as a legal and cartographic division between land and water. For the Inuit and Australian indigenous peoples, the coast unites rather than divides water and land. See also Mulrennan and Scott (Chapter 6, this volume).
18 Rhys Jones (1991, 29) notes that a hunter's perspective on the landscape depends on both ecological and linguistic structures. Certain Aboriginal taxonomies correspond with those of Linneas; others are superior, based on an appreciation of the amino-acids shared by certain species that are only now being mapped by modern science. See also Buege (1995). The issue of knowledge systems that are referred to as "traditional" is hardly limited to the Inuit or the Aborigines. Martha Johnson (1992) treats the problems of capturing oral traditions.
19 See Jacobs (1994).
20 For a full study of the implications of the scoping process used in this review, see Mulvihill (1997).
21 See the comments in Adin Steinsaltz's (1995) chapter, "Formed from the Dust." See also Sanhedrin 38a-b *Soncino Talmud* (London: Soncino Press, 1995).
22 A recent project for the Village of Verchères attempts to address these issues, focusing on the shared metaphors of the village community. See Jacobs (1996).
23 See Buber's (1955) *The Legend of the Baal Shem*. The *Baal Shem Tov*, the master of the Good Name, is considered the fountainhead of the eighteenth-century Hasidism in Eastern Europe. Rabbi Israel Ben Eliezer lived from 1700 to 1760. Martin Buber, in his introduction, argues that "myth is the expression of the fullness of existence, its image, its sign; it drinks incessantly from the gushing fountain of life" (11). Interestingly, the Greek construct of the labyrinth posits darkness at the centre, while the Hasidic tale posits light – both surround these goals with Ovid's illusions. In the first, liberty is achieved through return; in the second, liberty is achieved through suppression of illusion.
24 See Mulvihill and Jacobs (1991).

References

Adams, Ann Jensen. 1994. "Competing Communities in the 'Great Bog of Europe': Identity and Seventeenth Century Dutch Landscape Painting." In *Landscape and Power*, ed. W.J.T. Mitchell, 35-76. Chicago: University of Chicago Press.

Adelson, N. 1992. "'Being Alive Well': Indigenous Belief as Opposition among the Whapmagoostui Cree." PhD diss. McGill University, Montreal.

Bachelard, Gaston. 1942. *L'eau et les rêves: Essai sur l'imagination de la matière; livre de poche*. Paris: Librairie José Corti.

Berkes, Fikret. 1989. *Common Property Resources: Ecology and Community-Based Sustainable Development*. London: Belhaven Press.

Bord, Janet. 1975. *Mazes and Labyrinths of the World*. New York: E.P. Dutton.

Bord, Janet, et Jean-Clarence Lambert. 1977. *Labyrinthes et dédales du monde*. Paris: Les Presses de la Connaissance.

Buber, Martin. 1955. *The Legend of the Baal Shem*. Edinburgh: T. J. Clark Ltd.

Buege, Douglas J. 1995. "Confessions of an Eco-Colonialist: Responsible Knowing among the Inuit." In *Wild Ideas*, ed. David Rothenberg, 81-93. Minneapolis: University of Minnesota Press.

Bullfinch, Thomas. 1898. *The Age of Fable*. David McKay Publishers.

Commission de la qualité de l'environnement Kativik. 1992. *Directive: Étude des impacts sur l'environnement du projet hydro-électrique Grande Baleine*. Montréal.

Freeman, Milton. 1976. *Inuit Land-use and Occupancy Project*, 3 vols. Ottawa: Indian and Northern Affairs Canada.

Havnen, Peg. 1994. "The Mabo Decision and Its Implications." In *Surviving Columbus*, ed. P. Jull, M. Mulrennan, M. Sullivan, G. Crough, and D. Lea, 88-93. Darwin: North Australia Research Unit.

Herbert, Robert L., ed. 1964. *The Art and Criticism of John Ruskin.* 145-51. New York: Da Capo Press.

Hydro-Québec. 1991. Complexe Grande Baleine, Bulletin 5, Novembre.

–. 1993. *Feasibility Study: Complexe Grande Baleine.* 34 vols. Montréal.

Illich, Ivan. 1985. *H_2O: Les eaux de l'oubli.* France: Lieu commun.

Jacobs, Peter. 1991. "Proposed Definition of Landscape Architecture." Unpublished paper commissioned by the American Society of Landscape Architects, Washington, DC.

–. 1994. "À propos de l'Arcadie." *Trames* 9: 7-12. Faculté de l'aménagement, Université de Montréal.

–. 1996. "Environmental Parentheses and Design Metaphors." In *Nature Outside Protected Areas,* ed. Dusan Ogrin, 56-71. Ljubjana: University of Ljubjana and the Council of Europe.

Jacobs, Peter, and Peter Mulvihill. 1995. "Ancient Lands, New Perspectives: Towards Multi-Cultural Literacy in Landscape Management." *Landscape and Urban Planning* 32: 7-17.

Johnson, Martha. 1992. *Lore: Capturing Traditional Environmental Knowledge.* Yellowknife/Ottawa: Dene Cultural Institute/IDRC.

Jones, Rhys. 1991. "Landscapes of the Mind: Aboriginal Perceptions of the Natural World." In *Humanities and the Australian Environment: Papers from the Australian Academy of the Humanities Symposium,* ed. D.J. Mulvaney, occasional paper no. 11, Canberra, Australia.

Joyce, James. 1934. *Ulysses.* New York: Modern Library Edition. (With a forward by Morris L. Ernst and decision by Judge John M. Woolsey not to prohibit publishing the book in the United States of America.)

Melzack, Ronald. 1970. *Raven, Creator of the World: Eskimo Legends Retold by Ronald Melzack.* Toronto: Little, Brown and Company.

Metayer, Ronald, ed. 1972. *Tales from the Igloo,* transl. R. Metayer. Edmonton: Hurtig Publishers.

Mitchell, W.J.T., ed. 1994. *Landscape and Power.* Chicago: University of Chicago Press.

Mulrennan, Monica E. 1994. "Mare Nullius: The Extension of Co-management Arrangements into Coastal and Marine Environments." Paper prepared for the Canadian Anthropology and Society/Canadian Association of Geographers, joint session on Environmental and Development Issues in the Canadian North. Learned Society Meetings, Montreal, May.

Mulvihill, Peter. 1997. "Environmental Assessment and Viable Interdependence: The Great Whale River Case." PhD diss., Université de Montréal.

Mulvihill, Peter, and Peter Jacobs. 1991. "Towards New North-South Development Strategies in Canada." *Alternatives* 18, 2: 34-9.

Penn, Allen. 1995. "Protecting the Traditional Way of Life: Strategies in Hydro-Electric Development." Unpublished paper. Montréal: Cree Regional Authority,.

Richardson, Boyce. 1993. *People of Terra Nullius: Betrayal and Rebirth in Aboriginal Canada.* Vancouver: Douglas and McIntyre.

Roger, Alain. 1989. "Esthétique du paysage au siècle des lumières." In *Composer le paysage: Constructions et crises de l'espace (1789-1992),* ed. Odile Marcel, 61-82. Champ Vallon, France: Collection Milieux.

Schama, Simon. 1995. *Landscape and Memory.* Toronto: Random House.

Seddon, George. 1986. "Landscape Planning: A Conceptual Perspective." *Landscape and Urban Planning* 13, 5-6: 335-47.

Steinsaltz, Adin. 1995. "Formed from the Dust." In *In the Beginning: Discourse on Chasidic Thought.* 19-27. New Jersey: Jason Aronson Publishers.

Sweet, Frederick A. 1945. *The Hudson River School and Early American Landscape Tradition.* Chicago: The Art Institute of Chicago.

Turner, J.H.D. 1982/3. "Landscape Planning: A Linguistic and Historical Analysis of the Term's Use." *Landscape and Urban Planning* 9, 3-4: 179-92.

Weiner, David R. 1962. *City and Country in America.* New York: Appleton Century Crafts.

6
Aboriginal Rights and Interests in Canadian Northern Seas

Monica E. Mulrennan and Colin H. Scott

Although territorial identification with a continuum of homelands and home-seas is a defining characteristic of many Aboriginal peoples, Europeans have generally failed to understand or accept this concept. In Canada, for example, central governments have adopted various principles for the discussion and negotiation of Aboriginal land claims, and these principles often ignore or underrate the central importance of estuaries, coastal areas, offshore islands, seas, and the seabed to Aboriginal peoples. Inuit, on the other hand, in common with the Cree of James Bay and Hudson Bay and other coastal indigenous peoples,

> view their right to use the seas and the land as one that is fundamental and woven into the fabric of their lives. They view their environment and their own place in it as a whole. They do not make the arbitrary distinctions made by scientists or administrators in the European tradition. (Jull and Bankes 1984, 562)

Seemingly in an attempt to address this problem, in 1986 the federal government extended its comprehensive land claims policy to include offshore areas traditionally used for harvesting, as well as Aboriginal participation in the resource and environmental management of such areas. According to this federal policy, Aboriginal claims to offshore areas are to be settled following the same general principles as are those that apply to land areas:

> In many cases, the areas traditionally used by Aboriginal groups to pursue their way of life include offshore areas. In such cases, negotiations concerning harvesting rights in offshore areas will be conducted, to the extent possible, in accordance with the same principles as those which apply to terrestrial areas. Participation in environmental management regimes and resource revenue-sharing arrangements may also be negotiated with respect to offshore areas. (DIAND 1986, 13)

Notwithstanding the significance of these policy developments, the federal government (1) has not recognized Aboriginal property rights to sea space as being as strong or complete as those applying to portions of traditionally owned lands, and (2) despite a willingness in practice to share decision making in resource and environmental management, it stubbornly holds to the claim that its own jurisdiction is paramount. This claim is not benign. The strategy of federal claims policy is to reduce the scope of a vaguely defined Aboriginal title and remove "uncertainty" with respect to the disposition of resource rights. The continued use of language calling on Aboriginal peoples to "cede, release and surrender" signals a federal strategy of blanket extinguishment of Aboriginal title that does not differ fundamentally from the intent of nineteenth- and early twentieth-century treaties.[1] If anything, the language of contemporary claims settlements today is more careful to erase any doubt that rights not specifically affirmed by these settlements, including rights of self-governmental territorial jurisdiction, are extinguished. And what Aboriginal claimants, in exchange, are able to retain of their authority for marine areas has been even more fragmentary than what they have been able to retain for land areas.

In this chapter we examine the extent to which comprehensive land claims agreements, as a primary vehicle for resolving Aboriginal rights, have accommodated the offshore interests of Aboriginal peoples. Two agreements – the James Bay and Northern Québec Agreement, 1975, and the Nunavut Final Agreement, 1993 – are reviewed in some detail, with more cursory reference to the Inuvialuit Final Agreement, 1984. Between them, these three agreements span the quarter century of modern treaty making (i.e., comprehensive land claims) in Canada and reflect the changing policy and legal context within which Aboriginal claims have been and are currently negotiated.

James Bay and Northern Québec Agreement (JBNQA)

Before reviewing the JBNQA, it is worthwhile outlining, briefly, the significance of the coast and offshore to the Aboriginal communities covered by the agreement – the James Bay Cree of Eeyou Istchee and the Inuit of Nunavik (see Figure 6.1).

The Inuit reside in fifteen villages near estuaries along the arctic coast, on offshore islands, in Hudson Bay, Hudson Strait, and Ungava Bay. Collectively, the Inuit of northern Quebec have adopted the name *Nunavik* to designate their homeland and sea. Nunavik is comprised of the totality of culturalized land- and sea-space whose places are named by Inuit, which they have used historically, and to which they enjoy customary rights (Müller-Wille 1993). Cree communities occupy the subarctic areas, with five villages located near estuaries along the coast and four located inland, mainly on the larger rivers flowing into James Bay and Hudson Bay. Their regional territorial designation, *Eeyou Istchee*, refers, similarly, to a cultural complex of land- and sea-space built up of significant and named places, richly imbued with the mythical, historical, and personal events of oral tradition, and regulated by a sophisticated customary tenure system (Scott 1986, 1988).

As a marine people, Inuit extensively use the arctic waters and depend for subsistence on the resources in those waters. Research indicates that approximately 70 percent of Nunavik Inuit food is harvested in the offshore zone (JBNQHRC 1982). Coastal and marine resources are also central to the subsistence economy and cultural continuity of the Cree, with coastal wildfowl and fish species comprising a significant part of the Cree diet. Wild goose harvests alone – from coastal bays, peninsulas, and offshore islands – have accounted for up to one-quarter of the annual subsistence foodweight harvests of coastal James Bay Cree communities, depending on the size of fall and spring migrations (Scott 1987). Coastal ducks and loons are also important contributors to diet. Seals and polar bear are occasionally taken in coastal areas, though less frequently by Cree than by Inuit hunters. Saltwater fish, particularly whitefish and sea-run brook trout, are also major contributors to diet.

The JBNQA was signed in 1975 and is often regarded as the first modern comprehensive agreement under the then new federal policy of addressing outstanding Aboriginal land rights.[2] The circumstances surrounding the signing and implementation of the agreement have been described elsewhere (Richardson 1975; LaRusic 1979; Salisbury 1986; Peters 1989; Penn 1994). Signed in November 1975, the JBNQA was intended to serve as a charter for relations between the Aboriginal and central government parties with regard to a broad range of environmental, economic, social, and cultural matters (Quebec 1976; Morantz 1992; Peters 1992). Under the agreement, the Cree and Inuit surrendered title to 980,000 square kilometres of territory in return for certain rights and benefits (Hamley 1993). These include ownership and control of a limited area of land in addition to provisions for the management of fisheries and wildlife, and environmental and social impact assessments. Several reviews have detailed the fisheries and wildlife provisions of the agreement (Feit and Scott 1979; Berkes 1989; Feit 1989; Penn 1994). These include exclusive and preferential Aboriginal harvesting rights; recognition of local authority in wildlife management; deregulation of Aboriginal fishing and hunting rights, subject only to the principle of conservation; and creation of the Hunting, Fishing and Trapping Coordinating Committee, a co-management body with primary wildlife policy-making authority.

Several classes of land are distinguished with respect to allocation of title, resources, interest, and jurisdiction (Figure 6.1).[3] Category I lands are relatively small tracts in the vicinity of permanent settlements that are held by the Cree and Inuit in a collective form of fee simple title (representing about 1.3 percent of the traditional territory). Category II lands are larger tracts over which Cree and Inuit have exclusive rights to the harvest of wildlife resources for subsistence purposes but over which they have no surface rights. The remaining 83 percent of the territory comes under Category III lands, which are open to Aborignals and non-Aboriginals but where Cree and Inuit subsistence takes priority. Quebec, according to the JBNQA, has a "right to develop" on Category II and III lands (subject to environmental assessment), with a provision for replacement of any Category II lands permanently removed from subsistence production.

The agreement does not apply beyond the low tide mark, and no provision is made for Cree or Inuit interests in the offshore. Under the agreement, "the seashore, beds and shores" of the principal lakes and rivers in the region are excluded from lands set aside for the Cree and Inuit (i.e., Category I lands), along with a 200-foot strip backing the shores of the lakes, rivers, and the James Bay coast. All those lands, including the intertidal zone in front of Category I lands, are held by the Crown in the right of Quebec as Category II lands. The intertidal zone fronting Category II and III lands also forms part of those land categories, respectively, and a limit of 50 percent of the coastline (later revised to 55 percent) could be included in Category II lands. There is no provision in the agreement specifically indicating the powers and duties of the Cree and Inuit with respect to offshore resources. For example, the agreement does not deal with the right to harvest marine mammals and migratory birds. Thus, although their Aboriginal claims within Quebec were settled in 1975, the JBNQA did not deal with the Aboriginal rights, interests, and titles of James Bay Cree and Nunavik Inuit in the offshore area. Both the Cree and the Inuit retain undiminished Aboriginal rights and titles to the coast, estuaries, islands, waters, and seabeds of Hudson Bay and James Bay – protected, in principle, by Section 35 of the Constitution Act, 1982.

The unresolved status of Aboriginal rights and interests below the low tide mark is incongruous in view of the importance of offshore resources to the Cree and Inuit, whose rights derive from the use of the coast and adjacent offshore areas over millennia. To continue exercizing these rights into the future, they must retain a central role in the management of the offshore area and its resources. Attempts to negotiate offshore rights led to commitments on the part of the federal government at the time of the signing of the JBNQA. A letter-of-undertaking, dated 15 November 1974, commits the federal government to negotiate Cree and Inuit claims in and to the islands offshore of Quebec, on the understanding that any future legal regimes applicable in the offshore would be brought into harmony with the regimes applicable under the agreement: "the Inuit communities of Québec and the James Bay Cree communities ... would have the right

80°00′W
75°00′W
70°00′W
65°00′W
60°00′N
60°00′N
Mansel Island
Ivujivik
Salluit
Baffin Island
Nunavik Inuit Offshore Claim
Hudson Strait
Kangiqsujuaq
Quaqtaq
Taqpangayuk
Akulivik
Kangirsuk
Ungava Bay
Aupaluk
Tasuijaq
Kuujjuak
Kangiqsualujjuaq
Inukjuaq
Hudson Bay
Nunavik Inuit Offshore Claim
Sanikiluaq
Umiujaq
Belcher
Nunavik
study area
NWT
NVT
Canada
United States

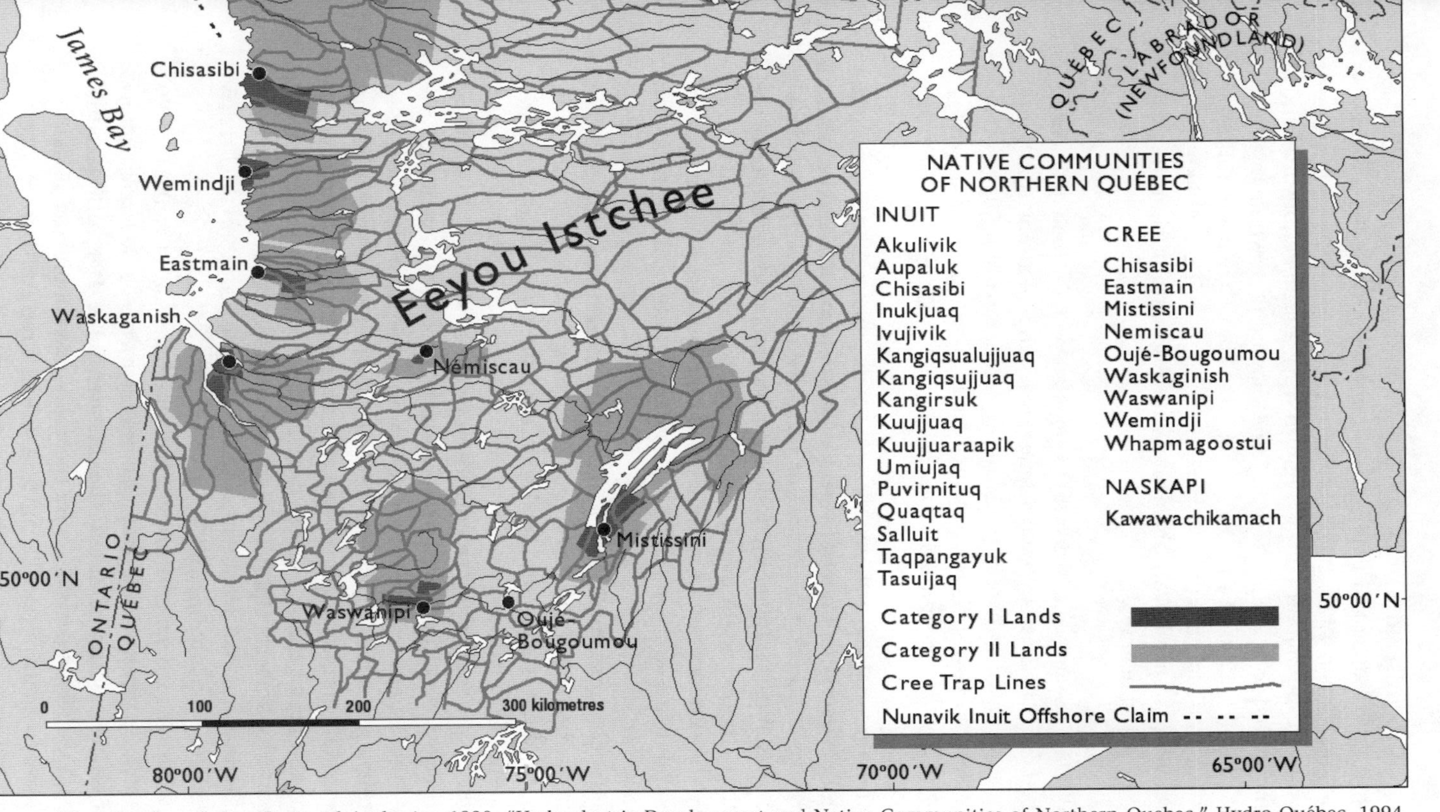

Source: "Cree Traplines," Cree Regional Authority. 1990; "Hydroelectric Development and Native Communities of Northern Quebec," Hydro-Québec, 1994. *Cartography:* David Widgington – Nimbus Carto.

Figure 6.1 Territorial lands and seas of James Bay Cree and Northern Quebec Inuit

to select on such islands, lands under a regime substantially similar to that applying to Category I lands, as contemplated in the Agreement-in-Principle" (Buchanan 1974, 3).

According to Buchanan (sub-paragraph 5[i]), the selection of islands would be limited to those islands "in James Bay lying in whole or in part within a 10-mile radius of the recognised James Bay Cree communities in the case of the Québec James Bay Cree." The letter-of-undertaking also makes reference to parallel arrangements with respect to the hunting, fishing, and trapping regime:

> In addition, Canada would undertake to negotiate with the Inuit of Québec and the James Bay Crees, the establishment of a hunting, fishing, and trapping regime on all or part of the islands ... substantially similar to the regime negotiated to apply to Category II lands as contemplated in schedule "B" of the Agreement-in-Principle (3).

A further undertaking included discussions on "the application of local and regional government powers as far as is possible to such land but under the exclusive jurisdiction of Canada or the Government of the Northwest Territories" (sub-paragraph 5[iii]). Indeed, Buchanan makes it clear from the outset that "the negotiations relating to the offshore islands have as an objective the surrender of any native rights and interests which may exist in respect to such islands on such terms and conditions as might be agreed upon" (Section 5).

These undertakings, made in the mid-1970s, indicate a commitment in principle on the part of the federal government to establishing coherence between the administrative and legal regimes applicable in the offshore and the onshore areas. Negotiations with the Cree and Inuit took place and were close to producing an agreement-in-principle when the Cree pulled out of the process (Hutchins 1990). Despite the fact that many of the resources that interested the Cree were marine, they had been unable to extend the negotiations to include offshore waters along with islands (Alan Penn, personal communication, 1996). The Cree withdrawal from negotiations was also prompted by a fear that entry into a new treaty arrangement while major hydroelectric projects were taking place would pose a greater risk and limitation than would arguing unextinguished Aboriginal rights and titles later on (Hutchins 1990).

Meanwhile, the federal government has taken measures to substantially change offshore jurisdictional and legal arrangements while largely ignoring the issue of Aboriginal title in the offshore. Bill C-104, introduced in 1986, proposed federal legislation for the application of provincial and territorial laws to their respective offshore areas. Cree and Inuit concerns about the bill have been summarized as follows:[4] (1) their insistence on compatibility between the legal regime in the offshore and the legal regime established under the JBNQA and incorporating legislation; (2) their dissatisfaction with the confirmation of Northwest Territories jurisdiction (transferred to Nunavut as of April 1999) over the islands in James Bay, Hudson Bay, and Ungava Bay;[5] and (3) their desire for adequate consultation and participation in the implementation of any laws applied to the offshore area (Grand Council of the Crees of Quebec and Makivik Corporation, 1986).

Bill C-104 did not progress beyond first reading. However, a later version of the bill was introduced in 1989 as Bill C-39, with some minor amendments. Assent to this bill as the Canadian Laws Offshore Application Act was given on 17 December 1990, and the act came into force on 4 February 1991. Section 7 of the act, which concerns the offshore area adjacent to a province, is not yet in force. The effect of Section 7 would be to divide jurisdiction for the waters of James Bay and Hudson Bay between the three provinces of Quebec, Ontario, and Manitoba, while the islands in James Bay, Hudson Bay, and Ungava Bay would remain in Nunavut and be subject to Nunavut laws and regulations. Under this arrangement, the land-sea continua that figure in Aboriginal resource management and tenure arrangements would be subject to even worse jurisdictional division and fragmentation than at present. For the Cree and Inuit this would constitute a serious threat both to any future treaty process involving the offshore and to the natural environment of James Bay and Hudson Bay (Grand Council of the Crees of Quebec and the Cree Regional Authority 1990; Makivik Corporation 1990). Section 7 of the act, by giving Quebec legislative presence in the offshore, would add another layer of law and bring another player – and hence more governmental interests – into the region. This would inevitably complicate the working out of an offshore treaty. The inclusion of a standard non-derogation clause in the act purports to protect Aboriginal and treaty rights; but this clause rings hollow, given a federal government prone to accede to the demands of provinces on issues of environment and development.

The Cree have expressed concern that the act would hinder Canada from respecting and implementing its international obligations regarding the protection of wildlife species and wildlife habitat in northern and arctic regions (Grand Council of the Crees of Quebec and the Cree Regional Authority 1990). The prospect of domestic jurisdictional wrangling impeding efforts to protect the environment seems all too likely. The lack of political will to fulfill its legal commitments was demonstrated by the refusal of the federal government, in support of Quebec, to comply with environmental assessment requirements in connection with Hydro-Québec's proposed Great Whale project until forced to do so by an order obtained by the Cree from the Federal Court of Canada in September 1991. This federal reluctance persisted in the face of well documented impacts in offshore areas, including impacts on wildlife species and wildlife habitat presently under exclusive federal jurisdiction (Hutchins 1990). It continued even after the assessment was under way, with federal agencies avoiding the "scoping" hearings and going to extraordinary lengths to limit their involvement in the process (Fenge 1992).

While the Canadian Laws Offshore Application Act could enhance a provincial sense of responsibility for downstream cumulative impacts of developments, there is the danger that Section 7 of the act will simply provide federal authority with an excuse to extend the application of the Québec Environmental Quality Act to the offshore and then claim that no federal process is needed. Revised arrangements under the act seem likely to create an unworkably complex legislative and juridical environment in James Bay and Hudson Bay (Grand Council of the Crees of Quebec and the Cree Regional Authority 1990). The waters of James Bay and Hudson Bay would be subject to federal law as well as three bodies of provincial law – making it both practically and politically very complicated to determine what combination of provincial and federal laws applies and in which specific areas. More important, any attempt to rearrange legal or jurisdictional regimes in the offshore without providing for the settlement of Aboriginal claims and titles will inevitably prejudice the rights and interests of Aboriginal groups in those areas. The achievement of a comprehensive, coordinated approach to environmental and resource management would be hindered rather than helped.

In June 1991 the northern Quebec Inuit filed the Inuit of Nunavik Statement of Claim to the Offshore, which represented the first exclusively offshore Aboriginal claim with the federal government. The offshore claim includes "all islands, marine waters, and sea ice where Inuit from Nunavik continue to hunt, fish, trap, and where they are now developing offshore commercial fishing" (*Makivik News* 1991, 21). The claim includes overlapping areas of use in the offshore with the Inuit of Nunavut and with the Labrador Inuit (Makivik Corporation 1990) as well as with the James Bay Cree. At the time of writing, the basis for an agreement-in-principle had been negotiated between the federal government and the Inuit. Significant gains made by Inuit negotiators included a recognition of the authority of the various boards responsible for environmental and resource management, and stricter limitations on the ability of the minister to override the decisions of these boards, particularly within the context of marine protected areas proposed under the Nunavut Final Agreement (Lorraine Brooke, personal communication, 1999). Negotiations had, however, reached an impasse on the issue of financial compensation, and there was no schedule in place for their resumption. Inuit were focusing on lobbying efforts to further their cause, but there seemed to be no particular urgency to settle the claim. In the absence of any immediate development proposals, and given federal government unwillingness to meet their demands, the Inuit had taken the position that the best option for the time being was to hold on to their unsurrendered Aboriginal rights and titles to the offshore.

The Grand Council of the Crees, for its part, was defending offshore rights through legal action and negotiations with the federal government that took issue with the unilateral inclusion of Cree offshore islands in the new territorial jurisdiction of Nunavut. The federal government had refused to negotiate while the Cree were in active litigation. The Cree had then withdrawn their original legal action and were developing a more substantial case based on Cree rights and targeting issues vis-à-vis Nunavut. In the interim, negotiations on offshore rights were expected to proceed, conditional on a federal government commitment to a moratorium on development and a suspension of Nunavut wildlife and environmental protection regimes pertaining to Cree islands (Brian Craik, Alan Penn, personal communications, June 1999).[6]

Litigation and negotiations, should they result in a significant clarification and reinforcement of Cree and Inuit rights to the offshore, would address the vacuum left by the JBNQA in providing an adequate framework for managing coastal and marine environments. Currently, the only security the JBNQA offers with respect to participation in environmental assessment is advisory in nature. Furthermore, the various boards and committees created to protect the regional environment are concerned only with the impact of a development project within the province and have no mandate to consider the impact on the province of outside projects (Lanari 1991). Since the low tide mark appears to define the Quebec provincial boundary,[7] offshore islands, even those immediately adjacent to the low tide mark, have been outside the jurisdiction of the JBNQA, while the waters fall within federal jurisdiction. This poses a significant limitation to the effectiveness of the environmental regime because, while the Constitution (Section 92a) asserts the exclusive jurisdiction of the provinces over non-renewable resource exploitation and development, the waters of Hudson Bay and James Bay, which are heavily affected by Quebec-based development decisions, fall within exclusive federal jurisdiction (Section 91). Meanwhile, jurisdiction over the offshore islands has, as of 1 April 1999, been transferred from the Northwest Territories to a comparably remote Nunavut administration.

No single level of government has either the constitutional responsibility or the political will to implement a management regime throughout the Hudson Bay and James Bay region. Given that the provinces hold exclusive jurisdiction over the development, conservation, and management of non-renewable resources, including forestry and hydroelectric facilities upstream of Hudson Bay and James Bay, it becomes impossible, in practical terms, for the federal government alone to exercise its constitutional responsibility over the waters of the bays (not to mention the broader ecosystemic considerations of the James Bay and Hudson Bay bioregion). The need for a coordinated approach to the management of the region can only become more urgent. Until recently, inaccessibility served to buffer the coasts of James Bay and Hudson Bay from "direct" development impacts (although impacts through disruptions to fluvial discharge related to hydroelectric generation have certainly been "direct"). This situation is now changing as a result of the construction of access roads to coastal communities, which threaten to bring a rapid increase in the number of southern hunters and recreational fishers to the coast, along with possible disruption to locally sensitive waterfowl bays and islands. Rumours of mineral deposit development and the implied development of coastal transport and harbour facilities, in addition to the continuing impacts of hydroelectric development on estuaries and marine environments, remind local communities that the relative isolation of coastal areas may not last. The Cree and Inuit have direct vested interests in land and sea as an ecological continuum; more comprehensive recognition of their jurisdiction and ownership in the region would seem the most promising basis for coordinated, environmentally responsible approaches to development.

Nunavut Final Agreement (NFA)

The NFA is a comprehensive land claim agreement concluded in April 1992 (Ottawa 1993) by the federal government of Canada and the Inuit of the central, eastern, and high Arctic of the Northwest Territories. The agreement, which represents the largest comprehensive land claim in Canada, applies to an area of almost 450,000 square kilometres – an area that is home to 17,500 Inuit (representing 80 percent of the population) (Morrison 1992).

Inuit use of the land and sea has been well documented in the Inuit Land Use and Occupancy Study, which was conducted in the mid-1970s (Freeman 1976). The Inuit maintain a strong dependence on marine and terrestrial resources and currently use or did use approximately 3.8 million square kilometres of land and ocean in the Northwest Territories. The land- and seascapes, as well as Inuit use of these environments, vary dramatically from one part of Nunavut to another, according to diversity in topography, ice conditions, and natural resources (Riewe 1991). However, the importance of the coast and marine resources is ubiquitous; only one of the twenty-seven Inuit communities is not located on the coast, and most hunting occurs in the marine environment (Fenge 1994).[8] The offshore is used as an extension of the land for most of the year, and land-fast ice, in particular, is central to travel and camping as well as to the hunting of sea mammals (Freeman 1986). Given the significance of the offshore and the fact that these areas are also the main impact zone for development

(Nunavut Constitutional Forum 1985), the Inuit insisted that the protection and management of the marine environment be a central element of their land claim negotiations.

The NFA, although finalized in 1993, was more than twenty years in the making. The Inuit of Nunavut, like the Cree and Inuit of northern Quebec, were among the first Aboriginal peoples in Canada to commence land rights negotiations under the federal government's "comprehensive land claims" policy (announced in August 1973, amended in 1986). Under this policy the federal government insisted that the Inuit relinquish Aboriginal title to their traditional lands, which were comprised of roughly two million square kilometres. In return the Inuit received certain rights and benefits, including: the creation of a semi-autonomous Nunavut Territory with its own territorial government and legislative assembly; fee simple title to approximately 350,000 square kilometres, of which 35,000 square kilometres includes title to subsurface areas; $580 million in compensation, payable over fourteen years (thereby equivalent to $1.2 billion); and specific economic rights, such as a share of federal rents and royalties from oil, gas, and mineral development, including the offshore.[9] The Inuit are also guaranteed the right to harvest marine and terrestrial wildlife to meet subsistence needs as well as the right of representation on new institutions to manage land, water, and wildlife and to evaluate and mitigate the impacts of resource development throughout Nunavut (Fenge 1993).

The agreement differs from earlier land claims settlements in several respects. Especially notable is the degree of recognition given to offshore rights, responsibilities, and jurisdiction (Jull 1993). For example, several of the guiding principles of the agreement acknowledge Inuit interests in the marine environment:

- Inuit are traditional and current users of certain marine areas, especially the land-fast ice zones;
- Inuit harvest wildlife that might migrate beyond the marine areas;
- there is a need to develop and coordinate policies regarding marine areas; and
- there is a need for Inuit involvement in aspects of Arctic marine management, including research.

In addition to Section 15, "Marine Areas," which sets out a number of marine management provisions, several other articles, including conservation, land-use planning, development impacts, and employment matters, also apply to marine areas.

Management of the arctic marine environment has, in the past, been criticized for its project-driven approach and its ad hoc, fragmentary character (Rees 1978; Mills 1984; Fenge 1993, 1994). For example, a large number of federal and territorial departments and agencies have been involved in the management of terrestrial and marine resources without having any mechanism to coordinate and direct the various roles and responsibilities;[10] instead, "a confusing array" of more than fifty committees has shaped policy in a piecemeal way without any single department having a clear mandate to coordinate the various policies and programs (Mills 1984). Even within the Department of Fisheries and Oceans and the Department of the Environment – the two departments with primary responsibility for the marine environment – there has been no coordinated jurisdiction for the preservation and enhancement of the marine environment.

A key objective of Inuit negotiators was to improve the existing regime for land, sea, and resource management in Nunavut. While the NFA gives fee simple title to less than 20 percent of the land traditionally used and occupied by Inuit, and gives no recognition of Inuit ownership of marine areas, the Inuit did succeed in using the land claim to create institutional structures – quasi-judicial boards with equal representation from Inuit and the federal government – that would provide them with constitutionally guaranteed rights to participate in managing natural resources in Nunavut, both on the land and offshore (Fenge 1994). According to Fenge (1993, 27), "the goal has been to put in place a resource management system that is, unlike current arrangements, comprehensive, integrative and unified."

Five institutional structures are described within the agreement, along with details of their purposes, jurisdiction, composition, powers, and decision-making processes and procedures: A Nunavut wildlife management board (NWMB), a surface rights tribunal (SRT), a Nunavut impact review board (NIRB), a Nunavut planning commission (NPC), and a Nunavut review board (NWB). With respect to natural resource management, the wildlife provisions of the NFA are designed to integrate the management of all wildlife, with the NWMB being the primary institutional vehicle in this integrated approach. Regional land-use plans are to provide the basis for decision making with regard to land and water use.

More specific provisions for marine management are made under Article 15.4.1, and a Nunavut marine council has been proposed, largely as an add-on to the NFA, to manage marine matters (Fenge, personal communication, 1997).[11] A further provision to accommodate the marine interests of the Inuit, specifically their dependence on migratory marine species, has established two special zones outside of the settlement area. "Zone I" includes the east coast of Baffin Island, while "Zone II" is comprised of James Bay, Hudson Bay, and Hudson Strait. The government is required to promote coordinated management of migratory species in these zones and to seek the advice of the NWMB with respect to any wildlife management decisions that would affect Inuit harvesting rights and opportunities within the marine areas of the Nunavut Settlement Area.

Other NFA innovations also strengthen the management of land and sea as a continuum. While the definition of "lands" in Article 1 excludes water, it "includes lands covered by water whether in the onshore or offshore." As a result, several provisions within the agreement, including those outlined under the articles on land-use planning, development impacts, land and resource management institutions, and resource royalty payments, extend to offshore areas. In this respect, the inclusion of the offshore represents a significant departure from the conventional Euro-Canadian practice of delimiting land according to high and low water marks. However, while the Inuit can acquire fee simple title to certain onshore lands and offshore islands, the boundary of Inuit Owned Lands is located at the ordinary high water mark; in other words, Inuit Owned Lands exclude marine areas (Article 19.2.6).

The NFA also provides Inuit with the exclusive rights to the use of water on Inuit lands as well as the right to have water "flow through Inuit lands substantially unaffected in quality, quantity and flow" (Article 20). A problem arises, however, with the definition of "water" under the agreement because it excludes water or ice in marine areas and, thereby, fails to embrace the ecosystemic realities of water as a medium and the integral connection between inland and marine waters (Article 1). The provisions of Article 20 regarding the impact of projects outside of Nunavut on "the quality, quantity and flow of water" are rendered meaningless if, for example, they exclude the downstream impact of hydro developments on the marine environment. Furthermore, if there is to be any meaningful attempt to establish a coordinated, cooperative approach to managing the marine environment (particularly the wider bioregion, including Zones I and II), then it is essential to have management roles for the Cree, Inuit, and Chipewyan peoples of northern Quebec, Ontario, and Manitoba.

A coordinated and cooperative land-and-sea management regime is being attempted under the auspices of the NFA. While some observers refer to it glowingly as a model of integrated planning and management that other parts of the country should emulate (Gillies 1995), it will be much more difficult for Aboriginal peoples in other parts of Canada to turn consultative status into real decision-making authority. Provisions for the management of the Nunavut marine environment, coupled with the political majority status of Inuit in the new territory of Nunavut, should help to ensure that the federal government engages in meaningful collaboration with them. In no other province or territory in Canada do Aboriginal populations constitute such a majority (though they may do so regionally within the northern portions of some provinces).

Discussion

In all cases of comprehensive claims agreements settled since the 1970s, the Canadian government has won its basic demand – blanket extinguishment of Aboriginal title in exchange for the narrower, but more "certain," rights and benefits specified in the agreements. The rights and benefits vary significantly from one agreement to another with respect to co-management arrangements, wildlife and environmental regulations, economic development strategies, subsurface rights, and so on. Consistently, however, federally recognized rights to marine areas (notwithstanding progress made in recent years) remain significantly weaker than do rights to land.

There can be little doubt that the circumstances surrounding the negotiation of the JBNQA affected the content and structure of that agreement (Peters 1989; Hamley 1993; Penn 1994). It was negotiated under pressure of rigid deadlines and without the benefit of precedents or models that the Cree and Inuit could compare and assess. Furthermore, at the time, the Cree numbered about 6,000 people divided among eight bands, and they had only incipient regional political organization and poor infrastructure (Morantz 1992). Provincial interests in the region were extensive, powerful, and uncompromising. The urgent priority was to deal first with the territory claimed by Quebec to the low water mark. At the same time, the fact that no process of extinguishment has diminished Cree and Inuit rights and titles to the offshore has kept some options open: Cree and Inuit have come to expect better terms regarding offshore rights in the 1990s than were attainable in the 1970s and 1980s.

In the western Arctic, the federal government found it comparatively easy to reserve substantial tracts of land for the Inuvialuit: non-Aboriginal stakeholders were few and and not very entrenched, and no other level of government had any real control over the outcome of negotiations (Morrison 1992). As a result, the Inuvialuit Final Agreement (IFA) (Ottawa 1984) provided for the largest proportion of traditional land reserved, set apart, or granted to Aboriginal peoples in Canada up to that time, and it included the "beds of all lakes, rivers and other water bodies found in Inuvialuit lands" (Section 7.2). However, the IFA excluded offshore areas. It provided the Inuvialuit with preferential, rather than exclusive, rights to fish the offshore; and the denial of Inuvialuit rights to the oil and gas resources in the Beaufort Sea was a major precedent in the development of federal comprehensive claims policy. The Inuvialuit are, therefore, dependent upon the powers that they may exercise generally with respect to development in the settlement region, relying on the operation of any land-use planning agency on which they have representation and on their advisory powers through the Wildlife Advisory Council and the Fisheries Joint Management Committee (Bartlett 1988). Neither the Environmental Screening

Committee nor the review board has jurisdiction with respect to offshore development.

The Inuit of Nunavut, though widely scattered and relative newcomers to politics, had the great advantage of making up 80 percent of the population of their region. They could, therefore, count on controlling public government institutions in Nunavut (in addition to institutions defined under the NFA as exclusively Inuit) or at least having a guaranteed ratio of Inuit membership. The NFA is regarded as the largest, most far-reaching and comprehensive of the modern-day treaties negotiated between the Crown and Aboriginal peoples (Fenge 1993). It differs from its predecessors in that it gives considerably greater weight to environmental factors and provides for the establishment of statutory bodies, with substantial Aboriginal representation, to supervise use of natural resources and development in the settlement area (Fenge 1990; Crowe 1990, 1991). The NFA also differs from earlier agreements in the recognition it gives to marine environments. Aboriginal title to the Nunavut Settlement Area is based on "traditional and current use and occupation of the lands, waters and land-fast ice therein" (Ottawa 1993, 1), whereas the Inuvialuit Agreement was based on their claim to "traditional use and occupancy of the land [only]" (Ottawa 1984, 2). The NFA sets some targets for subsequent agreements to match or exceed. Its inclusion of responsibility for offshore resources in joint government-Aboriginal administration was in line with recommendations made eight years earlier, with respect to the offshore, by the Task Force to Review Comprehensive Claims:

> Recognizing the natural and legal differences between land and sea, topics for negotiation could include access to wildlife and fishery resources, participation in decision-making for conservation and resource allocation, and a sharing of the benefits from sub-sea minerals and hydrocarbons. The sharing of benefits from non-renewable offshore resources will have to be discussed in light of proposals regarding offshore resources. (Canada 1985, 60)

Of the contemporary agreements (the "modern treaties"), only the NFA seeks to establish a cohesive, integrated structure for the administration and management of marine resources and expressly provides for Aboriginal participation in that structure. Whether future claims agreements can go further in addressing the marine estates of Aboriginal peoples – in the full sense of combining rights of ownership and jurisdiction – remains to be seen. In May 1999 a comprehensive agreement-in-principle between the federal government, the Government of Newfoundland, and the Labrador Inuit Association was reached. This agreement is significant in this connection because it is the first to include clearly defined rights for an Aboriginal commercial fishery in addition to a marine management component within a Labrador Inuit marine zone.[12] Within that zone, Labrador Inuit are guaranteed a majority of new licences for commercially fished species as well as smaller proportions of new licences for fisheries in adjacent areas and for offshore shrimp (interview, Toby Anderson, LIA Land Claims Director, CBN-AM, 5 May 1999).

Aboriginal marine rights need to be more broadly accommodated in both state-level and international legal regimes dealing with human rights and with environmental management and protection. At the national level, two recently proposed initiatives – Canada's Oceans Act and the National Marine Conservation Strategy – offer further opportunities to develop policies for the participation of Aboriginal peoples in marine management. Recognition of Aboriginal rights and interests in marine areas by international legal regimes, such as is manifested in the 1982 United Nations Convention on the Law of the Sea, could erode the federal government's sovereignty rationale for limiting the recognition of these rights domestically.

European law and policy have applied the conceptual division between rights of property and of jurisdiction to the ontological boundary between land and sea. Property does not apply to sea space but jurisdiction does. Hence, Aboriginal claimants have recently found it easier to win recognized roles in resource management (conceived as a jurisdictional matter) than in the ownership of their marine estates. The fragmentation and rebundling of rights of property and jurisdiction that occurs in negotiation, however, offers opportunities on both fronts. It has become thinkable for central governments to share decision making through constitutionally protected treaties with Aboriginal claimants. Royalties and preferential harvesting rights are ways of acknowledging Aboriginal property rights in offshore resources. Strategies by Aboriginal negotiators to secure greater control represent, in general, a blurring and erosion of the distinctions between property and jurisdiction, and between land and sea. They were, from Aboriginal perspectives, artificial divisions from the outset.

Acknowledgments

The authors appreciate generous commentary received from Lorraine Brooke, Brian Craik, Terry Fenge, Peter Hutchins, Peter Jull, and Alan Penn.

Notes

1 As Usher, Tough, and Galois (1992, 129) state: "There is continuity between the earlier treaty-making era and the current round of litigation and negotiations of comprehensive claims. Canada insists on linking the recognition of Aboriginal title with the extinguishment of Aboriginal rights in exchange for compensation. Native people continue to insist on retaining the basic elements of their Aboriginal land systems and ensuring some measure of control over their own lives and livelihoods."

2 Yet, like its historical predecessors and subsequent comprehensive claims agreements, it is predicated on the principle of extinguishment of Aboriginal title in exchange for specified rights and benefits.

3 Penn (1994) explains that the designation of these land classes was based on considerations of future hydroelectric, forestry, and mining development rather than Cree needs with regard to productivity or ecology. Not surprisingly, these land categories "appear to hold no relevance at all to the contemporary territorial organisation of Cree hunting" (28).
4 An interesting parallel discussion of the implications of Bill C-104 for the Northwest Territories is provided by Bankes (1987).
5 The Northwest Territories Act states that the jurisdiction of the Northwest Territories includes "the islands in Hudson Bay, James Bay and Ungava Bay, except those islands that are within the Province of Manitoba, the Province of Ontario or the Province of Quebec" (R.S.C. 1970 c.N-22).
6 Nunavut only has jurisdiction over islands; the federal government maintains jurisdiction over waters (see main text, *infra*).
7 The question of whether Quebec's boundaries extend to the low water mark or high water mark may still be unresolved. See Assemblée Nationale, Journal des débats, Commission d'étude des questions afférentes à l'accession du Québec à la souveraineté, 17 October 1991, no. 6, pp. CEAS-153, where it is said by Henri Dorian that the position of the Quebec government used to be that Quebec's boundaries only extended as far as the high water mark. A subsequent federal/Quebec/Northwest Territories Agreement established that the boundary would be the low water mark.
8 As much as 82 percent of the hunting territory of Grise Fiord in the North Baffin region is marine, and 90 percent of the country food harvested comes from the sea (Pattimore n.d.).
9 The agreement is largely silent on social and cultural issues such as education, health, justice, and so on because these areas were to fall within the jurisdiction of the Nunavut government (Fenge 1993).
10 Management of terrestrial species of wildlife in the Northwest Territories has been the responsibility of the territorial government, while marine species have come under the jurisdiction of federal agencies.
11 The proposed structure is to be comprised of members from the various co-management bodies, including the Nunavut Impact Review Board (NIRB), the Nunavut Water Board (NWB), the Nunavut Planning Commission (NPC), and the NWMB. These bodies, which have equal government and Inuit representation, may jointly (as the Nunavut Marine Council) or severally advise and make recommendations to other government agencies regarding marine areas.
12 This zone extends twelve miles beyond the outer islands in the area from Cape Chidley in the north to Fish Cove Point in the south.

References

Bankes, N. 1987. "The Status of Hudson Bay." *Northern Perspectives* 15, 3: 14-15.

Bartlett, R.H. 1988. *Aboriginal Water Rights in Canada: A Study of Aboriginal Title to Water and Indian Water Rights*. Calgary: Canadian Institute of Resources Law, University of Calgary.

Berkes, F. 1989. "Co-management and the James Bay Agreement." In *Co-operative Management of Local Fisheries: New Directions for Improved Management and Community Development*, ed. E. Pinkerton, 189-208. Vancouver: UBC Press.

Buchanan, J. 1974. Ministerial letter to Mr. Charlie Watt, President, Northern Québec Inuit Association, 15 November.

Canada, 1985. *Living Treaties: Lasting Agreements. Report of the Task Force to Review Comprehensive Claims Policy*. Ottawa: Department of Indian Affairs and Northern Development.

Crowe, K.J. 1990. "Claims on the Land, part 1." *Arctic Circle* 1, 3: 14-23.

–. 1991. "Claims on the Land, part 2." *Arctic Circle* 1, 4: 31-5.

DIAND. 1986. Federal Policy for the Settlement of Native Claims. Ottawa: Department of Indian Affairs and Northern Development, March.

Feit, H. 1989. "James Bay Cree Self-governance and Land Management." In *We Are Here: Politics of Aboriginal Land Tenure*, ed. E.M. Wilmsen, 68-98. Berkeley: University of California Press.

Feit, H., and C. Scott. 1979. *Information Needs Concerning Wildlife, the Cree, and Development in the James Bay Region*. Québec: Bureau de la Baie James et du Nord québecois, Environment Canada.

Fenge, T. 1990. "Toward Environmentally Sustainable Economic Development in the Canadian Arctic: The Potential Contribution of the Inuit Land Claim Settlement." Unpublished paper. Ottawa.

–. 1992. "The Great Whale Review and the Federal Government's Disappearing Act." *Northern Perspectives* 20, 2: 2-5.

–. 1993. "Political Development and Environmental Management in Northern Canada: The Case of the Nunavut Agreement." Discussion Paper Series. Darwin: North Australia Research Unit, Australian National University.

–. 1994. "Managing the Arctic Ocean in Nunavut: The Inuit Land-Claim Settlement." In *The Sea Has Many Voices: Oceans Policy for a Complex World*, ed. C. Lamson, 185-206. Montreal and Kingston: McGill-Queen's University Press.

Freeman, M. 1976. *Inuit Land Use and Occupancy Project: A Report*. 3 vols. Ottawa: Department of Indian Affairs and Northern Development/Supply and Services Canada.

–. 1986. "Contemporary Inuit Exploitation of the Sea-Ice Environment." In *Sikumiut: People Who Use the Sea-Ice*, ed. A. Cooke and E. Van Alstine, 73-96. Ottawa: Canadian Arctic Resources Committee.

Gillies, B. 1995. "The Nunavut Final Agreement and Marine Management in the North." *Northern Perspectives* 23, 1: 17-19.

Grand Council of the Crees of Quebec and Makivik Corporation. 1986. Preliminary Comments of Makivik Corporation and the Grand Council of the Crees of Quebec on Proposed Bill C-104: Canadian Laws Offshore Application Act. Nemaska/Montreal: GCCQ/Makivik Corporation.

Grand Council of the Crees of Quebec and Cree Regional Authority. 1990. Submission of the Grand Council of the Crees of Quebec/Cree Regional Authority to the Legislative Committee on Proposed Bill C-39: "An Act to Apply Federal Laws and Provincial Laws to Offshore Areas and to Amend Certain Acts in Consequence thereof." May.

Hamley, W. 1993. "Native Land Claims in Quebec Considered in a Canadian Context." *Geografiska Annaler* 75B, 2: 93-109.

Hutchins, P. 1990. Minutes of proceedings and evidence of the Legislative Committee on Bill C-39. House of Commons, Issue No. 2, 31 May.

JBNQHRC. 1982. *The Wealth of the Land: Harvests of James Bay Cree, 1972-73 to 1978-79*. Québec City: James Bay and Northern Québec Native Harvesting Research Committee.

Jull, P. 1993. "A Sea Change: Overseas Indigenous-Government Relations in the Coastal Zone." Report to the Resource Assessment Commission, Canberra. Unpublished.

Jull, P., and N. Bankes. 1984. "Inuit Interests in the Arctic Offshore." In *National and Regional Interests in the North: Third National Workshop on People, Resources, and the Environment North of 60°*, ed. Canadian Arctic Resources Committee, 557-86. Ottawa: Canadian Arctic Resources Committee.

Lanari, R. 1991. "Environmental Protection and the James Bay Agreement: Rethinking the Committee Approach." *Northern Perspectives* 19: 10-12.

LaRusic, I. 1979. *Negotiating a Way of Life*. Montreal: SSDCC, report prepared for Research Division, Department of Indian and Northern Affairs.

Makivik Corporation. 1990. Submission to the Legislative Committee regarding Bill C-39: "Canadian Laws Offshore Application Act." 29 May.

Makivik News. 1991. "Filing a Claim to Nunavik's Offshore." *Makivik News* 20: 20-3.

Mills, H. 1984. "Ocean Policy Making in the Canadian Arctic." In *National and Regional Interests in the North: Third National Workshop on People, Resources, and the Environment North of 60°*, ed. Canadian Arctic Resources Committee, 491-528. Ottawa: Canadian Arctic Resources Committee.

Morantz, T. 1992. "Aboriginal Land Claims in Québec." In *Aboriginal Land Claims in Canada: A Regional Perspective*, ed. K. Coates, 101-30. Toronto: Copp Clark Pitman.

Morrison, W.R. 1992. "Aboriginal Land Claims in the Canadian North." In *Aboriginal Land Claims in Canada: A Regional Perspective*, ed. K. Coates, 167-94. Toronto: Copp Clark Pitman.

Müller-Wille, L. 1993. "Placenames, Territoriality and Sovereignty: Inuit Perception of Space in Nunavik (Canadian Eastern Arctic)." *Bulletin de la Société suisse des américanistes* 53/4: 17-21.

Nunavut Constitutional Forum. 1985. *Building Nunavut: Today and Tomorrow.* Yellowknife: Nunavut Constitutional Forum.

Ottawa. 1984. *The Western Arctic Claim: The Inuvialuit Final Agreement.* Ottawa: Minister of Indian Affairs and Northern Development.

–. 1993. *Agreement between the Inuit of the Nunavut Settlement Area and Her Majesty the Queen in Right of Canada.* Ottawa: Minister of Indian Affairs and Northern Development and the Tungavik Federation of Nunavut.

Pattimore, J. N.d. Unpublished 1983 harvest data for the Baffin Region. Baffin Regional Inuit Association.

Penn, A. 1994. "The James Bay and Northern Québec Agreement: Natural Resources, Public Lands, and the Implementation of a Native Land Claim Settlement." Unpublished paper prepared for the Royal Commission on Aboriginal Peoples, 63 pp.

Peters, E.J. 1989. "Federal and Provincial Responsibilities for the Cree, Naskapi and Inuit under the James Bay and Northern Québec, and Northeastern Québec Agreements." In *Aboriginal Peoples and Government Responsibility: Exploring Federal and Provincial Roles,* ed. D.C. Hawkes, 142-242. Ottawa: Carleton University Press.

–. 1992. "Protecting the Land under Modern Land Claims Agreements: The Effectiveness of the Environmental Regime Negotiated by the James Bay Cree in the James Bay and Northern Québec Agreement." *Applied Geography* 12: 133-45.

Quebec. 1976. The James Bay and Northern Québec Agreement. Québec: Editeur officiel du Québec.

Rees, W.E. 1978. "Development and Planning North of 60: Past and Future." In *Northern Transitions: Second National Workshop on People, Resources and the Environment North of 60°,* ed. R.F. Keith and J.B. Wright, 42-62. Ottawa: Canadian Arctic Resources Committee.

Richardson, B. 1975. *Strangers Devour the Land.* Toronto: McMillan.

Riewe, R. 1991. "Inuit Land Use Studies and the Native Claims Process." In *Aboriginal Resource Use in Canada: Historical and Legal Aspects,* ed. K. Abel and J. Friesen, 287-300. Winnipeg: University of Manitoba Press.

Salisbury, R.F. 1986. *A Homeland for the Cree: Regional Development in James Bay, 1971-1981.* Montreal: McGill-Queen's University Press.

Scott, C.H. 1986. "Hunting Territories, Hunting Bosses and Communal Production among Coastal James Bay Cree." *Anthropologica* 28, 1-2: 163-73.

–. 1987. "The Socio-economic Significance of Waterfowl among Canada's Aboriginal Cree: Native Use and Local Management." In *The Value of Birds,* ed. A.W. Diamond and F.L. Filion, 49-62, ICBP Technical Publication No. 6. Cambridge: International Council for Bird Preservation.

–. 1988. "Property, Practice and Aboriginal Rights among Quebec Cree Hunters." In *Hunters and Gatherers: Property, Power and Ideology,* vol. 2, ed. James Woodburn, Tim Ingold, and David Riches, 35-51. London: Berg Publishers.

Usher, P.J., F.J. Tough, and R.M. Galois. 1992. "Reclaiming the Land: Aboriginal Title, Treaty Rights and Land Claims in Canada." *Applied Geography* 12: 109-32.

Territories, Identity, and Modernity among the Atikamekw (Haut St-Maurice, Quebec)

Sylvie Poirier

> Tell them we have never given up our territory [Kitaskino]. Tell them we have never sold or traded it. Tell them that we have never reached any other sort of agreement concerning our territory.
>
> – César Néwashish (1903-94)

From a non-Aboriginal perspective, the colonial history of the Atikamekw is similar to that of the other groups forming the great Algonquian language family. The ancestral territory of the Atikamekw is located in the Haut St-Maurice region (north-central Quebec), and its rich watershed lies in the midst of the boreal forest. The Atikamekw number approximately 5,000 members in three communities – Wemotaci, Manawan, and Opitciwan – and their territory largely corresponds to that of their traditional semi-nomadic bands. Their territory borders that of the Innu of Lac St-Jean to the east, that of the Cree of Mistissini to the northeast, that of the Cree of Waswanipi to the north, and that of the Algonquins to the west.[1]

Since the 1970s, and following the federal government's determination to negotiate comprehensive claims agreements (Asch and Zlotkin 1997), the Atikamekw have embarked upon the process of making political and territorial claims and negotiating with the federal and provincial (Quebec) governments. Likewise, they have met with all the obstacles, paradoxes, misunderstandings, and disillusionments that characterize this process. César Néwashish's declaration, which serves as this chapter's epigraph, is emblematic of Atikamekw territorial claims. It evokes their determination and will as well as their hope that they will finally be heard and recognized.

In this chapter, I analyze a number of facets of the contemporary Atikamekw relationship to ancestral territories and show its ongoing evolution. I describe how they are faced with two representations of territory, or two cartographies: their own and that of the *Kawapisit* (the Whites). The first representation derives from customary ways of dividing, sharing, and transferring areas with which families have been entrusted. The second representation is founded on property and a certain obsession with administrative delimitations. In addition, I deal with two modes of experiencing territory, each of which is founded on strong, albeit opposing, cultural ontologies, knowledge systems, practices, and values. Kawapisit-imposed administrative delimitations and modes of resource development, coupled with dilatory policies and, indeed, the absence of a political will to recognize Aboriginal rights, are all elements that have contributed to transforming the Atikamekw people's relationship to their ancestral lands. Nevertheless, this relationship has retained enough authenticity to safeguard Atikamekw practices.

The interpretation I propose with regard to Atikamekw authenticity and its relationship to territory does not attempt to circumvent the historical context and the power relations within which these people have transformed and reproduced their relationship to the world, their social order, and their cultural consciousness. Land is something that the Atikamekw live, tell, and transmit on the basis of a language, a culture, an endogenous history, and their current experience as hunters enmeshed within a global system. Weaver (1984) has brought out how various public discourses on "Indian-ness" and "Native-ness" tend to disregard and, indeed, mask how Aboriginal peoples visualize and construct their experiences and identities, and, it seems, their history. It is on just these sorts of issues that I focus my comments.

In the language of anthropology, authenticity has become a highly problematical concept. This is due to the impact of postmodernism, particularly as it concerns the dialectical and dialogical relationships between the global and the local. Following the example of the Comaroffs (1992), Ortner (1995, 176) conceives of authenticity as a process "in which the pieces of reality, however much borrowed from or imposed by others, are woven together through the logic of a group's own locally and historically evolved bricolage." As Sahlins (1993, 4) has written, in postcolonial contexts, cultural consciousness "entails the people's attempt to control their relationships with the dominant society, including control of the technical and political means that up to now have been used to victimize them" (see also Turner 1991). He adds, "The very ways society change have their own authenticity."

In this chapter, which is devoted to examining the Atikamekw relationship to ancestral territories – or, I should say, the identity of a territory marked by the Atikamekw presence – I give special weight to three interrelated approaches. The first approach serves to bring out the relevance of considering the traditional dynamic of societies within the contemporary context (Scott 1993) – the way in which "traditional forms of cultural expressions are developed into distinctive contemporary Aboriginal cultures with their own creative roots and dynamics" (Bennett and Blundell 1995, 5). The second approach stems from the first and highlights the question of resistance in terms of cultural persistence (Valaskakis 1993). In other words, it looks at how the Atikamekw, like other Aboriginal groups, have rethought and reinterpreted (Turner 1991) their relationship to ancestral territory. The last approach addresses being traditional hunters within the present-day context.

Atikamekw Nation

Anderson (1991) has shown how, throughout the world, nationalisms (what he calls "imagined communities") are the historical products of colonialism and the imperial order; they are, in short, creations of modernity. The Aboriginal nationalisms that, in Canada as elsewhere, came into being and took shape during the 1960s are part of this development. Whereas numerous analyses have taken up the relations between the First Nations and the Canadian government as a whole, few have inquired into how, locally, Aboriginal groups picture their own imagined communities in relation to themselves. The Atikamekw offer a worthwhile example of how, with regard to societies stemming from a nomadic, clan-based tradition, the concept of "nation" remains, at best, ambiguous.

In historical terms, it is possible to locate the modern emergence of the Atikamekw Nation as a distinct political entity towards the end of the nineteenth century. In 1881, faced with the gradual invasion of their territories by the Kawapisit, the chiefs of the then four Atikamekw bands – namely, the Wemotaci, Manawan, Kokokac, and Kikentatch (the present-day Opitciwan) – decided to make common cause. As the designated representatives of the *Kice Okimaw* (grand chieftancy), or the territorial government of that period, these men collectively petitioned the federal government to set aside lands for them. The modern expression of the Atikamekw nation came into being with this action. However, this nation did not acquire the attributes of a distinct, permanent political entity until the 1970s.

It should be pointed out that, in its traditional form, the Kice Okimaw was not always or necessarily made up of the chiefs of the four Atikamekw bands;[2] it was not a homogeneous, permanent political body. Flexibility rather than rigidity was the outstanding feature of this territorial government, whose composition could vary according to circumstances, contingencies, and needs. Thus, for a given period and space, the Kice Okimaw could include the Atikamekw chief of Opitciwan, the Innu chief from the Lac St-Jean area, and the Cree chief from Waswanipi (pursuant, for example, to a dispute over territory). The Kice Okimaw was thus a flexible decision-making body that served to manage the territory as well as the relations of exchange and alliance between several bands of distinct Aboriginal groups.

The 1881 petition by the Atikamekw Kice Okimaw was heard, and four communities ("reserves") were surveyed shortly thereafter. In 1930 one of these four, Kokokac, was flooded subsequent to the construction of the Rapide Blanc Dam (see below). In the following decades, various petitions were filed with the federal and provincial governments. The Atikamekw continued to pursue a semi-nomadic and autonomous type of existence, but they also had to deal with an increasingly strong non-Aboriginal presence on their territory (logging, railroad building, dam building, non-Aboriginal trappers, etc.). The 1950s were witness to the gradual abandonment of a semi-nomadic way of life. Among the various factors that, each in its own way, served to shape Atikamekw history were: off-reserve boarding schools for youths; settlement in sedentary communities; the revised Indian Act; the delineation of beaver reserves; and the reduction of hunting areas.

In keeping with the spirit of the 1970s and following the example of other Aboriginal groups in Canada, the Atikamekw embarked upon a process of reasserting and reappropriating their culture and identity. It was also during this period that they initiated territorial claims and negotiations. They founded a political body, *Atikamekw Sipi* (*Sipi* = river); that is, the Council of the Atikamekw Nation. In the following years, the *Nehiorwisiw Wasikahikan* (Atikamekw language institute) and the *Mamo Atoskewin* (Atikamekw trappers' association) came into being. These various institutions have enabled the Atikamekw to assert themselves as a distinct social, cultural, historical, and political entity. Through them, the Atikamekw are able to represent themselves vis-à-vis the Other.

As a rule, however, from the Atikamekw point of view the very concept of "nation," as an imagined community and as a product of modernity, remains somewhat ambiguous – at least when it comes to translating such a concept into the Atikamekw language. The difficulty is not so much one of representing themselves vis-à-vis the Other as it is one of translating a modern, non-Aboriginal concept in such a way that it is representative of the Atikamekw experience and identity (particularly with respect to modes of affiliation). Among other activities that occurred during the fall 1996 *Aski* (land) Summit, which drew nearly 200 Atikamekw, there was a debate concerning the best translation of the term "nation." Translation in this case was something of an approximation, for, to begin with, the Atikamekw language does not contain a term that is capable of rendering all the abstract connotations of this word.

I should point out that, since the founding of the Atikamekw Nation Council, *Atikamekw Iriniw* (the Atikamekw people) is the term used to denote the entire population. However, not everyone is comfortable with this appellation. Actually, the terms *Manawani Iriniw* (the people of Manawan), *Wemotaci Iriniw* (the people of Wemotaci), or *Opitcino Iriniw* (the people of Opitciwan),[3] which suggest a territory- and community-based identity, are more representative of Atikamekw experience and modes of affiliation. This being said, out of a desire to arrive at some consensus regarding a term that is capable of denoting the nation as a whole, a number of elders suggested the traditional expression *Ei nictweikisinanok*, or *Ei nictokweisinanok*, (three joined communities). Other elders preferred *nicto otenaw atikamekw* (three Atikamekw communities). Still others suggested *Mamo Itiwin* (all experiences and events shared by the Atikamekw). The expression *Atikamekw Niherosiw* (first inhabitants) has also been proposed. Finally, support was most general for *Ototew Isiwin* (original group or assembly). However, with regard to the appropriate term for the Atikamekw government, consensus was rapid and decisive: *Atikamekw Kice Okimaw*.

What appears as an ambiguity arising in connection with the inherent difficulty of translating a modern concept into the Atikamekw language shows up Atikamekw specificity – their desire to categorize phenomena in terms of local modes of constructing experience and identity. Among the Atikamekw there are two modes of identification: one that they use among themselves (which is founded on territorial and communitarian affiliation) and one that they use as a nation when dealing with the Other (i.e., non-Atikamekw). This distinction is also apparent in the terminology used to denote the Atikamekw territorial entity. The Atikamekw language distinguishes between an inclusive "us," which encompasses the person speaking, the listener, and other related people, and an exclusive "us," which includes the speaker and related persons but not the listener. Whenever the Atikamekw speak to Kawapisit, particularly within the framework of negotiations, or to the members of other Aboriginal groups, the Atikamekw territorial entity is referred to by the word *Nitaskinan* (in other words, the listener is excluded from territorial affiliation). When, on the other hand, they speak among themselves of their home territory (as evidenced in the statement by César Néwashish quoted above), *Kitaskino* is the word they use.

In the context of claims and negotiations, the Atikamekw are aware of the usefulness and necessity of being represented to the Other as a nation. Such are the dictates of modernity. In that connection, the Atikamekw Nation Council (*Atikamekw Sipi*) is an undeniable political force whose mandate is regularly renewed during general assemblies or special conventions (such as the Aski Summit). This does indicate, however, that the Atikamekw have fully incorporated the meaning of a "national" identity and affiliation.

Thus, for the Atikamekw, the ambiguity of the concept "nation" does not lie in how they are represented to the Other but, rather, in how they represent themselves to themselves. Actually, all the ambiguities relating to "nation" reveal the present-day persistence and pervading influence of a mode of individual and collective identification that is constructed according to a social organization within which affiliation with the family group and ancestral territory, coupled with responsibility for this territory, takes precedence over an "imagined" political entity. There is, in fact, no nationalism that is devoid of these ambiguities. However, the Atikamekw are dealing with both non-modern and modern modes of identity. And therein lies one of the original features of their cultural dynamic, authenticity, and resistance.

Kawapisit on Atikamekw Territory

From the Nineteenth Century to 1950

No research into the present-day territorial identity of the Atikamekw can afford to disregard non-Aboriginal presence, activities, and interests. During most of the nineteenth century White incursions were sporadic and, hence, manageable; but by the end of that century and the beginning of the twentieth century encroachment had gathered impetus and has since continued to do so. The Atikamekw have had to learn how, on the one hand, to deal with two systems of management and jurisdiction, two cartographies, and two representations of territory; on the other hand, they have also had to attempt to synthesize these two systems. The following historical overview presents a number of major phenomena that have become inscribed in the local history of the Manawani Iriniw, Wemotaci Iriniw, and the Opitcino Iriniw. It also highlights not only the flexibility and the resistance of the Atikamekw, but also the way in which they continually rethink and reinterpret their relation to territory.

The establishment of a trading post at Wemotaci (not far from the current community) in 1821 marks the first tangible advance of the Kawapisit into Atikamekw territory.[4] Not long afterwards, other posts were set up in Manawan (1838), Kokokac (1863), Kikentatch (1840)(under water since the construction of the Gouin Dam), and, eventually, Opitciwan (1914). In 1837, the first regular missions in the region appeared (Clermont 1977, 17).[5] Logging also commenced during this period, with the first timber concessions being granted to the Brown Corporation in the 1850s. It was within this context of an increasing non-Aboriginal presence that the four chiefs presented the government with a petition for lands.

During the twentieth century, construction of the railroad made access to Atikamekw territories easier for the Kawapisit, thus provoking multiple repercussions for Atikamekw. Nevertheless, the Atikamekw were able to cope with this new reality, and, in fact, used the railroad to reach various trading and supply posts. Logging, on the other hand, has grown steadily since the beginning of the twentieth century, thus altering the Atikamekw forest-scape. It is not for nothing that the White man is referred to as *Memitcikocic* – "he who uses the woods," or, more pejoratively, "the wood-eater." Willingly or not, the Atikamekw once again adapted to a White presence, and several of their number worked as lumberjacks in seasonal logging camps until the introduction of heavy equipment in the 1970s.

Alongside the loggers and railroad builders, the traders and the missionaries, another non-Aboriginal presence emerged at the beginning of the twentieth century: hunting and fishing sports enthusiasts. Private clubs were founded, whose clients were primarily American.[6] Control over a number of Atikamekw territories was compromised by these people. But, once again, the Atikamekw were able to adjust to a new presence, and their territorial expertise proved invaluable to this particular group of clients. Until the 1970s, at which time the clubs were abolished, several Atikamekw men worked as guides, and a number of women were able to earn an income by housekeeping in the camps, cleaning fish, or selling blueberries and locally produced products.

In any event, until the 1950s, the Atikamekw maintained a relatively autonomous semi-nomadic way of life based mainly on hunting, fishing, trapping, and gathering. From fall until spring the Atikamekw spread out over and lived off of various family territories. During the summer months, they would come together either at Manawan, Kikentatch (later Opitciwan), Kokokac, or Wemotaci, where they sold their furs or partook of the services offered by the mission. I would like to emphasize how the Atikamekw adapted to these new realities, how flexible they were. Down through the decades, the Atikamekw, sequentially or simultaneously, engaged in the fur trade, logged, or served as guides while continuing to maintain a semi-nomadic existence based on hunting, fishing, trapping, and gathering. Thanks to their capacity for diversifying their activities, the Atikamekw were able to maintain their autonomy within their territory.

During the first half of the twentieth century, two major events altered the configuration of Atikamekw territory forever: the construction of the La Loutre hydroelectric dam (which created the Gouin Reservoir) in 1918 and the construction of the Rapide Blanc Dam in 1930. The La Loutre Dam, whose construction marked the first instance of the flooding of broad areas of Aboriginal land, was built at a time when the rights of "sauvages" (savages) – as they were still referred to in French legal texts – counted for very little in decision-making processes. Among those areas that were flooded was that of Kikentatch, a summer gathering point for the Atikamekw of the region and the site of the former Hudson's Bay Company trading post. The Atikamekw, and the trading post, moved north to Opitciwan. The flooding itself, the suddenness with which it occurred, but also and above all the fact that, since that time, ancestral territories have lain under several metres of water, are all elements that permeate the history of Opitcino Iriniw and that have become an integral part of the Atikamekw oral tradition.

Western observers have evaluated this loss of territory mostly in quantitative terms; that is, in terms of loss of beaver pelts or game.

The Atikamekw view the scope of these losses differently. For these hunters and gatherers, the animal and plant resources that were subjected to flooding undeniably represent a loss that continues to be lamented. But, just as important, this event represents a loss in terms of Atikamekw values and representations, the scope of which can only be grasped through an understanding of the type of relationships that the Atikamekw have with their territory, the animal and plant worlds, and their ancestors. It was not merely the territory and the resources, in the Western sense of these words, that were subjected to flooding, it was also places, camping and portaging areas, locations of happy and unhappy events, and burial grounds. These places were named, narrated, lived, and passed on from one generation to the next; they were permeated with the traces, the presence, and the memory of the ancestors. The Atikamekw relocated further to the north, on the site of Opitciwan, which was selected because of its strategic position at the confluence of several waterways, thus providing access to various family territories.

The construction of the Rapide Blanc Dam in 1930, though not as large a project as was the construction of the La Loutre Dam, nevertheless subjected the better portion of the Kokokac reserve to flooding.[7] The Kokokac Band was simply left to fend for itself as best it could; government authorities no longer considered it as existing. Nevertheless, family groups affiliated with this band continued to use and occupy their respective territories and would meet with the people from Wemotaci during the summer period. Even today, they continue to maintain strong relationships with their ancestral territories (Poirier 1992).

From 1950 to the Present

The 1950s marked the gradual abandonment of a semi-nomadic way of life but not the abandonment of family territories, which the Atikamekw continue to frequent on a sporadic basis whenever they have the opportunity. In addition to logging, and the construction of the Rapide Blanc Dam and the La Loutre Dam, another event was to have an impact on the Atikamekw's relationship to their ancestral territories – the delineation of the Abitibi beaver reserve during the 1950s. The creation of the beaver reserves was a mixed blessing, to say the least. At a time when the fur trade was in full swing, and the beaver was declining dramatically subsequent to the abuses of non-Aboriginal trappers,[8] the Quebec government decided to intervene and delineate the areas where only Aboriginal people would be entitled to hunt and fish. There should be no misunderstanding as to the government's intentions: as the name suggests, the beaver reserves were created primarily in order to manage the reproduction of the beaver and not to protect territories for the Atikamekw or other Aboriginal hunters. Trapping lots were granted to the chiefs of family groups, or at least to those who were present in the communities of Wemotaci, Manawan, and Opitciwan when the Department of Indian Affairs representative happened to be passing through. Only slightly more than half of all the territories frequented by various family groups at that time were considered in the delimitation of the beaver reserve. For the first time, the Atikamekw were confronted with a Western cartography that all but ignored their customary ways of dividing and transferring family territories. Without entirely acceding to the territorial delimitation that had been imposed on them, the Atikamekw were nevertheless forced to redefine their traditional modes of occupying and using their territory.

Following the abolition of the private sports clubs in the 1970s, all Atikamekw territories located outside of the beaver reserve were subjected to an administrative delimitation that placed them in one of four categories: (1) a "zone d'exploitation contrôlée" (ZEC) or controlled harvesting zone; (2) outfitting camps (having exclusive or non-exclusive rights); (3) resort leases; or (4) logging leases ("contrat d'aménagement et d'approvisionnement forestier" [CAAF]). These administrative delineations and non-Native presence have clearly alienated the Atikamekw relationship to ancestral territories and, indeed, have become daily realities for the Atikamekw.

Today logging, particularly clear-cutting, represents one of the main concerns of the Atikamekw. They are justifiably worried about the negative impact of logging on all their territory and on the animal and plant world. It is a concern that the provincial government and the forest industry apparently do not share, despite the adoption of a new discourse on "sustainable development" and "integrated resource management." Interestingly, since the early 1990s, it is the Atikamekw hunters and trappers association, *Mamo Atoskewin*, that has been actively preparing for the proposed implementation of integrated resource management policies. Association members have banked on state-of-the-art technologies such as geomatics and remote sensing to take advantage of Atikamekw knowledge of the entire territory. Thus armed with a base of geo-referenced data for areas of activity and animal and plant resources, the association, the band councils and the Council of the Atikamekw Nation have begun negotiations with the forestry companies with a view to improved resource management. Owing to their lack of political influence, however, the Atikamekw have not been well received by the companies and the provincial government. In recent times, however, the nature and the extent of the dynamics of the relationship between the Atikamekw and the forest industry have, with the construction of a sawmill at Opitciwan under a joint partnership between the band council and the companies, significantly changed. It is too early yet to tell to what extent this new endeavour will prove satisfactory to the Atikamekw's multifaceted expectations.

As for the beaver reserve, it has become a space that the Atikamekw can frequent without encountering excessive interference or restrictions on the part of the Kawapisit. Nevertheless, Kawapisit encroachments upon the reserve land, in the form of resorts, outfitter camps, and logging, have increased from year to year.

In short, until the 1950s, and in spite of ever-growing restrictions, the Manawani Iriniw, Wemotaci Iriniw, and Opitcino Iriniw were able to maintain a certain autonomy over their respective territories. Today, despite the continual shrinkage of these territories and the decline of resources, the Atikamekw have preserved a strong link to their ancestral lands and have thus safeguarded their traditional system of values, knowledge, and practices.

Transmission and Guardianship of Ancestral Territories

> Even if it's levelled, it will always be my territory.
>
> – an elder, Manawan

Regardless of the administrative delineation it has been subjected to, regardless of whether it is located inside or outside the beaver reserve, every parcel of Atikamekw territory continues to be identified with a family group and is governed by a transfer process in accordance with Atikamekw customary law. Like the Innu (Mailhot and Vincent 1980), the Atikamekw do not consider themselves to be the "owners" of territories but, rather, the "guardians" or "trustees" of what has been passed on to them. In addition, these areas of responsibility, which are usually bordered by waterways, are viewed as forming a set of places, camping sites, and hunting grounds that are interconnected by means of land-based (*icawiṇ*, or *motewin*) or river-based (*itohiin*) routes and itineraries. An Atikamekw elder will never indicate the perimeter of his/her territory on a map but will, instead, point out the sites and itineraries making up this territory and his/her experiences of it. An itinerary entails a specific mode of "engagement" with the forest and named places that brings into play narratives, events, and experiences. If there are any borders at all between these areas of responsibility, they are essentially flexible and permeable, and they are reevaluated according to needs and events; here, the principle and logic at stake centres on networks of shared responsibility towards a living land.

On the subject of the transfer of territories, an elder from Manawan stated that "you don't give the territory itself, but everything that lives and grows on the territory." Hence, it is not only a territory and its resources that are passed on but, indeed, a living environment and a series of named, meaning-laden places and camping sites – all of which are permeated with the presence, traces, and activities of the ancestors (*kimocomnok*). This same elder added that "you give your *onerisiwin*"; that is, a way of living and being, or a path towards maturity and autonomy.

As a rule, responsibility for the territory – that is, for a series of sites and the surrounding area of occupation – is passed on to the eldest son of the family, although this is not an absolute. The eldest son thus takes on the responsibility for indicating to his brothers, brothers-in-law, sons, or others their respective hunting and trapping areas. However, responsibility for a territory may also be given to a younger brother, a nephew, or a grandson. In all cases, the decisive factor in the transfer process appears to be knowledge of the said territory. Another criterion used in the customary mode of territorial transfer is the number of children. Between two equally knowledgeable sons, an elder may choose to transfer the territory to the one who has the most children. In cases where responsibility for a territory is transferred to a son-in-law, the latter will be entrusted with this area until his own son (or the grandson of the elder) has reached an age at which he may take over. The son-in-law may not transfer the territory to his own brother. The chief role of the guardian, or *kanikaniwitc* (the one in front, the one at the head), is to respect and to compel respect for the custom governing the modes of resource management that he himself was taught. He must also ensure that all members of his family have an area of land that is sufficient for conducting their hunting, trapping, and other activities. It is also his responsibility to settle disputes concerning the said territory.

The entire Atikamekw territory has been named and has thus been endowed with meaning. The Atikamekw entertain an intimate, intrinsic link with the places they have named: there is no overemphasizing the importance of Atikamekw toponymy, which coexists with Kawapisit toponymy (just as Atekamekw cartography coexists with Kawapisit cartography). Places may be named according to a variety of criteria: topography, available resources, the behaviour of a particular animal, an event (be it happy, unhappy, or peculiar), a person who lived in the area, and so on. These place names serve to reveal not only a territory, but also the generations and events that have shaped Atikamekw history. Toponyms serve to continually renew cultural memory and the field of individual experiences. The place-naming process testifies to the ongoing and dynamic relationships between the Atikamekw and their ancestral territories. While most of the older toponyms are still used, other place names (which are better-suited to contemporary reality) have been added over the years. In addition to toponyms, there is a whole range of other signs that express Atikamekw presence on and engagement with the land: markers of camping sites (*matikan*), food caches (*tecipitakan*), and the notches made on trees (*wasikahikan*) to indicate and delineate seasonal trapping grounds.

On the territory, relationships between Atikamekw hunters and non-Aboriginal sport hunters are often tense, although not fundamentally so.

Two modes of relationship with the territory and the plant and animal worlds stand face to face. Obviously, there is much that could be written about the difference between the Atikamekw hunter and the sport hunter, but a single example will suffice. The principle of reciprocity serves as the foundation of the relationship between the Atikamekw themselves as well as between them, the territory, and the animal world. This reciprocity has not always been matched by the Québécois. In the past, a number of Atikamekw were surprised when the Québécois whom they had invited onto their territory to trap for a single winter proceeded to come back the following winters without having been invited. This presumption was contrary to Atikamekw ethics. Although the principle of inviting (*Wicakemowin*) is quite widespread among the Atikamekw, it is understood that an invitation applies only during the season within which it is extended. During the following season, it is up to the guardian of the territory (*kanikaniwitc*) to evaluate the state of the resources and to determine whether or not the invitation will be renewed. The Québécois who were invited by Atikamekw friends to trap for one season mistakenly believed that they had received an invitation to trap for an indeterminate period.

A number of elders prefer to abstain from frequenting the ancestral territory rather than run the risk of encountering non-resident non-Aboriginals who would ask them to justify their presence in these places – the places where they were born and raised and where their parents lie buried. A female elder from Opitciwan made the following revealing comments: "From Oskélanéo up to Opitciwan, you used to see a lot of camping sites. Nowadays, I no longer see the traces of where people camped, like I so often used to. Now, I only see the summer cottages that the Whites built on our camping sites. I only see traces of White land" (June 1994).

This type of nostalgia is an understandable reaction on the part of the Atikamekw elders. But it is an entirely different matter for the younger Atikamekw, who have no choice but to deal with the presence of the Kawapisit if they wish to practise their traditional activities and preserve their affiliation with their ancestral territories. As a rule, the Atikamekw do not allow themselves to be easily intimidated by the prohibitions and administrative delimitations imposed by the Kawapisit. Moreover, many of them continue to frequent family territories whether these lie inside or outside the beaver reserve, provided, of course, that logging has not despoiled these lands. They quite readily establish their camps on their family territories close to the cottages of the summer residents, track moose on the territory over which an outfitter camp holds exclusive rights, lay traps outside of the beaver reserve, and so on. When they have the opportunity to do so, the Atikamekw will visit their respective family territories and carry on their traditional activities, even if this means being insulted or arrested by the Kawapisit. Obviously, this behaviour on the part of the

Atikamekw represents a certain form of cultural resistance and consciousness. However, this is expressed even more clearly in the preservation of customary ways of dividing and passing on ancestral territories.

The current generations of Atikamekw must deal with two ways of representing territory. The first and oldest – and the one most relevant from the Atikamekw point of view – derives from ancestral modes of division and transmission of areas of territorial guardianship; the second has gradually taken root since the end of the nineteenth century and derives from various administrative delineations. The latter way of representing territory has been superimposed upon the former. While the second way of representing territory is scarcely conceivable to the Atikamekw elders, the younger people are able to understand its limitations without ascribing to its primacy.

Dynamic Tradition, or the Atikamekw as "Modern Hunter-Gatherers"

Waterways – that is, the numerous tributaries of the St-Maurice River – once constituted the traditional travel routes within Atikamekw territory. Today, all routes into Atikamekw territory, whether one is headed for Wemotaci, Manawan, or Opitciwan, are logging roads. The Atikamekw have adapted to this new reality, which has by no means ruled out the still frequent use of the canoe. As proof, most present-day camping sites are no longer located along waterways, as was traditionally the case, but, rather, are located along these logging roads (provided, of course, that a river or a lake is nearby). Whether temporary or permanent, these camping sites testify to the persistence and presence of Atikamekw activities on the territory.

All categorizations of socio-cultural worlds are guilty of oversimplification, and that known as "modern hunter-gatherers" is no exception. Nevertheless, this appellation is adequate for my purposes because it accounts for the contemporary identity of the Atikamekw insofar as it emphasizes the dynamic character of tradition as well as the appropriation of modernity. Some people, including a number of Atikamekw, would justifiably object that they no longer practise a way of life based essentially on hunting, fishing, trapping, and gathering. I, for one, couldn't agree more. My intention is neither to reify a past that has disappeared forever nor to pigeonhole the Atikamekw within a category that is too often freighted with oversimplified, evolutionist connotations; rather, I use the term "hunter-gatherers" in order to bring out the pervading influence of social practices and cultural values that are specific to hunter societies and to underscore the relationship between Atikamekw representations, knowledge, and symbolizing practices and their ancestral territories. As for the adjective "modern," it highlights the hybrid character of contemporary Atikamekw culture and the fact that the Atikamekw have become irremediably integrated within the world system and the market economy.

Classical models of hunter-gatherer societies were often inspired by evolutionist anthropology and cultural ecology – as such, they conveyed an essentially instrumental approach to "subsistence economy." In more recent times, these models have been supplanted by types of inquiry that are more sensitive to the epistemological and ontological foundations of hunter-gatherer cultures (Ingold 1996; Bird-David 1990, 1992, 1999) and/or to the contemporary mechanisms by which these societies link practices, knowledge, and identities (Povinelli 1993).

In ontological terms, and like several other hunter-gatherer cultures, the Atikamekw maintain a relationship with their territories that Bird-David (1992) refers to as intimate, reciprocal, and communicative (see also Feit 1994; Scott 1989; Tanner 1979; and Brightman 1993). Accordingly, the territory is viewed as a living and, indeed, personalized entity within which human and non-human beings, or "neighboring others" (Bird-David 1999, S78), coexist and interact. Moreover, the values expressing reciprocity with the animal world were at one time, and still are to a certain degree, well articulated during hunting rituals. An example of one such ritual consists in burning the first beaver pelt of the season so that the beaver (and its spirit) know that it has not been killed primarily for its pelt but, rather, for its flesh. This treatment of the beaver pelt is in keeping with traditional Atikamekw notions of ethics and sharing.

The expression "traditional activities," as it is used within the Canadian political and legal systems, simply refers to subsistence activities. Conceived of in this fashion, the expression also reflects a Western mode of relating to territory and resources as well as a Western vision of hunter-gatherers – a vision based on evolutionist, ecological, and quantitative paradigms. However, when understood in a broader sense, "traditional activities" clearly suggest knowledge, a code of ethics, social rules, cultural values, symbolic systems, and an oral tradition – all of which extend far beyond the needs relating to subsistence. In addition, the transfer and guardianship of territories, according to Atikamekw custom, are also traditional activities.

The question of knowledge is of capital importance. All systems of knowledge must be placed within their social, cultural, and historical context; for that reason, they are necessarily dynamic. As Bird-David (1992) has pointed out, the knowledge of hunter-gatherers "is expressed in a multi-stranded idiom – political, ecological, symbolic and social." It would obviously be a mistake to reduce Atikamekw knowledge to its ecological dimension alone. Atikamekw knowledge must be seen within the context of the type of relations that these hunters-gatherers have with their environment. The bear (*masko*), the moose (*mos*), and the beaver (*amiskw*) do not merely represent animals that may be killed; they are, first and foremost, the sentient beings and "neighbouring others" that the Atikamekw hunter is required to know and respect.

It would be wrong and, indeed, naive to think that traditional knowledge could have eroded completely in only two generations (i.e., since the 1950s). There is no denying that some knowledge and practices have become obsolete; the Atikamekw would be the first to say so. However, just because the Atikamekw no longer practise a semi-nomadic way of life does not mean that they have totally abandoned the practices, knowledge, and values of their ancestors. Furthermore, despite current restrictions, the Atikamekw continue to have access to ancestral territories and to frequent them whenever they have the opportunity. Even today the resources of the territory provide a considerable portion of their diet. Hides, particularly moose hides, continue to be used in the fabrication of items used in everyday life (moccasins, gloves, drums, etc.). Medicinal plants continue to be harvested and used. Not surprisingly, considering the strong Atikamekw ethic of sharing, the resources of the territory play an important role in maintaining and strengthening local networks of social exchanges and relationships. Far from representing a residual way of life that is condemned to disintegrate under the pressure of non-Aboriginal territorial interests, the Atikamekw hunter-gatherer culture remains alive, even as it is undergoing transformation.

Moreover, the majority of Atikamekw hunt, fish, or gather according to the season (or intermittently); during certain weeks in spring and fall, they engage in these activities more intensively. Beginning about ten years ago, the Atikamekw instituted "cultural weeks." For two weeks during spring and fall (the exact schedule varies from year to year) schools and offices are closed. During this time, families set up their camps on the ancestral territories. Within the current context, these sorts of events are undoubtedly crucial to the transmission of knowledge. In the communities, the younger generations have other opportunities to come in contact with the hunter-gatherer tradition. For example, when a hunter returns to the community with game, the younger Atikamekw are likely to hear the story of the hunt; to witness the process of the cutting up and preparing of the meat; and to be involved in the process of sharing it with relatives, friends, and neighbours. This knowledge and these practices are thus still accessible to the younger generations.

It is not so much a case of knowledge having disappeared or transformed as it is a shift in the processes by which it is transmitted and the frequency with which it is put into practice. The elders, both men and women, had to acquire a strong degree of autonomy in the forest by the time they reached puberty, and they are the first to deplore the loss of traditional knowledge among the younger generations. Theirs is a totally understandable point of view. With young people now having to attend school, it is clear that they will need additional time to acquire knowledge of hunting, fishing, trapping, and gathering. Eventually, however, this knowledge will be acquired and put into practice, at least by those who choose to do so. These practices and this knowledge have remained as relevant as ever; they are an integral part of present-day reality and represent a specific way of being in the world. It should also be added that the oral tradition plays a major role in transmitting the events that have shaped Atikamekw history as well as the knowledge and values associated with their territory. For example, the hunting tales that hunters tell after bringing game home or to the camp are part of the experience of Atikamekw youngsters. The story (*atsokan*) itself is a sign of respect for the animal who gave its life.

With respect to hunter-gatherer societies, the question of flexibility, which is raised by Bird-David (1992), merits several comments. This flexibility was traditionally reflected in the nomadic way of life. Hunter-gatherer societies were not chaotic and unorganized, as several Western observers have claimed; rather, they were constructed and reproduced on the basis of an open, flexible order that was continually negotiated between humans as well as between humans and non-human others. Flexibility refers to the capacity of hunter-gatherers to regularly reevaluate the resources and potentialities of a territory. Flexibility implies knowledge and sensitivity that is attuned to territorial, seasonal, and climatic variations. Hunters are not essentially limited by an ecological and seasonal order, as has often been suggested by studies in cultural ecology. On the contrary, their flexibility offers them ways of opening on to the world (Ingold 1996).

Atikamekw knowledge, being dynamic, encompasses the Atikamekw understanding of the world of the Kawapisit – a world with which they have learned to cope and to coexist. Whereas a number of elders have chosen to refrain from frequenting their territory on account of the presence of Kawapisit, the younger generations have learned to deal with this presence despite its annoyances. Furthermore, as an Atikamekw friend of mine commented, many of them have to deal with three living environments – the forest (*Notcimik*, "where I come from"), the community, and the city, each of which requires specific knowledge and practices.

The example of a young man from Wemotaci, in his mid-twenties and the father of two children, is particularly enlightening. This young man is a hunter. Having learned the requisite knowledge as a youngster, he often comes back to the community with game, which he then shares with his extended family. In the community, he works as a facilitator with the *Projet Migoun*, a project aimed at preventing suicide among Atikamekw youth. He is also an avid chess player, playing regularly with friends and on the computer. Finally, he plays traditional drum with other young men of his generation. Several time a year, they travel to powwows organized across Canada (and the United States) in order to share their art with others.

Conclusion

The Manawani Iriniw, Wemotaci Iriniw, and Opitcino Iriniw who make up the Atikamekw Nation have maintained strong links to their respective ancestral territories. In spite of increasing restrictions and a non-Aboriginal presence on their territory, the Atikamekw still consider themselves to be the "guardians" of these lands. The relative autonomy that previous generations had been able to preserve was lost with the gradual abandonment of a semi-nomadic way of life. It has given way, however, to a certain form of political recognition and, on the national level, to a level of bargaining power that was unknown to previous generations. Just as their elders once developed strategies for adapting to the new realities occurring on their territory, so the members of today's generation have been attempting to develop strategies that will enable them to combine their knowledge and values with a type of economic development that will be capable of safeguarding their autonomy within the contemporary context.

As all cultures are inscribed in history and laden with a broad spectrum of occasionally contradictory messages, they are necessarily dynamic and heterogeneous (Comaroff 1992). Throughout this chapter I have spoken of the "Atikamekw," but I am aware that this refers to a heterogeneous whole within which it is possible to differentiate several groups. One distinction may be identified in generational terms. The elders were born in the forest (*notcimik*) and experienced a semi-nomadic type of existence; in Western representations of the time, they were referred to as "Savages." The current generation of adults came of age during the period of boarding schools, when the policy towards "Indians" was one of assimilation. The younger generations were raised and educated within the communities; they have put forward claims for recognition by the dominant society and demands for social justice (which has yet to become a reality). Nevertheless, all groups share a history that has been embodied in their individual experiences, realizations, and sufferings and that has served to buttress their cultural resistance.

In this chapter I have explored various facets of the Atikamekw people's relation to their ancestral lands within the contemporary context. Over the last fifteen years, the Atikamekw have instituted a whole series of local initiatives in connection with the processes of reappropriating their history, reasserting their identity, healing their society, and renewing their rituals. It is true that these initiatives are part of a larger movement involving several Aboriginal nations and communities. Nevertheless, the forms and expressions of these initiatives are rooted locally. The Atikamekw are no longer the guides of sport hunters; rather, they are attempting to become, once again, the guides of their own future.

Acknowledgments

Research in the three Atikamekw communities was made possible through a grant from the Social Sciences and Humanities Research Council of Canada. I am also grateful to the Atikamekw Nation Council and to all the Atikamekw who expressed their confidence in my work. Special thanks go to Gaétanne Petiquay, Jean-Marc Niquay, Marcel Boivin, and Mary Coon (among others), who assisted and guided me in one way or another on my journey into the Atikamekw world.

Notes

1 In contrast to their Cree or Innu neighbours, the Atikamekw have rarely been the subject of any anthropological surveys. Of the few that exist, the work of Davidson (1928) and Clermont (1977) should be mentioned as well as, more recently, that of Gelinas (1998).

2 Traditionally, the Atikamekw band was made up of several family groups that were distributed over territories that were more or less bounded by the main waterways. Each family group had a spokesperson, who in all cases was a hunter of advanced years. One of these people was *Okimaw*, or chief, of the band. This was often a hereditary position.

3 In the same vein, the Innu of Lac St-Jean were referred to by the expression *Peikwakimikw Iriniw*.

4 Prior to this date, the Atikamekw travelled primarily to Trois-Rivières to sell their furs. Gélinas (1988) also mentions a few small, short-lived trading posts on Atikamekw lands prior to 1820.

5 The first missionary to visit the region (in the second half of the seventeenth century), Father Buteux, was killed during an attack by the Iroquois, who made frequent raids during this period. Until the nineteenth century, apparently no missionary ventured into the Haut St-Maurice; but by the end of the century the great majority of Atikamekw had converted to Roman Catholicism.

6 The Atikamekw call them the "Pactonew"; that is, the Bostoners (Suzie Basile, personal communication).

7 The Atikamekw never received any compensation for the reserve lands that were flooded. Today, Kokokac is the subject of specific claims by the Wemotaci band, with whom band members from Kokokac are affiliated.

8 The Atikamekw plied the fur trade for close to 300 years, and they had hunted beaver since time immemorial. Hence, it was not they who were guilty of over-trapping, for, had they done so, there would not have been any beaver on Atikamekw territory for quite some time. As early as the 1930s, the Atikamekw, accompanied by Father Guinard, brought the abuses of the non-Aboriginal trappers to the attention of Quebec premier Taschereau.

References

Anderson, B. 1991. *Imagined Communities*. London/New York: Verso.

Asch, M., and N. Zlotkin 1997. "Affirming Aboriginal Title: A New Basis for Comprehensive Claims Negotiations." In *Aboriginal and Treaty Rights in Canada*, ed. M. Asch, 208-30. Vancouver: UBC Press.

Bennett, T., and V. Blundell. 1995. "First Peoples." *Cultural Studies* 9, 1: 1-10.

Bird-David, N. 1990. "The Giving Environment: Another Perspective on the Economic System of Hunter-Gatherers." *Current Anthropology* 31: 189-96.

–. 1992. "Beyond the Hunting and Gathering Mode of Subsistence: Culture-sensitive Observations on the Nayaka and Other Modern Hunter-Gatherers." *Man* 27: 19-44.

–. 1999. "Animism Revisited." *Current Anthropology* 40 (Supplement): S67-S91.

Brightman, R. 1993. *Grateful Prey: Rock Cree Human-Animal Relationships*. Berkeley: University of California Press.

Clermont, N. 1977. *Ma femme, ma hache et mon couteau croche: Deux siècles d'histoire à Weymontachie*. Québec: Ministère des Affaires Culturelles.

Comaroff, J., and J. Comaroff. 1992. *Ethnography and the Historical Imagination*. Boulder: Westview Press.

Davidson, D.S. 1928. "Notes on Tête de Boule Ethnology." *American Anthropologist* 30, 1: 18-46.

Feit, H. 1994. "Dreaming of Animals: The Waswanipi Cree Shaking Tent Ceremony in Relation to Environment, Hunting and Missionization." In *Circumpolar Religion and Ecology: An Anthropology of the North*, ed. T. Irimoto and T. Yamada, 289-316. Tokyo: University of Tokyo Press.

Gélinas, C. 1998. "Les autochtones et la présence occidentale en Haute-mauricie (Québec), 1760-1910." PhD diss., Université de Montréal.

Ingold, T. 1996. "Hunting and Gathering as Ways of Perceiving the Environment." In *Redefining Nature: Ecology, Culture and Domestication*, ed. R. Ellen and K. Fukui, 117-55. Oxford: Berg.

Mailhot, J., and S. Vincent. 1980. *Le discours montagnais sur le territoire*. Report filed with the Conseil Atikamekw et Montagnais, Québec.

Ortner, S. 1995. "Resistance and the Problem of Ethnographic Refusal." *Comparative Studies in Society and History* 37, 1: 173-93.

Poirier, S. 1992. *L'occupation et l'utilisation du territoire dans la région du Lac Flamand, McTavis et Windigo*. Report filed with Conseil Atikamekw et Montagnais, Québec.

Povinelli, E.A. 1993. *Labor's Lot: The Power, History and Culture of Aboriginal Action*. Chicago: University of Chicago Press.

Sahlins, M. 1993. "Goodbye to *Tristes Tropes*: Ethnography in the Context of Modern World History." *Journal of Modern History* 65: 1-25.

Scott, C. 1989. "Knowledge Construction among Cree Hunters: Metaphors and Literal Understanding." *Journal de la Société des Américanistes* 75: 193-208.

–. 1993. "Customs, Tradition, and the Politics of Culture: Aboriginal Self-Government in Canada." In *Anthropology, Public Policy and Native Peoples in Canada*, ed. N. Dyck and B. Waldram, 311-33. Montreal and Kingston: McGill-Queen's University Press.

Tanner, A. 1979. *Bringing Home Animals*. London: Hurst.

Turner, T. 1991. "Representing, Resisting, Rethinking: Historical Transformation of Kayapo Culture and Anthropological Consciousness." In *Colonial Situations: Essays on the Contextualization of Ethnographic Knowledge*, ed. G. Stocking, 285-313. Madison: University of Wisconsin Press.

Valaskakis, G. 1993. "Parallel Voices: Indians and Others." Guest editor's introduction to *Canadian Journal of Communication* 18: 283-98.

Weaver, S. 1984. "Struggles of the Nation-State to Define Aboriginal Ethnicity: Canada and Australia." In *Minorities and Mother Country Imagery*, ed. G.L. Gold, Social and Economics Papers 13, 182-210. St. John's: Institute of Social and Economic Research, Memorial University.

Part 3
Resource Management and Development Conflicts

8

Voices from a Disappearing Forest: Government, Corporate, and Cree Participatory Forestry Management Practices

Harvey A. Feit and Robert Beaulieu[1]

Participation: A New Discourse of Control and Exclusion?

Participation has become a cornerstone of the new solutions to problems of the management of resources and the legitimation of their exploitation. Sustainable development, economic development planning, and "post-colonial" Aboriginal policies all claim to give varous sectors of the public specific forms of participating in resource-use decisions that will benefit all of society as well as the environment. But under this new rubric the opportunities to participate, and the means and conditions of participation, are being offered on the terms set by government authorities and the corporate sector. As a result, some analysts assert that the goal may be more to get citizens groups to comply with government and corporate uses of resources than to actually give them an effective voice. Nevertheless, compliance cannot be taken for granted, for these new arenas of participatory discourse and action are sites of contestation that may also serve as resources for autonomous demands for change. Some studies show that participation can contest and sometimes change the hierarchy of authoritative voices; the structure, scope, and definition of the processes of development; and the political context within which it occurs (see Richardson et al. 1993; and Pinkerton and Weinstein 1995 for examples).[2]

This chapter explores the significance of participation in the new forestry management regimes that have emerged in Canada and, especially, in northern Quebec. Participation has become the rhetoric of all those who want to use the resources of James Bay. Hydro-Québec has told James Bay Cree organizations that they may become partners, and co-owners, of its newly planned dams. Forestry companies and Quebec's Ministry of Natural Resources say that new opportunities for participation will give a voice to both the broad public concern for conservation and the particular needs and interests of communities and groups that use and value the forests in diverse ways and that are affected by commercial logging operations. Can these changes create new forms of decision making and resource use? Or are they being made without relinquishing government or corporate control? Is it possible for participation to work both ways in different situations? Or even in the same situation? For example, would the Cree have stopped the Great Whale project, even though they had no effective voice through the planning processes, without broadly based public support for the view that they should have a say in what happened on their lands? In short, how has participation worked? We begin with a brief review of recent contests for control of public forests.

How "Direct Action" Led to "Participation"

Protests against the ways in which Canada's forests have been exploited, and the intensity of this exploitation, have burgeoned over the last three decades, as have forestry protests in other countries, from South America to Southeast Asia (Devall 1993; Drengson and Duncan 1997; M'Gonigle and Parfitt 1994). Some of these public movements have affected the international economic marketplace through successful boycotts. Consider, for example, the decision by some British supermarket chains not to buy MacMillan Bloedel paper shopping bags and the banning in Germany of paper produced by using elemental chlorine. In the early 1990s, in Clayoquot Sound on Vancouver Island in British Columbia, several thousand people demonstrated and over 800 were arrested for civil disobedience while blocking forestry operations that threatened to clear-cut the forests of the region. It was a campaign that surprised provincial and federal governments by its intensity and the wide publicity it received, and they could control neither its development nor its consequences. Both the public protesters and the boycotts had impacts on how investors viewed the risk of putting capital into forestry stocks.

Partly as a result of these activities on the part of alliances of environmentalist and Aboriginal social movements – although these movements were not always in agreement – Canadian public opinion shifted and began to oppose the way governments and large corporations were managing public forests. By the late 1980s nearly 70 percent of Canadians thought the governments were not managing forests in the public interest (May 1998; Frisque 1996; Drushka et al. 1993; Marchak 1995). In the 1990s both the federal government and the majority of provinces, with the consent and (usually) the close cooperation of the industry, have made changes in policies, regulations, and/or legislation in order to make room for some public participation in forestry management decisions and to acknowledge that the multiple use of forests should play a greater role in planning commercial operations. At the same time, the forestry industry, responding both to public perceptions and to the boycotts, has substantially revised how it says it will manage the forest resources that have been allocated to it, largely from Crown lands, and it has mounted a series of publicity and public relations campaigns.

Foresters and forestry analysts have differed dramatically in their assessments of these changes: some call this a revolution in the forestry sector; others declare the changes a sham that merely obscures the continuing dominant alliance of government and corporations; and still others maintain that we should adopt a wait-and-see attitude (see Cantin and Potvin 1996; Dubois 1995; Poissant 1998; May 1998; Frisque 1996). Whichever view one adopts, these new regimes of participation are now part of the context within which organizations and communities are trying to claim an active voice and to contest those features of forestry policy that restrict their fuller participation.

New Quebec Regime of Participation Brings a New Rhetoric of Exclusion

In the last decade, Quebec's attempts to create a requirement for public participation in forestry policy and allocation decisions have been significant. Some analysts say that, in its official documents, Quebec now has some of the best principles for forestry management of any government or jurisdiction in the world. However, even favourable commentators have noted that "[I]l nous reste à passer du rêve à la réalité (we still must go from dream to reality)" (Frisque 1996, 33).

What is of concern is whether these changes signal a real shift towards practices that will facilitate broad and meaningful public participation in important forestry policy and allocation decisions. The very limited participation of the public in the processes for developing the new participatory regime has been questioned by professionals in the forestry sector and by activists. And some government reports have acknowledged failure in this regard (Dubois 1995; May 1998; and citations in Grand Council of the Crees of Quebec 2000).

The extent to which there is an as yet unfulfilled public interest for more participation, even after the policy changes, was recently indicated by the public response to a documentary video scripted by Richard Desjardins (a Quebec composer and singer) called *L'Erreur boréale* (Desjardins 1999).[3] The video is highly critical of the type of clear-cut forestry still being practised in the northern forests of Quebec, where Desjardins grew up and where his family still lives, and it has provoked widespread public support for change. Desjardins has been interviewed widely in the Quebec media, and he has been selected as "L'homme de l'année" (Man of the Year) of 1999 by the Quebec newsmagazine *L'Actualité* (vol. 24, no. 20, pp. 25-47), which said that the last such "pamphlet" to have as wide an impact in Quebec appeared some forty years ago.[4] A 1999 public opinion poll conducted for the newspaper *Le Devoir* found that 75 percent of Quebecers are convinced that "les grandes entreprises d'exploitation sacagent les forêts du Nord (large resource exploitation businesses are destroying the forests in the North)" (*L'Actualité* vol. 24, no. 20, p. 32).

The treatment of the Cree by the Quebec government also raises concerns about the meaning and implementation of participatory mechanisms. In 1996 the then Quebec assistant deputy minister of natural resources, Jacques Robitaille, said in an interview with the independent Cree magazine *The Nation* that nothing would now be done in forestry without consultation (Roslin 1996). But, in the same interview, Mr. Robitaille said, in response to a question about whether the impacts of forestry policies on the rights of Aboriginal peoples were a concern for the government:

> What we see is there is the political discourse, which to me is one thing, but there is also the reality on the ground where what is happening with local trappers and communities – I'm not sure it is as bad as certain people would have us believe for the ends of giving themselves a bit of political capital or publicity. (Roslin 1996)

We will examine what is happening locally to Cree hunters and trappers below. It is true that their politics are involved in assertions of impacts and in claiming the right to participate. However, this is an inevitable part of all policy-making mechanisms. Decisions that involve competing claims and different uses of resources are never purely technical: they involve economic and political allocations. All groups that make claims on the forests – forestry companies, the Cree, or the government itself – are involved in decisions that are to some degree political. But the assistant deputy minister's use of the term "political" with reference to the Cree does not acknowledge this; instead, it implies that Cree concerns are "political" rather than "real." Thus the subtext of his statement is that the Cree have no concerns that the government need take into account. At the same time, it implies that it is only the government that can be objective (i.e., non-political) and, hence, "real."[5]

Thus when the government declares that there will be no decisions without consultations, it also initiates a means of excluding groups from, or of diminishing the legitimacy of their participation in, the process. It denies that they have concerns that would legitimate their having an effective voice. It also implies that its own decision making is apolitical and realistic and, therefore, sufficient. These perspectives are not limited to the government: they are echoed in various forms by other groups at the core of the process, including scientists.[6]

Professional views are expressed in a book by l'Association des écologistes du Québec entitled *L'utilisation durable des forêts québécoises: De l'exploitation à la protection,* which is intended as a reference work for diverse audiences (Potvin, in Cantin and Potvin 1966, 2). In this collection Gilles Frisque reviews the changes in Quebec forestry politics and policies, and the public protests against Quebec forestry management in the past, under the title "Politiques forestières québécoises: *Le Québec est-il un Brésil du nord?"* (Frisque 1996, italics in original). The author is both critical and hopeful about the implementation of the new policies, and he recognizes the contributions of public protests to the creation of conditions of change, while rejecting what he argues are the extreme claims of environmental organizations, such as the analogy between Quebec's forestry practices and Brazil's.[7]

Frisque (1996, 30) also addresses Aboriginal issues and views, acknowledging that "le désir des populations autochtones de profiter de la ressource forestière et de protéger leur territoire afin d'assurer leur développement est parfaitement justifié." He goes on: "Cependant, l'absence de données factuelles et les réponses légalistes aux attaques souvent exagérées des représentants autochtones ne conduisent pas à un dialogue constructif" (30). Thus, while Aboriginal peoples have a just claim to benefit from forestry resources and to protect their lands for their own development, they do not have the factual knowledge to participate effectively. Their strategy, he says, has been to turn legalistic and to engage in exaggerated attacks. As a result, he believes that they have failed to contribute to a constructive dialogue. He implies that they themselves are responsible for not effectively participating in forestry decision making. The solution he proposes is as follows:

> La stratégie de protection des forêts du Québec préconise une approche préventive et holistique. Ceci devrait permettre de solutionner des problèmes qui, jusqu'à présent, avaient été abordés d'une façon strictement sectorielle, ponctuelle ou même conflictuelle ... Tout ingénieur forestier sait maintenant qu'il doit tenir compte de l'ensemble des ressources du milieu forestier et faire participer à ses décisions les spécialistes des autres disciplines, y compris les spécialistes en sciences sociales. (30)

Here participation would be extended from forestry engineers to experts from other disciplines, especially the social sciences. But recognition of the contributions that the knowledge and experience of citizens and Aboriginal peoples could make, alongside that of the scientists, is missing. Also missing from the decision-making process are the communities of people affected by commercial forestry. The policy recommendation calls for a holistic approach that seeks to avoid sectorialism and that, therefore, should recognize diverse peoples' interests in forestry resources. Yet it omits them from decision making. The implication is that professional social scientists will represent the interests of those groups. The argument expands upon, and, in many important respects, runs parallel to, the one made by Roslin. In both cases a regime of participation is used to exclude, to leave decision making in the hands of government or professional experts.

The rest of this chapter suggests both that there is Aboriginal knowledge that should play a role in forestry regime decision making and that the James Bay Cree have been constructively trying to participate in forestry decision making for several decades. It also asks whether the new participatory policy and regime are leading to a more effective public voice within the forestry regime.

Cree Initiatives for Participation

Knowing Forestry through Experience

James Bay Cree concerns about the way industrial forestry is being conducted and the impacts it is having on land, vegetation, animals, and Cree hunters and their families have been expressed throughout the last forty years. They have been expressed with increasing vigour and by more and more hunters. The following notes, taken from a series of interviews with Waswanipi Cree hunters recorded by Feit in the early 1980s, pre-date the revision of Quebec legislation. What he finds is that the same concerns were being expressed in the late 1960s and the late 1990s.

> They can't really kill as many moose as before, because they are cutting too close and scaring the moose. Moose usually go away when they hear noise ...
>
> After cutting, moose comes back, but he just passes through, looks for some wooded area to stay in. From where they first started cutting a long time ago, there are some high [bushes] there, but not trees, just shrubs ... When they get taller probably [moose will] stay, can't stay there [now] because it's too open. Beaver not affected [that way] by forestry.
>
> Nobody asked [him if he wanted them] to leave [some] trees, [or] mark on map [areas he did not want cut]. Wants some areas left uncut, if [they] only leave small yards [for] moose [the moose] won't stay long. (Sydney Otter, 30/8/1983)[8]

Many other hunters echoed these concerns, although not all comments were negative. Hunters often said that the forestry road network was a benefit, giving them increased access to their hunting territories. Cree hunters generally preferred to speak from experience rather than from what they had heard from others. When they did speak of things they had heard but not seen, they usually identified the source of the information.

> Q:[9] What will happen when forestry operations [reach your hunting territory]?
>
> I can't really tell now what will happen. Because [in] the area where they will be cutting there is not very much logging ... done. (William Gull, Jr., 27/8/1981)

By comparison, on hunting territories on which, by the early 1880s, extensive logging had occurred, there was clear experience to draw upon, as Sydney Otter did above and his brother does below:

> Several roads go through [the] trapline[10] that interfere with his hunting. They [non-Aboriginal hunters] come in at all seasons on his hunting ground. In winter [they] come in on skidoos to fish. There are a lot of [non-Aboriginal] cabins situated on [his] hunting ground. They kill almost any animal that they see, geese, ducks. Most of time animals that they kill they throw away, he finds them in plastic bags. A lot of times when we go away overnight they come and take our things, took our chainsaws and gas one time. [At] mileage 60 on [the] James Bay road [where] he was trapping one time, they took 20 of his [family's] rifles and their [outboard] motor. We didn't try to find who took them. They didn't decide to look because they thought they won't find it anyway. Last winter where he trapped he didn't get anything because there was no game around ... From fall to spring only got five beaver. It has been over a year since he hunted on his [own] trapline where he hunted before, [but] he does know how it is ... He is going to still be hunting [the next year] where he hunted on the old man's hunting ground [i.e., not his own].
>
> Q: Why not go back to own ground?
>
> He was invited over to hunt where he is hunting now, because his dad hunts in that area. He said there is not that much moose around where he used to hunt [on his own hunting territory] because of the forest being cut, it goes where there are more trees. There just seems to be moose around the streams and rivers where the trees have [not] been cut down into the streams. Beaver seems to be scarce around that area because there are streams drying up because of the dam[s] made by roads [i.e., poor culvert installations – H.F.]. If there is no vegetation for it to feed [near] the streams the beaver doesn't stay around. A beaver only seems to stay around where he can feed, and if he can't feed he leaves the area. Most of his trapline has already been cut except along the shoreline ... All trees are not cut down along the shoreline, for 100 feet they are not cut ...

> Q: Is it getting harder to hunt and be a hunter?
>
> It is hard for a hunter to hunt when there is nothing to hunt, when there is plenty to hunt that's when a hunter enjoys to hunt, but when there is not much then he has to go far to hunt. (Jossie Otter, 27/8/1981)

Another hunter who had experienced extensive logging, although stretched out over a two-decade period, expressed his experience as follows:

> Where I hunt I find a lot of change in animal life from what it was several years ago, a lot of [wild]life has been destroyed. A lot of times we find beaver along the shores that have died. And this must be caused by the development, because where he hunts that is where the log cutting is going on.
>
> Q: What kind of effects [does] cutting have on animals [and] on hunters?
>
> Cutting too much forest around the area, which cuts the supply of animals' feeding and the environment where they live ...
>
> Q: How does cutting ruin things for animals in water like fish?
>
> From the fumes of machine[s] and gasoline being used it destroys the fish. And sometimes because of various chemicals the water tends to smell, and this causes beaver to die. It has been twenty years now that forest industry has been working inside his trapline. The government tells him to hunt there, this is his trapline, and expects him to survive there even with all the work there ...
>
> Q: How much of trapline [has been] cut, a quarter, a half, more than half?
>
> Over half has been cut, but here are several patches left that are not desirable to be cut.
>
> Q: After cutting does beaver come back?
>
> After cutting beaver doesn't intend to come back, goes to where it is better.
>
> Q: [Can you] continue to hunt, trap in [the] cut trapline [in the future]?
>
> In my trapline I don't think I'll be able to stay too long, because of industry invited to stay [by the government]. But if I was invited by another [Cree] group I would stay [on their trapline].
>
> Q: Is it right to cut forest?
>
> The only way I can see it, they are really over me, because they want to get the development over forestry, and there is no way I can stop it. I feel it is not only my own land that they will take over, from what I hear they will be able to take over any territory they wish to cut. (Antoine Icebound, 25/8/1981)

When he was interviewed again two years later, Antoine Icebound reaffirmed his knowledge.

> [His trapline] is [n]ot very good for beaver because it's all affected by forestry. About half cut. It was affected by forestry. There is nothing left where trees were taken. But where they leave an island not cut there is some game. The beaver stays along the lake, but they don't stay on streams, that's where they all come [to the lake] when they leave their home ... He'll find it hard to look after things. Because they think the moose goes away from there when they hear that noise, sometimes they don't see any tracks in summer and fall. Lot [of] sport hunters go there in fall. He hunts with his son-in-law, [t]hey don't have enough for all of them to hunt. [There is] still cutting.
>
> Q: Be better to leave rest [uncut]?
>
> Yes ... Sometimes they take all the trees in a moose yard. Sometimes they take all the trees along the river or stream, and some of those trees are pushed into the river. Maybe they have an effect on the water [quality], because sometimes they find a dead beaver. Also when they set their nets, on the pole to [hold the] net you can see green stuff on pole, from work [being done for logging].
>
> Maybe later in the future it will be the same as before, maybe 30 years. Maybe he won't be able to hunt by that time, he'll be an old man.
>
> [He w]on't go [to his trapline] this year. He is going up north ... He's not going to let anyone hunt there this year.
>
> Q: Anything he wants said?
>
> The only thing is that he didn't like all the trees being cut down where they hunt, and they are destroying all the animals. (Antoine Icebound, 6/9/1983)

When his son-in-law was interviewed, he compared hunting on Antoine's land with hunting on his own family's land further north where there was little forestry at that time:

> He finds it really different this side [Antoine's], the moose, beaver, rabbits, food is not really good, not as good as up north. Like you know moose meat and internal organs are good, [but it is] not like that now, leaves are dead, their food is not good. He found a beaver last fall, it was dead shortly before, and it was like the moose [another hunter had found], it was all swollen on neck and chest. I know it will be hard for us to find something to eat if we go back there for years and years ... When he eats beaver he gets sick. That's the thing he eats a lot. (Abel Gull, 1/9/1982)

Trying to Participate from the Land

Hunters whose lands were in the early stages of being cut over often made an effort to communicate their concerns to government officials and forestry company representatives in the field. Initially, they understood that their experience and concerns would be taken into account.

> They can hear forestry already, probably it will come, maybe this winter, that's the white man for you. There will be a lot less game, it will ruin the ground for trapping. Those forestry people asked where there are a lot of moose, maybe they will leave that part alone, [we] asked them to leave it alone. They asked him when would be best time to cut down trees, he said winter, then they won't kill many young animals. They said they'd try to leave trees along streams especially if there is beaver. The road they are building is supposed to go right up north.
>
> [Cree translator]: [It will be] good for my father ...
>
> Q: [How would you like it cut?]
>
> Cut half of the trapline, [then] wait ten years. That would be good, that would be a lot better. If they would just cut a little section each time they cut trees. If somebody could control that it would be good.
>
> White sport hunters come, but only ones he invites, usually only invites two. These white people, even if both have a license, they are only allowed one moose between them ... Probably sport hunters will increase when road is built for forestry.
>
> [Another hunter told me] it takes 20 years for hunting to be good again. This area [where we were talking was covered in brush not high trees – H.F.] was cut 20 years ago, [there] was a sawmill here, then a fire. He'll probably be dead by then. Probably his sons and grandchildren will use it, but he doesn't know if he will live to see that. (Noah Eagle, 4/9/1982)

When Noah Eagle was interviewed again two years later he was not asked about the earlier conversation, but he returned to the subject to report the results of his efforts to have logging operations on his hunting territory modified:

> Another thing I want talk about is the log cutting. They cut down trees close to the rivers and creeks. When they first started that business, they said they'd get the logs just in the bush not close to the river or creeks. But that is not true. They even cut down the beavers' food, poplar. What tree or logs they don't have use of they just push them into the creek or river. I see today too, where beavers loved to lodge, is now all damaged, all their food is cut down and they can't stay there anymore. I see that everywhere I go. They don't do what they said, just to cut down the trees from far in the bush. That's how everyone's ground is ...
>
> Maybe in years ahead, we'll just be like the Indians in the old days, they were so poor, or before the Indian Agent came to help us, or when the

Income Security stops ... We won't have nothing left if they keep on cutting down our trees, damaging our land ...

If anyone doesn't believe what we say, we could take them there to see or we'd take pictures of what we're talking about. We're not too happy about that, our hunting ground being damaged like that. Some Indians that hunt up north say they have a lot of moose there, where their ground is not yet damaged. I guess the moose just takes off and goes to where the land is good and plenty of their food there. It can't stay where the ground is damaged, it's the same way with all the other animals.

I don't know what will happen to us in the future, but right now we're okay, the way we're living. In the olden days I remember we didn't have any tea or sugar, all we had to drink was [the broth] from what we cooked, fish, rabbit and other game, we never had anything to make soup. And I think it's going to turn out that way pretty soon, by the way things look, in the past two years. (Noah Eagle, 5/8/1984)

Negotiating Participation with the Government

Concerns about the long-term future of the land and of hunting were expressed by the Cree throughout the 1970s and were part of the negotiations leading to the James Bay and Northern Québec Agreement (JBNQA) in 1974-5. In order to ensure protection of the lands and resources, the Cree and Inuit insisted on negotiating an environmental and social impact assessment regime that would apply to all future development in the region.[11] Land was also essential to the continuation of Cree hunting, which various provisions of the JBNQA recognized and supported as a goal. Forestry was to be considered as part of these environmental protection provisions, with specific means of participation set out in the agreement (see Section 22).[12] These provisions did not fully satisfy Cree concerns; nevertheless, the Cree were to have a definite role in the processes of forestry policy making and in allocation decisions.

Quebec tried to limit this role in various ways, for example by insisting on inserting a clause in the JBNQA on Category II Lands – lands on which wildlife is reserved exclusively for the Cree but on which development is also permitted. This clause states: "Forestry operations are compatible with hunting, fishing and trapping activities" (Section 5.2.5.c). Interpretations of this clause differ; however, Quebec spokespersons have sometimes used it to argue that forestry has no negative impacts and, thus, to diminish any consideration of Cree concerns. Feit was involved in some of these discussions, and he interpreted the clause as an insistence by the Government of Quebec that the Cree agree not to oppose forestry operations in principle by claiming that they were all incompatible with hunting. In other words, the Cree would have to specify impacts in any hearings about forestry, even where their rights had priority over those of other wildlife users. Feit firmly holds that a strictly factual interpretation of this clause – as a statement that forestry and Cree hunting are always compatible regardless of how each is conducted – is clearly counterfactual and counterintuitive.

The Grand Council of the Crees claims that the implementation of the JBNQA has been incomplete and seriously flawed (Diamond 1990; Grand Council of the Crees of Quebec 1996; Vincent and Bowers 1988). When Quebec revised its Forestry Act in 1986, and again when it brought in new regulations and policies for participation in the 1990s, it ignored the obligations it had undertaken to ensure Cree participation under the JBNQA. The Cree claim that they do not have an effective voice in forestry policy or decision making today, despite having negotiated and signed the JBNQA in 1975 and despite new participatory provisions put forward in the 1990s. They insist that Quebec is ignoring its obligations to them (Grand Council of the Crees of Quebec 1999).

Cree Forestry Concerns

Over the course of the last three decades forestry has become an increasingly important concern among Cree of all ages as logging has spread and efforts to have a say in its planning both at the hunting territory level and in legal agreements have not succeeded. However, the majority of Waswanipi also support Cree forestry operations as a means to create employment for those Cree, especially sectors of the youth, who want and need jobs. To this end the Waswanipi Cree have run their own logging operation for over a decade, auctioning the wood to local mills; and, in recent years, they have built and run a small joint-venture sawmill with a major forestry company. Nevertheless, concerns for how logging operations are conducted in the region are widespread among Waswanipi of all ages and occupations.

Impacts of Forestry Operations: A Synthesis

Cree concerns about forestry impacts include but go beyond the immediate effect of forestry operations on game animals; they extend to the economic, health, and socio-cultural implications for Cree society. The impacts reported below have been identified from field notes, interviews, and responses to questionnaires provided by Cree hunters over the last three decades. The review begins with the kinds of information cited in the quotations above, but it is based on discussions with many hunters on extended topics.

Many hunters reported that several species of game tend to be encountered less frequently because they "move away" after the forests have been cut. The noise created by forestry operations was repeatedly said to scare moose and make them more skittish and harder to hunt. Moose and some of the other species might later increase when appropriate vegetation is reestablished, but this would take at least one or more decades. And there was a general sense of uncertainty about the timing and sequences of animal repopulation.

Many hunters indicated that they caught fewer moose and fewer members of some other species due to the effects of forestry. Beaver populations were reduced because of changes in the streams and water systems due to poor culvert construction, increased soil erosion and siltation, and/or from trees falling in the streams. Even when a tree border was left standing along the shore, interviewees said that strong winds would sometimes throw down trees when there was no adjacent forest cover. As a result beaver also often "move away." Moose and beaver were the two most abundant harvests in the Waswanipi Cree hunt (as measured by food weight produced). Hunters said that these reduced harvests caused many to experience economic hardships. Because animals were often seen to be in poor health in logging areas, health problems for hunters and their families were a repeated concern.

Hunters reported that forestry roads provide easier access for them but that they also increase the number and the dispersal of non-Cree sports hunters. This increased access was associated with increases in thefts of equipment and vandalism of camps. This creates added economic burdens, for not only must stolen or damaged property be replaced, but goods must also be protected. For example, some hunters now have to transport their snowmobiles and canoes out of the bush each summer in order to protect them, and so they incurred increased transportation costs. In cases of loss of equipment people do not usually have rapid access to sufficient additional cash or credit to replace them and refinance travel, so the entire hunting year is sometimes either foregone or substantially truncated.

Some hunters indicated that supplies of the particular types of trees that were needed to make certain kinds of equipment were no longer readily accessible. This sometimes also reduced available plots of plants and bushes that served a variety of medicinal or herbal needs or provided materials for equipment and/or crafts. While people acknowledged that there were usually other plots available, they were not always accessible to a particular campsite.

The disruption of animal populations has spiritual implications for most Cree hunters. In saying that the animals "move away," the hunters are reflecting the Cree worldview the animals do not just die off, they leave because they do not like what has been done to the land; they go to where it is better. In the view of some hunters, the animals' souls survive their bodies, and they are aware of what is done to the land. In many Cree hunters' views, the way forestry operations are conducted is disrespectful to the land and the animals, and the animals see and respond to this disrespect as would persons with intelligence: they "leave." Cree hunters believe that such disrespect may mean that they themselves can be given bad luck and ill fortune by the spirits of the animals and the land.

Because of reduced harvests of game on hunting territories that have undergone significant forestry activity, some stewards explained that they had to reduce the invitations they could offer to other hunters. Comments also indicated a reduction in the amount of "bush food" that could be shared with others. These patterns of exchange are how the Cree affirm their social ties to one another and express their caring for one another. A reduced ability to express social ties and personal generosity can create a sense of social and moral loss.

The changes in the land, vegetation, and game make it hard for stewards to continue to manage and conserve their territories. Knowing whether or not you are killing too many of any given species depends on your knowledge of how many indicators of that species you should expect to see in a given area. Many factors can alter game populations, so a steward needs to know how game has responded to particular terrains, vegetation, and microclimates. With such knowledge a steward can have an idea of whether changes in game populations are due to such factors or to the number of animals being harvested.

Forestry cutting transforms the area and eliminates the applicability of past knowledge. There is no location-specific knowledge about what will follow cutting, about what vegetation will return and when, and about how animals will respond over the next years and decades. This makes it difficult if not impossible to adjust the intensity of today's hunt to levels that might enhance future game populations, which is the essence of conservation in Cree hunting.

The stewards serve as models of expertise in hunting and as examples of how important it is for others to learn these skills. Young hunters learn basic hunting and bush survival skills from older hunters; however, more sophisticated stewardship skills require long-term learning. A vital part of the knowledge needed to manage game and land depends on learning to understand the particular history of game populations on a particular piece of land. To effectively teach this to a young hunter one cannot reduce it to a set of rules or principles. Extensive cutting of hunting territories, therefore, threatens the transmission of complex hunting knowledge and skills to the next generation of stewards and hunters.

This has broad implications for culture and identity. Many stewards whose hunting territories have been extensively cut over express sadness that their own sons and daughters will not experience fully the way of life that they have had. They know that most will not be able to learn the more complex stewardship skills. They express both sadness and uncertainty about the future of Cree culture.

He started hunting when he was thirteen, and all the hunting was good, the animals were all healthy, and they aren't now. There was all kinds of game. And the things that used to be there, half of them are not there ...

Q: [Does it] make him bitter?

He is bitter because they come to his land to destroy his land, they never go to their land to destroy their land. He's been hunting for fifty years, and he has been keeping track of his land, and he finally realizes how much damage the white man has been doing on his land. He thinks all the damage that has been done it's irreversible, the land will never be the same as it's been before ...

Q: [Will his] children and grandchildren be able to live [on the land]?

It's gonna be really different, won't be able to survive as good as before. Like when he was hunting he used to live alone in the bush, and they would have their children alone in the bush, and when the bush was good, that's how they managed to survive. Since he was born he has never had a job and he has never worked, and he has still raised his sons and daughters to be full grown from the bush. Now that the land has been ruined, he doesn't think any of his sons could raise their families like he did when the land was still good.

What he did before on the land he wasn't thinking about himself but about the younger generation, so they could survive as he did. What he learned from the bush, he didn't learn from his father he taught himself in the bush.[13] When he was just growing up for his family, many times he used to think about that, and thought about times he didn't see his dad. Sometimes when he's out hunting he just stood there and thought about his dad, and he used to cry. Then he finally got better and better at hunting. Then he finally [learned(?)].

When he looked at tracks of other people and he knew they didn't have no food, and he went to their camp and it was true they didn't have no food, and he went to his camp to get a toboggan load of food and he took it to them. He can't do that he's too old, and he's getting sick. Sometimes when he looks at his son he wishes his son could do the same thing he did in his younger days. (Jacob Happyjack, 30/8/1983)

These uncertainties also affect how Cree youth think about the pattern of life they want for the future. In some cases, families whose hunting territories have been extensively cut over have no children in young adulthood who have chosen to learn stewardship skills. The extensive forestry cutting reduces the willingness of young Cree adults to choose intensive hunting as a long-term economic and lifestyle commitment.

These uncertainties are not just individual, they are also collective. In the interviews conducted in 1997, there was widespread worry about the future of the land, hunting, and the Cree way of life among all groups of people. This uncertainty was often explicitly tied to the extent of forestry operations.

Quantitative Exploration

Up to now this chapter has stressed the knowledge and concerns that Cree hunters have expressed, in discussions with outsiders, over the effects of forestry. We also want to consider the substantial quantitative information that Cree hunters have and use, and that they have shared with outsiders. Information on Cree harvests of wildlife has been repeatedly shared with government agencies, Cree organizations, and independent researchers, and these unique data provide one of the most detailed records of a hunting society that is available anywhere in the world.

The literature on the quantitative impacts of forestry on subsistence hunters is virtually non-existent, whereas the impacts of forestry on animal populations, such as moose, have been reasonably well studied. We have, therefore, set out to examine whether the impact of logging can be demonstrated through looking at the information on Cree harvests of moose.

As the Cree hunters cited above indicate, forestry can affect moose hunting in diverse and complex ways. For example, we cannot separate the effects of cutting the forest per se from those of building roads and increasing non-Aboriginal hunts. Nor have we tried to do so. Both cutting and road building are necessary to commercial logging operations. Our goal is to explore the overall and combined effects, if any, of these operations (and all of their component activities) on Cree moose harvests.

In different years, there are many factors that more or less randomly affect the levels of moose harvest on a hunting territory and that create a high variability in harvest numbers. We also know that there are a number of things, independent of forestry, that have been changing during the recent decades that could also affect the Cree moose harvest. These include the rapid demographic growth of the Cree population, an increase in the incomes of settlement-based hunters, and the increase in the number of Cree who hunt intensively (thanks to the JBNQA). Many hunters were generally spending more time in the bush and could afford more equipment and services, such as transportation from the settlement to hunting territories, during the period covered by this research. Most of these factors would tend to increase moose harvests over the years and could, therefore, have effects that would be the opposite of those expected in logging areas. While these factors would, in principle, be felt on all hunting territories at the same time, logging would not. The effects of more people with more cash travelling more regularly from the settlement to hunting camps is more pronounced where road access is readily available. Although this increased hunting effort is not caused by the growth of the road network per se, the geographical distribution of the effects of these demographic and economic changes is affected by where logging has expanded the road network. Therefore these changes, which, as has been said, would have the opposite potential effects on Cree moose harvests from those expected from logging, are particularly difficult to separate from the latter. This made it difficult to identify the effects of logging.

Some other changes worked to reduce moose harvests, having effects similar to those expected of logging over time, particularly those associated with other forms of forest disturbance, such as forest fires. We assumed, therefore, that clear-cutting and forest fires would have cumulative impacts on moose harvesting and that it might be difficult to separate them. We incorporated burning into our analysis,[14] and we sought to examine whether there was a relationship between the percentage of the forested lands of a hunting territory that had been disturbed, by being cut or by being burned, and the number of moose that were harvested by Cree hunters on that territory.

Feit aggregated the information available on Cree moose harvests by territory by year from almost twenty studies that had been conducted in the Waswanipi region, covering the period from 1969 to 1985. Where a hunting territory was not used during a given year we did not include it in the data set because the lack of a harvest was ostensibly the result of no hunter effort rather than a failure to find moose. The actual circumstance is, however, more complicated: hunters may not use a hunting territory precisely because there are few moose, and such declines and choices can result from forestry. In these instances the lack of a harvest and the absence of a hunting effort are both the result of perceived impacts of forestry. Thus our decision to exclude all cases in which a territory was not used actually excludes some cases in which the consequences of forestry cutting might be expected to be most clear. This choice could not be avoided given the information available to us.

Beaulieu used Quebec forestry records and calculated the extent of the disturbed area on each trapline. We grouped both sets of data into five-year blocks (1969-75; 1976-80; 1981-5) in order to smooth annual variations. The first block covers a seven-year period, but, as no harvest data were available for 1970-1 or 1971-2, each block includes data on five years of harvests.

We were unable to run tests for more recent periods because fewer and less complete sources of data on Cree moose harvests are available after 1985. The cumulative areas that had been subject to commercial forest cutting were considerably more extensive by the 1990s than they were in the earlier years of this series, so our inability to include this period was unfortunate because the relationship of logging and moose harvests would be expected to be most clear during the latter period.

We explored the relationship between logging and Cree moose harvests by plotting the two variables on a scattergram graph and by running tests for the statistical significance of the relationships.

Social Data Methodology

The data on Cree moose harvests by trapline are drawn from the results of studies of Waswanipi Cree land-use and harvesting activities. The most extensive data are from two studies conducted by Feit from 1968 to 1970 and from 1981 to 1983. During the first period he met and interviewed nearly all of the Waswanipi Cree hunters, including nearly all the hunting territory "bosses," or stewards. Many were interviewed more than once. In the 1980s Feit worked with a team of Waswanipi interviewers to complete questionnaire-based interviews with nearly all the hunting territory stewards and all but a few of the Waswanipi adult males. The information from the hunting territory stewards included whether a territory was used in each of the last five years, which hunters used it, and the number of big game harvests taken by the hunters during the last one to three years before the interviews.

We also examined information that had been systematically collected, for which research methodologies had been reported, and that was considered reliable by those who had conducted the original research. The information collected by Feit primarily covers the periods from 1969 to 1970, and from 1979 to 1981. The other sources provided information that addressed hunting territory use and moose harvests during the years not covered by Feit's research. They also provided information that filled in gaps in Feit's information on hunting territories. Finally, they provided overlapping information with which to examine the consistency and plausibility of the different sources. This information was collected by a variety of organizations: two were Cree, three were government-based, and eleven were joint Cree-government agencies. Two of Feit's shorter field research projects were also used.

The most common research methodology relied upon hunter recall, although hunters' diaries were used as well. We reviewed the results of the evaluative research on harvest recall information conducted for the James Bay and Northern Québec Native Harvesting Research Committee (JBNQ-NHRC), which was a joint initiative of the Grand Council of the Crees, the Northern Quebec Inuit Association, the Governments of Canada and Quebec, Hydro-Québec, and the James Bay Development Corporation. Those studies found strong reliability and validity for interviewee recall and records of harvests for several years back in the case of big game and for one year back in the case of less important species. They also found evidence that Cree reports of harvests have a tendency towards being conservative; that is, hunters tend to report lower harvests than do observers, and their reports tend to decline the further back individuals are asked to recall information.[15]

Where there were overlapping reports available to us we made comparisons between hunting territory stewards' reports and data from those interviewed by different research groups in order to examine the quality of the studies and the interviewees. This comparison allowed us to identify a few interview results that did not seem consistent and that we removed from the database. On the basis of these analyses we also identified the studies to which we would give priority when two sources of information from other organizations overlapped and when we had no information from our own research.

While the great majority of information came from hunting stewards' reports, when these were unavailable some was also drawn from individual interviews with hunters.[16] For the quantitative analyses we have only used information on the number of moose killed per trapline per hunting year.[17] The average annual moose harvest was calculated for each territory for each block of years. We excluded from the final data set territories for which there was no harvest information for more than a single year because single-year harvests can be inaccurate measures of general levels. These and the earlier exclusions on the side of caution limited the number of cases to just over 100. We then calculated the average annual moose harvest per 100 square kilometres of land on each territory in order to adjust for the different sizes of hunting territories. These data were then examined in relation to the average percentage of the hunting territory that had been disturbed by cutting and/or forest fires during each five-year segment.

Forest Disturbance Data Methodology

The first two provincial forestry surveys that were carried out by the Quebec Ministry of Natural Resources (MNR) in the mid-1970s and the mid-1980s did not integrate ecological and social data. Since 1993, the third forest inventory survey has integrated some ecological variables, but this information was not available at the time we gathered our data. We have therefore extracted the forestry disturbance data we use in the present study from the second forest survey database (1985), whose structure was set up in the 1970s.[18] It is not the purpose of the present study to describe in detail the MNR forestry inventory and accounting system. However, we believe that presenting a summary description of information that we used to characterize forest within the Waswanipi hunting territories is useful.

Forest contours are presented on forestry maps at 1:20,000 scale, and there are more than 125 maps for Waswanipi hunting territories under commercial forest operations. These maps resulted from interpretation of aerial photographs at 1:15,000 scale. The smallest forest entity interpreted is more than one hectare for forest disturbance areas and four hectares for forested areas. A forestry map at 1:20,000 scale contains between 1,000 and 2,000 such areas, or polygons. Each polygon can represent a forest or a non-forested area. A forest stand is composed of a group of trees of different species having the same origin. Within Waswanipi hunting territories, a large part of the mature forest originates from forest fires. Forest stands could also originate from human disturbances such as clear-cuts.

Robert Beaulieu carried out a preliminary analysis of the forest database corresponding to Waswanipi hunting territories. Forest data have been grouped based on the following criteria: forest cover type, origin, forest disturbance, and biophysical land class. This process has served to create a forest classification system mainly based on forest disturbance. A program has been developed to group data per parcel. A parcel is a subdivision of the forest management unit; it generally aligns with biophysical entities and it contains between twenty and fifty forest stands. The database compiled by the Cree Regional Authority (CRA) contains the following information on each parcel: parcel number, the management unit to which it belongs, land categories, forest development stages, forest disturbance per period (1969-75, 1976-80, 1981-5), forest canopy density, forest canopy tree height, and nature of forest disturbance (natural or human).[19]

Findings

The distribution of the available data did not allow a sensitive statistical testing, and statistical test results were not significant. A more sensitive statistical testing would require additional data. It is especially unfortunate that appropriate moose harvest data do not extend into the 1990s, when the cumulative effect of commercial forest cutting could have been tested.

Nevertheless, the graph of percentage of hunting territory cut for forestry or otherwise disturbed by fires, plotted with the average annual Cree moose harvests per 100 square kilometres of hunting territory for each of the periods, indicates a clear tendency towards a linear and negative relationship (Figure 8.1). These data show a tendency for the moose harvest to decline as the percentage of the hunting territory that is disturbed increases. Beaulieu notes that the slope of the line that predicts the relationship can be interpreted as indicating that for each 1 percent increase in the area disturbed on a hunting territory, there is a 1 percent reduction in the moose harvests on the trapline.

This tendency is consistent with the statements of Cree hunters that forestry cutting and fires adversely affect their moose hunting. This tendency also complements Cree hunters' own statements about how important it is for everyone involved to continue to explore ways of changing forestry practices in the region. In the mid-1990s these efforts were renewed.

Figure 8.1

Waswanipi moose harvests vs. forest area cut and burned, 1969-85

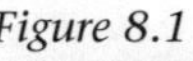

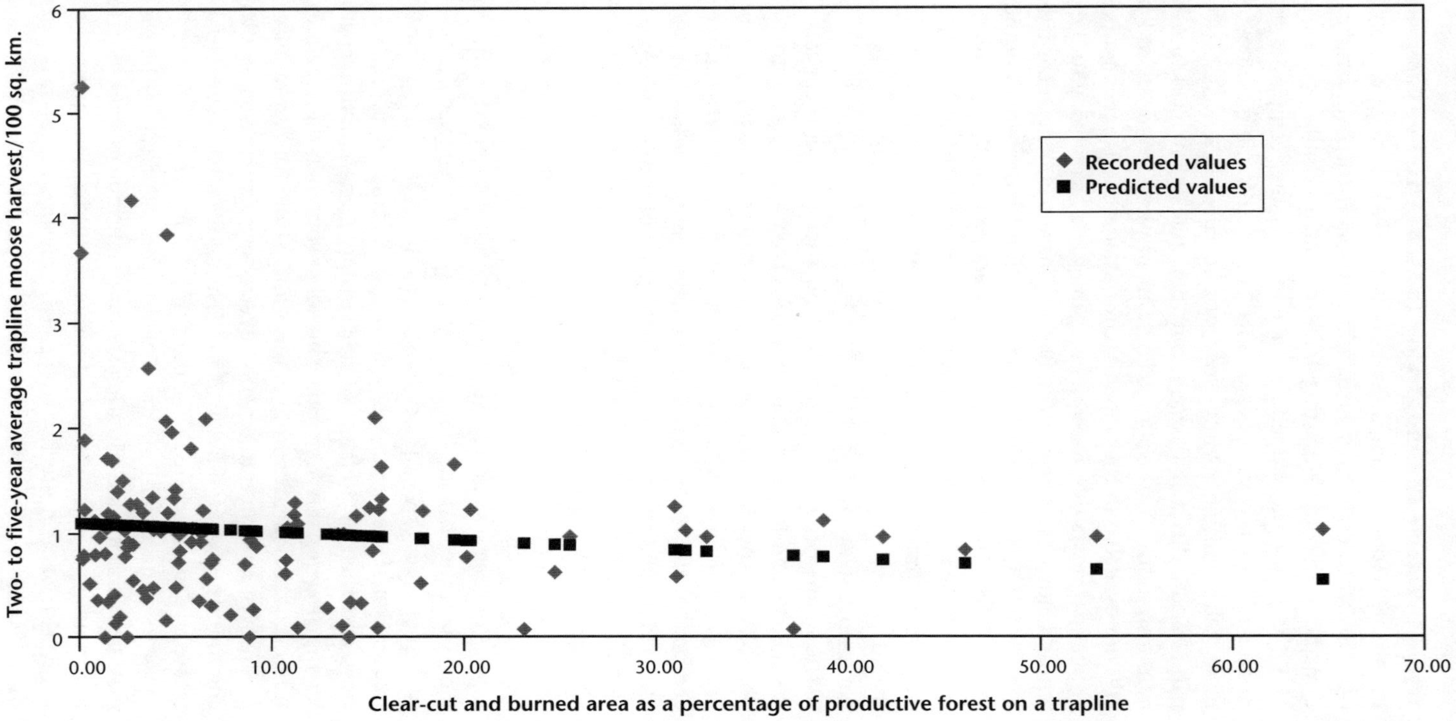

Trying to Finesse Consent, Trying to Make Effective Compromises

In the 1990s forestry companies have had to seek ways to comply with the new Quebec forestry procedures, which enjoin them to undertake consultation and demonstrate that they have consulted with the concerned public. The key strategy developed by some of the larger companies in areas of Aboriginal land use, such as James Bay, involved signing contractual agreements with hunting territory stewards. Initially, these were between companies and individual stewards, but they quickly changed to involve the administration of First Nations. These are private agreements and are generally not available to the public.[20] On the one hand, agreements specified annual payments that forestry companies were to provide to the stewards whose lands were being cut that year. These payments were either to go directly to the stewards or to the First Nation for the benefit of the individual stewards. These payments have reportedly varied in size, but they were often sufficiently large that they made a significant contribution to the disposable incomes of Cree households. Many of these agreements also include a clause indicating that there would be consultations between companies and stewards.

The companies' motivation for making such payments appears to be that it enables them to claim that they consulted with Cree hunters. It is also possible that they intend to say that they had received the consent of stewards to cut the forests on their hunting territories (given that these stewards accepted payments specified in the agreements). In fact, no such claims have been publicly made, and, initially, the companies called no consultation meetings.

The agreements generated diverse responses in Cree society and inevitably caused divisiveness. Many Cree fear the agreements and payments would legally compromise Cree land rights in general – especially the collective aspects of Cree systems of tenure. Many hunting stewards think the agreements indicate that the forest companies have recognized Cree authority, and, therefore, they support these documents as being at least a partial recognition of Cree rights. They also appreciate the needed cash. Some Cree reasserted their own claims of stewardship; some sought recognition for having arranged the payments; and some contested the very unequal distribution of payments within families and within the community.[21]

However, after an initial period of strongly conflicting views within the community, several individuals in Waswanipi started a concerted effort to create a local consensus. They did this by using an unexpected feature of the agreements and of the new Quebec forestry policies – the clauses that mandate participation. Hunting stewards continue to want to have a voice in forestry operations on their hunting territories. The critics of the agreements also want an effective Cree role in forestry decision making. By using the agreements as a basis to insist that companies fulfill their obligations to consult with Cree stewards, a group of Cree leaders and administrators have brought about some unity between both those Cree who support and those who oppose the agreements. Thus dialogues and some common vision of what is desirable are again being explored.

This led to the community hiring Cree staff members to work with stewards to help them to negotiate how forestry was being conducted on their hunting territories. Cree staff pressured forestry companies to fulfill their contractual obligations to consult stewards. They thus also succeeded in opening a new area of participation.

It is less clear what is emerging in the new negotiations with the forestry companies. A few companies have resisted dealing with community representatives and have tried to continue dealing only with individual stewards. But the benefits of having community staff advise them in negotiations are clear to most stewards, and so they have exerted pressure on the companies to involve First Nations staff. The Cree administrative staff members, for their part, have made it clear to the companies that they will face more protests and direct action opposition if they do not work through the community-initiated process for consultations. Most companies have, therefore, entered into consultations.[22] In addition, the Grand Council of the Crees has set up a fund to pay hunting territory stewards whose lands are being cut and to reduce the pressure on them to sign agreements with forestry companies.

Initially, forestry companies expected the consultations to be pro forma. Most stewards wanted their territories to be managed as distinct units for forestry, and they wanted some areas of cultural importance and of ecological significance excluded from forestry cutting. Managing smaller forestry units is part of the new provincial and national forestry policies, and Quebec officials attribute this change to pressure from Aboriginal communities. Indeed, by paying funds to the land stewards the companies had already implicitly acknowledged the hunting territory unit, whether they intended to do so or not. But companies have not agreed to manage forestry by trapline units.

However, a major disagreement in these consultations over specific hunting territories concerns whether meaningful areas are to be protected from forestry operations. In consultation discussions, company representatives said that they thought that sites of cultural and ecological significance could be dealt with if Cree stewards would put points on a map. The companies would then agree to establish cutting exclusion zones of several hundred metres around these points. The areas that stewards identified for protection covered tracts that included approximately 10 percent to 40 percent of a territory, and territories range from approximately 300 square kilometres to over 1,000 square kilometres. This was an entirely different scale of protection from the one the companies had offered. The implausibility of what the forest companies were proposing was easily pointed out by Cree negotiators, and the former quickly withdrew from their initial position. Areas of exclusion have now become the main topic for consultation, although other Cree concerns are being discussed as well.

Stewards generally begin the discussions by identifying the areas they wish to have protected in the current cutting plan. Forestry companies have generally replied at subsequent meetings that they would exclude some but not all of these areas from the cutting plans, and they have reduced the size of most of the areas to be excluded. The companies emphasize that they have agreed to protect most of the geographical units that the Cree stewards want protected, at least in part. Cree negotiators increasingly make the point that these protected areas cover only half or less of the 10 percent to 40 percent of the hunting territory that they had originally wanted excluded. However, stewards sometimes accept these areas because they can be better than no agreement at all.

The forest company then adopted the strategy of putting into their written approvals of protection (usually in minutes of meetings or letters pertaining to the results of discussions) that these involve temporary exclusions and that cutting on the lands in question is subject to further discussion in three to five years. The Cree have a different view of the temporary nature of exclusions. Many stewards emphasize that they do not want to discuss forestry cutting in the excluded areas until the areas currently being cut over have regenerated and again offer productive wildlife habitats (probably anywhere from ten to thirty or more years). Thus the 1999 discussions between forestry companies and the Cree resulted in very big differences, both spatial and temporal, between the two parties. And what had been agreed upon up to then does not satisfy most Cree stewards.

The Cree have been trying to make the consultation process work, whereas the forestry companies have made what could reasonably be called limited concessions (since any agreement is only binding for a few years). The risk to the Cree is that these discussions and documents will be accepted as adequate consultation if and when these processes are reviewed within the context of the new forestry procedures. The talks themselves could, therefore, compromise Cree participation. However, as the cutting is ongoing, some are willing to support taking the risk.

The Cree-initiated consultation process has created some unity among the Cree and has led to renewed resolve and initiative among Cree hunters and administrators. But consultations of this scale have not been sufficient for many Cree. Frustrations with the process led to renewed talks with the provincee in 1997-8 and again in 1999, and when these failed an injunction request was made to the courts in July 1999. In addition, strength has built in the community for the possibility of a public protest campaign and for making new alliances with environmentalists. The

Grand Council has started to take its case against Quebec forest products to major buyers such as Home Depot and to legislators in the United States (Grand Council of the Crees of Quebec 2000). But, in mid-2000, Cree political organizations have also renewed efforts to restart meaningful discussions with the province.[23] The eventual outcome of these complex initiatives for effective participation in forestry decisions pertaining to Cree lands remains unclear.

Conclusions

These conflicts, including the current direct negotiations between Cree stewards and forestry companies, and between Cree organizations and Quebec, concern whether or not effective participation has occurred, who has the right to such participation, and whether or not (and how) more effective participation might be established in the future.

Certain provisions of the JBNQA – the establishment of a new forestry regime in Quebec, company payments to stewards – can all be seen as efforts to create the appearance of effective Cree participation in forestry planning. However, to date, neither the provisions of the JBNQA nor those for provincewide public participation in forestry decision making have been effectively implemented. Indeed, the need for Cree involvement has been denied and subverted by statements and actions of senior government representatives. Forestry company proposals for protecting small areas around geographic points, or for negotiating cutting exclusion zones that only apply for a few years, are clearly of limited utility. Company initiatives have been concerned primarily with creating the appearance of consent (through the acceptance of payments and ongoing discussions) without negotiating effective protections. Each of these participatory initiatives has been shown to be more concerned with legitimating the existing decisions of governments and corporations than with creating effective participation for Cree or with changing environmental and social impacts on the ground.

These processes use participation as the key criterion for legitimating forestry resource allocations to the public and in the consumer marketplace. Thus participation, insofar as the forestry companies are concerned, has two goals: (1) to tie the Cree (and environmentalists) to a set of procedures and incentives that change forestry practices only very modestly, if at all and (2) to clear away public distrust, international protests, and marketplace anxieties by claiming that those groups who have legitimate claims have participated in and consented to what is happening.

But there is also another side to these processes. Participation in forestry decision making is not just a claim used by companies and governments; the demand for participation has been continuous from within the Cree community for over three decades. These local initiatives for representation do not have their origin solely in responses to the initiatives of companies or governments; local demands are not initiated by outside interests. Locally initiated projects for active participation take many forms. The Cree wood-cutting operation and the joint-venture sawmill allow the Cree to claim a share of the forestry resources. There are direct efforts aimed at creating pressures for effective participation in decision making, including extensive discussions on forestry plans (both informal and formal) and periodic high-level meetings with ministers during repeated crises. There have also been political strategies for increasing pressures, including long-term legal action; occasional protest demonstrations; and mobilization of American forestry products buyers, regulators, and social movements. These diverse initiatives have their roots in Cree daily life on the land and in Cree experiences of the impacts of commercial forestry. They include a Cree desire to share the land while enhancing autonomy. Furthermore, Cree initiatives take every opportunity to communicate to government, companies, and the public their knowledge of what can and should be done in the forests.

These complex strategies of action clearly have an effect on governments and corporations that have tried to force the Cree to give up their more autonomous forms of action. For example, Quebec insisted for nearly a year and a half that, before it could restart negotiations, the Cree would have to drop the forestry court case. Quebec also cut off government funding for already agreed-upon community development projects (such as a youth centre) (see Chevrette 1999, Quebec minister delegated for Aboriginal Affairs). These stances appear to have been dropped only after they came under increased public scrutiny as a result of the court case. Thus, Cree initiatives show that the Cree hold onto their autonomy even when under direct pressure.

However, there are contradictions at each level. Although the Cree community must now mobilize partly in response to the divisiveness created by the forest companies, it can do so in line with its traditional desire to protect land and wildlife through active cooperation. The governments and forestry companies want to appear to be responsive to citizens' concerns, so, having been forced into discussions they did not want, they offer token solutions. As a result, the public becomes more critical of the ability of governments to effectively protect forested lands from excessive exploitation and of the willingness of forest companies to manage their forest cutting so as to take into consideration the needs of diverse users.

Participation is being used effectively by governments and corporations to limit input into decision making on the part of the public and groups with specific rights and interests in forests. But the failure of that participation frustrates the participants, and it strengthens public opposition and motivates specific groups to develop diverse and complex strategies to seek meaningful changes. These strategies have as their goal effective participation, and those involved engage in legal challenges, public protests, social movement alliances, and interventions in the marketplace and international political arenas in order to attain it. Efforts to turn participation into a way of legitimatizing present practices and excluding those who should have a voice have not succeeded. Yet, the vision of effective participation backed up by political and legal action is still a valued goal. What is not yet clear is whether logging will be adequately regulated so that Waswanipi forests and hunting will be protected in the future.

Acknowledgments

The authors wish to acknowledge the support for this project given by the people of the Cree First Nation of Waswanipi and by the Cree Regional Authority. Harvey Feit specifically wants to thank: Fatima Amarshi, Mario Blaser, Diane Cooper, Brian Craik, Abraham Dixon, Paul Dixon, Stewart Gilby, Peter Gull, Sam C. Gull, Suzanne Hilton, Glenn McRae, Monica Mulrennan, Derek Neeposh, Alan Penn, Evelyn Pinkerton, Geoff Quaile, Alan Saganash, Colin Scott, and Wendy Russell for helpful comments. Financial support from the SSHRC-MCRI program to the AGREE team directed by Colin Scott, and from the Cree Regional Authority and the McMaster University Arts Research Board is appreciated. Harvey Feit's research was also funded by the Social Sciences and Humanities Research Council (SSHRC grants 410-99-1208, 410-96-0946, and 410-93-0505).

Notes

We prepared this chapter in our capacity as researchers, and it does not purport to speak for anyone other than ourselves as authors of the sections for which we are individually or jointly responsible (see Note 2). Our approaches are ethnographic, descriptive, comparative, analytical, and scholarly, and we do not intend this chapter as a commentary on the issues being presented in current court cases involving the Cree and the Governments of Quebec and Canada.

1 Robert Beaulieu, ingénieur forestier with the Cree Regional Authority, is the co-author of the section of this chapter entitled "A Quantitative Exploration," including "Social Data Methodology," "Forest Disturbance Data Methodology" (for which Beaulieu is the primary author), and "Findings." Other portions of the paper were written by and are the responsibility of Harvey Feit.

2 For recent literature on participation, see Escobar 1996a and b; Parajuli 1998; Pinkerton 1993; Povinelli 1993; Rahnema 1996; and Sachs 1996a and b. For one of a series of classifications of types of participation, in this case in the context of co-management discussions, see Berkes et al. 1991.

3 The video has been reissued in an English version called *Forest Alert.*

4 Richard Desjardins has followed up his video by starting a series of fundraising concerts, Action Boréale, to establish an organization to press for changes in current forestry practices in northern Quebec and also for an independent public inquiry into forestry practices (Nicholls 2000).

5 Mr. Robitaille later left the civil service to become president of the Association des Manufacturiers de Bois de Sciage du Québec (Nicholls 2000, 15).

6 The response of forestry companies to public participation policies will be discussed below.

7 An example of this comparison occurs in Roslin (1996).

8 The text of these interviews was written down at the time by Harvey Feit, who omitted common words in order to facilitate the speed of his note taking and the flow of the conversation. Most bracketed words and phrases in these quotations are Feit's reconstructions of his note-taking omissions. They are inserted here to create a more readable text. Most

discussions were conducted through a Cree interpreter, although some of the interviewees were multilingual (speaking Cree, English, and sometimes French), and they could follow and correct the translations where needed.

9 "Q" indicates a question asked by the interviewer.

10 "Trapline" is an alternative term for hunting territory.

11 At the time there was no general environmental and social impact or assessment legislation applying to Quebec.

12 The interpretations of these provisions of the JBNQA are among the key issues before the courts, and they will not be discussed here in detail.

13 The speaker lost his father while still a child.

14 These forest fires are of natural or accidental origin; there is no planned burning in the region.

15 See the methodological chapters and appendices in the JBNQ-NHRC's final report on its Cree research (1982).

16 Ninety percent of the cases are based on information from the stewards (421 cases), 7 percent (thirty-one cases) are based on reports from other hunters who were either leading or participating in the hunting groups that used the territory. Three percent (eleven cases) are based on individual interviews with each hunter who was using a territory (each reported their own harvests). In 1 percent of the cases (five cases) we had interviews with all but one of the hunters reported to be present.

17 In 3 percent of the cases (12/468), the reports of harvests indicated that more than one trapline was hunted by the same hunting group during the year, and, in these cases, we divided the reported moose harvests equally between the territories used.

18 Forest managers had the following objectives in mind when they designed the provincial public forest database: to establish the actual commercial stock (area and volume of timber) of the forest, to control commercial forestry activities within public lands, to maintain an up-to-date database on forests, and to evaluate forest stock depreciation attributable to natural disturbances (e.g., tree disease, insect epidemics, forest fires, etc.).

19 We have also created a geographical link between the parcel descriptive database and geographic data represented on MNR parcel maps at 1:250,000 scale. This has been done with the CRAGIS system. Simplification of the original forestry database implied that we reduced the number of variables in order to keep only the more significant ones. To prepare forest disturbance data through time per trapline, we have superimposed forestry parcel coverage with Cree Waswanipi traplines polygons (CRA 1990 map at 1:1,000,000 scale). Overlapping of the two layers of information has resulted in a coverage that contains information on both hunting territories and forests on a parcel basis. The resulting polygon attribute table has been used to generate statistics on forest disturbance per trapline.

20 The discussion of their contents is based on a copy that Feit was shown for his use, independently of his co-author.

21 Only those stewards whose lands were cut in a given year received payments, and payments were therefore difficult to predict. In addition, the amounts paid in later years were recalculated by some companies so that the same sums were divided among several stewards and their families. Therefore, later recipients often got less than early recipients. As smaller companies also started to make agreements, they tended to reduce the levels of payments.

22 A few smaller companies have refused to enter consultations or agreements at all.

23 There are also other initiatives in the Waswanipi community that are not touched on here. Waswanipi has explored cooperation with governments, companies, and forestry researchers by applying for and establishing a joint model forest based on its lands. The jointly run model forest has its offices at Waswanipi, and it employs several Cree and non-Cree staff members.

References

Berkes, Fikret, Peter George, Richard Preston. 1991. "Co-Management: The Evolution in Theory and Practice of the Joint Administration of Living Resources." *Alternatives* 18, 2: 13-17.

Cantin, Danielle, and Catherine Potvin. 1996. *L'Utilisation durable des forêts québécoises*. Ste-Foy: Les Presses de l'Université Laval.

Chevrette, Guy. 1999. Letter to Matthew Coon Come, 10 February 1999. Copy at: www.gcc.ca/news/forestrycase_update/correspondence_on_case.htm.

Desjardins, Richard. 1999. *L'Erreur boréale* (video). Montreal: National Film Board of Canada and ACPAV, Inc. (Also available as *Forest Alert*).

Devall, Bill, ed. 1993. *Clearcut: The Tragedy of Industrial Forestry*. San Francisco: Sierra Club Books and Earth Island Press.

Diamond, Billy. 1990. "Villages of the Damned: The James Bay Agreement Leaves a Trail of Broken Promises." *Arctic Circle* (November/December): 24-34.

Drengson, Alan, and Taylor Duncan, eds. 1997. *Ecoforestry*. Gabriola Island, BC: New Society Publishers.

Drushka, Ken, Bob Nixon, and Ray Travers, eds. 1993. *Touch Wood: BC Forests at the Crossroads*. Madeira Park, BC: Harbour Publishing.

Dubois, Pierre. 1995. *Les vrais maîtres de la forêt québécoise*. Montréal: Les Éditions Écosociété.

Escobar, Arturo. 1996a. "Planning." In *The Development Dictionary: A Guide to Knowledge as Power*, ed. Wolfgang Sachs, 132-44. London: Zed Books.

–. 1996b. "Constructing Nature: Elements for a Poststructural Political Ecology." In *Liberation Ecologies*, ed. R. Peet and M. Watts, 46-68. London: Routledge.

Feit, Harvey A. 1989. "James Bay Cree Self-Governance and Land Management." In *We Are Here: Politics of Aboriginal Land Tenure*, ed. Edwin N. Wilmsen, 69-98. Berkeley: University of California Press.

–. 1994. "Hunting and the Quest for Power, the James Bay Cree and Whitemen in the Twentieth Century." In *Native Peoples: The Canadian Experience*, second edition, ed. R.B. Morrison and C.R. Wilson, 181-223. Toronto: McClelland and Stewart.

Frisque, Gilles. 1996. "Politiques forestières québécoises: *Le Québec est-il un Brésil du nord?*" In *L'Utilisation durable des forêts québécoises*, ed. Danielle Cantin and Catherine Potvin, 27-33. Ste-Foy: Les Presses de l'Université Laval.

Grand Council of the Crees of Quebec (Eeyou Astchee). 1996. *Crees and Trees: An Introduction*. Ottawa: GCC(EA), Forestry Working Group.

–. 1999. The Case *Mario Lord et al. v. The Attorney General of Québec et al.*: Cree Forestry Litigation Checklist of Positions Taken in the Proceedings by Plaintiffs. On www.gcc.ca/News/forestrycase-update/thecase.htm.

–. 2000. "Forestry and Trade: The Social and Environmental Impacts on the Cree People of James Bay." Brief to the Office of the United States Trade Representative, 13 April 2000. On www.gcc.ca/Environment/forestry/ustr_submission.htm.

James Bay and Northern Quebec Native Harvesting Research Committee. 1982. *The Wealth of the Land: Wildlife Harvests by the James Bay Cree, 1972-73 to 1978-79*. Quebec: JBNQHNRC.

Marchak, Patricia M. 1995. *Logging the Globe*. Montreal: McGill-Queen's University Press.

Maser, Chris. 1994. *Sustainable Forestry: Philosophy, Science and Economics*. Boca Raton: St. Lucie Press.

May, Elizabeth. 1998. *At the Cutting Edge: The Crisis in Canada's Forests*. Toronto: Key Porter Books.

M'Gonigle, Michael, and Ben Parfitt. 1994. *Forestopia. A Practical Guide to the New Forest Economy*. Madeira Park, BC: Harbour Publishing.

Nicholls, William. 2000. "Action Boreale Off and Singing." *The Nation*, 30 June: 15.

Niezen, Ronald. 1998. *Defending the Land: Sovereignty and Forest Life in James Bay Cree Society*. Boston: Allyn and Bacon.

Parajuli, Pramod. 1998. "Beyond Capitalized Nature: Ecological Ethnicity as a New Arena of Conflict in the Global Capitalist Regime." *Ecumene* 5, 2: 186-217.

Parfitt, Ben. 1998. *Forest Follies: Adventures and Misadventures in the Great Canadian Forest*. Madeira Park, BC: Harbour Publishing.

Pinkerton, Evelyn. 1993. "Co-Management Efforts as Social Movements." *Alternatives* 19, 3: 33-8.

Pinkerton, Evelyn, and Martin Weinstein. 1995. *Fisheries That Work: Sustainability through Community-Based Management*. Vancouver: The David Suzuki Foundation.

Poissant, Charles-Albert. 1998. *Donohue. L'histoire d'un grand succès québécois de 50 000 dollars à 2 milliards de chiffre d'affaires*. Montréal: Québec Amérique.

Povinelli, Elizabeth A. 1993. *Labor's Lot: The Power, History, and Culture of Aboriginal Action*. Chicago: University of Chicago Press.

Quebec Superior Court. 1999. *Mario Lord et al.* v. *The Attorney General of Québec et al.*, S.C.M. 500-05-043203-981.

Rahnema, Majid. 1996. "Participation." In *The Development Dictionary: A Guide to Knowledge as Power*, ed. Wolfgang Sachs, 116-31. London: Zed Books.

Richardson, Mary, Joan Sherman, Michael Gismondi. 1993. *Winning Back the Words: Confronting Experts in an Environmental Public Hearing*. Toronto: Garamond Press.

Roslin, Alex. 1996. "'Dialogue of the Deaf': *The Nation* Goes Head-to-Head with Quebec's Main Man in the Forest." *The Nation*, 8 November: 12-17.

Sachs, Wolfgang, ed. 1996a. *The Development Dictionary: A Guide to Knowledge as Power*. London: Zed Books.

–. 1996b. "Environment." In *The Development Dictionary: A Guide to Knowledge as Power*, ed. Wolfgang Sachs, 26-37. London: Zed Books.

Scott, Colin H. 1992. *Political Spoils or Political Largesse? Regional Development in Northern Quebec, Canada and Australia's Northern Territory*. Canberra: Australian National University, Centre for Aboriginal Economic Policy Research, Discussion Paper No. 27.

Vincent, Sylvie, and Garry Bowers, eds. 1988. *Baie James et Nord québécois: Dix ans après*. Montréal: Recherches amérindiennes au Québec.

9

Conflicts between Cree Hunting and Sport Hunting: Co-Management Decision Making at James Bay

Colin H. Scott and Jeremy Webber

> We have a lot of respect for what we kill; and what we're trying to do is we're trying to avoid the people who just kill for the game and just being able to knock down something. That's not sport! They call it sport! They knocked down something. They knocked the life out of something. That's not necessary – it's not. There's no purpose to that. No purpose.
>
> – Wemindji Cree hunter

This chapter addresses the implementation of a controversial caribou sport hunt in northern Quebec. In particular, we examine the effectiveness of the Hunting, Fishing and Trapping Coordinating Committee (HFTCC), the wildlife co-management body established pursuant to the 1975 James Bay and Northern Québec Agreement (JBNQA)(Quebec 1976), in protecting and promoting the interests of Cree hunters. One of the main problems of co-management bodies in their many variations across subarctic and arctic North America is their tendency to adopt a culture of bureaucracy, to rely preponderantly on the idiom of scientific management, and to fail to connect with the knowledge and cultural priorities of those local people who have the most direct contact with – and often the most at stake in – lands, waters, and resources in their home areas. This problem is frequently exacerbated by the reluctance of central governments to accept a genuine sharing of decision making and by their impulse to overrule Aboriginal parties thanks to the strength of superior political resources.

In the case of the caribou sport hunt, the Quebec government undertook actions, with "majority-vote" endorsement by the HFTCC (achieved only with the chair's deciding vote, during a period when the Quebec government occupied the chair), that entailed profound conflict with Cree cultural values concerning right relationships to animals and local control of Cree homelands and waters. At the same time, there was local interest in economic opportunities that might be salvaged from a course of development authored by the government of Quebec, a dominant political force that would be influenced in minor respects but not dissuaded. We seek to convey the complexity of what transpired by interweaving three narratives: the first relates Scott's conversations with Cree hunters at the community of Wemindji; the second offers an abridged history of the encounter between Quebec and Aboriginal representatives at the HFTCC; and the third relates Webber's discussions with people at the community of Chisasibi, where interest in the entrepreneurial possibilities of Cree outfitting was highest.

Scott traces his involvement with the subject to an incident that occurred some years ago:

> In January of 1992 I drove the 1,400 kilometres from Montreal to Wemindji, and from there some 300 kilometres to the northeast to visit the hunting camp of an old friend and members of his family who were in the bush that winter. Johnnish was the senior elder in camp, while the head of a second family was *nituuhuu uuchimaau* (hunting boss) for the territory on which the camp was located. Johnnish had been a supporter of my research and one of my teachers since the later 1970s, when I began learning about Cree hunting knowledge. Travelling with me was a woman from Montreal who had been a nurse in Wemindji in the 1970s; both of us had been friends of one of Johnnish's daughters, Emma, since those years. This was a social visit.
>
> We turned off the highway onto some forty or fifty metres of snow-ploughed laneway that ended in the camp clearing, at the edge of which two vehicles were parked. The front ends of the vehicles were covered with heavy blankets and recycled wall-to-wall carpet, used to insulate the engines against severe cold. We were expected, but everyone was inside; the only sign of life was smoke rising vertically, as it does on cold calm days, from the stovepipes of the two lodges. We had long enough to step out of the car, stretch our legs, and note with surprise that a fully intact caribou, frozen solid, had been propped upside down against the side of the *mitutisaanikimikw* (a domed, oblong lodge with a frame of bent poles and canvas covering). It was obviously not a fresh kill. Yet my past experience had been that animals as large and important as caribou are dressed and butchered immediately. To do otherwise, to risk spoilage or waste, signifies disrespectful treatment of the animal, with misfortune in hunting or in other endeavours the normal consequence.
>
> Presently, Johnnish appeared out of the larger of the two lodges, a more permanent trapper's cabin, to greet us. After a few polite words, he gestured towards the frozen caribou and began to explain, quickly becoming more agitated than I had ever seen him. The act had been committed during the caribou sport hunt, while the Cree families using the territory had travelled to Wemindji for Christmas. Upon their return, they had discovered this

> caribou, discarded, at the campsite as well as a second one abandoned on the ice of a small lake nearby, the camp's water supply. There was nothing apparently wrong with the health of either animal, nothing to justify the waste! And what if the carcasses had not been found before spring? The water would have become contaminated! Such people should be banned from coming north! The Crees respected the animals – these problems were unknown before the flood of sport hunters had begun! (Colin Scott, field-notes)

The incident left a deep impression. Discussions at that camp, at Wemindji, and in Montreal with leadership of the local council and the Cree Trappers' Association, and in Ottawa at the office of the Grand Council of the Crees, motivated us to undertake a more systematic survey of responses to the caribou sport hunt. In important respects it was an unusual case of "resource-use conflict." The resource itself was plentiful, and no one claimed that kills by sport hunters were at the present time depriving the Cree of caribou. In cultural terms, the Cree were coping with a threat that was equally fundamental. Outsiders were treating animals, and the Cree, in ways that were profoundly disrespectful. For senior hunters, in particular, who bear the primary social responsibilities of stewardship, the sense of loss occasioned by this intrusion was more acute than outsiders could easily imagine.

One gets some sense of the religious character of this responsibility in the following statement by a Wemindji hunter:

> the Cree people respect the caribou and the bear ... They have a lot of respect for the food supply; you know, for the animal itself. They have been told by the ancestors throughout the generations that there are ways to respect especially the bear and the caribou. The bear and the caribou are the – I guess what you'd call at this time of the year – the food supply for the family; and if you respect the bear and the caribou as food supply they will always come back. If you do not, there is always a way the Creator will see that the bear doesn't come back. That's how you say in Cree. The bear or the caribou won't come back if you don't respect them. They know when they're insulted in a way, they know, they can tell. So that's one of the things that have happened.

The return of the caribou in large numbers is a major episode, literally a once-in-a-lifetime occurrence, in Cree hunting. It occurs almost in the nature of a prophecy fulfilled, for the elders have always said that the caribou would return. Most animals come and go in cycles. A standard Cree metaphor for the periodic disappearance and reappearance of animals is that they "submerge," as if vanishing beneath a surface of water, until they "resurface" some years later. The caribou vanish and return in the longest cycle of all.

In the mid-1880s only two or three Wemindji people were alive to remember the last time, at the beginning of the twentieth century, when migratory caribou were present in large numbers.[1] A modest increase in the sighting and killing of caribou had been noticed by the mid- to late 1970s, when Scott was first conducting research at Wemindji, but these were still isolated encounters. Hunters whose territories are at the northeastern extreme of Wemindji's range say that the herds again became truly plentiful around 1984. Each winter thereafter, the extent of the migration expanded so that hunters in the north-central Wemindji area had caribou in numbers by 1986; and by 1990 some herds were encountered as far west as the James Bay coast between Wemindji and Chisasibi. From that point until 1993, when Scott's main interviews for this chapter were conducted, caribou numbers and locations were seen to be fairly constant, though the trajectories of particular annual influxes varied somewhat – sometimes northeasterly and sometimes more northerly in issuance.

Migratory caribou appear in December, as soon as travel over ice is secure. Many cross the extensive hydro reservoirs – particularly, in the case of those bound for Wemindji territory, the LG-4 reservoir – and retreat eastward in March, before spring thaw. In 1993, Scott was told, their traffic had become so heavy that one could walk from lake to lake through the bush on their trails without wearing snowshoes. At the time of his research, there was no local sense that the caribou were in decline, though some biologists believed that the peak for the larger George River population had been reached by the late 1980s due, in part, to deteriorating summer range in eastern Quebec and Labrador.[2] Local people expected that signs of a decline would eventually occur. One younger hunter observed:

> You would notice places in the summer where they had been eating a lot of the white moss and other vegetation [the previous winter] ... a long time ago in my grandfather's time, at the peak numbers, they would have eaten out the vegetation to the point that the numbers would start to go down.

Hunters interviewed commented that the level of body fat on both male and female caribou seemed normal. Although they reported isolated instances of diseased animals, these were not interpreted as indicators of overpopulation or the deteriorating condition of the herd as a whole. There was, however, considerable apprehension about the unseen risks of industrial contamination. Most hunters claimed no longer to eat the liver, having heard public warnings about the possible toxicity of cadmium and other metals concentrated therein.

Biologists' concerns about peaking numbers and deteriorating range are an important piece in the story of the introduced sport hunt. By 1988, Quebec representatives at the HFTCC were arguing not only that caribou numbers in northern Quebec permitted increased hunting without damage to the herd, but also that such hunting might be beneficial. Culling the herd, it was reasoned, could modulate the deterioration of range and perhaps forestall the precipitous declines that characterize the natural cycle.[3] This management approach complemented the goals of the sport hunting lobby – to gain enhanced access to the James Bay territory – and of the Quebec government, who stood to gain popularity by such a measure while extending yet another layer of sovereign presence and economic integration into the northern landscape.

The JBNQA had contemplated the extensive use of outfitting – the provision of lodging and guiding services by Aboriginal hunters – as a means of controlling hunting behaviour and of returning economic benefits to Cree, Inuit, and Naskapi communities. But the new hunt would be a "free" hunt, conducted by individual parties of southern sport hunters who would gain access by road, without the use of guides or other services. Indeed, most southern sport hunters are unable to afford air travel and outfitters' fees to hunt caribou. If road access had remained closed and outfitters had been required, then the experience of hunting caribou would have remained beyond the reach of many hunters. And such hunting as existed would have had limited effect with regard to culling the herds. The area south of the La Grande River and the hydro reservoirs was, however, one of only two areas (the other being Fermont, near the Labrador border) where migratory caribou were potentially road-accessible. From the provincial government's perspective, an excellent solution, both politically and in management terms, was a sport hunt in Cree territory.

In meetings of the regional Hunting, Fishing and Trapping Coordinating Committee (HFTCC)[4] during late winter and spring of 1985, the Quebec members of the committee first gave notice of the intention of the Ministère du Loisir, de la Chasse et de la Pêche (MLCP) to implement a caribou hunt for a portion of Zone 22, the sport hunting management zone that includes the La Grande River Basin (where the hunt would be focused). The MLCP advocated a hunt for which Quebec residents in general could apply. They emphasized the claims of sport hunters in Radisson, the one non-Aboriginal community in the heart of Cree territory, where the small population servicing the La Grande hydroelectric complex resides. But they also noted the assertions of hunting associations in the Abitibi District, to the south of the territory of the James Bay Cree, whose numbers and political weight were much larger and more consequential than were those of the hunters of Radisson.

At the outset Quebec declared a quite restrictive interpretation of the JBNQA with regard to HFTCC authority in the matter. It claimed that the role of the HFTCC was merely consultative and that the government, not the HFTCC, was responsible for wildlife management (though the HFTCC could submit recommendations). Quebec representatives argued the limited jurisdiction of the HFTCC on other grounds as well – for example, that a management board contemplated in its Caribou Management Plan did not directly affect the HFTCC because the geographic scope of caribou management exceeded the boundaries of the territory as defined by the JBNQA.[5]

The language of the JBNQA (Quebec 1976), on the other hand, indicated that the HFTCC's role in the determination of wildlife policy was something stronger than the minimalist view advanced by Quebec:

> A Hunting, Fishing and Trapping Coordinating Committee ... an expert body made up of Native and government members, is established to review, manage and in certain cases, supervise and regulate the Hunting, Fishing and Trapping Regime. (paragraph 24.4)
>
> The Coordinating Committee shall be a consultative body to responsible governments, save where expressly stipulated in paragraph 24.4.30 [*infra*] and as such shall be the preferential and exclusive forum for Native people and governments jointly to formulate regulations and supervise the administration and management of the Hunting, Fishing and Trapping Regime. (paragraph 24.4.23)
>
> The Coordinating Committee shall have the right to initiate, discuss, review and propose all measures relating to the Hunting, Fishing and Trapping Regime in the Territory. The Coordinating Committee may propose regulations or other measures. (paragraph 24.4.25)
>
> All regulations relating to the Hunting, Fishing and Trapping Regime proposed by responsible governments shall be submitted to the Coordinating Committee for advice before enactment. (paragraph 24.4.26)

In the case of "big game" species, the powers of the HFTCC go beyond the above-quoted general rights and responsibilities of consultation:

> The Coordinating Committee may establish the upper limit of kill for moose and caribou for Native people and non-Natives and, with respect to black bear in the buffer area, make decisions relating to the non-Native hunting, the harvesting and the management of populations thereof. Subject to the principle of conservation, decisions of the Coordinating Committee pursuant to this paragraph shall bind the responsible Minister or

> government, who shall make such regulations as are necessary to give effect thereto and shall bind local and regional governments. (paragraph 24.4.30)

Even for species other than moose, caribou, and black bear, the authority of the provincial and/or federal minister should not under normal circumstances contradict the recommendations of the HFTCC. Before enacting regulations or refusing to enact the recommendations and decisions of the HFTCC,

> the responsible Provincial or Federal Minister shall consult with the Coordinating Committee and shall endeavor to respect the views and positions of the Coordinating Committee on any matter respecting the Hunting, Fishing and Trapping Regime. (paragraph 24.4.36)

> In all cases where the responsible Minister modifies or decides not to act upon the recommendations of the Coordinating Committee or decides to take new actions, he shall, before acting, consult with the Coordinating Committee when his decisions relate to Native and non-Native activities and the wildlife resources in the Territory except in the case of certain minor measures relating exclusively to non-Native activity and not affecting Native interests. (paragraph 24.4.37)

On decisions regarding caribou in the territory covered by the JBNQA, it seemed clear that the minister would be bound by the recommendation of the HFTCC, unless s/he could demonstrate that serious considerations of "conservation" demanded that s/he overrule an HFTCC decision. "Conservation" is itself defined by the JBNQA to protect both wildlife populations and Aboriginal hunting as a way of life, the latter taking precedence over non-Aboriginal sport hunting and fishing:

> "Conservation" means the pursuit of the optimum natural productivity of all living resources and the protection of the ecological systems of the Territory so as to protect endangered species and to ensure primarily the continuance of the traditional pursuits of the Native people, and secondarily the satisfaction of the needs of non-Native people for sport hunting and fishing. (paragraph 24.1.5)

The Cree members of the HFTCC responded to Quebec's intention to implement a caribou sport hunt by saying that they had no objection in principle to a non-Aboriginal hunt, provided it complied with Sections 24.8 and 24.9 of the JBNQA and that it be restricted to residents of Radisson (i.e., residents of the territory). Quebec members of the HFTCC objected to restricting the hunt to residents of the territory on the grounds that it would discriminate against other residents of the province and that the government was committed to improving access to Crown lands for all citizens of Quebec. The objection conformed to a view of provincial citizenship that was strongly held within Quebec – that all citizens should be in precisely the same position with respect to the state. But it had scant basis in law. The JBNQA explicitly distinguishes the rights of non-Aboriginal residents of the territory from those of residents in the rest of Quebec. Section 24.8.9 specifies that restrictions on non-Aboriginal hunting in the territory shall be imposed in the following order: first to non-residents of Quebec, second to non-residents of the territory, and third to non-Aboriginal residents of the territory. Cree members had only to remind the committee that JBNQA provisions are protected under Section 35(3) of the Canadian Constitution, which includes as treaty rights the terms of contemporary land claims agreements. As treaty rights, the JBNQA provision would withstand a challenge based on any anti-discriminatory law or policy subordinate to the Constitution.

Relations between the Quebec and the Cree were conflictual. The Cree accused the Quebec government of trying to rush the proposal through without due process and consideration – a 1985-6 sport hunt had already been announced in the magazine *Norditudes*. Quebec accused the Cree of obstruction and warned that it would not tolerate indefinite consultative delays. Cree representatives, while repeating that they did not object in principle to a sport hunt, insisted that the JBNQA principle of Aboriginal harvesting priority must be considered and that they must consult with their own hunters on feasibility and control. Otherwise, court action to block Quebec's proposal was a possibility. The HFTCC passed a resolution criticizing Quebec's attitude in the matter, although the resolution was annulled when the province undertook to delete the Zone 22 caribou hunt from the 1985 regulations.

Issues of adequate control and of compatibility with the legal priority of Aboriginal harvesting were keenly important to Cree hunters. The territory was being opened to public road vehicle access, with Quebec arguing that it would not indefinitely restrict public access to roads maintained with tax dollars. Up to this time, a control gate at Matagami had limited traffic to Hydro-Québec personnel, its contractors and subcontractors, residents of the territory, and others with authorized business in the territory. Cree authorities took the position that they were not opposed to road access but that they wanted adequate surveillance of non-Aboriginals as well as significant Cree involvement in administration. Cree hunters had experienced problems of theft and vandalism at their camps during LG-2 construction and insufficient control of hunting and fishing by non-Aboriginal employees of the hydro project.

The Cree members of the HFTCC, therefore, wanted controls contemplated in the JBNQA to be fully implemented. According to Section 24.8:

> A control shall be exercised by the responsible governments and the Coordinating Committee over the number of non-Natives permitted to hunt and fish in Category III and over the places therein and times where they may hunt and fish with a view to giving effect to the principle of conservation and the rights and guarantees in favour of the Native people. (paragraph 24.8.6)

> The use of outfitting facilities shall be considered as a principal means of controlling non-Native hunting and fishing activity in that portion of the Territory above the 50th parallel of latitude. (paragraph 24.8.7)

> Over and above other available means of controlling the numbers of non-Natives permitted to hunt and fish in the Territory and the places and times where and when they may hunt and fish and subject to paragraph 24.8.9, Québec shall endeavor, to the extent that outfitting facilities are available, to require non-Native hunters and fishermen to use such facilities. Such requirements shall provide, to the extent feasible, that non-Native hunters and fishermen be accompanied by Native guides. (paragraph 24.8.8)

The JBNQA also provided for the training and employment of a network of Cree conservation officers. Neither approach to enhancing Cree control of non-Aboriginal use of the territory, however, had been sufficiently developed even by the 1990s to do the job contemplated. The Crees "right of first refusal" on seven out of ten proposed outfitting operations was itself a bitterly contested matter, one that forced the Cree to take Quebec to court to have their priority enforced and that continued to be a matter of tactical manoeuvring and vigorous argument in the HFTCC during the mid- to late-1980s. The Cree cited the paucity of central government support for the economic development provisions of the JBNQA as a factor that limited their ability to develop outfitting enterprises. Quebec, meanwhile, had all but abandoned a program begun in the early years of JBNQA implementation to train and employ Cree conservation officers from each Cree community.

Like other subsistence species, caribou are subject to "guaranteed levels of harvesting" for the Aboriginal parties to the JBNQA (Section 24.6). The guarantees apply to the levels of harvesting prevalent at the time that the JBNQA was concluded. These, in turn, were to be determined by a multi-year harvesting study conducted in the 1970s (James Bay and Northern Quebec Native Harvesting Research Committee, 1976-82), while caribou were still scarce. In the specific case of caribou, then, the Cree were not in a particularly strong position to argue that sport hunting would impinge on guaranteed levels of caribou harvest per se, since there was now an abundance of caribou to support harvesting far beyond that of the Aboriginal kill of the 1970s. However, when considered in a broader sense, the hunt had a real potential to interfere with the historic levels of Cree game harvesting generally, which had already been disrupted, in the region of the reservoirs where the sport hunt would occur, by the flooding of extensive tracts of land and by other development activities. The sport hunt promised further disruption, both by direct competition for game and by the danger posed by large numbers of not well disciplined sport hunters on the land. At this stage, however, there was little direct experience to substantiate such a prediction.

The opposing positions taken by the Cree and Quebec, as outlined above, were reiterated at meetings of the HFTCC throughout 1985, 1986, and 1987. In September 1987, Quebec tabled a proposal for a hunt for which residents of Quebec at large would be eligible, with a long season running from 12 September to 15 April, ostensibly to accommodate the vagaries of the herd's movement. Each hunter would be permitted two caribou. A minority of the total area, Category II lands of Chisasibi, would be accessible only to hunters using the services of a Cree outfitter.[6] The MLCP was pushing for a quick endorsement from the HFTCC in order to implement a hunt for the 1987-8 season. All Aboriginal members responded negatively to the proposal, the Cree on the grounds of past experience with sport hunters and their opposition to extending the hunt to Quebec residents at large. The Naskapi were also concerned about this extension of the hunt and its effect on Aboriginal outfitting operations when combined with an enlarged Zone 24 (into which Naskapi homelands fall), as advocated by the MLCP.[7] The Inuit expressed general reservations about a large influx of sport hunters, while showing interest in an MLCP initiative to commercialize the harvest of caribou meat through Aboriginal enterprises.

In a bid to placate Aboriginal resistance, Quebec, in February 1988, promised that a long-awaited outfitting plan, which was to cover the whole province, would be released the next year and would address Aboriginal concerns. Meanwhile, Quebec argued somewhat implausibly that its support for Aboriginal outfitting development was not in conflict with its goal of enlarged public access for unguided sport hunting. Having already experienced delays in getting Quebec's commitment to a constructive course of action vis-à-vis Aboriginal outfitting, Aboriginal parties were not comforted by the prospect of a further delay in the tabling of its outfitting plan, while the province applied pressure for an immediate expansion of unguided sport hunting.

In July 1988, Quebec tabled its draft regulations on the caribou hunt, including permits to be issued to 1,000 hunters in Zone 22, each entitled to take two caribou. The season would be 1 December to 30 April, with hunters to register at Radisson. The existing conservation service would be responsible for control of the hunt; there would be no additional funding or hiring, only a temporary transfer to Radisson to cover needs. A brochure would be developed to inform sport hunters about Aboriginal rights, and the Cree might benefit by administering camping and parking. Aboriginal parties were asked to respond and to make recommendations by 1 September.

The response of the Cree Regional Authority (CRA), submitted on 14 September, raised concerns about the reliability of caribou population data. While the Cree had indicated no objection in principle to a limited sport hunt when estimates of the herd were at 700,000, estimates by biologists varying downward to as few as 350,000 were now noted. Aside from numbers, concern was expressed that concentrated sport hunting effort along the road corridor could stress the herd, causing it to shift its migration and deprive Cree hunters. Control of the hunt was a further concern. Because Category II lands do not follow natural boundaries, sport hunters, following skidoo trails, could easily stray onto areas set aside for exclusive Cree use. Sport hunters' perception of the area as uninhabited, combined with their relative inexperience, would pose a safety risk for Cree families on the land.

The CRA recommended a number of measures: (1) a western boundary for the hunt at LG-3 (thus eliminating hunting in areas adjacent to Category II lands); (2) no sport hunting along the road (instead, all hunting should be confined to an area north of the road, with a buffer zone between the road and the legal hunting area); (3) a boundary following natural demarcations that would be more recognizeable and enforceable; (4) an information campaign to acquaint sport hunters with Cree habitation sites; (5) a requirement that all sport hunters go through an outfitter, or at least the services of a Cree guide; (6) a more limited number of permits; and (7) compensation arrangements for theft and damage to Cree property. Absolute opposition to the hunt was promised unless Quebec provided sufficient personnel and resources to control it.

A letter from the president of the Cree Trappers' Association (CTA), also sent to the HFTCC on 14 September, summarized many of the same concerns stated in HFTCC discussions over the preceding three years: safety for Crees in their camps due to the "impatient and anxious" practices of non-Aboriginal hunters; lack of updated biological data; Quebec's mistaken assertion that lack of declared opposition in principle amounted to Cree support for its proposals; probable interference with Cree traditional activities; absence of an outfitting plan for the territory; non-implementation of guaranteed harvesting levels under the JBNQA; probability of theft, vandalism, and poaching with no provision of compensation for the Cree; insufficient guarantees of adequate sport hunting supervision and enforcement of regulations; problems of littering and garbage disposal; lack of communication with Cree communities other than Chisasibi (with which ministry officials had held bilateral consultations outside the HFTCC); and lack of confidence in Quebec's intentions in regard to the JBNQA-guaranteed rights of priority for Aboriginal outfitting enterprises.

Measures recommended by the council and local CTA of the community of Mistissini were in a similar vein: prevention of theft, vandalism, and conflicts with local hunters; protection of safety; a no-hunting radius of at least ten miles around Cree camps; a 200-foot no-hunting corridor along the highway; a season shortened to 1 December to 28 February; only 500, rather than 1,000, sport permits issued; caribou hunting limited to residents of the territory; a hunting zone boundary to follow easily identifiable features of the landscape; registration and access through Radisson only; organization of the hunt through outfitters; designation of the hunt as a pilot project, subject to review; establishment of an MLCP/Cree monitoring committee; and clarification of what the hunt implied for guaranteed harvesting levels.

The Inuit, meanwhile, reiterated their opposition in principle to the hunt on the grounds that the JBNQA required outfitting to be the principal means for controlling hunting in the territory as well as on grounds of their understanding (derived from the Big Game Working Group of the HFTCC) that there would be no new allocation of caribou until new caribou census results had been finalized. The Naskapi also repeated their strong reservations about the hunt.

Unanimous Aboriginal opposition at this stage, however, proved insufficient to block HFTCC endorsement of the MLCP's draft legislation. The annual rotation of non-Aboriginal government and Aboriginal members as HFTCC chair – the chair having a tie-breaking vote – meant that Quebec, with Canada's support, could enshrine its own agenda as HFTCC policy. In October 1988, the draft legislation was endorsed on the strength of the vote of then chair Despatie, an MLCP representative.

Implementation of the hunt was to be delayed, however, until 1989-90 in order to allow time to modify regulations and to consult further with the Cree on security and other issues. The MLCP proposed bilateral talks between the Cree and itself in order to discuss issues of control. On 21 December 1988, the MLCP issued a press release announcing the caribou sport hunt, with details of the lottery and permit conditions; and on 23 August 1989, the Zone 22 hunt received provincial approval by Order in Council. On 1 December 1989, the caribou "free" hunt was under way.

Conflicts on the hunting territories were quick to arise, as is related in a letter (7 December 1989) to the minister of the MLCP from Chief Pachanos of Chisasibi. Signs had not been erected, as promised, to alert sport hunters to the location of Cree camps. Safety concerns, the wounding and non-recovery of caribou, the careless disposal of remains, lack of enforcement, and interference with Cree customary practices had been the subjects of daily complaints by Cree hunters. Some Cree had left their camps during their main hunting period and returned to town, fearing for their safety. The Chisasibi local Cree Trappers' Association was recommending that the hunt henceforth be supervised by Cree hunters from the traditional territories concerned. On 13 December, the CRA passed a resolution asking that the hunt be stopped. A letter in February from Chief Matthew Coon Come of the Grand Council of the Crees to the minister of the MLCP, reviewing the hunt, reported specific incidents of sport hunters shooting along the line of the road when Cree were present. It decried the insufficiency of the MLCP's position that it was legal to hunt along the road but that criminal laws regarding the careless use of firearms would be enforced. Coon Come's letter also criticized the high density of sport hunters in the free zone, concentrated mainly in the December portion of the season, and reminded the MLCP that the hunt was to be regarded as a pilot project only.

The MLCP's immediate response to the Cree experience with the sport hunt was that time constraints would prevent changes to regulations in time for the 1990-1 hunt but that security measures could be modified. The MLCP claimed it did not intend to increase the number of permits to be issued in 1990-1 but that it was open to discussing supplementary permits requiring the use of guides. Signs had not been erected to indicate Cree camps, the MLCP claimed, because it was afraid of encouraging theft and vandalism. Those who abandoned caribou carcasses would be prosecuted, if apprehended. A clean-up of caribou entrails had been conducted, and an extra conservation officer had been assigned to Radisson (in addition to three permanent conservation officers in Radisson, whose duties included monitoring an area adjacent to 1,200 kilometres of main highway as well as numerous secondary and tertiary roads and snowmobile trails). Patrols, it was claimed – weather permitting – had been conducted daily. The Cree were encouraged to provide more information, such as licence plate numbers, to assist in the investigation and prosecution of criminal offences. In 1990-1, the MLCP would send researchers to examine the carcasses of sport hunter kills. Cree demands to close the road to hunting immediately, pending review of the hunt, were refused.

In May 1990, the MLCP released a document providing its overview of the 1989-90 hunt.[8] The report noted that the HFTCC had approved regulation of the hunt, but it did not mention the unanimous Aboriginal opposition. Cooperation with a range of (mostly non-Aboriginal) agencies, as well as individual Aboriginal and non-Aboriginal entrepreneurs, was claimed. During the 1989-90 season, 860 out of 1,000 sport hunters had exercised their permits, taking 1,410 caribou, mostly during December and January. With regard to local concerns about the impact of high concentrations of hunters, these concerns were deemed normal wherever hunting is permitted, and the situation was judged satisfactory, given daily patrols by conservation officers and the provision of information to sport hunters concerning Cree presence. When problems had developed, the MLCP had issued a press release encouraging respect for Cree practices and the environment. It noted that local Cree representatives had been consulted in February and March. Still, further improvements were promised for the future.

The document also reversed the MLCP's commitment of the previous winter not to increase the number of free hunt permits. The MLCP now recommended a lengthened season and a substantial increase in the number (1,500) of permits issued. Licences issued beyond this number would have to use the services of an outfitter. Outfitting should be developed beyond the zone of the free hunt to absorb some of the pressure; and zoning should be redefined to include some of Chisasibi's Category II land to enable the Cree to develop outfitting enterprises.

At HFTCC meetings over the ensuing months, the MLCP continued to claim success for the Zone 22 hunt – a success that it was determined to repeat. Yes, some sport hunters had shown a lack of respect for the environment, but quick action by the MLCP had solved any real problems. Consultations with Aboriginals and non-Aboriginals would continue, and draft regulation changes would shortly be tabled to include the expansion into Category II lands. A "shortened" season from 15 November to 15 February, though with 1,500 instead of 1,000 permits, would be implemented.[9] The number of conservation officers would be doubled, and signs would be posted to warn of the presence of Cree harvesters.

Cree opposition to the hunt was again voiced. Since JBNQA rights had not been fulfilled, the CRA declared its inability to support the Zone 22 hunt at this time. Chisasibi, meanwhile, rejected the proposal for inclusion of Category II lands in Zone 22 until adequate measures to ensure safer hunting conditions had been implemented. Further, Chisasibi held that the number of permits issued should not increase until safety and other monitoring issues had been resolved.[10]

At meetings of the HFTCC in November 1990, the MLCP emphasized the major economic opportunities available to the Cree through outfitting. While tabling regulation changes for 1991-2 in order to increase permits to 1,500, and to establish the 15 November to 15 February season, the MLCP stated its readiness to consider freezing the number of free hunting permits at the 1991-2 level. Increased police patrols were promised. Cree representatives accepted most modifications to the regulations, but with a request on record, ignored by the MLCP, that the decision to increase permits to 1,500 be reconsidered.

Meanwhile, discussion of Quebec's Outfitting Development Plan at the HFTCC during late 1990 and early 1991 occasioned expressions of Cree disappointment with the plan's neglect of JBNQA provisions that gave priority to Aboriginal outfitting. All Aboriginal members decried the lack of consultation during the development of the plan. The Naskapi perceived a bias in favour of economic returns over conservation. The Cree, Naskapi, and Inuit cited the lack of adequate knowledge about carrying capacity of the land as well as broad uncertainties with regard to estimates of the size of the George River herd. Cree representatives asked MLCP representatives to make oral presentations of the plan in Cree communities, but they were refused. In the MLCP's view, it was the responsibility of Cree representatives to the HFTCC to provide the links to local communities.[11]

In February 1993 Scott undertook more systematic visits to Wemindji hunters camped along the highways in order to hear about their experience, in situ, with sport hunting. The camps were located at intervals from Old Factory Lake northward along the highway that runs from Matagami to the LG-2 Hydro installation, and eastward to Caniapiscau on a connecting highway running several hundred kilometres along the southern periphery of the chain of reservoirs, dams, and generating stations of Hydro-Québec's La Grande Complex. Each winter, between 1,000 and 2,000 provincially licensed sport hunters, drawn by lottery, had come along this corridor of road, each authorized to kill two caribou. They vastly outnumbered the local Cree families – a few dozen from the communities of Wemindji, Chisasibi, and Mistissini – whose hunting territories are transected by the highways.

We learned that there were several dimensions to the sense of invasion occasioned by such a concentrated influx of sport hunters. The clash in values concerning the respectful use of animals was key, and it was occurring within the context of the steady erosion of the ability of the Cree to regulate harvesting on their hunting territories. In addition to caribou hunters, several thousand recreational fishers, and growing numbers of moose and goose hunters, were making their way onto the lands of the northerly Cree communities – communities that, unlike those on the southern periphery of the Cree region – had little experience of non-Aboriginal hunters. It was not the mere presence of sport hunters that was the problem; nor, as mentioned earlier, was it simply an economic matter of competition for scarce resources. It was the impossibility of incorporating the newcomers socially, of gaining respect in Cree terms for existing cultural and ecological relationships, or of getting central government agencies to respect Cree needs in this regard. Cree hunters were relegated to the guest room in their own house.

And there was the dimension of safety. Migrating caribou frequently make use of roadways, and the Cree witnessed sport hunters shooting along the highways in a manner that made them anxious for their safety.

A number of Cree reported outsiders shooting in the immediate vicinity of their camps and cabins. One hunting boss commented:

> Sometimes white hunters shoot just a few feet from here [the cabin where the interview occurred] ... they're not supposed to shoot between signs that show where native camps are, but they don't seem to follow that ... they shoot too close to the cabin.

A second *uuchimaau* concurred:

> There was so much shooting on the road, I couldn't go out [from his cabin, to hunt]. Cree hunters don't shoot the caribou close to our cabin, like the white hunters do ... I'm not allowed to hunt near the white man, around those [hydro] transmission lines; we expect the same kind of consideration from the white man, not to shoot close to our cabins.

A third hunting boss, a few dozen kilometres up the road, had similar experiences: "during the time when hunters are here, we can't do very much hunting, because we're afraid to get shot by these white hunters." Some people had vacated their camps and returned to the village until the sport hunt subsided rather than risk accidental shootings. Too large a portion of sport hunters were perceived to be trigger-happy, anxious, and inexperienced.

Entrails left by sport hunters at frequent intervals along the highway were condemned as further evidence of people who seemingly did not know, or care to learn, the right way to do things. There were exceptions, as one elder observed: "Some of these white people, especially the old people, they really care about the environment; somebody from Chisasibi saw an old white guy piling up caribou guts ... he didn't want to waste anything and didn't want to mess up the environment."

But such exceptions were too few to prevent the seasonal proliferation of roadside waste. The Cree repeatedly emphasized that entrails should not be left on display or be discarded on the ice where they would sink or get washed up somewhere following break-up. They should be gathered together and burned or taken to a swampy area where scavengers could clean them up in seclusion. Adding to the spectacle of carnage on the highway, long-distance, high velocity tractor-trailer drivers servicing the hydroelectric installations sometimes surprised herds of caribou walking on the roadway and were unable to brake in time. Local Cree recounted disturbing incidents of coming upon a dozen or more caribou left shattered on the roadway, survivors with smashed limbs staggering in the adjacent bush. Photographs were produced to prove the assertions. These images are in stark contrast to the considerable trouble to which Cree hunters routinely go to erase even bloodstains in the snow from animals they have killed. For people who apply so light a touch to the land, "carnage" is not too strong a term to describe the cumulative impression that has resulted from outsiders' practices.

The disrespect shown by some sport hunters towards the Cree was not always unintentional, the result of divergent cultural values or inexperience. Several Wemindji people had returned to their camps after Christmas break to find their cabins broken into and equipment stolen – snowshoes, traps, generators, outboard motors, canoes, all-terrain vehicles, and so on. Over the centuries, when the loss of vital equipment was a danger to survival, there developed a cultural ethos strongly prohibiting interference with others' stores. Hunters could freely cache equipment and provisions, returning months or even years later in full confidence that all would remain as they had left it. Within a few years, this has changed dramatically. Until the roads penetrated Cree territories there was no need for lock and key. Today, lock and key are poor defence. Break-ins at camps located along the highway have become commonplace. One territory boss reported being broken into every year for the past five years. With road vehicle access and bush radio communication, theft rarely represents a survival risk; but it is a serious hardship and unaffordable expense. Losses cannot be fully insured, and valuable equipment can now be protected only by hauling it back and forth between the settlement and the camps.[12]

Risks to personal safety and property loss, and resulting lost hunting time, were serious problems in themselves. But the careless disregard of sport hunters for the animals they killed was the dominant theme, and it brought the heaviest condemnation. At all of the Cree camps on territories frequented by non-Aboriginal caribou hunters, a number of healthy, intact caribou carcasses had been found abandoned during the current sport hunt. Other carcasses were found with only the antlers removed or sometimes with only choice portions of meat carved away. In cases where the animal had been more completely butchered, the hide was routinely discarded (this, in itself, was regarded by the Cree as careless, or at least uneducated, waste). In many cases, insufficient skill or effort had been invested in recovering wounded animals:

> I found one caribou shot and left on the lake here [next to camp]; there were a lot of tracks made by white hunters around ... and there were quite a few other places where we found caribou that had been shot, wounded and left to die later ... there might be a few more lying around; but I can't check every place where [the sport hunters] go.

Many sport hunters would get their limit of two caribou in the first day or two of their vacations. Subsequently, many would find themselves with the opportunity to kill larger ones, with better trophies. Exceeding the kill limit posed little risk for the felon, given the infrequency of patrols by a game warden: two Cree hunting bosses in prime caribou territories who spend much of the year at their camps along the road reported having seen a conservation officer only once and twice, respectively, during a four- to five-year period. But getting illegally killed caribou out of the territory is another matter. The risk of arrest increases dramatically when the animals are transported, since a single checkpoint near Matagami can monitor all out-going traffic. The solution adopted by several sport hunters, evidently, was to discard less valued caribou once more desireable ones had been obtained.

The conflict between sport hunters and the Cree was expressed by the latter as a fundamental divergence in worldview, ethics, and way of life. One elder explained:

> Cree hunters have always been very careful not to waste what we kill, what we caught from the caribou ... we've always been very thankful for what we got to survive through the years by hunting caribou and we wasted nothing; we have been taught very well by our parents not to waste anything, and we intend to follow that ... For many, many years we have survived by hunting and trapping; that's why we don't want to waste anything we kill from the wild.

Cree hunters routinely emphasized that, although they were regularly presented with opportunities to kill many caribou, they did so only occasionally, and selectively, choosing animals that were fat and disease-free, so that none would be wasted. Most families reported killing only one or two caribou for their own consumption, in addition to a small number for friends and relatives in the village.

No Cree with whom I spoke favoured continuence of the sport hunt under current conditions. Opinion was divided, however, between those who believed sport hunting should be banned altogether and those who thought it tolerable if placed under stricter control. The latter view was expressed by one hunting boss in the following terms: "Right now there's enough game for everyone to hunt, but they have to respect certain rules ... because they are in Indian territory ... they should have Indian guides who could watch them."

The James Bay Agreement contemplated two means for developing a sport hunt that was consistent with prior Cree use of the land: the use of Cree outfitting and the implementation of a system of Cree conservation officers. Neither condition has been adequately realized. Although conservation officer training for individuals from several communities was under way in the early 1980s, the province discontinued the initiative. Only one Cree person was working as a conservation officer at the time of the research. Local hunters were convinced that surveillance of the region, Aboriginal or non-Aboriginal, was too scanty to have much impact. Cree outfitting, on the other hand, was insufficient to provide an infrastructure for large numbers of sport hunters; and the province had made it clear that it was not prepared to wait for outfitting to develop.

The outfitting option is itself problematic in the view of many Cree hunters. Several Cree hunters with whom we spoke were negative towards the idea of serving as guides and outfitters. Not everyone has the personality needed to provide service to clients who are frequently both demanding and inexperienced. Many Cree hunters find commercial gain an insufficient incentive to endure the potential awkwardness of such an arrangement. Further, and more important, the relationship between hunter and land is an intensely personal one, and hunters are strongly protective of it.

Cree hunters who thought that sport hunting should be banned altogether regarded subsistence harvesting and sport hunting as irreconcileable on ethical and spiritual as well as on economic grounds. As an economic issue, there were those who felt that the relative abundance of caribou had to be viewed within a broader context. While it was true that caribou numbers were up, and that moose numbers had also been increasing over the past couple of decades, beaver numbers were down, and losses of Cree territory to hydroelectric flooding had left families on badly flooded areas with few alternatives:

> We've lost the best part of our territory to Hydro Quebec; this is where we used to trap and hunt ... the bear, the beaver ... now it's all been destroyed by Hydro-Quebec ... the best part of our trapline is under water ... We only have a small place here where we can hunt now. When the caribou go, we'll have nothing.

Was it too much to ask, this man wanted to know, to be left what remained of his land to use and care for according to his own understanding?

The overall impact of recreational hunting and fishing has been to cause serious economic losses for the Cree living along the road, even if, in the specific instance of caribou, game was relatively abundant. In the case of moose, central wildlife managers calculate sustainable harvests and sport hunting quotas on a regional basis. However, given its localization along the road corridor, the sport hunt is not sustainable on a trapline-by-trapline basis. Within units at this scale, according to local management knowledge, the sustainable annual harvest might only be two moose, particularly in the biologically less productive more northern areas. From this perspective, even one kill by a sport hunter on a Cree family's territory would inevitably deprive that family. Sport fishing, meanwhile, has depleted the available subsistence harvests on a number of the more road-accessible lakes, and territory bosses are worried about the increasing frequency of access to more remote lakes by sport fishers using light aircraft.

Some Cree hunters expressed concerns about the extent of disturbance that the caribou will tolerate in the long run – vehicle traffic compounded by intensive seasonal hunting along the road corridor – without altering their migration. The oral tradition emphasizes the theme of human responsibility with regard to the last retreat of the caribou early in the twentieth century.[13] According to one interpretation, hunting caribou every year at places where they crossed the river, and living too close to those crossings, encouraged them to avoid the territory. From this perspective, even though the caribou are present today in large numbers, and even though they seem relatively undeterred by human presence, it would be folly to take them for granted. The resource must be nurtured through the responsible relationship that binds the Cree to the animals they hunt; this is an inclusive relationship that is at once practical, ethical, and spiritual.

In the early years of the hunt, Aboriginal parties suffered intrusion and disruption without seeing any economic benefits. MLCP representatives frequently exhorted the Cree to capitalize on an expanded hunt and to develop better outfitting facilities, but, given the free character of the hunt and the consequent lack of local involvement in provisioning or guiding, these exhortations rang hollow.

In the mid-1990s, however, this began to change, although to a modest degree and chiefly for only a few Aboriginal entrepreneurs. There had long been a concern to secure greater economic development in the Cree communities, particularly in order to employ those residents who did not or could not base their lives on subsistence hunting. This concern was frequently combined with considerable soul-searching over what forms of development might be compatible with respect for the environment and the maintenance of Cree traditions. And there was also frustration at the general lack of opportunities. This led some Cree, especially from Chisasibi, to begin to investigate whether there might be employment opportunities associated with the caribou sport hunt. Since any benefits were likely to come from outfitting, and since outfitting also provided the best way of controlling the sport hunt, the economic-development and hunting-security agendas worked reasonably well together. There was, however, potential for friction, especially since economic development was often best undertaken by larger enterprises operating over a broad area – a structure that did not fit well with traditional Cree patterns of wildlife harvesting (which tended to focus on an individual hunting group leader's exclusive control over a trapline). Moreover, economic development might provide the rationale for an expanded sport hunt; subsistence hunters strenuously opposed the existing hunt, let alone any expansion of it.

As we have seen, the MLCP had previously encouraged the communities to accept an additional hunt, dependent upon Aboriginal outfitters, in the Category II lands. In March 1993, the Cree Nation of Chisasibi passed a resolution in support of controlled and managed caribou sport hunting in Cree traditional territory, and it requested 500 permits from the MLCP for the exclusive use of Cree outfitters, to be administered by the Chisasibi Mandow Agency (the agency established for the promotion of tourism in Chisasibi lands). The MLCP, affirming that it had always wanted Cree participation, promised to consider extending the hunt into Category II lands, making a fixed number of supplementary permits available for outfitters' clients. In June, the MLCP notified the HFTCC that it would table revised regulations to permit a sport hunt, available only with the use of outfitters, on an area extending well beyond the land covered by the existing free hunt, including the Category II lands of Chisasibi and Whapmagoostui (and Wemindji, if the community so requested). The hunt in this area would be open to nonresidents of Quebec, and there would be no limit on the number of permits for clients of outfitters. In addition, however, the MLCP proposed an expansion of the free hunt, increasing permits from 1,500 to 2,000 and expanding that hunt's limit southward to 53°N. These changes to the regulations were approved by the HFTCC in December 1993, with the Cree abstaining from the vote. They came into effect in the 1994-5 season. Henceforth there were two caribou hunting subzones in zone 22: zone 22A for the free hunt and zone 22B for the hunt with outfitters (in the end, zone 22B excluded the Category II lands of Wemindji).

At the same time, a group of Chisasibi Cree developed an outfitting operation at Lake Katatipawasakakamaw, near the LG-4 hydroelectric installations, in the free hunt zone but close to the eastern boundary between zones 22A and B. This operation was an initiative of Nouchimi Tourism Inc., an enterprise that had been formed as a cooperative venture by thirteen Cree trappers in 1989. It acquired an outfitting permit for the site near LG-4 in 1994-5 and met with rapid success. It quickly expanded its capacity in its original location from twenty-eight to forty-eight beds. In 1996, it applied successfully for outfitting permits for two additional sites (as principal outfitting bases) and for eight additional sites (as outpost camps). Along with two non-Aboriginal outfitters operating in the region, Nouchimi not only provided outfitting to hunters in zone 22B, but also to those engaged in the free hunt in zone 22A. Apparently, many hunters in the free hunt had discovered that they preferred the heated accommodation offered by the outfitters to camping in the subarctic winter!

The development of these operations created a new interest group. In 1995, the Aboriginal and non-Aboriginal outfitters joined together to oppose an expansion of zone 22A and the opening of the free hunt to non-residents of Quebec, arguing that this would undermine the nascent outfitting industry. In 1996, they pushed for more game wardens and for new regulations to create a corridor on either side of the road, within which shooting would not be permitted. The number of game wardens was increased, and the HFTCC approved a draft regulation establishing a 150-metre corridor on either side of the road. However, in later drafts, the government first reduced this corridor to ten metres and then eliminated it altogether.

The use of outfitters did permit some additional control on hunting activities. The outfitters' camps provided a place in which hunters could be informed of appropriate behaviour. This control was imperfect, however. In 1995-6, some non-Aboriginal outfitters simply sold permits for use in zone 22B, without insisting that the hunters use any lodging or guiding services. This practice was discontinued when the Chisasibi Mandow Agency complained. But even when hunters lodged with outfitters, they usually continued to hunt on their own. Complaints remained about unsafe practices, vandalism, and the improper disposal of animal remains, including improper disposal by the non-Aboriginal outfitters themselves.

The continued seriousness of these concerns was underlined in late 1996, when Quebec ministry officials began lobbying outfitters to support the extension of the caribou season. The representatives of subsistence hunters strongly opposed the extension. Edward Gilpin, the president of the Cree Trappers' Association, noted that, because of the sport hunters' actions, families were still leaving their camps and returning to town for the duration of the sport hunt, effectively shortening the period available for wildlife harvesting. Significantly, this position was strongly endorsed by the principal spokespersons of the Aboriginal outfitters, the Chisasibi Mandow Agency and Nouchimi Tourism. They argued that the hunt should not be extended until control had been improved. The Cree representatives on the HFTCC echoed their arguments, suggesting that an extension ran the risk of both prejudicing the quality of the outfitting services and feeding subsistence hunters' opposition to the sport hunt. In April 1997, the Cree Nation of Chisasibi passed a resolution opposing any extension of the duration of the sport hunt.

Conclusion

Quebec's decade-long campaign, from the mid-1980s to the mid-1990s, to expand public access to caribou on Cree lands leads to several observations and conclusions about the character of "co-management" at James Bay.

First, Quebec government representatives showed little concern for the sport hunt's profoundly disruptive impact on Cree harvesting activities, and the HFTCC was unable to block the changes that led to that disruption, even though the preservation of traditional patterns of Cree harvesting had been one of the chief aims of the JBNQA. The Cree were unsuccessful, for example, in limiting the hunt to residents of the territory, in resisting the MLCP's program to increase the number of permits and the area of the hunt, in securing the regulation of the hunt through mandatory outfitting and through the training and employment of Cree conservation officers, in shifting the hunt away from the road corridor and Cree hunting camps, and even in getting enough surveillance and control of the hunt to have MLCP's own regulations enforced. On some occasions, changes to the hunt were delayed; on others, alterations were made at the margins. However, by and large, the sport hunt was implemented as the Quebec government wished.

Perversely, some improvements were made only after outfitting began to take hold. The number of conservation officers was increased. Government representatives seriously considered, although in the end they did not adopt, measures to limit shooting along roads. The structure of outfitting permitted greater accountability over such matters as the disposal of carcasses. Throughout the period examined here, the Quebec government demonstrated scant respect for Cree subsistence harvesting. It was very attentive to the demands of the sport hunting lobby, and it acted in ways that plainly furthered that lobby's desire for a new hunting experience. But it could be swayed by arguments of economic development – arguments that it encouraged through its own exhortations to Cree communities to engage in the commercial exploitation of wildlife. As the operations of Nouchimi Tourism and the non-Aboriginal outfitters expanded, they provided their own rationale for the limitation or control of the free hunt. And their voices received more attention than had the voices of the subsistence hunters. That posed a potential problem, for the interests of the outfitters were not identical to those of the subsistence hunters, and the latter, who wanted to maintain traditional ways, continued to make up the more substantial proportion of the populations in the territory in question. But, at least during the period studied here, the Aboriginal outfitters were careful to maintain a substantial degree of solidarity with their compatriots involved in subsistence harvesting.

Why, it might be asked, when there would seem to be a clear case for noncompliance with JBNQA provisions in regard to a number of primary Cree goals, did these people not pursue legal action? The answer, in part, must be that the resources of local and regional Cree bodies are limited. During much of the period in question, the Cree had devoted major financial and personnel resources to court cases and political activity surrounding further development of hydro resources in the territory, in particular the proposed Great Whale Hydro-Electric Project. Only so many battles can be fought at a given time.

Why, it might also be asked, did the Cree not wait until an Aboriginal was chair of the HFTCC to win a vote to dismantle the sport hunt? Cree members of the HFTCC comment that it is considerably more difficult to undo what has been done than it is to do it in the first place. Institutions and vested interests, once in place, take on a life and political inertia of their own. Moreover, tit-for-tat retaliation, the partisan over-ruling of previous policy with each successive chair, is no basis for developing a relationship of joint management.

The real losses connected to this history took place neither in meeting rooms nor in court rooms. They took place on the land and in Cree hunters' sense of their declining authority to discharge age-old responsibilities free from interference, in the reminders of invasion that impinge daily upon ordinary experience, and in the sense of sacred places and relationships steadily eroded. Something precious is forfeit if the social pact between hunter and animal is denied; when those who care most – those whose connection amounts to something more palpable, more intimate than maps, graphs, or vacation time – are displaced in their role as keepers and leaders of the hunt.

Notes

1 Biologists' conclusions are congruent with Cree oral history. Harrington (1991, 2), summarizing several sources (Banfield and Tener 1958; Luttich 1983; Goudreault et al. 1986; Crête et al. 1987, Crête et al. 1989) states that "the George River population was quite high in the 1880s, declined to a low level by the 1920s, stayed very low until the 1950s, and then increased from probably less than 10,000 animals in the late 1950s to over 600,000 animals in the mid-1980s." The Leaf River population, numbering over 100,000, was possibly still expanding at the end of the 1980s.

2 Harrington (1991, 2), citing Couturier et al. (1990), Huot (1989), and Crête et al. (1987), attributes the decline, in part, to deteriorating forage on the summer range of the George River herd, though forage on the Leaf River herd's summer range was in much better condition.

3 The question of whether the cull by sport hunting of a few thousand animals is capable of arresting overgrazing or population decline is best left to others. The cultural expectation of the Cree with whom I spoke, however, was that little could or should be done to regulate a phenomenon of such magnitude and complexity. One elder remarked: "I'm sure that the caribou will be gone in a few years, as happened a long time ago ... I'm sure it's going to happen again in the future."

In May 1994, Serge Couturier (1994), for the Ministère de l'Environnement et de la Faune (MEF, formerly MLCP), presented a strategy for optimal exploitation of the caribou herds. George River herd numbers, according to this document, were stable at 740,000 animals, but degradation of the eastern section of the range, used for calving, was a major concern. The current exploitation of the George River and Leaf River herds was inadequate; a significant increase was needed for good management. Despite efforts to increase the sport hunt, exploitation of the George River herd was only 5.2 percent when up to 7 percent was sustainable for migratory caribou. While the order of priority should be to accommodate first subsistence hunting then sport hunting, commercial exploitation would be needed to reduce the herd to an optimum size of 500,000. During the period studied here, the Inuit and the Naskapi particularly sought to develop a commercial hunt in their areas of the territory.

4 Under the terms of the JBNQA, as amended in 1978, the committee is comprised of sixteen members, four each from the Governments of Canada and Quebec, and eight in total appointed by Aboriginal self-governing bodies. The voting regime differs, depending upon whether jurisdiction over the issue is provincial or federal and whether the issue affects all or only some of the Aboriginal parties. The total votes are, however, always equally divided between Aboriginal and non-Aboriginal parties. In case of a tie, the chair of the committee, which rotates on an annual basis between the non-Aboriginal governments and the Aboriginal parties, has a second and deciding vote.

5 The territory includes "the entire area of land contemplated by the 1912 Québec boundaries extension acts ... and by the 1898 acts" (JBNQA, paragraph 1.16); in short, all of northern Quebec north of the St. Lawrence watershed, which is comprised of the traditional lands of the Cree, Naskapi, and Inuit peoples of present-day northern Quebec. The area constitutes roughly two-thirds of the entire area of Quebec.

6 This in fact represented little concession on Quebec's part, since, under the JBNQA, Cree communities have authority to admit or exclude non-Aboriginal hunters and fishers from Category II lands, which make up roughly 20 percent of the Cree portion of the territory.

7 The Naskapi were further along in the development of outfitting enterprises than were the Cree.

8 Entitled "Caribou Hunting in Zone 22: Report and Recommendations," Doc. 90-91D:08E.

9 Given that sport hunters overwhelmingly preferred the early part of the season, the addition of two weeks in November probably more than offset the cancellation of the 15-February-to-30-April period. However, the move responded, in part, to the Aboriginal view that caribou were past prime after February and that harvesting should therefore cease.

10 Letter, Chisasibi chief Pachanos to Despatie, 30 October 1990. Despatie, in response (letter dated 12 December 1990), indicates his willingness to accept Chisasibi's decision regarding Category II lands as well as his openness to reconsider should positions change. He indicates the government's intention to open a zone for outfitting in which Cree outfitters might apply to operate, and he states that, although the number of free hunt permits will increase to 1,500, he expects to freeze the number at that level for several years, in favour of outfitting development.

11 The Canadian Wildlife Service, Quebec Regional Office, recently took a less bureaucratic approach to a crisis in the management of Atlantic flyway Canada geese. Rather than relying solely on official regional bodies, it engaged in direct consultation with Cree hunting bosses and community residents, thus generating substantial support for coping measures (see Mulrennan and Scott 1998).

12 Suspicions were expressed that not only non-Aboriginals, but also Cree from other communities, have sometimes been guilty of these thefts. The road networks have given greater regional access to other Aboriginals as well as non-Aboriginals, and several Wemindji Cree complained of poaching and other offences by members of adjacent communities.

13 See also Berkes 1998.

References

Banfield, A.W.F., and J.S. Tener. 1958. "A Preliminary Study of the Ungava Caribou." *Journal of Mammology* 39: 560-73.

Berkes, F. 1998. "Do Resource Users Learn from Management Disasters? Indigenous Management and Social Learning in James Bay." Paper presented in the Session on Cree Resource Management, Seventh Annual Conference of the International Association for the Study of Common Property, 1998, Vancouver, British Columbia, 10-14 June.

Couturier, S. 1994. *Modalités du suivi de l'exploitation commerciale du caribou au Nord-du-Québec*. Québec: Ministère de l'Environnement et de la Faune.

Couturier, S., J. Brunelle, D. Vandal, and G. St. Martin. 1990. "Changes in the Population Dynamics of the George River Caribou Herd, 1976-87." *Arctic* 43: 9-20.

Crête, M., D. Le Hénaff, R. Nault, D. Vandal, and N. Lizotte. 1987. *Estimation du nombre de caribous associés aux aires de mise bas de la rivière aux Feuilles et de la rivière George en 1986.* Unpublished. Québec: Ministère du Loisir, de la Chasse et de la Pêche.

Crête, M., D. Le Hénaff, R. Nault, L.P. Rivest, and S.N. Luttich. 1989. *Estimation du nombre de caribous associés à l'aire de mise bas de la rivière George en 1988 et révision des estimations antérieures.* Québec: Ministère du Loisir, de la Chasse et de la Pêche.

Goudreault, F., D. Le Hénaff, M. Crête, and S.N. Luttich. 1986. *The Counting of Caribou on the George River Calving Ground in June 1984 with the use of Vertical Aerial Photography.* Unpublished joint technical report. Quebec and Newfoundland-Labrador.

Harrington, F.H. 1992 (1991). "Caribou Populations in the James Bay Region. Hydro-Electric Development: Environmental Impacts." *James Bay Publication Series,* Paper No 1. Montreal: North Wind Information Services, Inc.

Huot, J. 1989. "Body Composition of the George River Caribou (*Rangifer tarandas caribou*) in Fall and Late Winter." *Canadian Journal of Zoology* 67: 103-7.

James Bay and Northern Quebec Native Harvesting Research Committee. 1976-82. *Research to Establish Present Levels of Harvests by Native Peoples of Northern Quebec.* 6 vols. Montreal: James Bay and Northern Quebec Native Harvesting Research Committee.

Luttich, S.N. 1983. *Historical Review of the Hudson Bay Company Journals for the Status of Caribou and Furbearers in the Ungava/Labrador Peninsula, 1925-1950* (Project Report No. 4904). Goose Bay: Newfoundland-Labrador Wildlife Division.

Mulrennan, M.E., and C.H. Scott. 1998. "Canada Geese: Joint Management on the Mid-Atlantic Flyway." In *A Casebook of Environmental Issues in Canada,* ed. M. Mulrennan, 111-26. New York: John Wiley and Sons.

Quebec. 1976. *James Bay and Northern Québec Agreement.* Québec: Editeur officiel du Québec.

10

Becoming a Mercury Dealer: Moral Implications and the Construction of Objective Knowledge for the James Bay Cree

Richard T. Scott

> Even though I'm not eating too much fish, I've still got a [mercury] level of 19.[1] The people, you know, they're telling different stories about mercury. It's not all the same information.
>
> – Cree Trapper, Chisasibi, August 1991

> There are no facts in themselves. For a fact to exist we must first introduce meaning.
>
> – Attributed to Friedrich Nietzsche by Roland Barthes

This chapter is concerned with the poisonous problem of the relationship between fact and value in epidemiological research into the effects of methylmercury contamination on the people of Chisasibi, a Cree community in northern Quebec. My aim here is to point to two politically significant paradoxes arising from that research. The first paradox is that, in spite of the fact that nobody in Chisasibi is free from the knowledge that she is contaminated by mercury, in spite of the prominence of media representations that portray the inhabitants of the village as afflicted by the *disease* caused by mercury contamination, and in spite of the presence of a conspicuous medical surveillance program in the community, nobody – neither the people who live there nor the doctors who run the local hospital and the mercury surveillance program – claims to know personally of anyone afflicted by methylmercury, nor, indeed, to know confidently what form of disease it might take.[2] The second paradox is that scientific attempts to extract an essential set of objective value-free facts about methylmercury have played a central role in producing methylmercury as a value-laden, fearful, and ambiguous object of knowledge for the people of the community.

I develop this argument via a close critical reading of the medical literature dealing with the problem of methylmercury contamination in Canada since 1972, when it was first raised as a potential hazard in relation to chlor-alkali plants at Grassy Narrows and White Dog in Ontario, and Mistissini and Waswanipi in Quebec. My aim is to trace the development of methylmercury as an object of medical knowledge by examining the discursive techniques used to elaborate it. I ask how the problem has been framed at any given point of time and what methodological and ideological resources researchers and writers draw upon to reach their conclusions and to elaborate their accounts. A brief historical sketch provides a bare framework for the main body of my argument, which follows it directly.

From Minamata to Chlor-Alkali Plants to Hydroelectricity Plants

The history of methylmercury contamination of Canadian First Nations begins, for all intents and purposes, in the late 1950s with the deaths of hundreds of Japanese people in Minamata and Niigata from the consumption of fish contaminated with methylmercury that had been released directly into the bay by the Chisso Plastics Company. With the gradual unfolding of the terrible neurological syndrome that came to be known as Minamata disease, and the publication of the stories and photographs of those who suffered from it, methylmercury came to be loaded with a moral significance that would prove hard to ignore.

Chlor-alkali is an industrial paper bleach, and mercury was one of the main chemicals used in its production. Over the course of the 1960s fifteen chlor-alkali plants were built across Canada. Prior to its closure in 1975, one of these plants had discharged 20,000 pounds of mercury into the English-Wabigoon River system and 10,000 to 16,000 pounds into the atmosphere. Another, built in the southern James Bay region of northwestern Quebec in 1967, had released 14,000 pounds of mercury into Lac Quevillon by 1978. This was allowed by the government of the day because it was *inorganic* mercury, which was supposed to be relatively inert and insoluble compared to *organic*, or methylmercury.

The beginning of the controversy over methylmercury contamination in Canada can be traced to the work of a Norwegian graduate student named Norwald Fimreite. He measured high levels of methylmercury in fish near chlor-alkali plants in industrialized regions of Saskatchewan and southern Ontario, and he pointed out that elevated methylmercury levels were potentially a problem for all of the chlor-alkali plants in Canada. Fimreite was subsequently recruited by the owner of a tourist camp in northwestern Ontario to test fish in the English-Wabigoon River adjacent to a chlor-alkali plant. He found levels as high as 27 ppm (parts per million), well above the limit of 0.5 ppm allowable in fish for commercial sale. The Canadian Department of Fisheries and Oceans then conducted tests for methylmercury in water bodies near chlor-alkali plants across Canada.

Although levels were high in several cases, it was at two plants in particular that the dumping of mercury led to a major controversy. In both cases there were First Nations communities near the chlor-alkali plant – Ojibwa people in reservations called Grassy Narrows and White Dog in the province of Ontario, and Cree people in the Matagami-Waswanipi-Mistissini region of Quebec. In both cases the communities relied heavily on fish as a source of food as well as for employment (in commercial and tourist fisheries).

The crucial decision that set off the controversies in both provinces was the closure of the commercial fishery by the Department of Fisheries on the grounds that mercury levels in fish exceeded the allowable level of 0.5 ppm. The closure of the fishery constituted an authoritative declaration of danger to the public health. However, because fishers, tour guides, and tourist fish camp operators immediately lost their jobs, the decision to close the fishery also created an economic injury.

The connection between methylmercury contamination and hydroelectric reservoirs was not established until 1986, when government surveillance of fish in the newly completed James Bay hydroelectric reservoir revealed a three- to fivefold increase over levels found prior to the construction of the project. Subsequently, the mechanism for this increase was explained by the microbial breakdown of large amounts of vegetation flooded by the reservoirs. Bacteria convert inorganic mercury in the vegetation into organic methylmercury. The flooding of large areas of forest produces sudden and dramatic increases in the mass of rotting vegetation from which methylmercury is liberated by microbial activity.[3]

Moral Imperatives, Models of Language and Scientific Authority

Scientific knowledge producers share a number of self-constituting moral imperatives. The philosopher Charles Taylor (1985; 1988) argues that scientific activity and modes of thought are associated with a particular moral framework that emerged from the natural science revolution of the seventeenth century. This naturalistic framework asserts that human beings are to be seen as part of nature and that nature is to be understood and described according to two principal edicts: (1) we must avoid anthropocentric "subjective" properties; and (2) we must give an account of things in absolute terms (Taylor 1985, 2). In this century this moral framework has been assimilated by the logical positivists of the Vienna School into a theory of language and knowledge that asserts, following the early Wittgenstein (1921), that it is possible to describe the world in terms of a single set of atomic sentences derived from observation and related logically to each other (Hacking 1973, 84). It is only over the last thirty years that referential language theory has come to be discarded in favour of holistic models of language in the history, philosophy, and sociology of science (Kuhn 1962;

Rorty 1979; Barnes 1982; Hacking 1982; Lakoff 1987; Latour and Woolgar 1986; Putnam 1988).

The social significance of this assimilation of scientific methodology into a referential theory of language has been enormous, for it has allowed scientists to see the quest for certainty as converging on a single valid account of the world – an account that is necessarily superior to all other accounts. The basic notion behind this is that it is possible to strip any phenomenon of its affective and moral significances to get at an unassailable core reality, which, though stripped of such significances, will, nonetheless, remain meaningful in practical terms. This delusion became particularly entrenched during the postwar period and has done much to bolster technocratic claims to authority, even over issues in which emotions run high and political interests are central.

One of the points I wish to make is that referential models of language make it impossible to take adequate account of the role of scientific researchers in creating the very objects that, methodologically, they see only themselves as capable of uncovering. Referential models of language make it hard to admit, for example, that at the end of twenty-five years of research into methylmercury contamination in Canada, millions of dollars might have been spent, and thousands of people discouraged from fishing and subjected to decades of surveillance, only to produce a vast quantity of virtually meaningless data. As John Dewey succinctly puts it from the point of view of pragmatist philosophy in the early twentieth century:

> All the techniques of observation employed in the advanced sciences may be conformed to, including the use of the best statistical methods to calculate probable errors, etc., and yet the material ascertained be scientifically "dead," i.e., irrelevant to a genuine issue, so that concern with it is hardly more than a form of intellectual busy work. That which is observed, no matter how carefully and no matter how accurate the record, is capable of being understood only in terms of projected consequences of activities. (Dewey 1981, 408-9)

Epidemiologist's Regress and Fact/Value Distinction

Methylmercury researchers are faced with the dual problems of constructing certain knowledge and of deciding what is to count as certain knowledge. As scientists they have to deal, in practice, with variants of the logical problem that Collins (1985) refers to as "the experimenter's regress." As far as methylmercury research is concerned, this might perhaps more appropriately be called "the epidemiologist's regress" or "the neurologist's regress."[4] The general form of this regress is that attempts to resolve a particular question (e.g., What disease does methylmercury cause?) lead the researcher into a field of related questions, some of which pertain to the definition of the general categories used in framing the original question (e.g., "What is to count as a disease?" or "What is to count as methylmercury?"). These, in turn, widen out and demand the resolution of other questions, which may lead to others, and so on. Although, in theory, the questions might widen out forever, in practice they must be stopped somewhere.

The practical resolution of a particular variant of this problem was the subject of a presidential address to the Section of Occupational Medicine of the British Royal Society of Medicine in 1965, now frequently cited as a classic in the field of epidemiology. Bradford-Hill (1965, 295) asks: "In what circumstances can we pass from this observed *association* [between a particular element of the environment and signs and symptoms of disease] to a verdict of *causation*?" In answer to this question, he lists nine second-order features that would tend to make an epidemiologist attribute causality to a putative toxin.[5] Almost as an afterthought, he adds:

> Finally, in passing from association to causation I believe in "real life" we shall have to consider what flows from that decision. On scientific grounds we should do no such thing. The evidence is there to be judged on its merits and the judgment (in that sense) should be utterly independent of what hangs upon it – or who hangs because of it. But in another and more practical sense, we may surely ask what is involved in our decision. (Bradford-Hill 1965, 300)

In practice, says Bradford-Hill, the construction of knowledge about environmental toxins has practical and moral consequences, and it is both impractical and immoral for epidemiologists to try to ignore them when they construct their epidemiological facts.

In effect, he is pointing to a contradiction that epidemiologists face in trying to see their own activity strictly in terms of an ideology and a model of language that asserts that the progress of scientific knowledge proceeds by accurately describing the world in terms of categories that correspond with reality, and then finding pre-existing causal connections between them (Hacking 1973; 1991, 261). This positivist account presupposes a categorical separation of fact from value so that only facts (and not, as Bradford-Hill argues, ethical choice) enter into determining the constitution of other facts. Bradford-Hill's formulation of the epidemiologist's dilemma stops short of absolutely rejecting the positivist account only because he draws a distinction between the exigencies of epidemiology in practice and the progress of science in general. Even as he ironically acknowledges cracks in the walls that keep fact and value apart, he suggests that advancing science will eventually repair them.

I maintain that the distinction between the role of ethical choice and epidemiological method is much cloudier even than Bradford-Hill's account suggests.

Sources of Medical Knowledge about Methylmercury in Canada

The Mercury Program was started by the Medical Services Branch (MSB) in 1972 in the wake of the controversy over mercury pollution from chloralkali plants in the Ojibwa communities of Grassy Narrows and White Dog in Ontario. It was later taken over in the James Bay region by the Cree Health Board. In 1986, it came under the purview of the joint Cree/Hydro-Québec Mercury Committee created by the Mercury Agreement. This Mercury Program, and the committees and subcommittees associated with it, became the central sites for the continuing production of knowledge about methylmercury in relation to the James Bay Cree.

Here I consider five major clinical studies that were involved in establishing the identity of methylmercury as a toxin in relation to Canadian Aboriginal peoples[6] during the 1970s and 1980s. These include: (1) the initial investigations by physicians recruited by the MSB in the early 1970s (Bernstein 1973; 1974); (2) investigations conducted by a task force of Japanese physicians in 1975 (Harada et al. 1976); (3) investigations of a committee struck by the Quebec provincial government in 1976 to look into the problem of methylmercury contamination in northwestern Quebec (Barbeau et al. 1976); (4) the epidemiological study transferred from Grassy Narrows, which was eventually conducted in several of the James Bay Cree communities in 1978 (McGill Methylmercury Study Group 1980; McKeown-Eyssen and Ruedy 1983; McKeown-Eyssen et al. 1983); and (5) an epidemiological study funded by Domtar Pulp and Paper in 1977 in order to settle questions related to litigation (Spitzer et al. 1988).

Shifting Responsibilities, Changing Moralities

Medical writing about the problem of methylmercury contamination in Canada changes dramatically over the decade between the discovery of elevated levels of methylmercury in fish in 1971 and the publication, in 1980, of the results of the first major epidemiological study of a First Nations population contaminated by methylmercury. In particular, references to Minamata disease, which are prominent at the beginning of this period, gradually dwindle away. With them, references to concerns related to responsibility for compensation and for measures to alleviate suffering give way to concerns related to accurate and objective representation of disease. I would like to suggest that there is nothing dispassionate, natural, inevitable, inherently rational, or unquestionably beneficial about this shift from political and humanitarian concerns to apparently scientific ones. In the next few pages, I describe how this discursive shift from overtly moral to apparently epistemological concerns about methylmercury came about. I argue that this shift is the outcome of a contested process in which one kind of morality gradually comes to take precedence over others within the context of disputes and debates that increasingly centre on issues related to professional and technocratic responsibility for knowledge production.

Moral Weight of Minamata

Although mercury has a long genealogy as a toxin, methylmercury poisoning was first described as an industrial occupational hazard in 1940 (Hunter et al. 1940). It attained notoriety as an environmental contaminant when it was identified as the cause of numerous deaths and severe neurological disease in the Japanese cities of Minamata and Niigata in the late 1950s and early 1960s. Altogether 187 people died at that time, and 1,419 people were eventually diagnosed with a new syndrome of epidemic methylmercury poisoning. This type of poisoning subsequently came to be known as Minamata disease.[7] After several years of investigation, the cause of the disease was established as methylmercury that had been dumped in large quantities directly into Minamata and Niigata Bays, along with waste from vinyl chloride factories. Throughout the 1960s the Minamata and Niigata epidemics were widely publicized. In Japan, Europe, and North America, Minamata disease was transformed into a disease emblematic of careless industrialization.[8]

Whereas at Minamata Japanese researchers and physicians had been faced with an unusual constellation of signs and symptoms of disease but had no cause, Canadian researchers began with a cause – unusually high levels of mercury in fish and humans – and had to look for a disease to go with it.

Although, after the Japanese experience, mercury poisoning came to be more or less synonymous with Minamata disease, the term is conspicuously absent from early MSB pronouncements on the problem of methylmercury contamination in Canada (e.g., Bernstein 1973, 1974). It was to physicians from Minamata, nonetheless, that the National Indian Brotherhood (NIB) and its allies turned for an alternative diagnosis to the official one. Contrary to the findings of the MSB, the Japanese task force recruited by the NIB stated that "the inhabitants of the regions concerned are polluted by mercury to an extraordinary extent" (Harada et al. 1976, 175). However, this categorical statement was hedged by doubts about the kind of clinical effects attributable to the extraordinary pollution of which the Japanese physicians spoke:

> Many neurological symptoms were identified and documented. It cannot be concluded that all of these symptoms resulted from methylmercury.

> Neurological symptoms caused by other diseases should be distinguished carefully. However, symptoms observed frequently in Minamata Disease – sensory disturbance, impaired hearing, contraction of visual fields, tremor and incoordination – were immediately recognized. (178)

Later in the same paper we find these statements:

> Neurological findings observed among the group were relatively slight. If congenital Minamata disease, or severe, typical Minamata disease had occurred, the patients were not found among this group. Perhaps those more seriously ill had already died or had been hospitalized. (182)

In the Japanese physicians' account, the situation at Grassy Narrows is characterized by tremendous ambiguity, uncertainty, and danger. The clinical signs they elicited, although not typical of Minamata disease, bear a disturbing family resemblance to it: "Certainly some differences exist, but there is no essential difference" (Harada et al. 1976, 182). The differences that do exist may be due to differences in the setting: "the mode of life, diet, and source of pollution," as well as differences in the kind and amount of mercury being discharged. "It is true," they suggest, "that there has been no mass outbreak of Minamata disease in the Canadian area under discussion, but this may be due to the sparseness of the population" (182).

The Japanese physicians also mentioned other ominous signs that, unrecognized at the time, had preceded the occurrence of death and severe disease in Minamata:

> When Minamata disease was first discovered in Japan, the cause was unknown. Not until two years after the mass outbreak was the cause, methylmercury, elucidated. If such serious cases had not been found in large numbers, the combination of symptoms could have been overlooked as a distinct disease. However, if one had observed carefully, various signs would have been visible. For example, fish floated to the surface of the sea, birds fell to the ground and cats went mad. The present situation of Canada is exactly like that of Minamata before the mass outbreak of the disease. I thought that I had indicated this similarity by means of fragmentary but reliable data. But although I have assembled the above mentioned facts, many people point out differences between Canada and Japan. (181)

In Minamata, the authors suggest, the connection between suffering and methylmercury was drawn only after serious and typical cases presented themselves: "in some patients, symptoms were so mild that only sensory disturbance was observed ... It is a mistake to ignore the effects of methylmercury until typical cases of poisoning are found" (182).

References to the human consequences of Minamata disease recur throughout the paper, and Minamata itself provides the implicit backdrop to the Japanese physicians' discussion of their findings at Grassy Narrows. Their message is essentially a moral one, guided by their own experience: action should be taken to avoid the possibility of repeating the tragedies of Minamata and Niigata.

A search for Minamata disease also prominently informed the inquiry of the Comité d'étude sur les effets médicaux et toxicologiques du mercure organique appointed by the Quebec provincial government to look into allegations of mercury poisoning in the James Bay region (hereafter referred to as the Comité). The nutritional section of this inquiry concluded, for example, with the claim that it had discovered "evidence that the dietary habits [*mode d'alimentation*] of the study population is sufficient to favour a new episode of Minamata type" (Barbeau et al. 1976, 121). Similarly, in his discussion of the ascription of numerical values to clinical signs for the purpose of diagnosis, the neurologist heading the inquiry stated: "In the case at hand, which is organic mercury poisoning, there is a constellation of signs which has been clearly identified by retrospective study in previous victims of poisoning, particularly at Minamata" (41). After a discussion of the difficulties inherent in making such a diagnosis because of the non-specificity of signs, he concludes: "In spite of everything, it is possible to arrive at an ensemble of symptoms more or less characteristic of mercury poisoning" (42). Thus, the Comité's final conclusion, that its study "confirms that several autochthones in North-West Quebec are already victims of the neurological effects of organic mercury poisoning" (149), relies on a gradual elision of meanings (mediated by numbers) between "Minamata disease" and the more generic "organic mercury poisoning." In the context of subsequent professional disputes over responsibility for the rationalization of medical knowledge, this elision was gradually repudiated and disqualified.

Disputes about Professional Responsibility

Following the publication of the Comité's report, disagreements among Japanese physicians, MSB physicians, and the neurologist heading the Comité created a minor legitimation crisis for the Canadian neurological community. One medical observer wrote: "Because of the sinister possibility of mercury-induced irreversible brain damage the current situation demands our full attention. Action is required" (Shephard 1976, 472). "What should be done?" he asked, and in reply to his own question he called, above all, for a consolidation of responsibility:

> The multidepartmental approach to mercury poisoning in Canadians should be replaced by one that is the responsibility of a single group ... What is required is a cohesive effort to synthesize this information and the approaches of the past so that the Indians, the group mainly affected, can be given a clearer indication that a constructive approach will be followed. (472)

It was "desirable that differences between Canadian and Japanese neurologists, and between Canadian neurologists be resolved" (472). However:

> This will not be easy because these differences stem from differences in interpretation of clinical findings relating to Canadian Indians examined. In part the differences are attributable to a fragmented and quasipolitical approach to the problem of mercury poisoning. (472)

The medical profession in general, he said, had a responsibility to provide First Nations with coherent and authoritative knowledge about the significance of the mercury problem. The quickest route to such coherence was to ensure that a single voice remained responsible for medical knowledge about methylmercury. There could be no public disagreement if there was only one public speaker.

The next paper to deal with the Canadian mercury problem did indeed resolve the voices of several of the main disputants into a single authorial voice: the medical spokespeople for the MSB and the Comité study as well as two other prominent mercury experts (Wheatley et al. 1979). It was entitled *Methylmercury Poisoning in Canadian Indians: The Elusive Diagnosis*, and it reported on the autopsy of "a male Cree Indian, aged 79 at the time of his death in 1977." Although he died five days after being admitted to hospital with diagnoses of intestinal obstruction and pulmonary tuberculosis, his case was said to be relevant to the problem of methylmercury poisoning because, during the course of blood screening in July 1975, it was noted that he had a high mercury blood level.[9] The patient was referred to Montreal for neurological examination in October and subsequently reexamined by a different team of neurologists in November. Whereas the discharge summary on the first occasion had stated that "no specific neurological abnormalities which could be clearly related to mercury intoxication" had been detected, the conclusion after the second examination was that he had "a degree of neurological involvement entirely compatible with definite signs of chronic mercury intoxication" (420).

What the article does not say (to do so would unnecessarily historicize its narrative) is that the first diagnosis was rendered in the course of the MSB mercury program and the second by the Comité team of neurologists headed by Barbeau. The case was significant mainly because it was indexical of the differences of medical opinion that had been causing so much controversy, and it was a case that supposedly gave itself up to a court of final appeal for such diagnostic disputes. Since there was a corpse, a pathologist could decide the case. As it turned out, his decision went against the findings of the Comité: "The patient whose case is presented did not exhibit the severe neurological damage associated with 'Minamata Disease'" (421). Perhaps it is significant that, for the first time in the professional literature, "Minamata Disease" is enclosed in quotation marks. It was losing its fact-like status with respect to the Canadian methylmercury problem.[10]

However, the article also contains several clauses that leave open the possibility that significant injury caused by methylmercury might be occurring nonetheless:

> Artifacts due to faulty preservation were numerous in this material ... Perhaps neurohistology is too blunt a tool at the levels of methylmercury being seen in Canada and the answers may lie in the fields of neurophysiology and biochemistry. Poisoning may be causing significant injury undetectable on pathological examination ... Evidence [unspecified] points to biochemical disturbances, which do not necessarily entail detectable histological damage, as the most likely basis for neurological effects which may be observed at the blood mercury levels being detected in Canadian Indians at the present time. (421)

Through the use of such interpretive exit clauses, an investigation that tended to undermine the assumption of neurological toxicity attributable to methylmercury in the Canadian situation could, in the end, be used as grounds to entrench professional and technocratic responsibilities predicated on an assumption of risk. The final conclusion contained in this article reads as follows: "Given the present problems in early detection, regulatory agencies should continue to allow a substantial safety factor in setting standards to protect the general population" (421).

Hidden in Wheatley et al.'s apparently apolitical, generalizing language are a number of historically very specific referents. The standards mentioned are those set by a particular federal government agency – the Medical Services Branch of National Health and Welfare – governing a "general population" living entirely on First Nations reserves.

Statistical and Clinical Significances

The search for Minamata disease also informed the a priori definition of what constitutes a *case* in the McGill Methylmercury Study, the first epidemiological study of the problem of methylmercury contamination in Canada (McGill Methylmercury Study Group 1980). Roughly speaking, the main research question in this study could be summarized thus: "Given an a priori definition of a case as a particular constellation of signs of disease which can be elicited by neurological examination, is there a statistically significant association between the level of methylmercury in the body and the probability of being a case?"

In epidemiological studies, case definition – the identification of a person in the study population as having the particular disease or disorder under investigation – is an important methodological issue. As an epidemiological dictionary points out, "The epidemiological definition of a case is not the same as the ordinary clinical definition" (Last 1988, 19). As far as methylmercury poisoning in Canada is concerned, however, there is no ordinary clinical definition of a case. Indeed, the study is supposed to ask if there is any disease present that might be attributable to methylmercury. It is worth noting, then, that the McGill study does not simply define a case according to the presence or absence of specified neurological signs. Even in the presence of such signs, an additional condition is required: "In order to ensure that subjects with mild abnormalities considered to be of no *clinical significance* were not included as cases, the definition of a case also required that the neurologist had recorded the presence of neurological *disease* in his overall assessment" (McGill Methylmercury Study Group 1980, 50, emphasis added).

Statistical, or epidemiological, significance thus comes to be predicated on the neurologist's ascription of *clinical* significance to a case. Clinical significance, in other words, is incorporated in an objectified form into statistical significance. In its emphasis on disease, clinical significance is, in turn, predicated on the observation of a *generally* disordered and injured body; the assumption is that we simply do not know what is causing the general injury. In the tension between these two kinds of significance – the clinical and the statistical – it is only just possible to note a tenuous link with the moral meanings that surrounded the allegations of injury associated with the controversy over the chlor-alkali plants.

It is not so much that moral or political significances are stripped away in the course of the contestation and investigation of methylmercury contamination; rather, these meanings come to be supplanted bit by bit by naturalistic, objectifying significances. The process is not one of simple substitution. It involves elisions and erosions of meaning as the signs of contamination are constructed and the voices and bodies of the people who bear those signs (they eat fish, their hair and blood contain methylmercury, they are First Nations people living on reserves, they are diseased) come to be represented and interpreted by others – first by those speaking a language of political morality and subsequently by professionals speaking dialects of a language of naturalistic morality. The question "What do these signs mean?" is asked and answered differently at each locus of representation. Although there is generally some overlap in the moral concerns that mediate these shifts in the sites and forms of representation, it is not a foregone conclusion that the overall contiguity of meaning will be maintained.

Techniques of Objectification

The production of an objective narrative requires above all the elimination of subjectivity. In the first place this means the elimination of the subjective interpretations of those whom epidemiological research designates as "subjects" (i.e., the objects of epidemiological research); and in the second place it means the researchers' own subjective interpretations. The first is relatively easily accomplished. The second requires a more sustained effort in order to paper over the contradictions inherent in trying to write a story that must seem to write itself. Barthes (1967) describes this problem with respect to what he terms the "so-called 'objective' mode of historical discourse," in which the author distances himself from his own discourse, never alluding directly to the originator of the text, so that the history seems to "write itself." The authorial subject is as evident as ever, but an objective subject replaces the human persona.

Neurological Examination

In all of the studies of methylmercury contamination, the central technique by which researchers materialize putative signs of methylmercury poisoning is a simple neurological examination. For example, the clinical examination performed for the Comité inquiry in Quebec included nineteen rapid tests of function, including six aspects of sensation and nine of "spino-cerebellar" function as well as evaluation of muscular force and normal and abnormal reflexes. In practice, the physical examination is brief, ranging from 10 to 30 minutes in length, and consists of a series of uncomplicated physical manoeuvres. The history taking is also usually brief, and consists of asking the patient if he has any physical complaints either in general or in response to a standardized list of symptoms pertaining to the nervous system (e.g., "Do you have any numbness or tingling in your legs?").

This process of clinical examination – the level at which signs are elicited from the human body – varies only in detail from one study to the next. There is no technique at this level that one could point to as conferring significantly greater power to one study rather than another. The differences here are details: an electronic hearing test replaces a ticking watch in one study; the procedure for measuring visual fields is slightly modified in another. All of the signs of disease that are eventually reported as bearing on the presence or absence of mercury poisoning are derived from the neurological examination.

It is perhaps worth noting, then, that the whole edifice of clinical and epidemiological knowledge about the effects of methylmercury on the human body is derived from a procedure that contains few tools for revealing secrets about the patient's body of which the patient him/herself is likely to be unaware. In spite of this, the patient's role in the procedure is a fundamentally passive one. It requires nothing of him/her but to submit to examination, to do as s/he is told, and to answer questions by indicating yes or no.

This is because the function of the examination is to materialize signs in relation to the patient's body *for the examiner* so that s/he may perform further operations on them, for example, assigning them numerical values and/or inscribing them on charts, tables, and maps of the patient's body. Through such operations, signs elicited from the patient's body can be translated and inscribed in a manner that can be incorporated into particular clinical forms of representation. These, in turn, can be made to stand for the functioning of a whole community of bodies relative to a standardized norm. In this way, the procedure transforms the examiner into an inscription device[11] that translates signs from the individual body into numerical values standardized according to notions of normality fixed by his/her training and clinical experience. The closer the procedure approaches the ideal of naturalistic objectivity, the more automatic the examination becomes and the less information passes consciously from the "subject" to the examiner. It is this *ideal* that differentiates scientific medical practices from other diagnostic practices. It is in the degree to which it is implemented that diagnosis in epidemiological research differentiates itself from everyday clinical practice.

This concern with stripping away all significances but objective ones is expressed in concerns with "*blinding*" the examiner to any knowledge that might distinguish one patient from another. "Blinding" is a commonplace conceptual tool used in epidemiology. Based on a theory that hypothesized that unconscious psychodynamic processes influence the evaluation of bodily sensations mediating human experience, blinding was introduced into experimental measurement by Pierce and Jastrow in 1884 (Hacking 1990, 205). In the McGill study we find statements such as this:

> All examinations pertinent to the collection of data for analysis were performed by individuals who were uninformed as to the results of previous methylmercury measurements of the subjects. Individuals were asked not to seek this or any related information from the subjects. (McGill Methylmercury Study Group 1980, 32)

Problems with blinding meant, for example, that the study design had to be modified to exclude the evaluations of any of the Cree paramedical observers who had been trained for this purpose:

> Neurological abnormalities detected during the screening examination were not considered in the case definition because it was probable that the Cree paramedical observer who evaluated the screening tests was aware of the life-style – although not the past methylmercury measurements of some subjects and was therefore not entirely blind to their methylmercury exposure. (McKeown-Eyssen and Ruedy 1983, 467)

Because they cannot be "blinded" to their own experiences, the accounts of the Cree "subjects" concerning their own bodies are also of no use to an objectifying epistemology. The rationale for this exclusion is based not only on a concern with unconscious psychodynamic processes, but also on a fear of conscious misrepresentation or bias. Thus, we read in the McGill study:

> Symptoms reported by the subjects were not considered because most subjects were aware of the measurements of their methylmercury exposure made in 1975 and 1976 and because some were litigants in a suit concerned with contamination of the environment with methylmercury. (467)

Interesting in this respect are some of the results of the Domtar Study. Because this study did not use an a priori definition of disease to separate *cases* from *controls*, it was able to treat "stated sickness" as one variable among others for statistical analysis. The Domtar Study divided its study population into four groups: (1) a "Self Designated Disease Group" of Cree individuals living in the river system contaminated by mercury from the chlor-alkali plant "who alleged that they had methylmercury intoxication"; (2) "Neighbourhood Controls ... who lived and fished in the same villages ... and yet who did not allege that they had methylmercury intoxication"; (3) "Ancestral Controls" – members of an Algonquian population living on "a water system free from industrial mercury contamination ... and who followed a traditional ancestral lifestyle where fish provided the major source of dietary protein"; and (4) a "General Comparison Group – White and Algonquin individuals living in the [contaminated river] system at varying distances from the local chlor-alkali plants" (Spitzer et al. 1988, 73).

The variable "stated sickness," which was defined as "the prevalence of any hospitalization, confinement to bed or other disability during the last six months, as stated by the subject" (89), was lower in the Self Designated Disease Group than in any of the control groups; that is, the people in the Self Designated Disease Group tended to designate themselves as diseased less often than did anybody else. The researchers concluded that "there was no evidence of conscious attempts to overstate illness or disability by the subjects" (95).

Other ways of eliminating the problem of subjectivity in this and the Domtar Study include the videotaping of all neurological examinations for separate blinded evaluation by each of the neurologists. A separate section of the McGill study is devoted to "Observer-Variation," the results of which are subsequently taken into account in trying to interpret the findings.[12] Still further possible refinement of objectification involves eliminating human examiners in favour of machines capable of measuring and quantifying particular signs.

Ideally, an objectifying study entails the gradual elimination of particular possibilities of interpretation so that, in the end, the observational method seems to speak for itself. What, then, is one to make of such an ideally objective utterance or inscription? Let us suppose that a study now in its planning stage manages to demonstrate a statistical correlation between bodily levels of mercury and a numerical variable derived from a sensitive laser-machine that registers the severity of otherwise undetectable tremor. What might the practical or moral significance of such a super-fine objective variable be? Even if subjective meanings are maximally stripped away through objectifying research techniques, the problem of interpreting the resultant facts in terms of subjective concerns eventually returns. It seems possible for the objectification of knowledge to proceed to the point of producing facts that are certain but meaningless in practical terms.

Making Up Numbers

In creating objective narratives, numerical values are frequently assigned to qualitative observations of a particular phenomenon. Indeterminate aspects of a phenomenon that do not lend themselves to being translated into numbers gradually fade from view in favour of a simplified numerical object. In this sense, numbers in the company of other numbers seem to take on a life of their own. With only a little effort they beget new numbers and tables of numbers. It is hard to imagine a faster way to move towards (if never quite arriving at) the creation of an "objective subject" capable of narrating itself.

Perhaps the most transparent case in which the ascription of numerical value is used in support of a claim of value-free objectivity occurs in the Comité study. The neurologist conducting the clinical inquiry divides neurological signs into six groups and assigns each a number based on his/her estimate of its value in making a diagnosis of "organic mercury poisoning" (e.g., one point for absent reflexes, four for constriction of the visual fields). The score for each positive sign is multiplied by a factor for severity (0 = normal, 3 = severe) to produce a "severity score." Peg board tests of manual dexterity are evaluated to produce a "performance score." The system of evaluation is tested on a "control group" of six "normal" men and women selected from among the people accompanying patients to appointments in the neurologist's urban practice in southern Quebec.

From the numerical criteria s/he creates, and based on criteria of abnormality s/he devises for mercury blood and hair levels, the neurologist then allocates each case into one of several categories of probability with respect to the diagnosis of organic mercury poisoning. These include *certain, probable,* and *suggestive* categories as well as a residual *asymptomatic* group. Because the neurologist has devised the whole scoring system de novo, there is little that s/he can say in defence of decisions to set a categorical limit here rather than there. The closest s/he gets to such justification is the statement: "It was decided not to consider a patient as presenting symptoms *suggestive* of organic mercury poisoning unless his 'mercury-neurologic' score exceeded, by a minimum factor of 2, the average score of the control group" (Barbeau et al. 1976, 43). Nonetheless, the numbers and tables accumulate, and in the end the inquiry claims to have "effectively revealed in a certain manner that *several individuals residing in Northwest Quebec demonstrate objective signs of neurological intoxication by organic mercury*" (170, emphasis in original).

The Trouble with Normal

> One can, then, use the word "normal" to say how things are, but also to say how they ought to be. The magic of the word is that we can use it to do both things at once. The norm may be what is usual or typical, yet our most powerful ethical constraints are also called norms ... Nothing is more commonplace than the distinction between fact and value. From the beginning of our language the word "normal" has been dancing and prancing all over it. (Hacking 1990, 163)

What the concept of normality does regularly for us, Hacking (1990, 63) suggests, is to "close the gap between 'is' and 'ought.'" It does so partly because it can mean so many things, and one can shift rather quietly between the various meanings of the word from one moment to the next. With respect to methylmercury contamination, normality is used to attribute particular positive or negative values to culturally specific habitual practices (e.g., dietary practices or subsistence harvesting) in the guise of objective, value-free description.

The most common meaning of "normal" in use today is that which is most closely allied to the statistical definition of the norm: for a given domain, what is normal is the most common, the usual, the standard, or the most regular. Hacking suggests that this meaning rose to prominence in the early nineteenth century when it began to take the place of the concept of "nature" in discussions about what is good or right for people. What might once have been defended or condemned in terms of what is "natural," we then learned to defend or condemn in terms of what is "normal." Natural was what was right by God; normal is now what is right by us or, perhaps, right by them.

Another meaning for normal was introduced into medical discourse as a central principle of Broussais's physiology in the nineteenth century and then into sociology through the positive philosophy of August Comte (Hacking 1990, 164). Broussais's principles defined pathological states of organs in terms of deviations along a continuum from a normal healthy state. In this conception what is diseased is that which deviates from the norm. Hacking argues that, in incorporating Broussais's ideas about physiology into his sociology, Comte expressed and strengthened "a fundamental tension in the idea of the normal – the normal as existing average, and the normal as figure of perfection to which we may progress" (168).

Hacking also points to a frequent elision of meaning created by attempts to apply the notion of categorical human-made *standards* of quality developed for human-made goods to continua of normality/abnormality or normality/pathology recorded from nature (165). By this elision, standards of normality could be imposed upon the natural world as easily as they came to be imposed on manufactured goods over the course of nineteenth-century industrialization.

Standards

It was trouble with standards that exploded the whole controversy regarding methylmercury contamination in Canada.[13] The running together of various connotations of normality with the idea of bureaucratic standards also contributed an air of objectivity and facticity to official pronouncements of danger. This elision between the notions of standards and norms is explicit, for example, in the Comité inquiry, which states, in a section headed "General philosophy": "In fish ... the concentration of organic mercury frequently surpasses the federal norm of .5 ppm. This constitutes a danger for those who regularly consume this fish" (Barbeau et al. 1976, 170). The next sentence claims that the inquiry has demonstrated the presence of "objective signs of organic mercury poisoning[,]" and the next paragraph assimilates the idea that mercury is physiologically unnatural with concepts of abnormality and pathogenicity:

> In effect, it is known that mercury, as a trace element, has no particular enzymatic function in living organisms, and hence in man. Any concentration of this metal in tissues, however weak it might be, becomes therefore an aggression against the enzymatic systems responsible for metabolic homeostasis ... *Any amount of mercury in man is therefore harmful to health.* (Barbeau et al. 1976:171, emphasis in original)

The only way this chain of propositions could seem syllogistically sound is if one takes for granted the validity of the implicit identifications it contains of the unnatural with the abnormal and with the pathological: no enzymatic function, *therefore* unnatural, *therefore* abnormal, *therefore* pathological, and *therefore* harmful. It is a style of reasoning based on categories of meaning embedded within a particular culture (scientific medicine) and wedded to a particular history (Broussais's notion of the pathological assimilated with Claude Bernard's notion of a homeostatic milieu interieur.) It is also a style of reasoning that is, at best, anachronistic. That it does not necessarily work empirically becomes immediately evident if one substitutes gold (which has some therapeutic use in the treatment of rheumatoid arthritis) or penicillin for mercury in the quoted passage.

Difference and Pathology

This style of reasoning in which observations are assimilated and identified with underlying categorical forms of difference, abnormality, and pathology is a recurrent one. Sometimes it is applied simultaneously to different aspects of the same phenomenon so as to create what Hacking (1990, 22) describes as "the standard feature of a risk portfolio, namely that at almost the same time opposite extremes are presented as dire perils."

This pattern of contradictory evaluations of normality coming together can be seen quite clearly, for example, in the "Nutritional Inquiry" of the Barbeau study. After a preamble in which the Cree are described as "the greatest experts of the ecology of their own region" by virtue of conservation practices embedded within "ancestral custom" (Barbeau et al. 1976, 92), the nutritional inquiry claims that the Cree regularly consume "on average, *one pound of fish per day per person in the summer!*" (94, emphasis and exclamation mark in original). It does not matter that the consumption practices described here are positively evaluated in the light of a romantic ideology that characterizes the "Indian" as timelessly pre-modern and in harmony with nature (cf. Berkhofer 1978, 47-9; Bieder 1986). Difference is difference, and it is liable to be translated into pathology whatever the other evaluations that may be attached to it. Because the Cree eat such a lot of fish, the situation is "*such that it is possible to place the nervous system in danger in a single summer*" (Barbeau et al. 1976, 102, emphasis in original).

The element of double jeopardy is introduced by the simultaneous nutritional evaluation of the overall Cree diet as abnormal by other standards. Thus, though in one sentence we are told that the Cree habitually consume enormous amounts of fish and game, in the next we are told that the Cree diet is generally poor: low in protein (!) relative to sugars and fats, and low in fresh fruits and vegetables. It does not help matters that the Cree apparently drink too much tea and alcohol (103).

With respect to the White population surveyed, on the other hand, the nutritionists conclude that the diet "is adequate, that is to say that it provides all the necessary nutritional elements. Each food group is well-represented, and the dietary habits are [predictably] almost identical with those of Quebecois in general" (114). Although the White people are also noted to consume alcohol, they do so "in a reasonable manner" (115).

A surplus of mercury via an abnormally high intake of fish relative to the White population is thus combined with a deficiency of just about everything else by other standards of normality. On both counts the translation of abnormality into pathology is a foregone conclusion, and the Cree come to be labelled as doubly susceptible to disease:

> In individuals subject to such a deficiency, the threshold of resistance to aggression against the cells of the nervous system is markedly diminished. The least exposure to toxic products such as mercury, would be necessary to cause signs and symptoms [of disease]. (Barbeau et al. 1976, 107, emphasis in original)

It is impossible to separate "facts" such as this from the meanings that constitute them: romantic stereotypes of difference, and professional and bureaucratic standards of normality.

Risk and Responsibility

Puzzle 1

In most medical encounters, the patient presents to the diagnostician with signs that she and/or her relatives consider to be candidates for a disease falling within that person's realm of competence (Young 1976, 16). The signs the patient presents identify him as "patient" in relation to a particular diagnostician. With respect to the problem of methylmercury contamination in Canada, on the other hand, the patient's designation as a member of a particular group "at risk" defines him as a "patient" in relation to a particular diagnostician. This designation had to be constructed before the search for signs of disease on the patient's body could begin. Almost without exception people "at risk" of methylmercury contamination in Canada have been members of Aboriginal communities, many of them living in reserves distant from centres of industrialization. One might well ask how this state of affairs came about.

Puzzle 2

In 1990, the *Activity Report* of the James Bay Mercury Committee (1990, 8) stated:

> After several years of intensive monitoring of the Cree population, the Cree Board of Health and Social Services of James Bay is now able to identify the individuals at greatest risk ... It has therefore optimized its program for monitoring mercury levels to include:
>
> - women of child-bearing age (15-39), particularly those with mercury levels in excess of 9 mg/kg;
> - persons over 40, in particular: regular trappers; participants in the guaranteed-income program [for hunters and trappers]; all those with previous levels over 30 mg/kg; those not previously sampled;
> - persons wishing to learn their mercury levels.

The same report also states that:

> An examination of the results of the past few years confirms that the majority of Crees have a level of mercury exposure that not only is not problematic for their health, but also permits a promoting of the nutritional value of fish in their diet. Only one woman of child-bearing age exceeded the Cree Board of Health and Social Services of James Bay standard of 9 mg/kg [ppm][14] measured in the hair, in 1989. Among adults over 40 years of age, who are therefore closer to traditional activities, only one person had a level greater than 60 mg/kg [ppm][15] in 1989, compared with 48 in 1984. (James Bay Mercury Committee 1990, 9)

We have a situation now, in which 1,500 people out of approximately 9,000 in the James Bay district are designated "at risk" from eating fish. However, the report also states that only two of those people at risk have blood levels of mercury that place them in danger, while the majority have a level of mercury exposure "that is not only not problematic for their health but also permits the promotion of the nutritional value of fish in their diet." We have come full circle here, from the recommendations of the Comité and the MSB programs that were predicated on the assumption that the least amount of mercury and hence of fish was harmful to human health. What does this language mean? This language that designates people "at risk" from something that at the same time ought to be promoted for its nutritional value? Perhaps it is easier to answer the complementary question: how have these concepts developed?

Risky Beginnings

I would like to suggest that the meaning of being "at risk" is inherently problematic and that it can be most adequately understood as a designation manufactured to justify the actions of one group of people upon another.

It always occurs within the context of particular relationships of power and difference: one corporate body is held responsible for and/or asserts its responsibility over another through claims of privileged knowledge about hidden dangers. In other words, you cannot understand risk unless you understand the social relationships that give rise to its deployment.

The phrase "at risk" appears early in MSB documents dealing with the problem of methylmercury in Canada. The report of the Health and Welfare Task Force on Organic Mercury in the Environment at Grassy Narrows and White Dog precedes its first use of the term with claims that it possesses privileged and authoritative knowledge about the people it subsequently designates "at risk":

> The Task Force was able to gather a considerable amount of information on the habits and life-style of the residents of both communities and concludes that mercury has created adverse effects by reducing opportunities for employment and by restricting a natural source of food from the diet. Up to the present time, the effects of the mercury contamination of the Wabigoon-English River system appear to have been mainly economic, social and cultural, and any adverse effects to the health of the Indian people apparently result from the elimination of fish as a source of animal protein in the native diet; or as a consequence of loss of employment opportunities which have brought about enforced idleness leading to dysfunctional behaviour patterns. (Bernstein 1973, 13)

Two faces of being at risk from an abnormal diet appear. First Nations people are not only at risk from eating abnormally large amounts of fish relative to that consumed by the White population, but they are also at risk from not eating fish because this is abnormal with respect to their "traditional" diet: "Store bought foods of dubious quality and nutritional value have largely replaced traditional foods, with a resulting reduction in protein and increase in carbohydrates. From the aspect of child and maternal health, this is perhaps the most serious problem" (14). "Fish" is here assimilated under the broader category of "traditional foods," a notion that implies its own standards of normality and, hence, of pathology.

In mercury research, we find the first use of the concept of a population being at risk under the heading "Future Program," where it is tied explicitly to the task force's proposals for distributing responsibility for the ongoing medical service program:

> - Responsibility for the on-going program relating to the health of the native people in White Dog and Grassy Narrows would revert from the Task Force to the Regional Director [of the MSB], Ontario Region.

- Because of the persistent nature of the mercury pollution in the Wabigoon-English River system, the populations of White Dog and Grassy Narrows must be considered at risk. For this reason, health programs must continue to exercise a high level of surveillance of the people, with particular emphasis to pregnant females and neonates.
- Because fish consumption persists, it will be necessary to continue the blood and hair sampling program started by the Provincial government. The Task Force understands that the Provincial Ministry of Health is willing to continue this program in close co-operation with the Department of National Health and Welfare. (Bernstein 1973, 14)

On the next page we find the first precursor of the Cree Health Board's notion of a "target population" – the hunters and trappers, those most "Indian" of "Indians." The people least at risk from assimilation to abnormal "modern" dietary practices by Cree standards are those who are most at risk from a form of industrial pollution that penetrates the wilderness. One way or another, difference of some kind brings "risk" to the First Nations person:

> Previous mercury testing programs have missed a vital subgroup of the Indian population, namely the hunters and guides and their families who are frequently absent from their communities. Future mercury-testing programs must take this high-risk group into account and field personnel taking samples should be prepared to seek out persons absent from their villages at the time of the survey. This may entail visits to fish camps, tourist lodges and hunting areas. (15)

There are echoes here, in the image of people bringing syringes, test-tubes, and claims of medical knowledge to the hunters and fishing guides, of missionaries penetrating the wilderness to bring religion to the "Savages." If only the First Nations would accept the message offered them, they might yet be saved from an invisible threat within. Risk, like sin, goes beneath the surface of the body.

Which, then, is the greater risk: eating fish, not eating fish, doing both at once, or being subject to the recommendations of a task force? Difficulties with the coherence of the message delivered by the MSB are papered over by attributing them to difficulties in communication and not too subtly casting the responsibility for incoherence back onto the community "at risk":

> The inhabitants of White Dog and Grassy Narrows are relatively well-informed on the subject of mercury poisoning, but information is subject

> to misinterpretation, hearsay and distortion. This problem is aggravated by the fact that there is no written native language in the area ... Ways and means to improve communications with the Indian people are necessary to impart knowledge of the mercury situation, to discourage fish eating and to encourage interest in diet and nutrition. (Bernstein 1973, 17)

This passage implies that the problem is neither with the message nor with the messenger but, rather, with the mode of communication by which it is transmitted to the First Nations people who are, though "well-informed," therefore liable to subject what they hear to "misinterpretation, hearsay and distortion."

Risky Generalizations

The relationship between structures of difference, power, responsibility, and the constitution of groups at risk is particularly apparent in the light of the MSB's decision two years later: "In view of the multiple potential sources of environmental mercury across Canada ... the mercury program should be expanded to cover all communities for which Medical Services Branch has health responsibilities" (Wheatley 1984, 51). The rationale for this is partly that "The Indian and Inuit people of Canada eat more fish, game, and sea mammals than do most other Canadian residents, and, therefore, are more exposed to the dangers of certain environmental contaminants than is the general population of Canada" (13). Again, the tacit style of reasoning that carries so much weight in the face of uncertainty (and within the context of an assumed responsibility for health) is the deeply embedded and, therefore, unexamined movement from the idea that what is not usual is abnormal and that what is abnormal is pathological.

By 1978, 35,683 tests for mercury had been carried out in the 350 Aboriginal communities for which the MSB had "health responsibilities," including urban communities such as Kahnawake, which is located across the St. Lawrence River from Montreal. Of these, approximately 25,000 (68.5 percent) were said to be "within acceptable normal limits (less than 20 ppb)," 10,400 (29 percent) were "in the range of increasing risk between 20 and 99 ppb," and 900 (2.5 percent) were "in the 'at risk' group with levels over 100 ppb" (Wheatley 1984, 63). These 900 at risk tests were recorded in approximately 550 people, only about 300 of whom lived in the four reserves adjacent to the chlor-alkali plants that had given rise to the concern in the first place. The remaining 250 people were scattered throughout thirty-nine of the 350 communities tested (141).

Having constructed all of the communities for which it has responsibility as at risk, the MSB then refined its definitions of risk on the basis of human blood mercury levels. Although there are federal standards for commercial fish, none exist for humans; so the MSB defined them. In consultation with "an internationally recognized expert on mercury" (51), and in accordance with recommendations from the World Health Organization and a "Swedish Expert Group" (97), the MSB physicians devised a table of standards for levels of mercury in blood (97):

< 20 ppb	Normal acceptable range
20-100 ppb	Increasing risk
> 100 ppb	At risk

The rationale for the construction of these categories goes as follows: the lowest blood levels at which neurological signs were documented during epidemics of mercury poisoning in Japan and Iraq was in the range of 200 to 500 ppb (54). The lower end of this range is divided by a factor of ten to allow for a margin of safety. The two ranges of risk – "increasing risk" and "at risk" – are established for separate purposes. All those "at risk" are advised to undergo neurological and ophthalmologic examination and to remain under chemical surveillance. The lower limit of the "increasing risk" range is used to develop fish consumption guidelines.

The MSB physician describes his own reasoning in devising these consumption guidelines:

> The standard of 0.5 ppm maximum acceptable level of mercury in fish, is based on an assumption of an individual average Canadian consumption of less than one pound of fish per week. The average Canadian Indian who consumes fish usually eats a considerably greater amount than this. Medical Services Branch, therefore, recommended in 1976 that, for Indians and others eating large quantities of fish, the maximum acceptable level of mercury in fish should be 0.2 ppm ... The standards applied are conservative but are felt to be realistic with the data available. (54)

The legal standard for selling fish to the "average Canadian" is taken for granted as providing a reasonable standard for deciding how much mercury and how much "risk" would be acceptable to the "average Canadian Indian." On this premise, the MSB develops stringent fish consumption guidelines for First Nations, allowing for a maximum weekly intake of 0.20 milligrams of methylmercury. This means, for example, that the weekly allowable consumption of fish containing 1 ppm of mercury (which, under FDA regulations in the United States, would have been allowed for commercial sale in unlimited quantities) was limited to 210 grams per week. Aboriginal people in northwestern Quebec and Ontario were advised to curtail their consumption of fish dramatically. Given the levels of mercury prevalent throughout the James Bay area, even at sites remote from any identified industrial source of mercury, literal application of these guidelines would have meant closing the Aboriginal fishery altogether in Quebec (Allan Penn, Cree Regional Authority Environmental Advisor, personal communication).

By the end of 1982, the number of people across Canada defined as at risk for the purposes of continued chemical and clinical surveillance had grown from 550 to 600 (Wheatley 1984, 18). In addition to at risk individuals, there were now at risk communities, which were formally defined as: "an area where an individual, at any time, was considered to be 'at risk' or where fish, game, or sea mammals have had levels in excess of 0.2 ppm" (18). Since levels above 0.2 ppm are common in piscivorous (fish-eating) fish that are sold commercially in urban Canada (e.g., pike, walleye, tuna, swordfish), it perhaps bears pointing out that, if such standards were applied to communities other than those that are Aboriginal, then most neighbourhoods with a fish market would find themselves at risk. As it is, fifty-two Aboriginal communities were so designated.

A further modification of the group designated as "high-risk" by the Grassy Narrows Task Force in 1973 occurred in 1984, when the term "Target population" formally entered the MSB lexicon. "Target populations" were so named in order "to identify those individuals who may be potentially 'at risk'" (18). This group, not necessarily yet "at risk" or even at "increasing risk" according to the MSB's blood or hair mercury standards, included "fishing guides and known heavy fish eaters," "heads of households," and "pregnant women because of the increased vulnerability of the fetus to methylmercury" (18).

Another distinction is superimposed on the category of people at risk. Because clinical examination in the first few years of the Mercury Program had revealed few neurological findings attributable to methylmercury contamination, only those with mercury blood levels above 200 ppb are now being recommended for neurological examination. Ironically, at the same time that the MSB acknowledges being unable to find evidence of mercury poisoning in most of those at risk on the grounds of blood mercury levels, it announces that, "because specific intakes give rise to somewhat higher blood values than previously thought, the safe weekly consumption rates have been revised downward by about 25%, so that the 20 ppb blood level is not exceeded" (18).

Application of Risk

How were the categories of knowledge of the MSB Mercury Program applied at the level of the communities and individuals designated at risk? I can only provide a sketchy answer to this question. A few "educational" meetings were held, including screenings of a film about Minamata disease in Japan. The taking of blood and hair samples for mercury testing became routine in many communities. In the James Bay communities, talk about "organic mercury poisoning" was translated into "neemasakusoon," or "fish sickness," a new term that presented its own problems of interpretation in the local vocabulary.

Those who had their hair or blood tested eventually received letters such as the following, sent to a resident of Fort George in July 1978 to inform him that his mercury blood level the previous October had been within the "normal" range:

> What does this [blood level] mean to you? The amount of mercury that you show is not known to give any trouble or disease to people but you could become sick if this amount in your blood shows any increase in the months to come. What are you to do in order to prevent this increase from occurring? First of all you have to recognize and accept the fact that the mercury found in your blood comes from eating fish that has been poisoned by mercury.
>
> The next thing to do is to have the nurse or mercury worker check your hair every year so that you [will] be informed of any increase in your body mercury level. A Mercury Worker will be in to see you when the time comes: your willingness to accept this further testing is very important for your own protection. In the event that any such increase in your body occurs, you will know that you have not been careful enough in eating only the good fish and that medical examination may become necessary. If this is so, you will be advised.
>
> The Cree Regional Health Board [in the process of taking over responsibility for the Mercury Program in the James Bay region] has recently named native mercury workers to help you in dealing with the mercury problem in your area; these persons will be meeting with you and will be able to answer questions that you might have on these matters.
>
> In this letter we have informed you of the many things that you have to do to protect yourself against this terrible disease of mercury poisoning. We will give all the help we can; to give you this help we need your collaboration and your understanding. The most important thing to do right now is to check how much fish you eat weekly and be careful not to increase that amount.
>
> Dr. ______________, M.D.
> Regional Director
> Medical Services Branch

Being at Risk Today

In the James Bay region, the Mercury Program of the Cree Board of Health has inherited many facts and categories from the MSB. These include a large body of assertions and statistics built up around the assumption of First

Nations people in general as being people at risk, and of "traditional Cree," in particular, as being a target population at special risk. Since taking over the program, the Cree Health Board has tried to narrow its definitions of the group at risk and to liberalize its own guidelines regarding fish consumption. This has produced the paradoxical result that the health board is now trying to encourage those who are at risk of mercury contamination because they eat fish to eat more fish for the sake of their health. Those running the program explicitly frame what they are trying to do in terms of reversing some of the harm caused by the MSB mercury program.

What, then, does the notion of being "at risk," mean? If I want to answer this question in terms of what it says about the people to whom it is applied, then I think I would have to admit that I don't know. It says very little of use about the quality or quantity of danger posed by methylmercury for the Cree in James Bay, for example. Perhaps the meaning of this particular designation can best be accounted for as the product of historical contingency, institutionalized practices, power relations, and culturally embedded styles of reasoning operating within the context of a particular local moral economy.[16]

It is entirely possible that many of the contradictions and paradoxes posed by the risk of mercury contamination for the James Bay Cree and other Aboriginal groups in Canada arise now not so much because of autonomous changes in an objective world but, rather, because of changes in the social relationships governing the production of the scientific language by which mercury is described. That this is conceivable suggests that mercury may have taken on its aura of phantom objectivity in Chisasibi to the extent that a single discourse devoted to stripping away social and moral significances has been allowed to usurp the voices of those for whom mercury has become a problem of the most personal and immediate significance.

Notes

1 Parts per million (ppm) in hair samples.

2 This assertion is based on repeated visits to the community as a replacement physician over a period of three years as well as interviews with residents of the community and medical and scientific researchers in charge of the mercury program. For details on this and other relevant points, see Scott (1993).

3 An account of the history and politics of the James Bay Agreement would be indispensable to any attempt at a full account of the methylmercury problem, particularly with respect to the incorporation of knowledge about methylmercury contamination into an emerging regional and national moral economy related to environmental injury. See Scott (1993).

4 Cambrosio and Keating (1992, 369) provide a succinct statement of this problem.

5 These include: (1) the strength of an association; (2) the consistency of an association; (3) the specificity of an association; (4) the temporal characteristics of an association; (5) the presence of a dose-response relationship; (6) plausibility according to current biological knowledge (though he argued that this was not strictly necessary as long as it did not seriously conflict with available knowledge – see next point); (7) coherence with current scientific knowledge; (8) consistency with experimental evidence, if available; and (9) consistency with analogous situations.

6 This, and the equivalent French-Canadian term "autochthones" (from the soil), are used to distinguish a heterogeneous collection of populations distinguished from the rest of the people in Canada on racial, ethnic, and political grounds. What these populations have in common is that they all claim descent from populations present prior to the arrival of Europeans in the fifteenth, sixteenth, and seventeenth centuries.

7 Signs and symptoms associated with this diagnosis included, in order of decreasing frequency: paraesthesia (disturbance of superficial and deep sensation); constriction of visual fields; hearing loss; speech disturbances; psychological disturbances; excessive salivation; excessive sweating; dysdiadochokinesia (inability to perform rapid alternating movements); disordered handwriting; unsteady gait; intention tremor; Rhomberg's sign (inability to stand steadily with feet together and arms at sides); chorea, ballismus, and athetosis (presence of abnormal involuntary movements); exaggerated deep tendon reflexes; reduced tendon reflexes; presence of pathological reflexes. Similarly, prenatal or neonatal exposure to high levels of methylmercury was associated with evidence of profound neurological damage. Such evidence included: lack of head control; inability to sit or walk; disturbances in chewing, swallowing, speech, gait, coordination, and mental development; enhanced tendon reflexes; presence of pathological reflexes; increased muscle tone; involuntary movements; salivation; incontinence (Kurland et al. 1977, 371; Harada 1977, 218).

8 For example, see D'Itri and D'Itri (1977) and Smith and Smith's (1975) photo essay on Minamata, many photos of which were reproduced in *Life* magazine.

9 Of 552 ppb. See below for a discussion of the meaning of mercury blood levels.

10 Latour and Woolgar (1986, 75-85) describe how statements about scientific entities are transformed from "artifact-like status" to "fact-like status" through the gradual elimination of modalities. Modalities are aspects of a statement that identify it as being about statements (so and so said the sky is blue) rather than about the world (the sky is blue).

11 "An inscription device is any item of apparatus or particular configuration of such items which can transform a material substance into a figure or diagram which is directly usable by one of the members of the office space" (Latour and Woolgar 1986, 51).

12 Roughly, the study reported finding an association between mild neurological symptoms and mercury blood and hair levels that was statistically significant in the community of Mistassini but not in Great Whale. The study of findings in children found a statistically significant association between a single finding – diminished tendon reflexes – which was clinically significant only in boys. Both studies contained provisos against drawing hard conclusions from the studies. In particular, the point was stressed that "the data do not permit the estimation of a threshold of methylmercury above which an excess of neurological abnormality might occur" (McKeown-Eyssen and Ruedy 1983, 468).

13 For details, see Scott (1993).

14 Equivalent to 30 ppb in blood.

15 Equivalent to 200 ppb in blood.

16 For a discussion of the concept of "moral economy," see Scott (1993).

References

Barbeau, A., A. Nantel, et al. 1976. *Étude sur les effets médicaux et toxicologiques du mercure organique dans le Nord-Ouest Québécois*. Québec: Ministère des affaires sociales du Québec.

Barnes, B. 1982. *T.S. Kuhn and Social Science*. New York: Columbia University Press.

Barthes, R. 1967. "Historical Discourse." *Social Science Information/Information sur les Sciences Sociales* 6, 4: 65-75.

Berkhofer, R.F. 1978. *The White Man's Indian: Images of the American Indian from Columbus to the Present*. New York: Vintage Books.

Bernstein, A.D. 1973. *Final Report of The Federal Task Force on Organic Mercury in The Environment*. Ottawa: Health and Welfare Canada.

–. 1974. "The Significance of Reports of Mercury in Various Body Tissues in the Perspective Studies in Various Canadian Populations." Paper presented at the Third International Symposium on Circumpolar Health, Yellowknife, NWT.

Bieder, R. 1986. *Science Encounters the Indian, 1820-1880: The Early Years of American Ethnology*. Norman and London: University of Oklahoma Press.

Bradford-Hill, A. 1965. "The Environment and Disease: Association or Causation." *Proceedings of the Royal Society of Medicine* 58: 295-300.

Cambrosio, A., and P. Keating. 1992. "A Matter of Facts: Constituting Novel Entities in Immunology." *Medical Anthropology Quarterly* 64: 362-84.

Collins, H.M. 1985. *Changing Order: Replication and Induction in Scientific Practice*. Chicago: Chicago University Press.

Dewey, J. 1981. *The Philosophy of John Dewey*. Chicago: University of Chicago Press.

D'Itri, P.A., and F.M. D'Itri. 1977. *Mercury Contamination: A Human Tragedy*. New York: John Wiley and Sons.

Foran, P., and T. Kosatsky. 1992. The Assessment and Management of Effects of Covariables in the Evaluation of Health Effects of Long Term Exposure to Methylmercury among James Bay Cree: A Proposed Study. Montreal: Cree Board Of Health And Social Services.

Hacking, I. 1973. *Why Does Language Matter to Philosophy?* Cambridge: Cambridge University Press.

–. 1982. "Language, Truth and Reason." In *Rationality and Relativism*, ed. M. Hollis and S. Lukes, 48-66. Cambridge, MA: MIT Press.

–. 1990. *The Taming of Chance*. Cambridge: Cambridge University Press.

–. 1991. "The Making and Molding of Child Abuse." *Critical Inquiry* 17: 253-88.

Harada, M. 1977. "Congenital Minamata Disease." In *Minamata Disease: Methylmercury Poisoning in Minamata and Niigata, Japan*, ed. T. Tsubaki and K. Irukayama, 209-39. New York: Elsevier Scientific Publishing Company.

Harada, M., T. Fujino, T. Akagi, and S. Nishigaki. 1976. "Epidemiological and Clinical Study and Historical Background of Mercury Pollution on Indian Reservations in Northwest Ontario, Canada." *Bulletin of the Institute of Constitutional Medicine* (Kumamoto, Japan) 26, 3-4: 169-84.

Hunter, D., R.R. Bomford, and D.S. Russell. 1940. "Poisoning by Methylmercury Compounds." *Quarterly Journal of Medicine* 9: 193-219.

James Bay Mercury Committee. 1990. Report of Activities, 1989-1990. Montreal: James Bay Mercury Committee.

Kosatsky, T. 1992. Feasibility of Applying Available Human Exposure Data to a Proposed Study of the Health Effects of Long-Term Ingestion of Methylmercury among the James Bay Cree. Montreal: Cree Board of Health and Social Services.

Kuhn, T.S. 1962. *The Structure of Scientific Revolutions*. Chicago: University of Chicago Press.

Kurland, L.T., S.N. Faro, and H. Siedler. 1977. "Minamata Disease: The Outbreak of a Neurological Disorder in Minamata, Japan, and Its Relationship to the Ingestion of Seafood Contaminated by Mercurial Compounds." *World Neurology* 1: 370-90.

Lakoff, G. 1987. *Women, Fire and Dangerous Things*. Berkeley: University Of California Press.

Last, J.M. 1988. *A Dictionary of Epidemiology*. Oxford and Toronto: Oxford University Press.

Latour, B., and S. Woolgar. 1986. *Laboratory Life: The Construction of Scientific Facts*. Princeton, NJ: Princeton University Press.

McGill Methylmercury Study Group. 1980. *McGill Methylmercury Study: A Study of the Effects of Exposure to Methylmercury on the Health of Individuals Living in Certain Areas of the Province of Quebec*. Montreal: McGill University.

McKeown-Eyssen, G.E., and J. Ruedy. 1983. "Methyl Mercury Exposure in Northern Quebec: I. Neurological Findings in Adults." *American Journal of Epidemiology* 118, 4: 461-69.

McKeown-Eyssen, G.E., J. Ruedy, and A. Neims. 1983. "Methyl Mercury Exposure in Northern Quebec: II. Neurological Findings in Children." *American Journal of Epidemiology* 118, 4: 470-79.

Putnam, H. 1988. *Representation and Reality*. Cambridge: MIT Press.

Rorty, R. 1979. *Philosophy and the Mirror of Nature*. Oxford: Basil Blackwell.

Scott, R. 1993. "Bringing Home Methylmercury: The Construction of an Authoritative Object of Knowledge for a Cree Community in Northern Quebec." MA thesis, McGill University.

Shephard, D.A.E. 1976. "Methyl Mercury Poisoning in Canada." *Canadian Medical Association Journal* 114: 463-72.

Smith, W.E., and A.M. Smith. 1975. *Minamata/Words and Photos*. New York: Holt, Rhinehart and Winston.

Spitzer, W.O., D.W. Baxter, H.S. Barrows, D.C. Thomas, R. Tamblyn, C.M. Wolfson, H.B. Dinsdale, W.D. Dauphinee, D.P. Anderson, and R.S. Robertson. 1988. "Methylmercury and the Health of Autochthones in Northwestern Quebec." *Clinical and Investigative Medicine* 11, 2: 71-98.

Taylor, C. 1985. *Sources of the Self: The Making of the Modern Identity*. Cambridge: Harvard University Press.

–. 1988. "The Moral Topography of the Self." In *Hermeneutics and Psychological Theory*, ed. A. Messer, L. Sass, and R. Woolfolk, 299-320. New Brunswick: Rutgers University Press.

Wheatley, B. 1984. *Methylmercury in Canada: Exposure of Indian and Inuit Residents to Methylmercury in the Canadian Environment*. Ottawa: Health and Welfare Canada.

Wheatley, B., A. Barbeau, T.W. Clarkson, and L.W. Lapham. 1979. "Methylmercury Poisoning in Canadian Indians: The Elusive Diagnosis." *Canadian Journal of Neurological Sciences* 6, 4: 417-22.

Wittgenstein, L. 1921. *Tractatus-Logico-Philosophicus*. London: Routledge and Kegan Paul.

Young, A. 1976. "Some Implications of Medical Beliefs and Practices for Social Anthropology." *American Anthropologist* 78: 5-24.

11
Media Contestation of the James Bay and Northern Québec Agreement: The Social Construction of the "Cree Problem"

Donna Patrick and Peter Armitage

> Deux petites armées d'avocats s'affrontent cette semaine devant la Cour supérieure du Québec sur les multiples interprétations possibles d'une bible de 500 pages appelée la Convention de la Baie James et du Nord québécois.
>
> Two small armies of lawyers are confronting each other before the Supreme Court of Quebec this week, debating the numerous possible interpretations of a 500-page bible called the James Bay and Northern Québec Agreement.
>
> – Catherine Leconte

Since the announcement of the first phase of the James Bay hydroelectric development project in 1971, there has been intense public debate in Quebec about Aboriginal land rights, about the impact of industrial development on the fragile northern environment, and about Quebec's energy needs and its energy exports to the United States. To a great extent, this debate has been played out in the news media, which have had an important role in formulating public attitudes towards the environment, Aboriginal issues, and other matters of public policy, particularly when such matters become "public problems" (Miller 1992; van Dijk 1991). The James Bay and Northern Québec Agreement (JBNQA) has functioned as an authoritative text in this debate – a "bible" to which contestants have made reference in seeking to give greater credibility to their claims.

In Quebec, debate over these issues started to intensify in the mid-1970s, when the Cree and Inuit attempted to stop hydroelectric development on what they considered to be their ancestral lands. When the first phase of hydroelectric development (James Bay I) was announced, the Cree and Inuit initiated a complex legal and political process that led to the signing of the JBNQA in 1975 (Quebec 1976). A second phase of hydroelectric development – James Bay II, or the Great Whale project – was announced in 1989 and met with stiff opposition from the Cree and Inuit of Great

Whale River, many of whom expressed great concern about the cultural and environmental impact of the project. Like its predecessor, this second phase of development and protest generated a great deal of coverage in the Quebec news media.

News media are important sites in the production of political discourse because they provide ways of representing political issues and events, and the key players involved. News coverage constructs topics in particular ways and – like other forms of discourse – in turn "limits the other ways in which the topic can be constructed" (Hall 1992, 291). Through news texts and other forms of discourse, public knowledge is socially produced and opinions about minority groups and public problems formed, circulated, and reproduced (van Dijk 1991). Although media reproduce dominant ideologies or preferred meanings in order to make sense of the world (Hall 1980), political discourse is contested terrain and "above all, [one] in which social meanings are produced or challenged" (Seidel 1985, 44).

This chapter deals with one aspect of the representation of Aboriginal peoples and minority perspectives in the mainstream Quebec press. It focuses on the discursive construction of the JBNQA through analyzing key propositions about the agreement as they appeared in three Montreal daily newspapers – *Le Devoir*, the *Gazette*, and *La Presse* – between 1989 and 1994. These propositions, which concern the question of rights, advantages, and disadvantages of the JBNQA, and the environmental review process, are produced by political players in the land claims debate and reproduced by journalists and editors in various news texts. Some of these propositions become dominant when they appear more frequently than others and when, despite challenges from key players in the debate, they are eventually accepted as true by the editors or journalists themselves. There are other propositions that coexist alongside these dominant ones; together, these propositions reveal the contested nature of the JBNQA. Ultimately, our findings challenge the prevailing attitude within Quebec and the rest of Canada – that land claims agreements are *the* solution to the "Native problem" (Dyck 1993, 200; Dyck 1991; Coates 1992).

In Canada the "Indian problem," or "Native problem," like all "public problems," is socially constructed through historical representation, government policy, reports, and bureaucratic practices. In the latter half of the twentieth century, the media have played a large role in how the "Native problem" (including Native and Euro-Canadian relations) has been constructed and presented for public consumption. Our analysis of how the JBNQA is represented in the print media suggests that the agreement itself has become a "public problem." Rather than providing a definitive answer to particular issues, this text has become a point of reference open to various interpretations and judgments regarding its legal authority. In addition, our analysis reveals a number of "second-order problems," which can be understood as "problems about the problem," or problems resulting from the JBNQA. These include the environmental, social, and economic effects of the agreement and hydroelectric development, and the Cree themselves, who quickly became a "problem" in the eyes of the Quebec government and Hydro-Québec as the controversy over the Great Whale project unfolded.

Using several propositions as examples, our analysis shows how preferred readings of the JBNQA are inserted through discursive journalistic techniques and how various actors in the controversy insert their own readings into the news discourse. As we shall see, journalists often rely on authoritative sources for the legitimization of claims made within the text (Ericson et al. 1989). In the media coverage of the Great Whale controversy, virtually all of the sources that journalists refer to are produced by Cree representatives, Hydro-Québec officials, federal and provincial government ministers, and spokespeople for various lobby and protest groups. In other words, the discourse constructed by the Quebec journalists in our sample is largely an "official" discourse, whether from opponents or proponents of the Great Whale project.[1]

The propositions concerning the JBNQA and the news texts within which they are embedded are produced not only within the politically charged context of hydroelectric development, but also within a broader political context defined by Aboriginal issues (including the Oka controversy of 1990; see Sauvageau et al. 1995), constitutional affairs, Canadian and Quebec nationalism, and worldwide environmental degradation. We shall demonstrate how, within this larger context, the text of the JBNQA has been understood, as we have said, as a "bible," which contestants have invoked in support of their own positions.

Historical Context

In April 1971, Quebec premier Robert Bourassa announced the James Bay hydroelectric development project at a Liberal party gathering. At the time, the Cree and Inuit of northern Quebec lacked bureaucratic political structures as well as the kind of community infrastructure that most Canadians take for granted (e.g., airports, roads, telephones, television). Within a year of Bourassa's announcement, however, the two Aboriginal groups had joined forces to begin legal proceedings to halt the project. They argued that they had never given their consent to hydroelectric development, had not been consulted, and had not ceded their title to the land. After a series of unfruitful meetings with federal and Quebec government leaders, and with construction of the project under way in August 1972, the Cree and Inuit filed a motion for an interlocutory injunction to stop the project.

In December 1972, Judge Albert Malouf of the Quebec Superior Court began hearings into the injunction; 167 witnesses appeared, over 100 of them Cree and Inuit hunters. In November 1973, Judge Malouf granted an interlocutory injunction and ordered the construction halted on the basis of Cree and Inuit land rights. These, he agreed, had been recognized by the Government of Canada and had never been extinguished. The Cree and Inuit, Malouf concluded, "have had since time immemorial, and continue to exercise, personal and usufructuary rights, including rights of hunting, fishing and trapping" (O'Reilly 1988, 34). A week later, the Quebec Court of Appeal suspended the injunction on the basis of the "balance of inconvenience," without dealing with the issue of land rights (Vincent and Bowers 1988, 221). In short, the Court held that the interests of six million Québécois represented by the National Assembly took precedence over the interests of the 6,000 Cree and Inuit people of northern Quebec (Morantz 1992, 112). With the threat of an appeal to the Supreme Court of Canada, and with construction of the project under way once again, negotiations between the federal and Quebec governments and the Cree and Inuit intensified. These negotiations resulted in the signing of the JBNQA on 15 November 1975.

The JBNQA is a political, legal text that, in Quebec, has become central to discussions of how natural resources in the James Bay region are to be exploited as well as to what rights Aboriginal and non-Aboriginal groups have with regard to halting or promoting such exploitation. The text of the agreement gives great latitude to the divergent, often contradictory, interpretations of the various players in Quebec political affairs. As Arcand notes:

> La Convention de la Baie James et du Nord québécois ... demeure un texte qui peut être lu, compris, commenté et vécu de façons très diverses et parfois contradictoires. Et ces contradictions temoignent de la diversité des intervenants dans un dossier terriblement vaste et complexe. La Convention n'a pas le même sens pour ceux et celles qui l'ont signée que pour ceux et celles qui ne l'ont pas signée. Et elle sera comprise autrement encore par les signataires gouvernementaux, qui étaient à l'epoque membres du parti au pouvoir dans une assemblée qui est dite nationale, mais qui ne peut jamais représenter que certains secteurs de la population. La Convention de la Baie James ça veut dire des choses fort différentes si vous êtes un travailleur de la construction membre de la F.T.Q. ou si vous êtes un joueur de la finance internationale. Le texte a un sens en ingénierie et un tout autre sens en termes de géo-politique de l'État québécois. (Arcand 1988, 167-8)

> The James Bay and Northern Québec Agreement ... remains a text that can be read, understood, commented upon, and lived in very different and sometimes contradictory ways. These contradictions attest to the diversity of interventions in a terribly vast and complex case. The agreement does

> not have the same meaning for those who signed it as it does for those who did not. And it will be interpreted in yet a different way by the government signatories, who at the time were members of the party in power in an assembly said to be national, but which can truly only represent certain sectors of the population. The James Bay agreement means something very different to a construction worker than it does to an international financier. The text has one meaning in engineering and a completely different one in the geo-politics of the Quebec state.

In the analysis of the JBNQA, as it is described in Quebec print media, the agreement is a very "open" text that permits multiple readings; this "openness" has been a basic source of disagreement among those involved in the struggle over the Great Whale project. The multiple readings emerge clearly in the print media, as we shall demonstrate below.

Method

The following analysis is based on newspaper articles, editorials, opposite editorial pieces, and letters to the editor obtained from two French-language Montreal dailies – *La Presse* and *Le Devoir* – and one English-language daily – the *Gazette*. The articles used in this study make reference to the JBNQA and appeared over a five-year period: from 1 January 1989 to 31 December 1994. This period spans the years between the announcement by Hydro-Québec of the Great Whale project in early 1989 and its suspension by Premier Jacques Parizeau on 18 November 1994.

In attempting to compile as complete a sample as possible, we gathered articles from newspaper clipping files at Makivik Corporation, the Grand Council of the Crees, the Great Whale Public Review Support Office, Hydro-Québec, university libraries, and CD-ROM databases.[2] We then did a preliminary reading of each newspaper item to determine if any reference was made to the JBNQA. In total we looked at 1,179 relevant news items in the *Gazette*, of which 123 (10.4 percent) referred to the JBNQA. From *Le Devoir*, we had a total of 670 news items, of which 109 (16.3 percent) referred to the JBNQA; and in *La Presse* we had a total of 913 news items, of which 146 (16.0 percent) referred to the JBNQA.

Based on these articles, we extracted themes and propositions relating to the JBNQA. We took note of which propositions were contested and which emerged as dominant in the discourse. Whether a proposition is considered dominant or not is based on how frequently it appeared and/or whether the journalist or editor has presented it as a fact (that is, without attributing the statement to a specific actor or source). The latter indicates that the journalist or newspaper editor accepts the validity of the proposition and thereby dismisses opposing interpretations.

In presenting our data, we shall not attempt to compare the coverage of the JBNQA in each of the three newspapers. In addition, we wish to emphasize the importance of distinguishing between news media discourse and the statements of actors to whom propositions are attributed. When Matthew Coon Come (former grand chief of the Grand Council of the Crees) or Guy Versailles (spokesperson for Hydro-Québec) is quoted in print media, we are not reading their actual discourse but that of the journalist reporting what they allegedly said.[3]

Analysis

Three main themes emerged from the articles that refer to the JBNQA: (1) rights, (2) advantages and disadvantages of the agreement, and (3) the environmental impact assessment of hydroelectric development. Each theme, in turn, encompasses a variety of propositions dealing in some way or another with the agreement. These propositions are listed below:

Themes and propositions found in Québec print news discourse regarding the JBNQA, 1989-1994.

(1) Rights
- (a) The JBNQA extinguished Cree and Inuit rights.
- (b) It did not extinguish Cree and Inuit rights.
- (c) It gives Quebec and Hydro-Québec the right to develop Great Whale, etc. (Cree and Inuit consented to further development).
- (d) It does not give Quebec and Hydro-Québec the right to develop Great Whale, etc.
- (e) It gives Quebec rights to the territory; that is, it guarantees the territorial integrity of Quebec.
- (f) It does not provide such rights or guarantee territorial integrity.
- (g) It gave the Cree and Inuit exclusive harvesting rights in certain portions of northern Quebec.

(2) Advantages and Disadvantages of the Agreement for the Cree and Inuit

Advantages:
- (a) It recognizes Aboriginal peoples as nations.
- (b) It made the Cree and Inuit politically stronger (political autonomy, more powers).
- (c) It made the Cree and Inuit prosperous (provided compensation, business preferences, schools, clinics, etc.).
- (d) It led to conditions that improved Cree health.
- (e) It allows the Cree and Inuit a say in development.
- (f) It allows the Cree to hunt, fish, and trap (income security, promotes or sustains harvesting).

Disadvantages:
(a) Social and health problems mushroomed in its wake.
(b) The flooding to create reservoirs caused mercury pollution.
(c) Harvesting territory was lost to the flooding.
(d) Cultural erosion intensified after the signing of the agreement.
(e) Obligations under the agreement were not honoured by the federal and Quebec governments.
(f) The agreement accelerated modernization.

(3) Environmental Impact Assessment of Dam Construction
(a) The federal government must be involved in the impact assessment.
(b) The federal government is invading Quebec's jurisdiction by implementing its Environmental Assessment Review Process.
(c) The impact of dam construction should not be assessed separately from the impact of project infrastructure (roads, airports, etc.).
(d) Eastmain River Dam environmental assessment is required.
(e) Laforge I environmental assessment is required.
(f) Public hearings are not required for the impact assessment apart from those required by the Inuit-Cree committees (COMEX, etc.).

In what follows, we provide examples of these propositions from each of the three newspapers in our sample.

Rights

The JBNQA very quickly became both the object of opposing interpretations and a rhetorical resource for the Cree, the Quebec government, Hydro-Québec, and others involved in the debate about the construction of the Great Whale hydroelectric project. All three newspapers in our sample contain examples of reports and editorials that demonstrate the contested status of Cree rights in the wake of the JBNQA.

Extinguishment of Rights

Two propositions emerged early in our sampling that concerned the JBNQA and the Oujé-Bougoumou Cree of northern Quebec. The Oujé-Bougoumou Cree did not sign the agreement and wanted to settle a land claim with the Canadian and Quebec governments. These propositions are found in the following statements, where they are indicated in italics:

> The Ouje-Bougoumou Cree were left out of the James Bay and Northern Quebec Agreement of 1975, which *addressed the Aboriginal rights of other Cree and Inuit.* (A. Norris, *G*, 13 September 1989, a4)[4]

> The land belongs to the [Oujé-Bougoumou Cree] band because *it was never conquered or ceded as part of an agreement.* (E. Thompson and C. Buckie, *G*, 26 July 1989, a4)

The first proposition is that Aboriginal rights were "addressed" in the JBNQA. While "right" is never defined as a political or legal concept, there is still a suggestion that the rights of the Cree (with the exception of the Oujé-Bougoumou people) and Inuit have been taken seriously and dealt with appropriately.

The second proposition refers to "agreement" in an unspecific way. However, this brings to mind the JBNQA, which had been in the news earlier the same month within the context of the claim that the Oujé-Bougoumou Cree were not signatories of the JBNQA. This proposition is interesting on two counts. First, it contains a presupposition that, while promoted by many Aboriginal peoples across Canada, has never been accepted by Canadian courts; namely, that land can belong to Aboriginal people in a pre-treaty period.[5] Second, it asserts that land is "ceded" by Aboriginal peoples through land claims agreements – a claim that is challenged in some news media discourse in our sample. In 1990, spokespeople for the Grand Council of the Crees advanced the proposition that the Cree had not renounced their rights in signing the agreement. This claim appeared within the context of news coverage of Cree efforts to obtain an injunction in the Quebec Superior Court to halt construction of the Great Whale project.

> "*Nous n'avons jamais cédé nos droits ancestraux dans le nord,*" a declaré le Grand chef Matthew Coon Come, en faisant allusion à la signature de la Convention de la Baie James en 1975.

> "*We never gave up our ancestral rights in the North,*" stated Grand Chief Matthew Coon Come, alluding to the signing of the James Bay and Northern Québec Agreement in 1975. (*P*, 4 April 1990, a2)

> "We are the owner. We have jurisdiction over the land," Grand Chief Matthew Coon Come said at a news conference. "We are trying to protect our main economic base – hunting, fishing and trapping as a way of life" ... *The Cree argue they have never surrendered rights to the natural resources on that land.* (G. Hamilton, *G*, 4 April 1990, a6)

Cree leaders expounded this view right up until the end of our sample period in 1994. In a speech given at a Quebec Studies conference, Matthew Coon Come,

> rappelle que son peuple occupe ces terres depuis 5000 ans et rejette l'affirmation selon laquelle les droits de son peuple sur ces terres ont été éteints avec la signature de la Convention de la Baie James. M. Coon Come qualifie cette convention "d'instrument d'oppression et de dépossession."
>
> reminds us that his people have occupied this land for over 5000 years and rejects the claim that their rights to the land were extinguished with the signing of the James Bay and Northern Québec Agreement. Mr. Coon Come characterizes this agreement as "an instrument of oppression and of dispossession." (M. Venne, *D*, 18 November 1994, a12)

While the Cree maintained their position that land rights were not ceded through the JBNQA, various advocates of dam construction claimed the opposite; namely, that in signing the JBNQA, the Cree had forever given up their rights to the land and any claims flowing from it. For example, regarding the issue of whether the federal government would subject the Great Whale project to the federal Environmental Assessment Review Process (EARP), Richard Le Hir of the Quebec Manufacturers Association was quoted as saying:

> Les règles du jeu relatives au développement de Grande-Baleine ... étaient entièrement prévues par la Convention de la Baie James. Convention que les autochtones ont d'ailleurs signée, *renonçant ainsi à leurs droits sur les terres de la Baie James.*
>
> The ground rules concerning the development of the Great Whale project ... were explicitly contemplated in the James Bay and Northern Québec Agreement. What's more, the Aboriginals signed the agreement, *ceding their rights to the James Bay land.* (Paré, *D*, 18 July 1991, a2)

Parti Québécois leader Jacques Parizeau was also a frequent defender (in all three newspapers) of the extinguishment interpretation within the context of questions about the territorial integrity of Quebec in the event of the province's separation from Canada. He suggested that the Cree should appear before the Quebec Parliamentary Commission on Sovereignty to explain their claims to northern Quebec in the event of Quebec separation, and he was quoted as saying that the Cree have ceded their territories "avec tous leurs titres et droits à la province en 1975 lors de la signature de la Convention de la Baie James (with all their titles and rights to the province in 1975 upon the signing of the James Bay Agreement)" (L.-G. Francoeur, *D*, 23 October 1991, a1).

> [Parizeau] also blamed Ottawa for failing to challenge Cree threats to separate from an independent Quebec. Those threats are absurd *because the Cree relinquished Aboriginal claims to northern Quebec when they signed the James Bay Agreement* in 1975, he said. (B. Aubin, *G*, 17 August 1991, a4)

Reference to the extinguishment provision in the agreement, as in the Le Hir and Parizeau quotations above, emerged as a dominant proposition in all three newspapers in our sample. Apart from frequency of appearance (it appeared in twenty-three different news texts in the sample period),[6] the most obvious indicator of this dominance is the dropping of attribution by journalists in referring to the "extinguishment clause" and, hence, their reference to extinguishment as a fact. Thus, according to one *Gazette* journalist:

> Namagoose said that if Quebec separates ... the landmark 1975 James Bay agreement signed between Ottawa, Quebec and the Cree and the Inuit would have to be scrapped. The agreement, which made possible the first phase of James Bay hydroelectric development, saw natives *surrender land claims* in return for promises of $232.5 million in compensation. (G. Hamilton, *G*, 11 March 1991, a4)[7]

In 1991, a background article on the JBNQA, "L'accord source de tous les désaccords," explained how the agreement constituted a compromise accepted by all parties in 1975:

> Grosso modo, les gouvernements du Québec et du Canada l'ont signée pour permettre l'exploitation économique des ressources des deux tiers de la province de Québec. Ce qui supposait, d'une part, qu'on établisse les conditions d'une paix sociale avec les quelques 10 000 autochtones qui habitaient cette region et d'autre part, qu'on supprime tous les doutes qui subsistaient quant aux droits du Québec sur ce territoire. C'est-à-dire, selon la méthode préconisée par le fédéral, *qu'on éteigne tous les droits ancestraux des autochtones sur les terres* (reconnus par le Roi d'Angleterre en 1670 mais jamais bien définis) et qu'on les remplace par des droits et garantis précisément – croyat-on! – délimités.

> Broadly speaking, the governments of Quebec and Canada signed it to allow for the economic exploitation of two-thirds of Quebec's resources. This presupposes, on the one hand, that social peace be established with the Aboriginals living in the region, and on the other hand, that any remaining doubts regarding Quebec's rights on this territory be resolved. In other words, according to the method advocated by the federal government, *all*

> *Aboriginal ancestral rights on this land (recognized by the King of England in 1670 but never clearly defined) are to be extinguished* and replaced with precisely defined rights and garantees. (C. Leconte, *D*, 18 September 1991, b1)

In the *Gazette* an author of an editorial (26 October 1991, b2) is emphatic about the extinguishiment matter; and, claiming to provide a "cool, dispassionate look at the Great Whale power project," cites a "key provision of the agreement":

> In consideration of the rights and benefits herein set forth in favor of the James Bay Crees and the Inuit of Quebec, the James Bay Crees and the Inuit of Quebec hereby cede, release, surrender and convey all their native claims, rights, titles and interests, whatever they may be, in and to land in the Territory and in Quebec and Canada.

In conclusion, the editorial states:

> It may be argued that the James Bay agreement was no good for the natives, that they sold their rights for a song. But the agreement is there, and it is clear that under its terms, Hydro-Québec has the right to proceed with Great Whale, provided it proceeds in the right way.

The evidence suggests, then, that a claim regarding the Cree – namely, that the Cree lost their ancestral rights to the land in northern Quebec when they signed the JBNQA – had become a dominant proposition. The verbatim quotation of the "extinguishment clause" in the agreement by some journalists left little doubt about the validity of the proposition in the minds of advocates of the hydroelectric dam project. Nonetheless, the print media paid little attention to the ongoing legal dispute over the issue of extinguishment at that time, and they gave little credence to the counter-proposition that the Cree did not "bargain away their rights" when they signed the JBNQA. This counter-proposition – that the preservation of Cree rights to hunt and fish on the lands covered by the JBNQA entailed the preservation of rights over water and other natural resources tied to this land – was both reasonable and grounded in the text of the JBNQA. Yet news articles that present the legal arguments in response to the dominant proposition of extinguishment, put forth by the Cree leadership and their legal advisors in a court case at the time, are rare.

Hydro-Québec and Government Rights to Develop

According to most print media sources, the Cree and Inuit lost rights by signing the JBNQA. Related to this is the proposition that Hydro-Québec and the Quebec government gained rights to development in the territory or, rather, achieved a greater degree of certainty concerning their development rights.[8] The extent of these rights and the degree to which they are constrained by the JBNQA and Aboriginal rights were highly contested in the discourse represented by our sample.

> One proponent of the right to development, Richard Le Hir, described the Cree land threatened by the project as "barren" and "bare as a knuckle." [...] Le Hir said Quebec has every right to develop the area under the 1975 JBA – signed by the Inuit, Cree, Ottawa and Quebec. (G. Baker, *G*, 18 July 1991, a4)

In the same vein, a lawyer acting for Hydro-Québec was said to insist that "a careful reading of the 1975 agreement shows that hunting and fishing rights must give way to development – once the precondition of environmental assessment is met" (R. Laurent, *G*, 18 July 1991, a4). In *La Presse*, Premier Robert Bourassa also cited the agreement to justify Quebec's right to proceed with Great Whale: "'Ils ont signé la Convention de la Baie James qui, à l'article 7, prévoit la construction de Grande-Baleine. Doit-on conclure que les Cris ne respecteront pas leur parole?' ('They signed the James Bay Agreement which, under article 7, anticipates the construction of the Great Whale. Are we to believe that the Crees did not keep their word?')" (A. Pépin, *P*, 28 August 1991, a2). Statements countering this view rarely appeared; when they did, they were attributed to James O'Reilly, a lawyer representing the Cree:

> O'Reilly said the James Bay agreement has left the Cree with several possible ways of challenging further development in the court. He said the Cree had conceded rights over land, "but no mention is ever made of conceding rights over water or natural resources in the area," he said. "Our terminology was carefully chosen (in 1975) and no title was transferred to Quebec over water or other natural resources," he said. (B. Aubin, *G*, 9 November 1991, b3)

Thus, although there has been legal opposition on the part of the Cree concerning the rights to further hydroelectric development, this claim is given little coverage in the print media. This lack of coverage plays a role in shaping the public perception that the JBNQA is clear on the issue of relinquishment of Cree and Inuit rights, and the right of Hydro-Québec to pursue hydroelectric development at Great Whale.

Quebec's Rights to Territory Post-Separation

The proposition attributed to Cree leaders that gave rise to the most vitriolic rebuttals from the Quebec government and Parti Québécois representatives concerned the possibility of Cree separation from Quebec should the latter attempt to leave Canada. There were only six references to this proposition in our sample. Debate on this topic surfaced sporadically in newspaper coverage from mid-1991 through to the fall of 1994, when Matthew Coon Come broached the subject before American audiences. In August 1991 Coon Come was quoted as saying that:

> Any attempt by Quebec to secede unilaterally would put the province's Cree in a stronger legal position to take unilateral action themselves ... That's because the JBNQA which the Cree signed in 1975 was concluded with both Quebec and Ottawa – and any unilateral change to Quebec's position in confederation would affect the treaty and thus the Cree's rights, he said. "When we approved the agreement in 1975, the people understood that it was within the parameters of confederation," he said ... The Cree's decision would affect the 373,000 square kilometers of land to which they have title under the 1975 accord, Coon Come said. (A. Norris, G, 8 August 1991, a4)

Bourassa located Quebec's rights to the north in the Boundary Extension Acts of 1898 and 1912, and he claimed that the JBNQA had eliminated any obligations to the Cree that flowed from these acts (G. Normand, *P*, 23 October 1991, a5). Jacques Parizeau was equally emphatic:

> Quand le chef Cri Billy Diamond déclare que les Cris ont de très sérieux arguments juridiques pour retenir "les deux tiers du Québec dans le Canada," M. Parizeau s'emporte. "C'est faux! Tout ça est illégal et inconstitutionnel!" Le chef péquiste brandit l'entente de la Baie James (1975), par laquelle les Cris ont renoncé à leurs droits sur la quasi totalité du territoire québécois ... en échange de 225 millions de dollars et de droits sur certaines parcelles de territoire ... [ces groupes] n'ont aucune "existence constitutionnelle" sur laquelle s'appuyer pour tenter d'accroître leur autonomie, comme c'est le cas du Québec. Les Cris auraient pu y prétendre, mais ils y ont renoncé en 1975, dit-il.
>
> When Cree chief Billy Diamond declared that the Crees had very convincing legal arguments to keep "the two-thirds of Quebec in Canada," Mr. Parizeau exclaimed, "That's not true! All this is illegal and unconstitutional!" The PQ leader brandished the James Bay agreement (1975), whereby the Crees renounced their rights to nearly the entire Quebec territory ... in exchange for $225 million and rights to certain parcels of land ... [these groups] have no "constitutional existence" on which to base an increase in their autonomy, as is the case of Quebec. The Crees could have had a claim to it, but they gave it up in 1975, he said. (*P*, 24 August 1991, b4)

While there are opposing views on the territorial integrity of Quebec in the event of Quebec's separation from Canada, both arguments are supported with reference to the JBNQA. Cree and Quebec political leaders alike appeal to the "authority" of the agreement, highlighting once again the contested nature of the interpretations given to the text.

Aboriginal Rights

While the propositions concerning land rights (extinguishment, development, and territorial integrity) were contested, there was a consensus amongst political leaders and journalists regarding the rights that the Cree gained in the agreement. These include, inter alia, exclusive wildlife harvesting rights. The notion that the Cree gained rights is advanced by Cree spokespeople, advocates of dam construction, and journalists themselves. For example, in a background piece in *La Presse*, a journalist notes that the Cree and Inuit have no hunting restrictions on all the territory covered by the agreement (B. Bisson, *P*, 7 January 1991, a6). An article in the *Gazette* quotes Matthew Mukash ("a community activist in Great Whale River" and, later, chief) as saying:

> "The James Bay Agreement recognizes our strength and our powers to defend our traditional way of life." The agreement, he says, recognizes the Cree right to hunt, fish and trap in their territory, to control their own institutions and the means for their economic development, and to maintain their traditional way of life. (B. Aubin, *G*, 9 November 1991, b3).

In *Le Devoir*, a journalist notes that the Cree "sont conventionnés. En vertu du traité de la Baie James signé en 1975, une grande partie du territoire nordique leur est concedée aujourd'hui. Ils ont reçu de l'argent en partage, en plus des droits de trappe, de chasse et pêche (... in accordance with the James Bay treaty signed in 1975, a large part of the northern territory has been granted to them. They have received their share of money, in addition to trapping, hunting and fishing rights)" (*D*, 27 July 1993, a9). Such rights and other "benefits" for the Cree and Inuit that flow from the JBNQA are discussed in more detail below.

Advantages and Disadvantages of the Agreement

Numerous assertions about the advantages and disadvantages of the JBNQA were made during the Great Whale controversy. Proponents of the Great Whale project were generally presented as supporting the agreement and attributing a variety of benefits to it as far as the Cree and Inuit were concerned. For proponents, the JBNQA provided cash compensation, hunting rights, land, economic development opportunities, an invigorated hunting economy (through the Income Security Program), improved housing, education, and health care. The agreement has also helped the Cree and Inuit to become political forces to be reckoned with (see also Salisbury 1986). Reduced infant mortality, a greater lifespan, and increased population were all linked in some way to the JBNQA. The JBNQA had, in effect, helped push the Cree and Inuit into the modern era.

While Great Whale proponents and media pundits were willing to admit that so-called "modernization" had a dark side in the form of higher suicide and alcohol rates, they did not link such problems to the agreement or to hydroelectric development. These problems, they asserted, were the inevitable consequences of rapid culture change that all Aboriginal peoples are experiencing with or without hydroelectric dams and treaties.

On the other hand, according to press accounts, opponents of the Great Whale project, particularly the Cree, were generally negative in their evaluation of the JBNQA. Multiple social and health problems had followed in the wake of the agreement; mercury pollution in the reservoirs built with the blessing of the agreement had poisoned fish and other aquatic creatures, making them unfit for human consumption; and valuable harvesting territory had been lost forever. Processes of modernization had been accelerated by the agreement and were eroding Cree culture and alienating Cree youth from their elders and traditions. Cree leaders were quoted as saying that the federal and Quebec governments had not lived up to many of their obligations under the agreement; self-government, economic development, and control over resources had not been adequately addressed.

Federal member of parliament (NDP) Phil Edmonston indirectly praised the Agreement following "inflammatory" statements by his colleague, Jim Fulton, to the effect that Hydro-Québec had blood on its hands from the drowning of 10,000 caribou on the Caniapiscau River in 1984: "Edmonston noted that the James Bay agreement was one of the first modern treaties between Aboriginal and non-Aboriginal governments and that the Quebec government was the first to recognize Aboriginal peoples as nations" (P. Curran, *G*, 16 February 1993, a6).

Following the anti-Great Whale hydroelectric development advertisement in the *New York Times* in October 1991, Hydro-Québec placed its own advertisement there in order to rebut propositions by the James Bay Coalition.[9] *La Presse* immediately reprinted a translation of the advertisement, in which the utility remarked: "Les 31 chapitres qu'elle contient permettent aux 17 000 Cris et Inuit du Québec de disposer d'un degré d'autonomie politique sans equivalent sur le continent nord-américain (the 31 chapters it contains allow the 17,000 Crees and Inuit of Quebec to exercise a degree of political autonomy unparalled in North America)" (28 October 1991, b3). The Hydro-Québec advertisement also claimed that the agreement had given the Cree and Inuit tools for economic development and diversification and that, since its signing, infant mortality among the Cree has been reduced by half, while life expectancy had increased by more than twenty years.

The proposition that Cree health improved after the signing of the JBNQA was cited frequently in our newspaper sample. It should be noted, however, that no journalist investigated the link between particular terms of the agreement and improved health; that is, no one asked the question whether improvements in health had occurred in other Aboriginal communities that did not have modern treaties in place or whether they would likely have occurred among the Cree due to the funds and services that were being provided to Aboriginal people across Canada during the same period. At the same time, the link inferred by certain Cree leaders between the JBNQA and health and social problems went similarly uninvestigated by journalists.[10]

Another proposition, which surfaced in print media discourse between 1989 and 1994, is that the Cree and Inuit prospered economically from the agreement. This developed into a dominant proposition, given the frequency with which it is mentioned and the failure of journalists to attribute a source to it. There were thirty-three references to this proposition in our sample. For example, in her long exposé on the agreement, a *Le Devoir* reporter, Catherine Leconte, states that

> au fil des ans, de dix amendements à la Convention initiale et de diverses ententes ont progressivement porté la valeur totale des dédommagements concédés à plus de 500 millions dollars ... Ces chiffres ne prennent cependant pas en compte le coût des services publics qui sont fournis aux autochtones bénéficiaires de la Convention comme à tous citoyens canadiens et québécois. En incluant ces coûts, le ministère canadien des Affaires indiennes calculait, dans son rapport annuel 1990, que depuis la signature de la Convention, quelque 18 000 autochtones ont reçu plus d'un milliard dollars.

> over the years, ten amendments to the initial agreement and various understandings have gradually raised the total value of compensation awarded to more than $500 million ... These figures do not take into account, however, the cost of the public services provided to the Aboriginals benefiting from the agreement, as to Canadian and Québécois citizens alike. By including these costs, the Canadian Ministry of Indian Affairs, in its 1990 annual report, calculated that some 18,000 Aboriginals received more than a billion dollars since the signing of the accord. (18 September 1991, b2)

In reference to a controversy involving the company Beaver Asphalt and a highway paving contract between Matagami-LG2 and Chisasibi, *La Presse* reporter André Pepin states that, besides providing the Cree with cash compensation, the JBNQA also provided them with business opportunities:

> La Convention de la Baie James (art. 8.14.4), conclue en 1975 entre le gouvernement du Québec et la population autochtone, prévoit que des dispositions doivent être prises pour permettre aux bandes et entreprises cris de faire des offres pour des travaux de construction et des services correspondant à leurs qualifications et expérience ... L'interprétation de cet article oblige la SEBJ à faire appel aux Cris pour la construction de la route en question.

> The James Bay and Northern Québec Agreement (art. 8.14.4), entered into in 1975 by the government of Quebec and the Aboriginal population, asserts that provisions must be made in order to enable Cree bands and businesses to submit tenders for construction work and other services corresponding to their qualifications and experience ... The interpretation of this article obliges the SEBJ [James Bay Power Company] to call on the Crees for the construction of the road in question. (14 June 1989, a1)

The notion that the agreement gave the Cree a say in the development of their territory also surfaced in our sample, although infrequently. In the Hydro-Québec advertisement in the *New York Times*, the utility claimed that the JBNQA "leur donne une voix importante lorsque vient l'heure d'approuver les projets d'aménagement ... Enfin, elle en fait des partenaires importants du développement du térritoire sub-arctique au Québec (gives them a crucial voice when the time comes to approve the development projects ... It makes them important partners in the development of the sub-Arctic territories of Quebec)" (*P*, 28 October 1991, b3). In *Le Devoir*, Catherine Leconte stated that

> Les Cris et Inuit, eux, ont signé la Convention parce qu'ils voulaient contrôler leurs propres affaires. Ce qui supposait qu'ils aient une participation aux fruits du développement économique du territoire et un droit de regard sur la façon dont il serait mené, suffisamment larges pour qu'ils aient le choix d'y participer activement ou de continuer un mode de vie traditionnel qui reste viable.

> The Crees and the Inuit signed the Agreement because they wanted to control their own affairs. This presupposed their reaping the benefits of economic development and the inclusion of an inspection clause regarding the way in which it would be conducted, large enough for them to decide to actively participate or to continue with a more traditional, and still viable, way of life. (*D*, 18 September 1991, b1)

Finally, several references appeared in the news discourse regarding the beneficial effects of the JBNQA on Cree harvesting activities:

> The James Bay agreement ... brought the northern Cree a measure of autonomy and prosperity they had rarely known, and made it economically possible for many Indians to continue hunting, fishing and trapping. (Editorial, *G*, 10 August 1991, b2)

> "Les Cris font davantage de troc, de chasse et de pêche qu'ils ne le faisaient auparavant; ils le font pendant au moins 120 jours par année, grâce à la Convention de la Baie James," a lancé la ministre [Lise Bacon].

> "The Crees barter, hunt and fish more than ever – at least 120 days a year, thanks to the James Bay agreement," exclaimed the minister [Lise Bacon]. (G. Normand, *P*, 23 October 1991, a1)

> Hydro-Québec souligne aussi à quel point le Programme de sécurité du revenu, mis sur pied par la Convention de la Baie James, a aidé les Cris à passer à travers la crise qui a provoqué l'effondrement du marché de la fourrure, créé en grande partie par un certain écologisme.

> Hydro-Québec also emphasizes the extent to which the Income Security Programme, set up by the James Bay agreement, helped the Crees to get through the crisis that caused the collapse of the fur market, which resulted in large part from enviromentalism. (L.-G. Francoeur, *D*, 24 October 1991, a1)

Opponents of the Great Whale development did not speak as glowingly about the benefits of the agreement, but they did note some positive aspects, such as the Income Security Program and the political strength it gave to the Aboriginal peoples of northern Quebec. For example, one news report paraphrased Romeo Diom Saganash, vice-president of the Grand Council of the Crees, as follows: "ce programme de sécurité du revenu a eu un effet stabilisateur sur la pratique des activités traditionnelles qui étaient en declin au moment de la signature de la Convention de la Baie James, en 1975 (this Income Security Programme helped stabilize the practice of traditional activities which were in decline at the time of the signing of the James Bay agreement, in 1975)" (B. Bisson, *P*, 7 January 1991, a1). In another article, Matthew Mukash from the Cree community of Whapmagoostui (Great Whale) was quoted as saying "'the agreement has made us stronger than any other native community in Canada'" (B. Aubin, *G*, 9 November 1991, b3).

For the most part, however, opponents of Great Whale development have emphasized the problems associated with the agreement. Saganash was quoted in the context of an interview with *La Presse* as saying:

> "Nous vivons aussi depuis 15 ans avec une Convention qui ne nous a rien apporté sans que nous ayions à harceler le gouvernement." [...] Selon lui, les désillusions accumulées depuis la signature de la CBJNQA expliquent pourquoi le mouvement de contestation gronde si fort dans les communautés cries du Québec. Au cours de cette période, la pratique du mode de vie des Cris s'est maintenue artificiellement grâce à un programme de sécurité du revenu. L'inondation de milliers de kilomètres carrés, lors de l'aménagement du complexe La Grande, a perturbé la division des territoires de chasse et de pêche ancestraux, ce qui a entraîné de vives tensions dans certaines communautés. Les jeunes qui ont grandi sous le régime de la Convention sont aussi moins enclins à perpétuer les activités traditionnelles de leurs parents. Et pour eux, l'absence d'alternative économique a créé de sérieux problèmes d'intégration. Les cas de dépendance à l'alcool et aux drogues ont décuplé en moins de 10 ans.
>
> "For 15 years we have lived with the agreement and yet we have had to fight for everything we got from the government." [...] According to him, the disappointments accumulated since the signing of the JBNQA explain why the protest movement resonates so strongly in the Quebec Cree communities. During this period, the lifestyle practised by the Crees was artificially maintained thanks to an income security programme. The flooding of thousands of square kilometres, during the development of the La Grande complex, disrupted the division of the ancestral hunting and fishing lands, which led to serious tension in some communities. Those who grew up under the agreement are also less inclined to perpetuate their parents' traditional activities. And for them, the absence of economic alternatives created a serious integration problem. Cases of drug and alcohol addiction have increased tenfold in less than 10 years. (B. Bisson, *P*, 5 January 1991, a6)

In a direct challenge to statements attributed to Guy Versailles, a spokesperson for Hydro-Québec, Matthew Mukash wrote the following in a letter to the editor of the *Gazette* (26 January 1993, b2):

> I would like to clarify Mr. Versailles' propaganda that Hydro-Québec has provided benefits for the natives – "economic development and easier access to modern education and health-care services." The Cree had to sign the JBNQA that allowed the construction of the La Grande complex, disrupted

> their traditional way of life and increased social problems dramatically, in exchange for modern housing, education and health care that Canadians had enjoyed for centuries. What did Hydro-Québec give up? Nothing!

Here, Mukuash establishes a direct causal link between the agreement, environmental impacts, and "increased social problems."

> Since [the Cree signed the James Bay and Northern Québec Agreement] ... mercury pollution has made fish in neighbouring lakes inedible. The death of 10,000 caribou crossing the Caniapiscau River in 1984 has been blamed on poor reservoir management by Hydro-Québec. (P. Curran, *G*, 15 July 1989, b5)

Addressing the possibility of renegotiating the JBNQA, Brian Craik, an adviser to the Grand Council of the Crees, was quoted in the *Gazette* as saying, "the Cree see the negotiations as a chance to solve problems that the 1975 James Bay and Northern Quebec Agreement failed to address, such as regional government and economic development" (*G*, 21 January 1993, a6). This point was clarified in *La Presse* as follows:

> Parmi les problèmes les plus concrets on trouve encore 1200 familles cries qui "n'ont pas de maison" et qui vivent chez d'autres ou dans des abris, explique M. Craik. Deux des neuf communautés cries du Québec ne sont toujours pas approvisionnées par le réseau d'Hydro-Québec. Finalement on ne trouve qu'un centre communautaire pour toute la communauté de 12 000 personnes, dans un seul village. Or toutes ces situations sont en contradiction directe avec ce qui était prévu dans la convention de la Baie-James en 1975, explique M. Craik.

> Among the most concrete problems, there are still 1,200 Cree families who "have no home" and who live with others or in shelters, explains Mr. Craik. Two of the nine Cree communities in Quebec are still not supplied by Hydro-Québec. Finally, there is only one community centre for the whole population of 12,000 people, in one single village. All these situations are in direct contradiction with what was stipulated in the James Bay agreement in 1975, explains M. Craik. (*P*, 30 October 1992, b1)

It appears that the JBNQA, initiated as a "solution" to the Cree "problem," has failed to improve the living conditions in Cree communities. In this respect, the "problematic" agreement appears to have created a series of "second-order problems" – increased social problems, loss of traditional way of life, mercury pollution in fish, and an increase in housing shortages.

The representations by journalists in the news media serve to construct these problems by representing the effects of the agreement as both "beneficial" and "destructive" to the Cree way of life.

Propositions Dealing with the JBNQA and Environmental Impact Assessment

A third major topic in the news discourse surrounding the JBNQA is the environmental review of the Great Whale complex and other hydroelectric projects further south, including Laforge I and Eastmain I. We found ninety-two propositions that dealt with this topic in our sample and another fifty-seven references to environmental assessment that did not properly state propositions.

The exact nature of environmental impact assessment and the extent to which its terms are determined by the JBNQA were contested in the courts and in the news media throughout 1990 and most of 1991. The issue of whether the Canadian or Quebec governments, or both, were responsible for environmental impact hearings was introduced early on in the debate (*G*, 15 March 1990, a7). Journalists said that the JBNQA was "complicated" and "special" because it was signed by the Cree, Inuit, Canadian, and Quebec governments, and it was passed by both the federal and Quebec legislatures. Any assumption that the agreement would clarify responsibilities for the environmental review was frustrated by the apparent complexity of the agreement and the conflicting interests of the signatories.

As the debate over the Environmental Assessment Review Process (EARP) unfolded, a compromise was struck between the federal and Quebec governments to split the review into two parts – one dealing with the impact of project infrastructure (e.g., roads, airports), the other with the hydroelectric complex itself. Cree representatives successfully contested this position and won a court injunction preventing this division of the review process.

Both the Cree and defenders of dam construction made references to the JBNQA as a way of legitimizing their positions regarding the EARP. The agreement was used as an authoritative text to which opponents and proponents made reference in seeking support for their views: "The Cree contend that splitting the process is illegal. They say that the James Bay agreement calls for a full, independent environmental-impact hearing" (P. Authier, *G*, 19 September 1990, a6). Quebec environment minister, Pierre Paradis, at first vacillated, and then supported the proposition that the EARP could be split.

> Récemment, le ministre Paradis avait soutenu qu'il faudrait une étude globale sur tout le projet. Maintenant, il reconnaît qu'en vertu de la Conven-

> tion de la Baie James, un projet et ses infrastructures sont des projets distincts et doivent être évalués comme tel.
>
> Minister Paradis recently maintained that a comprehensive study would be needed for the whole project. Now he admits that, in light of the James Bay agreement, a project and its infrastructures are distinct projects and must be evaluated as such. (D. Lessard, *P*, 24 October 1990, a2)

At the time, the Parti Québécois took the same position as did the Cree. Parti Québécois critic for the environment, Denis Lazure, was quoted as saying: "'Le gros bon sens et l'esprit de la Convention de la Baie James, quoi qu'en dise le gouvernement libéral, dictent de procéder à une évaluation globale du projet et un consensus social s'est developée sur cette idée' ('Common sense and the spirit of the James Bay agreement, regardless of what the Liberal government says about it, direct us to proceed to a comprehensive evaluation of the project and a social consensus was developed from this idea')" (*D*, 12 July 1991, a4). With the exception of Pierre Paradis's change of position, both Cree and government-Hydro-Québec representatives asserted that the JBNQA was clear and unambiguous on the matter of splitting the EARP. When juxtaposed, however, their competing assertions served only to reaffirm the vagueness and ambiguity of the text of the agreement.

In addition to appeals to the JBNQA by government, Hydro-Québec, and Cree representatives were those put forth by journalists, who made consistent rhetorical use of the agreement in such a way as to legitimize the various committees overseeing the review process. The terms defining the structure and composition of the environmental assessment commissions, like the review process itself, are repeatedly referred to as being set by or stipulated in the JBNQA, pointing once again to an authoritative role for the agreement. From articles dating to the latter part of 1990 and throughout 1991, we are told that environmental commissions owe their origin to the JBNQA: the Kativik Environmental Quality Commission is "a body set up for the Inuit under the 1975 Agreement"; the Cree Review Committee was "set up for the Cree under the 1975 agreement and has three members from Quebec, and two Cree members" (*G*, 27 March 1991, a1, a2). In addition, we are told of the special rules and provisions stipulated under the agreement, such as the rotation of a committee chairperson from Ottawa, Quebec, and the Cree.

It is far beyond the scope of this study to determine how such details concerning the EARP and the JBNQA are read by the average news consumer. However, if such a reader understands anything about the environmental review provisions of the agreement, it is that they are extremely complex and open to multiple interpretations. That the Cree interpretation won out, and became the dominant one in the print media,[11] was facilitated by Judge Rouleau's judgment requiring a single assessment process. In this case, both the JBNQA and Rouleau's interpretation of it made the Cree proposition regarding the EARP the dominant one.

Conclusion

Media accounts play a crucial role in the construction of knowledge of particular events and policies concerning Aboriginal peoples and Canadian judicial and political processes. As van Dijk (1991, 7) notes, media in general "convey public knowledge, as well as expressed or implicit opinions, about social groups and events most majority group members have little direct knowledge about." Media, and those who control the means of symbolic production, provide "ideological frameworks" for the interpretation of events and play "a decisive role in the development of the ideologies of the population at large" (37-8; see also Herman and Chomsky 1988). However, as we have attempted to demonstrate in this chapter, the news media can be a highly conflictual political arena, wherein the players in public controversies attempt to insert preferred meanings into public discourse. Given this observation, the preferred meanings of the key players in these controversies will find some form of expression in news texts; however, the degree to which a given meaning prevails is determined by a host of factors. Given the limits of the present discussion, we can only note that these factors might include the relative skill of the players in developing and exploiting financial, communicative, and other resources; the practical limits of news work; and the ideologies of the media personnel themselves.

Our analysis of Quebec news media coverage of the JBNQA has, we hope, shed light on the role of authoritative texts – in this case, the agreement – in the social construction of public "problems." Given the great legal significance of the JBNQA, the vast territory, natural resources, and peoples it encompasses, it is not at all surprising that it should lend itself to divergent interpretations and that it should constitute a foundational, authoritative text upon which political combatants will stake the credibility of one or another proposition.

The data presented in this chapter show how the JBNQA has been constructed as a public "problem" in its own right because of the numerous failings attributed to it by Cree representatives. News texts have presented the Cree as seeking solutions to this problem in the form of a renegotiation of the agreement and litigation to force governments to respect its provisions (e.g., EARP). But our data also point to the role of the agreement in the construction of other public problems, which we have referred to as second-order problems. These include the potential environmental, social, and economic impacts of the Great Whale hydroelectric project, which require intervention and corrective action. They also include the Cree themselves because of their vocal opposition to this project – their international campaigning, challenges to the Parti Québécois sovereignty project, and threats to Hydro-Québec's financial markets in the United States.

Within this context the JBNQA is used by opponents and defenders of Great Whale as a rhetorical device to give credibility to their arguments. In effect, they argue that a given proposition must be valid because it appears in the JBNQA. Thus the agreement serves as an authoritative text, a "bible" used to legitimize various claims in the debate over Great Whale. The news texts are but the surface manifestations of rhetorical strategies designed to shape public attitudes about the issue.

Our data also reveal that the JBNQA has not ended the "Indian problem" in northern Quebec. Land claims agreements have been conceived of as a way of settling grievances and working within a system of fair exchange; that is, of compensating Aboriginal peoples for ceding their land. Historically, the signing of treaties and land claims agreements has been considered a peaceful means of reconciling radically different aspirations and models about how land should be used. From a Euro-Canadian perspective, treaties have been seen as a means to (1) clear the way for peaceful occupation of Aboriginal lands, (2) help Aboriginal peoples to make the transition to "civilized" society, (3) provide some measure of protection for Aboriginal harvesting practices, and (4) provide a measure of compensation for the extinguishment of Aboriginal rights to the land. In sum, land claims agreements have been seen as an equitable solution to the "Indian problem" in this country (Dyck 1991).

Treaty making involving Aboriginal peoples, however, has always been based on a fundamental power imbalance between the state and the Aboriginal peoples who find themselves caught within the bounds of expanding nation-states. The processes that underlie the negotiation, interpretation, and implementation of treaties or agreements depend on what the terms of these agreements mean in practice. Given divergent expectations about what an agreement should provide in the way of rights, benefits, and constraints, it is not surprising that signatories quickly end up with very different interpretations of the agreement's provisions. From the government's perspective, the main purpose of a land claims agreement is to eliminate any lingering doubts about ownership of land so that it may be freed up for resource development and settlement. Aboriginal peoples, on the other hand, hope that such agreements will protect their land, wildlife, and culture for future generations.

Since the famous 1969 White Paper on Indian Affairs, Aboriginal peoples have increasingly had to mobilize, using the political rules of Euro-Canadian society in order to protect their lands and cultures, and to obtain access to services provided to non-Aboriginal groups throughout the country. In response, federal and provincial governments have channelled Aboriginal demands into land claims negotiations and the bureaucratic structures that flow from them. In the case of the James Bay Cree, evidence of the bureaucratization of their efforts to defend their rights, land, and culture is found in the great number of news texts in our sample that dealt with the environmental assessment of hydroelectric developments and the legal wrangling underlying it. The news texts also show that the JBNQA became a gigantic legal battleground on which the Cree, federal and Quebec governments, Hydro-Québec, and other players strive to impose their interpretations of the agreement's provisions.

Our data have revealed that the JBNQA gives rise not only to multiple, competing interpretations, but also to the emergence of certain dominant propositions regarding the agreement and the rights, benefits, and problems that have resulted from it. What this means is that the reading public will be inclined to conclude that the JBNQA extinguished Cree and Inuit rights in northern Quebec and that it provided them with huge amounts of money, services, and special hunting rights. What this public will tend not to recognize, however, are the great social costs that the agreement itself has brought to Aboriginal communities, not to mention the very real difficulties that its language has created for the resolution of future conflicts. Not least of these, as alluded to above, is the question of Aboriginal sovereignty within a sovereign Quebec.

Notes

An earlier version of this chapter was presented at the Canadian Anthropology Society (CASCA) conference, Université du Québec à Montréal, May 1995. The order of the authors' names does not reflect the amount of time devoted to this chapter; it was written as a collaborative effort, and the work was shared equally. The authors would like to thank Cathy James and Benjamin Shaer for comments on an earlier draft of this chapter.

1 Since the Grand Council of the Crees has reached institutional status and has an institutional presence in the news media, we consider discourse from this source to be "official" rather than "marginal" (in contrast, for example, to that produced by grassroots protest organizations).

2 Limiting our search to files of clippings might conceivably have biased our database towards the preoccupations of the organizations for which the original clipping was made. However, by searching the files of a range of organizations that hold various positions in the debate, we have minimized such bias.

3 We have attempted to alert the reader to this distinction throughout our analysis by making use of such formulae as "statements were attributed to" or "according to journalist." These formulae are, of course, cumbersome, and we have abandoned them in favour of direct attribution wherever a particular actor is reported to have made a particular statement (e.g., "Robert Bourassa stated that").

4 Emphasis in all quotations is ours. References to individual newspapers are abbreviated as follows: *D* = *Le Devoir*, *P* = *La Presse*, and *G* = the *Gazette*.

5 Even in such ground-breaking Supreme Court decisions as *Sparrow*, Canadian jurisprudence has steadfastly adhered to a "settlement thesis," which holds that whatever rights Aboriginal peoples held after contact existed at the pleasure of the Crown and were

usufructuary. Their sovereignty, if such a thing existed in pre-contact times, was automatically extinguished when their lands were claimed for European sovereigns (see Asch and Macklem 1991).

6 In the frequency analysis we conducted, the maximum number of occurrences of any one proposition was thirty-six, so that the sum of twenty-three for the extinguishment proposition is not unusually low; rather, its frequency was on the high end of the scale.

7 Hamilton conflates land claims and land rights. The JBNQA presumably extinguished Cree land rights thereby preventing any future legal claims (assertions of ownership) that would interfere with the Crown's jurisdiction. Paradoxically, Aboriginal rights to the land are recognized only to the extent that they are extinguished in a land claims agreement and replaced with "legislated" rights enshrined in the Canadian Constitution.

8 Our sample contained fourteen references to this proposition.

9 The coalition consisted of the Grand Council of the Crees, Greenpeace, and other environmental organizations.

10 However, the assertion by Cree leaders that the James Bay I hydroelectric development had caused such social and health problems was challenged by Université Laval sociologist Jean-Jacques Simard and certain proponents of Great Whale (see below). They argued that the problems were inevitable consequences of modernization and that Aboriginal peoples across Canada were experiencing them.

11 The dominance of this interpretation is demonstrated by editorial opinion, the dropping of attribution by journalists, and so on. Thirty-six texts in our sample contained propositions dealing with the necessity for federal involvement in the EARP, while another twenty-four dealt with the issue of splitting the review between infrastructure and the dam complex (including opposition and support for splitting).

References

Arcand, Bernard. 1988. "Un dossier aux multiples intervenants." In *Baie James et Nord Québécois: Dix ans après*, ed. S. Vincent and G. Bowers, 167-8. Montréal: Recherches amérindiennes au Québec.

Asch, Michael, and Patrick Macklem. 1991. "Aboriginal Rights and Canadian Sovereignty: An Essay on *R. v. Sparrow*." *Alberta Law Review* 29, 2: 500-20.

Coates, Ken, ed. 1992. *Aboriginal Land Claims in Canada: A Regional Perspective*. Toronto: Copp Clark Pitman.

Dyck, Noel. 1986. "Negotiating the Indian 'Problem.'" *Culture* 6, 1: 31-42.

–. 1991. *What Is the Indian "Problem": Tutelage and Resistance in Canadian Indian Administration*. St. John's: Institute of Social and Economic Research, Memorial University of Newfoundland.

–. 1993. "'Telling It Like It Is': Some Dilemmas of Fourth World Ethnography and Advocacy." In *Anthropology, Public Policy and Native Peoples in Canada*, ed. N. Dyck and J. Waldram, 192-212. Montreal/Kingston: McGill-Queen's University Press.

Ericson, R.V., P.M. Baranek, and J.B.L. Chan. 1989. *Negotiating Control: A Study of News Sources*. Toronto: University of Toronto Press.

Feit, Harvey. 1985. "Legitimation and Autonomy in James Bay Cree Responses to Hydro-Electric Development." In *Indigenous Peoples and the Nation-State: Fourth World Politics in Canada, Australia and Norway*, ed. Noel Dyck, 27-66. St. John's, NF: Institute of Social and Economic Research, Memorial University of Newfoundland.

Hall, Stuart, 1980. "Encoding/Decoding," In *Culture, Media, Language: Working Papers in Cultural Studies, 1972-79*, ed. S. Baron, M. Denning, S. Hall, D. Hobson, A. Lowe, and P. Willis, 128-38. London: Hutchison.

–. 1992. "The West and the Rest: Discourse and Power." In *Formations of Modernity*, ed. Stuart Hall and Bram Gieben, 275-332. Cambridge: Polity Press.

Herman, Edward S., and Noam Chomsky. 1988. *Manufacturing Consent: The Political Economy of the Mass Media*. New York: Pantheon Books.

Miller, Karen. 1992. "Smoking up a Storm: Public Relations and Advertising in the Construction of the Cigarette Problem, 1953-1954." *Journalism Monographs* 136 (December): 1-35.

Morantz, Toby. 1992. "Aboriginal Land Claims in Quebec." In *Aboriginal Land Claims in Canada: A Regional Perspective*, ed. K. Coates, 101-30. Toronto: Copp Clark Pitman.

O'Reilly, James. 1988. "The Role of the Courts in the Evolution of the James Bay Hydroelectric Project." In *Baie James et Nord Québécois: Dix ans après*, ed. S. Vincent and G. Bowers, 34. Montréal: Recherches amérindiennes au Québec.

Quebec. 1976. *The James Bay and Northern Québec Agreement*. Quebec: Editeur officiel du Québec.

Salisbury, Richard F. 1986. *A Homeland for the Cree: Regional Development in James Bay 1971-1981*. Montreal: McGill-Queen's University Press.

Sauvageau, Florian, Pierre Trudel, and Marie-Hélène Lavoie. 1995. *Les tribuns de la radio: Echos de la crise d'Oka*. Québec: Institut québécois de recherche sur la culture.

Seidel, Gill. 1985. "Political Discourse Analysis." In *Handbook of Discourse Analysis*, vol. 4, ed. Teun A. van Dijk, 43-60. London: Academic Press.

van Dijk, Teun A. 1991. *Racism and the Press*. London: Routledge.

Vincent, Sylvie, and Garry Bowers, eds. 1988. *Baie James et Nord Québécois: Dix ans après*. Montréal: Recherches amérindiennes au Québec.

12
Low-Level Military Flight Training in Quebec-Labrador: The Anatomy of a Northern Development Conflict

Mary Barker

Vocal public protests and logistical airspace constraints have prompted three of Canada's European NATO partners to transfer some low-level flight training activities from their own densely populated nations to the thinly settled Quebec-Labrador peninsula. There, the perception (shared by Canadian military planners and most Europeans) of wide open, empty terrain ideal for flying low-level sorties, along with the current dependency of the local wage economy on the military presence, is juxtaposed with concerns about environmental, health, and socio-cultural impacts; the efforts of regional Aboriginal organizations to assert rights to land, resources, and self-determination; and the protests of Canadian church, peace, and Aboriginal support groups opposed to military activities in the North. For some local supporters and opponents the conflict is existential because livelihoods are seen to be threatened. Among other, more distant, less issue-specific protagonists, the outcome of the dispute will not be felt so directly. This chapter describes the low-level flight training project and the decision-making process determining its future; defines the regional context within which the conflict has developed; and explores the range of issues, stakeholders, and viewpoints involved at the local, regional, and national levels within Canada.

The central themes of the conceptual framework used to identify and assess components of the conflict are shown in Figure 12.1. (This chapter focuses on some but not all of these elements.) At the macro-scale, the fundamental issues concern sustainable resource use, centre-periphery relations, and the relations between Euro-Canadian and Aboriginal cultures and economies: an issue-complex common to many resource developments in the northern frontier-homeland (Berger 1977; Saunders 1990; Bone 1992). At the supra-regional scale, the origin, dynamics, and outcomes of resource conflicts are influenced by a complex interplay of factors revolving around the legal-institutional framework governing ownership and access to resources and the relative political empowerment of stakeholder groups.

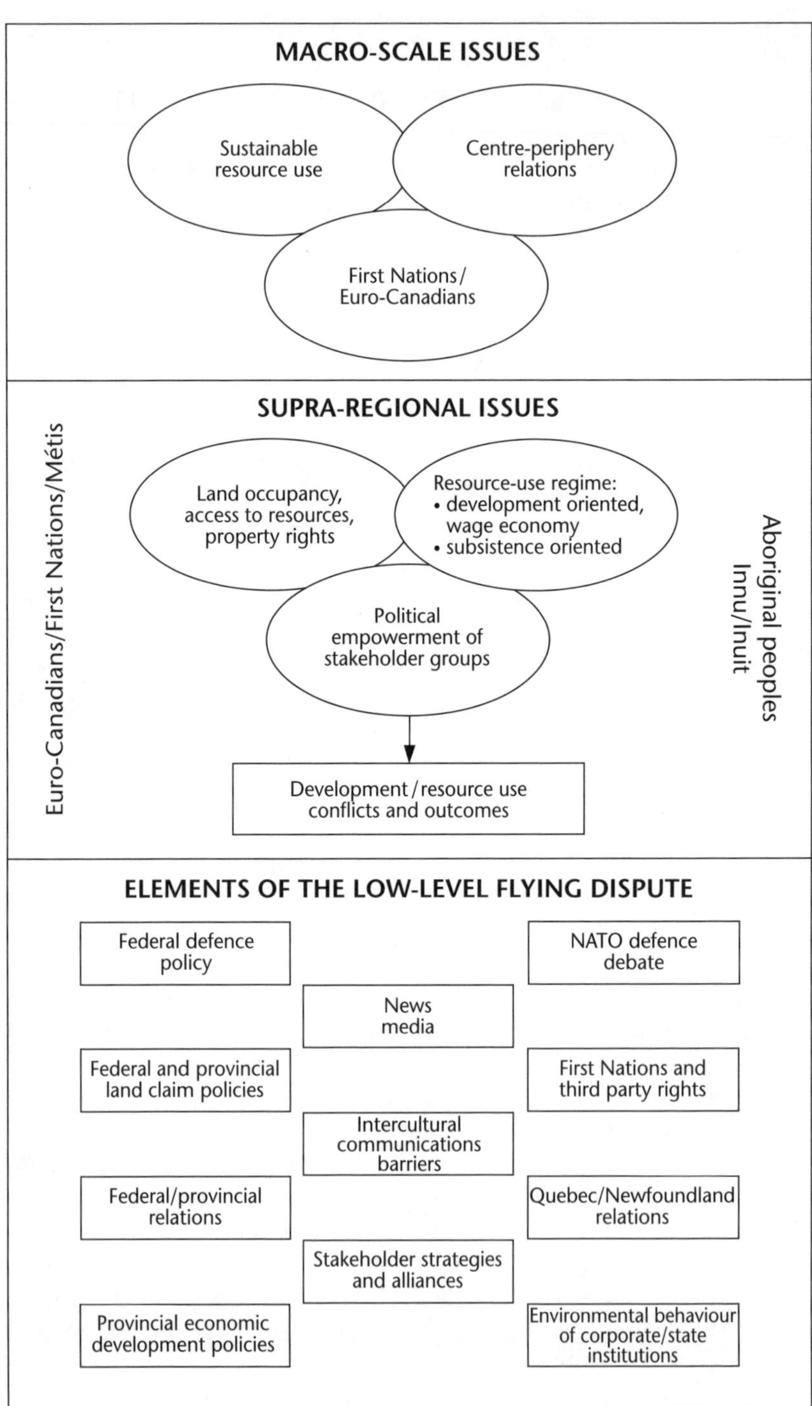

Figure 12.1 Conceptual framework

In this particular case, an array of local, regional, national, and even transnational factors is involved. Some themes, for example Canadian defence policy and the debate over the future role of NATO in the new world security relations, are specific to the military flight training conflict. Most others, however, are shared in common with many resource-use and development conflicts, ranging from the clear-cut logging of first-growth forest stands on the west coast and the boreal forest throughout the Canadian provincial subarctic to the construction of the Oldman River Dam in Alberta and the James Bay hydroelectric project in Quebec.[1] All of these cases have involved the question of defining and balancing Aboriginal rights with those of other Canadians; the environmental behaviour of corporations and state institutions (in this particular example, the Canadian Department of National Defence); the role of the news media; the strategies adopted by stakeholders in the dispute; and intercultural communication barriers stemming from differences in language, values, and knowledge systems (Freeman/Carbyn 1988; Lalonde 1991). Within this context it is important not to focus exclusively on the gaps between Aboriginals and non-Aboriginals at the expense of neglecting variation (relating to perceptions, values, and aspirations) within Euro-Canadian, Aboriginal, and Métis populations.

Regional Context

Military planners see the Quebec-Labrador peninsula and the Canadian Forces Base at Goose Bay (Labrador) as offering suitable terrain and the necessary infrastructure for low-level flight training. In particular, the absence of permanent settlements within the two designated training areas (100,000 square kilometres in total) is seen as a great advantage over densely populated Europe. The river valleys incised into the Canadian Shield landscape, shifting gradually from boreal forest cover in the south to subarctic tundra in the north, are particularly attractive for military flight training at heights as low as thirty metres above the surface.

Biological productivity and species diversity are generally limited by the harsh physical conditions (Luttich 1986): soils are poorly developed and acidic and the winters are cold and long (with up to eight months of snow-ice cover). Some wildlife species are characterized by large populations, albeit subject to dramatic periodic fluctuations. For example, the George River caribou herd is currently one of the largest in North America. Accurate long-term records are lacking, but the herd is thought to have grown from 15,000 animals in the late 1950s to over 600,000 by the late 1980s (Bergerud 1967; Canada, Department of National Defence 1989). Based on the most recent census data, the herd population is currently estimated to be over 500,000 (Canada, Department of National Defence 1994; Labrador Institute of Northern Studies 1994). The herd has calving grounds on the northern Labrador peninsula but follows a seasonal migration across the entire Quebec-Labrador peninsula (Figure 12.2). Other smaller caribou herds occupy more confined ranges, mainly in the southern boreal forest zone.

The caribou were a key component of traditional Aboriginal subsistence culture. Small nomadic First Nations bands belonging to the Algonquian language group (and now known as the Montagnais and Naskapi in Quebec, and the Innu in Labrador) pursued a hunting-gathering economy with seasonal camps in the interior and near river mouths along the coast (Henriksen 1973; Mailhot 1986; Quebec 1984). Along the coast of Labrador and northern Quebec, the Inuit population had a subsistence culture tied to fishing as well as hunting sea mammals and caribou (Brice-Bennett 1977). Their seasonal coastal occupancy means that the Inuit have had a long history of contact with whalers and coastal missionary stations. Many of the interior Aboriginal peoples have been sedentary only since the federal government settlement policies of the 1950s and 1960s. Approximately 9,000

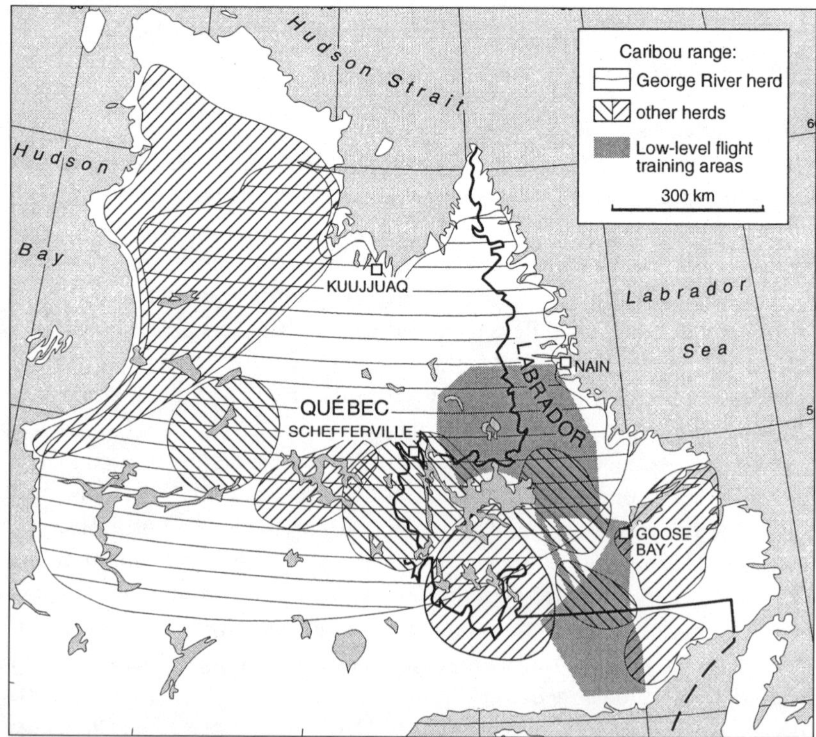

Figure 12.2 The Quebec-Labrador Peninsula (after Canada, Department of National Defence, 1994, p. S-23)

Montagnais now live in nine communities along the Quebec North Shore, the small Naskapi band lives in a community near Schefferville (Quebec), and the 1,100 Labrador Innu live in two communities, Sheshatshiu (fifty kilometres from Goose Bay) and Davis Inlet on the coast. Over 4,500 Inuit and *Kablunangajuit* ("not quite Whites") live in coastal Labrador communities and in Happy Valley-Goose Bay. Three Aboriginal organizations, the Conseil Attikamek-Montagnais (in Quebec), the Innu Nation (in Labrador), and the Labrador Inuit Association, are currently conducting separate negotiations with the federal and respective provincial governments over their comprehensive land claims based on traditional land use and occupancy of the Quebec-Labrador peninsula (Figure 12.3).[2] While the Aboriginal population now lives in permanent settlements along the coast (with the exception of the Naskapi near Schefferville), a proportion continues to pursue seasonal hunting, fishing, and gathering activities from temporary camps in the interior, where low-level flying takes place (Armitage 1992; Rowell 1992). Other long-term residents, both Euro-Canadians and Métis (known locally in Labrador as "Settlers") also hunt, fish, and trap in the country.

Labrador alone has a total population of 30,000 (of which 8,000 live in Labrador City and 7,500 in Happy Valley-Goose Bay). The region has a dual economy: resource projects and related services keyed into the southern industrial economy (e.g., mining, logging, hydroelectric power development, military flying) and a subsistence economy that provides country food (e.g., game) and plays an important cultural role but that depends on wages and transfer payments to cover the costs of equipment and transport (Usher 1982; Brice-Bennett 1986). A similar general pattern exists in the Quebec portion of the peninsula, although the North Shore (of the St. Lawrence River) tends to be more accessible and large tracts have been alienated for forestry and hydroelectric projects (Charest 1982). The first mega-project development began in the 1950s, with iron-ore mining at Schefferville (mine closure 1983), Labrador City, and Wabush. A second phase occurred in the 1970s, with the construction of the Churchill Falls hydroelectric project (including flooding of land to create the Smallwood Reservoir) in Labrador and the expansion of large-scale logging operations into the interior of Quebec. Oil and gas exploration offshore in the Labrador Sea and uranium exploration in central Labrador proved short-lived. Both the capital requirements and market responsiveness of large resource projects and the reliance of the subsistence sector of the dual economy on wage and transfer payments underline the dependency relationship between the Quebec-Labrador peninsula and southern Canada. In Labrador alone, over the last fifteen years, changes have been brought about by improved transportation access, the establishment of commercial hunting and fishing camps, mineral exploration activities, and the construction of North Warning System radar stations along the coast (e.g., at Saglek). There is a long-term plan for another large-scale hydroelectric development (the Lower Churchill project). Most recently, there have been improvements to the Trans-Labrador Highway linking Sept Îles and Goose Bay, proposals to extend this road and to construct a snowmobile trail link to the coast, to build a small wood processing plant at Cartwright to exploit local timber

Figure 12.3 Comprehensive land claims (after Canada, Department of Indian and Northern Affairs, 1994)

reserves, and to create two new national parks in the Mealy and Torngat Mountains (Figure 12.4). A massive mineral discovery at Voisey Bay (on the Labrador coast south of Nain) was announced in November 1994. This rich nickel-copper-cobalt find resulted in an exploration and claim-staking boom in the region, with the prospect of large-scale mining operations should the reserves prove to be feasible at prevailing world mineral prices. Many developments and project proposals involve questions about resource ownership and user rights as well as about balancing economic benefits against cumulative impacts (e.g., threat of critical habitat loss, pollution, increased hunting competition). Although military flight training does not fit neatly into the category of a resource-construction project, this particular activity should be viewed within the broader context of developments resulting in cumulative environmental and cultural changes.

Low-Level Flight Training

A military base was established at Goose Bay (Labrador) as a wartime staging post. It was used for Allied flight training in the 1950s, but its strategic role had shrunk by the 1960s (Canada, Department of National Defence 1989, S-l). This changed in 1979-80, when the British expanded and the German airforce began low-level flight training at Goose Bay. In 1986, Canada formalized this arrangement by signing a Multinational Memorandum of Understanding (MMOU) with the United States, the United Kingdom, and the Federal Republic of Germany, permitting them to station personnel and aircraft at Goose Bay for low-altitude flight training. In 1987, the Netherlands joined the MMOU, while the United States withdrew a few years later. The rationale for allowing the European partners to fly in Canada is twofold: First, NATO's earlier Follow-On Forces Attack (FOFA), or Deep Strike strategy, designed to penetrate behind Warsaw Pact forces in a European combat arena, would have required low-level flights to avoid ground-based radar detection. In the 1990s, low-level flight training was still considered to be indispensable by military planners who cite the need to guarantee European security and to support global peace-keeping interventions. Second, public safety considerations and growing protests against low-level flight training in western Europe led to the search for alternative locations in less densely populated regions (Spaven 1991; Mende 1994).

In the early 1980s, two Low-Level Training Areas (67,000 square kilometres and 32,000 square kilometres, respectively, and linked by airspace corridors) were designated in Labrador and eastern Quebec (Figures 12.2 and 12.4). Low-level training sorties, defined as flights flown at less than 300 metres above ground level, focus on navigation, manoeuvering, and target-bombing with non-explosive weapons in two Practice Target Areas. In designated areas, sorties are flown as low as thirty metres above the surface.

The MMOU permits a training season of up to thirty-six weeks between March and October/November. A maximum of 18,000 sorties is allowed under the agreement, but the current number varies between 6,000 and 8,000 per year. In 1992, for example, 8,400 training sorties were flown, 87 percent at low levels and a small proportion at night (Canada, Department of National Defence 1994, S-6). Noise levels may exceed 125 decibels,

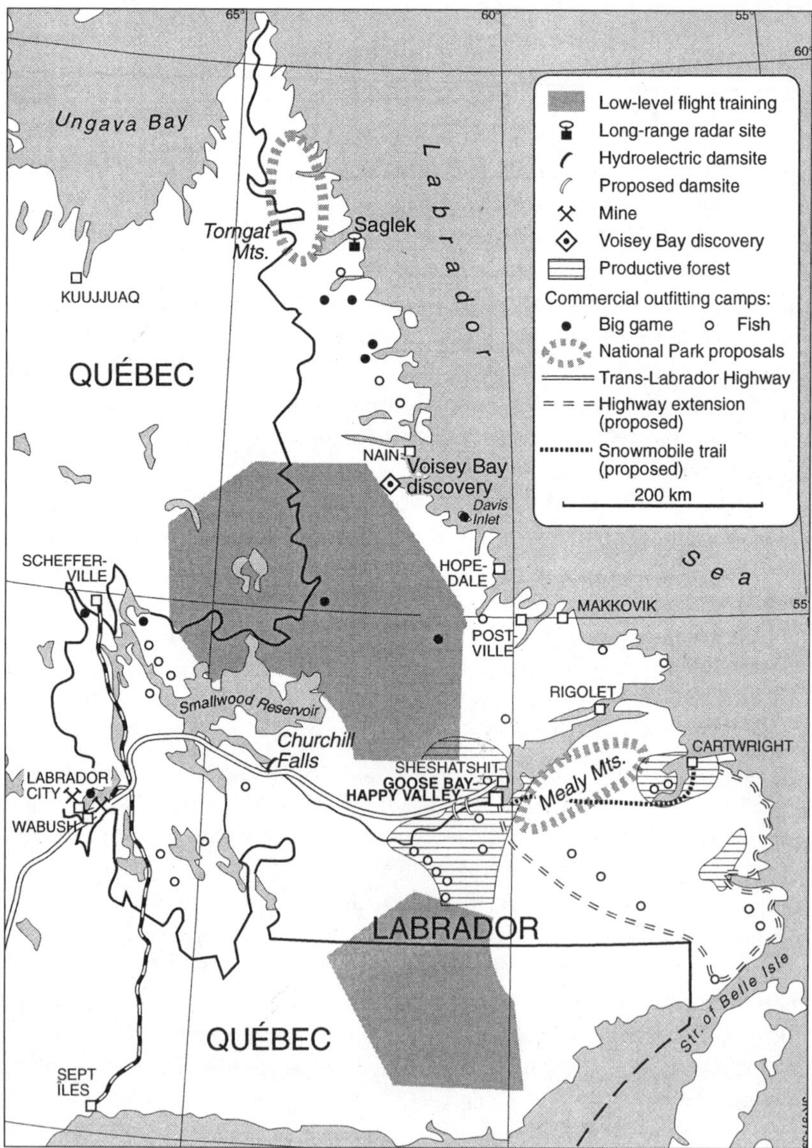

Figure 12.4 Resource use and development initiatives in Labrador

depending on the height of the fighter aircraft and distance from the observer. By the early 1980s, Canada was under pressure from other NATO members to increase its commitment to the organization. In 1984, it submitted a bid to locate a proposed NATO tactical training centre at Goose Bay in competition with another bid for an alternative location at Konya, Turkey. The tactical training centre, if located at Goose Bay, would have involved up to 40,000 training flights a year, an offshore bombing range in the Labrador Sea, and the use of live weapons. NATO dropped this proposal in 1991 in response to profound shifts in the world strategic balance of power. The Canadian Department of National Defence abandoned this second component but continued to provide logistical support for low-level flight training in Labrador and eastern Quebec.

In 1990, the proponent introduced a set of mitigative measures designed to avoid low-level overflights of people and sensitive wildlife species (e.g., caribou, waterfowl, and raptors) and critical habitats (e.g., calving grounds in season). It developed a satellite monitoring program designed to track the seasonal movements of caribou; a GIS mapping system to plot flight patterns, land uses, and wildlife distributions as well as standardized criteria for avoiding sensitive species: once a designated threshold had been reached, the affected area was to be closed to low-level overflights. Two toll-free telephone lines were provided for resource users to notify the Department of National Defence when they intended to enter the flight training areas: hunting and fishing camps, for example, were not to be overflown at low-levels within a radius of 4.6 kilometres (2.5 nautical miles). A resource user advisory group was set up at Goose Bay as a forum for exchanging information before and after (but not during) each training season. A memorandum of understanding (MOU) was also signed with the Labrador Inuit Association, aimed primarily at improving and formalizing an exchange of information about flights, wildlife habitat and movements, and land-use activities.

In 1992, the airspace closures resulting from the mitigation-avoidance program ranged from 6 percent of the low-level training areas in April to 38 percent in October. These restrictions have been heavily criticized by the European flyers – to the point where they have questioned the cost effectiveness and operational viability of the entire program. In 1994, the Department of National Defence proposed two alternatives: either to reduce the scope of the avoidance program within the two existing training areas or to retain the current avoidance standards and redesign the configuration of the training areas by expanding some boundaries and contracting others.

At the present level of activity, the flight training program is a major contributor to the regional economy of Labrador. In 1992, 1,600 military and civilian personnel were employed at the Canadian Forces Base at Goose Bay, and base expenditures reached almost $130 million, approximately 65 percent of which were contributed by the three Allied nations (Canada, Department of National Defence 1994; Newfoundland and Labrador 1993). The proponent and key project supporters, such as the provincial government, the local chamber of commerce, and the Town Council of Happy Valley-Goose Bay, warned that the economic future would be bleak if this source of employment, direct revenues, business, and infrastructural spin-offs in central Labrador were to be lost as a result of the withdrawal of the low-level flight training activities.

Deciding the Future of Low-Level Flight Training

In 1986, the Department of National Defence, in its role as project proponent, referred the military flight training program to the federal minister of the environment. This step conformed to the much criticized federal Environmental Assessment and Review Guidelines Order-in-Council (1984), which called for a public review of all federal projects that had potentially significant environmental impacts or that generated sufficient public concern (Barker 1990). The weakness of these guidelines lay in their discretionary nature and in their emphasis on the self-assessment of the proponent. The Department of National Defence had already conducted an internal self-assessment of the project (Landry 1981), but, by the mid-80s, public concerns and opposition had received considerable media attention. On 21 March 1986, the minister of the environment announced a full public review to assess the environmental and socio-economic impacts of the project and to recommend measures to minimize any negative effects. Two issues, Aboriginal land claims and Canada's defence policy, were excluded from the terms of reference. An independent environmental assessment panel was appointed and charged with preparing guidelines for the preparation of an environmental impact study by the proponent, conducting the public review process, and submitting recommendations to the minister of the environment. According to the Guidelines Order-in-Council (1984), the minister of national defence had the ultimate responsibility for accepting or rejecting the recommendations of the minister of the environment; however, in the case of disagreement, the matter was to be referred to Cabinet for decision.

After a series of community meetings in Labrador and Quebec, the Environmental Assessment Panel released comprehensive guidelines for the environmental impact study. On 7 January 1987, the panel chair requested clarification of the panel mandate and proposed two interim steps: (1) if the impacts could not be mitigated, then the panel sought the right to recommend severe restrictions even to the point of stopping the project; and (2) the ongoing flight program was not to exceed the 1986 level, with minimum altitude and timing restrictions for certain areas (Barnes 1987). The minister of national defence objected to any prejudgments on the basis of unsubstantiated evidence and the minister of the environment subsequently reaffirmed the original mandate limited to making recommendations on mitigative measures; however, he expressed the hope that the panel would identify any effects that could not be mitigated in order to assist the government in making its final decision on the project (Beatty 1987; McMillan 1987). On 31 October 1989, the Department of National Defence released the environmental impact study prepared by its consultants. After a three-month public review period, during which 120 written submissions were filed, the panel rejected the study as inadequate and released a list of deficiencies along with recommendations for capping the 1990 flights at the 1986 level and for setting up an impact monitoring program. Later, at the end of 1990, the minister of national defence announced that the NATO tactical training centre proposal had been withdrawn and requested that the public review address only the low-level flight training activities permissible under the MMOU signed in 1986. In mid-1991, the minister of the environment instructed the panel accordingly; it issued a revised deficiency statement calling for an overhaul of the 1989 environmental impact study, dealing only with this first component.

The revised study was released on 21 April 1994, and the ninety-day public review period began. After assessing the study and receiving over 850 public comments on it, the panel announced a round of hearings with sixteen community sessions in Labrador and Quebec planned for the fall of 1994. The Department of National Defence was anxious that the environmental assessment and review process be concluded: it had agreed not to increase the flight activities, not to enter into agreements with other interested partners (e.g., Italy and Belgium), and not to begin negotiating the renewal of the ten-year MMOU (due to run out in 1996) until the review was completed. Germany, Britain, and the Netherlands were also awaiting the outcome. Time was running short.

Issues and Stakeholders

There is a recognizable interplay between the specific nature of the project and its setting; the issues raised and how the interests and concerns have been articulated; and the nature, motives, and strategies of the various actors involved in the conflict.[3] The protagonists include, on the one hand, those in favour of the project because of military and regional economic benefits (e.g., the Department of National Defence as project proponent, the three NATO partners, the provincial government of Newfoundland and Labrador, and the Town Council of Happy Valley-Goose Bay) and, on the other hand, critics and opponents of the project, ranging from regional Aboriginal organizations, Aboriginal support groups, church organizations, and the Canadian peace movement to women's groups and representatives of selected legal and medical associations. Interestingly, the environmental movement in Canada has played a conspicuously minor role. Once again, care should be taken not to label all the participants as either totally for or totally against the project: the conflict has become highly politicized, and it is far easier to identify the pole positions among the protagonists than to recognize the undertones, particularly at the local level.

As the dispute has evolved over the last ten years, the key issues have concerned questions about:

(1) peace and security requirements (i.e., NATO policy and the justification for low-level flight training in Canada);
(2) Aboriginal rights and comprehensive land claims;
(3) future viability of the regional economy;
(4) health impacts of noise, particularly the "startle effect" of low-flying aircraft;
(5) environmental impacts, especially the effects of noise on wildlife and the accumulation of pollutants in the food-chain;
(6) socio-cultural impacts on Aboriginal, Métis, and Euro-Canadian populations (the military presence and the role of women has become one component of the debate); and
(7) the proponent's program to mitigate or avoid impacts.

The objective of the environmental assessment process has been to address all of these issues except defence policy and Aboriginal land claims. Nevertheless, some critics and opponents have focused on these very aspects: the peace movement has attacked NATO policy and the justification for low-level flight training in Canada. Some peace, church, and Aboriginal support groups have identified the project as another example of the "militarization of the North" and have called for a broader definition of security – one that includes the well-being of Aboriginal peoples (Regehr and Robinson 1989; Armitage 1991). The Aboriginal Rights Coalition (an affiliation of church organizations formerly known as Project North) labelled Canada as the "Amazon of the North" in its lobbying campaign, which tried to draw parallels between the pattern of development in Brazil and the impacts of energy projects, logging, and military activities on Aboriginal populations in Canada (Angus 1991; Aboriginal Rights Coalition 1992). Aboriginal organizations and some support groups have raised moral arguments about unceded territorial rights and the legal question of whether the ongoing project might prejudice any future land claims settlements (Armitage 1989; Andersen 1990; Rowell 1990). The debate over economic, environmental, and socio-cultural impacts as well as the proponent's impact avoidance program has tended to focus on basic differences in values and on substantive questions about the quality of data, standards of evidence, and the relative value of scientific and traditional knowledge.

Groups, organizations, and individuals with both project-specific interests and broader agendas have been involved in the conflict; the authorship and spatial distribution of the 120 submissions to the Environmental Assessment Panel commenting on the first environmental impact study (1989) are symptomatic (Figure 12.5). Of the fifty-six organizations and interest groups that submitted comments, 39 percent were affiliated with the Canadian peace movement, 9 percent were regional Aboriginal organizations (the Inuit and Innu in Labrador; the Inuit, Montagnais, and Naskapi in Quebec), and 7 percent were national or regionally based Aboriginal support groups with academic, church, or professional memberships. A smaller proportion came from groups and organizations representing the medical profession, women, and local communities in Labrador. One-third of the fifty-six organizations were based in Newfoundland and Labrador, one-third in Ontario, and a smaller proportion in the Prairie provinces, Quebec, and the Maritimes. A major group of submissions came from urban centres in the South (e.g., St. John's, Halifax, Montreal, and Toronto).[4] These tended to be from national and regional Aboriginal support groups; churches; national peace movement groups (with their regional branches); and organizations concerned with legal, women's, or medical issues. The predominance of church and peace groups in Ontario and the Prairies largely reflects the headquarters of organizations such as the Mennonite Central Committee (in Winnipeg) and the distribution of regional branches (e.g., of Project Ploughshares). In Labrador, the submissions dealt with a wide range of topics. In southern Canada, peace and Aboriginal rights issues dominated and specific, project-related criticisms tended to be grafted onto the broader interests and agendas of the interest groups involved.

When the Environmental Assessment Panel called for public comments on the second, revised Environmental Impact Statement (released in April 1994), the sources and regional distribution of written submissions had altered radically from the first round in 1989 (compare Figure 12.5 maps). In 1994, there were 858 public and government submissions commenting on the adequacy of the revised impact statement but arguing, more often than not, for or against military flight training. An index of submissions failed to identify the location of 11 percent of the individual respondents, but it seems fair to assume that many of these came from the Happy Valley-Goose Bay area. Nevertheless these were not included in the following analysis, which is based on the 766 responses from identifiable locations. In stark contrast to 1989, 84 percent of the public comments in the second phase, mostly from individuals, came from the Happy Valley-Goose Bay area, followed far behind by the rest of Labrador, Newfoundland, the Quebec North Shore, Ontario, and the rest of Canada (Figure 12.5). Of the thirty-six organizations and groups that submitted comments in 1994, 17 percent were regional Aboriginal organizations (those from 1989 plus the newly created Labrador Métis Association); 25 percent were community representatives from south/central Labrador and the Quebec North Shore; and 22 percent were local, regional, and national union representatives. In comparison to 1989, the peace movement, church groups, and organizations representing the medical and legal professions, women, Aboriginal peoples, and the environment were greatly underrepresented. Once again, the organized environmental groups across Canada failed to participate (with the exception of a joint submission – Sierra Club/Cultural Survival). A most striking shift was the absence of church and peace groups that had mounted a nationwide letter-writing campaign in 1989. The predominance

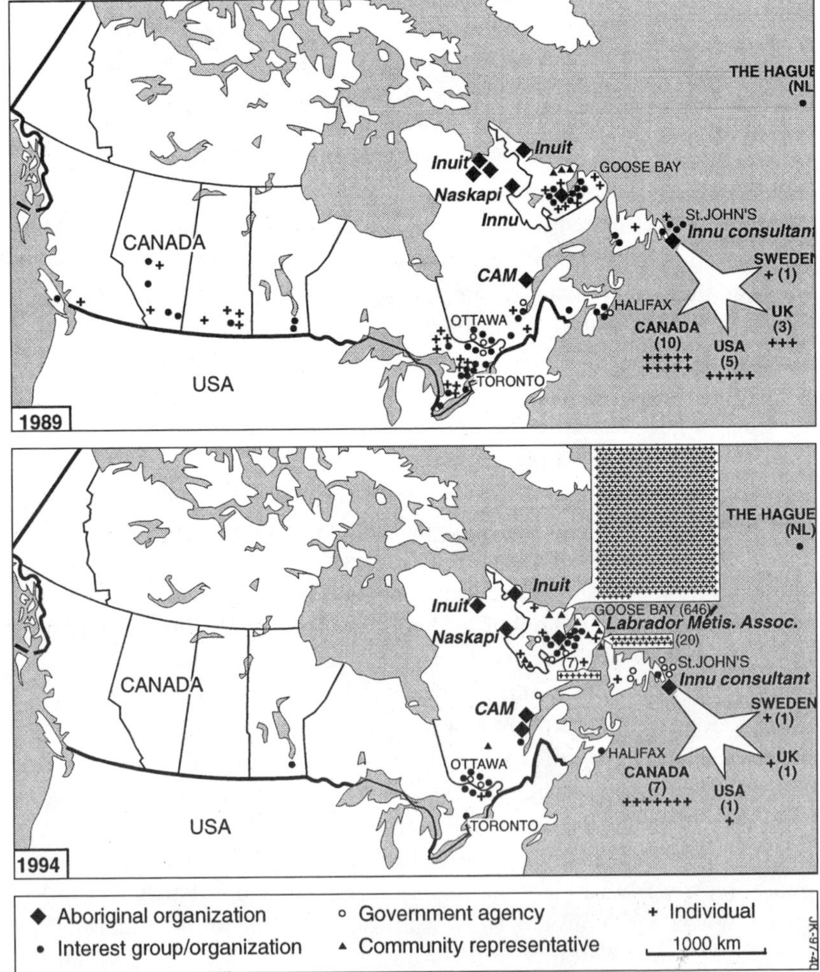

Figure 12.5 Regional distribution of public submissions commenting on the first (1989) and second (1994) Goose Bay Environmental Impact Statements

of local responses (with many submissions from businesses, their employees, and union representatives) reflected a concerted public mobilization by key project supporters who aimed to correct what had been, in their view, a slanted negative campaign in 1989 and in the intervening years. Many of the earlier opponent groups had not kept in close contact with events and assumed that, with the cancellation of the NATO tactical base proposal, the problem had gone away. Subsequently, they diverted their limited resources to other issues. The strength of the proponent, the federal Department of Defence, may have led some opponent groups to conclude that further action was futile. The key remaining opponents did not form strong strategic alliances with other groups while key supporters embarked on an intensive public campaign to demonstrate local support, a strategy adopted by other resource-use alliances and share groups across North America. In this particular conflict, unlike in other resource disputes (Soyez 1995; Princen and Finger 1994), the opponents were unable to broaden the playing field and mobilize national and international support for their cause. Rather than this being an example of the globalization of a resource conflict, the balance of public responses shrank back to a predominantly local/regional arena.

The strikingly low profile of the environmental movement during both public review phases and throughout the entire dispute may be explained by a number of factors. The conflict was defined in political and moral rather than in environmental terms, despite the question of potential impacts on caribou and endangered bird species. Other environmental campaigns were assigned a higher priority because, outside the region, the issue was perceived largely in terms of peace and Aboriginal rights. The conflict arena was remote, low-level flying activities were not seen as a project per se, and some thought that the matter was resolved once the plan for a NATO tactical training centre had been dropped. The dispute may have been too controversial for some middle-class, conservative environmental groups, given the nature of the (military) proponent and the civil disobedience campaign of the most vocal opponents (i.e., the Innu and the peace movement). There were severe obstacles to forming effective linkages between regional interests and national environmental organizations: the environmental movement in Newfoundland is weak, and there are strong regional antagonisms towards Greenpeace since the political battle over the offshore seal-hunt in the 1970s.[5]

Regional Resource Values and Aboriginal Interests

Since the early 1980s, the Inuit, Innu, Montagnais, and Naskapi leaderships in Labrador and Quebec have all been critical of the low-level flight training. At the risk of grossly oversimplifying the matter, it can be said that Aboriginal peoples differ in the degree to which impacts are experienced, their responses, their relationship to federal and provincial governments, and their strategies in negotiating comprehensive land claims. As will be seen, they also have a number of common key interests and concerns. The wider implications of low-level flight training activities cannot be assessed in isolation but, rather, must be seen within the broader context of regional resource values, other development initiatives, the resource management regimes currently in place, and policies with respect to Aboriginal land claims. This approach leads inevitably to the larger question of how to balance the rights, values, and interests of all northern inhabitants. A brief look at government resource management policies in Labrador and the comprehensive claims of the Innu Nation and Labrador Inuit Association serves to illustrate some of the complexities involved.[6]

In its landmark decision in the *Calder* case in 1973, the Supreme Court of Canada formally recognized the existence of inherent Aboriginal rights. After this crucial decision the federal government adopted a policy of negotiating comprehensive settlements in areas where traditional land use and occupancy could be documented and where Aboriginal title had not been extinguished by treaty (Fleras and Elliott 1992, 33). In 1980, the Government of Newfoundland and Labrador agreed to participate in tripartite negotiations to settle the outstanding claims of the Labrador Inuit and Innu. The Labrador Inuit Association is the only Canadian Inuit group that has not reached a land claim settlement. The fact that only two comprehensive claim settlements (the James Bay Northern Québec Agreement [JBNQA] in 1975 and, more recently, the Nisga'a treaty in British Columbia) have been made in Canada south of 60° latitude underlines the difficulties involved in shared federal-provincial jurisdictions, particularly in more populated areas where there are more third-party interests. Until recently in Newfoundland and Labrador, provincial wildlife regulations were based on the premise established when Newfoundland joined Confederation in 1949: Aboriginals and non-Aboriginals were to be treated alike (Tompkins 1988). The Innu and Inuit opposed the equal application of provincial game laws, which, they argued, were an unacceptable imposition because territorial rights had not been extinguished by treaty (Tanner and Henderson 1992). In 1992, after another landmark Supreme Court decision in the *Sparrow* case (1990), the provincial government reconsidered its policy regarding the application of hunting regulations (Bartlett 1990; Nolan 1993).

The Innu Nation (formerly known as the Naskapi-Montagnais Innu Association) has always opposed military flight training, which it sees as a fundamental infringement upon unceded territory. The flight activities are seen as a severe threat to the Innu culture, which is based on a strong attachment to their land – Nitassinan. This ran headlong into the military viewpoint that only a small number of Innu engaged in seasonal hunting in the interior and that unoccupied land not in immediate use by Aboriginal harvesters could be used for other purposes (Weick 1990, 58). In critiques of the proponent's impact statements and avoidance strategy, the Innu have stressed the importance of spiritual values attached to the land independent of use, and they have documented the mobility of hunting parties that range well beyond the 4.6-kilometre flight avoidance radius around known camp locations (Armitage 1989, 1992). In 1990, the Innu were unsuccessful in the federal court action that they brought against the Department of National Defence – an action that aimed at stopping flight training while the federal environmental review was under way. (According to environmentalists and other critics, this court ruling weakened the federal guidelines [1984] regulating environmental impact assessments, and it certainly had direct implications for other projects where construction continued during the environmental review phase [Hood 1994, 167]). For many years the Innu leadership focused on opposing the flight training, and it did not enter into land claim negotiations with the federal and provincial governments until 1991. The Innu state that they are not anti-development but that they want to stop those development initiatives (e.g., the Lower Churchill hydroelectric scheme, new logging plans, and proposals for improved road and trail access) that are not based on sustainable-use principles and that lead to critical habitat loss, threaten their cultural attachment to the land, and increase pressures on wildlife resources in traditional hunting areas (Ashini 1992). A key issue in the land claim negotiations is the question of interim measures to protect resources and land until a settlement is reached (Ashini 1994).

The Labrador Inuit Association made an earlier decision to focus on the strategy of negotiating their comprehensive land claim based on a study of traditional land use and occupancy completed in 1977 (Brice-Bennett). This was seen as the best available vehicle for resolving development encroachments (Haysom 1990; Andersen and Rowell 1991). In a land claim settlement proposal submitted to the provincial government in early 1993, the Labrador Inuit Association sought greater political empowerment via co-management rights to protect habitat and wildlife populations as well as the right to veto projects and resource uses seen as a threat to their future livelihood. In a counter-offer proposal made in November 1993, the provincial government emphasized the importance of protecting third-party rights, particularly in areas outside the proposed Labrador Inuit Lands. It was generally unwilling to cede its jurisdictional authority over resources and their management, including its responsibilities to other long-established (but non-Aboriginal) resource users. The Inuit argue, however, that they should have a say in how resources are allocated and managed, particularly wildlife resources migrating beyond the borders of Labrador (e.g., the George River caribou) (Andersen and Rowell 1991). In

1992, Newfoundland Premier Wells announced that there would be no development in the claim areas without seeking advice and providing the opportunity for comments (Warren 1992). Both the Innu and the Inuit in Labrador want more than a consultation role in this process. Thus, the balance of rights question is a pivotal issue in the negotiations.

Both the Labrador Inuit Association and the Innu Nation have emphasized the need for a holistic approach that would guarantee Aboriginal rights, would take into account the cumulative effects of development (rather than simply reacting to single-project proposals), and would have long-term sustainability as its main goal. Seeking a balance between Aboriginal and third-party interests will be a major challenge in the future, as competition for resources increases and as new developments (e.g., large-scale mining at Voisey Bay, Labrador) are proposed. The federal environmental assessment and review process, which looked at ongoing military flight training activities in Labrador and Quebec, did not have such a mandate, nor was it the appropriate vehicle for solving all of the issues at stake. However, the public review that began in 1986 and ended in spring 1995 became the forum within which it was possible to air strongly opposing viewpoints. This public environmental review, heavily criticized for being the longest in Canadian experience, could address substantive project-specific issues; but it could neither resolve questions about the cumulative distributional effects of overall development nor provide an effective framework for managing wildlife species and their habitat. Other processes, such as the ongoing comprehensive land claim negotiations and discussions about resource co-management, appear to be more appropriate vehicles for resolving the more fundamental issues that underlie this and other development conflicts on the Quebec-Labrador peninsula.

Postscript

On 2 March 1995, the federal government publicly released the panel report on military flight training in Labrador and Quebec (Environmental Assessment Panel 1995). The panel concluded that, at the moment, there was little evidence confirming negative environmental, health, or social effects and that termination of the military flying program would result in severe economic impacts. It recommended that low-level flight training continue, subject to a number of conditions, including: (1) creation of an independent body of resource users and government representatives to manage the research, monitoring, and impact mitigation program currently run by the Department of National Defence; (2) acceptance of the revised flight training boundaries proposed by the proponents as the basis for renegotiating the MMOU (which expires in 1996) with Canada's NATO partners. (However, the panel argued that flight training should continue in the two existing designated areas until adequate baseline studies have been completed in the new areas); (3) creation of a joint Canada-Labrador-Quebec caribou management board for the George River herd; and (4) settlement of Aboriginal land claims as soon as possible. The panel did not recommend limiting the number of flights below the proposed level but advised that flying activities be restricted or phased out if monitoring studies indicated severe impacts that could be neither justified nor mitigated or that could not be avoided without threatening the viability of the flying operations. Under the federal guidelines in effect when this project was referred for environmental assessment and review in 1986, none of the panel recommendations is binding. (New federal environmental assessment legislation partly addresses this issue and other shortcomings, but this act is applicable to new projects and not to those already under review.)

The minister of national defence announced, on 1 May 1995, the federal government's general acceptance of most of the panel's fifty-eight recommendations, including the creation of an institute for environmental monitoring and research, in which Aboriginal groups and other major stakeholders could participate. (An external consultant was asked to submit a proposal for such a body by 31 August 1995.) The Department of National Defence was anxious to renegotiate the MMOU with its existing European partners. In the meantime, France, Italy, and Belgium have expressed interest in low-level flight training in Labrador and Quebec. Alone, the renegotiation of the MMOU with Germany, Britain, and the Netherlands will likely involve a doubling of low-level flights from the current level of 7,000 to 15,000 to 18,000 per year. This expansion will be seen as an even greater threat to the Aboriginal peoples using the existing and newly proposed flight training areas for seasonal subsistence activities. Project opponents have already expressed severe disappointment with the panel findings, and some, especially Innu Nation representatives, have condemned the public hearings process as a sham. The pressure is on and the protagonists' positions have hardened during the long drawn-out dispute. Fundamental issues remain to be resolved: even without its inherent shortcomings, the federal environmental review process could never have served as a single, all-encompassing vehicle for resolving an array of economic development-Aboriginal rights conflicts. Now that this decision has been made, it remains to be seen whether the federal and provincial governments move to accelerate the negotiation of comprehensive Aboriginal claims. Some critics already argue that the a priori approval of ongoing military flight training means that the basis for any future negotiations is inherently flawed. In the short term, the attention of the various stakeholders will jbe focused on how quickly and to what extent the non-binding panel recommendations will be implemented by the federal government. The proposed creation of a new body to monitor and mitigate the impacts of military flight training will certainly be a focal point. The Department of National Defence adopted a conciliatory stance in publicly announcing acceptance of the panel recommendations; but, in an atmosphere charged with mutual distrust and hardened positions, a great deal will ride on the role and responsibilities assigned to this new institute: representation and power-sharing will be two of the most important issues.

Acknowledgments
This research was supported by a grant from the Deutsche Forschungsgemeinschaft. Many people in Canada were generous in providing their time and access to information. Given the complexity of the issues and the intensity of the conflict, the author wishes to emphasize her responsibility for the interpretations presented in this chapter.

Notes

This chapter, first published in the *Zeitschrift für Kanada-Studien* 27 (1995): 25-46, has been modified to incorporate a brief analysis of public comments in the 1994 phase of the federal environmental review as well as updated information on new resource development activities in Labrador.

1 The conceptual framework presented in Figure 12.1 was developed by Dietrich Soyez and the author during collaborative research on the transnationalization of two northern development conflicts, James Bay II and military flight training. See Barker and Soyez 1994.

2 For an outline of federal policy, see Canada, Department of Indian and Northern Affairs 1993. The Naskapi-Montagnais Innu Association (NMIA, now known as the Innu Nation) in Labrador, the Labrador Inuit Association (LIA), and the Conseil Attikamek-Montagnais (CAM) in Quebec submitted land-use and occupancy studies in the late 1970s, and the federal government accepted the claims for negotiation. (The NMIA claim was accepted provisionally, pending submission of final documentation.) Formal negotiations began with CAM and the LIA in 1989, and with the Innu Nation in 1991. The two sets of tripartite negotiations in Labrador broke down in 1992 when the federal government and the Government of Newfoundland and Labrador failed to reach a separate agreement on cost-sharing; these negotiations resumed in 1994, but, in the meantime, the LIA and the provincial government had exchanged proposals for an accelerated settlement process.

3 The range of issues and stakeholders defining the conflict has been distilled from an analysis of public briefs presented to the Environmental Assessment Panel, federal and provincial government documents, the publications (including newsletters and press releases) of public organizations and interest groups as well as media coverage. These sources have been supplemented by interviews conducted in 1992-3 with representatives of the proponents, supporters, critics, and opponents.

4 The Innu submissions from St. John's (Newfoundland) were coordinated by their environmental advisor, Peter Armitage, and included a compendium of comments from Canadian and international experts. See Figure 12.5.

5 These ideas draw on discussions with representatives of Aboriginal organizations, Aboriginal support groups, and national peace and environmental organizations.

6 The decision to focus on Labrador in this chapter does not mean that the low-level flying activities are not an issue in eastern Quebec.

References

Aboriginal Rights Coalition. 1992. *Amazon North: The Assault on Aboriginal Lands in Canada*. Ottawa: Aboriginal Rights Coalition.

Andersen, C., and I. Rowell. 1991. "Joint Management Inaction: George River Caribou Herd." *Rangifer* (Special Issue) 7: 67-72.

Andersen, T. 1990. "Position of the Labrador Inuit Association re: The Adequacy of the Goose Bay EIS." Position paper submitted to the Environmental Assessment Panel. Nain, Labrador: Labrador Inuit Association.

Andersen, T., and J. Rowell. 1991. "Environmental Implications for the Labrador Inuit of Canada's and Newfoundland's Land Claim Policies." Paper presented at the Memorial University of Newfoundland, St. John's.

Angus, M. 1991. *And the Last Shall Not Be First: Native Policy in an Era of Cutbacks*. Toronto: NC Press.

Armitage, P. 1989. *Homeland or Wasteland? Contemporary Land Use and Occupancy among the Innu of Utshimassit and Sheshatshit and the Impact of Military Expansion*. Sheshatshiu, Labrador: NMIA.

–. 1991. "Indigenous Homelands and the Security Requirements of Western Nation-States: Innu Opposition to Military Flight Training in Eastern Quebec and Labrador." In *The Pentagon and the Cities*, ed. A. Kirby, 126-53. London: Sage.

–. 1992. *Contemporary Land Use in Military Flight Training Areas in Labrador-Quebec*. Report prepared for the Innu Nation, Sheshatshiu, Labrador.

Ashini, D. (Director of Innu Rights and the Environment). 1992. Interview, 15 October 1992, Happy Valley, Labrador.

–. 1994, quoted in "Innu Anxious to Get on with Land-claims Talks." *Labradorian*, 11 April, 1.

Barker, M.L. 1990. "Umweltverträglichkeitsprüfung in Kanada." *UVP-Report* 4, 1: 39-43.

Barker, M.L., and D. Soyez. 1991. "Think Locally – Act Globally: the Transnationalization of Canadian Resource Development Conflicts." *Environment* 36, 5: 12-20, 32-6.

Barnes, D.H. 1987. Letter from D.H. Barnes, Chairman of the Canadian Environmental Assessment Agency to T. McMillan, Minister of the Environment, Ottawa, 11 January. Unpublished.

Bartlett, R. 1990. "Indian Summer in the Supreme Court: the Sparrow Quartet." *Canadian Institute of Resources Law Newsletter* 32: 6-7.

Beatty, P. 1987. Letter from P. Beatty, Minister of National Defence to D.H. Barnes, Chairman of the Canadian Environmental Assessment Agency, Ottawa, 15 January. Unpublished.

Berger, T. 1977. *Northern Frontier, Northern Homeland: The Report of the Mackenzie Valley Pipeline Inquiry*. Ottawa: Supply and Services Canada.

Bergerud, A.T. 1967. "Management of Labrador Caribou." *Journal of Wildlife Management* 31: 621-42.

Bone, R.M. 1992. *The Geography of the Canadian North: Issues and Challenges*. Oxford/ Toronto: Oxford University Press.

Brice-Bennett, C., ed. 1977. *Our Footprints Are Everywhere: Inuit Land Use and Occupancy*. Nain, Labrador: Labrador Inuit Association.

–. 1986, *Renewable Resource Use and Wage Employment in the Economy of Northern Labrador*. Background report, Royal Commission on Employment and Unemployment, Newfoundland and Labrador, St. John's, Newfoundland.

Canada, Department of Indian and Northern Affairs. 1993. *Federal Policy for the Settlement of Native Claims*. Ottawa: Department of Indian and Northern Affairs.

Canada, Department of National Defence. 1989. *Goose Bay EIS: An Environmental Impact Statement on Military Flying Activities in Labrador and Quebec*. Ottawa: Department of National Defence.

–. 1994. *EIS: Military Flight Training: An Environmental Impact Statement on Military Flying Activities in Labrador and Quebec*. Ottawa: Department of National Defence.

Charest, P. 1982. "Hydroelectric Dam Construction and the Foraging Activities of Eastern Quebec Montagnais." In *Politics and History in Band Societies*, ed. E. Leacock and R.B. Lee, 413-25. Cambridge: Cambridge University Press.

Environmental Assessment Panel Reviewing Military Flying Activities in Labrador and Quebec (Canada). 1995. *Military Flying Activities in Labrador and Quebec: Report of the Environmental Assessment Panel*. Ottawa: Canadian Environmental Assessment Agency.

Fleras, A., and J. Elliott. 1992. *The Nations within: Aboriginal-State Relations in Canada, the United States and New Zealand*. Toronto: Oxford University Press.

Freeman, M., and L.N. Carbyn, eds. 1988. *Traditional Knowledge and Renewable Resource Management.* Edmonton: Boreal Institute.

Haysom, V. 1990. "Labrador Inuit Land Claims: Aboriginal Rights and Interests v. Federal and Provincial Responsibilities and Authorities." *Northern Perspectives* 18, 2: 6-10.

Henriksen, G. 1973. *Hunters in the Barrens: The Naskapi on the Edge of the White Man's World.* St. John's, Newfoundland: Institute of Social and Economic Research.

Hood, G.N. 1994. *Against the Flow: Rafferty-Alameda and the Politics of Environment.* Saskatoon: Fifth House.

Labrador Institute of Northern Studies. 1994. George River Caribou Workshop, Labrador City, 27-9 January.

Lalonde, P. 1991. *Applied Traditional Knowledge.* Report prepared for the Canadian Environmental Assessment Research Council, Ottawa.

Landry, G. 1981. *An Initial Environmental Evaluation on a Proposal to Conduct Low-Level Flying from Goose Bay, Labrador.* Ottawa: Department of National Defence.

Luttich, S.N. 1986. *Issues in the Management of Ungava/Labrador Caribou.* Newfoundland-Labrador Wildlife Division, Labrador, Internal Report No. 4010.

Mailhot, J. 1986. "Beyond Everyone's Horizon Stand the Naskapi." *Ethnohistory* 33: 383-418.

McMillan. T. 1987. Letter from T. McMillan, Minister of the Environment to D.H. Barnes, Chairman of the Canadian Environmental Assessment Agency, Ottawa, 20 July.

Mende, B. 1994. Interview "Tiefflugverzicht unverantwortlich," *Focus* 41: 86-8.

Newfoundland and Labrador. 1993. *Low-Level Flying in Labrador.* St. John's, Newfoundland: Government of Newfoundland and Labrador.

Nolan, P. (Solicitor, Department of Justice, Government of Newfoundland and Labrador). 1993. Correspondence, 27 January.

Princen, T., and M. Finger. 1994. *Environmental NGOs in World Politics: Linking the Local and the Global.* London: Routledge.

Quebec, Secrétariat aux Affaires Autochtones. 1984. *Native Peoples of Quebec.* Quebec City: Secrétariat aux Affaires Autochtones.

Regehr, E., and B. Robinson. 1989. "Real Sovereignty." *Ploughshares Monitor* (September): 13-16.

Rowell, J. 1990. "Northern Labrador's Biggest Developer: The Department of National Defence." *Northern Perspectives* 18, 2: 11-17.

–. (Environmental Advisor, Labrador Inuit Association). 1992. Interview, Nain, Labrador, 18 October.

Saunders, J.O., ed. 1990. *The Legal Challenge of Sustainable Development.* Calgary: Canadian Institute of Resource Law.

Soyez, D. 1995. "Industrial Resource Use and Transnational Conflict Patterns: Geographical Implications of the James Bay Hydropower Schemes (Canada)." In *Environmental Change: Industry, Power and Policy*, ed. M. Taylor, 107-26. Aldershot, UK: Avebury.

Spaven, M. 1991. "Environmental State, Military State and Society: the Goose Bay Low Flying Controversy." *British Journal of Canadian Studies* 6: 155-71.

Tanner, A., and S. Henderson. 1992. "Aboriginal Land Claims in the Atlantic Provinces." In *Aboriginal Land Claims in Canada: A Regional Perspective*, ed. K. Coates, 131-65. Toronto: Copp Clark Pittman.

Tompkins, E. 1988. *Pencilled Out: Newfoundland and Labrador's Native People and Canadian Confederation, 1947-1954.* Ottawa: House of Commons.

Usher, P. 1982. *Renewable Resources in the Future of Northern Labrador.* Report prepared for the Labrador Inuit Association, Nain.

Warren, R. (Chief Negotiator, LIA Land Claim, Province of Newfoundland and Labrador). 1992. Interview, St. John's, Newfoundland, 6 October.

Weick, E. 1990. *A Review of the Socio-Cultural Effects of Low-Level Flights on Aboriginal Peoples in Quebec and Labrador.* Report prepared for Indian and Northern Affairs Canada, Ottawa.

13

The Land Claims Negotiations of the Montagnais, or Innu, of the Province of Quebec and the Management of Natural Resources

Paul Charest

In April 1979, the Conseil Attikamek-Montagnais (CAM) presented a statement of its comprehensive land claim to the minister of Indian Affairs and Northern Development (Conseil Attikamek-Montagnais 1979). Fifteen years later, in December 1994, CAM was dissolved without having signed a final agreement with the provincial and federal governments. Nonetheless, during those years there were substantive negotiations, and two preliminary agreements were signed with the governments of Canada and Quebec. Ironically, at the moment the dissolution of CAM was announced, the Government of Quebec made public a proposal of settlement.

As with comprehensive claims negotiations conducted elsewhere in Canada under the federal policy first adopted in 1973 and modified in 1986 (Canada 1987), the objective of CAM and the governments had been a lasting settlement of the land issue, on the basis of the Aboriginal rights of the Montagnais. The rights of property and management pertaining to land-based natural resources were also a major issue of the negotiations, and they gave rise to questions that I tackle more specifically in this chapter. Among the many resources that can be found in Montagnais territories (forests, wildlife, minerals, hydro) I have chosen forests and wildlife for the following reasons: (1) limitations on chapter length; (2) the particular interests of the Montagnais; (3) my recent research and publications on the subjects of forest and wildlife exploitation by the Montagnais (Charest 1994a, 1995; Charest, Huot, McNulty 1990; Charest and Walsh 1997); and (4) the great interest among anthropologists (and other researchers working in Canadian arctic and subarctic regions) in the management of wildlife by, or in cooperation with, Aboriginal peoples – a field developed mainly in the 1980s (Freeman and Carbyn 1988; Feit 1988a, 1988b; Osherenko 1988a, 1988b).

I try to answer the following question: in the current state of their negotiations, can the Montagnais achieve their original goal; that is, the control

– in the sense of decisional power and exercise of responsibilities (Feit 1988a) – over substantial parts of their ancestral lands and the natural resources they contain (Conseil Attikamek-Montagnais 1979, 182)? My response is based on an analysis of official documents that have issued from the negotiation process in which CAM has participated (the statement of claims, the framework agreement, the interim measures agreement, the settlement proposal by the Government of Quebec) and of newspapers articles concerning Quebec. I also make reference to three other texts: two specific agreements between Hydro-Québec and the Innu communities of Mashteuiatsh and Uashat Mani-Utenam, and an agreement-in-principle proposal made public recently by the Mamuitun Tribal Council, one of the three associations that has replaced CAM for land claims negotiations purposes. My role as research advisor and/or director for CAM between 1976 and 1990 gave me inside knowledge of the overall context within which the negotiations took place – a context that I should explain briefly before turning to the examination of the documents just mentioned.

Short History of the Land Claims Negotiations of the Montagnais

The Conseil Attikamek-Montagnais (the name was changed in 1988 to the Conseil des Atikamekw et des Montagnais), or CAM, was founded in 1975 following the break-up of the former Indians of Quebec Association. Its original members were the three Atikamekw communities of the Upper St. Maurice region (Manawan, Wemotaci, Opitciwan) and eight of the nine Montagnais communities of the Lake St. John and North Shore regions (Mashteuiatsh, Essipit, Pessamit, Matimekosh, Ekuanshit, Nutashkuan, Unaman Shipit, Paquashipi), with the community of Uashat mak Mani-Utenam joining the others just two years later. Its primary function was essentially political; that is, the representation of its members before the federal and provincial governments and other authorities, and the initiation and pursuit of the land claims negotiation process. Through the years the council also developed an administrative function within the context of the devolution, on the part of the federal Department of Indian Affairs, of responsibility for certain programs (e.g., education, health, housing) to representative associations or band councils (Charest 1992). This move, however, led to internal disputes and was completely abandoned in 1990. There were also debates over negotiation issues and process, between the Atikamekw and the Montagnais and among the Montagnais themselves, that led to the dissolution of CAM at the end of 1994. The negotiating role was immediately assumed by the Conseil de la Nation Atikamekw for the three Atikamekw communities; by the Mamuitun Tribal Council for the communities of Mashteuiatsh, Essipit, Pessamit, and Uashat mak Mani-Utenam; and by the Mamit Innuat Tribal Council for four of the other five

Innu communities. Considering itself to be in a somewhat unique situation, because the majority of its lands had been included in the James Bay and Northern Québec Agreement (JBNQA), the community of Matimekosh has decided to negotiate a separate agreement.

CAM's land claim statement of 1979 was addressed to "the Government and People of Canada" under the following title: "*Nishastanan Nitasinan* (Notre terre, nous l'aimons et nous y tenons)." The statement concerned mainly the justification of the land claim according to federal policy on non-extinguished Aboriginal rights. Its conclusion took the form of eleven basic principles summarizing the main objectives and orientations that the council hoped to fulfill through the negotiation process. Four of those objectives concerned the management of natural resources:[1]

> (5) We are opposed to any project for the exploitation of the resources on our lands by members of the dominant society as long as our rights are not acknowledged.
> (6) We seek to control the future exploitation of our lands and our resources.
> (7) We seek to prioritize the development of renewable resources over non-renewable resource development.
> (8) We seek an economic base, stemming from our control over the exploitation of our lands, that ensures our economic, social and cultural well-being into future generations, as was the case before the invasion of our lands by merchants, colonizers and industrial enterprises. (Conseil Attikamek-Montagnais 1979, 182)

The validity of the land claim of the Atikamekw and the Montagnais was acknowledged by the federal government in September 1979, and in January 1980 the Government of Quebec agreed to participate in a tripartite negotiation process. There were slow beginnings, and little progress was registered over the first five years, during which time information and opinions were exchanged between two successive CAM negotiating teams and frequently changing government representatives. Up to the present, the process has been marked by a series of ups and downs, advances and setbacks, as likewise occurred in the cases of negotiations with the Dene of the Northwest Territories and the Inuit of Nunavut. Indeed, besides the internal disputes mentioned earlier, CAM has known four different negotiation structures and teams, to which we can add the three present ones. In point of fact, real negotiations began only after Bernard Cleary was named chief negotiator in 1985. Under his direction written proposals were presented and discussed at the central negotiating table, and two preliminary agreements were signed, in 1987 and 1988, respectively (Cleary 1989, 1993). In spite of these achievements, major internal disputes over the objectives and the leadership of the negotiations were instrumental in Cleary's departure at the beginning of 1990. The negotiation process was then stalled for more than a year until the naming of a new chief negotiator, Jacques Kurtness, from Mashteuiasht (as was Bernard Cleary). There were no further changes in the negotiation structure until the dissolution of CAM and the presentation of the Quebec government's proposal in December 1994.

Two Agreements Signed by CAM

The federal comprehensive land claims policy published in January 1987 included in its procedures for negotiation the signing of a framework agreement early in the process in order to avoid interminable discussions over non-pertinent issues (Canada 1987, 24). CAM's negotiators readily accepted this new requirement, even though their negotiations had begun under the previous policy. The framework agreement was signed by the three parties to the negotiation on 13 September 1988 ("Entente-Cadre" 1989). Among the "subjects to be negotiated," this agreement includes the following items:

> (A) Interim measures to protect the interests of the Atikamekw and the Montagnais pertaining to territory and to the exercise of their activities during the negotiation period
> (B) The territory on which the Atikamekw and the Montagnais have based their comprehensive land claim ...
> (D) The traditional activities of hunting, fishing, trapping and collecting. (62)

In an appendix to the agreement the following aspects are included in the explanation of "territory" and "traditional activities":

> (B) Territory
> - (e) Management of lands and of renewable and non-renewable resources: use, development, protection, access and planning.
>
> (D) The traditional activities of hunting, fishing, trapping and collecting
> - (a) Conservation principle
> - (b) Zones for the practice of activities
> - (c) Ways of exploiting the renewable and non-renewable resources
> - (d) Implementation. (63)

Although the procedure of the federal policy does not include an agreement on interim measures, such measures were insisted on by CAM's negotiators in exchange for concluding the framework agreement, signed on 25 April 1989 ("Entente sur les mesures provisoires" 1989). Interim measures relate to the sixth principle of the statement of claim; that is, the right of veto over development projects during the negotiation period. The content of the agreement, however, is far from the original intention because the Government of Quebec was categorically opposed to any veto right.

The "object" of the agreement on interim measures is phrased in the following terms: "to establish interim measures for the protection of the interests of the Atikamekw and Montagnais in relation to the territory and the practice of their activities during the negotiation period; and to facilitate their participation in the different stages of the elaboration and realization of the development projects, wholly in accordance with the terms described hereunder" (64). In the absence of a veto right on development projects, the agreement offered the possibility of participation by Aboriginal communities and individuals for economic benefit – an objective contained in the eight principles of the statement of claim. Part 2 of the agreement concerns mainly the so-called "regulated" development projects – those automatically submitted to the federal and provincial impact assessment procedures, as well as government projects in general (new parks and wildlife and ecological preserves; outfitters' enterprises; construction of roads, ports, airports, etc.).

Part 3 of the agreement concerns the important subject – important to the Atikamekw in particular – of forest exploitation. The main interim measure proposed is the formation of a bipartite working group "to promote discussion and to bring about solutions to the problems that could arise in relation to forestry activities" (66). For other matters, the Atikamekw and Montagnais communities are invited to deal with the usual administrative services of the Quebec administration; that is, the local management units and the regional offices of the MER (Ministry of Energy and Resources). Plainly, these measures are not very restrictive for the Government of Quebec or for the companies exploiting the forest resources on Aboriginal territories. The proposed working group met a few times without satisfactory results. Consequently, this part of the agreement was denounced by the Atikamekw representatives whose communities and hunters have suffered for decades from the impacts of clear-cutting on ancestral territories, and who are looking for greater control of forest companies' activities. The agreement became a further cause of dispute inside CAM, and for this reason it was not renewed when it expired on 30 April 1991, even though renewal was a possibility according to Article 3 (65).

Part 4 of the agreement creates a "Working group on hunting, fishing and trapping," the mandate of which is "to examine the problems pertaining to the traditional activities of hunting, fishing and trapping of the Atikamekw and the Montagnais on the territory under claim, and to propose appropriate solutions aiming to reduce the disruptions encountered in ractice of these activities" (66). This measure had more success than the preceding one, yielding concrete results through specific negotiations dealing with new ecological preserves (e.g., that of Babel on the territory of the Pessamit community and that of Matimek on the territory of Uashat mak Mani-Utenam), outfitting enterprises (e.g., for the community of Essipit), and so-called "zones of controlled exploitation" (ZEC)[2] (e.g., the salmon-fishing ZEC on the Escoumins River).

Finally, an appendix to the agreement set up a "working group" for negotiations over Hydro-Québec's project on the Ste. Marguerite River. This measure must be seen as a test case for the implementation of Part 2 of the agreement, concerning "regulated" development projects, which led to the signing of two specific agreements between Innu communities and Hydro-Québec. These represent tangible economic impacts stemming from the agreement on interim measures. They also signify a turnaround in relations between the Innu and Hydro-Québec – marked until then by non-collaboration and confrontation – as illustrated in the building of a small power station at Robertson Lake, on Lower North Shore, in Mamit Innuat territory (Charest 1994b; Québec 1992a, 1992b).

Mashteuiatsh/Hydro-Québec Covenant (1993) and Uashat Mak Mani-Utenam Agreement (1994)

The first of these agreements concerns the construction of the twelfth energy transport line, beginning in Cree territory and passing through the hunting territories of the Montagnais of the Mashteuiatsh community. The second one concerns the building of a hydroelectric complex on the Ste. Marguerite River in the territory of the Innu of Uashat mak Mani-Utenam. As mentioned in their respective preambles, these agreements have absolutely no effect on comprehensive land claims, which can be resolved only through tripartite negotiations. The objectives of these smaller, specific agreements are to ensure that the communities in question will take no measures to stop the projects, that the concerns of their members about the protection of their traditional activities will be taken into account, and that they will receive some economic benefits. In an information bulletin called "Info Ligne 12" (published in April 1994), under the title "Why Negotiate?" the following arguments were adopted by the band council:

> For lack of power and will to stop this type of development on the ancestral territory of the Lake St. John Montagnais, the Council decided that it was wise to negotiate measures with Hydro-Québec to mitigate the environmental and social impacts of the project, to derive economic benefits from it, and to compensate for its negative impacts. The objective of the agreement concerning the 12th line is to harmonize the respective interests

> of the two parties, the Montagnais of Lake St. John and Hydro-Québec, to reduce the impacts of the project on the physical environment and the activities of the Montagnais and to promote the community, economic and cultural development of the Montagnais. ("Info Ligne 12" 1994)

On the issue of renewable resource management, the twelfth line working group, together with the scientific committee born from it, enabled Mashteuiatsh community members to influence the planning and building of the line. This occurred through the active participation of Innu hunters in the impact study and through Hydro-Québec taking account of the environmental and economic impacts on Innu hunting territories and traditional activities when choosing the best corridor for line passage. Similarly, the interests of Innu users of areas of land affected by such construction activities as clearing, line maintenance, and increased traffic on the territory were protected by the agreement. Furthermore, Chapter 7 of the agreement provides for the establishment of a fund to support social, cultural, and economic development, totalling $2,900,000, which aims to "maintain and develop fishing, hunting and trapping activities" and "environmental enhancement" ("Convention Mashteuiatsh/Hydro-Québec 1993, Chapter 7).

The agreement on the Ste. Marguerite project is based on similar principles (Uashat mak Mani-Utenam 1994, 4). In legal terms, the band council, or Innu Takuaikan of Uashat mak Mani-Utenam, "undertakes to collaborate with Hydro-Québec for the elaboration and implementation of environmental and mitigative measures related to the project, and in any instance when its collaboration is required" ("Entente Uashat mak Mani-Utenam" 1994, Article 3.6). To compensate for the impacts of the project on the hunting, fishing, and trapping activities of the Aboriginal users of the territories affected, Hydro-Québec contributes an annually indexed amount of $308,268 to the *Innu Aitun* Fund over a period of fifty years. As with the Mashteuiatsh agreement, this money is to be used to maintain, promote, and develop traditional activities throughout the community territory. Finally, a budget of $10,000,000 is allotted for remedial works for which a company named SOTRAC is responsible – as under the JBNQA – aiming "to preserve the biological and visual quality of the environment together with its productivity," and "to contribute to the reconstruction of habitats" (Article 13.7).

Measures for the protection or rehabilitation of wildlife resources in the Innu territories affected by hydroelectric projects do not represent legal mechanisms whereby Montagnais hunters can control the exploitation of these resources on their lands. With these agreements, however, their present situation has taken a step forward from thirty years ago, when

Hydro-Québec proceeded to develop the Bersimis, aux Outardes, and Manicouagan watersheds with no consideration for the land use and occupancy of the Montagnais of Pessamit (Charest 1980). Nevertheless, pending settlement of the comprehensive land claims of the Montagnais, the interim measures described previously do not confer on Innu hunters of Mashteuiatsh and Uashat mak Mani-Utenam real management responsibilities for the wildlife resources of their territories. Consequently, they do not fulfill Montagnais objectives for land claims negotiations.

Government of Quebec Proposal, December 1994

The Government of Quebec's proposal to the Atikamekw and Montagnais for the settlement of their land claims came after many years of discussions at the central and sectoral tables, but it did not come at the right time. Indeed, it was presented just as CAM's dissolution was publicly announced by its leadership (Vigneault 1994a, 1994b). In the event, it seems that Quebec acted more out of political opportunism than cynicism inasmuch as the new separatist government was eager to show its good will towards the Aboriginal nations before the referendum on Quebec independence (Venne 1994). The settlement proposal was rejected unanimously, both by the two nations directly involved (the Atikamekw and the Montagnais) and by the representatives of the major non-Aboriginal users of natural resources in the territories under claim: the Association of Forest Industries of Quebec, the Association of Lumber Manufacturers of Quebec, and the Quebec Wildlife Federation. What was the content of Quebec's proposal, so unanimously rejected, in regard to the management of forest and wildlife resources?

The key elements of the government's proposal are Chapter 1 concerning the territory ("Atikamekw Lands and Montagnais Lands") and Chapters 3 and 8 concerning, respectively, the management of resources ("Rights Related to the Practice of Traditional Activities and to the Co-management of Resources") and economic development ("Measures Governing the Exploitation of Resources in Areas of Shared Jurisdiction"). Respecting land rights, the goverment's offer proposes constituting Atikamekw and Montagnais estates (to which they would hold full ownership [similar to Category 1 lands under the JBNQA]) of 4,000 square kilometres to "allow community and local development for each community" (Québec 1994, 6). In effect, it involves enlarging existing reserve lands to meet the current needs of communities for space and access to important resources. The communities' ownership of these lands would, however, be to the exclusion "of the beds and banks of water streams, the lakes, reservoirs, hydraulic powers, ... underground reservoirs ... and previously allocated titles and rights over minerals" (8). In addition, conservation areas not exceeding 10,000 square kilometres in total would be created in Montagnais territory only. Only wildlife harvesting and recreational and touristic activities would be authorized in these areas, and they would be under co-management.

In the chapter on resource management pertaining to the practice of traditional activities, the government's document does not make reference to land categories (as in the JBNQA), but it makes a clear distinction between "public lands at large" and "zones for traditional activities and the co-management of resources" (partly analogous to the distinction between Category III and Category II lands, respectively, under the JBNQA). In the first case, "the rights of Quebec to use, exploit and develop the lands and other resources and to have access to them are maintained" (10). In the second, "there will be given exclusive trapping rights, and hunting, fishing and collecting rights for subsistence purposes, following the revision of beaver preserve status" (10-11). The total surface of those co-management zones would be approximately 40,000 square kilometres (11). Article 41 of the proposal states that "in the zones for traditional activities, the Government of Quebec will share resource management and fiscal revenues with the Aboriginal governments concerned," and that a "mechanism allowing for concrete participation of the Montagnais in decisions pertaining to these territories will be set in place to take into account their interests and priorities" (11).

In the section on economic development, the government seeks to promote entrepreneurship, partnership, and job creation for the Montagnais in resource co-management zones through the following measures: (1) first priority for the set-up or purchase of outfitting enterprises, (2) financial assistance to establish new enterprises, and (3) priority in the management of "structured activities" (e.g., ZECs, parks, and wildlife preserves). In concrete terms, Chapter 9, "Support Measures for Specific Projects," proposes the allotment of 186,000 cubic metres of wood outside the Atikamekw and Montagnais estates "in (communal) forest areas under grant of forest exploitation and management contracts (CAAFs)"; and it promises financial support from existing programs to promote the establishment of Aboriginal enterprises (19). This part of the government's proposal raised negative comments from the big forest companies, who alleged that there were no additional wood resources available in the major part of the claimed territories and that jobs were in danger (*Le Devoir* 1994, B-4; Duchesne et Déry 1995, 9).

In the same chapter, under the heading "Wildlife Enhancement," the government offers the possibility of establishing on public lands "twelve (12) Atikamekw and Montagnais outfitting enterprises, with exclusive rights over a surface of 2,500 square kilometers, either by forming new ones or by buying existing ones" (Quebec 1994, 19). Together with the co-management of resources in beaver preserves, this proposal drew virulent criticism from the president of the Québec Wildlife Federation, who declared it contrary to the democratization of access to public lands and wildlife resources, adding that the "unreasonable appetite of the Attikameks and Montagnais" had to be stopped (Francoeur 1995, A-6).

Finally, in Chapter 13, "The Powers of Autonomous Governments," Quebec's proposal identifies six sectors in which Aboriginal self-government could be exercised, two of which concern our analysis: "the management of Atikamekw and Montagnais estates; [and] certain resources found in the Atikamekw and Montagnais estates" (Québec 1994, 25). The nature of these powers is explained in Article 86: they include the management of forest and wildlife resources, but with Aboriginal governments being obliged to harmonize their regulations with those of the province in regard to principles of conservation and security (33-4).

The settlement proposal presented by the Government of Quebec to the Atikamekw and the Montagnais made headlines in the major French newspapers on 16 September 1994, which especially emphasized the ownership of lands and monetary compensation in the amount of $342 million (Girard, in *Le Journal de Québec*, 8; Cantin, in *La Presse*, B-1; Lesage, in *Le Devoir*, A-1; Gagnon, in *Le Soleil*, A-5). The day after, political leaders of the two nations were already announcing that the offers seemed unsatisfactory, mainly because of the limited land base and because of self-governing powers confined to those of municipalities (Cantin 1994b, A-21; Gagnon 1994b, A-6). However, their final appraisal of the proposal was postponed to a later date, pending thorough examination of its contents. This appraisal was delivered by the new negotiating entities that succeeded CAM, who, one after the other, decisively rejected the government's offers (Vigneault 1995, G-5; Yakabuski 1995, A-1, A-10). Among Montagnais leaders, it was the chief of Mashteuiatsh, Remy Kurtness, who was most insistent on control of natural resources:

> The Amerindians ... want larger territories with control of natural resources and complete self-government. The government's proposal ... speaks mainly of co-management [with the MRC] on some parts of the territory and the Government keeps all of the rights over mineral resources.
>
> ... Our goal is to obtain enough territory with full control of natural resources to ensure our economic, cultural and spiritual development. If there is no territory and control of resources, there is no self-government. (L. Tremblay 1994)

This position is consistent with the objectives of CAM's original land claims statement. The representatives of the Montagnais considered –

rightly in my opinion – that the government's offer was far from meeting their objectives in terms of the quantity of lands and resources under their authority. Besides, the modalities of the co-management of resources were quite loosely explained in Quebec's proposal, and it is questionable whether they add up to an actual co-management structure. This issue, however – like others – might have been addressed more rigorously at the negotiation table while preparing a final agreement.

The Montagnais of the Mamit Innuat Tribal Council were categorical in their rejection of the proposal (Vigneault 1995, G-5). The leaders of the Mamuitun Tribal Council, for their part, deemed it "an interesting basis" for further negotiations and announced that a counter-proposal would be forthcoming in the near future (Venne 1995, A-11). This was presented to the Quebec government and made public in February 1997.

Agreement-in-Principle Proposal of the Mamuitun Tribal Council

In its counter-proposal, the negotiating team for Mamuitun takes an approach somewhat different from that of the Quebec government: no quantum of lands or sums of compensation money are mentioned. The chapter on the "territorial regime" states "that the areal extent and location of lands ... will be determined with certainty between ratification of the agreement-in-principle and the signing of the final agreement" (Conseil Mamuitun 1997, 14). Hence, during public presentations of the agreement-in-principle proposal, only a fictive map was produced to illustrate the "different territorial allotments":

- Innu-Montagnais lands in full ownership, or *Innu assi*, including ownership of "the natural resources found on them together with marine zones, intertidal zones and under water lands" (15);
- conservation territories (*Assi eka tshe pikunakan*) on which "no development or exploitation of natural resources is allowed excepting *Innu aitun*, activities associated with the interpretation and implementation of Innu-Montagnais culture and with recreational and touristic activities organized by registered Innu-Montagnais" (17);
- lands under joint jurisdiction (*Tshe aitapatet assi*) by the Government of Canada, the Government of Quebec, and the Innu-Montagnais government and on which the "Innu-Montagnais have exclusive rights and priority rights" (17).

The chapter on the jurisdiction and powers of the self-government bodies of the communities (called Innu-Montagnais First Nations) is centrally concerned with "the management of *Innu assi* and of activities thereon, as well as on *Tshe aitapatet assi*" (38). Regarding traditional activities, or *Innu aitun*, they would be under exclusive Innu control inside *Innu assi*, regulated by independent codes of practice and overseen by Innu territorial officers. In regard to natural resources, the following powers are enumerated:

- The exclusive control of the management, protection and harvest of fur animals inside *Tshe aitapatet assi*;
- The co-management of regulations for natural resource exploitation, land management and research and development activities inside *Tshe aitapatet assi* ...
- The exclusive management of the natural resources of which the Innu-Montagnais First Nations of Mamuitun are owners or on which they have exclusive rights, inside *Tshe aitapatet assi*. (32)

The section on economic development stipulates that the powers of Innu self-governments would encompass the regulation of forestry and of outfitting enterprises along with the control over wildlife resources and hunting activities (33). A short chapter dealing with "rights to natural resources" on shared jurisdiction territories (or *Tshe aitapatet assi*) and on municipal territories proposes that detailed measures be adopted before the signing of the final agreement concerning, inter alia, such matters as "respect for the collective and family rights of the Innu-Montagnais" and their exclusive access "to a fair portion of the total harvests for a specific natural resource" (48). Furthermore, a working committee on natural resources would be set up and mandated to propose scenarios in connection with natural resource rights on these same territories (48). Again, sound management of natural resources on these territories would be ensured by Innu-Montagnais codes of practice and by an intervention code (Chapter 7). The following principles would guide the formulation of these codes:

(a) respect for the ancestral right to practice *Innu Aitun*;
(b) respect for species;
(c) respect for other users;
(d) respect for traditional values;
(e) respect for the environment;
(f) respect for the regulations of the Code of Practice. (56)

In regard to the terms and conditions of the exercise of traditional activities, the following elements are listed:

(a) hunting seasons;
(b) issuance of identity certificates;
(c) harvesting reports;

(d) species;
(e) quotas to be respected;
(f) gear;
(g) family inheritance of places for the practice of *Innu Aitun*;
(h) community and intercommunity sharing rules;
(i) roles and responsibilities of territorial and peace officers;
(j) roles and responsibilities of members of the First Nations concerned;
(k) supervision rules;
(l) infractions and penalties;
(m) authority for the implementation of legislation;
(n) territorial allotments. (56-7)

The two main goals of the intervention code would be "to harmonize the activities of all the users inside *Innu assi*" and to "protect the traditional activities of the Innu-Montagnais within *Innu assi*" (57). It would entail the fundamental revision of existing governmental laws and regulations, and it would give a role and specific responsibilities to the Innu territorial and peace officers (57-8). Finally, the public would have the right to circulate freely on *Innu assi* lands as well as on those lands upon which the Innu would have exclusive rights to exploit natural resources (58).

In the chapter on economic development, the Mamuitun proposal includes two sections – one on enhancement of forest resources and one on the enhancement of wildlife, fish, and game resources. Regarding forest resources, the council claims from Quebec the allotment of significant quantities of wood outside *Innu assi*, the continuation of forest exploitation and management contracts (CAAFs), and financial and technical help to develop Montagnais enterprises in the forest sector (67). From the forest industry it also expects 50 percent of contracts negotiated for forest remedial works (67). The section on the enhancement of wildlife resources deals specifically with the set-up or purchase of outfitting enterprises by Innu entrepreneurs outside *Innu assi* as well as with the monetary assistance expected from provincial and federal governments. Another section on the enhancement of fish and game resources examines the possibility for commercial exploitation of certain species – crab and seal in particular – involving the setting of exclusive quotas for the Montagnais, the issuing of licences, and financial assistance (69-70).

Finally, in the chapter on "financial arrangements," the Mamuitun proposal envisions the financing of local self-government mainly through "taxation and income revenues from *Innu assi* and from certain resources and activities inside *Tshe aitapatet assi*; the sharing of royalties from natural resources, and the sharing of fiscal revenues of the governments from *Tshe aitapatet assi*; [and] financial agreements" (79).

Comparison between the Quebec Proposal and the Mamuitun Proposal

For lack of space this comparison can only be of a summary nature. The Mamuitun document (102 pages) is almost twice as long as is the Quebec document (fifty-seven pages). This is a first indication of the seriousness with which the Montagnais negotiating team prepared its settlement proposal. The chapters on economic development and self-governance, for example, stand at twenty-four and twenty-four pages for the Mamuitun proposal as opposed to five and fourteen for the Quebec proposal, respectively. This shows the importance the Central Innu place on these two areas of negotiation. The territorial issue is of similar weight in the two proposals, but it is differently developed. Passages dealing with the management of natural resources, the key subject of this chapter, are sprinkled through several chapters of the two texts, mainly those on territory, economic development, and self-government. Once again the Mamuitun proposal is much more detailed than is the Quebec proposal, particularly where the exercise and protection of traditional activities is concerned. Indeed, this issue is the sole subject of two chapters: "Rights to Natural Resources" and "Innu-Montagnais Codes of Practice and the Intervention Code."

A closer examination of the basic positions of the two proposals on jurisdiction for natural resources shows that they are quite compatible. Both parties identify three types of jurisdiction, associated, respectively, with three categories of lands: territories of full Innu ownership, territories of shared jurisdiction, and conservation territories. Important differences can be seen, however, in the way that Innu jurisdiction for natural resources and their management is conceived in each proposal. Thus, in Quebec's offer, hydraulic resources in their entirety, and a large part of mineral resources, are excluded from Innu jurisdiction, even in fully owned territories. Moreover, in territories of shared jurisdiction, the government text is ambiguous and does not explicitly extend true co-management responsibilities to the Innu. Conversely, for this same category of territory, the Mamuitun proposal claims a combination of exclusive and priority rights on quantities of lands and types of resources to be determined in the negotiation of the final agreement. These could include hydraulic resources as well as mineral, forest, or wildlife resources.

The Mamuitun proposal also gives detailed information about how the Central Innu want to control their exploitation of wildlife and other resources inside the different categories of territories through codes of practice and the intervention code. This innovative proposal is based on an ongoing project that began many years ago at Mashteuiatsh and that has been described in detail by the anthropologist Martin Côté (1994, 1997). On the conservation territories, co-management is proposed by Quebec but its terms and conditions are yet to be determined. The Innu text, for its part, is mute on the nature of self-government jurisdiction on these same territories.

In brief, in its settlement proposal the Mamuitun Tribal Council claims full jurisdiction, or self-management, of all resources inside territories under full Montagnais ownership; exclusive jurisdiction and self-management of certain resources located in the territories of shared jurisdiction (specifically relevant to the exercise of their traditional activities or *Innu aitun*); and a form of co-management ("participation in the exploitation of natural resources") of resources located on those lands over which they would not have exclusive rights.

Even if the two proposals coincide on some basic principles (full ownership on portions of land, shared jurisdiction for other resources, conservation territories), they differ widely on questions of the extent of land categories claimed or proposed and on the nature and importance of resources under exclusive and shared jurisdiction. Those differences are brought into sharp focus by the totally opposed reactions to the Quebec proposal on the part of forest industry and non-Aboriginal wildlife users' representatives, on the one hand, and on the part of the political leaders of the Innu, on the other. In their negotiation strategy, Mamuitun leaders have chosen to avoid specifying their claims in terms of surface area, jurisdiction for resources, and monetary compensation. As stated in a public meeting, they want first to discuss basic principles like shared jurisdiction for lands and resources and self-government powers before discussing in detail quanta of land, resources, and money. Quite obviously, these quanta are at least as important, if not more so, than are the principles – even if the latter are judged acceptable by both parties. In fact, it is very likely that the value of lands and resources claimed, rather than principles of shared power and authority, will wreck the negotiation if the Montagnais are considered too "greedy" – as overtly claimed in the media by an influential minister of the current government (Charest 1996, B-10), and by many economic leaders and representatives of the wildlife lobby. "Quebec-Montagnais Negotiations are Troubling," read a headline in *Le Quotidien*, the leading daily newspaper for the Saguenay-Lake St. John region (Tremblay 1994).

Conclusion

Will the Montagnais, or Innu, of the Province of Quebec (and particularly those of the Mamuitun Tribal Council, who are of central concern in this chapter) achieve the objective they set for themselves at the beginning of the long negotiation process eighteen years ago? That is the question motivating the foregoing description and analysis of official documents pertaining to Montagnais land claims negotiations and, more specifically, of sections dealing with the very important issues of territory and natural resources. More precisely, I have examined the possibility that the Central

Innu, through the settlement of their land claims, will regain at least some significant jurisdiction and control of their ancestral territories and their natural resources in order to ensure the viability of economic, social, and cultural development that benefits present and future generations. At the end of this exercise, it would be presumptuous to answer the question with a simple yes or no, as the negotiations are still ongoing. I have well founded doubts, however, about the possibility of a settlement that is satisfactory to the Montagnais, and this is because of the weight of economic interests involved for a very significant territorial and demographic portion of the Province of Quebec.

But we can also consider several scenarios that are both more and less pessimistic: (1) there will never be any comprehensive settlement and the Innu will satisfy themselves with some of the more important administrative tasks, following the present federal policy of devolution of responsibilities to the local level; (2) there will be two limited comprehensive settlements, following acceptance by the members of the Mamuitun and Mamit Innuat Tribal Councils of a considerable reduction in their expectations regarding lands, control of natural resources, and self-government (the former will prefer to share the benefits of exploiting renewable and non-renewable resources on their lands, while the latter will prefer control over the exploitation of wildlife resources and consultation on new development projects that could have impacts on their traditional activities); and (3) there will be further political fissioning and a multiplication of negotiation units to a limit of the current nine bands, or even ten, should the Nitassinan secessionist group of Mani-Utenam reach its objective. The small units mentioned in (3) would negotiate separately a multitude of specific agreements over certain parts of their territories, the exploitation of particular resources, or the administration of specific programs. This last scenario is the one favoured by the federal policy on self-government and also by the provincial government, which welcomes the potential municipalization of Aboriginal reserves. Moreover, most of the Innu communities have already signed a score of agreements and contracts with Hydro-Québec; different departments of the Governments of Canada and Quebec; and other administrative entities concerning hydroelectric developments, parks, ecological preserves, the hunting of migratory birds, the administration of schools, health services, welfare services, and so on.

This piecemeal strategy, based on divide-and-rule tactics, is seductive for both parties, especially for federal and provincial governments seeking to maximize their retention of powers and jurisdiction. Meanwhile, the exhaustion resulting from prolonged negotiations could lead many Innu communities to surrender ideals in exchange for more immediate concrete benefits, such as monetary compensation, budgetary decentralization, jobs, administrative control, and so on. These easier choices are favoured by many persons inside Innu communities, in particular by those who manage programs and budgets. The tendency towards an administrative solution has been present for at least two decades, pursuant to the devolution, or "prise en charge," policy of the Department of Indian Affairs (Charest 1992). This option weighs heavily, as my colleague Jean-Jacques Simard (1996) has demonstrated in the cases of the Cree and Inuit. I fear that the Montagnais will not be able to withstand it or, rather, that the governments will leave them no other choice. Even if the JBNQA has never been a model for them, it is difficult to see how the Innu could get more decision-making powers and self-management responsibility for their ancestral lands and resources than have the Inuit, Cree, and Naskapi. The Innu negotiate within a much less favourable territorial, demographic, and economic context. I hope that I am wrong in my prediction of possible scenarios – scenarios that might be characterized, following Cassidy and Dale (1988, 29-34), as "partners for development," in the case of the Central Montagnais of Mamuitun, and "allies and adversaries" in the case of the Eastern Montagnais of Mamit Innuat. The fundamental issue remains unanswered: will there be an Innu homeland?

Notes

1 There are no English translations of the documents quoted in this chapter, and the translations that I have provided are not official. Readers should refer to the original texts in French for the exact phrasing of quoted segments.

2 Public use of zones d'exploitation controllées (ZECs) for recreational hunting and fishing is regulated by the elected representatives of associations to which members of the public may adhere through the payment of fees.

References

Bellemarre, André A. 1995. "L'offre du Québec aux Montagnais et Attikameks inquiète la Fédération." *Le Soleil*, 26 janvier, S-7.

Canada, Affaires indiennes et du Nord. 1986. *La politique des revendications territoriales globales*. Ottawa: Approvisionnements et Services Canada.

Cantin, Philippe. 1994a. "Québec offre aux Montagnais et Atikamekw la pleine propriété de 4000 km de terre: Les communautés pourront exercer, à leur rythme, de nouveaux pouvoirs." *La Presse*, 16 décembre, B-1.

–. 1994b. "Les Atikamekw et les Montagnais jugent exiguës les terres que leur offre Québec." *La Presse*, 17 décembre, A-21.

Cassidy, Frank, and Norman Dale. 1988. *After Native Claims? The Implications of Comprehensive Claims Settlements for Natural Resources in British Columbia*. Vancouver: Oolichan Books and the Institute for Research on Public Policy.

Charest, Paul. 1980. "Les barrages en territoire montagnais et leurs effets sur les communautés amérindiennes." *Recherches amérindiennes au Québec* 9, 4: 323-38.

–. 1990. "Les Montagnais, le gestion des ressources fauniques et le soutien aux activités traditionnelles." In *Les Montagnais et la faune: Rapport de recherche*, ed. Paul Charest, Jean Huot, et Gerry McNulty, 1-33, Ste-Foy: Département d'anthropologie, Université Laval.

–. 1992. "La prise en charge donne-t-elle du pouvoir? L'exemple des Atikamekw et des Montagnais." *Anthropologie et sociétés* 16, 3: 55-76.

–. 1994a. "Solutions de rechange aux grands projets en territoires autochtones: Impacts socio-environnementaux et développement durable." In *Evaluation des impacts sociaux: Vers un développement viable*, ed. Christiane Gagnon, 105-28. Chicoutimi: GRIR.
–. 1994b. "Dans l'ombre de la Baie James: Les Innus montagnais du Québec et les nouveaux projets hydroélectriques sur leurs terres ancestrales." Communication présentée au Symposium Indigenous Peoples and Hydroelectric Development dans le cadre du 48ème Congrès International des Américanistes, Stockholm, 4-9 juillet.
–. 1995. "Aboriginal Alternatives to Megaprojects and their Environmental and Social Impacts." *Impact Assessment* 13, 4: 371-86.
–. 1996. "La supposée disparition des Atikamekw et des Montagnais." *Le Soleil*, 25 mars, B-10.
Charest, Paul, Jean Huot, and Gerry McNulty. 1990. *Les Montagnais et la faune: Rapport de recherche*. Sainte-Foy: Département d'anthropologie, Université Laval.
Charest, Paul, and Gordon Walsh. 1997. "La récolte faunique des Mamit Innuat." *Recherches amérindiennes au Québec* 27, 1: 39-48.
Charette, Donald. 1996. "Québec veut une entente rapidement avec les Attikameks et les Montagnais." *Le Soleil*, 11 avril, A-6.
Cleary, Bernard. 1989. *L'enfant de 7000 ans: Le long portage vers la délivrance*. Québec: Septentrion.
–. 1993. "Le long et difficile portage d'une négociation territoriale." *Recherches amérindiennes au Québec* 23, 1: 49-60.
Conseil Attikamek-Montagnais. 1979. "Nishastanan nitasinan (Notre terre, nous l'aimons et nous y tenons)." *Recherches amérindiennes au Québec* 9, 3: 171-82.
Conseil tribal Mamuitun. 1997. Proposition d'entente de principe du Conseil tribal Mamuitun préparée en vue de la conclusion d'une entente de principe et d'une entente finale entre d'une part le Conseil tribal Mamuitun et d'autre part le Gouvernement du Canada et le Gouvernement du Québec. Mashteuiatsh: Mashteuiatsh Band Council.
"Convention Mashteuiatsh/Hydro-Québec 1993." 1993. Unpublished. Mashteuiatsh: Mashteuiatsh Band Council.
Côté, Martin. 1994. "Le bureau des services territoriaux de Mashteuiatsh: Une implication autochtone dans la gestion des ressources fauniques." MA thesis, Department of Anthropology, Université Laval.
–. 1997. "Les Services territoriaux de Mashteuiatsh: Un soutien aux activités de récolte montagnaise et une participation à la gestion des ressources fauniques." *Recherches amérindiennes au Québec* 27, 1: 63-76.
Le Devoir. 1994. "L'industrie du bois de sciage critique l'offre faite aux Attikameks et aux Montagnais." 22 décembre, B-4.
Duchesne, André, and Gaston Déry. 1995. "Des emplois menacés: L'industrie forestière s'inquète des répercussions économiques de l'offre territoriale du gouvernement aux autochtones." *Le Devoir*, 11 janvier, 9.
"Entente sur les mesures provisoires." 1989. *Recherches amérindiennes au Québec* 19, 4: 64-7.
"Entente Uashat mak Mani-Utenam." 1994. Unpublished. Uashat mak Mani-Utenam: Innu Takuaikan.
"Entente-cadre." 1989. *Recherches amérindiennes au Québec* 14, 4: 62-4.
Feit, Harvey A. 1988a. "The Power and the Responsibility: Implementation of the Wildlife and Hunting Provisions of the James Bay and Northern Quebec Agreement." In *Baie James et Nord québécois dix ans après*, ed. Sylvie Vincent and Gary Bowers, 74-88. Montreal: Recherches amérindiennes au Québec.
–. 1988b. "Self Management and State Management: Forms of Knowing and Managing Northern Wildlife." In *Traditional Knowledge and Renewable Resources Management in Northern Regions*, ed. Milton M.R. Freeman and Ludwig N. Carbyn, 72-91. Edmonton: IUCN Commission on Ecology and Boreal Institute for Northern Studies.
Francoeur, Louis-Gilles. 1995. "Chasseurs et pêcheurs contre l'entente avec les Attikameks." *Le Devoir*, 21-2 janvier, A-6.
Freeman, Milton M.R., and Ludwig N. Carbyn, eds. 1988. *Traditional Knowledge and Renewable Resources Management in Northern Regions*. Edmonton: IUCN Commission on Ecology and Boreal Institute for Northern Studies.

Gagnon, Katia. 1994a. "Parizeau présente ses offres aux Atikamekw-Montagnais." *Le Soleil*, 16 décembre, A-5.

–. 1994b. "Les Montagnais se disent déçus des dernières offres du Québec." *Le Soleil*, 17 décembre, A-6.

Girard, Normand. 1994. "De l'argent et des terres pour les Attikameks et les Montagnais." *Le Journal de Québec*, 16 décembre, 8.

Giroux, Raymond. 1994. "Des terres et un peu de pouvoir." *Le Devoir*, 19 décembre, A-6.

"Info Ligne 12. Mashteuiatsh-Ligne de transport d'électricité." 1994. No 12. Mashteuiatsh: Mashteuiatsh Band Council.

Lesage, Gilles. 1994. "342 millions $ et 4000 km^2 de territoires pour les Attikameks et les Montagnais." *Le Devoir*, 16 décembre, A-1, A-10.

Osherenko, Gail. 1988a. *Sharing Power with Native Users: Co-management Regimes for Arctic Wildlife*. Ottawa: Canadian Arctic Resources Committee.

–. 1988b. "Wildlife Management in North American Arctic: The Case for Co-Management." In *Traditional Knowledge and Renewable Resources Management in Northern Regions*, ed. Milton M.R. Freeman and Ludwig N. Carbyn, 92-104. Edmonton: IUCN Commission on Ecology and Boreal Institute for Northern Studies.

Québec. 1994. "Revendications territoriales des nations atikamekw et montagnais." Offre du Gouvernement du Québec, Québec, s.é.

Québec, District de Mingan, Cour Supérieure. 1992a. "Hydro-Québec vs le Conseil des Atikamekw et des Montagnais et autres: Jugement sur requête en injonction interlocutoire provisoire." Honorable Robert Pidgeon, 4 novembre.

–. 1992b. "Hydro-Québec vs le Conseil des Atikamekw et des Montagnais Inc et autres: Jugement en injonction interlocutoire." Honorable Robert Pidgeon, 27 novembre.

Simard, Jean-Jacques. 1996. *Tendances nordiques: Les changements sociaux (1970-1990) chez les Cris et les Inuit du Québec. Une enquête statistique exploratoire*. 2 vols. Sainte-Foy: GETIC, Université Laval, (Collection MétriNord, No 5).

Le Soleil. 1995. "... et craint qu'on paye cher 'la paix' avec les autochtones." 21 février, A-5.

Tremblay, Bertrand. 1994. "Les négociations Québec-Montagnais inquiètent." *Le Quotidien*, 27 décembre, 8.

Tremblay, Louis. 1994. "Selon Rémy Kurtness: Base intéressante mais insuffisante." *Le Quotidien*, 17 décembre, 9.

Uashat mak Mani-Utenam. 1994. Info SM 3. Uashat mak Mani-Utenam: Innu Takuaikan.

Usher, Peter. 1984. "Property Rights: The Basis of Wildlife Management." In *National and Regional Interests in the North: Third National Workshop on People, Resources, and the Environment North of 60°*, ed. Canadian Arctic Resource Committee, 389-415. Ottawa: CARC.

Venne, Michel. 1994a. "Des terres, des pouvoirs et des droits pour les Atikamekw et les Montagnais: Parizeau promet de leur faire une offre 'globale' avant Noël." *Le Devoir*, 30 octobre, A-1.

–. 1995. "Les Montagnais en veulent plus: Décus de l'offre de Québec, ils déposeront probablement une contre-proposition en janvier." *Le Devoir*, 17-18 décembre, A-11.

Vigneault, Nicolas. 1994a. "C'est quasi la fin du Conseil des Attikameks et Montagnais." *Le Soleil*, 26 novembre, B-8.

–. 1994b. "Disparition du Conseil attikamek-montagnais: Deux groupes négocieront avec les gouvernements." *Le Soleil*, 1 décembre, A-12.

–. 1995. "Les offres péquistes déplaisent aux nations Mamit Innuat." *Le Devoir*, 28 janvier, G-5.

Yakabuski, Konrad. 1995. "Les Attikameks rejettent l'offre du Québec." *Le Devoir*, 10 février, A-1, A-10.

Part 4
Community, Identity, and Governance

14
Community Dispersal and Organization: The Case of Oujé-Bougoumou

Abel Bosum

In 1992-3 we began to see the tangible results of many years of work. As members of the community will recall, we spent many years in meetings and assemblies with very little that we could point to as a successful outcome. We spent years developing political strategies together, years thinking about what kind of village we would like to one day see, and years sharing our dreams with one another.

We talked about creating a village in which we could take pride, a village that would be viable, that would be a place in which we could all grow and where, once we were together again, we could heal ourselves from the many years of difficulty we have experienced. I believe it is fair to say that our dreams are coming true. The effort we put into thinking and planning for the kind of village we would build has now borne fruit. During the past year we saw the completion of a number of important parts of the village. Our first homes were completed; we finalized our housing program, which, we hope, will address the needs of our people on into the future; our district heating system was completed and now provides us with comfortable and inexpensive heating. We have all worked together to create what is now a beautiful village that has the potential to be successful economically, environmentally, and culturally.

Our History in This Region

The people of Oujé-Bougoumou, now a population of 500 and growing, have historically resided in this region of James Bay. To trace part of our history and some of the problems confronting us today, we need to go back to 1926, when we first encountered the prospectors and non-Aboriginal people from the South. Our people, during those days, were not familiar with these new visitors and, not knowing what would happen in the future, became guides for local prospectors. They took them around and showed them different mineral outcrops.

This whole region has great potential as a mineral belt for both gold and copper. Between 1926 and 1970, our people were forced to relocate seven times due to mineral discoveries. These relocations were forced upon them. They knew of no alternative. It was only in 1960 that we realized there were government structures with which we could deal. Before that there was a form of local government that dealt with management of the land and its resources. In 1970, we were moved to our last community, which was located on Dore Lake. I have strong memories of this location as it was there that I grew up. Much of my time as a young boy was spent there, until I was sent off to residential school. The conditions there were poor because we were just building camps and tents with whatever we could find, whether it was scraps from the dump, cardboard, paper, or whatever. The lodging facilities were, of course, not very good.

In 1970, efforts were made by our former chief, Jimmy Mianscum, to obtain housing. He noticed that funds were being provided to neighbouring communities, particularly for the construction of log cabins, and so he began his efforts to try to get some suitable housing for our people. I guess it was at that point that he was informed that we were not recognized as a distinct band and, therefore, not registered with Indian Affairs. However, some members of our community had been registered under the Mistissini Band, which was about ninety kilometres away from us. The absence of band status and a land base made it very difficult for us to get anyone's attention. These were the first efforts made by our former chief.

In 1972, the community was asked to relocate either to Chibougamau or Mistissini. These were the two options given to them. Many thought that moving to Mistissini might be a better solution. However, this did not work out for a number of reasons. The main reason was that several people had already established residences in the region where they had grown up. They had already developed an attachment to the land in this area. Another concern was that, with the development of the municipalities of Chibougamau and Chapais, there was a greater need to move back to the land in order to protect it. And many people did move back, and those who were on welfare or could live in Chibougamau moved into the town. But there were not too many who chose this option. The majority continued their life of just hunting, fishing, and trapping, and they lived on their traplines.

Gathering Political Will

During the negotiations surrounding the James Bay and Northern Québec Agreement (JBNQA), our former chief was invited to participate in the discussions with the Mistissini Council. He made some requests during those meetings. At the time he realized that the land issue was perhaps the most complicated aspect of the JBNQA. He tried to obtain at least one square mile for the community. Unfortunately, he did not get very far. There was a lot of opposition to our request from the neighbouring municipalities and the mining and forestry companies. This made it very difficult for the negotiators. As a result we were left out of the JBNQA and were not identified as a community in the agreement.

Shortly after the agreement was signed, there was a change in the Quebec government, and the Parti Québécois (PQ) came to power. The first challenge we faced under the PQ was the impact of Quebec nationalism on Quebec's Aboriginal policy. They were trying to minimize federal land in the province and adopt a policy regarding Aboriginal lands. These political developments forced us to develop our own strategies because we realized that we had no status and that nobody recognized us. So the first step was to make sure we were on everybody's agenda, whether it was the Government of Quebec, or the Government of Canada, the Grand Council of the Crees, or the municipalities in the region.

One thing that helped us was that, through the friendship centre in Chibougamau, we managed to secure some funding to get a student of anthropology to come in and document the history of our people. She came in and interviewed the elders who had been through various relocations, and she also compiled existing studies done by other anthropologists in this region. From this study we developed a proposal, that was submitted to both federal and provincial governments, seeking recognition and discussions around the provision of a land base. During this time we had no resources, but we were lucky in that we received some funding through the Grand Council of the Crees to continue some of the research. But the struggles continued, and we still had to fight to get on the agenda and to reach a point where even other Cree would take us seriously.

In those days we held a lot of community meetings to discuss what was happening, what people wanted, and how far they were willing to go to reach their objective. A lot of our discussions were based on what it would be like to live as a community and whether or not this was what we wanted. Our elders played an important role in sharing our history with us. They spoke of the importance of the land, the importance of the resources, and the need to come together. This encouraged the younger generation, regardless of their education, to work together to put pressure on the government so that we could one day reach our objective.

One of the first things we had to do in the early days was to begin to act like a band. We had been dispersed throughout so many different campsites for so long that we had lost our sense of being a band. I often look back and think that organizing as a band was an act of faith on our part because nobody recognized us as such. We could not wait until someone else said, "Well, you are a band." We decided that we were going to declare the name of our nation, which was Oujé-Bougoumou, and establish an office. So that is how we began as an organized political group.

Long Trail of Government Negotiations

We made some attempts to get recognition from both the federal and provincial governments. The first response we got from the federal government was that if we wanted recognition we would first have to secure a land base. Of course, the PQ had just adopted a policy on the creation of reserves and strongly opposed the establishment of any new federal lands in Quebec. We received a letter from the federal government stating that if we were able to obtain a land base, then they would give us formal recognition and assume their responsibilities. We took this letter to the provincial government. After much effort, and to everyone's surprise, René Levesque agreed to set aside one square mile for our village. We went back to the federal government with this promise, and it agreed to begin negotiations.

Shortly after this, a tri-party committee was set up with the federal government, the provincial governments, and the Cree. Each of these groups had quite separate agendas. We were hoping that, through these negotiations, we would both establish ourselves and eventually become full participants in the JBNQA. We were hoping to get the agreement amended so that we could receive land under the land regime on terms similar to those of other Cree communities.

The province's agenda, of which we later became aware, was to put us on one square mile of land that had no real value. We were first asked to look at all the mining claims in the region and to select a spot that was not subject to such a claim. Second, they said that we had to deal with the interests of the forestry companies. So we had to choose a piece of land that did not have forestry concessions attached to it. Third, we had to deal with the local municipalities and their boundaries as well as any other registered activities in the region. At the time there were over 200 registered cottages around the lake (on the shores of which Oujé-Bougoumou is now built).

While Quebec was trying to put us in an area that had little or no commercial value, the federal government wanted to save money and have us located in the town of Chibougamau. The army base there was being dismantled, so they offered this to our community and said: "All you have to do is move in and you have got your community." Our people did not agree to this offer. Then the federal government decided to put us on the outskirts of Chibougamau, with the hope that all it would need to do would be to connect the infrastructure to the municipality and then we would be treated as non-reserve "Indians" with off-reserve programs.

These efforts on the part of the federal government never materialized. This was the first time that we had direct dealings with governments, and our people had hoped that such dealings would be productive. However, through a series of ups and downs we began to see how different our respective agendas were. These were difficult times for all of us, and we began to question whether we would ever get beyond where we were at that time. I guess what helped us was our own faith and our own religion. What we believed in held us together. People came together, and we got spiritual strength in a number of forms. While we were hurting on the inside from all these obstacles, our faith played an important role in keeping us together.

In 1985 there was a change in the government; Robert Bourassa and his Liberal party defeated the PQ. We had a meeting with Bourassa, and he asked us if we would support the James Bay II project. We said "No," and he just walked out on us. As soon as we said "No," he was out the door. Then we decided to go back and find out what happened during the JBNQA negotiations. We dug through the notes of the negotiators and people who were involved. At that time we realized that the person we should be approaching was John Ciaccia, who was the negotiator for the province. So we talked to him and, sure enough, he said that he recollected the discussions on the Dore Lake issue. He then explained the problems he had and the obstacles to resolution. When we learned this, it gave us hope again. Sure enough, here was someone who was a senior minister and who remembered what happened. With the elections a few months away, we asked if he would put this in writing so that we would have something documented. In his mind, he thought the Liberals were going to win the election, and he did not want to commit his government beforehand. Then he gave us a verbal commitment that they would deal with us as soon as they got in.

One of the first things that had to be done at this point was to change the mandate of the Province of Quebec. This was because, as I mentioned earlier, the original mandate dealt only with one square mile. The Liberals agreed to negotiate a land regime similar to the ones negotiated with other Cree communities. One of the problems they had was that they did not want to reopen the JBNQA, so the only way to facilitate this was to get Mistissini to agree to transfer lands based on a population of 275, which was the number of people from the Oujé-Bougoumou Band who were registered under the Mistissini. So that seemed to be the solution to that problem. John Ciaccia went back and got the agreement amended.

Another thing that helped us was the fact that, in 1986, there were negotiations being held on the La Grande Project, Phase II. This was the first time we received formal recognition. We supported the Grand Council of the Crees and insisted that the Cree not sign another agreement until we were included in one way or another. That was the first time we were included as a group in an agreement. After that there were some commitments from the province and from Hydro-Québec. We then started going after the federal government, and, after several meetings with the prime minister, we began to get a few more commitments. That was when the process of site selection began.

Site Selection

Site selection involved going through a fairly elaborate process with all our members. First we approached all our tallymen;[1] there were fourteen in all. We asked each of them and their families to identify community sites that they thought would be suitable. We also developed criteria regarding what we would be looking for in each site. Each trapper identified one or two locations and outlined their advantages and disadvantages. We went through a process of elimination until we got down to six sites. Then we conducted a few more technical studies. Finally we took all this information and asked the band members to decide where they wanted to relocate. They chose a site on Opataca Lake, about forty kilometres north of here. This site was chosen because it was a reserve and a protected area, and people felt that this would be untouched land. There was no mining or forestry there at that time, so it was an ideal site.

We then resumed negotiations with Quebec, and once again Quebec had some objections to our chosen location. Mainly there was opposition from the Ministère du Loisir, de la Chasse et de la Pêche (MLCP). It thought that we would be invading the area by putting our reserve there and, therefore, managing the area. And Energy Resources Quebec said that it would be too expensive to build a road up there and that we would be isolating ourselves. So, after a number of negotiations and going back and forth, we realized that we were not going to get very far. We then went back to the band members and asked what other options we had. It was during the course of the second consultation that, for a number of reasons, we chose this place on the shores of Lake Opemiska. It was then that we decided to occupy this place. At that time there was only a temporary camp where the lodge is right now.

Dealing with Ongoing Social Problems

It was around the same time that we had to deal with the problems plaguing the people along the highway. The conditions were so poor and dangerous that there was an urgent need for us to do something. So while we were working on the larger picture, there were also a lot of local issues that had to be confronted. We managed to get some funding for remedial measures, and we installed trailers with washrooms and running water in six main camps. That was the first improvement program available to our members.

We then started to involve the media. They began to come in and look at the conditions. We were also documenting the living conditions of the people through pictures. Through the involvement of the media we started to attend various conferences dealing with human rights and housing (indeed, we went wherever we could get our foot in) just to raise the issues. We wanted the public to be aware of the conditions of our people. Through that effort, both governments started to get a little more serious about discussions, and we had another round of negotiations. There was also a change in the federal negotiations. Andrew Croll came in and he seemed determined to get the agreement settled.

Changing Our Strategy

In these early discussions we were just looking for some recognition, money for technical studies, and access to formal programs. That was our only agenda. But the federal government insisted that what it wanted was to get an agreement that would cap everything, an agreement whereby we would have no claims over the past. It wanted us to totally release all claims in the past, present, and future. We could never understand why it wanted a release for the future, so we turned that down. Then the offers began to come in; the government offered us $5 million and went up as far as $14 million. At $14 million even our local MP, Benoît Bouchard, came and told us: "Well, it's $14 million, take it or leave it." So we had a very difficult decision to make, one that created problems within our own band. We had one group that said: "Take it, you know we're not going to get another chance." We were also looking at what was happening with the MoCreebec, who had been offered $10 million; and the government, to this day, has not gone back to the table. So there was that lesson that we had to look at, and we had to make our decision. But the majority of the people, including the elders, said: "If you want to build a community, you have got to build it the way you want. If you feel that you are going to get money to build something small, then the children are not going to like it. We are talking about moving people. It has got to be something that you want, something that is good." We refused the offer. For almost a year nobody called us, nobody talked to us. There were a number of changes in the ministers, and so we approached each one and each said that we had had an opportunity and had missed it.

When the young people started to get more involved, our strategies began to change from a more structured approach to anything that would put pressure on the government. This is when we began to discuss blockades and other strategies. This posed some difficulties in the group because many people held very strong religious convictions. They could not see the wisdom in these approaches or understand why we would get very far blocking roads. "Why would you block the roads?" they would ask, "You know it isn't Cree nature to obstruct things." In the final analysis, after the pros and cons were reviewed, we agreed to give it a try.

One of the first things we did was to march out of the places we were living and to occupy this site. We started to construct various facilities here. Shortly after we did this, Energy Resources Quebec came in and asked us to dismantle everything. It told us to go back to where we had come from, that we had no right to the land and so forth. But the people had made a choice; they were not going to move. Camps were erected on the site. Our presence here put pressure on the government and created some momentum, which, in turn, produced some action. We then resorted to blocking one of the forestry roads nearby, which created a lot of tension for the region. We did this just as the fishing season was about to open. This meant that people who had permits and who normally enjoyed going up to the Assinica River to fish could no longer get through. There were also a few mining companies doing some drilling north of here. We stopped them as well, and they became very upset and started calling the government. The forestry industry was also being hurt by the blockade, so we were able to hit three sectors with that strategy.

Towards a Final Agreement

We then got a call from Raymond Savoie, the provincial Liberal minister of natural resources, asking for a meeting. The meeting took place here in one of the shacks. Quebec came in with a delegation of maybe fifteen people, the federal government came in with just a negotiator. We tried to hammer out the principles for a more comprehensive agreement. At 2:30 AM we reached an agreement whereby Quebec and Canada would agree to contribute to the construction of the village and to provide a social and economic development fund that would allow us to develop businesses and create jobs. So we signed a deal that night at 2:30 AM. Two weeks later, when we sat down to negotiate the details, the federal negotiator walked in and said: "You know I never agreed to the social and economic development fund." Then he started cursing everyone at the table and walked out. That was the end of that federal negotiator; we never saw him again. Then we waited another six months, and finally the government appointed another negotiator to resume those discussions.

The governments offered us a choice at that time: we could either go with one government or try to keep working with both of them. The Quebec government was willing to negotiate because it felt that it had something at stake here. There was a lot of pressure on it from within the region to settle things, so it wanted to negotiate. We decided to go ahead and negotiate with the province and see what we could get out of it. Finally, in the summer of 1989 we reached an agreement whereby the provincial government agreed to contribute towards part of our infrastructure. It also said that it had an agreement with Hydro-Québec, so that the hydro line would be part of the deal. And it agreed to approximately $20 million for social and economic development. So we signed the agreement.

We then used this agreement with the Quebec government to put pressure on the federal government. We had to employ media campaigns as well. Eventually, the federal government decided to appoint a negotiator. Andrew Croll was brought in to deal with other Cree issues, particularly operation, maintenance, and capital funding, for some of the eight Cree bands. We managed to slip in as part of a test to see whether the federal government was serious enough in its attempt to resolve some of these other issues. That is how we got in on the negotiations, and our file was treated as the main file. The other Cree communities waited until there was some resolution. This is something we will not forget; the support that they gave us when they allowed our case to be in the forefront.

Back in 1980 we had put together a shopping list. In our community meetings we would talk about what we wanted to see, what kind of community we wanted and how we wanted to build it, and who we wanted to involve. As we began negotiating, we kept these plans and objectives in mind so that what we ended up with would allow us the flexibility to achieve them.

After many ups and downs an agreement was finally signed in 1992. It did not include everything we wanted, but we decided that, at that point, the most important thing was to get a community and to improve living conditions. We would wait for another time to deal with some of the more political issues concerning land and past damages – issues that still needed to be resolved. So those two items were left out of our agreement with the federal government. It was not easy to take past damages and land claims out of the agreement because we had hoped to have an agreement that was comprehensive. We thought we were taking a risk, but at the same time we did not know whether we would ever again have a chance to get back to the negotiating table. The government could just say: "We've done our job, you have got your community and that's it." But it was a decision we took, and today we are back at the table with Quebec trying to deal with the implementation of the JBNQA. We are also trying to establish the next table to deal with the larger issues.

During all these processes we held a lot of meetings with the band members, and this was extremely important. Most of the councillors and the leaders had to show that they believed in what they were fighting for, regardless of what was happening.

Lessons Learned

I guess some of the major lessons we learned were, first of all, to take advantage of all opportunities, to look around and see what is happening and find out what we could do. Second, we learned to never stop working; if we had stopped, then our people would have started to question our leadership and our desire to build a community. Third, we learned to keep the issues alive. We could not just stick to one strategy; we had to develop a whole bunch of different approaches and they all had to have some movement. That helped us locally because when people got a "No" in one area they knew that we were already working on some other angle. So they never lost hope.

In an effort to remain sensitive to the immediate needs of the people, we set up a remedial measures program and tried to get access to some of the other regular programs available to Cree communities – programs for which we had previously been ineligible due to our lack of recognition. As leaders we could not just focus on the political issues or on the larger issues. We had to be concerned about what was happening with the health of the people, the education of our children, the youth, and the social problems. We tried not to let political victories overshadow the need to deal with local problems. We always reminded ourselves that people are complex and have many needs and that the solutions we were looking for were not all to be found in the political arena. We had to deal with individual families as well as community needs. With our limited resources we had to tackle these issues, and this is what helped bring us together.

Another thing we did was involve people in the decision-making process. Although we had a council, it never made decisions; the decisions went back to the members. Every time there was a change in local strategy we would talk to the people. Every time there was a change in government position, we went back to the people. So they felt involved and remained part of every decision.

We also learned the importance of having a fallback position on every issue, and we learned to avoid all-or-nothing strategies that might have resulted in people being in even worse positions than they were before. Of course, this meant that we had to be ready to receive advice from many different perspectives. The community decided on what actions were necessary for its own long-term interests, with the full knowledge of the options available and the consequences of each one of them. Whenever we were faced with the decision to take an offer or leave it, we looked at each other and asked ourselves about the advantages and disadvantages. We also listened to people from the outside. We centralized communication and tried to maintain control over all the major communications with governments so that our story would come out and it would always be consistent.

There were a lot of things happening not only here, but also across Canada in many other reserves. We looked to what was happening in the Cree camp and with the Mohawk in Quebec. We watched what was happening with the Lubicon out west and with the Innu in Labrador. We tried to stay on top of government strategy because we realized that the government was doing the same thing over and over. When Katie Rich, the chief of Davis Inlet, came up here recently she told me how the government initially wanted to move their community to an old abandoned army base. I said: "That's funny. Back in 1984-85, that is what their strategy was. They still haven't changed. They're not offering anything new."

Planning the Community

The agreement that we signed allows us to be innovative in our approach to community development and planning. It gives us the decision-making power. There are a number of innovative projects that we are working on right now and others that we want to pursue in the future.

We have some but not all of the resources we need to deal with economic development. The most important resources are the natural resources. We have financial resources but not natural resources, and that is an area we want to develop. We have established a relationship with the region and are now a group with some status. We might not have formal recognition but we have recognition nonetheless. Governments, municipalities, and companies have come to respect us and accept that we are here and that we can be partners and co-exist.

Part of our vision involves trying to create a win-win situation. Our youth have been very involved in the planning of the community, as have the elders. At times they played different roles, but attempts were made to encourage them as much as possible to participate in every stage of the process.

Some of the challenges that lie ahead of us will involve dealing with problems that stem from forced relocations and social issues that arise from people having lived in different camps. There are many adjustments for people to make. Some people have enjoyed living in cities and towns, and now they have to live in the community, which is a bit isolated. There are those who lived along the highway in shacks and who are now moving into new houses, which bring with them new responsibilities.

We were also looking at what was happening in other Cree communities: what was good, what was bad. We hope to learn from this. Ultimately our goal is to become self-sufficient, not to just accept what is there or what has been done but to look at it and see if that is what we want. As we were constructing the village, and as we became involved in issues of education with the Cree School Board as well as issues of health with the Cree Board of Health and Social Services, our approach was not to just take what they had to offer but to look at what is working and what is not working and try to make the appropriate changes wherever possible. So far we have been really pleased with the openness of these institutions. However, there is some reluctance on the part of the governments to make certain major changes.

Time will tell exactly what changes will take place among the people here. Right now it is exciting and we are living in an exciting time. We still have some internal issues to deal with in the community. We have issues to deal with within the region and we also have a role to play, with other Aboriginal groups, in the larger picture.

We want to build a community that emphasizes a local vision, a community that can serve as a model for other Aboriginal groups, and a community that can show the government that, when resources are given to Aboriginal peoples, they can be creative, they can do things to make their communities succeed.

The agreement we signed was new. For instance, with regard to housing, rather than getting Canadian Mortgage and Housing Commission programs, we received a lump sum of money and developed our own housing program, which involved home ownership. That is not an option in many of the programs governments usually offer.

What I have been trying to point out here is that the most important component in this whole process is the participation of the local people. Everything begins with them, and if we do not forget who they are and what they want, then they will continue to be very supportive of our efforts.

Notes

This chapter, transcribed by Hedda Schuurman, is based on a presentation delivered by Oujé-Bougoumou chief Abel Bosum at an AGREE Workshop in that community in March 1994. Oujé-Bougoumou is a newly established village on the shores of Lake Opemiska in James Bay. The completion of this village, whose architecture and layout are designed to reflect the values and culture of the Oujé-Bougoumou people, is a testament to their years of hard work, protests, negotiations, and solidarity. Abel Bosum describes the process the community has gone through and some of the insights they have gained from the experience of establishing this village.

1 "Tallyman" is the English term given to the leaders of Cree hunting territories when these territories were registered as "traplines." The lead "trapper" on these "lines" was expected to keep count of the number of beaver lodges and so on, and report these to the government. Though still used by the Cree as a gloss when speaking English, the term is discouraged because it diminishes the actual role and status of the Cree hunting territory leader.

15

Gathering Knowledge: Reflections on the Anthropology of Identity, Aboriginality, and the Annual Gatherings in Whapmagoostui, Quebec

Naomi Adelson

The work that originally brought me to Whapmagoostui (Great Whale River) nine years ago still informs the research that I am conducting and is the basis for my thinking about the tremendous changes that have taken place since my first arrival to this small Cree community (Adelson 2000a). What I want to discuss in this chapter are some of the ideas that many anthropologists are mulling over these days. We have come to agree, I think, on the contingency of culture and the relative importance of the ethnographic enterprise in negotiating or mediating our "grounded" understanding of the lives and practices of the people with whom we work.

Over the last few years the questions that I have asked as a medical anthropologist have shifted from "what is health?" to "how is health linked to resistance?" to "what is resistance and how is it tied to identity and, more specifically, Aboriginal identity and its implications and meanings?" What, in other words, is "Aboriginality" within the Cree context? (Adelson 2000a, b). At first I thought that each of these questions was separate and unrelated, having little in common except my work in the community of Whapmagoostui. In rethinking my initial research on the politics of health, I am beginning to see the links and connections – the evolution of my line of thinking as I simultaneously reflect on my original data, the new events and activities in Whapmagoostui, and, of course, the subtle and not so subtle shifts in thought within the discipline of anthropology itself. Within anthropology, I am both pleased and troubled by the recent explosion of interest around issues of hybridity, voice, power, authenticity, intentionality, and identity. I am pleased because I see room for my ideas within the context of the poststructuralist enterprise – a perspective that asserts that we must endeavour to reveal, if not necessarily to revel in, the complexity, the ambiguity, and the contradictions "out there." I am troubled, however, by the risk of obfuscation that may result when – in the process of presenting the complex and the ambiguous – we forget the lived experiences, multitextured as they are, of the people with whom we work. Sherry Ortner

(1995, 185) spells it out in this way: "The question here is how to get around the ideological construct [of de-essentialism] and yet retain some sense of human agency, the capacity of social beings to interpret and morally evaluate their situation and to formulate projects and try to enact them." She goes on to say that "the answer to the reified and romanticized subject must be an actor understood as more fully socially and culturally constructed from top to bottom" (186). It is in understanding the "constructedness" of the subject, of culture, and, ultimately, of agency that we come to understand the potency of the process linking identity to political action. Power, I contend, lies in contingency and, to some extent, in ambiguity. This is the strength both of the argument and of the process. People use various resources, manipulate their realities, formulate their projects to "both become and transform who they are, [to] sustain or [to] transform their social and cultural universe" (187). The creative and transformative aspects of resistance to which Ortner refers incorporate notions of hybridity and speak directly to the ways in which "culture" is used to authenticate or contest group identity.

My own work on issues of Aboriginality speaks to this same process of "authentication," of identity, and of "culture," yet in a particular way. I am not looking at, or at this point particularly interested in, the question of the rhetorical integration of non-Aboriginal material or ideological matters. This is certainly an interesting avenue of study and has been explored by Comaroff (1985) and others. However, my interests lie in the concept of Aboriginality and the particularities of local-level efforts of cultural (re)construction. Increasingly, but by no means invariably, those efforts incorporate "traditional" Aboriginal values and practices – values and practices that are being reinvigorated across North America (O'Neil 1993).[1]

From the Northwest Territories to central and coastal towns, villages, and communities, there are examples of community-based programs of "healing" that are either in place or in the works (Royal Commission on Aboriginal Peoples 1995). Many of these efforts are government- or locally sponsored and endorsed programs that incorporate particular ideals of "cultural self-esteem" and a concomitant return to traditional values and practices. The notion of "tradition" is being used by healers and communities alike in their respective efforts to respond to social ills and to encourage self-esteem. When I speak of "traditional" practices, I am referring specifically to practices that are viewed as "healing," such as the Medicine Wheel teachings, sweat lodges, and traditional powwows. These teachings, practices, and beliefs have flourished in western Canada for over two decades now and have spread to the northern regions of eastern Canada in the last five to ten years.[2]

But what of the idea of "cultural self-esteem"? And what does "traditional" mean? Is there a cultural "renewal" taking place and, if so, what does that mean? I do not challenge the importance of the tremendous healing programs and initiatives that are having real effects across the country. I am curious, however, about ideas of culture, tradition, and identity; and, in particular, about that malleable, contingent process that Aboriginal artist and scholar Gerald McMaster refers to as contentious and mutable across time and place (1995).

When talking about those processes amongst historically internally colonized populations, I prefer to use the term "Aboriginality" because I think it offers a particularly useful way of understanding the negotiated reality of the First Nations peoples of Canada. Aboriginality, for the Cree as for Aboriginal populations elsewhere in the world, is a claim to distinctiveness based on the assertion of original occupancy, of land rights, and the concomitant spurning of colonial influences. Aboriginality occurs within the constraints of current political and social relations linking representations of the past with identity constructions in the present. Thus, Aboriginality – however it is locally defined – is the negotiation of the political, cultural, and social space of Aboriginal First Nations peoples within the nation-state (Archer 1991). Aboriginality is a critical political tool – and, as Beckett says, a vital "space of otherness that is shifting, complex, and dynamic [yet] in which Aboriginal imagination can produce an identity" (Beckett 1992, 167; Bennett and Blundell 1995).

It is that inventive and vitally political process that I address in this discussion of the Whapmagoostui Cree of Great Whale River, Quebec. In this community there has been a relatively new annual event, the summer gathering. The gathering can be described at one level as an interlude, a time when and a place where people can come together as a group and revel in "community." The gathering has also evolved into an occasion during which people can, by extension, reflect on issues such as interpersonal violence or substance abuse. The gathering does not directly address these social ills, nor, for that matter, does it seek to cure the fundamental problems of chronic unemployment, poverty, or related social pathologies that people return home to once it is over. The gathering is not a panacea. It is, however, an important local initiative aimed at improving, in the long term, the community's welfare. It is also a time and place for "culture" and "tradition" to be actively negotiated as part and parcel of the larger project of social response. This chapter draws from ethnographic fieldwork conducted at the three gatherings that were held between 1993 and 1995, along with discussions with members of the community about the gatherings that were held at other times of the year.

The village of Whapmagoostui, located approximately 1,400 kilometres north of Montreal, Quebec, is in the taiga region of the subarctic Canadian boreal forest and sits on the northern edge of the mouth of the Great Whale River. Like many remote Aboriginal communities in Canada, today's village site is the product of a history of contact. Great Whale River, to be more specific, consists of two official municipalities – Whapmagoostui (Cree) and Kuujjuarapik (Inuit) – and three unofficial communities – Cree, Inuit, and non-Aboriginal.[3] Whapmagoostui's village borders are circumscribed by the limits of Cree and Inuit designated lands, as set out by the James Bay and Northern Québec Agreement (JBNQA). Cree and Inuktitut are the first languages of the Cree and Inuit communities, respectively.[4]

Whapmagoostui, by comparison to many other communities in Canada, is doing well. Services, schooling, and warm homes are available and there is local government control of many of the immediate aspects of peoples' lives. Many, but by no means all, of the adults have over the last decade moved away from alcohol. There has not been a single "successful" suicide in Whapmagoostui. Yet there are still far too many women and men who are physically and emotionally traumatized or abused, who drink to excess, who hurt their children, or who were themselves hurt as children – people whose lives are scarred by what has aptly been called the pain of being Aboriginal (Gilbert 1995). Personal conflict was exacerbated by the highly publicized struggle that took place between 1989 and 1994 when community members fought to save their river, their land, and themselves from a massive hydroelectric project (Adelson 2000a).

In the next section I describe Whapmagoostui's gatherings, the first of which coincided with the final year of battle against the hydroelectric project originally slated for this region. The gathering has since changed its primary focus somewhat but remains a compelling example of cultural assertion as collective response. It is in the assertion and expression of "culture" as "tradition" and as "product" that one sees the ways in which culture is simultaneously contingent, negotiated, and dynamic.

Whapmagoostui Gatherings, 1993-5

The annual summer gathering began, in part, as a local initiative in the prolonged fight against a hydroelectric project slated for the Great Whale River's waterways. The premise of the first gathering was to promote Cree cultural values in light of the protracted political struggles with Hydro-Québec. After all, the Great Whale hydroelectric project and Cree opposition to it stand today as the most notable recent processes that have directly and indirectly affected this community's overall sense of what it means "to be Cree." That first gathering was described as a way to take stock, to reconsider what "being Cree" means. As then chief Matthew Mukash said at the opening ceremonies: "This gathering is a result of a resolution of the Whapmagoostui First Nation who called for a gathering of this kind to be able to assess the influence of modern impacts on our culture ... There are many reasons for this gathering but the most important is to revisit our culture." And, as another member of the community expressed to me:

> The first summer, 1993, was a very exciting time because it was something new to do and was for a special and specific reason which was to show the outside world that we are still alive and well and practising our way of life. [The first gathering] was quite the learning experience, everybody was there. Because you understood how confused you were and that it was the political fight for the river, but in turn you were going across on the river ... it made it more real; that if this river is gone you won't be able to go across it.[5]

This first gathering was relatively large and was organized in every detail to accommodate the hundreds of Whapmagoostui Cree as well as the more than 100 primarily First Nations guests. In attendance were many of the 600 Whapmagoostui Cree; visitors from Chisasibi who travelled by canoe to attend the event; Inuit from Kuujjuarapik and Povungnituk; professional photographers; film, television, and radio crews; and anthropologists/observers.[6] Other guests included the spiritual leaders, or elders, brought in from the provinces of Manitoba, Ontario, and New Brunswick.[7]

This first week-long gathering officially opened on the afternoon of 26 July 1993 with an honour song by local drummers; a prayer by catechist Joseph Masty Sr.; and speeches by the event coordinator Robbie Dick, Chief Matthew Mukash, and Kuujjuarapik mayor Anthony Ittoshat. Speeches were also made by representatives of the Chisasibi Caravan and the group of Povungnituk Inuit. The majority of the speeches revolved around the general themes of the gathering: to teach and learn about the ways of the Cree people; that ideas and practices need to be rekindled, not lost – brought out, not suppressed. The hydro issue was explicitly raised by some of the speakers. Politics and media attention were central, but they were not the exclusive focus of this first gathering. The gatherings, from the outset, have always constituted a time and place for the young people to learn from the old, a time for people to relax and enjoy themselves away from the village, a time and a place for them to "revisit their culture." The gatherings are, as one woman eloquently stated, "rejuvenating to the spirit and to the history of the Whapmagoostui [people] and other indigenous peoples who join our gatherings. It is a peaceful and an exciting time."

The gathering was held across from the village on the south shore of the mouth of the Great Whale River, within easy view of massive Hudson Bay. This particular site was selected because it was the traditional summer meeting site of the ancestors of the Cree of this northeastern region of Quebec. A recent archeological survey as well as all sorts of old debris found around the campsites attest to the numerous past dwellings in and around this area, as people discovered when, in the process of preparing the ground for their tents, they uncovered such things as an old pipe, a copper nail, and desiccated whale bone. Family camps were set up around the entire gathering site, with tents accommodating in excess of 300 people. Many people spent the entire time at the gathering, perhaps returning by canoe to the village to briefly shower or shop.

The scheduled events of the 1993 gathering began in the early hours of the morning for those who attended the daily sunrise ceremonies. The next event, usually conducted between 9:00 AM and 10:00 AM, was the opening drumming honour song, followed by a Christian prayer recited by a church elder. The rest of the morning was often taken up with speeches and the afternoons were filled with a variety of scheduled workshops. The workshops were conducted by both local and visiting elders, and, more often than not, were divided by gender. Some of the workshop sessions included traditional trap building, making spruce gum glue, traditional lodge building, or carving tools out of wood (all men's work) as well as the proper handling and tanning of caribou hides, knotting fishnets, or making moss diapering (all women's work). Other workshops included sessions on the proper use of language, legends from the past, medicine from plants or animals, or teachings about respect. Geared specifically towards the youth were a number of sessions on married life, traditional versus modern ways, information on alcohol and drugs, spiritual and physical healing, and the problems of peer pressure. Workshops were held either out in the open or in one of the several *iyiyuukimikw* (Cree dwelling, teepee) built for that purpose. A typical craft workshop consisted of an elder member of the community talking about and demonstrating to those present how to go about making a particular item, be it a wooden snow shovel, a diaper of absorbent sphagnum moss, or spruce gum glue. These workshops were, for the most part, well attended in this first year of the gatherings.

Evening and night activities were real crowd pleasers and included some powwow dancing, a concert by the popular Innu duo Kashtin,[8] Cree versions of softball or soccer, and square dancing. An elder's feast was held for all present at the gathering on the last evening of the event. And, of course, there were the closing speeches, an integral – if at times lengthy – part of the event. Thus the first gathering ended successfully and served its dual purpose of bringing the community together and demonstrating its unity to the outside world via the various media who were recording the entire event.

The two gatherings that have taken place since 1993 differ somewhat from that original event. With the shelving of the hydroelectric project in 1994, the gathering no longer had to be a production for anyone but the Whapmagoostui people themselves. The band council and community at large felt that the gatherings had to continue, however, since they had become integral to "the revival of culture here." Locally, this resolute attention to things Cree is unequivocally viewed as beneficial to the long-term and broadly based social health of the community at large. The annual summer gathering has thus evolved into an event that provides a forum for a self-conscious affirmation of particular notions of Aboriginal identity. It has become a time and a place for rethinking and reconstructing cultural practices within the contemporary context of Aboriginal identity in Quebec.

Thus the second and third gatherings were, for the most part, "quieter" than the first in that there were virtually no media – only this anthropologist – as explicit witnesses to the events. Within Whapmagoostui, however, the gatherings have become anything but quieter. In particular, formal discussions by elders about which events should or should not be included as well as general planning and preparations for the gatherings now occur months before the actual event. One woman with whom I discussed the local preparations explained it to me in this way:

> I have noticed when I am at the store, I hear people talking of buying something that they will need for the gathering, things like pots, foam mattresses, sleeping bags, new canvas for a teepee or a new tent. The people seem to prepare for the gathering all year round ... The people start getting firewood and poles for the tents and teepees when the weather starts to warm up, in March. As soon as the river is navigable, in early June, some people will already be putting up their tents and teepees and spend weekends there. People will start packing their stuff as soon as they can to be ready to go at a moment's notice for the actual gathering, which takes place sometime in the middle or near the end of July ... The families will urge the young people to participate in the preparation of the camps. The youth are employed to make ready the guest tents and teepees. They help to erect the dwelling, gather firewood and the [fir] boughs [for the floors]. They get and chop firewood for the elders long before the gathering. When the time comes, everything is ready. All the tents and teepees have already been made.

The second and third summer gatherings were held at a site on the southern shore of the river as well but somewhat closer to the village – just across from the Kuujjuarapik boat docks. This new site, still a place where previous generations camped and lived, was selected primarily because it was considerably more accessible than was the first site. Boats could easily dock on the these shores and people could readily climb the sandy incline or drive an all-terrain vehicle up to the camps. As well, it was felt that there was a larger area for tents to be set up and a natural dell provided an ideal, protected space to build a stage for the speeches and dances.

Both the 1994 and 1995 gatherings were well attended by the Whapmagoostui Cree and Chisasibi Caravan visitors. More than sixty tents and teepees were set up in and around the new location, with at least 300 people living at the gathering site. In accord with the request of the Whapmagoostui elder's council, scheduled events were planned somewhat differently than they were the first year. Specifically, there were fewer speeches and no honour drumming in the mornings. Workshops were scheduled throughout the day, and speeches were relegated to the 6:00 PM to 8:00 PM time slot. Between 8:00 PM and 11:00 PM there were social activities, square dancing, and games. Church services, held at the gathering site, were incorporated into the 1994 and 1995 schedules. Also included in the second and third gatherings, as "other daily activities," were morning and evening sweat lodges conducted by visiting elders, who were also available for individual healing sessions.

The theme of the 1995 gathering was "Protecting our Lands and Traditional Way of Life." Tradition, however, was rethought at this gathering since it was here that the community organized its first formal "traditional powwow." Traditional powwows are large, non-competitive dance and drumming events with specific features such as honour songs, healing dances, and give-aways. In Whapmagoostui, as is normally the case elsewhere, drumming groups, dancers, an elder, and a master of ceremonies were invited in from various other Canadian Aboriginal communities in order to enhance the local event. Powwow dancing activities have, in the last decade in particular, become a growing part of Aboriginal cultural practices across North America. The kind of formalized dancing and drumming that is so familiar at powwows is quite new to Whapmagoostui, however, and, along with Aboriginal spirituality, is growing in popularity and importance for some members of this community. While hardly uncontested locally, the official opening of that first traditional powwow most assuredly confirmed the incorporation of transnational "traditional culture" into Whapmagoostui.[9]

Despite all of the advance planning, late summer wind and rain storms in both 1994 and 1995 ultimately dictated a rather curtailed schedule of outdoor activities. Any indoor workshops that were planned were also not that well attended, although this was for another reason entirely. People were content, it seemed, to just spend a great deal of time at the gathering site visiting with one another. Indeed, a general comment heard often was that the best thing about the 1994 gathering was the time it afforded people to just enjoy each other's company in familiar camp surroundings in a way that is structurally impossible back in the village. The time of the gathering was used to cook and eat bush foods, talk, and listen to or tell stories; in other words, it was a time to just relax and enjoy oneself. People may have been conscious of doing "Cree things" at scheduled events or activities, but, for the most part, many spent their days as they might typically at any hunting camp – collecting and splitting wood, getting water or fir boughs, relaxing, playing checkers, eating, drinking tea, or enjoying a good story or two. There is, simply put, a particular enjoyment derived from being together and socializing in this communal camp setting, which is so familiar to families who regularly live in the bush during hunting seasons. At the gatherings, though, there is also a conscious focus on the past and on what will be lost with the passing of the elder members of the community, including the (oral) histories of the people as well as the language in which they are told:

> When people are at these gatherings they visit each other more often and they see each other at the outdoor events. They help each other out. Some will get water and chop firewood and cook food to share with all the family members. It is a time of getting closer to your own family members because you are living in the same tent with them. Some family groups will even join their tents together. In this way, there are more open discussions about things in general and personal family member things ... When I was there with my mother, she would start telling us a story that she had heard her mother tell her about her parents – an event that happened right there on those [gathering] grounds. It made my ancestors more real and I felt closer to them and wanted to know about them when they were alive.
>
> It is at these events where our language comes out strong as well, living here in [the village] without associating with the nature half of our language means that [so much] is not used. Whereas if we live in the bush or at camp, words and expressions in Cree come out, which we don't normally use here in the community. Best of all the teachings from our elders come out so strong, they have so much to teach us and we have so much that we need to learn.

The proximity of one family dwelling to the next and the soft, permeable walls of a canvas tent are, as people note, far more conducive to communication than are the permanent houses back in town.

> Then there is the community togetherness that is not here [in the village]. Because it's very hard. Even with my next door neighbour – we have walls ... [on] both sides, we would live this close if we were in a tent side by side. All those barriers that were put around us, barriers that isolate us from one another, are taken away when we live in our traditional way, on the traditional site ... Just the setting is different because if you are in a school or in a – even a community home, you're being taught – there is a constant reminder of what was taken away.

The permeable walls also mean something else for members of the community: "You look around and people are happy ... you don't hear – one of the things that I am very glad about because there are no physical outbursts of family violence in the tents." Linked to this is the fact that the gathering is a "dry" event: no alcohol is allowed at the site.

To summarize, the gatherings bring people together at a historically important site where they can opt to participate in various specific cultural events and activities. Along with the (moderately attended) workshops, there are feasts, ceremonies, and speeches. There are square dances and powwow dances. There are caribou, geese, bannock, and tea along with soft drinks, fried foods, chocolate, and cakes. There is a ceremonial fire and tobacco offerings. There are mugs, sweatshirts, and key chains made specifically to commemorate and subsidize the event. There are visiting healers and visiting anthropologists. There are stories about the past and gossip about the present and future. There are church services. There are sweat lodges and healing ceremonies.

Reflections on Aboriginality and Tradition at the Gatherings

For the Whapmagoostui *Iiyiyuu'ch* ("Cree people") the issue of hydroelectric development was undoubtedly the impetus for the first gathering. It was, to a large extent, the seemingly interminable and unblinking eye of the cameras on the community during their lengthy opposition to the hydroelectric project that instigated this search for, and affirmation of, Cree identity. That first gathering, in turn, became a media event itself because the band wanted to record how people went about "revisiting their culture." The second and third gatherings were no longer public displays for the outside world but, rather, time set aside for the people of Whapmagoostui to draw from their past and from the present, to reflect upon their contemporary situation while living in a communal setting away from the village.

The planned "cultural" activities – the workshops – were not all that successful, however. These events mattered but were not central to the success of the second and third gatherings. Indeed, despite the gatherings being organized to highlight specific material cultural artefacts and practices, those programs lost out to checkers, storytelling, cooking, relaxation, square dancing, and, for some, sweat lodges and healing sessions. The opportunity to be amongst extended families, whether learning from them or simply relaxing with them, was viewed as being more significant than any of the planned activities. In living at the gathering site, recounting stories of the past, and eating bush foods such as goose or caribou, and in enacting newly invigorated practices such as sweat lodges or powwows, there is a conscious melding of old and new. People are not so much "revisiting the past" as they are negotiating and constructing a new sense of themselves as Aboriginal Canadians. The people of Whapmagoostui are making their own history – melding influences, commodities, practices, and products (Clifford 1995) – as they create and define their collective sense of Aboriginality.

To be sure, part and parcel of the negotiation of Aboriginality is the telling of and acting upon a particular historical identity (Friedman 1992). What it means to be Cree draws, to a large extent, on the oral historical record and interpretations of the past as it is constituted through the retelling of stories of hunting and survival. The temporal and social space of the gathering are thus significant and evocative. The planning, preparing, the readying of the site itself with stage, tents, wood, fir boughs, and even adequate waste facilities signify the importance of this place. Having the gathering both near the end of the summer and at this site establishes a temporal link to the congregations of family ancestors who travelled to this very spot for their summer respite from harsh winter work and travel.

As well, the move away from the village is viewed as particularly important. The village is recognized as a useful but imposed structure and a reminder of a colonial history. Home has far less to do with village houses than it does with family and the expanse of land to the north, south, and east of the Whapmagoostui. Thus one might argue that the short-lived week-long gathering instills more of a sense of permanence than do the concrete-based houses of the village. We clearly see in this an expressed opposition between village and land-based dwellings. There are, in fact, numerous dualisms at play here. People speak of the impermeability of the walls of the village homes versus the permeable canvas tents, isolation versus connection, present versus past, and, of course, alcohol versus dry. These are without doubt potent symbolic oppositions that all locate Cree against non-Cree, or "Whitemen."

The claim to cultural authenticity is made, more specifically, in contradistinction to what is summarized through the conceptual figure of "Whiteman"; that is, the industrial, individualistic, overly secular governing society that perpetually marginalizes Aboriginal Canadians (Légaré 1995, Adelson 2000a). Yet herein lies the provenance of Aboriginality. It is through those oppositions that identity is constructed, that a sense of Aboriginality is developed and ultimately expressed. And yet Aboriginality is not simply a rejection of all things non-Aboriginal. It is a melding of concepts and practices – powwows, dancing, playing checkers, living in tents, hearing stories from the past, videotaping the present, scraping hides, eating bush foods, along with purchasing gathering memorabilia such as t-shirts or mugs – that authenticates a particular identity. Further, it is in the assertion of a particular and particularly political stance – however it is defined – that we find the basis of local strength. To defer to Ortner (1995, 186) one last time, "every culture, sub-culture, every historical moment, constructs its own forms of agency, its own modes of enacting the process of reflecting on the self and the world and of acting simultaneously within and upon what one finds there." Salée (1995, 293) puts it slightly differently:

> The ancestral customs and practices, however thin they may wear in some cases, serve as ideological mooring where the collective imagination can anchor and elaborate a concrete identity. This identity, even if invented, even if tainted by borrowings from the very culture it claims to oppose politically, constitutes the impregnable rock on which Aboriginal [peoples] lay their territorial claims, mobilize themselves, and express their desire to gain autonomous control of their collective destiny.

And, I would emphatically add, even if borrowed from near and distant Aboriginal neighbours, the question of authenticity is moot. It is not important to ask whether powwow dancing is authentically Cree or how much people choose to integrate Aboriginal and non-Aboriginal materials or practices but, rather, to ask what purpose Aboriginality serves and, in particular, to what ends? The analytic task, in other words, is "not to strip away the invented portions of culture as inauthentic, but to understand the process by which they acquire authenticity" (Hanson 1989, 198). All traditions are invented in as much as they are reproduced from year to year: and the gathering exemplifies that process by which traditions "present and reflect contemporary concerns and purposes rather than a passively inherited legacy" (Linnekin 1991, 446). Aboriginality is increasingly constructed as an exchange, layering, and intermingling of old, new, adopted, and created Cree practices. Practices such as powwows and sweat lodges, both rooted in various Aboriginal histories across the Americas, are coming increasingly to symbolize transnational Aboriginal unity as well as local potential in Whapmagoostui. Thus, "being Cree" is actively negotiated and lived in Whapmagoostui today; yet, as Clifford (1995, 100), paraphrasing Marx, similarly notes for the Wahgi, "not in conditions of their choosing."

It is, I think, sadly ironic that the Whapmagoostui *Iiyiyuu'ch* must strive to build, let alone assert, cultural identity. Yet it is that sense of Aboriginality – what was not that long ago either forbidden or trounced right out of people – that now serves as one of the incremental stepping stones towards social and political awareness, strength and social healing. Culture does not "cure" (cf. Santiago-Irizarry 1996), but, in negotiating what it means "to be Cree," people have some control over their identity and its significance and implications. There is no one particular configuration of being Cree, or Aboriginal, for that matter. This is part of the "historical reality and agency of human diversity" (Clifford 1995, 100) that ultimately defines Aboriginality. That active, conscious, and imaginative process finds points of convergence and resonance at the summer gatherings where people have the opportunity to reflect upon and negotiate their cultural and political identities.

Conclusion

Writing about commodification and the individuation of tradition in Papua New Guinea (PNG), Errington and Gewertz (1996) reflect upon the shifting uses of culture. They examine culture as both source and resource; that is, as a dynamic commodity that gets redefined depending upon how it is used and by whom. They reflect on the ironic circumstance of how "traditional culture" is commodified in a fight to regain "traditional" cultural values. Writing about the Chambri of PNG, Errington and Gewertz (1996, 124) note that, "rather than peripheral in a global village, the Chambri home communities would become models of a globe of villages. Not bad work, if the government or PepsiCo ... would help them get it." Culture as source and resource has, according to these two anthropologists, become the central aspect of modernity everywhere from Eastern Europe to the Amazon (114). I would, for the most part, agree with their assessment. In Whapmagoostui, culture is undeniably growing as source – if not resource – and as a means of mediating the fragmenting effects of the neocolonial enterprise. There is undeniable political efficacy in the use of "culture" (equated with "tradition") as people in Whapmagoostui attempt to locally renegotiate the terms and conditions of identity in the face of direct and indirect threats to their land, lives, and livelihoods. The annual summer gathering, as a (re-)new(ed) event, links this community not just to a precolonial past but to a present and future that include a growing range of what will constitute Aboriginal beliefs and practices.

Notes

This chapter – an earlier version of which appears as an AGREE Discussion Paper (Adelson 1997) – arose out of a 1996 presentation to the Aboriginal Government, Resources, Economy and Environment (AGREE) Research Group at McGill University and draws from my research on social suffering, social health, and Aboriginality. I thank the Social Sciences and Humanities Research Council of Canada (Strategic Grants Program), the US Social Science and Research Council's Committee on Culture, Health and Human Development, and the Faculty of Arts of York University for generously funding the first three years of my research at the Whapmagoostui gatherings. I graciously thank the Whapmagoostui First Nation Band Council for their continued support of my work in their community. An untold number of heady and rewarding discussions have led to the production of this chapter. I thank, in particular, Colin Scott, Margaret Lock, Arthur Kleinman, Lisa M. Mitchell, J. Teresa Holmes, Cathrine Degnen, Liz Fajber, and, especially, Emily Masty and Arthur Cheechoo for their insights and comments on various earlier drafts of this work.

1 The people of Whapmagoostui have only in the last few years begun to regularly invite elders/healers into the community. Specifically, their work includes performing ceremonies (blessing homes, feasts for the departed), running sweat lodges, individualized

healing sessions, and group teachings on the Medicine Wheel. They are often invited in as part of alcohol and drug abuse or related social service programs. To be sure, the community has not extended wholesale acceptance to the "traditional" practices, but the healers are playing a larger and larger role in the processes of "social healing."

2 This should not be surprising, as one elder who teaches the traditions explained to me, since the prophecies indicated that the return to traditional Aboriginal practices would spread from west to east.

3 There are approximately 300 Inuit living in Kuujjuarapik and 150 non-Aboriginal Francophones living primarily on Inuit 1A lands. It is only in the last few years, since many Inuit moved to the newly created village of Umiujaq, that the Cree outnumber the Inuit. Umiujaq, located about 100 kilometres north of Great Whale, is a village that was petitioned for by Kuujjuarapik Inuit as part of the compensation package in the JBNQA. The construction and eventual move to this new coastal village took place in the early 1980s. The non-Aboriginal teachers, government employees, hydro workers, police, employment officer, postal employees, aviation workers, and engineers all live near their respective offices. This entire section is literally "up the hill" from the two Aboriginal communities. For the most part there is very little social interaction between those who live up the hill and those who live in the Aboriginal communities. There are, of course, other layers of political import here, as those who live "up the hill" are primarily well employed French Quebecers. They are what I would refer to as "sovereignty pioneers," perhaps inadvertently asserting Quebec's nationalist agenda (e.g., celebrating St. Jean Baptiste, a particular national[ist] holiday) on Aboriginal lands. These issues are relevant but tangential to those raised in this chapter (see, for example, Salée 1995).

4 Communication between the three (unofficial) communities occurs most often in a fourth language – English. Since Cree and Inuit speak different mother tongues and hunt in different areas, and since people tend to socialize largely within their own extended kin groups, there tends to be only limited socializing between the two communities.

5 Whapmagoostui is the real name of this very small community. For this reason, and for reasons of practical ethics, I do not disclose the identity of the men and women who shared their time and stories with me. While this does a disservice to those individuals, I am bound by the rules that govern the ethical conduct of research and must forego the nuance of detail for the larger narrative that is being told here.

6 Approximately fifty members of the Cree village of Chisasibi, about 100 kilometres to the south, paddled up to Great Whale in a caravan of seven canoes in order to participate in the gathering. The Caravan trip and the stay at the gathering were recorded on video by a Chisasibi production crew. In addition, Inuit guests had come by trawler from Povungnituk, a community further up the Hudson Bay coast, in order to actively show their alliance with the Cree and Inuit of Great Whale in their struggle against Hydro-Québec. This was an exceptionally welcome act, given that the provincial Inuit leadership had already resolved themselves to the (apparent) inevitability of the hydroelectric project.

7 Aboriginal spirituality was certainly a part of the 1993 gathering and an even greater part of the 1994 and 1995 events. The elders were active participants in the gatherings, leading various teaching sessions as well as performing the sunrise ceremonies, conducting sweat lodges, and delivering healing services as requested. As noted earlier, this shift to – and friction around – increasing Aboriginal spirituality in Whapmagoostui is a separate but related issue.

8 The Kashtin concert was held at the large gym in the village and was attended by hundreds of Cree and Inuit. The Cree elders complained, however, that the people should not have left the gathering site en masse as they did. All activities in 1994 were kept at the site. In 1995, the powwow was postponed so often due to inclement weather that the decision was finally taken to move it to the village band hall.

9 Because of inclement weather the opening ceremonies of this powwow were held early Sunday evening, conflicting with church services. Those who attended the powwow commented that there would likely have been a better turnout if there had not been this scheduling conflict. This may or may not be true. My current research specifically addresses the conflicts surrounding the incorporation of "traditional" practices in Whapmagoostui.

References

Adelson, N. 1997. "Gathering Knowledge: Reflections on the Anthropology of Identity, Aboriginality, and the Annual Gatherings in Whapmagoostui, Québec." AGREE Discussion Paper No 1. Montreal: McGill University.

–. 2000a. *Being Alive Well: Health and the Politics of Cree Well-Being*. Toronto: University of Toronto Press.

–. 2000b. "Re-imagining Aboriginality: An Indigenous Peoples' Response to Social Suffering." *Transcultural Psychiatry* 37, 1: 11-34.

Archer, Jeff. 1991. "Ambiguity in Political Ideology: Aboriginality as Nationalism." *TAJA* 2, 2: 161-9.

Beckett, Jeremy. 1992. "Comment on Hollinsworth." *Oceania* 63: 165-7.

Bennett, Tony, and Valda Blundell. 1995. "First Peoples." *Cultural Studies* 9, 1: 1-10.

Clifford, James. 1995. "Paradise." *Visual Anthropology Review* 11, 1: 93-117.

Comaroff, Jean. 1985. *Body of Power, Spirit of Resistance*. Chicago: University of Chicago Press.

Errington, Frederick, and Deborah Gewertz. 1996. "The Individuation of Tradition in a Papua New Guinean Modernity." *American Anthropologist* 98, 1: 114-26.

Friedman, Jonathan. 1992. "Myth, History, and Political Identity." *Cultural Anthropology* 7, 2: 194-210.

Gilbert, Stephanie. 1995. "Postcolonial Aboriginal Identity." *Cultural Studies* 9, 1: 145-9.

Hanson, Allan. 1989. "The Making of the Maori: Culture Invention and Its Logic." *American Anthropologist* 91, 4: 890-902.

Légaré, Evelyn I. 1995. "Canadian Multiculturalism and Aboriginal People: Negotiating a Place in the Nation." *Identities* 1, 4: 347-66.

Linnekin, Jocelyn. 1991. "Cultural Invention and the Dilemma of Authenticity." *American Anthropologist* 93, 2: 446-9.

McMaster, Gerald R. 1995. "Border Zones: The 'Injun-uity' of Aesthetic Tricks." *Cultural Studies* 9, 1: 74-90.

O'Neil, John. 1993. "Report from the Round Table Rapporteur." In *The Path to Healing: Report of the National Round Table on Aboriginal Health and Social Issues*, ed. Royal Commission on Aboriginal Peoples, 13-24. Ottawa: Ministry of Supply and Services Canada.

Ortner, Sherry. 1995. "Resistance and the Problem of Ethnographic Refusal." *Comparative Studies in Society and History* 37, 1: 173-93.

Royal Commission on Aboriginal Peoples (RCAP). 1995. *Choosing Life: Special Report on Suicide Among Aboriginal People*. Ottawa: Canada Communication Group.

Salée, Daniel. 1995. "Identities in Conflict: The Aboriginal Question and the Politics of Recognition in Quebec." *Ethnic and Racial Studies* 18, 2: 277-314.

Santiago-Irizarry, Vilma. 1996. "Culture as Cure." *Cultural Anthropology* 11, 1: 3-24.

16
Building a Community in the Town of Chisasibi

Susan Jacobs

In 1980, 1,500 Cree people were relocated from Fort George Island to a nearby site on the mainland of northern Quebec. The move to the new town of Chisasibi was prompted by the expected effects of the James Bay power project, which would engineer increased flows of the La Grande River and significant erosion of the island. At the time of this research in 1992, more than a decade after families and houses were resettled, the Cree still did not feel at home in Chisasibi. Although careful plans allowed houses literally to be lifted from the island and placed upon new foundations in the mainland town just a few kilometres away, the sense of community known to the people of Fort George did not cross the river with them to Chisasibi.

The move to Chisasibi was made in the name of development – of North America's hydroelectric resources, of Canadian economic power, of infrastructure in Northern Quebec, of a stronger mixed economy for James Bay Cree communities. Why then, has the development of a sense of community been so difficult in Chisasibi? To what extent do women feel it is their responsibility to build community? How will they do it? What obstacles stand in their way? This chapter, based on fieldwork conducted in Chisasibi, explores the answers the Cree women offered to these questions.

My approach to data collection and analysis assumes that, in Chisasibi, women's relationships and responsibilities are linked in a complex network and that research must therefore begin with an understanding of women's everyday world and realities. This approach is similar to that taken by Youngs (1991) and Poelzer (1991), both of whom worked with Aboriginal women in Saskatchewan. Poelzer, in turn, borrowed from Smith (1987).

My definition of "community" is adopted from Blythe, Brizinski, and Preston's (1985) work with Cree women as well as from their work in Moosonee and Moose Factory. These authors use the fluid concepts of "family" and "community" to describe networks of affiliation between people and responsibilities according to those relationships. The concepts of family and community are overlapping rather than exclusive: women create networks that "have meaning because they represent an investment in community through family, and a support of family through community" (Blythe, Brizinski, and Preston 1985, 150).

Chisasibi in Context

Chisasibi has been perched on the banks of La Grande River where it meets James Bay since 1980, when construction of the new town was sufficiently complete for people to be relocated from the island of Fort George. The move was effected according to a plan negotiated by the Cree and the Quebec government pursuant to the 1975 James Bay and Northern Québec Agreement (JBNQA). The ancestors of Chisasibi's people have lived on and near the eastern coast of James Bay since before recorded history, subsisting on harvests from their hunting, fishing, and trapping activities. Cree history teaches us that, in summer, many nomadic Cree people would gather for summer festivities on an island located where La Grande River flows into James Bay.

That island was given the name Fort George in 1803 by European traders who established a Hudson's Bay Company post there. Along with a new name for the island, the traders brought a number of new institutions to the region. The flourishing fur trade brought early diversity to the Cree economy. Europeans and Euro-Canadians instituted an Anglican mission (1852) and school (1907) and, later, a Roman Catholic mission (1927). Throughout this period, Cree families continued to spend the majority of the year on their hunting territories, and they continued to camp and trade on the island during midsummer. During the 1960s, government services grew to the point that significant numbers of Cree people could settle into wage employment or sustain themselves, in part, through transfer payments (C. Scott, personal communication, 1997). In 1980, the 2,000 or so permanent residents of Fort George[1] – 1,558 Cree, 150 non-status "Indians," 53 Inuit, and 200 non-Aboriginals – were relocated to Chisasibi on the mainland due to the expected erosion from the rerouting of the water systems for the James Bay Power Project (Shaw 1982, 6).

The new town of Chisasibi is fairly isolated from even its nearest neighbours. The second northernmost of the nine Quebec Cree communities, its coastal location allows residents access to the nearby islands and waters of James Bay and Hudson Bay, including Fort George Island. Sixteen hundred kilometres north of Montreal, Chisasibi is at the northern extreme of the 700-kilometre Route de la Baie James, which has provided road access to northern Quebec via Matagami since 1973. Chisasibi's nearest neighbour, Radisson, is a Hydro-Québec town 100 kilometres to the east along the

Route de la Baie James. A small airstrip in Chisasibi allows access by plane, but the majority of air traffic terminates at the larger airport near Radisson and Hydro-Québec's LG-2 complex.

An estimated 3,000 people currently reside in Chisasibi. The 2,500 permanent residents are mostly Cree, including descendants of both Coastal and Inland Cree "cultural groups" – a distinction based on whether ancestors lived, hunted, and trapped along the coast or along the river systems of the inland forests.[2] Permanent residents also include several Inuit families as well as Aboriginal and non-Aboriginal people from other regions who have married into Cree families.

Chisasibi, a deliberately landscaped modern town with a sprawling residential zone filled with clusters of houses arranged in culs-de-sac, is markedly different from the old residential pattern of Fort George, where houses and teepees stood together in much larger groups. In addition to the 200 houses that were hauled by barge from Fort George to Chisasibi in 1980, some 125 new houses have been built. During the summer of 1992, two more clusters of homes were being constructed along La Grande River to meet the needs of a growing resident population. With these two new clusters, Chisasibi approaches the outer limits of land suitable for residences, as housing clusters fan out from the centralized commercial buildings.

Landscaped gravel paths wind between housing clusters, alongside scattered teepees and around Chisasibi. More direct dirt paths forged by residents' consistent use, and unplanned by outside architects, cut directly from house to house or lead from housing clusters into the commercial zone sometimes referred to as "town." The commercial and social infrastructure is built along Chisasibi's central road, where residents can easily gain access to the hospital, the school, the arena (with a craft shop and a restaurant), the community centre (unfinished and unusable as of 1992), the daycare centre, the construction offices, an Anglican church, a Roman Catholic church, an additional convenience store, the local police station, the newly constructed women's shelter, and the multipurpose commercial centre.

Employment in Chisasibi takes many forms: wages are available through both market-based economic activity and subsistence-based activity (in the latter case through the Income Security Program for Cree Hunters and Trappers, or ISP[3]). The school board, the health board, and the band office are the three main sources of non-ISP wages in Chisasibi, as they are in other James Bay communities. Many people are employed in formal and informal private enterprises, such as small businesses and restaurants, craft work, sale of bush food, and babysitting. Seasonal employment ranges from clearing roads in winter, to making and flooding ponds for better waterfowl hunting, to escorting tourists around the nearby islands by canoe. Many people work at home, managing households and families, carving, quilting, or doing bead work to be sold privately or in one of the local shops. It is difficult to meet the high cost of living in this remote northern region; fresh food in the supermarket can cost double what it does in Montreal. Having a family member who harvests bush food on the ISP is a definite advantage, particularly for those households whose other occupational options are limited.

Educational opportunities in Chisasibi are sufficiently diverse to meet the needs of potential students at all levels. The James Bay Eeyou School (JBES) falls under the regional jurisdiction of the Cree School Board (CSB). Estimated enrolment for the 1992-3 school year was 550 elementary and 320 secondary students (personal communication, JBES main office staff). At the JBES, primary students are taught in Cree during the early grades; by the secondary level they are well into either the French or English curriculum and are taught mostly by non-Cree teachers. Courses that teach Cree culture are offered throughout primary and secondary grades. The school year schedule incorporates seasonal Goose Breaks in October and May, during which families may leave town together, go to the bush, and participate in another fundamental system of education. While some students attend school outside Chisasibi at primary and secondary levels, all those who attend CEGEP and university must leave Chisasibi to do so, as neither level of schooling is available locally.

Dislocation Effect of Relocation

Why, with all this well-developed infrastructure and opportunity, do so few people presently feel at home in the town of Chisasibi? The reasons given are diverse, but the two most commonly cited concern the relocation experience and the difference in physical layout of Chisasibi as compared with Fort George.

Some people were away from Fort George (in school, hospital, etc.) while their homes were transported across the water and pulled by flatbeds to new locations in Chisasibi. Families whose homes were moved in the early stages of the several-month moving process found themselves across the river in a partially completed community, surrounded by different neighbours than they had before. Families who were moved during the final phases of the schedule watched the systematic demolition of familiar buildings of Fort George buildings that, for many of them, held several generations of memories. A woman who left Chisasibi for school and returned to work in the band office, with the express goal of helping to rebuild the community, explained the impact of relocation on Chisasibi's residents:

> We were one of the last families to move, so I slowly saw the community disappear. It was like a ghost town – that's what it felt like. It was in the fall, in November. When I first got here I was totally lost, I couldn't even leave

> the house, I was totally insecure. Even today here, it doesn't seem like a community here. People do their own thing. I guess it's all spread out. You live in this little cluster with your own family, people don't visit each other. It's not the same.

She also taps into the commonly expressed perception that something about Chisasibi's physical layout prevents the growth of community spirit:

> I find it quite – I think it's – mmmm – going to take a long – and also – well – with everything going on in our community today [it] has a lot to do with moving over here. They uprooted an entire community, moved it into an entirely new structure. The way it's set up here, nobody likes it, everybody complains about it.

Another woman elaborates on this point, providing an explanation of how the town layout affects behaviour:

> Our lifestyle has changed and the way we behave towards each other it's completely different. We don't visit each other. Even though your relatives are right next door, they don't come and visit. I heard about a study that if the houses are like that, in clusters, people behave that way. Our lifestyle before – we would find a nice place and put your tent there. No zoning. Now there will be zoning – this is for commercial, this is for housing. Our lives will be more structured, and that's the way we're geared to work now – they're laying down more policy.

The difference in the layout of Fort George and that of Chisasibi was intentional. The permanent settlement at Fort George had grown around a trading post and a mission, it had been constructed by non-Aboriginal people to draw Aboriginal people into the fur trade and to acculturate them to Euro-Canadian society, and its configuration reflected the needs of institutions and governments foreign to the James Bay region.

In contrast, over 170 years later, Chisasibi was planned collaboratively by the local Cree government, the Fort George residents who were to be relocated, and hired consultants and planners. Brainstorming sessions and detailed surveys sought to determine residents' preferences on a range of issues. A local housing group was formed to submit potential design and layout plans for new homes.

Much of this planning effort could not be implemented in actual construction. Environmental factors narrowed opportunities for the extension of necessary utilities to homes, and the remaining options would have been too costly to execute and maintain. As a result, housing group designs that had been developed during collaborative planning sessions were abandoned. Families live in closer proximity than would have been preferable; clusters of homes often do not house residents' expressed choices of neighbours; and there is much less room for children to play or tents to be set up away from roads than people suggested was necessary (Shaw 1982, 107-26). The planning process for Chisasibi gave residents a welcome opportunity to participate, but compromising on their preferences has left them living in a place that does not feel like their own.

Extent of Women's Responsibilities

Of course, everyone has a part in building a community. But women explain why, as women, they feel responsible for rebuilding their families and the community. Responsibilities for their families have been handed down to women from the generations before them.

> And with my mother, like she had a duty with our family, I tried to learn from that. When we moved over [from Fort George], we sort of lost track of that. Even if we live in a cluster, I'm the only one who goes into other houses. My brothers have passed away, and I told my sisters-in-law that I won't treat them any differently ... Cooking food, including love in it, the best, and sending it over.

And they are being carried out for the sake of those that follow.

> I have a purpose in life – it's my kids' future also I have to worry about. I tell them this is for them, it's their community and I want to make it as healthy and as positive as I can for them instead of moving away.

Strengthening the family, as women see it, also means ensuring the welfare of men. One woman explained the mandate that was handed to her by an elder at a conference:

> She said "us women, we have to get up and carry our men, to lead them – us – to have their rightful place back as protectors of our communities, women and children." I believed her a hundred percent. It could do a lot for the community. Our community is a good community, our children can grow up to be anybody that they want. We as adults have to clean our households up and be able to face any obstacle in the community, I know it's possible. That's one goal I haven't accomplished yet – but before I leave this earth I will. Many of the women elders I met, they went through their life as volunteers. That inspired me. I've still got a lot to learn, to share, as a woman, to the community and for my family. Because we have a lot of

> power, and it's very important to play your role as a woman in the community ... That's the most important role in life, as a woman.

Another woman articulated her sense that, in the face of social problems, it is women especially who are expected to continue to respond to the immediate needs of community and family:

> I still don't understand the men's perception of what's going on. There's a phenomenon of men in their fifties who are unable to work [in office jobs]. They have a block. While women do whatever it takes to keep the family going.

Moving Towards Home

Women speak with great concern about family welfare and community relations because these are the key institutions that determine the future of Chisasibi's young people. When asked to list the major events of Chisasibi's brief history, people list the tragic deaths by suicide, fire, and car accidents, and the looming spectres of alcohol and abuse. With respect to these tragedies, nobody is concerned with assigning blame: everyone is busy trying to find solutions. In recent years residents have seen a concerted effort to organize community activities such as concerts, dances, sports, and community service projects. But in addition to staging new events, Chisasibi's women are talking about the importance of returning to where people feel at ease and of redoubling their efforts to educate youth about Cree values.

Returning to Fort George

One way Chisasibi's residents are recapturing, perhaps regenerating, what they lost in the move is by returning to Fort George. Intermittently throughout the summer months, people cross over from Chisasibi to Fort George, some to walk among the fireweed or to camp in a quiet spot, others to attend church services, still others to clean up after the celebrations. During the summer of 1992, these families were joined at Fort George by most of the residents of Chisasibi on two occasions. In July, the celebration of Mamowedow, the traditional return to the island, brought most residents across for a few days. The August powwow offered occasion to return again to Fort George, and the festive island population for those three days included visitors, dancers, and craftspeople from around the world. Adelson (1997; also Chapter 15, this volume) describes similar summer gatherings of the Whapmagoostui Cree as deliberate acts of healing. The annual Whapmagoostui gatherings are held in a site where their ancestors met during long-ago summers. That is true of the Fort George site as well, though its use continued up until the 1980 move. One woman explains how people, even children who are too young to remember Fort George as it was before the move, act and feel better when they are spending time on the island. "Many people feel that way [they prefer Fort George]. My kids like it there, during Mamowedow and the powwow. They like it, it's more free, no trucks, safer there. People are more relaxed." Going back to Fort George for these traditional gatherings seems to revive people, and when they later return to Chisasibi, they bring that new energy with them.

Reinforcing Cree Values through Education

One of women's roles is to ensure that their children learn Cree values: "Especially the Cree values – making bannock, [etc.]. I try to teach that to my kids. I don't want to rob my kids of that part of their lives."

Women talked about sharing, and its noticeable absence, with great concern. Sharing has also been a favourite topic among scholars of the Cree, beginning with Flannery (1935), E. Rogers (1963), and P. Rogers (1965) in their discussion of complementarity and reciprocal relationships brought about by "divisions" of labour. The importance of the principle and practice of generalized reciprocity among Cree people of the James Bay region has been taken up more recently by Scott (1989, 1988) and Scott and Feit (1992). Symbolic associations between reciprocity and the complementarity of men's and women's roles have also been addressed (see, for instance, Scott [1983] and Tanner [1979]). Today it is simply referred to as an essential building block for community: "We have our values, we've lost them – the young people. Living together, sharing. We've got to teach them that."

The local school could be a key medium through which to learn about values and about Cree culture in general, but women explain that the school system does not adequately meet the needs of Cree communities. The Cree School Board (CSB) curriculum used at the James Bay Eeyou School is largely based on the standard Quebec curriculum, a portion of which has been adapted specifically to the James Bay region. On the one hand, CSB schools must prepare students to continue their education at postsecondary institutions outside the Cree school system. On the other hand, they must also incorporate Cree content in order to prepare students for life in the region. Parents feel that the school system has been unable to teach traditional Cree values such as honesty, respect for fellow humans (especially for older members of the community), self-reliance, hard work, friendliness, and good manners. These are among the Cree values that parents discuss, along with the importance of learning to do things not for reward but for the sake of doing them (Chisasibi Band Council 1991, 10).

Parents have voiced their concerns that the school system does not sufficiently integrate the teaching of Cree culture and values. At the former Sand Park School at Fort George, parents requested that more hunting, trapping, and related bush skills be incorporated into the school curriculum (Kilfoil 1977, 22-3). This incorporation has been neither easy nor adequate since relocation and the adoption of a new school system.

The process of establishing a curriculum at the JBES – one that satisfactorily meets provincial standards and the unique needs of local people – is largely one of studied trial and error. Women mentioned several factors that contribute to the difficulties of learning Cree culture through the school system. Primarily, classroom-based education presents Cree students with a learning process that promotes learning by reading or listening rather than by experiencing or apprenticing.

> People relate more now to doing things, rather than sitting back in a classroom. Yes they have to learn theory, but is it better that they practice what they learn in theory so they can relate better? Something more concrete and less abstract, and why do we have to do formal schooling and all that? Why do we have to finish at a certain age? Why do we have to do that? If you want to take your kids and go when they're ten in the bush, they're learning skills, how do you evaluate that? How do you mark it?

Cree people continue to place high value on learning by example. Parents would like the school to hire a Cree elder who would be available to help students learn about Cree values and to try to incorporate into the school system the tradition of learning by apprenticeship.

Learning in the Bush

Women feel confident that the bush will continue to be an important venue for enabling students to learn, with their families, the essential values that they are expected to know and to use throughout their lives. "I've always encouraged education and bush life. [My] son finished his exams in May and was in the bush the next day." In fact, many women indicate that the bush is superior to school as a place to learn because bush life furnishes students with vital skills and with Cree values.

> About learning discipline, planning, management, preparation in the bush – this is what I mean in terms of life skills – it is a discipline too, taking seasons into account, preparing, ensure not to overlap. Managing – wildlife management, rotating areas. We have the best managers.

> For me, I think the best education, when you think about how you live life, is the bush life. Say for instance a man – he has to learn humility – you can't be a real hunter unless you're humble. Not a true Cree hunter. [In the bush, you] learn so much about life. Women too – I still plan to learn that.

> One of my goals is to find the time to learn that. I told myself that in university, "now I have learned that, [later I will go back to learn from the bush]."

Frustrated that their children are not learning these values in the town or at school, women look to the bush as a necessary educational resource. "I think of sending my boy in the bush with elders so they can teach him to respect others, animals – my parents did that to me when I was still running around, being bad. I took my books with me from school, did it in the evenings. In the day I'd help my grandmother and grandfather."

Obstacles to Living and Learning in the Bush

The time schedule of the school year is one of the main obstacles to students having the opportunity to go to the bush for extended periods of time. Parents must choose one educational forum or the other for their children. One effort to integrate the school year with the seasonal calendar involves the biannual Goose Break, during which families are able to go together to the bush. Even then, the tensions between the two systems of education can be a source of conflict. One mother explains:

> [This past] Goose Break, [my] youngest daughter brought homework out to the camp. We live there for two or three weeks. Traditional Break is not a holiday – people are busy, even kids, you're forever busy, even kids. [My daughter's] school bag is there, full and heavy. I said, "What is that doing here?" [Her response was] "I have homework." [After the Goose Break I asked my daughter] "Well, when did you do it?" What were the teachers doing – thinking – giving homework? [Later] the guidance counsellor called and said [my daughter] didn't do her homework so she had to stay in late for the week and hand it in by Friday. What was the teacher thinking, giving homework over the Goose Break? I'll bring it up at school night.

Women describe the bush as a place where children and families learn life skills that are applicable anywhere as well as hunting and trapping skills particular to the region. It provides a chance for generations and families to spend meaningful time together. The bush is a place for haven, for overcoming problems, and for being able to pursue a lifestyle that is comfortable, familiar, and rejuvenating. For many whose lives are rooted in town, the bush represents an ideal way of living. One mother who has been working for more than fifteen years said: "Since I was working, I've never had the chance to go away to the bush except for traditional breaks. Maybe eventually I'll take some time off and live in the bush." A young mother of two stated: "If I had the chance, I would go for a year." Another woman explains how community-based demands keep them from the bush: "We've been talking about taking a year off and going to the bush ... my husband used to be in road maintenance in the winter, so we couldn't even go for the weekend, he was always working, ploughing the snow off the highway. [Our son] didn't like [not being able to go to the bush]."

In order to go to the bush, families must take "time off" from the responsibilities, such as jobs and school, that tie them to town. They must be lucky enough to find the "chance" to go. They do not expect to have this option under normal circumstances. To participate fully in bush life, women and their families would need to do the impossible – to reconcile the schedule and time clock of the work and school year with those of the seasons, the weather, and the animals.

What Next?

At the time of this research, the community of Chisasibi was tapping into its diverse resources in order to meet the challenge of living lives that strengthen family and community by balancing life in the bush, on the Island of Fort George, and in town. As it has become more difficult for families to go to the bush, creative programs have emerged to foster apprenticeship relations in town (Chisasibi Band Council 1991). Alongside activities such as career workshops, work-study programs, and a speaker series inviting Chisasibi's adults to school to discuss their jobs with students, parents and teachers have suggested hiring an elder to speak to students at the school and continuing classes in Cree culture. These resolute efforts by the men and women of Chisasibi – to rebuild a community respectful of Cree values – aim to strengthen young people for the future by reminding them of the past.

Acknowledgments

I would like to thank the Chisasibi Band Council and the generous, thoughtful people of Chisasibi who worked with me in 1992. Financial assistance for the research came from the Max Bell Foundation Fellowship in Canadian and Northern Studies, from Social Studies and Humanities Research Council Strategic Grant # 803-91-0035, and from the Graduate Research Award of the McGill Centre for Research and Teaching on Women. Many thanks as well to the Department of Anthropology at McGill, particularly to Professor Carmen Lambert for insight and encouragement while supervising my research and to Professor Colin Scott for very useful comments on this chapter.

Notes

1 A few Cree families who pursue their livelihood in the bush have remained residents of Fort George despite the 1980 resettlement. Bush activities keep these families away from the island for a good part of the year, and they occupy their island homes throughout the summer months.

2 For discussion of the Coaster-Inlander distinction, see Morantz (1983).

3 Pursuant to the James Bay and Northern Québec Agreement, the ISP was established to guarantee income to Cree people who pursue their livelihood in the bush by hunting, trapping, and/or fishing. In this way, intensive subsistence production generates cash income as well as harvested food. Useful analysis of the ISP can be found in LaRusic et al. (1979) and Scott and Feit (1992).

References

Adelson, N. 1997. "Gathering Knowledge: Reflections on the Anthropology of Identity, Aboriginality, and the Annual Gatherings in Whapmagoostui, Quebec." Montreal: McGill University AGREE Discussion Paper No. 1.

Blythe, J.M., P.M. Brizinski, and S.Preston. 1985. *"I Was Never Idle": Women and Work in Moosonee and Moose Factory*. TASO Report No. 21. Hamilton: Research Program for Technology Assessment in Subarctic Ontario, McMaster University.

Chisasibi Band Council. 1991. *Dialogue on Education/ Dialogue sur l'éducation*. Chisasibi: Chisasibi Band Council.

Feit, H. 1982. "The Future of Hunters within Nation-States: Anthropology and the James Bay Cree." In *Politics and History in Band Societies*, ed. Eleanor Leacock and Richard Lee, 373-411. Cambridge: Cambridge University Press.

Flannery, R. 1935. "The Position of Woman among Eastern Cree." *Primitive Man* 8: 81-86.

Jacobs, S. 1992. "No Time in the Bush." Paper presented at the International Congress of Arctic Social Scientists, Laval University, Quebec.

–. 1993. "Expectations, Experience and Life Choices: Analysing the Aspirations of Cree Women in Chisasibi, James Bay." MA thesis, McGill University, Montreal.

Kilfoil, C. 1977 "A Survey of Community Attitudes toward Curriculum Content in the Sand Park School, Fort George." Brief Communication Series No. 42. Montreal: Programme in the Anthropology of Development, McGill University.

LaRusic, I.E., S. Bouchard, A. Penn, T. Brelsford, and J.-G. Deschênes. 1979. *Negotiating a Way of Life*. Montreal: ssDcc.

Leacock, E. and H.I. Safa, eds. 1986. *Women's Work*. South Hadley: Bergin and Garvey.

Morantz, T. 1983. *An Ethnohistoric Study of Eastern James Bay Cree Social Organization, 1700-1850*. Mercury Series, Paper No. 88. Ottawa: Canadian Ethnology Service, National Museum of Man.

Poelzer, I.A. 1991. "Métis Women and the Economy of Northern Saskatchewan." In *Race, Class, Genders: Bonds and Barriers*, ed. J. Vorst and The Editorial Collective, 201-26. Toronto: Garamond Press.

Rogers, E. 1963. *The Hunting Group-Hunting Territory Complex among the Mistassini Indians*. Bulletin 195, Anthropological Series 63. Ottawa: National Museum of Canada.

Rogers, P. 1965. "Aspirations and Acculturation of Cree Women at Great Whale River." MA thesis, University of North Carolina, Chapel Hill.

Salisbury, R. 1986. *A Homeland for the Cree: Regional Development in James Bay, 1971-1981*. Kingston: McGill-Queens University Press.

Scott, C. 1983. "The Semiotics of Material Life among Wemindji Cree Hunters." PhD diss., McGill University, Montreal.

–. 1988. "Property, Practice and Aboriginal Rights among Quebec Cree Hunters." In *Hunters and Gatherers: Property, Power and Ideology*, vol. 2., eds. J. Woodburn, T. Ingold, and D. Riches, 35-51. London: Berg Publishers.

–. 1989. "Ideology of Reciprocity between the James Bay Cree and the Whiteman State." In *Outwitting the State*, ed. Peter Skalnik, 81-108. New Brunswick, NJ: Transaction Publishers.

Scott, C. and H. Feit. 1992. *Income Security for Cree Hunters*. Montreal: McGill Programme in the Anthropology of Development Monograph Series.

Shaw, P. 1982. "Town Planning in Consultation with and Participation from a Native Community: A Case study of the Relocation of the Cree Indian Community of Fort George to Chisasibi, Quebec." MA thesis, McGill University School of Urban Planning, Montreal.

Smith, D.E. 1987. *The Everyday World as Problematic: A Feminist Sociology*. Boston: Northeastern University Press.

Tanner, A. 1979. *Bringing Home Animals*. London: C. Hurst and Company.

–. 1990. "Northern Indigenous Cultures in the Face of Development." In *The Legal Challenge of Sustainable Development*, ed. J. Owen Saunders, 253-68. Calgary: Canadian Institute of Resources Law.

Youngs, C. 1991. "Woods Cree Women's Labour within the Subsistence-Based Mixed Economy of Pelican Narrows, Saskatchewan." MA thesis, University of Saskatchewan, Saskatoon.

17
Cultural Change in Mistissini: Implications for Self-Determination and Cultural Survival

Catherine James

The ideas that form the basis of this chapter were sparked by interviews that I conducted with Cree women as part of a study of teenage pregnancy in the community of Mistissini. The research offered some insights into how, among different generations of Cree women, identity and culture were negotiated and perpetuated over time: it suggested that the nature of cultural change in Mistissini was a complex process not easily categorized as assimilation or cultural loss per se. The interviews chart the progress of cultural change in Mistissini at the level of individuals, revealing a process of exchange and critical evaluation on the part of Cree women and teenagers.

This chapter explores what significance these observations of cultural change may have for the models and concepts of Aboriginal culture that operate within the discourse of Aboriginal self-determination and cultural survival. Specifically, I argue that employing essentialized depictions of Aboriginal culture in order to support claims to a right to cultural survival or self-determination is problematic. By defining what is "Aboriginal" solely in terms of opposition or contrast to what is White, or European, essentialized depictions of Aboriginal culture encourage the inference that any cultural change that appears to move away from what was traditionally Aboriginal amounts to cultural loss. This inference encourages lack of attention to such issues as how and why social or cultural change in Aboriginal communities may be necessary or relevant. Essentialized depictions of Aboriginal culture fail to trigger debate over questions about how new beliefs and norms of social relations, as well as poverty and exposure to modern life, have transformed contemporary Aboriginal cultures into social systems that are quite distinct from their historical counterparts.

If cultural survival and self-determination are to be jointly realized, then social and economic institutions in Aboriginal communities must express ideals of culture that embody community values. Overly rigid notions of what is Aboriginal constrain designs for workable social and economic institutions in Aboriginal communities. One of the keys to creating viable social and economic institutions involves deflating the perceived importance of essentialized notions of the "authentic," or "traditional," as standards for judgment of things Aboriginal. These standards tend to categorize *all* change as cultural loss or assimilation rather than to promote critical analysis of how and in what ways change may sometimes be beneficial.

The construction of what is Aboriginal or Cree in Mistissini offers one example of how the ongoing invention of culture incorporates as well as departs from long-standing Cree traditions. One facet of the process of cultural change in Mistissini is the growth of an increasingly pluralistic notion of Cree identity and culture. The introduction of housing, birth control, changes in marriage practices, and a shift to a wage economy did transform some traditions, yet the new norms and practices that appeared were not always perceived as irreconcilable with "being" Cree. A second feature of cultural change in Mistissini is a thread of continuity with respect to some aspects of Cree life. This is evident in the continued valuation and practice of hunting, fishing, and living off the land. These activities formed the basis of Cree society and identity for hundreds of years, and successive generations have embraced and valued them.

In contrast to the above examples, change experienced as cultural loss in Mistissini occurs when a new practice appears and does not adequately replace the ethics or values that imbued the disappearing traditional practice. For example, the emergence of a notion of adolescence and the concomitant rise in power of the teenage peer group as a socializing agent of youth has been problematic for the community. To the extent that the peer group subverts past norms of personal responsibility, respect for the authority of elders, and perseverance in acquiring productive economic skills, it directly contributes to the loss of Cree culture – at least in the eyes of older members of the Cree community.

Whether the phenomenon of the peer group represents a loss for the adolescents themselves raises questions that address the crux of the hypothesized difference between cultural change and cultural loss. If the norms the peer group introduces "work" in the sense that they provide skills that allow these teenagers to function in meaningful, productive ways that express the community's ethics and values, then it may be that the new norms will come to represent new ways of being Cree. If things do not unfold so positively, then the teenagers also experience a cultural loss. Thus far, as replacements for the norms of parental and broadly based communal authority, the adolescent peer group and the set of social relations it generates only partially reproduce the ethics and philosophies formerly communicated within the context of small, semi-nomadic hunting groups.

In light of these observations of cultural change and continuity in Mistissini, it is difficult to construe the struggle for cultural survival and self-determination solely as a fight to preserve traditional ways of life. The characterization is partially correct because some traditions continue to represent values and ethics, widely accepted both now and fifty years ago, that are still considered fundamental to being Cree. Nonetheless, a more accurate characterization of cultural survival is that it is an effort to create "Cree" approaches to the modern world – some of which will be new, and some of which will be long-standing norms and practices perpetuated by successive generations. The crux of cultural survival involves meeting two contingencies: (1) the process of cultural transformation must be one in which the community participates and over which it exercises some control; and (2) the new norm must be one that assists the community in maintaining its chosen values and ethics.

These observations about cultural change suggest that attempts to base social and economic institutions of self-determination upon essentialized notions of Aboriginal culture will ultimately be counterproductive. A second, more implicit point, is that "culture" is no longer a tacit, uncritically accepted notion within the Aboriginal community itself; rather, it is a political, often contested, topic, potentially accessible to manipulation by most members of the Aboriginal community. Given this situation, there is justification for turning the negotiation of Aboriginal culture into a process whereby the community can expressly cultivate norms and ideologies that further its needs and goals.

Rhetoric: Essentialist Concepts of Culture and Self-Determination

The concept of culture figures prominently in the literature on self-determination. Cultural difference, in addition to supporting historical claims of autonomy, provides the moral imperative to allow peoples to determine their futures. The concept of culture is an increasingly important political vehicle for mobilizing against "central political authorities and hegemonic national cultures[,]" as Turner (1993, 423) notes. When culture is essentialized it is represented as something somewhat akin to a form of property, a thing that belongs to an ethnic group, often reified as a separate entity with a bounded, distinctive and homogenous content (411).

Reified, essentialized depictions of culture, employed at a macro-social level, have some positive effects. For example, positivist reifications of culture may help to highlight gross disparities between dominant versus minority ways of life, thus helping to justify demands for dialogue between colonizing and colonized cultures (Kymlicka 1989). A positivist notion of culture, as a bounded object experienced and "possessed" by groups, is implicit in international declarations of human rights. Reifying culture makes it possible to elucidate an important cause-and-effect relationship: suppressing different ideological or religious views amounts to suppressing the peoples who hold them. Membership in a cultural community necessitates some articulation of the "essential" beliefs and characteristics of the group of which one is a member.

In the discourse on self-determination, essentialist depictions of Aboriginal culture refer to the most well known traditional ideologies and symbols. The Aboriginal and non-Aboriginal are paired off in sets of opposites, for example: cyclical versus linear concepts of time, matriarchal versus patriarchal societies, egalitarian versus hierarchical social structures, spirituality based on a view of living in harmony with the natural world versus spirituality based on a view of dominating the natural world. These contrasting pairs emphasize the differences between Aboriginal and non-Aboriginal worldviews; they also emphasize the definition of culture as difference. Throughout the twentieth century, such essentialist notions of culture have been used to stereotype and denigrate as well as to legitimate. This has led to critiques of the essentialist concepts of culture.

Just as the historically silent subjects of anthropological study are invoking this model of culture in order to achieve political goals, so the discipline of anthropology is dismantling it (see, for example, Boon 1990; Clifford 1988; Geertz 1988; Marcus and Fischer 1986). One purpose of this line of thinking is to question the monolithic status of culture as an explanatory framework. For example, Turner (1993, 417) notes that multiculturalist discourse that frequently reifies and essentializes culture fails to identify issues that divide along lines of power, gender, or economics.

Other problems with essentializing and reification appear. Discourse that employs essentialized representations of Aboriginal peoples frames the problems and solutions of Aboriginal and non-Aboriginal relations as a series of choices between glaring dichotomies such as Aboriginal/White, authentic/inauthentic. This conceptualization of culture fails to capture the dynamic, changeable nature of cultures, particularly the role of individuals in clashing with, contradicting, and changing their cultures as well as reproducing them. Elevating ideological and material practices as constitutive of culture downplays the more generic but equally essential function of culture as a system that generates values and creates a social context within which meaning, belief, social relations, economic activities, and so forth are embedded.

In short, Aboriginal culture consists of more than a collection of beliefs and practices that express outstanding differences between Aboriginal and non-Aboriginal ways of life. Boldt (1993, 180) perceives a disjuncture between traditionalist ritual enactments and circumstances of modern Aboriginal life.

> Indian expressive-ritualistic culture no longer serves to celebrate the success of their traditional way of surviving and living ... it serves only a segmented function as a basis for spiritual identity and fraternity ... Although a totem can elicit powerful emotions, it cannot serve as a practical design for living and surviving in the modern world.

Boldt's observation leads into a more general point: reifying and essentializing Aboriginal culture produces the tautology that Aboriginal culture is important because it is Aboriginal. The latter observation is misleading because it fails to make explicit the point that material and ideological aspects of culture derive significance from the value they hold for individuals within a culture. If one entirely severs from the concept of culture any notion of its role in providing people with the means to get along socially and materially, then it becomes easy to equate cultural survival with the maintenance of mere forms and "totems."

Espousing essentialized concepts of Aboriginal culture while disregarding the practical organizing effect of culture distorts the significance of cultural difference. Within this incomplete framework, cultural change is easily equated with cultural loss. What in fact renders cultural difference either salient or inconsequential is the level of relevance and meaning it has for the person in daily life. Because culture is functional in this sense, cultural change is only destructive – that is, tantamount to cultural loss – when the transformed or changed practice/value ceases to be germane to, or actively undermines, other cultural values or ethics. For these reasons, a sense of the contingency, adaptability, and "created" nature of culture must temper the significance accorded to cultural difference within the discourse on self-determination.

Cultural Change and Continuity in Mistissini

The narratives of three generations of women in Mistissini illuminate the processes of cultural survival, cultural change, and cultural loss. The current construction of Aboriginal culture and identity in Mistissini is evolving in two directions. While the meaning of what is Aboriginal or Cree in many areas is expanding, some traditional values – such as the bush as a source of spiritual and economic sustenance or the value of family and children – continue to be reaffirmed by successive generations. Several specific examples of conflicts and consensus that surround Aboriginal ideologies regarding gender, fertility, and the ethics of social behaviour in the community help illustrate this.

In discussing ideologies of gender and fertility, I rely on Young's (1980) definition of ideology as a set of beliefs, consciously or unconsciously held, that people take to be real (i.e., to describe "the way the world is").

Understood in this sense, ideologies are a means for interpreting specific areas of experience. For example, in Mistissini, the topic of reproduction and childbearing is understood through a framework of ideologies (beliefs or assumptions) that express "facts" about becoming a woman, the significance of fertility, the value of children, and so forth.

The findings offered below are drawn from informal interviews that covered the perceptions of teenage life and teenage childbearing, birth control, residential schooling, and whether women's perceptions of teenage childbearing had changed in the last fifty years. Along with band council statistics, the interviews support the hypothesis that practices as well as perceptions of marriage and out-of-wedlock childbearing have indeed changed. In contrast to practices of fifty years ago, informants stated that today more teenagers have children in their early teens (ages thirteen to seventeen), social pressure to marry has decreased, and the stigma of out-of-wedlock childbearing (premarital sex that did not produce a pregnancy was not so stigmatized) has diminished.

Rates of teenage pregnancy rose when the previously stable practices of marriage, childbearing, and socialization began to change. Archival and oral history research on genealogy indicates that, among the Cree, first pregnancies out-of-wedlock fifty to 100 years ago were very common, but pregnancy led quickly to community recognition of the couple as marriage partners. With the appearance of Christianity, people formalized these marriages in the church as soon as possible (Colin Scott, personal communication, 1997). For women born after 1940, the residential school, the growth of a permanent community, and the shift towards a cash economy changed not only marriage practices, but also Cree social and cultural life generally. These factors ultimately stimulated Cree youth to contest the social order in order to modify traditional customs. As a social trend that developed with these changes, teenage pregnancy provides an example of the multidimensional nature of cultural change, and the internal forces and conflicts shaping Cree culture in Mistissini.

A significant factor influencing the rate of teenage pregnancy is the teenage peer group. Bourdieu's (1977) theory of the habitus and of practice offers one framework within which to interpret the emergence of the teenage peer group and the effect it has had as a powerful social force frequently associated with a loss of Cree culture. This model conceptualizes how individuals both reproduce and modify the ideological constructs that inform their perceptions of the world (163-70). Bourdieu argues that individual perceptions of the world can be characterized either as doxic, where the individual construes the social order as natural, or as heterodox, where the person is cognizant that the reigning social order is one of many possible orders. Comaroff (1985, 5) modifies Bourdieu's model by suggesting that perception fluctuates between doxic and heterodox awareness and that, in both cases, the individual continually engages in interpreting, critiquing, and modifying this social order.

The material and social changes of the last fifty years in Mistissini catalyzed a shift in how Cree youth viewed some, but not all, aspects of the traditional culture of their elders. Once the status quo was understood as arbitrary rather than natural, alternatives to it appeared; at the very least, teenagers contested or resisted traditional practices in both speech and action.

One effect of the new category of "adolescence" was that marriage came to be less practical. According to the old way, a boy of fourteen or fifteen could be counted a man, and a girl of similar age, a woman. The temporal "space" occupied by adolescence today pushes back the age of maturity and affords greater scope for young people to resist the conventions of their elders. Such shifts prompted the contest of elders' authority and generated alternatives to norms of indigenous Cree practices, at once expanding and modifying the definition of what was Cree and, sometimes, changing it.

As the notion of "teenage years" and a separate set of teenage practices developed, teenagers began to modify the formerly taken-for-granted practices of marriage, childbearing, and socialization. Previously powerful sources of social control over youth, such as respect for parental authority and the force of social opinion, weakened. In their place, the teenage peer group emerged as an influential force shaping teenage behaviour and generating a separate set of teenage activities. Today the teenage peer group is a preeminent agent of socialization, generating pressure to oppose adult authority, to become sexually active, to party, to drink, to experiment with drugs, and to participate in other social or recreational activities. Such peer group activities increase the likelihood of pregnancy.

The peer group exerts a powerful influence in the lives of adolescents in Mistissini for two reasons. A cultural ethic of conforming to the group rather than distinguishing oneself from others discourages teenagers from choosing alternatives to the contemporary trends in teenage activities. Many teenagers remarked on the heavy pressure they felt to drink, smoke, sniff gas, party, dress in a particular way, or become sexually active. Teenagers and some informants in their twenties mentioned that to be different – in dress, mannerisms, interests, or activities – is to raise suspicion and to sometimes be ostracized by one's friends. Among adolescents, restraint in expressing individuality appears to constitute a ground rule of socially acceptable ways of interacting.

An additional reason for the pressure to conform may be teenagers' subordinate position to adults (as possessors of cultural and social knowledge, students in the school system, or labourers in the economy). Power relations within subordinate groups may generate intense pressures to conform

(Scott 1990, 26). To the extent that teenagers reject cultural/social imperatives about who they must become or how they should behave, they resist adults and the perceived status quo. The peer group, reproducing notions of teenage identity and activities, generates pressure to conform to its internal rules. Conformity then confirms teenage solidarity as peers, affirms their teenage Cree identity, and legitimates their sometimes confrontational stance.

Yet although the teenage peer group modifies some ethics of Cree social practices, it reproduces others, such as not calling attention to oneself. Family life and early socialization practices generate a set of shared experiences that cross generational boundaries and reinforce the cultural valuation of family, conformity to the group, individual autonomy and competence, and the ethic of non-interference in the affairs of others. Located within this shared terrain of culture and social relations, the teenage peer group is not only a source of deviance and change, but also of cultural continuity between generations. The domains of adult and teenage activity do not separate cleanly.

In comparison to fifty years ago, contemporary Cree culture is less often perceived as "natural" and is far more likely to be contested and modified. Generational differences between Cree teenagers, their parents, and their grandparents occur because aspects of Cree life and ideologies (involving gender, reproduction, and marriage practices) are increasingly subject to modification. The dynamics of teenage social relations exemplify teenage responses to cultural and social imperatives from peers and parents. Over time the creation of a teenage habitus has helped to generate change in marriage and childbearing practices.

Teenage pregnancy is an event embedded within a particular set of social relationships and norms of interaction that evolves over time. Earlier studies posited that Cree youth experienced a cultural conflict between the White and Cree worlds (see Chance 1970; Wintrob and Sindell 1970) and that this generated anxiety and confusion; today, however, passage into adulthood involves more than resolving a clash between two cultures. Cree adolescents are equally engaged in managing multiple, sometimes conflicting, aspects of Cree culture: the social ethics of group harmony and behaviour, valuation of parenting and family, and the ethics and practices of bush life. Other potentially debilitating practices, notoriously the consumption of alcohol, also play a role in this process.

When they interact with their peers, teenagers may or may not be deviant, but in either case they are engaged in interpreting perceived social and cultural imperatives about being Cree. The phenomenon of the teenage peer group illustrates a complex constellation of factors, operating in the lives of Aboriginal teenagers, that is not easily identified as belonging to categories that line up with notions of Aboriginal versus non-Aboriginal culture. As an example of how cultural change has occurred over time, the peer group in Mistissini cannot be adequately described or accounted for by an essentialized concept of Cree culture.

Gender and Fertility

The emergence of adolescence entailed departures from traditional norms that informants frequently labelled as signs of cultural loss or social disintegration. In contrast, the cultural construction of gender and fertility in Mistissini exemplifies more neutral trajectories of cultural change. For example, work is no longer as heavily gendered an activity as it was historically (although men and women could routinely take on each other's tasks in the bush, there was an explicit division between men's and women's roles). A transition to more gender neutral roles for women and men has arisen with the entry of women into the workforce and with the growth of a cash economy. It may even be that women more often become the principal breadwinners, at least in cash terms. Insofar as involvement in the wage economy is concerned, the link between productive activity and gender has been greatly weakened: the construction of one's gendered identity is no longer determined by a tacit division of male versus female spheres of activity.

On the other hand, Cree ideologies of fertility that reinforce the values of family and children have tended to retain their doxic, or tacit, character. The dominant ideology relates fertility and childbirth to becoming a woman or man, and it symbolically links a woman's reproductive capacity to the transition to womanhood and accepted norms of male/female relations. Female informants of every age perceived and accepted ideological "truths" that identified childbearing as the main event in the transition to womanhood. Although the exact nature of individual awareness varies, conscious or explicit contestations of prevailing norms, whether verbal or symbolic, are recent and relatively rare. Somewhat more frequently, informants recognized and consciously accepted these ideologies as part of "being Cree."

Marital and parental status also remain closely associated with social maturity and one's status as a man or woman. Generally, pregnancy and childbearing are pivotal events in the construction of identity as a Cree woman. As a source of cultural generativity and motherhood, a woman's fertility is highly valued. Childless couples are often referred to as "poor" or "unfortunate."

Although it continues to be significant in Cree culture, the event of childbearing has not escaped the effects of modern reproductive technology. Birth control does affect Cree notions of fertility and sexuality in several ways. The advent of the pill coincides with a decrease in the average number of children born per family. Informants under twenty and those between the ages of twenty and thirty expressed the desire for two or three children, unlike their grandmothers, who were very likely to have had between four and seven children. In contrast to its use as a means of postponing childbirth, contraception in Mistissini is more likely to be used to limit family size after the desired number of children has been born.

The effect of the introduction of birth control, and the tension it has created between old and new attitudes towards childbearing, emerges in informants' statements about the pill. Middle-aged and elderly informants stated that some parents felt that if they approved of contraception they were condoning premarital sex, and a number of women felt that it was morally or religiously wrong to regulate one's fertility artificially. According to teenage informants, some mothers warned against using the pill because it could cause future infertility and/or damage reproductive organs; these informants said this was why some sexually active teenagers did not take the pill. Why do girls who "transgress" against parental wishes in other contexts heed parental advice in this case? Among other reasons (e.g., girls are embarrassed to go to the clinic, lack of forethought, ignorance of the pill as a birth control option, or religious beliefs), it seems plausible that the pill is avoided because it threatens childbearing – a source of social status and gender identity for women.

Despite their interest in learning more about contraception, many teenage informants stated that the pill was harmful to one's health and might prevent conception at a later date. Statements made by young women in their teens included such comments as: "I knew about birth control but my friends told me it can be bad for you."

Thus the seeming consensus about the importance of fertility and childbearing does not translate into a set of unproblematic choices for young women. Although they voiced distrust of the birth control pill, all of the teenagers interviewed stated that, if young women knew more about contraception and the biological facts about how pregnancy occurs, then at least some teenage pregnancies would be avoided.

> I didn't have a very good idea of when you could get pregnant. My mother knew but she didn't tell me. I could never understand that. Why didn't she tell me how you get pregnant?
>
> I got pregnant when I was eighteen. Parents don't want to put their daughters on birth control. If I had a daughter, I would put her on birth control the day she got her first period! (a teenage informant)

The informants' statements demonstrate that fertility is an integral but thorny aspect of their identities as Cree women.

Significantly, a small group of informants explicitly rejected the dominant ideology surrounding marriage and childbearing. Of these informants, several had not had children and did not view childbearing as the natural event that would usher them into womanhood. These few young women were attempting to formulate alternative definitions of womanhood. In so attempting, the informants were more articulate in identifying what they rejected (childbearing or marriage as threshold steps into womanhood) than in expressing what their personal notions of womanhood might include, although they mentioned such alternative personal goals as achieving financial independence or reaching a certain level of education. A second group of women in this category had children as teenagers or before marriage but explicitly criticized communal and parental expectations for women and men to marry as well as conventional norms of womanly behaviour that they perceived as too passive. Women in these groups expressly noted, and sometimes rejected, what they identified as an expectation in the community and among the majority of their peers; that is, that childbearing was an integral aspect of womanhood.

The responses of the informants demonstrate a range of contradictory opinions about reproduction and childbearing in Mistissini. For some women, the link between fertility and achieving adult status in the community is a powerful, self-evident fact, as analogous comparisons between fertile/barren, adult/child, and maturity/inexperience suggest. One informant linked reproduction and fertility of female bodies with the strengthening and "reproduction" of Cree culture, saying that a male member of the community regarded contraception as a threat to Cree culture and society because it would reduce the rate of population growth.

Along similar lines, some informants contrasted Cree reproduction to reproduction controlled by contraception and identified the difference in approaches as analogous to other oppositions, such as Aboriginal/White, natural/artificial, and familiar/foreign. The latter comments came principally from women over forty, who stated that family planning was a White way of doing things and that it was not natural to try to plan for children. Several informants stated that Cree women are less likely to use contraception in the "White" way of planning for, or postponing, the first child and that they prefer to use it to space their pregnancies or to limit family size. Other women, particularly those in the younger generations, often recognized these ideological norms as "cultural," or created, but as nonetheless central to a Cree identity. A very few rejected these constructs explicitly and articulated alternative visions of womanhood, remaining childless or behaving in other ways that contested prevailing standards of womanly behaviour. The production of gender ideologies and social mechanisms pertaining to the control of fertility helps to sustain assertions (or perceived truths) about Cree culture and social order, and it articulates widely perceived differences between Cree and White society.

Fertility and childbearing play a key role in the construction of womanhood. In turn, contemporary perceptions of teenage pregnancy in Mistissini involve a complex mix of both old and new ideas. Although teenagers accept these cultural ideations, they modify them as well. If in the future more young women recognize and question the ideological link made between gender and fertility, as do a few of their peers now, then the dominant ideology may begin to change. Regardless of their significance at any one time, these ideologies are open to potential scrutiny and modification by members of the Mistissini community. The evolution of the cultural significance of reproduction and gender, along with the changing landscape of teenage activities and social relations, will continue to act as forces that shape the event of teenage pregnancy and illustrate the process of cultural change.

Analysis

The narratives of the informants express subtleties and contradictions pertaining to the construction of Cree identity and culture that elude blunt categorization. In contrast, the rhetoric of self-determination often relies on blunt categories; it tends to construe culture so narrowly that the hypothetical range of institutions and laws apparently required to support it appears unrealizable. This research suggests alternative conclusions about the nature of cultural change and, therefore, implies a different vision of what cultural survival and self-determination might entail.

The first of these conclusions, as the phenomenon of the teenage peer group illustrates, is that Cree ideologies only retain vitality and significance if they attract the loyalty of each generation. The simplicity of this statement belies the range of outcomes that the process of cultural change may stimulate. On the one hand, some aspects of culture appear destined to decline without causing much disruption. The eventual disappearance of the practice of arranged marriage seems to fall into this category; its demise was seen, by at least half of the elder women who themselves experienced it, as an inevitable and ultimately desirable consequence of exposure to the "modern" method of choosing one's partner.

Likewise, although the introduction of the birth control pill has met with controversy in the community (involving religious as much as cultural opposition, as is the case elsewhere), the overall trend among the younger generations of women seems to indicate that regulating one's fertility is becoming increasingly common. The frequency with which young mothers choose to have one or two children and then return to school in order to become the main wage earner constitutes a pattern in Mistissini that will only reinforce use of the pill to limit family size.

On the other end of the spectrum of cultural change, it is possible to isolate a core of ideologies and practices that continues to be perceived as central to Cree culture. For example, the bush holds a preeminent place in both the spiritual and material life of most of the informants. Elder informants used their substantial experience of living in the bush as a standard by which to measure the failings and pitfalls of the younger generation. Young unwed mothers were perceived as a source of instability in Cree culture not because they were young but because they were unschooled in the necessary skills of home-making and lacked the maturity that a life in the bush, "a hard life," would have taught them.

Women in their twenties, thirties, and forties also referred to the bush as a source of spiritual nourishment and strength that had especially therapeutic effects for troubled teenagers who needed to "learn how to work," get over a drug dependency, or regain self-confidence. The bush was also a place to experience tranquillity and peace as well as personal growth. Many middle-aged informants had often returned to the bush for several years during or after residential school, and they spoke from personal experience about the significance of the bush in Cree culture as well as in their personal lives.

The importance of the bush to Cree culture raises the issue of whether it may be something "essential," something upon which Cree cultural survival depends. This is perhaps the case from the viewpoint of a particular generation of individuals. Although practices, beliefs, and, therefore, cultures change over time, the capability of an individual to negotiate the values and practices by which s/he lives is undoubtedly limited. For example, the testimony of Cree elders in the hearings that preceded the first James Bay Agreement expressed a deep, elemental relationship to their way of life and suggested that some practices, such as hunting and trapping, were constitutive of, and indeed essential to, Cree culture.

From the perspective of individuals such as those who testified at the hearings, it is probably true that loss of the bush does mean loss of Cree culture. This possibility legitimates, in a limited sense, the validity of an essentialist notion of culture and leads into the more general possibility that cultures do die, in a way, with the passing of each generation. To identify a loss from this perspective and to understand that it exacts a deep emotional toll on the persons who experience it, however, is something quite different from categorically denying the existence or value of the contemporary forms that Cree culture has assumed.

Although it is possible to argue that the bush, hunting, trapping, and so forth are essential to the survival of Cree culture (and so support an essentialized representation of Cree culture), this discussion proposes that such an interpretation offers an incomplete picture of the process of cultural change. Beliefs and practices associated with hunting and the bush continue not because they are quintessentially Cree or Aboriginal but because they continue to be embraced by successive generations of Cree, who perceive them as helping perpetuate values and ethics that the community affirms.

Cultural survival is threatened when there is no opportunity to assess or debate the relevance of ideologies or practices that are in jeopardy. In place of a process where contact with other societies produces scrutiny of traditions and stimulates some degree of communal discussion, Aboriginal communities historically experienced very little control over the pace or content of the changes they underwent. As the emergence of the teenage peer group in Mistissini exemplifies, cultural change becomes a confusing, disruptive phenomenon when the community experiences little control (in this case, over some aspects of teenage life). The peer group has prompted the abandonment of old traditions but has offered inadequate substitutes for parental authority and other means by which the ethics of personal responsibility and productivity were formerly communicated. From this perspective, the emergence of the teenage peer group has caused cultural loss.

These observations suggest the simple and self-evident inference that the level of communal participation in the process of change, rather than the change itself, is the more significant factor in determining whether cultural change is experienced as positive or negative. As perceptions of traditional life change due to the shift from doxic to heterodox awareness among members of a cultural community, culture is opened up to explicit criticism. The shift in perception constitutes a central feature of cultural change; it follows from this that what makes or breaks the cultural vitality of a community is not its level of exposure but, rather, its cohesiveness and ability to affirm certain values collectively. A community becomes vulnerable once it loses its cohesiveness or is not allowed any opportunity to control the nature and pace of change.

The phenomenon of the teenage peer group in Mistissini provides a case in point. The strength of the peer group arises in part because of the absence of any countervailing force (i.e., parental authority or the force of social opinion). Mobilizing the community in purposive ways to counter the pressure the teenage peer group asserts upon its members might overcome some of the negative effects the peer group produces (e.g., peer group pressure to skip school and devalue high academic achievement might be countered by positive reinforcement of education from within the community). The point implies that cultural survival and self-determination may be realizable to the degree that a community has the internal capacity to maintain consensus about the social values and ethics that sustain the traditions it wishes to keep.

The latter point remains hidden when an essentialized notion of Cree culture subsumes Cree ethics and values within a framework of reified, idealized narratives that narrowly define Cree culture. It is indeed important to recognize culture as a source of difference that sustains community and individual identity; however, this can be affirmed without granting culture privileged status as a flawless explanatory framework from within which to approach the issue of Aboriginal self-determination. While culture is clearly important, it also dovetails with economic and political factors that may effectively override its power or transform its effects.

Conclusion

I have attempted to explore the problem of cultural survival and self-determination by questioning the current emphasis placed on preserving essentialized notions of Aboriginal culture and Aboriginal "difference." Several basic points form the foundation for the discussion. One contention is that concepts of culture must reflect the contingency and adaptability of culture as a system; a corollary of this is that essentialist depictions of culture are never fully accurate and that most cultural boundaries are permeable and dynamic (unless entry and exit is expressly controlled by the community). It follows from these points that essentialist depictions of Aboriginal culture are based on an inaccurate understanding of the inherently dynamic and changeable nature of culture as a human invention. These contentions are, I hope, illustrated by the discussion of adolescence and changes in marriage and childbearing that have occurred in Mistissini.

A second basic point has been to try to define when and why cultural change is problematic. In responding to this issue, the discussion points to two factors: (1) whether a community has participated in debating the relevance or value of any particular ideology or practice (the more heterodox or politicized the concept of culture becomes, the more contested certain dimensions of cultural practice become and the greater the need for explicit articulation and debate); and (2) the importance of the degree to which the community can coalesce to maintain consensus, through collective action and discussion, about the philosophies and values it wants to support.

Self-determination implicates cultural survival because it requires that communities collectively engage in an internal process of negotiation, persuasion, discussion, and the pursuit of goals. This process may prove the best way to sort out, at a pragmatic level, how abstract concepts such as culture and self-determination will translate into meaningful actions as well as what understanding of "Aboriginal" and "culture" will inform these efforts. How will the preservation and encouragement of Aboriginal culture be achieved through the process of economic development and institution building in Aboriginal communities? This chapter suggests that reference to essentialized and narrow notions of Aboriginal identity and culture will prove inadequate for answering these and other questions.

A final caveat to the discussion is that the topic of self-determination is multidimensional. The local scale of the chapter should not be taken to imply that self-determination is somehow entirely in the hands of the Aboriginal community. Cultural survival and self-determination, by definition, implicate the need for economic and political contact with other actors – namely, federal and provincial governments as well as business and other social institutions. The process will necessarily require the joint efforts of these groups. Self-determination requires Aboriginal peoples to determine how to build economies and institutions that are self-sustaining without tying these solely to past, essentialized idealizations of Aboriginal tradition. It requires, on the part of the Canadian government and society, a willingness to release preconceived and essentialized notions of what an Aboriginal person is.

Acknowledgments

The research on which this chapter is based took place in 1990 and could not have been accomplished without the permission of the community of Mistissini as well as the participation of all the women who agreed to be interviewed. The project was funded by the Department of Community Health at the Montreal General Hospital (MGH) and was part of a larger study conducted by Dr. Joyce Pickering of the MGH.

I owe a large thanks to Colin Scott, Jeremy Webber, and Rod Mcdonald for their critical input as I developed the ideas and analysis contained in this chapter.

References

Boldt, M. 1993. *Surviving as Indians: The Challenge of Self-Government.* Toronto: University of Toronto Press.

Boon, J. 1990. *Affinities and Extremes: Crisscrossing the Bittersweet Ethnology of East Indies History, Hindu Balinese Culture and Indo-European Allure.* Chicago: University of Chicago Press.

Bourdieu, P. 1977. *Outline of a Theory of Practice.* Cambridge: Cambridge University Press.

Chance, N. 1970. *Developmental Change among Cree Indians of Quebec.* Summary Report, McGill Cree Project. Ottawa: Queens Printer for Canada.

Clifford, J. 1988. *The Predicament of Culture.* Cambridge: Harvard University Press.

Comaroff, J. 1985. *Body of Power, Spirit of Resistance: The Culture and History of South African People.* Chicago: University of Chicago Press.

Geertz, C. 1988. *Works and Lives: The Anthropologist as Author.* Stanford: Stanford University Press.

Kymlicka, W. 1989. *Liberalism, Community and Culture.* Oxford: Oxford University Press.

Marcus, G., and M. Fischer. 1986. *Anthropology as Cultural Critique.* Chicago: University of Chicago Press.

Scott, J. 1990. *Domination and the Arts of Resistance: Hidden Transcripts.* New Haven: Yale University Press.

Turner, T. 1993. "Anthropology and Multiculturalism: What Is Anthropology that Multiculturalists Should be Mindful of It?" *Cultural Anthropology* 8: 411-29.

Wintrob, R. and P. Sindell. 1970. "Education and Identity Conflict among Cree Indians of Quebec." In *Developmental Change among the Cree Indians of Quebec,* ed. N. Chance, C1-C116. Ottawa: Department of Regional Expansion.

Young, A. "The Discourse on Stress and the Reproduction of Conventional Knowledge." *Social Science and Medicine* 14B, 3: 133-46.

18

The Decolonization of the Self and the Recolonization of Knowledge: The Politics of Nunavik Health Care

Josée G. Lavoie

In recent years, self-determination has become a major focus for Inuit, provincial and federal governments, and scholars. Often times this avenue is presented as a matter of fact cure-all for social problems and political tensions. Likewise, self-determination in health care has been presented as a solution, perhaps the only possible solution, to inequities and shortcomings claimed to exist in northern health care services.[1] The established system has been called "une vraie farce (a real farce)" (*La Presse* 1986, A8), has been accused of marginalizing Inuit (Julien 1987), and has been qualified as "une structure centralisée et blanche (a centralized and white structure)" (Tremblay 1991, 15). It is characterized as top heavy, not adapted to local needs, and impervious to local participation, while its professionals have been characterized as living in a cultural ghetto (Kativik Regional Council of Health and Social Services 1986; Simard 1988; Weller and Pranga 1987). Labbé (1981b) claims that northern health services promote Inuit dependence on the South. Dufour (1989) states that the model of health care delivery needs to be adapted to the northern context, that in some cases it has replaced or weakened local resources of self-help, and that it remains inaccessible culturally because practitioners and clients do not share a common cognitive base. O'Neil (1988, 47) argues that "health services remain one of the most powerful symbols of the colonial relationship between northern peoples and the nation state, and the pervasiveness of this symbol in the intimacies of everyday life undermines further development in other institutional areas."

Theorists, politicians, Inuit political authorities, community leaders, and anthropologists, as well as health practitioners, all seem to want the Inuit to secure greater involvement in their health care services. Termed self-determination, "l'autochtonization," or local control, it is assumed that this greater involvement would lead to the resolution of the problems, conflicts, and shortcomings of services delivered by the dominant society.

What self-determination, l'autochtonization, or local control actually *mean*, however, remains obscure. The terms are rarely defined, either as ideological stances or with reference to the structural changes they imply. This "omission" permits an aura of convergent efforts, of consensus. In fact the terms are used loosely to signify an array of options that vary considerably in scope and complexity. Similarly, the discourse supporting self-determination in health care invariably draws on concepts of community health in the construction of its arguments. These concepts are, however, constructed and used in a variety of ways, reflecting differing political agendas.

This chapter focuses on the production and use of the community health discourse in relation to self-determination in Nunavik health care.[2] In 1975 the James Bay and Northern Québec Agreement (JBNQA) was signed by the Inuit, the Cree, the Government of Quebec and the Government of Canada. A comprehensive land claim settlement, the agreement was intended to put an end to federal and provincial jurisdictional debates and to allow for the development of coherent services in the North. Building on existing provincial structures, the agreement was expected to promote the regionalization of decision making in a number of areas, including health care.

The JBNQA provided for the establishment of the Kativik Regional Council of Health and Social Services[3] (hereafter referred to as Kativik Council) located in Kuujjuaq. The Kativik Council receives political direction from its board and, ultimately, from the Makivik Corporation,[4] and its budgets and operational direction come from the Quebec Ministry of Health and Social Services. The Kativik Council's task is to define regional health priorities for Nunavik as well as to allocate the budgets for regional strategies and the two hospitals located in Kuujjuaq and Puvirnituk.[5] The Département de Santé Communautaire du Nord (hereafter referred to as DSC du Nord), an affiliate of the Centre Hospitalier de l'Université Laval and located in Quebec City, was given an ambiguous role in the Nunavik health care structure. Provincially, the Ministry has paired each regional council with what is commonly known as a DSC, which is attached to a university hospital. Whereas the Kativik Council is mandated to define local priorities, the DSC is the site of "expert knowledge" and is mandated to provide highly specialized technical assistance in program planning and delivery and in time of crisis (i.e., an outbreak). The location of the DSC in Quebec City has been an ongoing source of debate and tension within the Kativik Council, which wants this organization relocated to Kuujjuaq.

In areas of health care, as in others, the JBNQA was to be the starting point for yet more debate. This continuing debate hinges on how Inuit political leaders, and the Quebec government, define "significant control" and "autonomy" – concepts that are now inscribed in the current national discussions over Aboriginal political self-determination and self-determination in health care. The first section of this chapter provides a synopsis of these debates through a review of the literature on political self-determination, self-determination in health care, and linkages to the community health model. Current paradigms tend to rely on the community health model to formulate self-determination in health care. This is often justified on the grounds that the community health model is "closer to the way Aboriginals think about health." There are obvious limitations to inscribing such a political process in a model that evolved from a Western medical tradition. Such limitations will be reviewed, and an alternative model will be offered – one that proposes that self-determination in health care is not a "public health movement," as O'Neil (1988, 48) suggests[6] but, rather, a political process that relies on this discourse to achieve its own ends.

The question of self-determination in health care in northern Quebec is of particular interest for a medical anthropological analysis because both sides of the debate use a common vocabulary in the construction of their arguments: the language of community health. On one side, Aboriginal leaders use the language of health to formulate what might otherwise appear as dissent from and rejection of medical services or as a simple quest for greater power and control. The reformulation of criticism in community health terms allows for increased credibility, giving statements a meaning apparently divorced from political agendas and imbuing them with an aura of righteousness typical of prevention-oriented health care. On the other side, government representatives and practitioners use the community health discourse as a way to shift responsibility for health and, to a certain extent, health care delivery onto the shoulders of individuals and communities. Here, community criticisms of the services are coopted and reformulated in community health terms to give an impression of convergence of efforts, thus giving legitimacy to the planners.[7] This integration of a political discourse within the boundaries of the community health discourse also has the advantage of side-stepping the larger question of the role of Western health care as the instrument of a continued colonial endeavour.

The second section provides an overview of the manner in which the community health discourse is produced and utilized to satisfy divergent interests in Nunavik. The community health model offers avenues through which Inuit pursue greater control over health care. The trend towards para-professionalism in community health has promoted the entry of Inuit into a structure that had been largely impervious to their involvement; deprofessionalization has led a greater number of Inuit to gain access to higher levels of decision making. While some claim that, as a result, the content of the structure is now slowly being "decolonized," the community health model has also facilitated the recolonization of Inuit knowledge. The alleged Inuit ownership over health care provides a mechanism through which certain aspects of Inuit know-how can be reconstructed through the biomedical model. Despite an apparent contradiction, the two processes can be understood as complementary.

Contextualizing Nunavik Health Care

Regardless of the actual terminology used, Inuit self-determination in health care seems to refer to at least three (not mutually exclusive) paradigms: the first utilizes individual Inuit interactions within the health structure in order to sustain arguments *against* a transfer of control; the second focuses on difficulties of communication in order to justify Inuit employment in health care; and the third looks at the the relationship between Inuit society and the nation-state in order to justify the latter transferring control of health services to the former.

The first paradigm revolves around the concept of dependency:

> La dépendance est devenue l'une des caractéristiques du Nouveau-Québec actuel et le secteur de la santé n'y fait pas exception ... La responsabilité de la santé n'appartient *plus* aux individus mais aux "spécialistes de la santé" que l'on viendra consulter au moindre bobo. Les méthodes traditionnelles pour faire face aux problèmes de santé ont été mises au rancart, ainsi que les initiatives personnelles ...
>
> En raison de système de "colonialisme d'assistance" auquel on les a habitués, *les Inuit ne perçoivent pas la responsabilité qu'ils ont quant à leur santé et les améliorations qu'ils pourraient y apporter individuellement en modifiant leurs habitudes de vie et collectivement en améliorant leur environnement.*
>
> Dependence has become one of Nouveau-Québec's current characteristics and the health sector is no exception ... The responsibility for health *no longer* belongs to the individual but to "health specialists" who are consulted for the teeniest scratch. Traditional treatments for health problems have been scrapped, as have personal initiatives ...
>
> Due to the system of "colonial health care" they have become used to, *the Inuit do not take responsibility for their health or consider the improvements they could make, individually, by modifying their habits and, collectively, by improving their environment.* (Labbé 1981a, 73, emphasis added)

Thus it appears that dependency, an artefact of the colonial encounter of which biotechnical medicine is an integral part, is now responsible for (some of) the health problems encountered in the North. To palliate this dependency, health advocates, taking inspiration from community development, have attempted to foster a genre of community participation:

communities are now expected to be able to define their own concept of health as well as to prioritize their needs and take their health care into their own hands. Gradually, control will be transferred as people learn to take responsibility for their own health. While rhetorically attractive, the means of action, and the responsibility for defining what constitutes appropriate interventions, have remained mostly in the hands, and minds, of professionals. The new "approche communautaire" has not resolved the dilemma of populations defining (even partially) their health in non-biomedical terms. This approach leads people to be treated as if they were "empty vessels," the relevance of their beliefs, needs, and expectations being excluded from the medical encounter.

It is not so much the first paradigm itself (i.e., incorporating Inuit into the health structure in order to sustain arguments against a transfer of control) that is of interest here as the way it is used. Although this paradigm does not often appear in written works, whether academic, professional, or governmental (Julien 1987 being a rare example[8]), it remains part of the "popular medical discourse" and has been brought forth by some practitioners and bureaucrats[9] as an argument against Inuit being given greater control over their health care: if individuals cannot take care of themselves by adopting healthy lifestyles, then how can they manage their health care services? Alternatively, if Inuit have not yet internalized the basic precepts of "good health" as defined by biomedicine,[10] then how can they operate the services that hinge on these precepts?

The second and more prevalent paradigm to be found in the literature (i.e., which focuses on difficulties of communication in order to justify Inuit employment in health care) defends the need for Inuit to secure greater involvement in the delivery of health care, drawing either on the difficulties of effective cross-cultural communication or, more simply, on the undefined rationale of protecting their "culture." Hence a number of authors stress the need to employ Inuit so that their presence can resolve problems of communication and professional obtuseness with regard to local community dynamics and to Inuit beliefs as well as improve the cultural appropriateness of programs (Crago et al. 1990), and address problems of high staff turnover (Labbé 1987; Simard 1988; Weller 1981; Weller and Pranga 1987). Expressed more succinctly: "Training is the means to autonomy" (Kativik Regional Council of Health and Social Services 1990, 2).

The gap between two cultures (the Inuit and the Euro-Canadian) and their assumed inability to communicate are blamed for the lack of success and popularity of health services. This gap curtails "l'accessibilité culturelle" (Dufour 1990). Improving cultural accessibility entails attempting to close the gap between Western health care and Inuit culture. Solutions must go beyond merely hiring more Inuit staff; they must address issues related to differences in medical ideology and practice. Dufour (1990, 13) proposes "[de] cesser de travailler sur une population pour travailler avec elle, à lui reconnaître la compétence et la capacité de se prendre en charge par l'intégration du système médical populaire au système médical professionnel (to stop working on a population to work with it, to acknowledge its competence and ability to take care of itself through the integration of the popular medical system to the professional medical system)." In other words, health services must be integrated into the fabric of the community and attuned to Inuit culture. Dufour (1989, 1990) does not operationalize her stance in terms of health care reform beyond supporting the employment of Inuit within the (northern) structure.[11] However, it often appears as if the services are first to be elaborated and then adapted through the inclusion of Inuit, thus the relevance of asking questions concerning cultural accessibility. It is at the level of health care services that attention must be paid to "culture" rather than at the level of ideology.

This argument tends to underplay the extent to which services are embedded within a coherent, albeit heterogeneous, whole that produces, maintains, and reproduces biomedical health services and within which Inuit medical ideology has little or no place. It appears overly optimistic to expect Inuit operating within the biomedical system, and having been socialized by this system, to be able to balance and articulate two distinct medical ideologies (often hinging on contradictory precepts) and to deliver coherent services that retain medical and cultural relevance for both parties. A second assumption inherent to this argument is that the biomedical culture merely "packages" underlying universal truths. These truths, it is further assumed, can be stripped of their biomedical cultural packaging and repackaged with Inuit culture. This paradigm neglects the fact that biomedical concepts are first and foremost cultural constructions (Hahn and Gaines 1985; Lock and Gordon 1988). Another assumption, which is even more problematic, is the belief that socially significant roles can be created by foreign institutions in isolation from community and cultural processes.

The third paradigm (which involves looking at the relationship between Inuit society and the nation-state in order to justify the latter transferring control of health services to the former) defines northern health services as an extension of the colonial system. For example, O'Neil (1986) talks about northern health care reflecting an internal colonial political economy, where the structural development of health services is an outgrowth of the dominant society and remains outside the realm of community control, isolated from issues of community development. "Self-determination in Native health care is a *public health movement* of historic proportions and the effective delivery of the full range of preventive, curative and educational health services in the North will not progress until the transfer is complete" (O'Neil 1988, 48, emphasis added). The message is clear: the problems identified with northern health services will not be resolved until health care is politically decolonized. Interestingly, decolonization is defined as a public health movement.

Broad in scope and quite compelling, this paradigm falls short due to its lack of specificity. While its ideological message is clear, its pragmatic application is problematic. Indeed, how much control is control? Given the actual political health care structure, how much change must it undergo in order for Inuit to be able to negotiate and/or create locally meaningful health care services? The political economy of health thesis,[12] which informs this paradigm, tends to collapse levels of analysis that would be better left distinct. In fact, the discourse of community health, and arguments revolving around dependency, is generated at three levels of analysis (and by different actors) to signify different processes. These levels are:

(1) the international and national levels, which focus on megatrends in medical ideology and on the relationship between Inuit society and the Canadian and Quebec societies;
(2) the provincial-regional level, which includes local politics and institutional debates generated in the communities; and
(3) the community level, which affects families and individuals.

Each level offers a multiplicity of perspectives that shape, albeit with different weight, the discourse of community health and arguments revolving around this discourse. Whereas the first level has been successfully analyzed through a political economy thesis (O'Neil 1986), this thesis serves to misinform other levels of analysis because it neglects "the periphery" that it aims to explain. At the meso- and micro-social levels, current paradigms in biomedical wisdom play an important and unexpected role: here the discourse is shared, both sides using community health concepts to formulate arguments, to seek political and pragmatic support, and to compete for continuity on the one hand and autonomy on the other.

The analysis presented above raises a number of questions. First, is the community health paradigm really conducive to true autonomy or is it a new manoeuvre to capitalize on the popular discourse of resistance by reintegrating it into a larger and institutionalized medical discourse? Second, what is the place of culture in northern health services? Must it provide a politico-culturally adapted structure that would then shape health care delivery? Must it be a component of health care delivery, a merging of two (or more) explanatory models? Or is the role of culture dynamic and in flux, depending on the political context and a cultural group's relationship with the dominant society? Third, what is control and what is the relationship between control, healing, and health? And fourth, what is the role of northern health services? Must it be defined strictly in terms of efficacy in improving Inuit health status? Or can it be redefined as serving other purposes that would include meanings beyond a biomedical concept of health?

Beyond the Community Health Model: Theoretical Framework

In his "Two Lectures," Foucault (1976) suggests that, beginning in the 1960s, "totalitarian theories" were increasingly challenged by the "insurrection of subjugated knowledge." By "subjugated knowledge," he means

> a whole set of knowledges that have been disqualified as inadequate to their task or insufficiently elaborated: naive knowledges, located down on the hierarchy, beneath the required level of cognition or scientificity ... A differential knowledge incapable of unanimity and which owes its force only to the harshness with which it is opposed by everything surrounding it. (82)

This subjugated knowledge acts as a local form of criticism, "an autonomous, non-centralized kind of theoretical production ... whose validity is not dependent on the approval of the established régimes of thought" (81). This resurgence of popular knowledge, however, opens the possibility of a recodification, or recolonization, of this knowledge. Comaroff and Comaroff (1989, 268) understand the southern Tswana's experience with colonialism as "the colonization of their consciousness and their consciousness of colonization," the former leading to the incorporation of Western concepts within the Tswana lifeworld, the latter giving rise to conflicts and movements of resistance. Thus, it is postulated that, since the implementation of the JBNQA, the development of Nunavik northern health care services involves two processes:

- the decolonization of the Inuit self, whereby the elaboration of certain structures and programs, following the signing of the JBNQA, provides the Inuit with mechanisms by which they can recover those elements of their culture that had been taken away by colonialism.
- the recolonization of local knowledge, whereby forms of knowledge and practices perceived as traditional are integrated into and redefined by the health care structure.

From this perspective, the political mobilization inherent in the negotiation process leading to the signing of the JBNQA, and the developments that followed it, provided the Inuit with a stepping stone from which to start reclaiming northern biomedical institutions. This can perhaps be best represented as the beginning of the decolonization of the Inuit self.[13] Indeed, this political mobilization gave rise to the formalization and reintegration of local knowledge, some of which, in effect, is being recolonized by the medical and, perhaps, other institutions.[14] But it also provided the opportunity for one dissident community (not a signatory of the JBNQA) to reclaim a Western institution – the hospital – in the pursuit of its own political aspirations. In this context then, the decolonization of the Inuit self is the process by which the Inuit can start representing a locally based Western and/or Westernized institution (i.e., the hospital) as an extension of their society that is embedded within and central to a contemporary community dynamic.

The above framework allows an examination of the relationship between tradition, culture, and the community health discourse, the latter being the mechanism by which the Inuit attempt to decolonize medical structures and by which practitioners realize a recolonization of Inuit knowledge. Again, both processes are symbiotic, depending on one another for legitimacy. A number of local informants perceive certain recent developments in Nunavik health care as attempts to give back the culture that has been eroded by the colonial process. This line of thinking, however, was often followed by discussions of the many hoops through which the Inuit now have to jump in order to have access to opportunities.

Decolonization of the Self and Recolonization of Knowledge

This section provides an overview of how the community health discourse is produced and utilized in order to satisfy divergent interests in Nunavik. It has been argued that self-determination is not a community health movement. In fact, the community health model offers opportunities for the Inuit to gain greater control over health care. From the "community's perspective,"[15] community health means anything that strengthens the relationship between the community and health care. This vision is coloured by the community's experience of health care and, thus, differs from community to community. For the purpose of this analysis, I review Puvirnituk's[16] perspective on community health and contrast it to the "regional perspective" on community health, which, in this case, refers to specific processes aimed at transferring to the Kativik Regional Council of Health and Social Services responsibilities and budgets controlled in Quebec City.

Puvirnituk: Community Health Belongs to the Community

Puvirnituk is a community of 1,100 (Quebec 1996), and Kuujjuaq residents often describe it as "traditional." Puvirnituk was selected in 1982 to be the location of a regional hospital – the Innuulitsivik Health Centre – following a consultation with the Hudson Bay communities. Its dissident stance vis-à-vis the JBNQA probably played a role in its selection. Politics aside,

Inukjuak would have been a more likely choice. The hospital is the biggest structure in town, the main local representation of government, and offers the most employment opportunities.

Community dynamics have played a major role in shaping Inuit involvement in health care in Puvirnituk (or POV, as it is commonly called). The community's stance against the JBNQA seems to have contributed to maintaining and/or strengthening community identity. From the time the hospital was announced, community groups sought involvement in its planning. The local women's group opted to refuse the hospital unless a maternity unit was included. The objective of integrating Inuit midwives into the health team was developed shortly thereafter,[17] and professionals opposed to this plan were slowly weeded out. The nomination of an Inuit director at the Innuulitsivik Health Centre in 1984 played a definite role in increasing Inuit employment opportunities: part of the hospital's mandate is to establish itself as a training centre for Inuit nurses (Groupe de Travail sur les Objectifs du CHCB 1984). Multiple efforts have also been made to train Inuit as para-professionals in a variety of roles.

The community's relationship with the hospital is a close one. In discussions of the community's role in health care, emphasis was placed on (1) the place of Inuit knowledge in health care, (2) the role of Inuit in shaping health care, and (3) the place of the hospital in the fulfillment of local political aspirations. I discuss each of these points in turn.

Place of Inuit Knowledge in Health Care

It is readily acknowledged within the community that the hospital's functioning hinges on "White," or "foreign," knowledge. This appears to run counter to the community's wishes. An Inuk leader involved in health care reported a discussion with a southern health professional as follows: "Don't give us your theories, your philosophy: we don't need them. We don't need your culture, we need the facts. We are part of our culture, born in it and raised in it. We get our information from other sources as well, from the elders, from other men and women." When asked about the place of traditional Inuit medical knowledge in the new order, elders generally explain how the Inuit used to help one another. They emphasize autonomy and self-reliance. And they readily refer to the role of the church and "White" health care in destroying the social context of healing.[18] Employing Inuit as health professionals is perceived as providing an opportunity to recover Aboriginal knowledge.

> There were some Inuit which had a "special touch," that could heal. The Whites did not know about it. When the Whites came, the Inuit tried to compromise with them, to live with them ... The knowledge is still here.

> Now that Inuit understand the rules more, they can bring that Inuit knowledge back. (An elder and former traditional midwife)

Role of Inuit in Shaping Health Care

The community health care model is an extension of biomedical ideology. While the model itself challenges some of the power relationships entrenched in the curative-oriented model of health care popular in the 1950s and 1960s, it remains faithful to a biomedical conceptualization of health. Furthermore, it remains faithful to the investment of power in professionals. In southern communities, boards of directors usually share the class culture of professionals. In the North, however, professionals and the Inuit Board of Directors constitute two distinct groups that do not share a common culture.[19] Community participation on the board of directors provides Inuit with a mechanism to shape northern health care that capitalizes on the knowledge acquired by Inuit health care workers and the power of the board.

> The nurses in the nursing stations have a lot of autonomy because they were let to have it. But we have to work so that the board of directors and local committees get more involved. We have to make the board of directors responsible for the care provided in the community: they have to ensure that [the nurse] works for the community. Inuit must provide the nurses with a framework to support the nurses in their involvement/work in the community ... It is for us to ensure that the health system is working for us. (An Inuk leader)

The services currently provided are deemed "not Inuit-like." The reason for this is attributed to powers beyond the reach of Inuit:

> This organization was given, no, introduced, by Whites. We should be able to give services the Inuit way. Because POV was dissident of the JBNQA, changes here were gradual rather than sudden. In other communities, they were suddenly given a lot of power, but no direction. In POV, it happened slowly. At the level of services, we should have as complete control first, but we will never have control, we will always be caught in between. (An Inuk health care worker)

Informants generally qualify "the Inuit way" as a non-institutionalized approach to caring. While the mechanisms called upon to address the shortcomings of the system are provided by the health care structure, comments emphasize the role of the community, Inuit health care workers, and board members in providing direction and shaping health care so as to reflect a culturally appropriate model.

Place of the Hospital in Fulfillment of Local Political Aspirations

Under the community health model, the hospital's role is to assist communities in achieving and/or maintaining their health status through broad-based participation in program design and decision making. In POV however, the hospital is part of a larger community process that is specific to this community. POV's rejection of the JBNQA has been empowering yet costly. It has focused the community on the common goal of resistance. The hospital, the community's largest employer, has been enlisted in this struggle:

> The hospital has a very important role to play in the community ... it has to work and build at the grassroots. It can't afford to alienate people. We do not need another institution that alienates our people ... There is little linkage [between Puvirnituk and the Kativik Regional Government] – we used them very little, unless sometimes for training funding. They are "disconnected," disoriented. We keep to ourselves as much as possible so that they can interfere as least as possible. All they want is money, KRG, KSB, Air Inuit, Avataq, Land Holding Corporation.[20] If they start seeing us as having money, they'll walk all over us. They destroy everything they touch for money. Nobody has been able to stand up to them. They don't think that people are more important than money. We will keep health separate as long as we do not have a fair and equitable government. The hospital is a means to train Inuit, to increase their self-confidence, to create a front which will be able to stand up to KRG. Nobody has been able to stand up to them yet. When they come for us, we will be ready. We will have thirty to forty people ready to stand up. The hospital is a way to prepare tomorrow's leaders. (An Inuk political leader)

The hospital as an institution is a vehicle through which the community may fulfill its political aspirations. I noted earlier that Inuit employment in health care is perceived as a way for Inuit to end their dependency on southern knowledge. Inuit health workers are given the task of learning southern medical knowledge, which they then integrate with Inuit knowledge. Inuit leadership sees this type of structure as providing a framework to ensure that health professionals are responsive to community needs and wants. One question remains: what is the linkage between these aspirations and the community health model?

Puvirnituk's perception of the role of health care does not fit neatly into the community health model. POV's vision of health care includes the assimilation of some technical biomedical knowledge, a precursor to the creation of a unique Inuit medical institution. It also includes the integration of the hospital into the political life of the community. The model proposed places the community at the core, where "subjugated knowledge" may find its expression once the structure becomes decolonized in terms of human resources. In this model, the hospital is part of a larger context of self-determination in Puvirnituk.

Community Health and the Regional Discourse

The discourse of community health, as used by health planners, hinges on a number of assumptions that inform the argument; namely, that the holistic, global, systemic approach or "l'approche communautaire" is best adapted to address northerner health care needs. A first assumption is that the North in general, and traditional Inuit society in particular, is communal – a characteristic lost or altered by modern life (Bédard and Baillargeon 1981; Bérubé et al. 1971; Choinière et al. 1988; Sampath 1988). This assumption is used to justify the use of a community health model (Labbé 1981b; Tremblay 1979).

A second assumption is that Inuit/northerners – unlike Qallunaat, Whites, allochtones, Euro-Canadians, outsiders,[21] and/or the government(s) – are assumed to be the only/preferred/sole legitimate providers of truly effective and/or culturally appropriate health care (Dufour 1983; Kativik Regional Council of Health and Social Services 1990, 1991; Tremblay 1978; Tremblay 1979). Again, holistic, global, systemic approaches ("approche[s] communautaire[s]") are presented as superior alternatives to biomedicine because they open the doors to "lay" practitioners and are believed to be closer to traditional Inuit concepts of health and illness (Dufour 1979, 1990; Tremblay 1979; Tulugak n.d.). It is through these oppositions that power and control over decision making are negotiated. A consultant working for the Kativik CRSSS argued, for example, that "the need for a Community Health Department [DSC du Nord] is evident but, it must be determined whether or not the needs of the region are met by an establishment based in the South. Dynamic community health programs are a necessity if the goal of optimal wellness through increased self-reliance is to be achieved." Or again:

> The Kativik CRSSS [Kativik Council] feels that the expertise of various establishments and organizations in the South should be used to establish priorities or to implement the required emergency measures [in case of epidemics]. But responsibility for the development of program policies and objectives must be kept within the region. (Kativik Regional Council of Health and Social Services 1986, 13)

The above comment is part of an introductory statement made during a presentation to Mrs. Thérèse Lavoie-Roux, then Quebec's minister of health. The arguments called upon here recur over and over.

According to the view of some planners, the allocation of control and power is also negotiated in terms of results: power and control will be passed on when desired results start to occur. In this model of tutelage, Inuit must first demonstrate their abilities: "Du côté des Inuit, on n'a pas une volonté de se prendre en charge, on est tellement gâté. Pour qu'il y ait une prise en charge, il faudrait qu'on les laisse faire leurs erreurs – on l'a jamais fait ... Les Inuit, de toute façon sont de grands parleurs, et de petits faiseurs (the Inuit don't have the desire to take charge, they're so spoiled. If they were to take control, we'd have to let them make their own mistakes – they've never done it ... Anyway, the Inuit are all talk, no action)" (a nurse-in-charge at one of the Health Centres).

Southern institutions involved in northern health care sometimes assume the role of experts who must "safeguard the Inuit and northern planners against themselves." A cultural argument is utilized, but control and resources are withheld until "the Inuit are ready." The ability of northern professionals to make appropriate decisions is even disputed on personal and professional grounds: "they could not get a job in the south."[22]

From the planners' perspective, then, the discourse of community health serves to define distinctions between inadequate and ideal planning, and to determine successes and failures. Their perception of community dynamics[23] may be utilized to explain community involvement, or the lack of it, within an institution, while the nature of the institution itself, its rapport with the community and the larger context of health politics, may become somewhat secondary. In cases of success, professional involvement is stressed over community involvement; in cases of failure, Inuit lack of commitment, northern politics, and individual personalities are stressed.

While communities appear to use community involvement in health care as a measure of success, the strengthening of a regional order through the allocation of greater power and control to the Kativik Council will not necessarily lead to a strengthening of community involvement. The linkage between the regional administration and the ministry, together with the control mechanisms involved in the provision of budgets, places limits on the Kativik Council's flexibility. Five- or ten-year plans are not likely to represent the diversity of various communities or to be responsive to spontaneous mobilizations. In other words:

> L'administration est souvent en retard sur les initiatives venant du terrain, des professionnels et de la communauté. On sent peut-être le besoin de se serrer les coudes, se sentant pris de cours, confronté ou mis devant un état de fait. Maintenant, on sent l'omniprésence de l'administration au nord. Avec le CRSSS [Kativik Council], il n'y a plus moyen de bouger sans avoir un gestionnaire dans son lit. Les professionnels sont scrutés à la loupe, pour

identifier les initiatives du terrain. Pour être efficace, l'administration devrait supporter les élans de la base. On tend plutôt vers le contraire ... On demande ... de faire une étude, qui serve de base au CRSSS pour établir ses objectifs et orientations. A partir de cela, on va établir un plan quinquénal. Pis les projets de base qui ne colleront pas se feront dire: concentrez-vous sur nos objectifs, votre projet n'est pas une priorité, veuillez respecter la grille ci-présente ... En subordonnant les problèmes identifiés localement à des grilles d'analyse, on ralentit le potentiel de changement. J'ai peur que la techno-bureaucratie reproduise le système de gestion. Au lieu d'un colonialisme blanc, c'est un colonialisme régional. On assiste maintenant à la formation de classes sociales, de stratification des collectivités. En essayant de standardiser les approches, on bureaucratise et subordonne les initiatives et besoins locaux à des plans quinquénaux. Le paradoxe du discours sur la santé communautaire, c'est qu'il conduit à la formation de gestionnaires à l'écoute de leur grille, pas du milieu.

The administration is often slow in dealing with initiatives from the region, professionals, and the community. We feel the need to stick together, feeling as though we've been caught unawares, confronted with or placed before an irrefutable fact. The administration's omnipresence is now felt in the north. With the Kativik Council, we can't roll over in bed without bumping into a bureaucrat. Professionals are put under a magnifying glass in order to identify field initiatives. To be efficient, the administration should support local efforts. The opposite tends to happen ... A study is requested to serve as a basis for the CRSSS, to establish its objectives and its direction. A five-year plan is then established. The design projects that won't fly are told: concentrate on our objectives, your project is not a priority, please adhere to the enclosed flowchart ... Subjecting locally identified problems to externally drawn flowcharts slows down the potential for change. I'm worried that the techno-bureaucracy will reproduce the administrative system. Instead of a white colonialism, there will be regional colonialism. We are now witnessing the creation of social classes, the stratification of communities. The attempt to standardize the approaches bureaucratizes and subjects the initiatives and the local needs to five-year plans. The paradox of a regional health care discourse is that it leads to the creation of administrators tuned in to their workplans, not to their community. (A consultant working for the Kativik CRSSS)

To summarize, the community health model provides interesting possibilities for the integration of the perspectives of various communities with regard to health care planning. However, the usefulness of this association is limited. POV is working towards the development of an outreach form of health care – one that is integrated with community activities. But POV also sees the hospital as having a role greater than that of "health care" in that it is an instrument that the community can use in its struggle for autonomy. At the regional level, broader political-cultural arguments are favoured to support relocating decision making in the North. Regional entities, however, appear to be fighting for the expansion of their own power[24] and are not necessarily interested in or able to respond to community needs. Nevertheless, the underlying themes in regional debates over self-determination in health care – culture, autonomy, and self-responsibility – were given greater legitimacy through the community health model. The agendas at work at both the community and regional levels go beyond the confines of the community health model; the northern health care system is absorbed into political debates linking Inuit to the dominant society.

Operationalizing Self-Determination in Nunavik Health Care

While self-determination is frequently called upon as a cure-all for disparities in health and problems encountered in or because of health care, the operationalization of self-determination within health care is rarely explored. In Nunavik, para-professionalism and Inuit employment are prized avenues through which the Inuit hope to take control of a foreign structure. In POV, these avenues allow the community to assert its independence from the regional government. But Inuit staffing alone is insufficient. The community agenda in pushing for a midwifery run by Inuit midwives – a goal shared by other Hudson Bay communities – opens the door for the hospital to become a vehicle that can bring back forbidden or forgotten knowledge.

Culture, Community Ownership, and Midwifery

"The grandmothers, the mothers, and the daughters got together. It was illegal, but we did it: we built our maternity" (an Inuk midwifery worker). The Puvirnituk midwifery program has been the most documented, discussed, filmed, studied, and envied of all the local training programs[25] (Dufour 1989; Gagnon 1989; Native Women's Association 1989). No doubt it was the existence of some commonality between Inuit and "southern" midwifery that made this project feasible, successful, and so visible.

The Innuulitsivik Health Centre opened its perinatal program in 1986 under the leadership of the local Native Women's Association and with the support of other community organizations (Dufour 1989). Its objectives were to: (1) keep as many deliveries as possible in the North, (2) encourage the reintegration of cultural know-how into obstetric and perinatal care, and (3) offer support in the prenatal and postnatal periods. The perinatal committee is formed by doctors, dentists, pharmacists, and professional and student midwives (the latter are Inuit who, upon graduation, will replace non-Inuit midwives). Dufour (1989) suggests that these Inuit student midwives take an active role on the committee and in planning strategies and interventions. The learning process involves apprenticeship. Strategies and interventions are also shared with the community at meetings that aim at what Dufour describes as a "communication symétrique et complémentaire" (9), where knowledge is exchanged between all parties, including health care workers, nurses, social service employees, maternity workers, school-age children, elders, pregnant women, the community council, and so on.

This project has achieved what no other program could: its role extends beyond the health centre and addresses the needs of a population that it has defined. Its impact has been much deeper than has that of midwifery: it appears to have brought back a desire to integrate local knowledge into the health care structure.[26]

> They came and took over everything, even delivering. We did not need the nurses but they insisted. For TB, it was different. But they took for granted that we could not look after ourselves because we needed pills for TB. They took over birthing ... It was not the first time that White people started coming in. The first time was around 1920. People then used to share. They did not take everything. Only the nurses did. White people in the 1920[s] used to share, help people with their home remedies. Earlier than 1960, White people helped with what they could and what they had. We hardly have home remedies any more – we lost a lot of things because [foreigners] started coming in. Now White people are starting to give our tradition back; i.e., Inuit midwives, and that is positive. (An Inuk midwifery worker)

This theme also arises in formal presentations:

> Having a maternity in our own community has given us a chance to make up our own goals. And for us right now, sharing information is a very big priority. We do it in our own language. We, as Inuit midwives, know our own people. We know things Qallunaaks [sic] can't know. We are being trained and we are bringing the knowledge back to our community. (Qumaluk 1988, 2)

What is being "given back," however, differs from what was "taken." Elders and former traditional midwives interviewed in POV all reported different protocols for birthing. In some camps, only women who had children themselves were helpers for delivery, whereas in others, youths, including young men, were invited to attend. Each midwife also reported different methods for dealing with complications related to birthing. As well, it appears that there was no "standard" Inuit medical practice: each camp seemed to have its own pattern for decision making and its own treatments. In some camps, decision making was made by the whole group; in others, it was the privilege of elders. In all interviews within which traditional medical knowledge and healing were discussed, Inuit emphasized the social context of birthing and healing. For example:

> Inuit tried to visit one another when they were sick. They tried to heal one another. They knew all sorts of things about how to take care of one another. They would search for what the problem was and try different natural substances to heal that person. Nurses knew how to do things, Inuit also knew, naturally. (An elder)

Or again: "Before the nurses, people used to visit one another, to help one another. They knew who was sick and would help. Now they just go to the nurses, they don't help each other anymore" (an elder).

The impact of colonialism has changed the social context of healing by placing decision making in the hands of a few. The impact of this change has remained despite the midwifery program, and can be seen in the changes the practice of *senayit* has undergone. "Senayit" means "being the maker, the one that makes the baby like that." Traditionally, the senayit would be the first one to dress the baby and, thus, define both gender and social role. With the midwifery program, Inuit midwives are being integrated into traditional roles in a novel way:

> For the time when deliveries were done outside the community, the senayit was decided by the mother, anyone, not necessarily related. She would tell them "I want you to have my baby as senayit." The ceremony would be done when the child was brought back: the senayit would dress the child, saying: "this will be what you will be when you grow up. You'll be helpful to your mother." Now I'm senayit to many babies. Now it is the person that cuts the cord. Although some still do it with clothing. (An Inuk midwifery worker)

The place given to local knowledge in midwifery and in the spatial arrangement of the clinic shows the difference between what was "taken" and what is "being given back." Professionals are making a conscious effort to "improve" what existed traditionally and to answer to perceived and expressed wants and needs from the women in the community: "Southern midwives introduced the concept of the uterus, why women get pregnant, a concept of the body. We have extended the role of the midwife, we are giving more than what the traditional midwife used to give"[27] (a non-Inuk midwife involved in the training of Inuit midwifery workers).

In contrast, when asked about the place of local knowledge in midwifery, an Inuk replied:

> You are right to be concerned about this. But the qallunaat are outnumbered here: 99 percent of patients speak Inuktitut, 75 percent of the care is in Inuktitut. Midwives are constantly bombarded by the community. Now their information is mostly White, but one day they will outgrow this. They will be in charge and it will be up to them to decide where the maternity should go. (An Inuit leader involved in the initial planning of the midwifery program)

There are clear intentions, as well, to modify the spatial arrangement of the midwifery program which, although very familial, is still perceived as too "southern":

> We have the dream birth centre from the South, now we need more Inuit physical props, ropes, the box to squat, different positions. It is not that it is forbidden, but the [double] bed takes a lot of space and there is no incentive for anything else. The woman that started this had a strong focus on "techniques." Now we need to move on, to relax this and let women decide what they want, to give them options. (A non-Inuk midwife involved in the training of Inuit midwifery workers)

Midwifery is soon to face a new challenge imposed by a southern tradition. In Western institutions, literacy is essential to leadership. In small governmental departments, it is customary for the coordinator, or the head, to do the administrative duties and the paperwork. This often means that the most competent people are taken away from their field of expertise to carry on administrative duties – a fact that will challenge Puvirnituk: "I am now the coordinator, which means a lot of paperwork. If [the Inuit midwife] who is now ready to graduate, although she still needs some direction with the paperwork, becomes coordinator, she will be plagued with paperwork. We will effectively take her away from what she is best at: being a midwife" (a non-Inuk midwife involved in the training of Inuit midwifery workers).

Conclusions

More than twenty years have passed since the signing of the JBNQA. In some ways, the context of health care in Nunavik has undergone dramatic changes. Substantial gains have been secured:

- Inuit employment in health care has grown beyond interpreting to include upper level management, paramedical roles, finance, support staff, and janitorial staff;
- some resources, dossiers, and budgets long administered from Quebec City are now controlled from Kuujjuaq;
- Hudson Bay Inuit women are no longer expected to travel to Moose Factory (Ontario) to give birth but can do so within a northern pilot maternity project.

The JBNQA created momentum, even in dissident communities, and enabled Inuit to assume a considerable part of decision making with regard to the northern biomedical system. Perhaps the major change in Nunavik since the JBNQA, at least with regard to health care, may be found in the way that Inuit formulate their demands. The JBNQA created an opportunity for Inuit to learn and master a powerful discourse: the discourse of community health. How this discourse has developed in Canada over the past twenty years has offered the Inuit new ways to justify setting their own agendas. The emergence of welfarism in the 1950s paved the way for the development of the community health discourse, facilitating its association with basic human rights. The Aboriginal rights discourse further enabled Inuit self-determination in health care to become embedded within a broad and powerful ideological context.[28] In a way, the convergence of discourses acted synergistically to facilitate a process of self-determination: arguments favouring para-medical employment opportunities, community involvement in health care, and reliance on cultural arguments to justify regional relocation of decision making are now vested with an aura of humanitarian legitimacy that has wide appeal. The development of para-medical roles is associated with a process that, Inuit believe, will enable them to integrate their traditional "subjugated" knowledge within the northern health care system. Puvirnituk's midwifery is perceived as the beginning of a process that involves southerners "giving back" Inuit culture. The changes brought about through the JBNQA facilitated both (1) the decolonization of the Inuit self, thus enabling Inuit to see the biomedical institution as their own and, consequently, to reshape it in their pursuit for cultural self-actualization; and (2) the recolonization of Inuit knowledge, whereby the biomedical institution, in its turn, reshapes Inuit knowledge.

The two processes are, at least for the time being, complementary. From the perspective of one informant (an Inuk health administrator), this situation is temporary: Inuit working in health care may have to replicate a foreign system for the time being. The influence of the community, Inuit culture, and the power of numbers is expected to change this situation over time. If this vision is accurate, then the operationalization of self-determination in health care in Nunavik may be a multi-phase process, where Inuit must (1) master foreign knowledge in order to be able to enter the field of health care, (2) ensure that Inuit employment in health care is facilitated, and (3) gain access to the decision-making level in order to finally bring about the decolonization of health services. During this process, Inuit knowledge may be temporarily recolonized and, perhaps, permanently modified. While it is difficult to assess whether significant decolonization is taking place, informants seem confident that a process of decolonization has begun and will eventually lead to true self-determination.

In Nunavik, health practitioners, bureaucrats, political leaders, and community members all capitalize on the discourse of community health in order to formulate arguments supporting or opposing Nunavik in securing greater control and autonomy over its health care decision making. Yet, what regional and community leaders are seeking goes beyond what the community health model has to offer. There are grounds for wondering whether integrating a political process into a biomedical model may be double edged. What will happen to Inuit aspirations as new biomedical paradigms develop? While the determining discourse of community health has favoured the quest of Aboriginal societies for self-determination, one may wonder about the future of this discourse. Land claim settlements are hard come by and have tended to become less generous. Social programs are eroding: given current trends in an increasingly conservative Canada, the fundamental social reforms this discourse demands may be a thing of the past.

Still, in sharp contrast to the current claims of Inuit dependency, acculturation, and apathy, my analysis shows how the northern biomedical system is being actively and purposively assimilated into the Inuit lifeworld and is, in fact, becoming part of the process of these peoples reclaiming their rightful place within Canadian society. Inuit are actors and consumers of various paradigms. This may not be a recent phenomenon, but it is certainly a requirement for self-determination:

> I have black in my sputum now. An elder told me to tie my finger like this.[29] If I went to the nurse, they would put a tube down my nose, and I feel that the finger works better. Some Inuit medicine works better. I'll try this one first. If it does not stop the bleeding, I'll go to the nursing station. (An elder)

Notes

This chapter is part of an MA degree completed at the Department of Anthropology at McGill University in 1993.

1 Under the label of self-determination in health care, I wish to also include what, in the French literature, is called "l'autochtonization des services de la santé" as well as the federal government's Health Program Transfer Policy. These terms are generally associated with distinct models and may have very different implications in terms of their outcomes. However, they do share one very important quality: all treat health care services more or less as a black box to be transferred from one authority to another. The transfer process

does not necessarily aim at giving Aboriginal peoples the ability to address the content of the box.

2 Nunavik corresponds roughly to "Nouveau-Québec," which lies north of the 55th parallel. The region is inhabited by 7,802 people, 91 percent of them Inuit, distributed over a region that constitutes 36 percent of Quebec's territory. The population is divided into fourteen villages along the coasts of Hudson Bay, Hudson Strait (58 percent), and Ungava Bay (42 percent) (Québec 1996).

3 In the health structure of the Ministère de la Santé et des Services Sociaux, each region has what is commonly known as a CRSSS (commonly referred to as "CR3S") tasked with determining regional priorities and making budgetary allocations to the *centres hospitaliers* (hospitals), *centres d'accueils* (nursing homes), *centres de soins prolongés* (long-term care facilities), and *centres de la santé et des services sociaux* (also known as CLSCs) who offer public health, outreach, and community clinic services. In this system, the CRSSS located in Kuujjuaq is known as the Conseil Régional de la Santé et des Services Sociaux Kativik, or Kativik CRSSS.

4 The Makivik Corporation, located in Kuujjuaq, is tasked with the implementation of the JBNQA.

5 In 1976, Ungava Bay residents made use of the hospital in Kuujjuaq when medical care was required. In contrast, Hudson Bay residents had to rely on a hospital located in Moose Factory. Part of the gains secured under the agreement was the building of a regional hospital on the Hudson Bay coast. The Innuulitsivik Health Centre opened its doors in Puvirnituk in 1982.

6 Public health and community health are often referred to interchangeably and rather loosely by social scientists. In biomedical parlance, however, public health generally refers to communicable diseases control strategies, such as immunization, contact tracing for sexually transmitted diseases, tuberculosis, and so on. Community health generally encompasses public health and refers to broad-based preventive strategies focused on community education, lifestyle changes, and access to primary health care. Since the WHO Declaration of Alma-Ata at the International Conference on Primary Health Care, Alma-Ata, USSR, on 6-12 September 1978, "community participation" has been promoted as an essential component of community health. In practice, community participation has been pursued at two main levels: first, health structures (such as those described in this chapter) have generally been managed through seeking the participation of non-professional community members (either as members of a board of directors or as part of an advisory committee); second, community participation has been sought through group health education activities such as workshops and health fairs.

7 And, incidentally, leaving the local health centre and the hospital to carry the burden of all criticisms.

8 "Récemment, une volonté s'est exprimée pour reprendre contrôle de la santé à travers divers éléments significatifs: les femmes Inuit de la Baie d'Hudson ont manifesté leur désir de reprendre en main la périnatalité ... De nombreuses personnes inuit [sic] ont participé à l'élaboration et à la mise en place du programme de contrôle de l'otite et de l'audition (recently, the wish to take back control of health care has been expressed: Inuit women from Hudson's Bay have demonstrated their desire to take charge of prenatal care ... Many Inuit people participated in the drafting and establishing of an ear infection and hearing examination program)" (Julien 1987, 19). Julien goes on to associate "la santé communautaire (community health)" with autonomy.

9 O'Neil (1988, 80) makes a similar claim.

10 The choice of an appropriate terminology to depict "Western" health care is problematic in this case. The term "biomedicine" recalls the technologically oriented curative form of medicine so highly criticized by national and provincial ministries of health, perhaps for economic reasons, and obscures the social surveillance mechanisms now inscribed in the health units (DSC and CLSC in Quebec). However, depictions of "northern Western health care depending on the South" are even more problematic. For my purposes, biomedicine and biomedical health care will be utilized as comprehensive terms for Western health care.

11 Her model is illustrated as two interlocked circles: the first represents the southern practitioners, the second the Inuit population. In the interface of these circles are the Inuit

health care givers (as trained by southerners), mediating the two systems. This paradigm has the disadvantage of leaving Inuit health care workers in the role of dual culture broker, while conceptualizing both circles as isolated, indeed impermeable, to exchange except through these brokers (Dufour 1989).

12 Morgan (1987, 132) defines the political economy of health thesis as a "macroanalytic, critical and historical perspective for analysing disease distribution and health services under a variety of economic systems, with particular emphasis on the effects of stratified social, political, and economic relations within the world economic system."

13 "The decolonization of the Inuit self" is defined as the process by which an Inuk becomes consciously aware of colonialism and its influence on Inuit culture and takes action either to benefit from or to curtail colonial influence.

14 The creation of the Hunters' Support Program, through which hunters can now be remunerated for the harvesting of country meat, can perhaps also be framed as an example of the dual processes of decolonizing the self and recolonizing knowledge.

15 There is obviously no such thing as a "community perspective," just as there is no unified "professional or southern perspective" on community health. For the purposes of this discussion, interviewees' input will be divided into two categories: (1) the "community's perspective," which includes local people who may also be health care workers as well as long-term residents; and (2) the "regional perspective," defined as the perspective of Nunavik political leaders.

16 At the time I conducted my fieldwork, "Puvirnituk" was still known as "Povungnituk," or POV.

17 See the Puvirnituk's Maternity Philosophy Statement, Inuulitsivik (n.d.).

18 The influence of missionaries, and the role they played in paving the way to formal medical services, was considerable. The establishment of nursing stations, along with tuberculosis epidemics and hunger, had much to do with the subsequent disintegration of the role of the Inuit midwife. Elders were affected by the epidemics, which hunger made even more acute. Many died, while a large number were evacuated to tuberculosis sanatoria. Accurate figures are lacking for many communities, yet it has been estimated that 70 percent of the Inuit population now over the age of thirty-five spent from one to nine years in southern sanatoria because of tuberculosis. The displacement of Inuit midwifery, the curtailment of visiting the sick in times of epidemics, and the substitution of medical confidentiality for group decision making added to the ongoing social disarticulation caused by epidemics and famine.

19 An implication of this comment is that Inuit communities are unified and homogenous. That is obviously not the case. A regional centre such as Kuujjuaq is made up of clusters of communities, with Inuit identifying themselves by the community in which they were born. These clusters act as mechanisms of exclusion and inclusion. Smaller communities, like POV, are less liable to this degree of fragmentation because of the scarcity of employment. However, northern communities, including POV, are stratified, although not necessarily or exclusively on the basis of wealth.

20 KRG stands for Kativik Regional Government, KSB stands for Kativik Regional School Board. The KRG, the KSB, and the Land Holding Corporation are all Kuujjuaq-based institutions that evolved from the JBNQA. Avataq (the Northern Quebec Inuit Cultural Institute) is an exception, being based in Inukjuak.

21 These words are often used in the literature as though they were synonymous.

22 A quote that was heard many times.

23 Inuit culture, gender relations, family relationships, political processes, and so on.

24 The Kativik Council wants to be the link to the Quebec Ministry of Health, and it promotes the adoption of five- and ten-year plans for regional health development in the hope that these will provide a framework within which to develop the two hospitals and the health centres. With this objective in mind, local initiatives and spontaneous mobilizations are less likely to be supported with funding and resources.

25 It is beyond the purpose of this section to present a comprehensive evaluation of Inuulitsivik maternity. Such an evaluation, however, is available and very informative (Meyer and Bélanger 1991; Tourigny et al. 1991a, 1991b, and 1991c).

26 The impact of the program has, however, been much more positive for POV than it has for other Hudson Bay and Hudson Strait communities. The goal is to extend the program to

other communities located on Hudson Bay, although an actual time frame has not yet been established. It is, however, a priority because of the importance given to birthing and to the community of origin: "White man took away the most important thing, we used to deliver our babies, it used to be a joyful thing. It's not the same now, when they arrive by plane ... Even when they go to Inuit midwives at POV, it is not the same as when the delivery was at home. Family and friends all used to visit when the new baby came. Now it does not happen any more. They don't see the baby any more. They don't even visit when the new baby comes back ... The White man does not trust us on our own efforts" (an elder).

27 It is doubtful that southern midwives introduced the concept of the uterus and pregnancy to Inuit culture, although southern professionals commonly assume that Inuit culture had little knowledge of biology prior to contact. The role of the midwife has, however, grown under the influence of southern midwifery to include the promotion of biomedical notions of prevention (sexual education, awareness of sexually transmitted diseases, etc.) and postpartum care.

28 Perhaps it is the larger context that made self-determination in health care conceivable.

29 A red string was tied around one of her fingers, keeping it folded.

References

Bédard, Denis, and Jacques Baillargeon. 1981. "Inuit du Nouveau-Québec: La pratique médicale." *Le Médecin du Québec* 16: 78-82.

Bérubé, Réjean, Monique Bolduc, and Jean-François Proulx. 1971. *Grossesse et services de santé chez les Esquimaux de l'Ungava*. Québec: Direction Générale du Nouveau-Québec. (Ms.)

Choinière, Robert, Marco Levasseur, and Norbert Robitaille. 1988. "La Mortalité des Inuits du Nouveau-Québec de 1944 à 1983: Évolution selon l'âge et la cause du décès." *Recherches amérindiennes au Québec* 18, 1: 29-37.

Comaroff, Jean, and John L. Comaroff. 1989. "The Colonization of Consciousness in South Africa." *Economy and Society* 18, 3: 267-96.

Crago, Martha, Anne Marie Hurteau, and Hannah Ayukawa. 1990. "Culturally Based Audiological Services for Hearing-Impaired Inuit in Northern Quebec." *Journal of Speech and Language Pathology* 14, 2: 33-46.

Dufour, Marie-Josée. 1983. "La Santé des Inuit: Préoccupation humanitaire ou enjeu politique?" MA thesis, Département d'anthropologie, Université Laval, Québec.

Dufour, Rose. 1979. *Rapport de la tournée dans les villages de la Baie d'Ungava*, Québec: DSC du CHUL.

–. 1989. "Maternité et prise en charge dans la Baie d'Hudson." Communication presented at the Sixth Conference of the Canadian Association for Medical Anthropology, University of Ottawa, 19-22 May.

–. 1990. *L'Intervention en santé au nord du 55e parallèle ou quand l'observé devient l'enseignant*. Québec: Projet Nord, DSC du CHUL.

Foucault, Michel. 1976. "Two Lectures." In *Power/Knowledge, Selected Interviews and Other Writings 1972-1977, Michel Foucault*, ed. Colin Gordon, 78-108. New York: Pantheon Books.

Gagnon, Johanne. 1989. "A Joint Venture by People and Professionals on Hudson Coast in Northern Quebec: The Povungnituk Maternity." Paper presented at the Forty-Fifth Annual Meeting of the Society of Obstetrics and Gynecology of Canada (SOGC).

Groupe de Travail sur les Objectifs du CHCB. 1984. *Objectifs généraux: Centre hospitalier de la Baie d'Hudson, secteur santé*. Puvirnituk. (Ms.)

Hahn, R. and A. Gaines, eds. 1985. *Physicians of Western Medicine: Anthropological Approaches to Theory and Practice*. Dordrecht, Holland: D. Reidel Publishing Company.

Inuulitsivik Health Centre. N.d. *Philosophy of the Povungnituk Maternity*. Puvirnituk: Inuulitsivik Health Centre.

Julien, Gilles. 1987. "La santé communautaire en terre Inuit." *Le Devoir*, supplément, 18 mars, 19.

Kativik Regional Council of Health and Social Services (CRSSS-Kativik). 1986. *Brief to the Rochon Commission: Health and Social Services Delivery System in Region 10A*. Kuujjuak: KRCHSS.

–. 1990. Letter to Marc-Yvon Côté, Minister, Ministère de la Santé et des Services Sociaux. Kuujjuaq: KRCHSS.
–. 1991. *Additional Brief Tabled to the Parliamentary Commission on Draft Bill 120: An Act respecting Health Services and Social Services*. Kuujjuaq: KRCHSS.
Labbé, Jean. 1981a. "La santé au Nouveau-Québec Inuit." *Études Inuit Studies* 5, 2: 63-81.
–. 1981b. "Inuit du Nouveau-Québec, les services de santé: Hier et aujourd'hui." *Le Médecin du Québec* 16: 61-7.
–. 1987. *Les Inuit du Nord Québécois et leur santé*. Québec: DSC du CHUL.
Lock, Margaret, and D.R. Gordon. 1988. *Biomedicine Examined*. Dordrecht: Kluwer Academic Publishers.
Meyer, François, and Diane Bélanger. 1991. *Grossesses et naissances dans deux populations Inuit du Nouveau-Québec: Évaluation des soins et services en périnatalité, Hudson et Ungava, volet epidémiologie*. Québec: Département de Santé Communautaire du Centre hospitalier de l'Université Laval.
Morgan, Lynn M. 1987. "Dependency Theory in the Political Economy of Health: An Anthropological Critique." *Medical Anthropology Quarterly* 1, 2: 131-54.
Native Women's Association. 1989. *Inuit Midwifery in the Inuulitsivik Maternity*. Puvirnituk: Native Women's Association.
O'Neil, John D. 1986. "The Politics of Indian Health in the Fourth World: A Northern Example." *Human Organization* 45, 2: 119-28.
–. 1988. "Self-determination, Medical Ideology and Health Services in Inuit Communities." In *Northern Communities: The Prospects for Empowerment,* ed. Gurston Dacks and Ken Coates, 33-50. Edmonton: Boreal Institute for Northern Studies.
La Presse. 1986. "Les Hôpitaux du grand-nord veulent un statut particulier." 16 août, A8.
Québec, Ministère des Affaires Municipales. 1996. Information sur les affaires municipales. <www/bsq.gouv.qc.ca.bsq.muni.reg10.htm> [26 March 1997].
Qumaluk, Akinisie. 1988. Address to Northern Obstetrics Research Conference, Innuulitsivik Health Centre, Puvirnituk.
Sampath, H.M. 1988. "Missionaries, Medicine and Shamanism in the Canadian Eastern Arctic." *Arctic Medical Research* 47 (suppl. 1): 303-7.
Simard, Jean-Jacques. 1988. "Les services socio-sanitaires au Québec cri et Inuit." In *Le Développement des peuples du Nord: Actes du premier colloque Québec-Russie*, ed. G. Duhaime, 107-28. Québec: Université Laval.
Tourigny, André, Judy Ross, and Pierre Joubert. 1991a. *Évaluation des soins et services de périnatalité dans la région de la Baie d'Hudson, volet organisation*. Rapport final, tome 1. Québec: Département de Santé Communautaire du Centre Hospitalier de l'Université Laval.
–. 1991b. *Évaluation des soins et services de périnatalité dans la région de la Baie d'Hudson, volet organisation*. Annexes, tome 2. Québec: Département de Santé Communautaire du Centre Hospitalier de l'Université Laval.
–. 1991c. *Évaluation des soins et services de périnatalité dans la région de la Baie d'Hudson, volet organisation*. Appendice, tome 3. Québec: Département de Santé Communautaire du Centre Hospitalier de l'Université Laval.
Tremblay, Francine. 1979. *Travail de recherche et de réflexion sur les expériences d'intervention collective au Nouveau-Québec, région de l'Ungava, de 1971 à 1978*. École des Gradués, Université Laval, Québec. (Ms.)
Tremblay, Normand. 1978. "Rapport concernant mon stage en santé communautaire à Québec." Présenté au Département de Santé communautaire du Centre Hopitalier de l'Université Laval, Québec.
–. 1991. "Les Médecins vont être mis dans le coup," *L'Actualité Médicale*, 20 mars, 15.
Tulugak, Aani. N.d. *Inuit Aspirations*. Innuulisivik Health Centre, POV. (Ms.)
Weller, Geoffrey R. 1981. "The Delivery of Health Services in the Canadian North." *Journal of Canadian Studies* 16, 2: 69-80.
Weller, Geoffrey R., and Pranlal Pranga. 1987. "The Politics of Health in the Circumpolar North." *Arctic Medical Research* 46, 2: 52-63.

19
Country Space as a Healing Place: Community Healing at Sheshatshiu

Cathrine Degnen

Most of the research done on "healing" and "health" in Aboriginal communities focuses either on the poor health status of Aboriginal peoples, emphasizing the disproportionally high incidences of mortality, suicide, infant mortality, alcohol abuse, and substance abuse found in Aboriginal populations (see, for example, Bagley 1991; Jarvis and Boldt 1982; Trovato 1991; Young 1994), or on ethnomedicine, "traditional medicine," and "shamanism" (see, for example, Descent 1986; Hultkrantz 1985; Malloch 1989; Morse et al. 1991; Young et al. 1989). When I raised the subject of traditional medicine (my initial research interest) with members of the Sheshatshiu community and with several researchers working with Aborignal groups, conversation often turned instead to the concept of "community healing" or "healing"[1] – a salient issue today in many Aboriginal communities across Canada.[2] The works mentioned above share a common conceptual point of departure in that they understand healing to mean curative practices for physical ailments. In comparison, what is meant by "community healing" in many contemporary Aboriginal communities entails a much wider sense of the word "healing" – one that very little published scholarly work has yet considered.[3] This piqued my curiosity: volumes have been written about Aboriginal peoples in Canada, yet anthropologists have largely neglected this highly relevant and current topic of discussion in Aboriginal communities.

"Community Healing"

Community healing especially appealed to me as a topic of inquiry for two reasons. First, initial conversations I shared with members of the Sheshatshiu community showed this concept to be of growing local importance. Additionally, studying community healing offered a chance to highlight positive initiatives arising internally within an Aboriginal community rather than perpetuating the negative image of an Aboriginal community in decline and despair. I began this project by asking: What does it mean to heal a community? This question led to others and gradually expanded to include: How are people addressing such difficult social problems? Who is involved in this process? What are the differing discourses among community members in Sheshatshiu concerning community healing? How does community healing relate to larger root issues such as the continual renegotiation of cultural identity?

I was fortunate enough to spend three months during the spring and summer of 1995 in an Innu community in Sheshatshiu, Labrador, exploring these issues. A number of the residents there are searching for effective and appropriate ways to reorder lives, which have been profoundly disrupted by rapid cultural change compounded by both substance abuse and family violence. For many Innu with whom I spoke, healing has come to signify a move towards new social meaning and coherence as well as towards regaining control of their lives by addressing the acute social problems that face their community. Within this context, healing goes far deeper than mending and medicating physical hurts. It also speaks to the residue of colonialism and its terrible effects on morale and self-confidence. Community healing involves, in part, a network of social service programs geared towards helping community members mend lives and the family fabric damaged by abuse and violence. Community healing also involves a forum for talking about the history of colonialism and assimilation, and the profound pain stemming from it. It also allows the Innu to look towards a better future while enabling them to take pride in being a contemproary Aboriginal person. This is not to say that community members are moving as one on these issues, nor is it to say that each individual in the community is eager to "heal." Opinions in Sheshatshiu about community healing vary widely, and it is not my intention in this chapter to attempt a bounded definition of healing for the Innu; instead, I offer one perspective on community healing that has been deeply informed by both my research questions and by my impressions, associations, and experiences within the community. Another point of entry would no doubt have differently nuanced my understanding of community healing and its place in Sheshatshiu today, for, as writers such as Clifford (1988), Crapanzano (1992), and Marcus and Fischer (1986) have made clear, ethnography is not neutral.

Going in Country

The day after my arrival in Sheshatshiu, I was having a conversation with a middle-aged man in the community with whom I had spoken a few times before and who was familiar with my interest in community healing. We began to speak of healing and of my research. Two things he said during the course of this discussion lodged themselves in my memory: "People's way of thinking is different when out in the country ... people are healthier"; and "the healing for the Innu, I think, is in the country." Going "in country" (or *nutshimit* in Innu-aimun) means going to live on the land with one's family in hunting and fishing camps for a period of two or three months in the spring or autumn. This involves living in tents and away from the community. Recently, after a period when few families went in country, more and more are doing so. During the spring of 1995 almost half the community went in country. But this man also told me that it has been eight or nine years since he had spent time out in country and that he feels guilty about not having been out more recently. Even so, this yearning he expressed had not been forceful enough for him to leave the community with his family and go in country. In subsequent discussions with other community members, similar and related themes emerged: the importance of being in country as well as the difficulty of escaping the community; how different life is when away from the community; how people always have things to do when in country; how alcohol is no longer important to people when they go in country. Why were people talking to me about being in country when I had asked them about community healing?

Preliminary Landmarks

This then became another important element of my research. Even though Sheshatshiu is today a permanent community, many people's living space is not limited to it alone but, rather, extends to life in country in hunting camps. Both the atmosphere and lifestyle in these two settings – community[4] and country – are markedly different, and the people with whom I spoke were quite explicit about distinguishing between the two settings. It is within this context of contrast between community and country that I situate community healing because the contrast represents a number of issues critical to appreciating the importance of community healing in Sheshatshiu. First, Innu people have experienced dramatic cultural change over the past fifty years: living circumstances and priorities have shifted from self-sufficient mobile hunting linked with some activity in the fur trade (only two generations ago) to settlement and assimilation into a cash-based economy. This is due, in part, to the efforts of Roman Catholic missionaries and the provincial and federal governments to assimilate the Innu by suppressing Innu culture. This, of course, resulted in social upheaval. Without this colonial history, there would be no need for community healing.

Second, this colonial experience is not unique to the Innu but has been repeated innumerable times throughout Canada. Third, within the past twenty-five years there has been a powerful movement among Aboriginal groups in Canada towards self-determination and the assertion of Aboriginal rights. This arose in the 1970s in concurrence with the American Indian Movement in the United States and the National Indian Brotherhood in Canada, both of which triggered a surge of Aboriginal pride throughout North America. In Canada, this movement was particularly solidified by the Liberal government's 1969 White Paper – a piece of proposed legislation that helped to unify an Aboriginal response to a colonial-minded federal government and fostered a new activism among many Aboriginal peoples on both sides of the border (see also Crow Dog 1990; Levin 1993; Richardson 1989).

Aboriginal peoples of Canada have been engaged in taking a series of political and legal steps towards reclaiming control over their own communities, lands, resources, and ways of life. Community healing is a crucial element of this process for many Aboriginal groups, including the Innu. As Ovide Mercredi and Mary Ellen Turpell (1993, 245) write, self-government is "an end to the dominance of one group of people over another ... it is a beginning, not a solution." It is a beginning that equates self-government with self-respect, self-esteem, and "the future for our distinct cultures and identities" (245) and one that also emphasizes "the profoundly spiritual nature of the movement for the recognition of First Nations rights and the *healing* of First Nations peoples" (41, emphasis added). It is under these general conditions that discourse about community healing has begun to emerge in many Aboriginal communities in northern Canada, and I argue that it is within this general historical framework that this development must be situated in order to be understood. Healing is personal, it is communal, and it is political.

Furthermore, in the specific case of Sheshatshiu, the discourse surrounding community healing has become linked with going in country. This, in turn, is the epitome of Innu identity for many community members. Being in country emerged again and again in my discussions with people as a crucial element of Innu identity as well as a "place of healing." There, people could rise above the daily circumstances they encounter while in the community and, instead, be in country, on the land, where the pace of life and daily concerns are geared towards Innu knowledge and skills. Some people described to me how being in country was a way for them to live as their ancestors had "for thousands of years" before. Being in country was explained as a way of escaping the chronic boredom of the community and its underlying tensions. Being in country was to be in a place where every day brought something new and challenging and a sense of accomplishment. Being in country was a way of affirming pride in being Innu and being Aboriginal.

As much as being in country and issues of identity emerged in conversations about community healing, people also talked to me about healing specifically in terms of facing problems such as abuse and alcoholism. Within this context, emphasis was often placed on the community intervention programs and support systems that had been put in place to address these problems. At first I thought that people were talking about different things, but then I began to see that there was no simple dichotomy between discussing healing as being in country and discussing healing as intervention programs: it was as if the discourses were circling around and through one another, connecting at certain points and swinging away at others, only to be rejoined again. Other themes about community healing that emerged from these circlings included knowing one's history and roots as Innu, notions of healing as grieving, notions of healing as confrontation, and notions of healing through "talking." All of these orbiting discourses are integral parts of what community healing means and signifies to Innu people in Sheshatshiu today. I could never hope to encapsulate the notion of "healing" for the Innu because it is such a fluid and individualized concept; rather, I attempt to describe some of these orbits of discourse on healing and offer my reading of what is currently transpiring in Sheshatshiu as people live their lives and try to address some of these problems. Although the intervention programs deserve reflection, for the purposes of this chapter I focus my attention on the concept of country space.

My framework for approaching community healing centres on two main theoretical axes: (1) the social suffering of the community that has emerged within the past thirty years and that stems from its colonial history and (2) the assertion of Innu cultural identity and a remobilization of pride in being Innu. This second axis is itself situated both within the wider context of Aboriginal self-determination in Canada and within the recent political activism in Sheshatshiu. Ultimately, it is at the point of intersection between suffering and identity that the strength and vital importance of community healing truly emerge.

Social Suffering

Community healing is a multifaceted response to some extremely painful and serious issues that touch Sheshatshiu community members on many levels. In a recent collection of essays on social suffering and structural violence, Kleinman, Das, and Lock (1996, xii) call for an approach to such topics that understands how "forms of human suffering can be at the same time collective and individual ... [and that describes] what is at stake in human experiences of political catastrophe and social structural violence." These authors, and others writing on different aspects of social suffering in the same volume, do not directly consider the contemporary living conditions of Aboriginal groups, yet their work parallels my own as it covers many of the same conditions inherent in communities experiencing social trauma and severe social conditions[5] (such as abuse, alcoholism, and addictions). My original research objective was to focus on positive community-based programs aimed at resolving local problems. I soon found that simply describing the standard socio-economic factors that motivated the move towards community healing was insufficient. In order to show the significance of community healing, it was absolutely essential to go beyond statistics and history and to reach instead towards describing "what was at stake in [the] human experience." One principle that guided me through so much of the research involved asking what these events *mean* for people's lives. How are the experiences that are being recounted to me distributed among the different layers that make up this community? In other words, in both my research and my writing I have attempted always to remain attentive to what Kleinman et al. refer to as the way in which "suffering ... is experienced within nested contexts of embodiment: collective, intersubjective, individual" (xvii). My ultimate objective is to give an account of the deeply significant meaning of community healing in Sheshatshiu.

In the same collection of essays, Paul Farmer (1996, 261-2) asks the question: "by what mechanisms do social forces ranging from poverty to racism become embodied as individual experience?" The issues facing Sheshatshiu are also of this nature and must be contextualized as such in order to be fully appreciated. Social suffering permeates a multitude of layers that together constitute a community's fabric and affect it on all levels of social interaction: individual, interpersonal, and collective. Farmer goes further to suggest that recounting life stories and experiences is an effective way of portraying "the sharp, hard surfaces of individual suffering" (263). However, he goes on to say that, in order "to explain suffering, one must embed individual biography in the larger matrix of culture, history, and political economy" (272). I concur with Farmer that recounting life stories is a vivid way of communicating the experience of social violence on the phenomenological, lived level and that, at the same time, the individual must also be situated historically and politically. In my own work I am not attempting to *explain* the suffering in Sheshatshiu as much as I am attempting to make its poignancy felt, to situate it within a historical context, and then to look at what is being said and done on the community level in order to address it.

Reappropriation of Identity

> Some people now, they are on their way to healing – it took a lot of courage to walk on the runway – you feel proud, that there's something you can do

> and feel proud of being a Native person ... Once you know you have strength, you can go kill caribou in *Kanimesh* when you aren't supposed to and [you can] go walk on the runway.
>
> – Grace, a middle-aged woman working as a family counsellor in Sheshatshiu

Running alongside the axis of social pain that community healing is attempting to redress is the axis of Innu identity. The emergence of community healing as an active discourse in Sheshatshiu occurred in conjunction with a dramatic change in community politics. According to Adrian Tanner (1993, 77), for many years the community "seemed to have been overwhelmed by the impact of development, and unable to put up any effective resistance to this process." However, throughout the late 1970s and into the 1980s, the Innu leadership in Sheshatshiu became increasingly politicized. Tanner traces the growth of this development and examines it in light of the increase in Innu social isolation and marginalization from the surrounding non-Innu society. He identifies this marginalization as a central contributing factor in the development of the "relatively extreme form of ethnic nationalism" (94) that informs the political activity of the Innu Nation in comparison with other Aboriginal political groups in Canada. Although Innu ethnonationalism and what Tanner refers to as Innu "self-conscious identity" began to emerge over a number of years and through different political leaders, it was the well documented Innu resistance to NATO low-level military training flights originating from the Goose Bay airbase that signalled the deep politicization of Sheshatshiu community members. Unlike the majority of Aboriginal groups in Canada, the Innu of Labrador do not have registered federal or provincial Indian status, and they have never signed treaties with either government. As such, their homeland has never been ceded and they do not recognize "the authority that provincial and federal laws and courts assert over them and their lands" (76). However, NATO[6] began training flights in 1980 (as well as constructing bombing ranges) over the Quebec-Labrador peninsula and Innu hunting territories without consulting the Innu Nation or conducting any environmental impact studies. As the flights take place at extraordinarily low altitudes (sometimes as low as thirty metres) and produce intensely loud noise without any warning (Armitage and Kennedy 1989), their intrusion over Innu hunting camps has been extremely controversial and has provided the impetus for an Innu civil disobedience campaign consisting of protests and demonstrations. This is, in part, what Grace refers to above: over a period of months, beginning in 1988, many Innu were "walking on the runway" at the Goose Bay NATO airfield in large groups, thus preventing NATO bombers from taking off and conducting training drills.

Each time the protesters went out on the runway they were arrested, and a number of them have had to pay fines or serve time in jail for their participation[7] in the demonstrations.[8]

The other incident Grace refers to, "you can go kill caribou in *Kanimesh* when you aren't supposed to," is another element in the recent upsurge of Innu politizication. By the 1950s, governmental game laws began to restrict hunting and fishing rights in Labrador. By the 1970s, both Aboriginal and non-Aboriginal people were required by law to have hunting licences, which were available only by lottery (Tanner 1993, 83-4). This did not stop the Innu from pursuing their traditional hunting, but it did mean that increasing numbers of them were arrested for hunting violations in country (84). A growing resentment towards these game laws erupted in the spring of 1987 when the government announced that the Mealy Mountains[9] caribou herd, off-limits for a number of years, would be subjected to a limited hunt. Innu leaders and families decided to hunt and camp without the licences and before the season opened as a way of demonstrating their sovereignty over unceded land. The Mealy Mountains are the traditional hunting and fishing grounds of a number of Sheshatshiu families, and many Innu of all ages became involved in the "illegal" hunt even in the face of RCMP raids on both hunting camps and houses in Sheshatshiu (Tanner 1993, 83-5; Wadden 1991, 93-5). A wide variety of sources, both internal and external, identify these two protest actions as defining episodes in the life of Sheshatshiu. The community found issues it could rally around and concerns that unified it, and for many people this was an extremely empowering experience.

Nagel (1994, 166) has written about how political protest and mobilization reaffirm ethnic identity and pride as well as about the effectiveness of relying on highly charged cultural symbols in order to highlight protesters' demands. Both the NATO protests and the Mealy Mountains civil disobedience campaigns centred around the Innu right to maintain traditional ways of life, particularly the right to hunt caribou, a potent Innu cultural signifier. By protesting and protecting their ability to continue such activities – activities that are integral elements of their identity – the Innu were also reaffirming their right to self-determination. The politicization of Sheshatshiu around low-level flying and game laws emerged from a deep frustration with the surrounding Euro-Canadian population, which would not listen to Innu concerns and opinions. These civil disobedience campaigns were, essentially, an Innu attempt to reclaim and control Innu destiny. However, the implications of these protests reach beyond the political level. The protests also became a way to protect and assert Innu identity, which is interwoven with the land that was being overflown. Country space in community discourse is a "place of healing," a space with an extraordinary capacity to reanchor people and to make them strong again. Within the community discourse, by defending the land, people were also defending their right to maintain this refuge and haven, this space that is at the core of Innu identity.

"Ripples in a Pond"

Before becoming a permanent settlement in the early 1960s, the area surrounding Sheshatshiu[10] was, for many generations, a place where Innu families met up with each other for a few months in the summer to visit and fish.[11] As the season wore on, smaller family groupings would leave and return to their hunting camps in *nutshimit*, or "in country." This cyclical pattern of nomadic caribou hunting during the majority of the year, with summer visits to Sheshatshiu, has only come to a halt[12] within the past thirty-five years, but hunting and fishing remain extremely important to many families in Sheshatshiu. Almost half the community enjoys seasonal trips out in country in both the fall and spring for two to three months at a time[13] to harvest migrating caribou herds; but virtually no one lives entirely off the land any more, and every family has well established homes in the community.

Sheshatshiu is home now to about 1,000 people. Families live there; kids play there; people laugh, cry, grow, and love in Sheshatshiu like they do anywhere else. However, Sheshatshiu is also a place experiencing great turmoil on both community and individual levels, as people expressed quite clearly to me:

> There is not one family here that has not been touched by abuse, violence, fear. (Caroline, a mother working as a counsellor for the Innu Nation Healing Services)

> The community has evil in it ... drugs, alcohol, and something is wrong here. (Agnes, a middle-aged woman working as a counsellor for the Innu Nation Healing Services)

> There *is* no community here ... there are no shared goals, no shared worths, no common values. This is not a community ... it's a village. (Rita, a young mother working as a counsellor for the Innu Nation Healing Services)

> This community is like a casket. A casket that was buried and is now rising up again as people go through the healing process and all sorts of stuff starts coming out. (Alex, a young man and father)

These tensions are further exacerbated by the size and composition of Sheshatshiu, which is a small and intricately connected living space. Family networks are extensive, and blood, marriage, or adoption connects each individual person to a large number of relatives within the community.[14] Given the small size and relative isolation of the community, even people not directly related to one another are familiar with each other as they have spent their entire lives together. Consequently, as several people pointed out to me, the events, both positive and negative, experienced by one person or family are not limited to the individuals directly involved:

> Violence affects the community as a whole; people used to think that family violence [and] abuse was an individual problem, but then we started realizing that Innu in the past have tried to deal with problems as a collective and that family violence is not isolated to two individuals ... it's a community, not [an] individual, problem. (William, a middle-aged man and member of Innu Nation Staff)

> Whatever happens here affects me personally; everyone knows everyone here; it's like one big family. (Joe, in his mid-thirties and working for the Innu Nation)

"Everyone knows everyone": generally, this means that everyone also knows what everyone else is doing. There is no anonymity in Sheshatshiu. Many people in Sheshatshiu do *not* drink alcohol, and a significant percentage of the community has "gone dry" during the past ten years. Nonetheless, the drinking that does occur (and the actions that stem from it) affects everyone because it affects the community atmosphere in very real ways.

In Sheshatshiu, people are generally reserved with one another unless they are family members or close friends; confrontation is not the preferred tactic for conflict resolution. But when on a drinking binge, all sorts of underlying feelings and emotions that are normally hidden deep inside burst forth. This being the case, drinking becomes a highly charged event in Sheshatshiu, especially as so much *is* going on underneath the surface: family violence, childhood abuse, high levels of unemployment, and so on. Furthermore, Sheshatshiu is small: "everyone knows everyone." The person stumbling across the gravel in the dark as you are trying to get into the house, or the person pacing outside your home and rapping on the walls, is not "just some weirdo," as might be the case in a larger urban area. This person is someone you know, someone you might have grown up with or lived next door to your entire life. Or it might be a relative: your brother, your cousin, or your aunt. Thus a certain amount of tension and anticipation flows through the community, and this is due not only to the drinking, but also to the actions that result from drinking – fights, violence, abuse, suicides, and suicide attempts. As William and Joe said, these are not individual problems, they are problems that affect the entire community.

Country Living

When talking about life in country, people would often compare it with life in the community in order to explain how it was different:[15]

> In country I see a lot of personal respect for one another, which you don't see in the community as much. (Caroline)

> When in country, you're there with your extended family, and you see each other every day, you talk to each other every day, all day. It's not like here in the community where you see each other much less frequently and where everyone is more or less isolated. (Rita)

Life in country is described as communal and connecting, unlike life in the community, which is seen by some as "isolating." This seems, in part, to be a consequence of the living arrangements as well as a change in atmosphere. For example, people move from living in houses in the community to living in tents in country. Both offer shelter and warmth but entail distinctly unique living patterns. In Sheshatshiu, most of the houses are built high up off the ground, with a steep set of stairs leading to the front door. The sloping hill upon which the community is built increases this effect as the houses are set back from the road and rise above it due to the angle of the hill. Furthermore, the houses are generally spread out and not immediately adjacent to one another. The overall effect of this is that the houses are spread far across the length of the community so that it might be a twenty- or thirty-minute walk to a relative's home. A fair number of people own vehicles of some sort, and this minimizes this particular problem, but many others do not have access to vehicles and are not always inclined to venture out for a walk and a visit. Tents, on the other hand, are pitched close together and low to the ground. This permits a great deal of regular contact between family members, especially given that much work and activity takes place directly outside the living area (and, indeed, is part of it). There are no locks on tent openings. Tents are made of canvas and are much more permeable to sound and movement than are houses. Jokes and news travel quickly and easily between the thin canvas tent walls, and many of the tasks needed to keep the camp going are shared and public rather than individual and private. Given this, people interact differently, depending on whether they are in the community or in country. In the community, visiting is more difficult and entails an effort. Tasks like cooking are not often shared between households, and wage labour is of an independent nature. People will often go days without seeing each other, perhaps only talking on the phone in the interim. In country, visiting and working towards common goals are inherent aspects of being there; they are a part of the daily rhythm of life. People share fire-places and hearths, food, and the work involved in preparing and cleaning up after a meal. Chatting, visiting, and communicating flow in a way that is not possible in the community. This is evidenced both in community discourse about what it feels like to be in country and in lived practice.

Other differences between being in the community and being in country were not always easy for people to articulate, but their comments often centred around the distinctions in atmosphere and level of activity:

> Being there [in country] feels good ... it's hard to explain ... there are no worries in country. (Joe)

> I'm more busy being in camp and away from the community; there are more things to keep us busy and we are always doing things for ourselves – there's stuff to do all day long for both me and my husband ... I'm really happy away from the community and at peace with myself living away ... I don't see any drunks there like in the community. (Katnin, an elder woman and grandmother)

People described themselves as feeling relaxed and peaceful in country, and the atmosphere of country life reflected these sentiments. The tension and nervous anticipation of community life vanished; isolation was the exception rather than the rule.

"Concrete Shoes"

However, going in country is not as straightforward as it might seem. Not everyone goes in country, and not everyone thinks that spending time there is the answer to community issues:

> People say that going in country is going to help you, but I watch people using country as a way to run away from their problems – and that's not the answer either. You'll be in [the] same situation when you come back if you don't deal with it [here first]. (Grace)

Going in country means going far away, and this is less tempting when people who are important in the family cannot come along. People who work cannot always go in country and are faced with choosing between spending time in country and earning money. In addition, although the school now recognizes going in country as constituting a valid absence, parents still have to choose between being in country with their children and sending them to school. Conditions like this led one young mother to tell me that "there are concrete shoes here in the community ... it's not just easy to go."

Clearly, what going in country means and how life there can be lived is a source of debate in Sheshatshiu today. Yet, for many people, knowing how to live in country and spending time there remains an integral part of being Innu and maintaining cultural knowledge. Being in country also provides refuge from the tensions and problems in the community.

Ties That Bind and Nourish

Another essential element of country living, and another reason people anticipate going in country, is country food.[16] Country food is hunted food – such as caribou, partridge, trout, salmon, and beaver – prepared in the traditional way and eaten with *innu-pakueshikan* (bannock). When available, this food is also consumed in the community setting. For the family I stayed with, as well as many others, eating country food is still extremely important, and it composed a significant percentage of the weekly diet both in country and in the community. Lacasse (1982, 27) documents the same phenomenon in Moisie: "Même si les [Innu] ne sont plus à présent des chasseurs de profession, il y a chez eux un attachement extraordinaire à la viande de gibier comme source d'alimentation et une valorisation très grande de la cuisine traditionnelle (even if the [Innu] are no longer hunters by profession, there is still an extraordinary attachment to game meat as a source of food and a great appreciation of traditional cooking)."

Writing in a very different era, Speck (1935, 78) also mentions Innu food preferences, recounting that, at that time, Innu avoided eating domesticated animals such as lamb, chicken, beef, and pork whenever possible because "they realize ... the impurity of these viands, and attribute their bodily ills, even the decline of their race, to the eating of domestic animals. The use of salt is also avoided in preparing pure wild meat."[17]

Country food is spoken of as being stronger and healthier than other food:[18]

> In a country setting ... the trust and the food is there, *healthy* food in *nutshimit.* (Agnes)

> We pay less for our food in *nutshimit*, and many of us say that country food is stronger. If you have enough wild game, you are not hungry, but if you buy food at the stores, you are always hungry and you always want to eat as well. (Innu Nation 1993, 66)

> [Les vieux] considèrent que la nourriture indienne[19] maintenait les Indiens en santé et en forme (in the understanding of elders, Indian food keeps Indians healthy and fit). (Lacasse 1982, 27)

Although people in Sheshatshiu eat store foods and bring some supplies with them in country, "la nourriture indienne" is still significant, especially for older people. In fact, at least one elder in my host family not only preferred country food, but he would only drink spring water as tap water bothered him. The family would take trips out to a spring about ten miles from Sheshatshiu to collect large buckets of this water for him. No one questioned the necessity of this; rather, they understood that this was what was best for him and accepted that, as an older person who had lived many, many years in country, he needed to drink country water.

Sharing country food is also a way of reaffirming ties within the family.[20] People who have gone out in country will send caribou, fish, partridge, and beaver back to family members that have not been able to accompany them, and this is highly valued and appreciated by those left behind. This sharing becomes a way of connecting country space with community space.

Time and Space

> The medicine and food we need, trees, water, plants, are all in the country and all that we need to heal.
>
> – Agnes

Nostalgia for the past is a potent indicator of conditions in the present. How the past is remembered can dramatically affect how the present is perceived. The country setting itself is spoken of in terms of health. Country space takes on powerful qualities in terms of its capacity to heal on the personal and community levels, and this is spoken about in explicit terms by a wide range of community members. For example: "I see a lot of personal respect for one another which you don't see in the community as much"; "you see each other every day, you talk with each other every day, all day"; "It's different in country"; "being there feels good ... it's hard to explain"; "people's way of thinking is different when out in the country ... people are healthier ... the healing for the Innu, I think, is in the country." This association of country with health is particularly evident in the community discourse when people talk about the past. People would talk about how Innu who lived in country in the past used to be extremely strong and did not get sick, did not get cold easily, and could walk for long periods of time without becoming tired. Some people in the community described their ancestors who lived in "the old days" as having supernatural powers and skills to which people these days no longer have access because they do not have the requisite knowledge or spiritual strength. In general, the community discourse describes country as a space where people in the old days were healthier and happier:

> But it didn't matter what would happen in country – babies, people born in country, and we didn't need doctors – in the past people were able to take care of each other, to help and support each other. (Katnin)

> People were hardly ever sick in the old days because we ate good food. Another reason that we were not sick is because there was never drinking going on in those days like there is today. As well, all our families used to be in the country all the time; we were very strong in *nutshimit* because we were physically active. We used to travel always on foot, with the canoe or toboggan. We did a lot of hard work. (Innu Nation 1993, 14)

The past is often idealized in community discourse, and, as country life was an integral element of the past, it too has become idealized.[21] However, as the quotes above indicate, this association of "health" with "country living" is not limited to recollections about the past, but also extends to a present-day vision of the country as a healing, or healthy, place in opposition to the community, which is generally characterized as unhealthy and stagnant. In today's Sheshatshiu, people talk not only about how they interact differently within the two settings, but also about how the pace of life changes depending upon where one finds oneself. In community discourse there is an acute consciousness of these differences between the two spaces, and some people speak of feeling transformed while being in the country space. Thus people are building on an idealized vision of the past. This amounts to reanchoring the self and community by calling on the past to find new strength for the present.

Strathern's (1995) work on nostalgia helps us to critically assess these sentiments about country space. Strathern, basing her thoughts on concepts borrowed from Battaglia (1995), describes substantive nostalgia as a force that "evoke[s] the past" in such a way as to "recal[l] relationships already in place" (Strathern 1995, 111). As such, substantive nostalgia is more than a romanticization of what one "was" or what one had: it is a reconstruction of the past that is brought about by bringing it into the present – it is "an attachment that is and can only be realized in the present." The feelings that many Innu expressed to me about being in country are not limited to memories of the past but, instead, speak to how the past informs the present.

There is nothing traditional about going in country for the purposes of healing the wounds of social suffering, although today's trips in country echo the "old days" in form if not wholly in substance (formerly, families' subsistence depended entirely on the land and on country skills). Yet within the contemporary discourse that links country with healing, there is an explicit reference to the past and to tradition as a source of strength. The nostalgia for country and the past that can be found within the community discourse has been reshaped in conjunction with present-day problems (i.e., severe social conditions) and within a present-day context (i.e., seasonal trips in country) to offer something currently relevant (i.e., healing) while at the same time strengthening ties to the past.

Battaglia (1995) also discusses the notion of nostalgia and elaborates upon its potential for the future rather than its implications for conceptions of past or present. As she writes, "it is important ... to detach the notion of nostalgia from the merely sentimental attitude with which we may too easily associate it" (77). She insists that, instead, we should consider how "nostalgia may in fact be a vehicle of knowledge, rather than only a yearning for something lost" (77). For Battaglia, nostalgia is strength, and a

> nostalgia for a sense of future – for an experience, however imaginary, of possessing the means of controlling the future – may function as a powerful force for *social reconnection.* In permitting creative lapses from dominant realities, it is such a nostalgia that enables or recalls to practice more meaningful patterns of relationship and self-action. (78, emphasis added)

This insight is highly relevant to the nostalgia involved in the discourse about country space. Not only has the meaning of country living been reshaped and mobilized to address contemporary community concerns, but it is also most emphatically a movement for and towards the future. And it is a way of creating a space within which to escape from destructive patterns and to rebuild individual and interpersonal strength and reinforce social connections by referring to the past.

The notion of "space" itself is an enigmatic one, but it is clearly central to this discussion. Until a short while ago, limited anthropological attention had been paid to using space as an element of inquiry; however, two salient articles (Rodman 1992; Gupta and Ferguson 1992) introduce place and space as problematized concepts. Margaret Rodman (1992, 640) "explores ways in which place, like voice and time, is a politicized social and cultural construct." She emphasizes that

> places are not inert containers. They are politicized, culturally relative, historically specific, local and multiple constructions ... Places have multiple meanings that are constructed spatially. The physical, emotional, and experiential realities places hold for their inhabitants at particular times need to be understood apart from their creation as the locales of ethnography. (641)

In community discourse, country and settlement contexts are experientially and emotionally distinct spaces where the same social actors interact in vastly different ways. Rodman (652) asks us to "look 'through' these places, explore their links with others, consider why they are constructed as they are, see how places represent people, and begin to understand how people embody places." I would add that we must also look to how places embody and affect social relations because they are not "inert containers" but, indeed, can hold richly nuanced significance, as does country space for many Innu (i.e., as a sanctuary and a place of wellness).

Akhil Gupta and James Ferguson (1992, 7) are concerned with the various problems that arise from the "assumed isomorphism of space, place, and culture," and they posit that culture can no longer be conceptualized as though mapped onto physical spaces; rather, it demands a more flexible approach that includes "exploring the processes of production of difference in a world of culturally, socially, and economically interconnected and interdependent spaces" (14). They also begin to explore the power of space and place:

> Remembered places have often served as symbolic anchors of community for dispersed people ... "homeland" in this way remains one of the most powerful unifying symbols for mobile and displaced peoples ... we need to give up naive ideas of communities as literal entities ... but remain sensitive to the profound "bifocality" that characterizes locally lived lives in a globally interconnected world, and the powerful role of place in the "near view" of lived experience. (11)

Most Innu are neither transnationals nor "mobile and displaced peoples" in exactly the sense to which Gupta and Ferguson allude. However, they have in many ways been *dispossessed* of control over their own destiny and disenfranchised within the Euro-Canadian society that grew up around them and then, subsequently, marginalized them. In response, country *space*, a concrete but also symbolic place, is being mobilized in community discourse as an anchor capable of recentring and refocusing community strength. Community life and country life are not polar opposites but, rather, compose complementary parts of contemporary life in Sheshatshiu. People live in both settings and move between them, but when they talk about being in country, they speak of a wholly distinct time and space from that of the community. Communal, family, and individual lives are now subject to vastly different pressures than they were when living on the land was a necessity; however, because of the new ways in which it is being mobilized, country space is a deeply emotionally significant space in the life of many community members.

Within community discourse, country space takes on an extraordinary capacity to heal on both the personal and community levels, and it also offers a safe space within which to disentangle deeply painful issues. Through a nostalgia for the past, the Innu are rediscovering new strength for the present. They are doing this by evoking the perceived strength of country space in order to enable the rebuilding of individual and interpersonal relations and the reinforcement of social connections.

Much has been made of the "invention of tradition" (Hobsbawm and Ranger 1983) and "genuine" and "invented" traditions (Hobsbawm 1983). Others have challenged these static concepts and have described tradition as more fluid, as an "on-going interpretation of the past" (Handler and Linnekin 1984, 287). My discussion takes both identity and tradition to be fluid and ever-changing, but it also avoids trying to qualify "traditions" and "Innu traditions"; instead, I have chosen to describe country space and Innu identity in terms of a substantive nostalgia (Strathern 1995). "Nostalgia" should not be taken to mean something condescending or "invented" but, rather, as Battaglia (1995, 77-8) emphasizes, "a vehicle of knowledge, rather than only a yearning for something lost ... nostalgia for a sense of future." Indeed, the reshaping and remobilizing of country space within the context of community healing is part of a strongly positive and forward-looking movement – one that is reaching towards creating a better future for people living in Sheshatshiu.

In Sheshatshiu, political activity, identity, and community healing have all developed within a context of intercultural knowledge and influence. The key to their significance is that they offer a source of strength, a reservoir of sorts, that enables Innu to strategically recreate and redefine "Innuness" while addressing troubling community problems. However, alongside this socio-political dimension of identity linked with self-determination and community empowerment there is, equally, a vindication of identity on the individual level. Social suffering is a form of violence that attacks individuals at the core of their being, destabilizing their entire social world. Within such a context, the personal empowerment associated in community discourse with healing offers another form of identity renewal. However, in this case, it is on the level of the individual who is seeking to regain control over the conditions of her or his own life.

Acknowledgments

This chapter is based on my master's thesis. As ever, it is the people of Sheshatshiu who made my project possible: thank you for your interest and patience. Over the years my thinking and analysis have also benefited from invaluable feedback from the Aboriginal Government, Resources, Economy and Environment (AGREE) research team participants, and I would particularly like to thank Colin Scott, Elizabeth Fajber, Naomi Adelson, Audra Simpson, Robert Paine, and Adrian Tanner. It has also been my privilege to work with Ellen Corin, my thesis supervisor, and I thank her for her superb insight and support.

I received funding for this research from McGill University through two Max Bell Fellowships in Canadian and Northern Studies and a Faculty of Graduate Studies and Research Social Sciences Sub-Committee research grant. AGREE generously provided additional funding.

Notes

1 Initially, I distinguished between these two terms. Upon reflection, I believe that they are used in relatively synonymous ways in Sheshatshiu, with the distinction that "healing" is used more often to refer to an individual's health (both physical and emotional) and that "community healing" is used more often to talk more about the communal path towards health as a social body. I use both these terms through the course of this chapter but try to respect their nuanced differences.

2 Important exceptions to the general lack of resources available on community healing are the recent Royal Commission on Aboriginal Peoples (RCAP) publications, particularly the final report (1996) (see Volume 3, Chapter 3; and Volume 5, Chapter 1, Section 4.2), an RCAP-sponsored National Round Table on Aboriginal Health and Social Issues, published as *The Path to Healing* (Royal Commission on Aboriginal Peoples 1993b), and also the published public hearings of the royal commission (Royal Commission on Aboriginal Peoples 1993a). These documents clearly identify "personal and collective healing for Aboriginal peoples and communities" (Royal Commission on Aboriginal Peoples 1993a, 3) as one of four central themes emerging throughout the public hearings. The thoughts expressed at these meetings by a wide range of both Aboriginal and non-Aboriginal people involved in health development and delivery in Aboriginal communities across Canada confirm the extreme relevance and importance of community healing today as well as the wide range of local approaches to it. Given the general lack of resources available on the topic of community healing, these publications (and others written by various community organizations) are illuminating. However, terms such as "community healing," "community well-being," and "a healing perspective" remain unproblematized in these documents.

3 One exception to this trend is Adelson (1992), who first explored the concept of health as a holistic and collective "wellness" in Whapmagoostui, Quebec (a Cree community), rather than as the inverse of "disease." Fajber (1996), working in a Dene community (Fort Good Hope, NWT), is another exception.

4 Social scientists conventionally use the term "settlement" to refer to a geographically bounded locale, and the term "community" to indicate social relations that transcend the physical confines of a settlement (indeed, there are settlements that do not operate as communities). However, I do not distinguish between the Sheshatshiu settlement and the Sheshatshiu community. This is because people in Sheshatshiu use the term "community" to indicate both the geographical location of the town and to talk about the social relations of that place. I have chosen to maintain local usage.

5 See An Antane Kapesh (1976) for a powerful account of the social suffering of Innu in Schefferville, told from the perspective of a woman living there.

6 The NATO nations who have, at various times, sponsored training at the airbase in Goose Bay, Labrador, include Germany, Holland, England, Italy, the United States, and France.

7 Although the majority of these runway occupations and protests took place between 1988 and 1993, the ramifications are still being felt in Sheshatshiu. As recently as 15 July 1996 one of the political leaders of Sheshatshiu was imprisoned for ten days after refusing to pay a $250 fine that was assessed him by the Newfoundland-Labrador courts after he was convicted on charges stemming from the occupation of Dutch F-16's during a runway protest on 8 September 1993.

8 See Wadden (1991) for an excellent and highly detailed account of Innu protest actions against low-level flying.

9 The Mealy Mountains are located on the south shore of Lake Melville not far from Sheshatshiu.

10 This Innu word translates into English as "large mouth of the river," or (more elegantly) into French as "la Grande Embouchure" (Mailhot 1993, 19).

11 And, in more recent times, to stock up on supplies from the Hudson's Bay Company store in North West River.

12 See Henriksen (1973) for a similar account of social change concerning the Innu in Utshimassit (Davis Inlet).

13 Five years ago the Roman Catholic school board commenced a policy referring to absences from school during these periods as cultural or traditional leave for children, and they now no longer penalize or keep a child back for a year if her/his family goes in country. Indeed, when I visited the school in Sheshatshiu in early June 1995, some of the teachers remarked that there were not many students in school at that time because so many had gone in country. For instance, the kindergarten class had eighteen children on the class list, but only six were still attending class. The others were with their families in hunting camps.

14 And, as Mailhot (1993) documents, to a large network of relatives throughout the other Innu communities in Quebec and Labrador.

15 Tanner's (1979) work with the Mistissini Cree (another Algonquian group closely related to the Sheshatshiu Innu) also delves into this dichotomy of community and country settings and, indeed, discusses it as a structural opposition.

16 Compare Rushforth (1977).

17 Disdain for using salt with country meats has faded, and today it is an important seasoning in the preparation of most foods, both from the store and from the country. This dietary change, as well as a marked increase in the use of sugar, has led to such significant health problems as hypertension and diabetes (Lacasse 1982; Neuwelt et al. 1992).

18 See also Borré (1991) for a discussion of the importance of seal meat and blood in Inuit discourse regarding health maintenance. And see Adelson (1992) for examples of how the Whapmagoostui Cree conceptualize bush foods as "strong" foods.

19 Lacasse's (1982, 27) explanation of this term is: "[les animaux] qui se nourrissent dans la forêt sont appelés innu-ueshish, c'est-à-dire 'animaux indiens,' et les animaux domestiques sont appelés kakusseshiu-ueshish, ce qui veut dire 'animaux blancs' (animals that find sustenance in the forest are called innu-ueshish, or 'Indian animals,' and domestic animals are called kakusseshiu-ueshish, or 'Whiteman's animals')."

20 The deep social significance of food, sharing food, and identity is certainly not limited to Innu. Flinn's (1990, 123) account concerning Pulap identity demonstrates how "the production and exchange of local foods" (ibid., 123) is an essential element in the assertion of contemporary Pulapese identity. She shows that "sharing food both demonstrates kinship and symbolizes the sharing of land. In this way Pulapese are typical of Pacific Islanders, for whom kin relations and land are fundamental to identity."

21 Although country space is most often spoken of in highly positive terms, as are the excellent health and strength of ancestors who lived in country year round, the difficulties and dangers of life in country have not been forgotten. Stories of famine in "the old days" are still strongly present.

References

Adelson, Naomi. 1992. "Being Alive Well: Indigenous Belief as Opposition." PhD diss., Department of Anthropology, McGill University.

Armitage, Peter, and John C. Kennedy. 1989. "Redbaiting and Racism on Our Frontier: Military Expansion in Labrador and Quebec." *Canadian Review of Sociology and Anthropology* 26, 5: 798-817.

Bagley, C. 1991. "Poverty and Suicide among Native Canadians: A Replication." *Psychological Reports* 69: 149-50.

Battaglia, Debbora. 1995. "On Practical Nostalgia: Self-Prospecting among Urban Trobrianders." In *Rhetorics of Self-Making*, ed. Debbora Battaglia, 77-96. Berkeley: University of California Press.

Borré, Kristin. 1991. "Seal Blood, Inuit Blood, and Diet: A Biocultural Model of Physiology and Identity." *Medical Anthropological Quarterly* 5, 1: 48-62.

Clifford, James. 1988. *The Predicament of Culture: Twentieth-Century Ethnography, Literature, and Arts*. Cambridge, MA: Harvard University Press.

Crapanzano, Vincent. 1992. *Hermes' Dilemma and Hamlet's Desire: On the Epistemology of Interpretation*. Cambridge, MA: Harvard University Press.

Crow Dog, Mary, with Richard Erdoes. 1990. *Lakota Woman*. New York: Harper Perennial Press.

Descent, Micheline. 1986. "Traditional Approaches to Health in Nouveau-Québec." *Northern Issues* 1, 1: 23-6.

Fajber, Elizabeth. 1996. "The Power of Medicine: 'Healing' and 'Tradition' among Dene Women in Fort Good Hope, Northwest Territories." MA thesis, Social Studies of Medicine/Department of Anthropology, McGill University.

Farmer, Paul. 1996. "On Suffering and Structural Violence." *Daedalus* 125, 1: 261-83.

Flinn, Juliana. 1990. "We Still Have Our Customs: Being Pulapese in Truk." In *Cultural Identity and Ethnicity in the Pacific*, ed. Jocelyn Linnekin and Lin Poyer, 103-26. Honolulu: University of Hawaii Press.

Gupta, Akhil and James Ferguson. 1992. "Beyond 'Culture': Space, Identity, and the Politics of Difference." *Cultural Anthropology* 7, 1: 6-23.

Handler, Richard, and Jocelyn Linnekin. 1984. "Tradition, Genuine or Spurious." *Journal of American Folklore* 97, 385: 273-90.

Henriksen, Georg. 1973. *Hunters in the Barrens: The Naskapi on the Edge of the White Man's World.* St. John's: Institute for Social and Economic Research, Memorial University of Newfoundland.

Hobsbawm, Eric. 1983. "Introduction: Inventing Traditions." In *The Invention of Tradition,* ed. E. Hobsbawm and T. Ranger, 1-14. Cambridge: Cambridge University Press.

Hobsbawm, Eric, and Terence Ranger, eds. 1983. *The Invention of Tradition.* Cambridge: Cambridge University Press.

Hultkrantz, Ake. 1985. "The Shaman and the Medicine-man." *Social Science and Medicine* 20, 5: 511-15.

Innu Nation. 1993. *Kamamuetimak: Tshentusentimak Nte Steniunu Utat, Nitshish, Kie Nte Nikan/Gathering Voices: Discovering Our Past, Present and Future.* Innu Nation Community Research Project, funded by the Royal Commission on Aboriginal Peoples.

Jarvis, George K., and Menno Boldt. 1982. "Death Styles among Canada's Indians." *Social Science and Medicine* 16: 1345-52.

Kapesh, An Antane. 1976. *Eukuan Nin Matshimanitu Innu-iskueu (Je suis une maudite sauvagesse).* Ottawa: Éditions Leméac.

Kleinman, Arthur, Veena Das, and Margaret Lock. 1996. "Introduction." *Daedalus* 125, 1: xi-xx.

Lacasse, Fernande. 1982. "La conception de la santé chez les Indiens Montagnais." *Recherches amérindiennes au Québec* 7, 1: 25-8.

Levin, Michael D., ed. 1993. *Ethnicity and Aboriginality: Case Studies in Ethnonationalism.* Toronto: University of Toronto.

Mailhot, José. 1993. *Au Pays des Innus: les gens de Sheshatshit.* Montréal: Recherches amérindiennes au Québec.

Malloch, Lesley. 1989. "Indian Medicine, Indian Health: Study between Red and White Medicine." *Canadian Woman Studies* 10, 2-3: 105-12.

Marcus, George, and Michael Fischer, eds. 1986. *Anthropology as Cultural Critique: An Experimental Moment in the Human Sciences.* Chicago: University of Chicago Press.

Mercredi, Ovide, and Mary Ellen Turpel. 1993. *In the Rapids: Navigating the Future of First Nations.* Toronto: Viking Press.

Morse, J.M., D.E. Young and L. Swartz. 1991. "Cree Indian Healing Practices and Western Health Care: A Comparative Analysis." *Social Science and Medicine* 32, 12: 1361-6.

Nagel, Joane. 1994. "Constructing Ethnicity: Creating and Recreating Ethnic Identity and Culture." *Social Problems* 41, 1: 152-76.

Neuwelt, Pat, Robin Kearns, Duncan Hunter, and Jane Batten. 1992. "Ethnicity, Morbidity and Health Service Utilization in Two Labrador Communities." *Social Science of Medicine* 34, 2: 151-60.

Richardson, Boyce. 1989. *Drumbeat: Anger and Renewal in Indian Country.* Toronto: Summerhill Press.

Rodman, Margaret C. 1992. "Empowering Place: Multilocality and Multivocality." *American Anthropologist* 4, 3: 640-56.

Royal Commission on Aboriginal Peoples. 1993a. *Exploring the Options: Overview of the Third Round* (Public hearings). Ottawa: Royal Commission on Aboriginal Peoples.

–. 1993b. *The Path to Healing: Report of the National Round Table on Aboriginal Health and Social Issues*. Ottawa: Royal Commission on Aboriginal Peoples.

–. 1996. *Report of the Royal Commission on Aboriginal Peoples*. Ottawa: Minister of Supply and Services.

Rushforth, S. 1977. "Country Food." In *Dene Nation, the Colony within*, ed. Mel Watkins, 32-46. Toronto; Buffalo: University of Toronto Press.

Speck, Frank. 1935. *Naskapi: The Savage Hunters of the Labrador Peninsula*. Norman: University of Oklahoma Press.

Strathern, Marilyn. 1995. "Nostalgia and the New Genetics." In *Rhetorics of Self-Making*, ed. Debbora Battaglia, 97-120. Berkeley: University of California Press.

Tanner, Adrian. 1979. *Bringing Home Animals: Religious Ideology and Mode of Production of the Mistassini Cree Hunters*. St. John's: ISER, Memorial University of Newfoundland.

–. 1993. "History and Culture in the Generation of Ethnic Nationalism." In *Aboriginality and Ethnicity: Case Studies in Ethnonationalism*, ed. Michael Levin, 75-96. Toronto: University of Toronto Press.

Trovato, F. 1991. "Analysis of Native Mortality." *Journal of Indigenous Studies* 2, 1: 1-15.

Wadden, Marie. 1991. *Nitassinan: The Innu Struggle to Reclaim Their Land*. Toronto: Douglas and McIntyre.

Young, David, Grant Ingram, and Lise Swartz. 1989. *Cry of the Eagle: Encounters with a Cree Healer*. Toronto: University of Toronto Press.

Young, T. Kue. 1994. *The Health of Native Americans*. New York: Oxford University Press.

20
The Concept of Community and the Challenge for Self-Government

Hedda Schuurman

What do we really mean when we use the term "community"? The word is laden with cultural assumptions, making universal definition difficult. In arenas of development policy and planning, one encounters the uncritical belief that local populations do (or should) function as communities – a belief that often has more to do with the premises and stereotypes held by mainstream North Americans than it does with realities "on-the-ground." Let me attempt, however, to offer a general definition of the concept of community: for the purposes of this chapter, "community" refers to a conscious bond uniting people who share common cultural traditions, life experiences, language(s), and/or religious sentiments. Community can also be conceived of as a consciousness that motivates people to work for a common good.

The terms "community" and "village" are, in most people's minds, synonymous. However, for my purposes, the terms "village," "settlement," and "town" refer to the geographic location of Sheshatshiu in Labrador, while the term "community" embraces the intangible forces that unite people in a shared world of culture and experience. Clearly there is real overlap between location and experience. At the same time, the term "community" is something of an anthropological construct: it is not a term indigenous to the Innu language (though it is now in common use among the Innu). The idea of community as a cohesive social unit is somewhat elusive in its application to the Innu of Sheshatshiu. In the late 1960s, when the Innu first began to live year-round in the settlement of Sheshatshiu, a distinct community consciousness did not automatically result from the new geographic and social conditions introduced by settlement life. Traditional perceptions of geographic and social boundaries were fluid. The semi-nomadic Innu lived for most of the year in small loosely knit family groups. In the summer months these groups would gather together in Sheshatshiu to trade and celebrate marriages and baptisms performed by the visiting priest. In contrast, community life for the Innu today is fraught with the ambivalence of multiple kin identities relating on a more proximate and permanent basis.

Since the relatively recent settlement of the Sheshatshiu Innu in the 1960s, change has been constant. This chapter captures only a particular moment within this particular process of transformation. Contrary to many images of Aboriginal communities as egalitarian and culturally and linguistically homogeneous, Sheshatshiu is a small village containing several hierarchically divided groups that are identified by different dialects (Mailhot 1997). This chapter explores the contemporary experience of community for the Innu of Sheshatshiu, and it examines the threads of tension and change that both define and negate ideals of community. It seeks to understand the causes of the divisions as well as the factors that have contributed to the meaning of community for the people of Sheshatshiu. Upon closer examination of village life, it becomes clear that self-government has some way to go to adequately represent the diverse practical needs and aspirations of the people of Sheshatshiu.

I argue that the Innu, despite having the semblance of community within the public sphere, have displayed characteristics of what one might call an "anti-community": a group that is, in part, opposed to its own social formation. This condition poses additional challenges for the Innu leaders as they work towards self-government within a community that is still coming to terms with its own existence.

From Country to Settlement Life

The Labrador Innu were one of the last Aboriginal groups in Canada to make the transition from a nomadic life as caribou hunters to a largely sedentary life in the village of Sheshatshiu. Prior to 1968, Sheshatshiu remained a summer, and occasional winter, residence for many families. Housing was initially limited to the elderly, widows, and the disabled – those who were perceived as more needy, or who faced greater obstacles in accompanying family members into the country for the fall and winter months. The majority of families who continued a semi-nomadic existence would live in their tents while visiting the settlement. Those who remained in the settlement were able to collect welfare and government pensions (McGee 1961, 30).

By 1959, fourteen houses were built, twelve with government assistance, to accommodate the old and disabled; two were built by men (who provided their own lumber and labour) for their own families (Mailhot and Michaud 1965, 11). Until 1959, the school remained part of the mission.[1] After 1959, when the first school was built, a few more families took up year-round residence. The eventual settlement of the remaining Innu, who had maintained a semi-nomadic and independent existence, took place in

1968. This completion of sedentarization was influenced in part by enforced school attendance, upon which continued government assistance became conditional (McGee 1961, 31). In addition, a large housing project, responsible for building fifty-one houses in Sheshatshiu between 1965 and 1968, helped draw the last semi-nomadic families into permanent settlement (Armitage 1989, 10). The government-built houses were all without water and sewerage facilities. It was not until the late 1980s that the majority of residences were equipped with indoor toilets and running water.

Settlement introduced radical changes to the social and economic structure of Innu society, and this made adaptation particularly difficult. Traditional forms of egalitarianism and economic control lost much of their relevance within this context. Leadership models that pertained primarily to the caribou hunt and other subsistence pursuits could not be sustained within the social and economic environment of the settlement. The Innu were subjected to the frequently coercive influence and leadership of missionaries, traders, and government officers.

The missionaries and government officers saw education as the key to sedentization. McGee (1961, 147), a Roman Catholic student and missionary who spent two years in Sheshatshiu during the beginning of permanent settlement, suggested that "compulsory school attendance may well become the chief factor conducive to a change of Montagnais outlook and culture. This is partly because through school the Indians are forced to learn English, which is certainly a means to their being employed above the menial level." Though McGee saw the school as a means of improving the situation of the Innu, he also noted several aspects of the education system that were obviously inappropriate for Innu children:

> The curriculum of required studies, established in accord with what is suitable and necessary for white children in the capital city, shows little relevance to the needs of children, Indian or white, in the remoter areas. The required language of instruction is English and the texts and other class materials are virtually useless in the Lake Melville environment. This means that the missionary, in conjunction with the local school board, must make heroic efforts to maintain some semblance of instruction and to try to meet rather ridiculous standards. (145)

The incongruity of a Euro-Canadian education system imposed on the language, values, and culture of the Innu students was thus recognized fairly early on. Despite this, attempts to rectify the situation were unsuccessful and these conditions persisted for decades.

Spending less time on the land resulted in the consumption of less "wild" food. Caribou, which is considered "real" Innu food because it nourishes the body as well as the soul, ceased to be a staple. Like other country foods, it began to play a less prominent role in the daily Innu diet and was slowly supplanted by chips, cheesies, french fries, pizza, chicken, Coke, and prepared cereals. Wild foods like caribou, salmon, trout, ptarmigan, hare, goose, and beaver became occasional supplements to a diet of processed foods.[2] Some outside observers might argue that the Innu were still "on their land," since Sheshatshiu, especially in the 1960s, was located in quite remote wilderness. However, from my observations, many Sheshatshiu residents had a dualistic attitude towards country and settlement, and they did not see themselves as being connected to the land while living in town. Being in the country meant living in tents with their family and relatives, hunting and eating wild meat – a totally interactive experience between human and non-human environments.

The process of procuring food in the settlement became a unidimensional activity regulated primarily by the flow of cash. Families were now living in separate houses and receiving separate cheques to buy food, which was to be shared and eaten primarily within their immediate households.

Henriksen (1989, ix-xi) suggested that the "fundamental interdependence" of the Innu was required by the environment within which they lived and hunted. Settlement did not entail the equivalent degree of sharing and dependence upon one another and, thus, gave people the freedom to exercise their individual autonomy in ways never before possible in the country. The presence of Euro-Canadian institutions, fixed residence in houses (which inhibited social mobility), and participation in the cash economy of a consumer society have had "drastic repercussions for how the Innu organized their daily activities" (Henriksen 1993, 2). The social organization of community life has largely destroyed the ability of the Innu to "use their social relations and cultural apparatus as tools to maintain their self-respect and sense of self-hood" (2).

The physical health of the Innu suffered under the sedentary conditions of village life. Regular access to alcohol, in combination with a bad diet and inactivity, brought on weight gain and poor skin condition. The lack of clean running water in the village caused gastroenteritis, impetigo, and related infections. In 1966, the conditions in the village were described as "horrible" (Paddon, cited in Budgel 1984, 43). In 1967 water wells were drilled in Sheshatshiu; prior to this, clean drinking water had to be obtained from the mission house (Budgel 1984, 46).

Fur prices had dropped by 1968, and, as a result, trapping was no longer a viable means of obtaining cash. More important, the imposition of the Newfoundland provincial hunting laws severely restricted access to caribou. The delivery of social services, upon which everyone soon became dependant, restricted movements in the country as cheques could not be obtained if people were not residing in the village. Distribution of government cheques was made conditional upon school attendance. Compulsory schooling and an increasing dependency on social assistance restricted trips into the country and caused a breakdown in the traditional transmission of knowledge and skills from older to younger generations.

Village life had initially offered a sanctuary for many Innu who, at the time of settlement, were suffering from poverty, disease, loss of easy access to game, and diminishing cash for furs. Many were in need of assistance (Armitage 1989, 12). In the beginning, they were eager to settle and to send their children to a Roman Catholic school (Armitage 1989, 12; McGee 1961, 142). Yet the conditions of settlement life, with institutional controls exercised by church and government, served to sabotage the ability of the Innu to adapt. The Innu found themselves settled within the domain of Euro-Canadians without having access to their land, the primary arena of their identity.

Contemporary Experience of Community

Now, thirty years since the process of settlement began, Sheshatshiu, on the shores of Hamilton Inlet, is surrounded by expanding communities of Settlers[3] and more recent newcomers, with the military base in Goose Bay just thirty kilometres away. When the Innu speak of the past they represent it as synonymous with life in the country; it as an expression of cultural heritage. Today, the country life of the past is defined in juxtaposition to present life in the village.

The Innu name "Sheshatshiu" refers to the coming together of the shores of two lakes, Lake Melville and Grand Lake (Mailhot 1997, 2). It is a location of majestic scenery, one that has been used by the Innu for summer gatherings for hundreds, perhaps thousands, of years. The name has appeared on topographical maps as early as 1703 and was referred to in a document written by Louis Jolliet in 1694 (Mailhot 1997, 1).

Sheshatshiu lies along the beach-like shores of Lake Melville and faces east towards the Atlantic Ocean, just beyond the horizon. The settlement itself is spread out, with houses running along more than two kilometres of beach road, lining the steep hillside that rises above the shore, providing many residents with a view. A population of about 1,000 occupies 151 houses in town, several of which are in need of renovations.[4] There is a small store with inflated prices run by an entrepreneurial Settler family, an all-grade school, a church, a clinic, and a social services office that serves both Sheshatshiu and the adjacent town of Northwest River. It is ironic that this particular office should be located in Sheshatshiu as it is the only place in town that residents of Northwest River ever need to visit. Northwest River is otherwise quite self-sufficient, and it is the residents of Sheshatshiu who must cross the bridge into Northwest River or drive to Goose Bay for most of their service and shopping needs. Northwest River is a popular option as few people have cars. Every day, people from Sheshatshiu can be seen crossing the bridge to Northwest River, going to the post office, the food "takeout," and the Northern Store. This flow is unreciprocated by residents of Northwest River, who rarely set foot in Sheshatshiu.

Prior to 1979, a cable car linked Sheshatshiu, on the south side of the channel that connects the two lakes, with Northwest River. Today a bridge spans the channel but not the differences between the two towns. Northwest River has a population of approximately 750; the majority are Settlers, but many Inuit and newcomers also reside there. Northwest River includes a post office, a large "Northern" department and grocery store, a cafe and take-away, a school, a community college, a clinic and alcohol and drug rehabilitation centre, various recreation halls, and three churches. It is an affluent town in appearance, landscaped with walking paths, trees, and pretty gardens. All the paths and gravel roads are marked with signs and are lit-up with bright streetlights at night.

The physical appearance of Sheshatshiu is run down, and its dirt roads are devoid of streetlights. Physical differences reflect, to some extent, differences in access to material resources; but they may also, in part, signify an assertion of distinctive identity. Schwimmer (1972, 117-55) argues that marginalized Aboriginal groups often present themselves in opposition to the dominant White society through the "symbolic competition" of asserted difference (even superiority) in relation to the perceived value system of others (see also Kennedy 1982). In Northwest River, people are more affluent and take pride in their lawns, gardens, houses, and cars. In Sheshatshiu people are seemingly poorer and the services more limited. There are also messages of resistance to an imposed value system and an emphasis on caring about different things. An Innu informant told me that if he wears clean, new clothes, then other Innu might think he is "trying to be White." Though he has a nice new winter coat he will not wear it because he does not want to look like a "White man." Another time I jokingly told an employee of the Innu Nation that he should use the very sophisticated-looking briefcase that sat unused in his office for his papers as he was always carrying his files to meetings in old plastic "Co-op" store bags. He replied that he never used his briefcase even when he was travelling on business and negotiating with politicians in various places. The recycled plastic bags were more characteristically Innu, he said. Carrying them around with him while meeting with high-level government officials was a symbol of his Innu-ness. Sheshatshiu, in its rundown state, may similarly be a symbol of Innu-ness and non-conformity – a visual statement of difference and resistance to the dominant middle-class values of White society.

Though historically intertwined, then, Sheshatshiu and Northwest River maintain very distinct cultural identities. These differences have helped to maintain senses on both sides of being divided, and these have become mutually reinforcing.[5]

Since the 1960s, many of the central governments' attempts to promote economic growth have not been successful. Unemployment has remained high, leaving many families on social assistance. Meanwhile, younger people, in particular, are influenced by the material values of the secular consumer society, which is prospering in nearby Happy Valley-Goose Bay and which is ubiquitous via television and video programs.

The majority of families in the village are struggling with problems of low self-esteem and family lives overshadowed by alcoholism and violence. The stress accompanying these conditions hinders the ability of many individuals to participate in the formation and administration of community organizations aimed at improving matters (see also Degnen, Chapter 19, this volume).

The loss of values that were integral to life in the country has become a cause of explicit resentment and a great source of discouragement. The ethic of sharing, which characterized the relationship between hunters and their families in the country, transfers poorly to settlement life; though it is sometimes renewed when wild meat is brought into the village. Although the expectation that people should share what they have still lingers, the practice generally collapses when individuals and families struggle to manage within the constraints of a cash economy. One informant lamented the loss of caring and sharing between people in Sheshatshiu, and pointed out that its lack has led to the deterioration of relationships of interdependence and become a divisive force between family groups.

Innu leaders and community members feel somewhat ambiguous about the presence of non-Innu institutions. The Roman Catholic Church, despite its enduring influence historically, is now becoming increasingly marginalized. Its influence was more pervasive when year-round settlement began. Prior to that, long periods in the bush allowed the Innu to revive their traditional beliefs and practices, which were put on hold while visiting the mission during the summer months. During the early years of settlement, sacred practices – such as the shaking tent and drumming – were actively condemned by the priest. Innu were told that, by practising these rituals, they were not acting in accordance with God but with the devil. Physical punishment, administered by the priest for disobedience and school absenteeism in the early years of settlement, has left many adults with sour memories. Though the Church has now admitted its past mistakes, the changes currently being instituted by the mission seem to have come too late. Weddings, funerals, baptisms, and Christmas and Easter masses are well attended, but only a few faithful elders come to regular mass. Recently the Church has become the locus of blame for the erosion of culture and traditions. For many Innu, the Church and the school are seen as concrete representations of their colonization.

The Innu Nation is in the process of taking over the administration of several non-Innu institutions in the village. A local radio station was established, and it offers broadcasts for at least twelve to fourteen hours a day. It plays primarily Innu pop and rock music composed by local musicians and groups from Quebec. Throughout the day, most homes tune in this station. Its phone-in line enables people to air their views on various issues, deliver messages, and make announcements. The radio plays an important role as communication hub and audio meeting place. When land claims issues and political protests are being discussed, the radio is often used as a means for people to conduct lengthy debates. A phone-in session on a community issue will last as long as the calls keep coming in; sometimes heated discussion goes on for six to eight hours.

Another component in the effort to "indigenize" local institutions is the Innu Nation's lobby to involve more Innu staff in the administration of social services. It is hoped that the greater participation of Innu staff will ensure delivery of programs that can effectively address the specific cultural needs of Innu families. However, this is proving to be a complex and difficult process. As Lyla Andrew (1992) points out in a study on the delivery of social services in Sheshatshiu, the historical relationship between the Innu and the Department of Social Services has been one of domination and control. She argues that it is difficult for the Innu to recommend changes because the philosophical framework from which their suggestions for change would be generated is so fundamentally different from that of social services. Thus changes are often quite superficial.

Meaning of Community[6]

Both the experience and concept of living within a fixed settlement were foreign to the nomadic Innu. Today the experience of "community life" for most adults is associated with social and political divisions along the lines of territorial subgroups, the imposition of foreign institutions and values, and social and cultural breakdown. Today, the word "community," as a synonym for life in the village, has primarily negative connotations.

The elders, who lived most of their lives on the land, still prefer to dwell in their tents for most of the year. For convenience they tend to camp along the highways and roads – a compromise between country and settlement life. In the village, signs of collective despair are everywhere, and the vitality of country living is lost. One day I asked an elder who was living in a tent in the woods just off the road to Goose Bay what was missing in the community. "The country," she replied.

In the past, territorial and inter-band mobility allowed for a dynamic pattern of social organization (Mailhot 1986a, 106). Historically, Innu communities were composed of social units that had coherent self identities but shifting social and geographic boundaries:

> A basic attribute of group identity [among the Innu] is the shared perception of a commonly used environment and a shared knowledge of its resources. Such a knowledge would be as flexible as group membership. At any specific instance the perceptions of group identity and land use would vary depending on the group's composition and the pooled knowledge of experience of individuals. (Loring 1992, 30)

Sedentary life introduced a form of social organization starkly opposed to that of previous forms of social existence.

In analysis, the concept of "community" is linked to states of consciousness. The "consciousness of community is, then, encapsulated in [the] perception of its boundaries, boundaries which are themselves largely constituted by people in interaction" (Cohen 1985, 13). This consciousness of community is developed through shared values and symbols of meaning. In the past, the nomadic life of Innu hunters was profoundly connected to a consciousness of community, the boundaries of which were affirmed through rituals such as *makushan*[7] and, later, Holy Communion (which the Innu perceived as being essentially the same as makushan) (Henriksen 1989, 78). During these rituals Innu hunters collectively communed with the Caribou Spirit and/or Jesus Christ, affirming their culture and the symbolic boundaries of their community (Cohen 1985, 47; see also Henriksen 1989).

Although the idea of community has often been associated with wholeness and integration, Cohen (1985) addresses the meaning of community from a different angle, embracing its complexity and dualistic nature. The community of Sheshatshiu has what Cohen describes as public and private faces:

> The boundary as the community's public face is symbolically simple; but as the object of internal discourse it is symbolically complex. Thus, we can all attribute gross stereotypical features to whole groups: but, for the members of those groups such stereotypes applied to themselves as individuals would almost invariably be regarded as gross distortions, superficial, unfair and ridiculous ... In the public face internal variety disappears or coalesces into a simple statement. In its private mode, differentiation, variety and complexity proliferate. (74)

The private face of Sheshatshiu is a divided one in that it encompasses four distinct territorial subgroups. Mailhot (1997) suggests that the establishment of these subgroups occurred as recently as this century and that the crystallization of social and political division between them occurred at the time of settlement in the 1960s. Though similar social groupings existed in the past, the corresponding social stratification did not. The emergence of a hierarchy of subgroups within the community has its genesis in the contact period, during which time certain groups remained more isolated from trading posts, missions, and the forces of modernization than did others. The degree of acculturation through contact with Euro-Canadian society was a primary influence in the formation of these subgroups. There are three primary divisions of the *Sheshatshiunnuat,* or "Sheshatshiu Innu": (1) *Uashaunnuat,* "Sept-Iles People"; (2) *Mashkuanunnat,* "Musquaro People"; and (3) *Mushuaunnuat,* "Tundra People." The first group is subdivided into (4) *Mekenitsheuat,* "Mackenzies" and (5) *Uashaunnnuat,* "Sept-Iles People" (Mailhot 1997, 41). There are several dialects within the village that reflect the three main divisions. However, within the subdivision of the *Uashaunnuat,* the Sept-Iles People, there are no differences in dialect (58). It is through exogamy that social status is often improved.

Mailhot (1997, 68) makes an important distinction regarding the attribution of status and economic power:

> The social stratification in the community of Sheshatshit springs from a symbolic complex that obtains throughout the Innu area. It would be wrong, therefore, to confuse it with the system of social classes found in industrialized societies. Sheshatshit does indeed have a local élite endowed with prestige and power, enjoying certain economic privileges, and playing the dominant role in the internal and external affairs of the Innu people of Labrador. But the members of this élite are recruited according to family and territorial, rather than economic, criteria. Individuals do not rise in the hierarchy by acquiring wealth or a better education: they do so by joining a social group through marriage or adoption. Moreover, economic privileges are obtained through political power rather than the reverse.

This system, which governs status and social positions, also determines access to political leadership. This challenges the widely held notion that Aboriginal communities are socially cohesive and egalitarian. For most adults in Sheshatshiu, the experience of community has been shaped by these political and social divisions. These internal divisions may have less impact on contemporary Innu youth than on their elders as the former tend to identify less with past traditions and are more connected to other youth in neighbouring communities. Today's youth may be the first generation to have a sense of community that is not so attached to specific territorial groups. Mailhot (1997, 70) speculates that, in the future, they may eventually develop a two-class system not dissimilar to Canadian social classes – the elite and the others:

> A structure of this type already exists in some Innu communities of Quebec, where education has become a mechanism for access to jobs in the service sector, and hence to political power. But in that case the growing phenomenon of inter-ethnic marriages could, at some future time, result in Sheshatshit acquiring a social structure with a racial component, analogous to that of the Innu community of Lake St. John, where the métis are the dominant group and the "pure Indians" the dominated.

Paradoxically, year-round life in Sheshatshiu has given rise to a community consciousness that seems to be opposed to its own existence. I refer to this as an "anti-community" consciousness. Though more positive dimensions of the sense of community do exist both internally and in relation to the public world, a deep-seated antagonism is nonetheless evident. This paradoxical condition is not unique to the Innu; it can be found in many social relationships. For example, between two cohabiting individuals there may exist an intense degree of resentment and negative emotion whereby the couple dislike one another as well as the relationship; internally, the consciousness of the relationship is opposed, in part, to its own existence. However, if the couple remain together, they may still have a relationship that is, at least publicly, regarded as coherent.

The complexities of Sheshatshiu exist on a larger scale than the complexities of individual relationships. An anti-community consciousness reflects lives and memories fraught with angst and pain, loss, division, and antagonism. These sombre aspects of community consciousness have surely contributed to the symbolic markers and internal integument of Sheshatshiu. At the same time, there are currents of hope and expressions of healing and change. The sense of community shared by its members is "refracted through all the complexities of their lives and experience" (Cohen 1985, 74).

Political action over the past ten years has revived several concepts of Innu-ness from the past that have helped to create a growing sense of the potential of an organized community to bring about social and political change. Cohen (1985, 99) writes that myths and memories of the past can often serve as a "'charter' for contemporary action whose legitimacy derives from its very association with the cultural past." Political action has produced new symbols, which have served to constitute a more positive public presentation of community consciousness. The meanings that individuals within the community attach to these symbols, be they drawn from the past or elsewhere, may differ: what is important to the construction of community is that they be shared. A sense of community, aside from its internal coherence and importance, has become necessary in order to secure external political gains. In the public political sphere, expressions of community bear positive meanings, with primary recourse to symbols of

Innu-ness drawn from the past. Symbols such as caribou, country, land claims, and self-government provide people in Sheshatshiu with broadly acceptable common markers of collective identity. These symbols, joining traditional values to future goals, have infused the concept of community with hope, meaning, and solidarity, thus ameliorating the consciousness of a community opposed to its own existence.

Loss of the Sacred

Some of the social forces animating community life can be understood by looking at the changes undergone in Innu religious life since permanent settlement. The provincial game laws drastically reduced access to the hunting and consumption of Innu animals. These activities were the basis of an interdependence between Innu family groups as well as between humans and the animal spirits: hunting as a "holy occupation" (Speck 1935). The loss of hunting rights impeded the persistence of several religious practices and ritualized social forms. The spirituality of the past was practised and reinforced through an interactive relationship with the animals and the environment. The material culture of the past coexisted with the sacred spirits of the forest and the animals. Through these forces, the natural world was explained and a context was provided for survival. Life was held in balance and infused with a sense of the sacred. In Innu cosmology "nature and society coalesce ... The spirits are everywhere in nature and the Innu interact with the spirits all the time" (Henriksen 1993, 6).

Settlement created a dichotomy in which life in the country began to be perceived as representing the world of the Innu in its entirety. Life in the community came to be seen as the antithesis of Innu reality, uninhabited by the sacred forces that infuse life and social relationships in the country with meaning. The breakdown in social relationships in Sheshatshiu can, in part, be attributed to a loss of these sacred forces, which are no longer able to provide a charter for the concept of self in relation to others and to that which is sacred. As Pandian (1991, 2-3) explains: "Human beings acquire their humanness by becoming symbols to themselves and others; they exist as subject and object, and as self and other, in an interactional relationship in a world of symbols that involves taking the role of the other and organizing thoughts and feelings in a culturally coherent and appropriate manner."

Religion provides symbols through which the "supernatural" elements of human identity can be recognized and through which people can experience "self" in relation to and as part of a greater sacred whole. Pandian suggests that different cultural formulations can be examined through their representations of the supernatural (i.e., the "sacred other") and of human identity (i.e., the "symbolic self"). The identity of the self is constructed through its relationship with the sacred other.

Innu religious forms had provided a means through which the "symbolic self" interacted with the "sacred other." Sometimes mediated by shamans, rituals or activities such as hunting would provide fertile ground for religious thought and action while at the same time enabling the pursuit of the practical goals of everyday life (Tanner 1989, 208). Women, who did not necessarily participate directly in the hunt, were nevertheless mediums for the animals' spirits, as they dreamed about the location of the animals. Dreams provided the inspiration for the designs women embroidered onto hunting garments.

The conception of the "sacred other" in Innu religious thought has largely lost its role in the lives of many community members. It would be incorrect to suggest that there is no religious sense in the lives of the Sheshatshiu Innu. But community life has deprived the Innu of their access to spiritual power and has created a condition of spiritual powerlessness (Henriksen 1993, 8-9). Much of the social breakdown now occurring is a reflection of a crisis in religious thought. The sacred meanings of social interactions are fading as the old codes become mixed up with secular values. Many people in Sheshatshiu still believe in the power of rituals and sacred forms of the past, but they lack the necessary knowledge to practise them. Since certain rituals – for example, the use of the drum and the shaking tent – were forbidden by the Church, their knowledge now lies solely with the elders, many of whom have recently passed away.

It is important to note that two new religious ideologies have been introduced to the community and have provided several Innu families with coherent frameworks of belief. The members of the Pentecostal Church and active participants in the Alcoholics Anonymous (AA) program stand out for their ability to overcome addictive behaviours and to maintain improved social relationships. Antze (1987, 149) points out that "A.A. does far more than to help the compulsive drinker shake off a troublesome habit. It also draws him into a community that globally reorders his life." Though AA does not claim to be a religion, it teaches people that their recovery is dependant upon the assistance of a greater power, and, in the steps to recovery, reference is made directly to God. The Pentecostal Church in Northwest River has provided several Innu families with an entirely different perspective on life and has drawn them into a strong and cohesive spiritual community that has provided them with a new road map.[8]

Many of the narratives and myths of Innu religious traditions of the past, which used to accompany and inform the practices of daily life, are now silent. The old maps of reality have not worked here. New maps are gradually being introduced; some people are finding guidance through AA, others through the Pentecostal Church; and many are looking for political solutions. For some residents the political values embodied in the fight for self-government and autonomy from Euro-Canadian institutions are providing a new framework for action. Through the struggle for independent nation status, attempts are being made to integrate the past, overcome the present, and work out a plan for the future.

Community Politics: The Challenge for Innu Government

The symbolic power of Innu ethnic nationalism is relatively superficial to the private realm of community life, applying, as it does, predominantly in relation to the "other" – to outsiders, Whites, government, and the media. Internally, the meaning of ethnic nationalism is complex, producing dissonance between how people feel about their Innu identity individually and how it is collectively portrayed by politicians. This dissonance is often reflected in efforts to take control of institutions locally, where community participation is often undermined by political apathy, divisions, and antagonisms.

The leaders are caught in a double bind (Tanner 1993b; also Chapter 21, this volume). While attempting to revitalize the culture and economy by taking control of local institutions, the leaders often take on roles of tutelage and control previously associated with outside government agents or missionaries, thus creating divisions and giving rise to suspicions and resistance between community members.

Though Innu society did have traditional figures of authority within the context of hunting, this position was not static; and everyone had a strong sense of his or her own personal autonomy. People seldom asserted dominance over one another; a person would be free to speak his or her own mind despite the fact that the rest of the group may or may not be in agreement. If people disagreed they could move their camp elsewhere (Tanner 1993a, 82). The existence of distinct and established positions of leadership continues to be difficult to accept for many individuals who, themselves, are without access to political power. In order for individuals to maintain their leadership positions it is crucial that they continue to recognize and treat everyone in the community as leaders in their own right. This approach, however, is hard to maintain, as Innu leaders today are confronted with the bureaucratic structures, deadlines, and pressures that reinforce a tendancy to emulate the authoritarian practices of leaders elsewhere. Traditional models of leadership continue to determine the way in which leaders are evaluated by community members. However, within the public domain, Innu politicians are evaluated by a different set of standards – those that correspond with Western political values. Leaders walk a tightrope between an internal leadership style that reflects their Innu-ness and a public style that reflects the degree to which they have mastered the language and form essential to their dealings with provincial and federal bureaucrats. The latter tends to dominate, as Innu leaders spend more and more time in their offices and travelling to meetings in other parts of the country.

Several people in Sheshatshiu have expressed concern about the potential problems of accountability when self-government is fully established. However, the problem of centralized financial accountability is one that every democratically elected government must face. Although community members distinctly fear having too much responsibility placed in the hands of one person or family group, the majority of them do not want to take too much responsibility for fear of making mistakes, being held accountable, and being criticized. Thus the person in a position of leadership is covertly admired and overtly criticized.

In Sheshatshiu, community solidarity is produced in response to issues like school control but quickly breaks down upon consideration of what an Innu-run institution would involve. For example, a survey conducted around the community's expectations for an Innu-run school revealed many differences in opinion not only with regard to school control, but also with regard to self-government. Several dimensions of school control were at stake, and the political discourse of Innu leaders often failed to reflect the diversity of views in the village. For the leadership, political autonomy and local school control are strongly related. School control would enhance pride in Innu culture, further the ethno-nationalist agenda for self-government, and provide the village with a chance to unite in the creation of a new educational system for the upcoming generation of Innu children. However, community members do not always perceive it to be in their interest to buy into the Innu Nation's political agenda. It is true that, on an ideological level, strong nationalist sentiments are felt throughout the village. But when the rhetoric and promise of self-government is examined by people in Sheshatshiu, doubts and concerns come to the surface. The actual meaning of self-government is contested in a village where individuals are accustomed to, and have more confidence in, literally governing themselves. The Sheshatshiu Innu are, in keeping with practices of the past, much more interested in being personally "self"-governing, in being autonomous as individuals rather than in having power and authority vested in a single locus, whether this locus be the Canadian state or the Innu Nation. Ironically, the individual autonomy known to the Innu may be threatened by the power structure implicit in an Innu government rather than enhanced by it. This has important implications for Innu leaders who have to mediate the demands of the state and the needs of their constituents to be recognized as distinct and self-governing individuals.

Notes

1 A permanent Roman Catholic mission was established in Sheshatshiu in 1952.

2 Based on my observations in 1992, wild meat and berries would account for an average of 10 percent to 20 percent of food consumed in the village. However, in the country wild meat is often eaten at every meal and constitutes up to 80 percent of the diet.

3 Settlers are descendants of the early Europeans from Scotland, England, and France who came to Labrador on fishing or trading vessels or to work at trading posts. These men often married Inuit women and set themselves up as independent trappers.
4 With a birth rate of 5.6 percent (based on 1990 statistics from Mani Ashini Clinic).
5 Evelyn Plaice, in *The Native Game* (1991), describes how the ethnicity of the residents of Northwest River has been defined in relation to that of their Innu neighbours.
6 The term "community" refers to the forms of social interaction arising from residence in the settlement. Some forms of interaction, however, seem to reflect a sentiment that is the antithesis of community.
7 Sacred feasting.
8 I encountered no prejudices expressed towards members of the Pentecostal Church or the AA group. Members of both groups have had some form of "born again" experience. There seems to be a high degree of tolerance towards the autonomy of the individual within this context.

References

Andrew, Lyla. 1992. "Whose Life Is It Anyways? Report on the Delivery of Social Services in Sheshatshit." Jointly commissioned by the Innu Nation and the Department of Social Services, Government of Newfoundland, April.

Antze, Paul. 1987. "Symbolic Action in Alcoholics Anonymous." In *Constructive Drinking: Perspectives on Drink from Anthropology*, ed. Mary Douglas, 149-81. Cambridge: Cambridge University Press.

Armitage, Peter. 1989. "Homeland or Wasteland? Contemporary Land Use and Occupancy among the Innu of Utshimassit and Sheshatshit and the Impact of Military Expansion." Submission to the Federal Environmental Assessment Panel Reviewing Military Flying Activities in Nitassinan. Report prepared for the Naskapi Montagnais Innu Association, 31 January.

–. 1991. *The Innu (The Montagnais-Naskapi)*. New York: Chelsea House.

Budgel, Richard. 1984. "Canada, Newfoundland and the Labrador Indians, 1949-69." *Native Issues* 4 (October): 38-49.

Cohen, Anthony P. 1985. *The Symbolic Construction of Community*. Chichester, England: Ellis Horwood.

Henriksen, Georg. 1989. *Hunters in the Barrens: The Naskapi on the Edge of the White Man's World*. St. John's, NF: ISER Publications MUN.

–. 1993. *Life and Death among the Mushuau Innu of Northern Labrador*. St. John's NF: ISER Publications MUN.

Kennedy, John C. 1982. *Holding the Line: Ethnic Boundaries in a Northern Labrador Community*. St. John's, NF: ISER Publications MUN.

Loring, Stephen J. 1992. "Princes and Princesses of Ragged Fame: Innu Archaeology and Ethnohistory in Labrador." PhD diss., University of Massachusetts.

Mailhot, José. 1986a. Territorial Mobility among the Montagnais-Naskapi of Labrador. *Anthropologica N.S.* 17, 1-2: 92-107.

–. 1986b. "Beyond Everyone's Horizon Stand the Naskapi." *Ethnohistory* 33, 4: 384-419.

–. 1987. "Montagnais Opposition to the Militarization of Their Land: An Historical Perspective." *Native Issues* 7, 1: 47-53.

–. 1997. *The People of Sheshatshit: In the Land of the Innu*. St. John's, NF: ISER Publications MUN.

Mailhot, José, and Andrée Michaud. 1965. *North West River: Etude ethnographique*. Université Laval, Québec: Institut de Géographie.

McGee, John T. 1961. *Cultural Stability and Change among the Montagnais Indians of the Lake Melville Region of Labrador*. Washington, DC: The Catholic University of America Press.

Pandian, Jacob. 1991. *Culture, Religion, and the Sacred Self: A Critical Introduction to the Anthropological Study of Religion*. Englewood Cliffs, NJ: Prentice Hall.

Plaice, Evelyn. 1991. *The Native Game: Settler Perceptions of Indian/Settler Relations in Central Labrador*. St. John's, NF: ISER Publications MUN.

Schwimmer, E.G. 1972. "Symbolic Competition." *Anthropologica* 14, 2: 117-56.

Speck, Frank. 1935. *Naskapi: The Savage Hunters of the Labrador Penisula*. Norman: University of Oklahoma Press.

Tanner, Adrian. 1989. *Bringing Home Animals: Religious Ideology and Mode of Production of the Mistassini Cree Hunters*. St. John's, NF: ISER Publications MUN.

–. 1993a. "History and Culture in the Generation of Ethnic Nationalism." In *Ethnicity and Aboriginality: Case Studies in Ethnonationalism*, ed. Michael D. Levin, 75-96. Toronto: University of Toronto Press.

–. 1993b. "Community Crisis and Healing: The Implications for Self-Government." Paper presented at the annual meetings of the Canadian Anthropological Society, York University, Toronto, Ontario.

21
The Double Bind of Aboriginal Self-Government

Adrian Tanner

This chapter is based on research conducted for the Aboriginal Governance Project among the Innu of Labrador. Although the data cover a diverse range of events, together they raise a set of practical and conceptual problems around Aboriginal governance and its prospects within an advanced industrial state. While the promise of Aboriginal self-government, a policy recently endorsed by the Royal Commission on Aboriginal Peoples (1996), is a reversal of the earlier assimilationist policies, implementation within the context of the non-Aboriginal system of governance raises many difficult issues.

Since the Innu are a minority group, self-government for them comes up against the ideological principle of one law for all citizens. Moreover, without a separate state with protected geographic borders, it will be difficult to clearly define the areas of jurisdiction for the self-governing Aboriginal entity and to have these rules internalized and respected as a matter of course by state authorities and the public. There are also special difficulties for a demographically small Aboriginal self-governing entity like the Innu, such as being able to recruit from its own ranks enough trained and talented individuals to manage all of the various self-government functions. In this chapter I focus particularly on difficulties arising from the pursuit of Innu cultural ideals within an economy and state formation based on different values and principles.

My objectives in undertaking the research were to document and analyze progress towards, as well as barriers standing in the way of, the Innu achievement of meaningful self-government. The work includes both planned inquiries and incidental and unplanned observation of events relevant to the issue as these were encountered during the research. In general, my inquiries centre around issues of regional and community control, as these were being faced at the time by the Labrador regional Innu organization, the Innu Nation (IN), and the two Labrador Innu communities of Sheshatshiu and Utshimassit. The data I refer to come from four specific episodes: a series of small group discussions I organized in July 1992 on the ideals of Sheshatshiu community members regarding their collective future; a series of interviews I conducted at Utshimassit (Davis Inlet) in August and September 1992 concerning relocating the community; my observations around a gas-sniffing-suicide incident at Utshimassit – one that came under intensive press and political attention in early 1993; and, finally, observations made at the Innu Nation policy workshop on *ishinniuiyat nutshimit* (the "bush way of life") held at Sheshatshiu in March 1993. I also refer to work I conducted subsequently outside this project as well as to the findings of others.

I want to draw attention to common thematic concerns that emerge from these observations and that have implications for Innu Aboriginal governance. One of these relates to the ideology and the practice of Innu national sovereignty, adding additional dimensions to my earlier observations on this topic (Tanner 1993). While, as I noted in 1993, the Labrador Innu have a record of forcefully asserting their right to manage their own affairs, a number of internal debates are taking place concerning the more specific objectives entailed in acquiring self-government.

One general theme is a new acknowledgement of, or perhaps heightened urgency around, the need to address their own internal social problems, particularly those pertaining to dysfunctionality at the individual, family, and community levels. This situation stems from the epidemic of symptoms of social breakdown that have afflicted the Innu since the 1960s, when, by government fiat, they were settled into villages. While the source of these problems is held to lie in past interventions and the state mismanagement of Innu internal affairs, it is becoming generally accepted that only the Innu themselves can find the solution to the resulting difficulties. As a consequence, a number of initiatives, often referred to as the "healing movement," are being launched, with the objective of (1) prompting individuals and families to take control of their lives and (2) collectively building "community" (a topic with which Schuurman deals in Chapter 20 of this volume).

The Innu are also confronting the problem of the loss of parts of their culture, a matter seen by many of them as requiring the preservation of their hunting way of life in the face of the economic and social changes that are undermining it. The internal debates within the Innu communities, while part of a general evolution of their political ideas, are strongly influenced by immediate practical issues. One of these is the general demand for employment opportunities that will enable them to escape the poverty and welfare trap. Another is the current competition over the limited forms of community political power.

While my research failed to meet one of its initial objectives – to elicit any clear public consensus regarding the central goals towards which the ıu believe their leaders should direct land rights and self-government negotiations – the reason for this failure is itself of significance. My research suggests that, in attempting to negotiate practical solutions to their common problems, the Innu frequently find themselves facing a "double bind"; that is, a contradictory situation in which they are required to make what seem to them impossible choices – ones they simply do not wish to make. This double bind not only inhibits the ability to take actions needed in order to move towards meaningful autonomy, but it also initiates cycles of reform and relapse. These cycles begin when attempts at healing are undertaken at the personal, family, or community levels. Because of the kinds of double bind they face, however, these attempts tend to generate ambivalence and stress, and so they fall short of their objectives. They may be followed by periods of disappointment and relapse, in which alcohol abuse and other symptoms of social breakdown return to dominate and render dysfunctional personal, family, and/or community life. While further healing activities are usually intitiated in order to overcome this new situation, the cyclical nature of this process means that permanent gains towards autonomy are rare. In this chapter I examine some of the details that go into making up this kind of double bind.

Setting

The Innu of Labrador, together with those closely related to them and living in Quebec, are an Algonquian-speaking group of formerly nomadic hunters who, from Aboriginal times up until recently (and, to some degree, even today), depended both economically and spiritually on hunting in Nitassinan, the vast interior lands of Quebec-Labrador. Their quarry was primarily caribou, along with various small mammals, fish, and birds. Traditionally, a high value was placed on hunting success and on the subsequent sharing of meat, the distribution of which was particularly symbolized at a ceremonial feast. Innu social organization was based on small hunting groups of bilateral kin. Membership with these groups was flexible and frequently changing, and the male elder was the consensual leader. Land was not divided into individual territories, as it was among the James Bay Cree, but large areas were loosely associated with regional groupings, and mobility between these groupings was common. Elders controlled religious knowledge and were believed to influence the welfare of the group through shamanistic powers. Such power was based on respect for and offerings to animal masters and other entities as well as on various forms of divination. The northern regional grouping, known as the Mushuau Innu, or Barren Land People, was particularly mobile, as it spent part of the year following the migrations of the large George River caribou herd. Until this century the Mushuau Innu gathered each fall at Indian House Lake on the

Quebec side of the border, where many caribou were speared while crossing the George River. Many of the values appropriate to this former way of life have survived the transition to sedentary life in villages, including respect for the autonomy of the individual, a high value on sharing, respect for elders, and a strong spiritual attachment to and identification with the land and the animals.

While the Innu had centuries of intermittent contacts with fur traders and Roman Catholic missionaries, they did not become as heavily dependent on fur trapping as did most other Canadian subarctic Indians; instead, after about 1850, another group, the mixed Inuit-European "settlers," came to dominate trapping for the Hudson's Bay Company in the southern Labrador interior. When the George River herd failed around 1916 several Mushuau Innu starved to death, and the rest were forced to split up, with those who became the present-day Utshimassit group moving closer to the posts on the northern Labrador coast. Further south, those trading at the North West River post, being comprised of four distinct regional subgroups, formed the Sheshatshiu Band.

The Innu were not administered under the federal Indian Act when Newfoundland joined Confederation in 1949, and they were only subject to extensive administration after they were settled by the Newfoundland government into the villages of Sheshatshiu and Utshimassit (Davis Inlet) in the 1950s and 1960s. The main rationale for this settlement process was to ensure that Innu children could attend school; however, since no residences were provided, parents were forced to give up hunting and most ended up living in poverty on government subsidies. Until they formed a political organization in the early 1970s the Innu had few formal contacts with government. At times traders or missionaries acted as middlemen between them and the authorities.

For the Innu the new villages were not comparable to any social units they had known before. When disputes had arisen in the past it had been a simple matter for hunting groups to split up, but once settled in villages this was no longer possible. The sites of the villages, located at the margins of Innu hunting lands, made access to game resources difficult. Sheshatshiu was also close to the large military base and regional administrative centre of Goose Bay – a population next to whom the Innu found themselves to be a small minority, unable to compete successfully for the few game resources in the immediate area. The Newfoundland government established Utshimassit on an island on the north coast of Labrador, near the old Hudson's Bay Company trading post of Davis Inlet. But it gave little consideration to choosing the location, except to ensure that it had deep-water anchorage for supply ships. The inappropriateness of this location soon became apparent. The unstable ground was not suitable for building foundations, there was no adequate source of fresh water, and access to hunting in the interior was restricted for several months each year during freeze-up and break-up.

Unlike the Inuit, the Innu did not establish close relations or intermarry with Labradorians of European descent. Settlers, people of mixed Inuit and European descent, have come to constitute the core social and political group of the Labrador coastal-oriented industrial and fishing society. The Innu now often find themselves excluded or marginalized from this core, and they are often at odds with them over such issues as land rights and industrial development.

Beginnings of Innu Self-Government

For many Aboriginal groups across Canada, the present federal policy of self-government is the culmination of a long government-orchestrated tutelage process – one that, in many cases, has lasted for more than a century, structured by programs under the "reserve lands" and "band government" provisions of the Indian Act. By means of these provisions, limited and token forms of decision making were gradually advanced to bands, under paternalistic supervision, to be withdrawn at any time they were not exercised to the satisfaction of the authorities. While the motive for this process may have been the integration of "Indians" within mainstream Canadian society, the effect was, instead, to create a dependent group that was permanently separated from its non-Aboriginal neighbours.

The history of government relations with the Labrador Innu represents, in some ways, the extreme opposite of this situation. First, the Innu have only come under any kind of effective state colonial control since the 1950s and 1960s, when forcible settlement into villages began. Prior to that, authorities or missionaries only saw them, if at all, for the short periods each year when they visited trading posts. Second, even after settlement, federal Indian Act jurisdiction and administration was not extended to them; instead, they were placed under provincial government authority. While the province's aims may have been similar to those that underlay federal Aboriginal policy, they did not have the resources, the expertise, or the inclination to engage in intensive tutelage efforts. Only limited endeavours could be made to guide the Innu towards state-approved forms of self-administration, particularly as at this time the whole concept of local government was something new in Labrador and was only just being initiated in the non-Innu communities.

In establishing the settlements, provincial authorities seem to have made the ethnocentric assumption that simply by being settled in houses, with their children being sent to school, the Innu would quickly become like other Labradorians. A key component of this ideological assumption appears to be that the new Innu settlements would by themselves come to embody the ideal of "community" – of a functioning local social unit beyond the family. While Innu hunting groups have some of the features we generally associate with this term, including collective action, leadership, sharing, and social control, these function are carried out in ways that are appropriate to the small size of the group and the practicalities of the hunting way of life. However, in terms of the reality of settlement life, the ideals of community have yet to fully take root, and few mechanisms of social control and collective organization entailed by the concept have as yet emerged.

Instead of the Indian Act form of "band" leadership, at first token "chiefs" were appointed by the Church, largely as rewards for compliance to Church authority. Having been left to their own devices more than had "Indian Act bands," the Innu themselves took the first steps towards self-government in the new settlements. After some initial meetings starting in the late 1960s, in 1973 the Native Association of Newfoundland and Labrador (NANL) was founded on the island of Newfoundland with the participation of a few Innu leaders. Recruitment of individual Labrador Innu members began later that year. In 1976 the Labrador Innu broke from NANL to form the Naskapi Montagnais Innu Association (NMIA), later to be renamed the Innu Nation (IN). From the beginning NANL recognized local groups as bands, each headed by an elected chief and band council. These concepts were apparently inspired by the Indian Act versions of these terms, but because none of the NANL groups came under this legislation, the institutions associated with them do not have the same legal status as do their Indian Act equivalents. In fact, since the bands themselves are not incorporated under provincial law, it is unclear whether they have any formal legal status. Nevertheless, the provincial government has generally, in practice, recognized the authority of the chiefs and councils, with whom they conduct political negotiations.

The unique history of Labrador Innu political development has both its positive and negative implications. On the positive side, among the Innu there is little of the legacy of entrenched tutelage and dependency found elsewhere in Canada, and there is no history of the Indian Affairs form of authoritarian supervision. On the negative side, the Newfoundland government authorities, whose own cultural background is arguably one of the most "monocultural" in Canada, tend to find the Innu difficult to both comprehend and to deal with and are reluctant to make accommodations. They approach Innu on the basis of the ethnocentric assumption that their own familiar concepts of community and local government are "natural," and they are generally unwilling to accept that there are fundamental cultural differences or to adopt the kind of structures that would be more suitable to Innu realities.

Sheshatshiu: Negotiated Rights and Community Healing

The validity of Innu Aboriginal land rights was formally recognized in 1978, but it was not until 1991 that the Innu Nation began negotiations with the federal and the provincial governments regarding a framework agreement for a land rights settlement (what the government insensitively refers to as "land claims"). While both governments had dragged their feet, participation in these negotiations also represented a significant policy shift for the Innu Nation who had, up until then, uncompromisingly characterized all activities of the Canadian state and the province of Newfoundland as being in violation of Innu sovereignty. In 1992 I began making inquiries among Innu people who were not political leaders regarding ideas about the kind of future economic and political goals they thought should be pursued through these negotiations. I had support from officials of the Innu Nation, who were also interested in hearing the opinions of their constituents regarding what negotiators should be aiming for. I was interested in understanding the process by which new demands were formulated and how they related to ideas about the kind of future community the Innu wanted for themselves and their children. On this basis a series of three small group discussions were held, within which I focused on questions about the future.

These discussion groups were held at Sheshatshiu and produced a diverse set of outcomes. First, it must be said that this method was not particularly fruitful with regard to achieving my immediate objectives. None of the discussions turned out to be occasions where participants speculated much about a future in which, thanks to new forms of land rights and self-government, they saw the difficulties of the present being left behind. I was surprised that the prospect of a land claim did not provide Innu participants with a meaningful context within which to think about the future.

One of the groups rejected participation in land claims negotiations altogether, arguing that the Innu should first undergo a collective healing process in preparation for undertaking the new responsibilities inherent in these discussions. In another group the discussion did not get beyond current economic difficulties and the question of whether it would improve things if the Labrador Innu sought the same benefits as the Quebec Innu already have under Indian Act registration. The members of this group seemed to be unprepared to consider whether their problems might be dealt with by receiving additional benefits from their own land rights settlement. The third group focused on the situation of teenagers, complaining that they were confused and without direction. There was general agreement that, in the future, there should be steady jobs for all; however, at the same time, everyone felt that all Innu should be able to spend time every year in the bush hunting in order to maintain their traditional way of life. However, there were few specific suggestions as to how either of these objectives could be achieved.

The first group consisted of three people who were all active in the community alcohol treatment program. All of them thought it was premature for the Labrador Innu to be negotiating specific land rights or self-government arrangements. They argued that, under the current circumstances, the Labrador Innu collectively lacked the competence to take on the kind of responsibilities that decisions about land rights and self-government involved. They argued that it was necessary for the Innu to solve their own severe social problems before they would be in a position to take on new responsibilities. The social problems to which they referred included not only the issue of alcohol abuse and the difficulties that stemmed directly from it, but also issues such as the loss of Innu cultural knowledge among young people, the decline in respect for the elders in family and community matters, and the general lack of functional cooperation between community members. One person in the group said that even the limited health and social services responsibilities already under Innu community control were more than they could properly manage.

The members of this group concluded that, before new responsibilities could be undertaken, a whole range of social problems had to be dealt with through a process of "community healing." The rest of the discussion concerned the details of this healing process, a major element of which involved a return to living in the bush. They advocated a program of treatment that would have its own facility in an isolated bush location and within which Innu elders and traditional Innu culture would play a major part. Border Beacon, an isolated abandoned weather station, was suggested as a possible location for this proposed facility. Group members also spoke of the idea of Innu inmates and juvenile delinquents being sent to such an isolated bush facility, where they could learn the bush way of life, rather than being sent to standard correctional facilities and group homes.

In the second group, the main participants were two married men with growing children. Both said they took paid work whenever they could, but only one of them said he was able to support himself at other times by hunting. He said that, because there was a perennial need for cash, hunting was only something to be done when no paying job was available. Another suggested that his support for Innu Nation policies depended on whether they gave him a job; if they did not employ him he would not continue to support their political protest actions.

The idea of the Labrador Innu seeking registration under the federal Indian Act was raised and debated in the second group. As noted above, the Innu were never registered and, thus, do not have access to the programs offered by Indian Affairs; instead, starting in 1954, limited federal funding for Innu and Inuit communities has been administered by the province, although in recent years a few programs based on direct federal funding have been made available to the Innu. Most Labrador Innu have relatives in the Innu communities registered under the Indian Act across the border in Quebec, and they are familiar with conditions there, which, in terms of funding, are better than their own. Opinion as to whether the Labrador Innu should seek registration was divided, with one man opposed to acquiring federal funding through Indian Act registration mainly because such funds would be administered by Indian Affairs. The other man, who was in favour of registration, particularly wanted reserve status for the land of the Labrador Innu communities because he believed that this would result in preventing non-Innu from residing and taking jobs in these communities.

Both men looked to the school to provide their children with job qualifications. However, they also wanted half of the time spent in school to be conducted in the Innu language and devoted to Innu content so as to ensure the maintenance of Innu culture, which, they said, was not now being fully passed on to the younger generation.

Both men said that drinking was the main problem facing the Innu, and both admitted to having a drinking problem themselves. They gave several suggestions for dealing with this problem, including steps to limit public access to alcohol. One spoke admiringly about a system he had observed in a Quebec Innu community, where any adult householder has the right to prevent people from drinking in his or her house. This could even extend to the person's own spouse, so that if one spouse does not wish the other to drink, s/he can require her/him not to do so. He said that the band police could be called in to enforce this rule.

The third discussion group was comprised of six young and middle-aged people. All agreed that their own children, when they were grown, would still want to spend part of every year living and hunting in the bush. However, their offspring would also want to have a salaried job, for which they would need to have formal educational qualifications. As in the previous discussion group, one person complained about not being given a job by the Innu Nation, and there was general resentment over Whites being given jobs in the community.

This group believed that, at present, teenagers were confused and mixed up, torn between preparing for a job and life in the settlement and learning the Innu hunting way of life by living in the bush. It was said that some of these young people, when taken to the bush, wanted to leave after only a few weeks. It was felt that, since the Innu had become settled in houses, the elders were losing their role of advising and educating the youth and that this process needed to be reversed. While participants appeared to assume that all of these problems could be solved, there were few specific suggestions as to how this could be done, particularly through any new provisions coming from land rights or self-government talks.

It might be pointed out that this notion that teenagers are confused, torn between the settlement and the bush, and unsure of what they want, may represent a specifically adult view (Orchard 1998). Orchard shows that, while the Innu teenagers at Kawawachikamach, near Schefferville, Quebec, may not be following middle-class Euro-Canadian patterns for their age group, they are not confused over such matters as their ethnic identity or whether they should orient themselves towards White or Innu values. However, she also reports that Innu parents in Kawawachikamach make the same kind of claims as do Innu parents in Labrador regarding teenage children; that is, that they are confused. She believes that parents are projecting onto their children the contradictions they are facing in their own lives.

Utshimassit Relocation Plan

The leadership of Utshimassit had begun to seriously press for the relocation of the village during 1990 and 1991. Through the efforts of volunteers of the Mennonite Central Committee, an architect-planner conducted a study of the idea, which included a technical survey of the favoured site of Sango Bay, together with plans for a small hydro plant, a fresh water supply, and the outline of a village plan. The study was based on discussions held with community members, at which other potential sites were also considered.

In February 1992 a disastrous house fire occurred in Utshimassit as a result of children being left without adequate supervision while their parents were out drinking. As a response, the band council and the Innu Nation launched a public inquiry into the incident, which included an examination of many such deaths over the previous years, all of which were attributable to alcohol and to the general issue of what I refer to as "community dysfunction." A series of workshops were held, some of them while much of the community was camped in tents at the Shango Pond site.

The inquiry's published report (Fouillard 1995) quoted and paraphrased what was said at these workshops. Among many points contained in this remarkable document, two emerge most clearly. Over and again people said that they could no longer simply blame others; they had to start to take responsibility themselves for what had happened. Many also expressed their belief that the genesis of the dysfunction in their lives was to be found in the events leading to the government settling them in this particular location without their agreement or participation. For the Innu of Utshimassit, it seems perfectly logical that the prevention of future tragedies must involve moving the settlement and making a new beginning, this time at a site selected and planned by the people themselves. The present site was polluted materially (because the clay soil does not permit even pit toilets) as well as psychologically (because of the human tragedies that have occurred there). And so this most recent tragedy, the fire, became the impetus for what became a social movement to relocate the settlement to Sango Bay.

In seeing the campaign to relocate the village of Utshimassit as a social movement we need to acknowledge its connection to the alcohol treatment program. A small group of Utshimassit people undergoing treatment, people who had remained sober for about a year, made up the core personnel of this movement. Through the summer of 1992 this group, which included key people in the band council, petitioned both levels of government to fund the relocation. During that summer, to add political pressure in support of relocation, band-owned construction equipment was moved to the site. When building materials for new house construction at Utshimassit arrived by boat they were commandeered by the band and moved to the new site, much to the annoyance of the provincial government. Finally, in August the two governments agreed to fund a very rushed feasibility study, for which I was contracted to conduct three days of interviews and to write a section of the report on the social and cultural implications of the proposal.

In the eyes of the Newfoundland government, the reason the Innu gave for the move was not sufficient to warrant spending the substantial amounts of public money that would be required. However, there was a reason for the move that the government did find sufficient: the fact that government engineers had been unable to find an economically feasible source of fresh water that could deliver the specified number of litres per hour for a settlement of this size, as called for by the Newfoundland and Labrador municipal code. Thus the feasibility report was finally accepted, although not for the reasons the Innu had put forward. Engineers indicated that the costs of bringing adequate quantities of water to the present site would be as costly, over the next fifty years, as would moving the village to the new site. The province quietly left aside the Innu assertion that the relocation was necessary because of the flawed process of establishing the present site without the consent of the community and because of the need to reestablish community functionality. It helped that it was the federal government that paid for the relocation. However, the province's publicly stated misgivings about the move – that the Innu may simply take their problems with them – continue to hang over the project like a dark cloud.

The Utshimassit Gas-Sniffing Incident

Gas sniffing by Innu children at Utshimassit in January 1993 received worldwide press coverage. Just why German television, *Time*, and the *Globe and Mail*, along with a host of other media correspondents, found this particular incident (sadly typical in northern Canadian communities) so compelling remains for me something of a mystery. As part of their coverage the press also wrote about community plans to relocate the village to the mainland. I had been aware for some time, both from others and from my own observations while visiting Utshimassit, that a serious solvent abuse problem existed among the youth – a situation similar to those that have been reported in a number of other northern Aboriginal communities. While conducting research in 1992 on Innu ideas about the relocation I was made aware, in considerable detail, of the extent of the problem. I observed some of the evidence of gas sniffing and was given details by the head nurse in the community, who had been observing such events over a period of two years. She told me that the only positive development to have occurred regarding this problem had been the recent return to the community of two young men sent out for Aboriginal police training. Despite having the authority to officially act as police withheld from them by the provincial government, they were still making nightly patrols, which were having some success in discouraging the practice of solvent abuse. I determined that other officials in the community were also well aware of the extent of gas sniffing by children, including the social worker, the alcohol treatment worker, the priest, and the teachers.

With the Innu Nation's release the following January of a home-made video showing five children sniffing gas and saying they wanted to die, the press carried a story whose core remained unaltered for several weeks: five children had tried to commit suicide. The press failed to mention the abundant evidence of a far more widespread and well-entrenched problem than the suicidal wishes of five children – parental alcohol abuse and consequent child neglect. It may be that reporters felt obliged, as do many anthropologists, to leave out what they thought the Innu themselves did not want revealed. However, this allowed the province to tell the press they had not previously been aware of any problem, thus failing to acknowledge the information known to their own field staff.

The press story effectively assisted the Innu in publicly making their case for relocation. They included in their stories the history of how the village location had been selected without local approval, the lack of decent housing and sanitation (despite government promises), and the isolation of residents during break-up and freeze-up. But, unlike the Innu themselves, the press apparently found it difficult to openly confront evidence of a general state of social dysfunction, parental neglect, and alcohol abuse. Moreover, when government officials reacted with surprise at being told of the existence of the gas-sniffing crisis, no reporters bothered to ask local officials about the situation.

Out of the extensive press coverage came political pressure, with the result that crisis meetings were held with the government, positions were established, and commitments were made. One result was that a large group of Innu children and their parents was sent for treatment at the Poundmaker's Lodge in Alberta. The federal government made a general commitment to relocate the community, but, as the details were dependent upon a funding agreement being reached between Ottawa and Newfoundland, it was only finalized in 1996. In the initial negotiations the Innu produced a Seven Point Plan. Although the government never accepted this plan in its entirety, its wording is significant and I provide it in full.

(1) Creation of an Innu community off the island and on the mainland.
(2) Establish a Family and Cultural Renewal Centre in Nutshimit (the country), based on a holistic approach to healing and emphasizing Innu cultural values and spiritual beliefs.
(3) Set up a Community Resource team, building upon the abilities of Innu.
(4) Recognition of Innu government and land and resource rights.
(5) Canada's acknowledgement of its constitutional obligations to the Innu people and Nation.
(6) The youth who are chronic solvent abusers, their families and interpreters be immediately sent to Poundmaker's Lodge in Alberta for treatment.
(7) That a meeting be held in Utshimassit between Innu representatives, Health and Welfare minister Benoît Bouchard, Joe Clark as minister for Constitutional Affairs, Indian and Northern Affairs Minister Tom Siddon and Newfoundland Premier Clyde Wells to work out the implementation of this seven point plan. (Utshimassit Band Council and Innu Nation 1993, 1)

Innu Nation Policy Workshop

In March 1993 the Innu Nation held a two-day policy workshop in Sheshatshiu, during which much of the discussion revolved around the issue of supporting the bush way of life, referred to as *ishinniuiyat nutshimit*. Following the establishment of Labrador Innu settlements in the 1960s, most parents had to stay in the village while their children attended school. In the mid-1970s limited funds became available to subsidize transportation for the Innu so that they could spend time hunting in the bush. This program has gone through a number of crises and was, for a time, administered by the Innu Nation in Sheshatshiu; however, otherwise it has been administered by the Sheshatshiu and Utshimassit bands.

Attitudes towards the bush and hunting both unify and divide the Innu. Some believe the Innu should live in the bush for extended periods of time and that this should be supported by such things as rearranging schooling and setting up alcohol treatment centres in the bush. These steps are being advocated as necessary in order to save Innu culture from extinction. Settlement life is seen as having already undermined traditional Innu ways, thus necessitating this radical reversal.

Others, however, say that, while going to the bush should be an option, the practicalities of competing needs dictate that this cannot be expected of everyone and that, therefore, it cannot be imposed. These people argue that Innu culture can also be passed on within the village setting by modifying the school curriculum and through the use of radio and other media.

Discussion of this issue occupied much of the workshop. Much of the deliberation focused on the practical matters of funding bush living as well as the conflicts between requirements for cash (and thus the need for a job) and living in the bush. The meeting included many people who had full-time jobs with the band or with the Innu Nation as well as those who were teachers and so on. There was considerable discussion around changing the school curriculum, with specific proposals for reorganizing the school calendar so that children could go to the bush. Some discussion dealt with a feature of the James Bay Agreement – the Income Security Program for hunters. In all these discussions, a clear ideological division was evident between those who favoured spending more time living in the bush and those who favoured living in the settlement for most of the year.

A Theory of Community and Dysfunction

The Innu have worked remarkably persistently, and have achieved some significant political successes, in asserting their claim to sovereignty in their territory. And they have done this against the generally intransigent opposition presented by the state and many of their Labrador neighbours. Turning these political gains into meaningful improvements and day-to-day control over the important conditions of their lives is proving to be a major challenge. What implications for a useful conceptual approach to the issues of Aboriginal governance can be drawn from the above events?

I begin with the assumption that the complexity of social life cannot be contained within a single, watertight theoretical frame of reference. Given the ability of humans to simultaneously hold multiple interpretations, and the potential of human action to simultaneously embody multiple motivations, social analysis needs to be able to draw on multiple, distinct, and even logically incompatible theoretical models. Although such a process may be intellectually complex, even inelegant, I believe that it is, increasingly, essential – especially if one hopes to achieve pragmatic, policy-oriented approaches to real life issues.

One implication of such a multiple approach is that we may now be able to reconsider and reuse earlier discarded theoretical concepts. The idea of "social function," for instance, receives little attention today, and I certainly have no interest in returning to the self-fulfilling teleology that was part of some forms of this theoretical line of thought. Nevertheless, anthropolgy has never rejected the notion that cultural forms of action often have a social function, at least in some sense; rather, once all a priori assumptions about functional integration, and about which social functions are universal, have been set aside, then the fact that, under normal circumstances, the operation of institutions does have functional social implications can be accepted as self-evident.

This brings us to the idea of "social dysfunction" – a term that I use to refer to a phenomenon whereby, for more than a brief period of time, the forms of behaviour in which people regularly engage are not integrated smoothly within their social structure and, as a result, they are inhibited from achieving their goals. If we can demonstrate the existence of such situations, then we need not assume that all institutionalized behaviour is positively functional. Moreover, the fact that some societies may be seen to be partly dysfunctional does not rule out the possibility that other societies may be functional; that is, that there may be an absence of glaring social problems. In the latter instances we may assume that some kind of functional integration is actually taking place, whether or not we can actually understand how the process of such integration actually works. In this sense, cases of social dysfunction, particularly those that allow us to observe how social problems arise, may provide us with insight into social functioning in general.

In classic social-functional theory, participants need not be aware of how system functioning occurs. In fact, such awareness may be a marker of dysfunctionality. My allusion to Innu concerns about community dysfunctionality refers particularly to attempts to create or recover responsibility *within* the residential grouping as opposed to accepting forms of responsibility that have been imposed from outside. This concern may begin internally, with accusations directed at particular community members about their failure to carry out some responsibility (e.g., a family obligation). Later it may become clear that these are not individual failures but, rather, systemic failures. Accusations may also be directed towards such Innu-run institutions as the band council, the health council, or the Innu Nation. Most problematic for the Innu is the attempt to hold responsible those institutions that were initially set up and administered by the state (e.g., health, school, social services), particularly where they are now partially locally administered.

Conclusion: The Double Bind of Community Healing and Self-Government

In both Sheshatshiu and Utshimassit there is much current concern around issues of accountability, and this relates, in turn, to concerns over the current problems involving community dysfunction. My use of the concept of "community dysfunction" is to be taken as emically defined; that is, it refers to a particular class of systemic structural problems generally recognized as such by most participants in the social groups concerned.

One aspect of the dysfunctionality of Innu communities is that many social mechanisms now needed for the smooth operation of modern settlement life were, historically, not integral to Innu nomadic culture. For example, no preparations were made for the complexities of house maintenance. Moreover, in the 1960s authorities provided few mechanisms to ease the rapid transition from nomadic to sedentary life. While there are some indications that the Innu at first welcomed the prospect of living in houses, and that they welcomed the promise that, through schooling, their children would have wage employment, disillusionment quickly set in. By 1975, when I started to conduct land rights research with the Innu, most people told me they were convinced that the government was engaged in an orchestrated campaign to deprive them of their land and their hunting way of life. Under these circumstances the Innu were suspicious of, and therefore unsympathetic towards, the frequent government and Church admonitions to better adapt themselves to settlement life.

On the other hand, certain features of Innu bush culture were found to create difficulties for people living in the settlement. The material poverty experienced by most people living in the settlement stands in contrast to the satisfactions of the people living in the bush (something which Newfoundlanders and other Canadians, despite what the Innu tell them at every opportunity, appear to be unable to accept). These new conditions of poverty place unmanageable strains on the Innu ethic of sharing. The small quantities of game meat coming into the community are still distributed, but a household receiving a regular paycheque cannot live up to expectations to distribute its wealth in a similar way.

In the late 1970s a dispute broke out with the Newfoundland Department of Social Services over a set of situations that entailed two or more families on social assistance sharing the same dwelling. The department insisted that one of the families be designated the landlord, charge rent to the others, and that everyone's social assistance payments be adjusted accordingly. Such a practice was totally incompatible with the Innu egalitarian ethic and attitudes towards sharing and hospitality. Thus village life often has the effect of undermining even those Innu institutions which have managed to survive the transition to the settlement.

Because of the virtual absence of mind with which the Newfoundland government established both settlements, neither Sheshatshiu nor Utshimassit had the infrastructure or community services necessary to allow them to function effectively as collectivities. Moreover, many households are, to some degree, dysfunctional due to alcohol dependency and its various consequences.

Despite the similarity of the social conditions of numerous Aboriginal communities in such diverse places as the United States and Australia, endemic alcohol abuse and community dysfunction are not well researched, and the steps necessary to bring about a solution to these problems are not well understood. In the absence of any general cross-cultural understanding of community dysfunction, some aspects of how the Labrador Innu situation has emerged seem to be significant. Mandatory settlement into houses, imposed cultural change, and enforced idleness seem to have resulted in cultural collapse and alienation. Under these circumstances many people turned to alcohol to fill their time and, subsequently, became addicted. This, in turn, created situations of interpersonal abuse. Children were sometimes neglected, leading to family break-up and youth substance abuse. In some cases there emerged psychological symptoms of guilt as well as self-perpetuating cycles of pathology; there have even been "infections" of suicide (Henriksen 1993). With self-administration, individuals holding positions of responsibility periodically become dysfunctional, thus placing an extra load on the rest of the community and increasing the probability that some will buckle under the strain.

The result of all of this is that there are unpredictable periods during which many individuals, and the obligations and duties for which they are responsible, cannot be relied upon by those dependent upon them. While others in the community do what they can to pressure affected individuals to live up to their responsibilities, or try to shift some of the communal responsibility away from them, a degree of unpredictability and community dysfunction has to be tolerated by everyone. In short, there are periods when the local social group is not fully functional.

In recent years the Labrador Innu have begun to face up to the dysfunctionality of their settlement life. In doing so they find themselves confronted with another of the many double binds that seem to enclose them. For many years the Innu Nation leadership has developed an increasingly pointed set of analyses of the Innu situation. This includes an insistence that the state has, with regard to the Innu, engaged in theft, colonization, cultural genocide, and the denial of basic human rights. While these contentions have been successful in recruiting support among a network of allies, they have not been accepted by state officials. Moreover, even if the state were to acknowledge its responsibility for creating dysfunctional communities, its officials could not, without the Innu themselves getting involved, undo the situation. In the end, no matter who is to blame, the Innu have to depend mainly upon themselves for a solution.

This kind of analysis of the Innu predicament has now begun to acquire new relevance for the everyday issues of self-government. The Innu find themselves confronted with having to make their settlements into functional communities, of having to tackle problems of poverty and dependency, as part of the process of achieving self-government. For many years the Innu have struggled against the supervisory authority of the Newfoundland provincial government by asserting Innu national sovereignty. Only now are they beginning to gain some degree of influence, mainly through direct funding arrangements with the federal government. At this point their own dysfunctions, both individual and community, take on a new and critical significance.

In the recent past the Innu, when faced with how to make their communities function properly, have been told to conform to what appear to them to be the arbitrary requirements of externally imposed responsibilities. They are now engaged in a much more radical search for new self-governing institutional forms – ones consistent with their own ideals and with the existing settlement-based social context but still acceptable to the state. By contrast, with any takeovers of existing institutions the issues of smooth functioning and accountability have to be addressed as special problems since, as a minority, the pressure is constantly on the Innu to change their practices to suit institutional forms that are familiar to the state.

These concerns around issues of community and individual functionality have led the Innu to embrace a social movement based on an ideology of community healing and renewal. Examples of this are taking place independently in both Sheshatshiu (around the Alcohol Treatment Program) and in Utshimassit (also around the alcohol program but, more specifically, around establishing a new community). In both cases the Innu seek inspiration from the past, which offers few practical guides for dealing with outside institutions.

Thus the assertion of local control, especially over state-established institutions, places the Innu within a series of double binds. In the past the economy of the bush was similar to that of a family enterprise within which the family owned and controlled all the means of production. Now movement between the settlement and the bush poses a major problem. The economy of the settlement either means working for others or accepting welfare, both of which represent a considerable loss of responsibility. But most Innu do not want to have to choose between the two: in the settlement there is access to needed cash as well as health and educational services, while in the bush there is access to valued foods and the ability to maintain valued traditions.

In this chapter I have discussed various double binds. The prospect of Innu self-government means either taking control while, as yet, unprepared to do so or not taking control until education and community healing have succeeded in getting their communities adequately prepared. Self-government forces the Innu to choose between a kind of sovereignty that is sometimes little more than symbolic and being incorporated within and subservient to state structures. They are being asked to choose between a discredited Indian Act and a more familiar but generally unsympathetic provincial administration. In education the Innu often have to choose between job preparation and cultural continuity.

In the case of the Utshimassit relocation, the planning of the new site also embodies contradictory aims. Either the new village is designed to afford more access to the bush, in which case the design of the houses should be such that they can be left secure in winter while people are away, or it is designed with an infrastructure that focuses on an orientation towards a wage economy and entails a greater requirement for house maintenance.

Another form of the double bind involves the inescapable disjunction between *ishinniuiyat nutshimit* and settlement-based economic and social practice. While the Innu ideology of national sovereignty treats any such disjunction as a result of external restrictions placed on the bush way of life, those concerned with community renewal must confront internal practical and symbolic contradictions, including those that have emerged between the bush and settlement ways of life.

To conclude, each of the above processes entails the same kind of double bind: whatever choice the Innu make entails a downside. They cannot hold to account those who are responsible for this situation, and even if they could, these persons could not solve their difficulties. Self-government offers the Innu a practical means of addressing their problems, but this requires the building of a new notion of community – one based on Innu values yet acceptable to the larger Euro-Canadian society.

References

Fouillard, Camille, ed. 1995. *Gathering Voices: Finding Strength to Help Our Children*. Vancouver: Douglas and McIntyre.

Henriksen, G. 1993. *Life and Death among the Mushuau Innu of Northern Labrador*. ISER Policy papers No. 17, St. John's: Institute for Social and Economic Research, Memorial University of Newfoundland.

Orchard, Treena. 1998. "Teenagers of the Tundra: the Teenage Experience among the Naskapi of Kawawachikamach." MA thesis, Department of Anthropology, Memorial University of Newfoundland.

Royal Commission on Aboriginal Peoples. 1996. *Report of the Royal Commission on Aboriginal Peoples*. Ottawa: Libraxus Inc.

Tanner, Adrian. 1993. "History and Culture in the Generation of Ethnic Nationalism." In *Aboriginality and Ethnicity*, ed. Michael Levin, 75-96. Toronto: University of Toronto Press.

Utshimassit Band Council and Innu Nation. 1993. "Seven Point Plan for Community Relocation." Unpublished. Utshimassit: Utshimassit Band Council.

Part 5
In Conclusion

22
Ways Forward

Colin H. Scott

By what criteria are our relations with Aboriginal peoples and territories to be assessed? In international and domestic arenas, discourses of human rights, environment, and development have focused increasingly on standards of ecological sustainability, social equity, self-determination, and cultural continuity. These represent separate vectors of development, each with its own motive force and tendency; but, in practice, they are interdependent factors in overall, longer-term outcomes.

Resource development conflicts in Aboriginal homelands bring all of these factors into focus. The clear-cutting of the boreal forest or the damming of the last great unmodified rivers for hydroelectricity – with the most immediate and severest impacts typically endured by local Aboriginal peoples – may be quite logical from the standpoint of profits in the marketplace but insane from the standpoint of sustainable use and enjoyment of biodiverse environments. Sustainability demands that we conform to standards that would not countenance, for example, cutting the boreal forest faster than the rate at which it can replenish itself as mature natural forest. Such self-limitation is eagerly attacked as utopian in some quarters. Yet the eco-logic of definite limits to growth is inescapable, and there are sound arguments for complying sooner (with some flexibility) rather than later (when pressed by the crisis of diminishing options and returns). There are also strong reasons to believe, given their self-interest in homeland areas and their histories of environmental knowledge and stewardship, that Aboriginal peoples may be better monitors, judges, and regulators of acceptable impacts than state authorities have proven to be. Hence, Aboriginal self-government jurisdiction for traditional lands and waters is closely tied to the prospects for environmental sustainability.

Directly related to the issue of how much should be extracted from northern areas, and at what rate, is the issue of who benefits and in what proportion. By strict standards of social equity, no outsider's wealth should be enhanced through northern resource extraction or development at a rate faster than that accruing to people indigenous to the North. Indeed, given the history of dispossession of Aboriginal peoples, resource-extractive companies and royalties-collecting central governments are in serious deficit to them; therefore, any development should deliver superior benefits to indigenous northerners until past inequities are remedied. This standard is undoubtedly threatening to much capitalist economic thinking, which holds that some persons (those already in possession of superior levels of capital, technology, and political influence) must be allowed to become even richer so that society at large might benefit economically from the motor of material greed. A corollary of this logic is that others will be dispossessed and expected either to redistribute their labour effort to conform to shifting employment opportunities or settle for welfare hand-outs. In short, the necessity of out-migration from "resource hinterlands" becomes a self-fulfilling myth, conveniently completing the cycle of alienation that has separated Aboriginal peoples from their territories.

Through expanding state transfers of various kinds, local entrepreneurship based on the recirculation of "public expenditure," and limited concessions enabling Aboriginal entrepreneurs to participate (very modestly) in primary industries – and through continuing reliance on subsistence production – a majority of indigenous northerners have managed, so far, to stay at home. But socio-economic conditions in many Aboriginal communities in the provincial Subarctic and Arctic range from hard-pressed to intolerable; and rapid population growth threatens, for some decades still, to outstrip efforts at economic adaptation and to drive most young people elsewhere or into deepening poverty. Meanwhile, core structures of state control and capitalist intrusion, generating massive net outflows of wealth from northern indigenous regions, remain substantially intact.

Human rights standards of self-determination would require the consent of Aboriginal peoples to the terms on which they, their territories, and their resources will participate in the more inclusive social order of the state. By this criterion, a sharing of sovereign powers with Aboriginal peoples – involving a veto over policies affecting them – would be the minimal standard for any state claiming that it no longer exercises colonial control over Aboriginal peoples. The implicit logic of treaty negotiation is to discover terms upon which Aboriginal peoples may freely and collectively consent to participate in the Canadian state. When they demand that development projects on their territories occur only with their acceptance, they present us with the acid test for determining whether or not the condition of colonial domination persists. Central governments have generally refused to recognize the necessity of Aboriginal consent to resource management decisions and proposed development on their traditional lands and waters, even as a temporary measure pending the negotiation of comprehensive settlements. There is, as yet, little in the contemporary structural relationship between northern Aboriginal societies and the state that would warrant the label of *post*colonial.

A policy of Aboriginal consent would, of course, actualize demands for equity in regional inflows and outflows of wealth, thus threatening central governments' ability to decide issues in their own political interest, to the alleged "greater public good," or on behalf of sectoral elites who present themselves as societal benefactors. To counter this threat, the rhetoric of state authorities – and of those whose interests are best served by the state – clings tenaciously to the ideology that an Aboriginal veto in development decisions would be tantamount to societal chaos. Yet, given Aboriginal peoples' need to achieve development in a manner that is beneficial both to them and to the larger society, this is highly implausible. Why, instead, could one not reasonably anticipate negotiated forms of development that are more equitable, more compatible with the long-term social and environmental viability of northern regions, and more respectful of communities' needs to balance continuity and innovation in Aboriginal lifeways?

It is, in some ways, an unsatisfying moment for addressing the question, "What is to be done?" On the one hand, since the 1960s, we have witnessed a steady surge of Aboriginal political organizing; encouraging, if cautious, progress in Supreme Court jurisprudence; the abandonment of overtly assimilationist federal policies; increased federal and provincial attention to negotiating Aboriginal and treaty rights; and constitutional entrenchment of these rights. Yet progress on the ground has been glacial. In the provinces, comprehensive settlements have been reached with only four Aboriginal nations in the thirty years since the federal government first formulated its contemporary claims policy (three of them under the James Bay and Northern Québec Agreement and the complementary Northeastern Quebec Agreement). Constitutional progress on Aboriginal self-government has been stalled for several years. The deeper political and economic structures of assimilation remain largely intact. Meanwhile, conditions of unresolved conflict simmer and periodically erupt.

In the wake of the crisis at Oka and Kahnawake, the Royal Commission on Aboriginal Peoples focused many of the country's best-informed and creative minds on the challenge of policy reform. In their final report, the Commissioners called on federal, provincial, and territorial governments and aboriginal organizations to "commit themselves to building a renewed relationship based on the principles of mutual recognition, mutual respect, sharing and mutual responsibility" (Royal Commission on Aboriginal Peoples 1996, vol. 1, paragraph 1.16.1). More concretely – and here I select only the most general recommendations that bear on the concerns of the present volume – the Commission advocates:

(1) official disavowal of the doctrine of "terra nullius";
(2) restructuring of nation-to-nation relations on the basis of consensus;
(3) rejection of the idea that treaty-making, past, present or future, effects blanket extinguishment of rights and title, or extinguishes the inherent right of self-government;
(4) renewal of treaties in a manner appropriate to evolving conditions;
(5) self-government territorial and civil jurisdiction, also involving sharing of jurisdiction with federal and provincial governments in areas of overlap;
(6) negotiation of self-government treaties, endowed with constitutional protection;
(7) acceptance of Aboriginal governments as comprising a third order in the constitutional sharing of powers with federal and provincial governments;
(8) an enhanced share of territory, resources and revenues from resource development for Aboriginal peoples – together with compensation for past and present resource exploitation and social disruption, and provision of economic development funding; and
(9) inclusion of education, health and healing as core areas in self-government jurisdiction. (Ibid., Appendix 'A')

Several institutional innovations were recommended to give effect to the foregoing principles and goals. Key among these were the following:

(1) preparation by the federal government of a Royal Proclamation, supplementary to the Royal Proclamation 1863, affirming bilateral nation-to-nation relations, and principles for the process of treaty-making, implementation and renewal;
(2) companion federal treaty-making legislation, together with parallel provincial and territorial legislation;
(3) establishment of treaty commissions by federal, provincial and territorial governments and Aboriginal and treaty nations;
(4) creation through federal legislation of an Aboriginal Lands and Treaties Tribunal, providing monitoring, support and adjudication in treaty processes cross-Canada;
(5) federal enactment of an Aboriginal Nations Recognition and Government Act;
(6) federal, provincial, territorial and Aboriginal collaboration to develop a Canada-wide framework for self-government treaties; and
(7) creation of an Aboriginal Peoples Review Commission, headed by an Aboriginal commissioner, to review progress in the fulfilment of treaties, the implementation of self-government, the provision of adequate

> lands and resources for Aboriginal peoples, the improvement of social and economic well-being and government action on the Royal Commission's recommendations. (Ibid.)

In the years since the Royal Commission handed down its report, one is hard-pressed to identify federal or provincial leadership on the key recommendations. We appear to suffer not from a lack of well-considered policy prescriptions but from a deficit of political courage to execute them. Surely it is not beyond our means to achieve resolution. The creation of the self-governing jurisdiction of Nunavut, with its accompanying comprehensive settlement, while certainly not perfect, indicates some ability to move toward more equitable treatment of Aboriginal territorial, political, and cultural rights. True, Nunavut represents the "easy case" for Canada: relatively sparse external competing interests in a region whose population is overwhelmingly Inuit. Aboriginal inhabitants in the northern regions of Canadian provinces, though also often in the majority, have found progress to be more elusive, the compromises demanded of them much greater, and institutions of internal colonialism more stubbornly entrenched. Northern Quebec and Labrador, in these respects, reflect provincial experience elsewhere.

The conclusion of much combined wisdom and experience seems inescapable: unless one welcomes a return to the calamity of earlier assimilationist policies, the way forward involves the broad-spectrum acknowledgment of Aboriginal peoples' collective rights, including possession of homelands and waters, political self-determination, and cultural difference. These are not utopian goals. In parts of Australia, several Aboriginal groups have gained recognition of freehold title to much larger percentages of their homelands than any Aboriginal nation in Canada has done. The accommodation of "tribal" sovereignty in the United States is, as yet, unmatched in Canadian legal precedent or constitutional practice. "Home rule" in Greenland combines political, territorial, and cultural autonomy. Each system has its own limitations, but the key elements for practical progress *are* viable, with positive results for Aboriginal people, and without life becoming impossible for the "mainstream" citizens of states who dare to relinquish aspects of colonial domination.

Aboriginal cultural difference, an inherently collective phenomenon, can only effectively be expressed and negotiated by broadly self-governing nations. Constituted along lines of linguistic and cultural commonality and historical association, the most politically effective are those who organize regionally. They must command extensive terrestrial and aquatic resources. In the Canadian Arctic and Subarctic, the economic viability of Aboriginal nations demands a combination of resource rents, public administration funding devolved from federal and provincial governments, local and regional enterprise development, and fortified subsistence economies and lifeways. Northern provincial regions are rich in hydroelectric, forest, mineral, and other resources, yet patterns of capital investment and employment that we have come to see as "ordinary" now undermine the potential for self-sufficiency of Aboriginal communities. This cannot improve without fundamental reforms to a property system that enriches provincial government treasuries and licensed resource-extractive companies, leaving the original owners of these regions with meagre compensation for weakly respected Aboriginal rights and titles, and with social assistance payments.

It is urgent that federal and provincial authorities forsake the practice of "half-measures." The negotiation of comprehensive and specific claims must achieve genuine and substantial sharing of power and wealth. Narrowly legalistic construal of past treaties and agreements as instruments of extinguishment is self-defeating. Their renegotiation is needed to remedy social problems, and to fulfil their promise as evolving nation-to-nation contracts. Attempts to limit Aboriginal governments to municipal-like status, or to confer upon them only narrow jurisdictional functions that pose no threat of competition to provincial or federal governments, are similarly counterproductive. Delegated status is unacceptable, because it exposes Aboriginal governments to provincial and federal veto in matters where clear conflicts of interest (with respect to resource development, etc.) may arise. Therefore, the empowerment of Aboriginal polities within a "third order" of constitutionally empowered governance remains critical. Mere consultative "participation" of Aboriginal nations in decisions about resource development and environmental management, without a share of jurisdictional power and responsibility, will do little to remedy inequitable material outcomes, and will serve mainly to legitimate external governmental and industrial interests. The Supreme Court of Canada's *Delgamuukw* decision endorses the legal right of Aboriginal nations to develop resources within their traditional territories. Federal and provincial governments need to respect and promote this right in forestry, fisheries, and other resource sectors and to abandon antagonistic policies aimed at neutralizing this dimension of *Delgamuukw*.

Restructuring along these lines is no panacea; new wealth and enhanced autonomy will not automatically resolve problems of social suffering and community dysfunction. But one thing *is* certain: without such structural reform, these problems will remain endemic. The lessons of history are clear on another point: Aboriginal communities are tenacious in their determination to endure, and we can expect long-term resistance and chronic conflict in direct proportion to our neglect of their rights and aspirations. In recent decades, Aboriginal nations have steadily enlarged their self-government capacity and practice, despite daunting structural constraints. These gains will not willingly or peacefully be surrendered.

Calls from the political right to eliminate special status; to cut off fiscal transfers to Aboriginal communities; to refuse further recognition of collective ownership rights; and to individualize existing reserve property are policy non-starters, if only because hostility toward these positions among Aboriginal people is overwhelming. Attempts to enforce such measures would trigger a level of social strife unacceptable to most Canadians. Besides, as most Canadians realize, such measures are blind to history, to the role of colonial dispossession in creating Aboriginal poverty, and to the repeated failure in Canada and elsewhere of the assimilationist agenda.

Lasting reconciliation will depend on the favourable evolution of civil political and legal arrangements, but, sadly, it is as if progress in that direction depends on the incentive of periodic confrontation. The situation of many Aboriginal communities is so desperate, the need to defend against imminent losses so great, and the behaviour of central governments so frequently dishonourable that to trust only in "due process" and patient negotiation would be self-defeating. In recent years several subarctic communities have resorted to "direct action" tactics – the blocking of forestry roads, the obstruction of military runway traffic, the torching of logging facilities – to impede destructive and unwanted projects in their homelands. In all cases that we are aware of, these tactics were only resorted to after legal recourse and political negotiation had failed.

Physical action by Aboriginal peoples elsewhere in Canada in recent years has ranged from the carnivalesque pelting of fisheries officers with marshmallows, to the "monkey-wrenching" of industrial operations, to armed barricades against orchestrated police and military operations. But experience indicates that Aboriginal communities walk a political tightrope when they resort to the physical defence of their homelands and resource rights. Since Aboriginal protestors can be answered with overwhelming force by state officials, physical tactics are effective only insofar as they dramatize local determination in the face of daunting odds and, it is hoped, gain media and public attention and support. When state authorities overreact (and if the public itself is not badly inconvenienced by Aboriginal action), then public sympathy may be appreciably enhanced. When, however, Aboriginal actions provide their critics with opportunities to present them as public aggressors, state authorities can deploy armed force at greatly reduced political cost to themselves. Aboriginal self-control, timing, and the skillful combination of complementary negotiations are critical in achieving political gains through direct action.

Direct action taken by local people has rarely involved loss of life, but it has, on several occasions, provoked reprisals from state authorities in the form of arrests and physical intimidation. The costs to families of having their members arrested, interrogated, and subjected to lengthy court proceedings have all been steep – compounding the stress of years of publicizing, lobbying, litigating, and negotiating. In some parts of the country, federal and provincial government authorities have exploited and exacerbated local despair in efforts to break community resistance. The toll in personal suffering has persuaded some that the price of oppositional solidarity is too high. In the view of many community leaders and members, however, the costs of not taking action are even higher. The structural violence of the status quo offers chronic fresh injury; and the materially viable futures of communities and cultural lifeways hang in the balance.

For communities embroiled in crises of suffering stemming from a series of colonial dislocations, responses may vary. On the one hand, their circumstances have sometimes been incubators for the intense resolve born of collective desperation; on the other hand, it is supremely challenging for people haunted by ghosts of personal loss and violence to find the hope, energy, and resilience for sustained political action. Personal healing, on a day-to-day level, may be challenge enough. Community leadership, nevertheless, faces the reality that, without systemic improvement in Aboriginal control of homeland resources and development, healing is, at best, a patch-up, individualistic effort that cannot staunch increments of fresh suffering. Effective leadership in these circumstances, as Abel Bosum (Chapter 14, this volume) points out, demands operating on several fronts simultaneously, pursuing strategies that restructure relations with the wider economic and political system, while making provision for local social needs, attending to community problems, and ensuring that community membership is involved in each decision, at each step of the way, in the pursuit of political goals.

If direct action locally is one response to failures of state law and policy, another is recourse to transnational arenas. Through speaking tours, media campaigns, and representation at human rights and environmental organizations, Aboriginal groups are raising international consciousness of the ecological and human costs of urban-industrial development in remote peripheries. In opposing the Great Whale hydroelectric project, the James Bay Cree organized influential information campaigns beyond Quebec and Canadian borders in order to undermine investment in the project and markets for its product. Labrador Innu opposition to NATO overflights and Lubicon Cree boycotts of petroleum and forestry multinationals involved similar approaches. On a number of occasions these peoples have won sympathetic hearings before various bodies of the United Nations.

The redefinition of rights to property and jurisdiction is a function of power, and it has several aspects: the explanation and understanding of cultural differences, the argumentation of rights according to various criteria of legitimacy, and the search for a meeting of minds with one's adversaries through negotiated agreement. Yet, as we all know, talk and persuasion are only a part of the story.

There is no shortage of sound moral and practical arguments for recognizing a broad spectrum of Aboriginal rights to lands, waters, and resources. These include the historical priority of Aboriginal possession, governance, use, and occupancy of the land; human rights of self-determination, social equity, and justice; the internationally recognized obligation to decolonize; and the preservation of community and cultural diversity. Moreover, it seems probable that the self-interest of non-Aboriginal sectors of society overall would be best served if Aboriginal peoples could exercise property and governmental rights on a scale that would enable them to participate fully in the Euro-Canadian economy while shaping this participation through effective stewardship of their home resources and environments. Why does such reasoning so often fall on deaf ears?

First, the intrinsic interest of citizens in social reconciliation is not always shared by politically and materially advantaged elites. Second, while broad-scale intercultural dialogue and understanding is a necessary condition for reconciliation, it may prove insufficient in overcoming the self-interested defence of particular interests. We may understand one another perfectly, but if what you want in your cultural terms is not compatible with what I want in mine, then mutual understanding might actually *increase* the conflict between us. When courts and governments have imposed their own preferred definitions of property and jurisdiction on Aboriginal lives, they have not always done so through unreflective or uninformed ethnocentrism. Perhaps, as often, an ethnocentric position is deliberately adopted because to recognize the reality and right of Aboriginal institutions, laws, and values would be intolerable to particular dominant interests. Creative, pluralist policy and jurisprudence, as formulated by even the most liberally progressive courts and central governments, operates within very restrictive understandings of how much cultural difference is admissible. If the institutions of majority democracy are ever to accommodate a more genuine pluralism and become more accepting of arguments for Aboriginal equity and political autonomy, then the political sympathies of the non-Aboriginal public must be enlarged. And in order for this to happen, the public must be led to question the ideology of congruence between the wider public good and the narrow interests of resource-oriented multinational corporations and state elites.

Peter Penashue, president of the Innu Nation, remarked: "One of the things that we have learned is that you never get anything for free. However beautifully we argue our point of view, that is not enough for Aboriginal people. What we have learned is that if we want it bad enough we have to shake the system" (Chapter 2, this volume). But how to shake the system when there are enough police, soldiers, and jails to overpower those who refuse laws laid down in distant capitals?

For the Innu, as for many Aboriginal groups, the practice of power is a practice of creative representation, revealing human damage and suffering; unmasking official lies and secrets; exposing the corrupt and the contradictory; displaying the dignity and validity of indigenous cultural ways; and, at times, forcing state authorities to jail them for defending their truths (all in the eye of the media) – thus making it very costly for state authorities to ignore Aboriginal visions and realities. By forcing the state to officially and explicitly deny Aboriginal culture and homelands, the opportunism of state laws continues to become more apparent, and the naked reality of rule by might, rather than by reason or right, threatens to disgrace the established system. And perhaps, sometimes, it forces its leaders to negotiate. So that the "beautiful argument" might come, in the end, to inform new understandings and better institutions.

We hope this is not too optimistic. For words and visions are the chief stock-in-trade, too, of scholarship – defining the outer limits of our all-too-limited power as societal agents. We are in the game of maximizing the impact of information, of understanding, of moral reasoning, of re-envisioned societal futures. This circumstance we share with Aboriginal peoples, seeking to construct alternative worlds through processes of negotiation and mutual consent – the only durable alternative to domination and inequality.

Acknowledgments

I am grateful to Michael Asch, Harvey Feit, Peter Jull, Peter Kulchyski, Monica Mulrennan, Peter Russell, and Adrian Tanner for advice, insight, and encouragement relating to ideas presented here. I hope I have managed to do some justice to the lessons and feedback offered by contributors to this volume, and by others who participated in AGREE workshops and conference sessions. I am also thankful for discussions at two conferences where some of these ideas were presented: "In the Way of Development: Indigenous Peoples, Civil Society and the Environment" (McMaster University, November 1998) and "Anthropology in the Twenty-First Century: Beyond the Ivory Tower" (University of Alberta, February 2000). Lastly, and not leastly, I am very much indebted to numerous graduate students who have provided inspiration, particularly through my seminar at McGill on "Local Knowledge, Aboriginality and Territorial Identity."

References

Royal Commission on Aboriginal Peoples. 1996. *Report of the Royal Commission on Aboriginal Peoples*. 5 vols. Ottawa: Royal Commisssion on Aboriginal Peoples.

Contributors

Naomi Adelson, Department of Anthropology, York University

Peter Armitage, Innu Nation Research Unit, St. John's

Mary Barker, Karlsruhe, Germany

Robert Beaulieu, Forestry Engineer, Cree Regional Authority

Abel Bosum, former Chief, Oujé-Bougoumou Cree

Paul Charest, Département d'anthropologie, Université Laval

Cathrine Degnen, Department of Anthropology, McGill University

Susan Drummond, Osgoode Hall Law School, York University

Harvey A. Feit, Department of Anthropology, McMaster University

Peter Jacobs, Faculté de l'aménagement, École d'architecture de paysage, Université de Montréal

Susan Jacobs, The World Bank, Washington, DC

Catherine James, College of Law, University of Utah

Josée Lavoie, Department of Native Studies, University of Saskatchewan

Ludger Müller-Wille, Department of Geography, McGill University

Monica Mulrennan, Department of Geography, Concordia University

Donna Patrick, Department of Applied Language Studies, Brock University

Peter Penashue, President, Innu Nation

Sylvie Poirier, Département d'anthropologie, Université Laval

Hedda Schuurman, Department of Anthropology, Memorial University

Colin Scott, Department of Anthropology, McGill University

Richard Scott, R.T. Scott Medical Associates, Grimsby, Ontario

Adrian Tanner, Department of Anthropology, Memorial University

Jeremy Webber, Sydney Law School, Sydney University

Index

Note: All locations are in Northern Quebec or Labrador unless otherwise noted. "CAM" stands for Conseil Attikamek-Montagnais, "EIA" for Environmental Impact Assessment, and "JBNQA" for James Bay and Northern Québec Agreement. "(f)" after a page reference indicates a figure or map, and "n" indicates an endnote.

Aboriginal rights: Aboriginal consent for use of territory, 418-19; arguments for, moral and practical, 425; *Calder* case (1973), 248; *Delgamuukw* decision, 11, 422; direct action tactics, 423-24; human rights of self-determination, 418-19; and JBNQA (*see* JBNQA); lack of progress, 419, 421, 425; linked with self-determination and culture, 417; low-level military flights (*see* Low-level flight training); in other countries, 421; recommendations of Royal Commission on Aboriginal Peoples, 419-21; resource ownership, 417-18; self-government (*see* Autonomy and self-government); transnational actions, 424. *See also* Aboriginal title

Aboriginal Rights Coalition: opposition to low-level flight training, 244

Aboriginal title: American argument, 50; based on system of land use and occupancy, 50-51; concept of terra nullius, 66; Cree threat of separation from independent Quebec, 215, 217-19; Euro-Canadian perspective on land claim settlements, 229; Euro-Canadian view of land ownership, 49; extinguished in Nunavut Final Agreement, 89; extinguishment by federal government, 79, 92; injunction to stop James Bay I, 209; Innu of Labrador, sovereignty over land, 363-64; Inuit notion of land use vs. ownership, 49; and JBNQA (*see* JBNQA); land claims, 237, 238(f); land and water not separated, 8-9, 37; lex loci argument, 50-51; media coverage (*see* JBNQA, media coverage); Montagnais (*see* Mamuitun Tribal Council; Montagnais); in other countries, 421; place naming system as evidence of a lex loci, 52; Quebec's name changes in northern Quebec, to assert sovereignty, 53; self-government (*see* Autonomy and self-government). *See also* Inuvialuit Final Agreement; Land title; Nunavut Final Agreement

Aboriginal title to offshore areas. *See* Sea rights

Aboriginality: beliefs re gender and child-bearing as identity markers, 320-21, 324-27; concepts of culture and self-determination, 15, 318-20, 330-31; cultural change vs. cultural loss, 16, 316-18, 327-30; as cultural self-esteem, 289-90; culture threatened, 10; definition, 291; melding of concepts and practices, 299-300; new concepts, 298-99, 323; social dynamics, 15; and teenagers (*see* Teenagers)

Atikamekw Nation: Atikamekw Nation, Council of *(Atikamekw Sipi),* 101, 102; Atikamekw place-naming, 108; concept and naming of "nation," 100, 101-2; creation of Abitibi beaver reserve, 105-6, 107; cultural resistance to government edicts, 109-10; development as political entity, 100-101, 102; flexibility of hunter-gatherer societies, 113; government land categorization, 106;

guardianship/transmission of territory, 107-10, 114; *Kice Okimaw* (grand chieftancy), 100; La Loutre Dam, impact of, 104-5; land claims, 260; logging, concerns about, 103-4, 106; modern hunter-gatherers, 110, 112-13; non-Aboriginal activities (18th C. to 1950), 103-5; non-Aboriginal activities (1950 to present), 105-7; Quebec proposal (1994) re economic development, 14, 263-64; Quebec proposal (1994) re land claims, 262-65; Quebec proposal (1994) rejected, 264-65; Quebec proposal (1994) re resource management, 263-64; Rapide Blanc Dam, impact of, 104-5, 115n7; sport hunting and fishing by outsiders, 104, 107, 109; traditional knowledge, 111-12, 112-13; traditional relationship with territories, 102, 107-9, 111-12, 114

Australia: concept of terra nullius, 66

Authenticity: concept of, 99

Autonomy and self-government: accommodation of difference, 4, 421-22; community healing and, 15, 359-61, 413; concepts of culture and self-determination, 15, 318-20, 330-31; for cultural expression, 10-11, 421-22; *Delgamuukw* decision, 10-11, 422; direct action tactics, 423-24; in health care, Nunavik, 333-34, 335-36, 338, 340, 350-52; human rights of self-determination, 418-19; implications, 3; jurisdictional questions, 8-9, 396; Mamuitun Tribal Council proposals, 265-66, 268-69; means to address problems, 422-23; in other countries, 421; power and wealth sharing with Canadian government, 14-15, 422; rights/self-determination/culture linked, 417; "third-order" arrangement within government, 422; transnational actions, 424; ways of attaining, 6-7. *See also* Aboriginal rights; Aboriginal title; Self-government, Innu

Avataq Cultural Institute, 38

Barren Land People (Mushuau Innu), 398-99

Beaver Asphalt, 221-22

Beaver reserve (Atikamekw territory), 105-6, 107

Birth control, 324-25, 326-27

Bourassa, Robert, 208, 217, 281

Britain: pre-emptive land claims, 56-58

Brochu, Michel, 46, 52-53

C*alder* case re Aboriginal rights, 248

Canadian Laws Offshore Application Act (1990), 85-86

Caribou: Cree respect toward animals, 151; George River herd, 235-36, 399; importance to Aboriginal peoples, 236; population and migration, 151-53, 168, 235-36

Caribou sport hunt: Cree conservation officers, 157; Cree objections, 155-58, 159-60, 162-63; Cree responsibility toward land, 172; dismissal of Cree concerns, 149, 155-56, 160, 161-62, 171; disrespect toward animals, 150-51, 164-66; eligibility of hunters, 155-56, 158; first hunt (1989-90), conflicts, 160-61; first hunt (1989-90), review, 161-62; government arguments for culling, 153, 172n3; HFTCC and wildlife management, 154-55; HFTCC's overruling of Cree concerns, 149, 155-56, 160, 171; JBNQA conditions, 166-67; outfitters, Cree, 158, 162-63, 167, 168-70; priority of Aboriginal harvesting, 156, 157-58; safety concerns, 160-61, 163-64, 165, 170. *See also* Sport hunting

Childbearing as gender identity, 324-27

Chisasibi Cree: bush life, education in values, 312-13; bush life, obstacles to, 313-14; concepts of family and community, 304-5; economy and employment, 306-7; education in Cree values and culture, 311-12, 312-13; educational opportunities, 307; opposition to caribou sport hunt, 170; physical layout of town, 306, 308-9; population of town, 305-6; relocation from Fort George Island, 304, 305, 307-8; returning to Fort George for traditional gatherings, 310-11; sense of community, 304, 307-9, 314; women's role in building community, 309-10

Chisasibi Mandow Agency, 170

Chlor-alkali plants and mercury contamination, 176-77

Ciaccia, John, 281

Cleary, Bernard, 257-58

Cole, Thomas, 68

Co-management: of caribou sport hunt (*see* Caribou sport hunt); government attitude to shared decision making, 149; by HFTCC (*see* Hunting, Fishing and Trapping Coordinating Committee); JBNQA provisions, 11, 12-13; wildlife management boards, 12-13. *See also* Participation; Resource management

Comité d'étude sur les effets médicaux et toxicologiques du mercure organique: clinical examination, 187; nutritional study of Cree, 183, 193-94; objectification of situation, 190-91
Community: concepts, to Chisasibi Cree, 304-5, 307-9, 314; concepts, to Innu, 400-401; definitions, 16, 379-80, 387; experience of, in Sheshatshiu (*see* Sheshatshiu, Labrador); theory of social function/dysfunction, 17, 409-10; women's role in building, to Chisasibi Cree, 16-17, 309-10
Community healing: to promote autonomy, 15, 413; in Sheshatshiu (*see* Sheshatshiu, Labrador, community healing); in Utshimassit (Davis Inlet), Labrador, 28-29
Conseil Attikamek-Montagnais. *See* Montagnais
Coon Come, Matthew (Chief of the Grand Council of the Crees): on Aboriginal rights and JBNQA, 213-14; on Cree threat of separation from independent Quebec, 218; opposition to caribou sport hunt, 161
Craik, Brian, 225
Cree: Aboriginality as concept (*see* Aboriginality); beliefs re gender and fertility, 320-21, 324-27; bush life, obstacles to, 313-14; bush life as teacher of values, 312-13, 328-29; caribou sport hunt (*see* Caribou sport hunt); Chisasibi (*see* Chisasibi Cree); community healing, 290; concerns re Canadian Laws Offshore Application Act (1990), 84-86; concerns re the Great Whale Project, 71-73, 207, 212, 219-26, 228-29; culture (*see* Aboriginality); environmental assessment in JBNQA, 11-12, 129-30; forestry (*see* Forestry and logging); ISP (Income Security Program),14, 314n3; and JBNQA (*see* JBNQA; JBNQA, media coverage); mercury contamination (*see* Mercury contamination); Mistissini Cree (*see* Mistissini Cree); moose harvests, data collection, 135-37; Oujé-Bougoumou (*see* Oujé-Bougoumou Cree); respect toward caribou, 151, 164-66; role in JBNQA ignored by government, 129-30; teenage peer group (*see* Teenagers); Whapmagoostui (*see* Whapmagoostui Cree)
Cree Regional Authority, 159, 161
Cree Trappers' Association (CTA), 159-60, 161
Croll, Andrew, 283, 284
Culture, Aboriginal. *See* Aboriginality

Davis Inlet, Labrador. *See* Utshimassit, Labrador
Delgamuukw court decision, 10-11, 422
Desjardins, Richard, 121-22
Diamond, Billy, 218
Dick, Robbie, 293
Domtar mercury study, 180, 189-90
DSC (Département de Santé Communautaire du Nord). *See* Health care, Nunavik

Edmonston, Phil, 220
Education: and bush way of life, 28, 307, 358-59, 360-61, 408-9; in Chisasibi, 307; and cultural values, 28; Euro-Canadian system in Sheshatshiu, 381; Quebec control, 52-53
England: pre-emptive land claims, 56-58
Environmental assessment; government reluctance to comply with Great Whale Project EIA, 85-86; Great Whale Project, 71-73, 214; Great Whale Project, news coverage, 226-28; under JBNQA, 11-12, 129; of low-level flights, recommendations (1995), 250-51; of low-level flights (1989), 242-43, 245, 246(f), 250; of low-level flights (1994), 245-47, 250

Fimreite, Norwald, 176
Flight training. *See* Low-level flight training
Forestry and logging: appearance of consultation with Cree, 122, 129, 141, 143; areas of exclusion, 142-43; on Atikamekw territory, 103-4, 106; claimed "compatible" with hunting, 129; Cree involvement criticized, 122, 123-24; Cree participation in JBNQA ignored, 129-30, 143; Cree political strategies, 12-13, 140-41, 142-44; direct action, 120-21, 142-43; forest disturbance data, 137-38, 139(f); government policy of participation, 119, 121-23; impact on Cree hunting and trapping, 124-27, 130-31; logging roads and increased crime, 131; moose harvests, data collection, 135-37; moose harvests in Cree territory, impact on, 135, 138, 139(f); private companies' consultations with Cree (1990s), 140-42; private companies' contracts with Cree, 139, 140; public participation lacking, 121-22, 144-45; spiritual and cultural implications, 131-33

Fort George Island. *See* Chisasibi Cree
France: claims on overseas territories, 56
Fulton, Jim, 220

Gas sniffing (Utshimassit or Davis Inlet), 23-24, 406-8
Gatherings and visits, annual and summer: Chisasibi Cree on Fort George Island, 310-11; cultural assertion and renewal, 291-92, 293, 295; Whapmagoostui Cree (1993), 292-94; Whapmagoostui Cree (1994, 1995), 294-98
Gilpin, Edward, 170
Grand Council of the Crees of Quebec (GCCQ), 6. *See also* Coon Come, Matthew
Grassy Narrows Reservation. *See* Mercury contamination
Great Whale Project: Cree and Inuit concerns, 71-72, 207, 212, 219-26, 228-29; EIA, 71-73, 214; EIA, news coverage, 226-28; government reluctance to comply with EIA, 85-86; impact on Nunavik, 64-65; media coverage (*see* JBNQA, media coverage); permission for, interpretation of JBNQA, 211, 214, 216-17; transformation of landscape into territory, 69-73

Happy Valley-Goose Bay, Labrador, 243, 245
Healing: bush life as teacher of values, 28, 312-13, 328-29, 358-59, 360-61, 408-9; community healing (*see* Community healing; Sheshatshiu, Labrador, community healing); cultural qualities that assist, 15; cultural renewal, 15-16, 290-91, 293, 295, 298-300; and direct action, 24, 26-27, 423-24; education system requirements, 23, 28; through gatherings (*see* Gatherings and visits, annual and summer); need for, 15-16; by Oujé-Bougoumou (*see* Oujé-Bougoumou Cree); problems adjusting to settlement life, 379-80, 381-83, 397, 405, 412; role of church in social collapse, 22-23, 385-86; role of new groups, church, and AA, 391-92; role of women, 17, 309-10; self-determination through health care service (*see* Health care, Nunavik); and self-government (*see* Autonomy and self-government; Self-government, Innu); Seven Point Plan of Cree, 24-25, 408; social functioning, 409-10; social problems/dysfunction, 22-23, 27-29, 224-25, 361-62, 397, 405-6, 407-8, 412. *See also* Health care, Nunavik
Health care, Nunavik: community health model, 334-35, 338, 340, 346-47; community health model assumed suitable, 344-45; community health vs. outreach (Puvirnituk), 344-47; criticism of, 332-33; decolonization of health care, 337-38, 350-52; decolonization of Inuit self, 339-40, 351, 354n13; dependency as argument against local control, 335-36; health context used for wider objectives, 17, 334, 351; hospital and politics (Puvirnituk), 343-44; Inuit involvement needed for cross-cultural communication, 336-37, 338; Inuit involvement in planning (Puvirnituk), 341; Inuit knowledge in health care (Puvirnituk), 341-42, 351; Kativik Council, mandate and limits, 333, 345-46; midwifery program (Puvirnituk), 347-50; Puvirnituk's stance against JBNQA, 340-41; role of DSC (Département de Santé Communautaire du Nord), 333; self-determination of, 334, 335-36, 338, 340, 350-52; "subjugated knowledge," 339
HFTCC. *See* Hunting, Fishing and Trapping Coordinating Committee (HFTCC)
Hudson Bay: title to, 57-58
Hunting, Fishing and Trapping Coordinating Committee (HFTCC): creation, 80; Cree members overruled, 12-13, 149, 155, 160; role in wildlife management, 154-55
Hunting and trapping: caribou (*see* Caribou sport hunt); Cree moose harvests, data collection, 135-37; logging, impact in Cree territory, 124-27, 130-31; logging, impact on moose harvest in Cree territory, 135, 138, 139(f)
Hydro-electric projects: Great Whale Project (*see* Great Whale Project); Hydro-Québec agreements, 260-62; impact on Nunavik, 63-65, 75n4; James Bay Hydro-Electric Project, 208-9; JBNQA (*see* JBNQA; JBNQA, media coverage); on Ste. Marguerite River, 260
Hydro-Québec: Mashteuiatsh/Hydro-Québec Covenant (1993), 260-61; Uashat mak Mani-Utenam Agreement (1994), 260, 261-62. *See also* Great Whale Project; JBNQA; JBNQA, media coverage

Innu, Labrador: background, 398-99; basis of social problems, 412; bush life (going "in country") and traditional values, 28, 358-59, 360-61, 408-9; bush life, workshop, 408-9; community healing needed before autonomy, 15, 413; community healing (*see* Sheshatshiu, Labrador, Community healing); community mechanisms not part of Innu culture, 411; Davis Inlet (*see* Utshimassit, Labrador); education, role in social problems, 23; ethic of sharing, 370, 385, 398, 411; flight training areas, 236-37, 248-49; hydro-electric project on Ste. Marguerite River, 260; land claims negotiations, 237, 238(f), 248-49, 250; nostalgia for country space, 370-74; not covered by Indian Act, 21-22, 400; opposition to flight training, 247-49; protests vs. low-level flights, 363-64; provincial attitude toward, 401; under provincial, not federal, jurisdiction, 21-22; and Quebec Innu, 21; reaffirming Innu identity, 15, 363-65; sacred forces, 390-92; self-determination and community healing, 359-61; self-government (*see* Self-government, Innu); Sheshatshiu (*see* Sheshatshiu, Labrador; Sheshatshiu, Labrador, community healing); social problems, 22-23, 412; Uashat mak Mani-Utenam Agreement (1994), 260, 261-62

Innu, Quebec. *See* Montagnais

Innu Nation (*formerly* Naskapi Montagnais Innu Association): land claims, 237, 238(f), 248-49, 250; negotiations re land rights (1991 on), 402; opposition to flight training, 247-49, 363; workshop on bush life, 408-9

Inuit, Labrador: land claims negotiations, 237, 238(f), 248, 249-50; land use vs. ownership, 49; opposition to flight training, 247-48

Inuit, Quebec: Aboriginal title (*see* Aboriginal title); geography and culture, 41-42; health care (*see* Health Care, Nunavik); Kativik administrative region, 36-38; land claims negotiations, 237, 238(f); land use vs. ownership, 49; Nunavik cultural region (*see* Nunavik); opposition to flight training, 247-48; place names (*see* Inuit Place Name Project); territorial lands and seas, 79-80, 82-83(f); territorial recognition in hunting society, 36. *See also* JBNQA

Inuit Elders' Conference. *See* Inuit Place Name Project

Inuit of Nunavik Statement of Claim to the Offshore (1991), 86-87

Inuit Place Name Project: area changes with the seasons, 45-46; and Inuit cultural identity, 38-39; place names' complexity, 47; place names and sovereignty, 47-48, 51, 53; seen as compromise and cultural loss, 43-44. *See also* Aboriginal title; Land title

Inuvialuit Final Agreement (1984): denial of right to energy resources, 92; offshore areas not included, 92, 93; terms, 92

Ishinniuiyat nutshimit. *See* bush life *under* Innu, Labrador

ISP (Income Security Program for Cree Hunters and Trappers), 14, 314n3

Ittoshat, Anthony, 293

James Bay I. *See* James Bay Hydro-Electric Project

James Bay II. *See* Great Whale Project

James Bay Hydro-Electric Project: background, 208-9; Cree and Inuit injunction, 208-9; instigation for JBNQA (1975), 209; media coverage (*see* JBNQA, media coverage). *See also* Great Whale Project

James Bay and Northern Québec Agreement. *See* JBNQA

JBNQA (James Bay and Northern Québec Agreement) (1975): Aboriginal title, whether extinguished, 37, 61n10, 211, 212-16; assumed rights of Hydro-Québec and government, 216-17; authoritative text, 219, 226, 227, 228, 229; Chisasibi Cree relocation, 304, 305; circumstances around negotiations, 92, 209; classes of land, 80-81, 82-83(f); creation of HFTCC, 80; creation of Kativik, 37; creation of Kativik Health Council, 333; creation of second-order problems, 208, 225-26, 228-29; Cree role ignored by government, 129-30, 143; Cree threat of separation from independent Quebec, 215, 217-19; EIA regime, 11-12, 129; first modern agreement, 6-7, 80; HFTCC's role in wildlife management, 154-55; ISP (Income Security Program), 14, 314n3; media coverage (*see* JBNQA, media coverage); multiple interpretations, 209-10, 228, 229; offshore interests not included, 8-9, 81, 84; as a "public problem," 207, 225-26, 228; terms of agreement, 80-81. *See also* Caribou sport hunt

JBNQA, media coverage: advertisement in *New York Times*, 220-21, 222; assertions re advantages, 211, 219-23; assertions re disadvantages, 212, 223-26; assertions re economic benefits, 221-22; assertions re "extinguishment" of Aboriginal rights, 211, 212-16, 217;

assertions re improvements in Cree health, 221; assertions re rights of Hydro-Québec and government, 216-17; Cree threat of separation from independent Quebec, 215, 217-19; environmental impact of dam, 212, 226-28; formulation of public attitudes, 206-8, 228; importance of, 207; information sources, 208; many interpretations of JBNQA, 209-10, 228; method of analysis, 210-11; propositions become "truths," 207, 210-11, 212-13, 215, 230

Kativik administrative region, 36-38
Kativik Regional Council of Health and Social Services, 333
Kawapisit (white people, to Atikamekw Nation), 98
Kice Okimaw (grand chieftancy of Atikamekw Nation), 100
Kikentatch Band. *See* Atikamekw Nation
Kokokac Band, 105, 115n7. *See also* Atikamekw Nation
Kurtness, Jacques, 258
Kurtness, Remy, 264
Kuujjuarapik village. *See* Whapmagoostui Cree

La Loutre Dam: impact, 104-5
Labrador: economy, 237, 241-42; low-level flight training (*see* Low-level flight training); population, 237; resource use and development initiatives, 237-39, 240(f). *See also* Innu, Labrador; Inuit, Labrador; Sheshatshiu; Utshimassit
Labrador Inuit Association: land claims negotiations, 237, 238(f), 248, 249-50
Land claims. *See* Aboriginal title
Land title: Aboriginal (*see* Aboriginal title); British Empire and pre-emptive claims, 56-58; conditions to satisfy, 55-56; by domination, 54-55; France and dominative claims, 56; Hudson Bay, argument between French and British, 57-58; maps and sovereignty, 58-59; place naming, role of, 51, 53, 57-58, 59-60; by pre-emption, 54; real vs. symbolic, 55-56
Landscape: choice of development model, impact of, 73-75; definitions, 65-66; distinguished from territory, 8-9, 64-65, 66; transformation to another landscape, 67-69; transformation into territory (Great Whale Project), 69-73. *See also* Nunavik; Territory
Lazure, Denis, 227
Le Hir, Richard, 214, 217
Leconte, Catherine, 221
Lex loci, 50-51
Logging. *See* Forestry and logging
Low-level flight training: and Aboriginal land claims, 244, 248-50; Aboriginal opposition to, 247-49; background and rationale, 239-41; economic benefits, 241-42; economy of northern Quebec/Labrador, 237-39; EIA (1989), 242-43, 245, 246(f), 250; EIA (1994), 245-47, 250; EIA panel's recommendations (1995), 250-51; environmentalists' low profile, 246; George River caribou herd, 235-36; Innu civil disobedience campaign, 363-64; and Innu land, 363-64; key issues, 233, 234(f), 235, 244; mitigation-avoidance program, 241; population in northern Quebec, 236-37; severe disappointment in recommendations (1995), 251-52; stakeholders, 243-44; suitability of Quebec-Labrador terrain, 233, 235; training areas, 236(f), 240(f)

Makivik Corporation, 6
Malouf, Albert, 209
Mamit Innuat Tribal Council, 256, 265
Mamuitun Tribal Council and land claims: counter-proposal to Quebec proposal (1994), 265-67; possible outcomes of negotiations, 269-71; proposals re self-governing bodies of community, 265-66; reaction to Quebec proposal (1994), 265; responsibility after 1994, 256
Marine resources: Aboriginal rights in Nunavut Final Agreement, 89-90, 93; Aboriginal rights under JBNQA, 8-9, 80, 81, 84, 87, 92; importance to Inuit and Cree, 79-80, 88-89; in Nunavut Final Agreement (1993), 90-91, 93-94. *See also* Sea rights
Mashteuiatsh/Hydro-Québec Covenant (1993), 260-61
Masty, Joseph, Sr., 293
Matimekosh, 257
McGill Methylmercury Study, 180, 185-86, 188-89
Mealy Mountains, 364-65
Media. *See* JBNQA, media coverage
Mercury contamination: abnormal becomes pathological, 192-93, 193-94, 198; assumption of Aboriginal people "at risk," 194-95, 195-98, 201-2; "blinding" in epidemiological study, 188-89; causal connection to disease, 178-79; chlor-alkali plants, 176-77; diagnostic difficulties, 181-83, 183-85;

as environmental toxin, 179, 180; epidemiological case definition, 186; fact vs. belief, 175-76; and fish consumption, 193, 194, 196-97, 199-200, 201; little proof, 175-76, 195, 200; Minamata disease, 176-77, 181, 203n7; objectification of problem, 187-91; release of mercury by rotting vegetation, 177; report of Task Force on Organic Mercury, 196-98; scientific moral authority, 12, 177-78; standards for human blood mercury levels, 198-99; symptoms compared with Minamata disease, 181-83, 203n7
Mianscum, Jimmy, 278
Midwifery program at Puvirnituk, 347-50
Military flight training. *See* Low-level flight training
Minamata disease, 176-77, 181, 203n7
Mistissini Cree: beliefs re gender and fertility, 320-21, 324-27; bush life as teacher of values, 328-29; childbearing as gender identity, 324-27; concepts of culture and self-determination, 318-20, 330-31; cultural change vs. cultural loss, 316-18, 327-30; teenage peer group and conformity, 321-23; teenage peer group and traditional culture, 16, 317, 320-22, 323-24, 329; teenage pregnancies, 321
Montagnais: CAM and land claims, 237, 238(f), 255-56; CAM's dissolution, 256; CAM's 1979 statement of claim and negotiations, 14, 257-58; forest exploitation, 259; hydro-electric project on Ste. Marguerite River, 260; land claims framework agreement, 258-59; land claims, possible outcomes, 269-71; land claims policy, interim measures, 258-60; Mamuitun Tribal Council negotiations (*see* Mamuitun Tribal Council); Mashteuiatsh/Hydro-Québec Covenant (1993), 260-61; opposition to flight training, 236-37, 247-49; Quebec proposal (1994), 14, 262-65; Quebec proposal (1994) rejected, 264-65; Uashat mak Mani-Utenam Agreement (1994), 260, 261-62. *See also* Innu, Labrador
Moose. *See* Hunting and trapping
Mukash, Matthew: on Cree rights after JBNQA, 219, 223; JBNQA linked with social problems, 224-25; at Whapmagoostui gathering, 292, 293
Multinational Memorandum of Understanding (MMOU) (1986), 239, 250-51
Mushuau Innu (Barren Land People), 398-99

Naskapi: and flight training, 236-37, 247-49
Naskapi Montagnais Innu Association (*now* Innu Nation), 401. *See also* Innu Nation
National Indian Brotherhood (NIB), 181
Native Association of Newfoundland and Labrador (NANL), 401
NATO flight training. *See* Low-level flight training
Nouchimi Tourism Inc. and outfitting operation, 169
Nui, David, 28
Nunavik: borders seasonally dependent (land, water, and ice), 45-46; coast and offshore continuous, 9, 45; as a compromised cultural entity, 42-44; concerns re Canadian Laws Offshore Application Act (1990), 84-86; creation of concept, 38-39, 42; defined by "process" geography, 41-42; health care in (*see* Health Care, Nunavik); impact of hydro-electric development, 63-65, 75n4; Inuit cultural region, 33; landscape, not territory, 64-65; manifestation of intercultural history, 44-45; place names (*see* Aboriginal land title; Inuit Place Name Project); in the "trait" geography model, 44
Nunavut Final Agreement (1993): differences from earlier agreements, 89, 93-94; extinguishes Aboriginal title, 89; Inuit Land Use and Occupancy Study, 88-89; marine provisions, 90-91; offshore rights, 89-90, 93; quasi-judicial boards created, 90; water rights, 9, 91
Nunavut Impact Review Board (NIRB), 90
Nunavut Planning Commission (NPC), 90
Nunavut Review Board (NRB), 90
Nunavut Surface Rights Tribunal (SRT), 90
Nunavut Wildlife Management Board (NWMB), 90
Nutshimit. *See* bush life *under* Innu, Labrador

O'Reilly, James, 217
Oujé-Bougoumou Cree: forced relocations, 278; history in region, 277-78; land and status negotiations, 280-81; negotiating strategies (1989, 1992), 283-85, 285-86; opposition to Great Whale Project, 281; opposition to JBNQA, 212-13; organized politically, 279; site selection, for community, 282; social problems and publicity, 282-83; working to build new community, 287-88

Pachanos of Chisasibi, Chief, 160-61
Paradis, Pierre, 226-27
Parizeau, Jacques, 214-15, 218
Participation: contracts with private logging companies, 138, 140-42; Cree concerns re logging ignored, 127-29, 130-33; Cree knowledge of forests, 124-27; forestry and logging, government policy, 119, 121-23; government limitations, 13, 119, 121-23, 422; and human rights of Aboriginal peoples, 418-19; JBNQA provisions ignored, 129-30, 143; legitimization of resource development, 13, 119-20. *See also* Co-management; Resource management
Penashue, Peter, 28, 425-26
Pepin, André, 222
Place Name Project, Inuit. *See* Inuit Place Name Project
Povungnituk (POV). *See* Puvirnituk *under* Health care, Nunavik
Puvirnituk. *See under* Health care, Nunavik

Qallunat (non-Inuit peoples, to Inuit), 42
Quebec: Cree threat of separation from independent Quebec, 215, 217-19; forestry policies (*see* Forestry and logging); low-level flight training (*see* Low-level flight training); name changes in northern Quebec, to assert sovereignty, 53, 61n10; Nouveau-Québec (*see* Nunavik); takeover of administration of northern Quebec from federal government, 52-53

Rapide Blanc Dam, 105, 115n7
Relocation of communities: Chisasibi Cree from Fort George Island, 304, 305, 307-8; Oujé-Bougoumou Cree (*see* Oujé-Bougoumou Cree); Utshimassit (Davis Inlet), need for, 25-26, 27, 405-6
Resource development: Aboriginal consent required, 418-19; Aboriginal participation, to legitimize policies, 13, 119-20; Aboriginal rights, 417-18; forestry (*see* Forestry and logging); hydro-electric projects (*see* Hydro-electric projects); Innu-Montagnais proposals, 265-67, 268; outflows of wealth away from First Nations, 14; pace accelerating, 5
Resource management: and human rights of Aboriginal peoples, 418-19; JBNQA provisions, 11, 12, 13; Mamuitun Tribal Council proposals (1994), 265-67, 268-69; Mashteuiatsh/Hydro-Québec Covenant (1993), 260-61; and Montagnais interim agreement (1988), 258, 259; and Montagnais land claim (1979), 257, 258, 259, 262; in Nunavut Final Agreement, 90; Quebec Proposal (1994), 263-65, 268-69; transborder, 13-14; Uashat mak Mani-Utenam Agreement (1994), 260, 261-62; wildlife management boards, 12-13; wildlife protection, 261-62
Rich, Katie, 286
Robitaille, Jacques, 122
Roman Catholic Church and Labrador Innu, 22-23
Royal Commission on Aboriginal Peoples: recommendations, 419-21
Ruskin, John, 68-69

Saganash, Romeo Diom, 223, 224
Sango Bay, 25-26, 405-6
Schefferville iron-ore mine, 237
Sea rights: Aboriginal view of home-seas, 8-9, 45-46, 78, 88; borders of Nunavik seasonally dependent (ice cover), 45-46; coast and offshore, significance of, 79-80, 88-89; Canadian Laws Offshore Application Act (1990), 85-86; government attitude towards, 78-79, 84-85; international recognition, 94; Inuit Land Use and Occupancy Study, 88-89; Inuit of Nunavik Statement of Claim to the Offshore (1991), 86-87; Inuvialuit Final Agreement, 92-93; negotiations with government (mid-1970s), 81, 84; not addressed or extinguished by JBNQA, 8-9, 81, 84, 87, 92; in Nunavut Final Agreement (1993), 89-90, 93; offshore islands and Nunavut, 85, 87; waters of Hudson and James bays, 85, 86, 87; weakness compared with land rights, 79, 85, 92
Self-government, Innu: background of Innu settlement, 398-99; bush life vs. settlement economy, 16, 414; collection of data re, 396-97; community healing necessary, 413; debate re registration under Indian Act, 403-4; discussion groups re, 402-5; "double bind," traditions vs. local control, 17, 398, 410-14; early political groups, 400-401; jurisdictional questions, 8-9, 396; land rights negotiations (1991 on), 402; Newfoundland's attitude toward Innu, 401; social problem-solving part of process, 402-3, 412-14. *See also* Autonomy and self-government

Sexual abuse, 28
Sheshatshiu, Labrador: Alcoholics Anonymous program, 391; "anti-community" consciousness, 380, 389; background of Innu, 398-99; basis of social problems, 412; church marginalized, 385-86; community healing (*see* Sheshatshiu, Labrador, community healing); community infrastructure lacking, 411-12; community mechanisms not part of Innu culture, 411; compared with nearby town, Northwest River, 383-84; concept/sense of community, 379-80, 387, 389-90; description of village, 383-84; education system, 381, 383, 393; health problems from village life, 382; indigenization of village institutions, 386; land rights (*see* Self-government, Innu); leadership models, old and new, 381, 392-93; lifestyle changes, 381-82; loss of traditional values, 385; non-homogeneous, 16, 380, 386, 387-89; Pentecostal Church, impact of, 391; reliance on transfer payments, 382-83; sacred forces lost in town, 390-92; self-government, differing attitudes, 392-93; settlement of semi-nomadic Innu (1968), 380-81, 399-400; social problems, 385; theory of social function/dysfunction, 17, 409-10. *See also* Innu, Labrador
Sheshatshiu, Labrador, community healing: bush life (going "in country"), 28, 358-59, 360-61, 408-9; country food, 369-70; meanings, 357-58, 361; nostalgia for country space, 370-74; problems affect whole community, 365-66; and protest re hunting restrictions, 364; and protest re low-level flights, 363-64; reaffirming Innu identity, 15, 363-65; and self-determination, 359-61; for social suffering, 361-62
Sport hunting: on Atikamekw territory, 104, 107, 109; attitude toward animals and land, 109; caribou (*see* Caribou sport hunt); consistent with Cree use of land, JBNQA conditions, 166-67; impact on Cree subsistence harvesting, 167-68

Tee-Hit-Ton v. *The United States* (1954), 50
Teenagers: attitude toward childbearing, 324-27; attitude toward traditional culture, 320, 322, 323, 404-5; contesting and modifying culture, 16, 317, 323-24; cultural change vs. cultural loss, 16, 316-18, 327-30; teenage peer group, effect on traditional culture, 317, 321-22, 323-24, 329; teenage peer group, pressures to conform, 321-23; teenage pregnancies, 321
Terra nullius, 66
Territory: concept of terra nullius, 66; development model, impact of, 73-75; different concepts, 34-35, 39-40, 64-65, 66; distinguished from landscape, 8-9, 64-65, 66; Kativik administrative region, 36-38; land and water continuous to Aboriginal peoples, 8-9, 37; Nunavik (*see* Nunavik); significance of land to humankind, 35-36; territorial integrity, 35. *See also* Landscape; Nunavik

Uashat mak Mani-Utenam Agreement (1994), 260, 261-62
Utshimassit (Davis Inlet), Labrador: alcohol abuse, 27-28, 407; background of Innu, 398-99; basis of social problems, 412; community healing, 28-29; community infrastructure lacking, 411-12; community mechanisms not part of Innu culture, 411; gas-sniffing incidents, 23-24, 406-8; managing the media, 24; need for relocation, 25-26, 27, 405-6; negotiations with government (2000), 26-27; settlement process, 399; Seven Point Plan for social problems, 24-25, 408; social problems, 27-29, 405-6, 407-8; theory of social function/dysfunction, 17, 409-10. *See also* Innu, Labrador

Versailles, Guy, 222, 224
Voisey Bay mine, 239, 240(f)

Whapmagoostui Cree: components of village, 292; and concept of Aboriginality, 289-90, 291, 298-301; home is family, 299; location of village, 291-92; summer gathering to promote Cree values (1993), 292-94; summer gatherings (1994, 1995), 294-98; tents enhance communication, 297-98
White Dog Reservation. *See* Mercury contamination